THE POEMS
OF GEORGE CHAPMAN

The Poems.

of

GEORGE CHAPMAN

Edited by

PHYLLIS BROOKS BARTLETT

NEW YORK

RUSSELL & RUSSELL · INC

1962

This Edition of Chapman's Poems
is Dedicated to
LUCY PEARSON BARNARD

CORRIGENDA

p. 2	12th line from bottom, delete ", a mathematician,"
p. 5	10th line from bottom, for "Corrina" read "Corinna"
p. 64	stanza 45.2, for "her churlish" read "his churlish", misprint 1595
p. 75	stanza 86.7, for "league" read "leaue"
p. 250	gloss 5, for "*Absurdam*" read "*Absurdum*"
p. 266	line 525, for "on" read "one"
p. 376	line 113, for "Jacete" read "Facete"
p. 415	line 103, for "the gaspt" read "that gaspt"
p. 417	line 28, for "Froggs" read "Foggs"
p. 426	note to line 217, 7th line, for "*C*" read "*N*", for "38" read "36"
p. 428	6th line from top, for "they they" read "then they"
p. 434	4th line from bottom, read "16.6"
p. 448	11th line from bottom, for "auritam" read "auaritiam"
p. 456	last line, for "*Mortianeriados*" read "*Mortimeriados*"
p. 458	delete note on line 429
p. 466	6th line from bottom, for "*Richard*" read "*Edward*"
p. 468	note to line 19, 1st line, for "V" read "VI"

PREFACE

THIS book is the second collected edition of George Chapman's poems. The first appeared in 1875, edited by R. H. Shepherd, with an introduction by Swinburne. In the present edition the original texts are reproduced as closely as possible; editorial corrections of printers' errors in spelling and punctuation are noted, as well as the few emendations which have seemed necessary. Since most of Chapman's poems were never reprinted in his lifetime, and only one is known to exist in manuscript, there are few textual variants, but such as there are have been recorded. The poems are printed volume by volume in chronological order and there are both textual and critical notes to each volume. Dr. Tannenbaum's *George Chapman: A Concise Bibliography* (1938) has made it seem unnecessary to furnish bibliographical material in addition to that given in the notes.

My work in editing the poems of Chapman was begun in London in the year 1936–37, a year that I owe in part to the award of a post-doctoral traveling fellowship by the University of Wisconsin. The publication of the book by the Modern Language Association has been made possible by a generous grant from the American Council of Learned Societies, and I am most grateful to Professor Karl Young for his advice and encouragement.

The officers of the Oxford University Press have also been most kind. Not only have they given me permission to reprint Marlowe's two sestiads of *Hero and Leander*, as prepared by Professor Tucker Brooke for the Oxford Marlowe, but Mr. Charles Williams of the London branch was the first to make the publication of this edition seem a real possibility.

Among the many in England who have given me friendly aid, I want particularly to thank Miss Gladys Scott-Thomson for having secured the permission of the late Duke of Bedford for her to bring his rare copy of *Eugenia* from Woburn Abbey to London for my use, and to Mr. F. C. Nicholson, librarian of the University of Edinburgh Library, for having lent me the only other known copy of the same work. I am most warmly indebted to the entire staff of the King's Library in the British Museum for the hospitality they afforded me on the little balcony.

The names of several students of Chapman appear in the notes to the poems and they have all added their own encouragement to the undertaking. The work started with the approval of Monsieur Franck L. Schoell and Professor Thomas Marc Parrott, who at one time had themselves planned to prepare an edition of Chapman's poems. Monsieur Schoell's work has been my richest mine of information as to Chapman's sources. Professor Parrott has been the most careful reader and improver of my notes. I am also indebted to Professor Douglas Bush for his reading of the manuscript and consequent suggestions, and to Mr. George G. Loane for his useful pamphlets and letters. It is pleasant to think that the eccentricities of Chapman's diction can afford such a constant source of interest, both in peace and in war, to a classical scholar who bas retired to the lovely hills of Gloucestershire. In addition to Professor Parrott, Professor Abbie Findlay Potts and Dr. Leslie A. Rutledge were good enough to read the introduction of the book and to challenge it at many points.

Finally, I thank three of my friends and former students: Miss Louise Shiffman for having helped me to check my copy of the items in the Dyce collection, Miss Charlotte Presler for her aid in reading the proofs, and Miss Phyllis Dudley for her patience and care in assisting me in the exacting work of preparing the manuscript for the press.

PHYLLIS BROOKS BARTLETT

Troy, New York
March, 1941

TABLE OF CONTENTS

INTRODUCTION

A NEW edition of Chapman's poetry needs no apology. Any poet who is still read, however rarely and by however few, is best read in a version as near as possible to his own original production; and where his language has been obscured by time, or was originally obscure through the very nature of his talent, it is a help to have guides to its source and intention. Such guides are, in the present edition, collected in the form of notes to his various poems. By way of introduction, the editor has attempted only to relate the sequence of his poems and their most characteristic qualities of style to his own theory of poetry. Chapman has enjoyed somewhat of a renascence in the past decade or two, probably because the taste of our times has so largely turned to difficult poetry and we have been trained by our own contemporaries to read verse that requires a higher degree of intellectual concentration than poetry is usually able to command. As all his critics have acknowledged, Chapman is a knotty poet. That granted, one may examine the nature of his poems in the light of his own conception of poetry.

George Chapman was a convinced believer in the Platonic doctrine that poetry is divinely inspired. It was a belief congenial to his conviction that he, of all men in modern times, was best fitted to translate the greatest poet of all time, Homer; and he was led direct to the doctrine by his perusal of Ficino's *Epitomae* of Plato's *Ion*. The conviction that poetry is in part a *divinus furor* is reiterated in his introductory epistle to the *Odysseys*, in a note to the twelfth book of that poem, and in his epistle dedicatory to the *Hymns of Homer*. This last states his fundamental belief succinctly and is accompanied by a quotation from Ficino:

> And though our mere-learn'd men, & Modern wise,
> Taste not poore Poesies Ingenuities,
> Being crusted with their couetous Leprosies,
> But hold her paines worse then the spiders worke,
> And lighter then the shadowe of a Corke:
> Yet th'ancient learn'd, heat with celestiall fire,
> Affirmes her flames so sacred and entire
> That, not without Gods greatest grace she can
> Fall in the wid'st Capacitie of Man.
> *Vt non sine Maximo fauore Dei comparari queat. Pla. in Ione.*

These lines, addressed to Somerset, not only give the basis of Chapman's poetic creed, but also express another conviction which in his view was an important corollary to it: the conviction that men of his own day were unfit by their light-mindedness as well as by their education to understand

I

the true poetry of any age. This is a conviction which he states with almost tiresome iteration. The picture which he presents of his literate contemporaries is that of the satirist of every day and age: they are impudent and upstart worldlings whom the artist would do best to despise but who nevertheless seem to be worth his continued invective. It is interesting that he considers their ignorance to be the result of a spiritual incapacity rather than a failure on their part to read what is available—interesting particularly because of Chapman's reputation as a scholar, which might lead one to suppose that he would recommend study as a cure for their blindness. He admits that many of them have read, and read widely, but protests that the only effect of their reading has been to turn them into "mere-learn'd men," or—to quote the title of one of his paraphrases of Epictetus—"imaginaries in knowledge." Learning is not an illuminating process unless it has made a man "noble," for true nobility is of the spirit and is rarely attained; it is the nearest man can reach to the divine and hence Chapman calls it "sacred."[1] His doctrine and his invective have a logic of their own: if poetry is a medium for the expression of divinity and the poets are inspired by a supernatural *inflatus*, then the reader must experience a similar inspiration to be able to understand the import of the poetry. The experience of the reader need not be so immediate an inspiration as that of the poet, but the reader must have attained a sacred nobility of spirit, an inner light, which will illuminate what he reads and reveal to him its truth.

The hackneyed image of the "inner light" is not idly used in describing Chapman's theory of poetry and of the proper relationship between poet and reader. It derives straight from the requisites which he sets down for a reader and the accounts of his personal experience as a poet. The preface to Matthew Roydon affixed to *Ouids Banquet of Sence* in 1595 is the most quoted of Chapman's critical prefaces. In this epistle he identifies Roydon, a mathematician, with the kind of reader who he feels is best suited to penetrate to the truth of poetry because of his own inner light. After explaining the kind of obscurity in his poetry for which he feels no need to apologize, he concludes by resting his hopes on those readers who are themselves sufficiently illuminated to be able to understand what his poetry is saying:

I know, that empty, and dark spirits, wil complaine of palpable night: but those that before-hand haue a radiant, and light-bearing intellect, will say they can passe through *Corynnas* Garden without the helpe of a Lanterne.

These "light-bearing intellects," so named early in Chapman's career, are, therefore, his ideal readers.

Fourteen years later, in *The Teares of Peace* (1609), Chapman describes

[1] See Epistle to Roydon, *Ouids Banquet of Sence.*

in the same image what was undoubtedly his highest moment of inspiration as a poet. It would not be unduly evangelical to term this moment a "call." *The Teares of Peace* is an allegorical poem in which the vision is revealed to the poet by no less an agent than the spirit of Homer. At the beginning of the poem Chapman describes himself as having sought out a solitude in which to deliberate on what it is in man that leads him into warlike activities instead of the search for "inner peace." While he was thus deliberating,

> . . . sodainely, a comfortable light
> Brake through the shade; and, after it, the sight
> Of a most graue and goodly person shinde,
> With eys turnd vpwards, & was outward, blind;
> But inward, past and future things he sawe;
> And was to both, and present times, their lawe.
> His sacred bosome was so full of fire
> That t'was transparent; and made him expire
> His breath in flames, that did instruct (me thought)
> And (as my soule were then at full) they wrought.

This "goodly person" whose spirit is so aflame was Homer, who—it is explained a few lines later—had appeared to Chapman once before "on the hill Next *Hitchins* left hand" and inspired him with the "true sense" to "english" his poetry. These two appearances of Homer are Chapman's chief claim to genuine poetic inspiration; Homer's spirit is a-glow with light from which Chapman himself, at least temporarily, takes fire. Hence it is clear that he sees the gift of poetic imagination in terms of light and claims that the reader of his poetry must share something of the same light in order to be able to understand it.

Though Chapman makes this claim to have been inspired in his translation of Homer, on other occasions he lays little claim to the title of a true poet in the high sense in which he conceives it. Following the current fashion of prefatory self-depreciation, he describes his *Eugenia* as "these weake watches;" he tells Sir Edward Phillips that he would not have dared to submit his little volume of paraphrases, *Petrarchs Psalms . . . With other Philosophical Poems*, to Prince Henry; he characterizes his *Epicede* on the death of the prince as "this vnprofitable signe of my loue;" and in his preface to the Justification of *Andromeda Liberata* he refers to the *Andromeda* as the "poor mite" which he offered up to the Somerset nuptials. Once, in 1598, when addressing the fragment of the *Iliad*, *Achilles Shield*, to Harriot the astronomer, he frankly and rather pathetically explains that he has not enough true fire to be a lucid poet, and wishes that he could partake of what must have seemed to him the genuine clairvoyance of his scientific friend. This passage, which has often been quoted, is Chapman's most personal and perspicacious analysis of his poetic gifts.

> Rich mine of knowledge, ô that my straunge muse
> Without this bodies nourishment could vse
> Her zealous faculties, onely t'aspire
> Instructiue light from your whole Sphere of fire:
> But woe is me, what zeale or power soeuer
> My free soule hath, my body will be neuer
> Able t'attend: neuer shal I enioy,
> Th'end of my happles birth: neuer employ
> That smotherd feruour that in lothed embers
> Lyes swept from light, and no cleare howre remembers.
> O had your perfect eye Organs to pierce
> Into that Chaos whence this stiffled verse
> By violence breakes, where Gloweworme like doth shine
> In nights of sorrow this hid soule of mine,
> And how her genuine formes struggle for birth,
> Vnder the clawes of this fowle Panther earth;
> Then vnder all those formes you should discerne
> My loue to you in my desire to learne.

This avowal leads to the surmise that Chapman meant what he said when, however fashionably, he referred disparagingly to his own volumes of verse: always excepting the translations of Homer in which the spirit of the Greek poet had fanned the translator's "lothed embers" into a bright flame by direct inspiration. The slim quartos of Chapman's non-dramatic verse indicate that he was seldom writing what he most wanted to write, but rather attempting in this hasty and somewhat diffident way to keep alive his title of poet while he gave his main imaginative attention to his work as a tragic dramatist and as the interpreter of Homer. He doubtless hoped that some day his inspiration would burn bright enough for him to be able to write a great poem of his own; unfortunately it never did. There are splendid passages, genuinely emotional with the energy of a sustained figurative language, but there is no single poem that would have been likely to satisfy him more than us. Taken volume by volume, his poems can best be described as occasional.

Chapman's first extant published work is *The Shadow of Night* (1594), a title devised to cover the two allegorical poems: *Hymnus in Noctem* and *Hymnus in Cynthiam*. These two poems, which celebrate the intellect and lament worldly injustice and are probably the most difficult of Chapman's poems to interpret, appear at first sight to be the least timely. Perhaps it was because of their obscurity and consequent failure to win an audience that Chapman never again resorted to any quite such diffi-

cult use of allegory, though his *Eugenia* is a close rival to them. It may
be, however, that even these two poems were written in response to a
current interest. This has been the assumption in recent years of scholars
who argue that Chapman was one of a group of men, including Raleigh
and Marlowe, who were interested in pushing science and philosophy
beyond the bounds of contemporary beliefs and decorum, a group bound
together by a common curiosity, suspected of being atheists and hence
condemned by most of their fellows, but mocked by Shakespeare in his
Love's Labour's Lost as "the school of night."[2] To those who feel assured
that such an ascertainable group existed, Chapman's *Shadow of Night*
appears to be its poetic manifesto and hence a timely document.

In many ways the volume of poems which Chapman produced in the
following year, 1595, is a *volte-face*. Undoubtedly he had been reading the
manuscript of Marlowe's *Hero and Leander*, perhaps already with the
idea of completing it; and it may have been the stimulation of this poem
and Shakespeare's *Venus and Adonis* which turned him temporarily
away from the celebration of the contemplative faculties to try his hand
at a poem which he must have hoped would be popular: *Ouids Banquet of
Sence*. This poem, which is accompanied by many complimentary verses,
is an erotic poem founded in the Neoplatonic doctrine of love. It cele-
brates Ovid's feast of all the senses when he comes upon his Corinna
bathing. The doctrine is that man must partake to the full of sensual con-
tentment in order that his mind may be excited to a higher love. Chap-
man always keeps the lesson in the reader's mind as he describes the
various stimulations to his senses that Ovid receives. The double effort
to compose a poem in the current amatory mode and still be true to his
belief in the higher purposes of sensual gratification gives a disparate
effect. The difficulty with which Chapman must have felt himself faced
is most evident in the abrupt conclusion to the poem, where, after decid-
ing to write the *Art of Love*, Ovid is interrupted in his approach to Corrina
and Chapman suggests, without describing, the completed feast of love.
The poem proves that Chapman was susceptible to at least an academic
interest in bodily sensation, but it was an interest which never served
him successfully to artistic ends. Readers of the completed *Hero and
Leander* (1598) have always received a severe jolt when moving on to
the third sestiad, where Chapman's contribution begins.[3] Because it is
his duty to see the poem through to its tragic conclusion, he gives warn-
ing at the outset that "More harsh (at lest more hard) more graue and
hie" his subject runs, and he is happier in describing Hero's fears and

---

[2] See particularly M. C. Bradbrook, *The School of Night* (1936), and F. A. Yates, *A
Study of Love's Labour's Lost* (1936).

[3] The first two sestiads are reprinted here from the *Works* of Marlowe, edited by Dr.
Tucker Brooke, by permission of The Clarendon Press, Oxford.

fits of conscience than in the moments when he tries to recapture something of the erotic passion of Marlowe's verse. The continuation of *Hero and Leander* is better poetry than *Ouids Banquet* largely because Chapman was better fitted to describe the tragic end of love than he was to describe its happy consummation.

The sequence of ten linked sonnets, *A Coronet for his Mistresse Philosophie*, which follows the title-piece in *Ouids Banquet of Sence*, was written for its day only in that it is an experiment in the use of the sonnet form. Otherwise, it serves somewhat to balance the erotic *Banquet*, for it announces Chapman's condemnation of "Muses that sing loues sensuall Emperie." But the balance is uneven; *Ouids Banquet* not only gives a catching title to the volume, but it is a much longer poem and more in vogue. The *Coronet* is chiefly interesting for its last sonnet, which states Chapman's faith in the power of tragic drama as a vehicle for philosophic truth. He wishes that the stage of his own day would assume the same ethical importance that it had in ancient Athens and Rome: a significant forecast of the stoical doctrines which were to be revealed in his own tragedies.

The *Euthymiae Raptus, or the Teares of Peace*, Chapman's next poem apart from the completion of *Hero and Leander* and the beginning of his *Iliads*, appears fifteen years later than *Ouids Banquet*, in 1609. This poem is linked to contemporary events by its introductory reference to the twelve-year truce in the War in the Netherlands, which had been effected the spring of that year, partly through the mediation of King James. However, inasmuch as the main structure of the allegory shows Peace lamenting the funeral of Love, it is likely that the poem was written before the truce. It may properly be called an anti-war poem and is written to deplore the Continental war, of which the English were getting very weary. Characteristically, Chapman attacks war by trying to analyze its source. He concludes that war is possible among men only when Love is dead, and hence he shows Peace despairing at the death of Love and telling the poet, as interlocutor, the cause of her despair. She concludes that man's chief defect, the reason why Love could not keep alive in this world, is man's lack of learning. When man is no longer capable of original thought, as he must be if he is genuinely learned, he can never arrive at a knowledge of God;[4] and in a world where man no longer knows God, Love dies and Peace is overcome by War.

Except for the *Hymn to Our Sauiour on the Crosse*, the poems in Chapman's next collection of published verse hardly deserve to be classed

---

[4] See Janet Spens' analysis of the poem in "Chapman's Ethical Thought," *Essays and Studies of the English Association*, Vol. XI.

with his original poetry. The volume, an octavo extant so far as is known only in a single copy at the Bodleian Library, is entitled *Petrarchs Seuen Penitentiall Psalms, Paraphrastically Translated. With other Philosophical Poems, and a Hymne to Christ vpon the Crosse, . . . 1612.* The "other philosophical poems" in the volume are, for the most part, free translations of some Virgilian epigrams and of passages from Epictetus. The Virgilian epigrams are so titled; the paraphrases in verse from Epictetus might at first glance pass as his own. The original Hymn, a heavily annotated poem, is Chapman's most sustained expression of his own religious faith. The poem rests its chief argument in the relation of body and soul: the necessary subordination of substance to form if man is to lead a godly life. The poet finds himself able to say that he has succeeded, through his faith in Christ and the Scriptures, in freeing himself from the bondage of the body, and hopes that through his contemplation of Christ he will be able to continue free from bodily and worldly importunities. The poem, Platonic in its philosophical doctrine, and stoical in its ethical teaching, concludes with the motto, Ανέχου, καὶ Απέχου "Bear and forebear," the saying that was Epictetus' rule of life.

In the same year that *Petrarchs Psalms* appeared, the patron of Chapman's Homer, Prince Henry, died. His death opens the saddest chapter in the life of Chapman, whose biography might well be entitled "A Poet in Search of a Patron." He had never succeeded in gaining permanent patronage until he had won the prince's command to finish his Homer, and it can easily be supposed that no one of the many poets who mourned Henry's death was more sincere in his grief than Chapman. To him, as to all of them, the loss seemed a real one for English letters; in the gifted and attractive young man they had all seen a new Maecenas who was very much needed at the time. A simple and rather moving testimony of Chapman's genuine feeling on the occasion is his failure to seek out any other prospective noble patron to whom to dedicate his *Epicede;* on the contrary, he addressed the poem to a Mr. Henry Jones, evidently a personal friend, whose identity is yet unknown. The first half of the *Epicede* describes the Prince and his last illness with the kind of detail that Chapman as a minor servitor in his court might be expected to know. This poem is the only source known to give a name to the disease from which the prince suffered: the Hungarian fever. After three hundred and fifty lines of genuine feeling and accurate description, Chapman's muse failed him and he went on to double the length of his poem by paraphrasing a Latin elegy by Angelus Politianus written on the death of a fifteen-year-old girl. In the latter half of the poem there are a few digressions which bring the matter back to the talk of the time, but on the whole the second half appears as an attempt to swell the poem in length so that it would more nearly fit in importance the catastrophe which occasioned it.

Chapman's next volume of verse, 1614, was also a funeral poem: *Eugenia*, written on the death of William, Lord Russell. This is the only known record of Chapman's attachment to the Russell family, and the poem, lacking the imprint of a publisher, probably appeared in a very small issue. Only two copies of it are known today: that in the library of the Duke of Bedford, and Drummond of Hawthornden's copy at the University of Edinburgh. The poem is elaborately constructed. It is composed of three "vigils," each with its own "inductio," and a peroration. The third vigil takes the form of a hymn. In the dedicatory epistle to Francis Russell, son of the deceased, Chapman promises to write further vigils or "watches" on every anniversary of Lord Russell's death; but so far as we know this promise was not fulfilled. Very likely this is no great loss, for Chapman is not in his most felicitous vein in writing elegies, and the *Eugenia* is even stiffer than the *Epicede*, probably because he had less feeling about the death that occasioned it. The mechanism of the poem is contrived by having a mythologized Eugenia, the figure of true nobility, fall into a trance on the occasion of Russell's death; whereupon Fame and Religion address her. Thus in the course of the poem we learn of Russell's virtues as a military man and governor and of his great piety. Chapman leans on the text of the funeral sermon preached by the Reverend William Walker for the circumstances of the Lord's death and the state of his soul on departing this life, and he draws on Plutarch's *Moralia*, one of his best-loved books, for much of the moral adornment of the poem.

In the same year as the *Eugenia* (1614), Chapman published another long poem, the *Andromeda Liberata*, in celebration of the famous marriage of the Earl of Somerset with Lady Frances Howard, former wife of the Earl of Essex. Somerset had succeeded Prince Henry as patron to Chapman's translation of Homer, and the successful outcome of the litigation over the annulment of the Howard-Essex marriage evidently pleased instead of shocked him. The poem is cast in the form of an allegory which describes Perseus' release of the innocent Andromeda who has been chained to a rock. It was wrongly interpreted, according to Chapman, by that same vulgar herd of men who do not know how to read, and the rock was taken—quite literally and naturally—to be Essex. Consequently, Chapman felt called upon shortly afterwards to write a *Justification* of the poem consisting of a prose tract followed by a dialogue between the poet and Rumor (or false report).

The misinterpretation of *Andromeda* was the most serious difficulty into which Chapman's love of obscure "misteries and allegoricall fictions of Poesie" had plunged him. On all other occasions he could merely blame his stupid public for not having the "light-bearing intellect" to understand what he had written; but this time, although he still imputes the fault to the vulgar herd, he cannot afford to remain aloof from their misinterpretations and has to go out of his way to explain. Otherwise he would have run the risk, not only of offending Essex and his faction, but also of alienating Somerset, who might not have welcomed this unsolicited addition to his notoriety. Therefore the prose *Justification of ... Andromeda* is initially devoted to an explanation of the functions of allegory. Chapman explains that allegorical fictions have ever been held

in high Reuerence and Aucthority; as supposed to conceale within the vtter barke (as their Eternities approue) some sappe of hidden Truth: As either some dimme and obscure prints of diuinity and the sacred history; Or the grounds of naturall, or rules of morall Philosophie, for the recommending of some vertue, or curing some vice in generall ... Or else recording some memorable Examples for the vse of policie and state: euer (I say) enclosing within the Rinde some fruit of knowledge howsoeuer darkened; and (by reason of the obscurity) of ambiguous and different construction.

In the *Andromeda Liberata* the general rule of moral philosophy as well as of state which Chapman "darkened" by the shadows of his allegory was, following Ficino's argument in his commentary on the *Symposium*, that, if a marriage between great personages prove unfruitful, they be allowed to dissolve that marriage easily in the hope of producing children through a different union. The discussion of allegory in this *Justification* seems to explain his interest in the device and its particular appropriateness to his own conception of the functions of poetry. Going back to the statements quoted from the dedication to *Ouids Banquet* and the poem *To Harriots*, it becomes obvious that the "palpable night" which "empty, and dark spirits" found in his poetry, and which he himself once acknowledged as lying too thick over the "smothered feruour" of his poetic inspiration, was a night very adaptable to the form of allegory. By resorting to fable as the vehicle of expressing his philosophic convictions he had at hand what might almost be called a natural excuse for shrouding his teachings. Allegory implies at the outset an indirection of statement, and—since indirection was Chapman's natural mode of approach—it afforded him what was probably his favorite form. The obscurity of his verse is due fundamentally to other causes than his use of allegory. In fact, had he confined himself to established fables in all his allegorical poems, as he did in the *Andromeda*, the form would probably have been a help rather than a hindrance to the understanding

of his poetry; when the fable itself confuses, it is because Chapman has
invented it instead of following some classic story.

The *Andromeda* and its subsequent *Justification* conform to the state-
ment originally made: that most of Chapman's poetry is occasional in
nature. All the verses that remain to be considered are also occasional,
in the strictest sense. There is the *Pro Vere*, written to urge the govern-
ment to send supplies to Vere and his men who, in 1622, were being be-
sieged at Manheim. It is a short poem of persuasion, comparable to *De
Guiana*, the poem written in 1596 for inclusion in Lawrence Keymis'
Relation of the second Voyage to Guiana, in which Chapman is urging
Queen Elizabeth to take over Guiana. *De Guiana*, however, is a far more
successful poem and has been generally admired for its heroic quality.
There is the unpublished poem on Ben Jonson, an exasperated answer
to Jonson's *Execration upon Vulcan*. With the exception of *Pro Vere*,
which was printed as a separate pamphlet, and the unfinished and un-
published *Inuectiue against Ben Jonson*, all the rest of Chapman's oc-
casional pieces are collected in this volume under the heading, "Compli-
mentary and Occasional Verses," and are arranged chronologically ac-
cording to the dates of the various books in which they appeared. They
indicate a wide range of interest: from his espousal of Raleigh's cause
in wanting to appropriate Guiana to his approval of the music written
for the virginals by Byrd, Bull, and Gibbons. The specific occasions for
all these verses are described in the notes to this volume.

In addition to the verses written to celebrate some occasion or to
praise another author's book, there are included in the present edition
of Chapman's poetry all the verse prefaces and dedications which he
wrote to accompany the various editions of his translation of Homer.
These poems deserve to stand with the *corpus* of his original poetry as
sincere utterances on the subject that was nearest his heart: Homer and
his own responsibility to Homer as one who had been directly inspired
to translate him. The foolish prose *Justification of Nero* has been in-
cluded to make accessible as much of Chapman as is practicable. The
funeral oration of Nero on burying one of Poppaea's hairs would hardly
fit into an edition of Chapman's translations, and certainly not into an
edition of his plays!

The question of what constitutes Chapman's "original poetry" will
probably remain something of a puzzle to any editor of Chapman. Ever
since Franck L. Schoell, in his *Etudes sur l'Humanisme Continental en
Angelterre à la Fin de la Renaissance*, amassed such a weight of evidence
for Chapman's reliance in his poems as well as his plays on Comes'
Mythologiae (largely derived from Ovid), Ficino's Plato, Xylander's
Plutarch, and Wolfius' Epictetus, the mystery of many of Chapman's

strangest utterances has been resolved. Large portions of most of his poems are directly derived from whatever books he was most interested in at the time of writing. Tracing the sources of his imagery is an occupation as fascinating as getting the clues to T. S. Eliot's *Waste Land;* and, like Eliot, Chapman often helps us out with glosses that refer to the source from which he derived his analogy, his illustration, or his figure of speech. No wonder—with this similarity of approach—that Eliot, despite his vastly different talents, is so felicitous in phrasing critical remarks about Chapman. Eliot himself probably knows the experience of having his mode of feeling altered by his reading, and—in a quick definition of metaphysical poetry—explains the one quality in Chapman's poetry which is closest to that of much of the best poetry of our own day: "In Chapman especially there is a direct sensuous apprehension of thought, or a recreation of thought into feeling, which is exactly what we find in Donne." Several scholars have recently allied Chapman with Donne and the other metaphysical poets, and properly so. His way of transferring elaborately his reading or his own speculative thinking into an image so definitely allies him with that school, that it is strange that Samuel Johnson did not classify him with Donne, Crashaw, and the others. The likelihood is, however, that the only poem of Chapman which Johnson knew is the "epic song" in blank verse, *De Guiana,* and this poem he attributes to Raleigh.

Chapman's effort to recreate his thought into feeling is largely responsible for the extraordinary difficulty which the unenlightened reader of his poetry today feels in common with Chapman's despised contemporaries. Primarily, he would not have been interested in clarifying his manner of expression because of his unalterable theory that poetry must to some extent be "dark" in order that it may be understood only by the right people. Since he held to this belief that it took a special endowment on the part of the reader to penetrate the mysteries of verse, he wilfully endeavored to say what he had to say in such a way that his poetry would be understood only by the elect. "Obscuritie in affection of words, & indigested concets, is pedanticall and childish; but where it shroudeth it selfe in the hart of his subiect, vtterd with fitnes of figure, and expressiue Epethites; with that darknes wil J still labour to be shaddowed." This is his creed stated in the preface to *Ouids Banquet,* and he is faithful to it. It may fairly be said that wherever in Chapman's poetry a conceit strikes the reader at first glance as "indigest," it will, on further examination, be discovered rather to be a method of approach to the central subject. Chapman's speculative thinking is as complex as his allegorical or figurative, and when the two are mated, a shroud of darkness indeed envelopes his expression. Take two characteristic passages from early and late in his poetic career, and note the concentration necessary to grasp the thought.

> And what makes men without the parts of men,
> Or in their manhoods, lesse then childeren,
> But manlesse natures? all this world was namde
> A world of him for whom it first was framde,
> (Who (like a tender Cheurill,) shruncke with fire
> Of base ambition, and of selfe-desire,
> His armes into his shoulders crept for feare
> Bountie should vse them, and fierce rape forbeare,
> His legges into his greedie belly runne,
> The charge of hospitalitie to shunne)
> In him the world is to a lump reuerst,
> That shruncke from forme, that was by forme disperst,
> And nought in more then thanklesse auarice,
> Not rendring vertue her deserued price.
>
> *Hymnus in Noctem*, 91–104

This passage illustrates his use of a difficult simile to vivify one of his favorite doctrines: that man is losing his essential nature, or manliness, by departing from the original "forme" in which he was cast. Instead of helping the thought, the image is so difficult to grasp that it entirely distracts our attention from the main statement. The later passage is chosen as illustrative of Chapman's philosophical verse when he is relying entirely on his reading (here, on Ficino's commentary to the *Symposium*) and does not even make the added effort to elucidate his point by the use of imagery.

> And since not in himselfe, his minde hath Act
> (The mindes act chiefly being of thought compact),
> Who workes not in himselfe, himselfe not is:
> For, these two are in man ioynt properties,
> To worke, and Be; for *Being* can be neuer,
> But *Operation* is combined euer.
> Nor *Operation*, *Being* doth exceed,
> Nor workes man where he is not: still his deed
> His being, consorting, no true Louers minde
> He in himselfe can therefore euer finde
> Since in himselfe it workes not, if he giues
> Being from himselfe, not in himselfe he liues,
> And he that liues not, dead is; Truth then said
> That whosoeuer is in loue, is dead.
>
> *Andromeda Liberata*, 405–418

Chapman's favorite epithet "indigest" may well be applied to such passages as these in which the tangled thought is all too well expressed by the awkward phrasing.

Swinburne, in analyzing the quality of Chapman's obscurity, did a signal service to the description of poetic obscurity wherever it is found. He defined obscurity as "the natural product of turbid forces and confused ideas; of a feeble and clouded or of a vigorous but unfixed and chaotic intellect." Although Chapman's intellect was of the latter sort, his seemingly irrelevant conceits are created not so much for arbitrary pleasure of creating them and puzzling the public as to delay the moment of making a decisive statement. His images serve as qualifications of his idea and he had the kind of mind which is impeded rather than aided by qualifications. It is the familiar kind of subtlety that turns inward upon itself, not the rare subtlety that advances thought. It is characteristic of this kind of thinker that when he strikes an *impasse*, he breaks off and utters a "wise saying" (in Chapman's verse often in the form of a gnomic couplet) that is likely to be platitudinous.

The worst complications of Chapman's style occur in his religious and philosophical poetry, whether he is approaching his subject directly, as in the *Hymn to Our Sauiour on the Cross*, or through allegory, as in *The Shadow of Night* or *The Teares of Peace*. It should be added that there is one mode of composition and one subject in which he makes himself crystal clear. The mode is satiric verse and the subject is false learning; on no ground did he feel himself so sure.

Chapman was intolerant of academic degrees, intolerant of critics who made a pretense to scholarship, intolerant of the "general reader" who presumed in his own light-witted way to pass judgment on every literary piece that came along. He was afraid of criticism and always tried to bark first and bark loudest in the hope of frightening it off. He thought himself a scholar, but—considering the rudimentary lapses he is constantly guilty of in his treatment of the ancient tongues, and the severe judgment he passes on those who attempted to pass a scholarly judgment on his Homer—I am inclined to think he was almost entirely self-taught. His friend Jonson found that he did not even understand fully the precepts of Horace,[5] and I can only suppose this to have been the reason why Chapman turned so bitterly against him.

Save for the one well composed poem addressed *To Yong Imaginaries in Knowledge* and the description of "intellectiue men" in *The Teares of Peace*, most of Chapman's ardent declarations on the subject of false learning are appended to the various editions of his Homer. In this work,

[5] See Percy Simpson, *TLS*, March 3, 1932, p. 155.

because of mystic inspiration, he could rise up and most surely proclaim his own superiority. Had not Homer appeared to him in a vision, his bosom full of fire, to tell him that he, of all moderns, was the only one suited to penetrate and interpret the mysteries of his divine poetry? The epistles dedicatory to the different editions of the *Iliads*, the *Odysseys*, and the *Hymns* are probably the best, if not the most interesting, verses that Chapman ever wrote. Take, for instance, the concluding passage of the epistle "To the Reader," prefixed to the *Iliads*, which voices Chapman's familiar cry against the worldlings who are too ignorant to understand the sacredness of poesy:

> So men, beastly giuen,
> The manly soules voice (sacred Poesie,
> Whose Hymnes the Angels euer sing in heauen)
> Contemne, and heare not; but when brutish noises
> (For Gaine, Lust, Honour, in litigious Prose)
> Are bellow'd-out, and cracke the barbarous voices
> Of Turkish Stentors: O! ye leane to those,
> Like itching Horse to blockes or high May-poles,
> And breake nought but the wind of wealth, wealth, All
> In all your documents; your Asinine soules
> (Proud of their burthens) feele not how they gall.
> But as an Asse, that in a field of weeds
> Affects a thistle and falles fiercely to it,
> That pricks and gals him, yet he feeds and bleeds,
> Forbeares a while, and licks, but cannot woo it
> To leaue the sharpnes; when (to wreake his smart)
> He beates it with his foote, then backward kickes,
> Because the Thistle gald his forward part,
> Nor leaues till all be eate, for all the prickes;
> Then falles to others with as hote a strife,
> And in that honourable warre doth waste
> The tall heate of his stomacke and his life:
> So, in this world of weeds, you worldlings taste
> Your most-lou'd dainties with such warre, buy peace,
> Hunger for torments, vertue kicke for vice,
> Cares, for your states, do with your states increase;
> And though ye dreame ye feast in Paradise,
> Yet Reasons Day-light shewes ye at your meate,
> Asses at Thistles, bleeding as ye eate.

Here every word hits the mark; there is no obscurity, and the long simile perfectly illustrates the content. Take from the same epistle, too, his lines on the advantage of English monosyllables for the purpose of rhyme:

Our Monosyllables so kindly fall
And meete, opposde in rime, as they did kisse;
French and Italian, most immetricall,
Their many syllables, in harsh Collision,
Fall as they brake their necks; their bastard Rimes,
Saluting as they iustl'd in transition,
And set our teeth on edge, nor tunes, nor times
Kept in their falles.

Note how he suits the action to the word, the word to the action, with a dexterity that reminds one of Pope's in the *Essay on Criticism*.

On observing how clearly Chapman's critical convictions can be expressed in neat satiric verses, one is tempted to believe that he would have been a happier poet had he lived a century later. As it is, he can be taken as rather perfectly representative of his time: a true Englishman of the late renaissance. In doctrine, Chapman is a humanist, primarily interested in man and right conduct, who believes the good life to be the great prerequisite for art and who relies on classic, or neo-classic, doctrines for moral aid; in wit, he is a poet of the seventeenth-century metaphysical school, who naturally delights in expressing his convictions through devious figures of speech.

These, then, are a very few of the observations that come to mind after trying to reproduce Chapman's poetry in a form which should as closely as possible approximate the way in which he wanted it to stand. Always it is to be remembered that had there been any such demand for his poetry as to send it into second editions, he would doubtless have made many corrections and improvements; witness the careful work he did in revising certain books of the *Iliads* when his translation came out in instalments. He was not a careful craftsman in the first place, but popularity and some degree of worldly success would have inspired him to take more care. Impulsive, sanguine, irascible, he let things loose to the public just as they teemed from his energetic but somewhat disorganized brain.

Above all, anxious as he was to publish and to justify himself constantly by saying how much more intelligent he was than his contemporaries, he did not hold his poetry in an ultimately high regard. He believed fully in the high mission of poetry, he believed in the divine madness of its conception, as explained by Plato, but he was much too close to the great verse of Homer, even seen darkly through the glass of a line-by-line Latin version, not to realize that his own speculative poems fell far short of his own great standard for poetry. All he could do, or was even interested in doing, was to dignify them by shadowing them with similes and allusions which led to obscurity. Thus, of course, his very fidelity to his notion of "high poetry" worked together with his confused mode of philosophical speculation to limit his reading public *in perpetuo*. He thought of himself, and rightly, as the translator of Homer, not as a great poet in his own right; and the most simple, as well as the most moving line of poetry he ever wrote was the first line of his farewell to Homer in his epilogue to the *Hymns:*

The work that I was born to do is done.

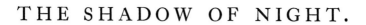

THE SHADOW OF NIGHT.

TO MY DEARE AND
MOST WORTHY FRIEND
MASTER MATHEW ROYDON.

IT IS an exceeding rapture of delight in the deepe search of knowledge, (none knoweth better then thy selfe sweet *Mathew*) that maketh men manfully indure th'extremes incident to that *Herculean* labour: from flints must the *Gorgonean* fount be smitten. Men must be shod by *Mercurie*, girt with *Saturnes* Adamantine sword, take the shield from Pallas, the helme from *Pluto*, and haue the eyes of *Graea* (as *Hesiodus armes Perseus* against *Medusa*) before they can cut of the viperous head of benumming ignorance, or subdue

10 their monstrous affections to most beautifull iudgement.

How then may a man stay his maruailing to see passion-driuen men, reading but to curtoll a tedious houre, and altogether hidebownd with affection to great mens fancies, take vpon them as killing censures as if they were iudgements Butchers, or as if the life of truth lay tottering in their verdits.

Now what a supererogation in wit this is, to thinke skil so mightilie pierst with their loues, that she should prostitutely shew them her secrets, when she will scarcely be lookt vpon by others but with inuocation, fasting, watching; yea not

20 without hauing drops of their soules like an heauenly familiar. Why then should our *Intonsi Catones* with their profit-rauisht grauitie esteeme her true fauours such questionlesse vanities, as with what part soeuer thereof they seeme to be something delighted, they queimishlie commende it for a pretie toy.

v Good Lord how serious and eternall are their Idolatrous platts for riches! no maruaile sure they here do so much good with them. And heauen no doubt will grouill on the earth (as they do) to imbrace them. But I stay this spleene when I remember my good *Mat.* how ioyfully oftentimes you reported vnto me,

30 that most ingenious *Darbie*, deepe searching *Northumberland*, and skill-imbracing *heire of Hunsdon* had most profitably entertained learning in themselues, to the vitall warmth of freezing science, & to the admirable luster of their true Nobili-tie, whose high deseruing vertues may cause me hereafter strike that fire out of darknesse, which the brightest Day shall enuie for beautie. I should write more, but my hasting out of towne taketh me from the paper, so preferring thy allowance in this poore and strange trifle, to the passport of a whole Cittie of others, I rest as resolute as *Seneca*, satisfying

40 my selfe if but a few, if one, or if none like it.

By the true admirour of thy vertues
and perfectly vowed friend.
G. Chapman.

G REAT Goddesse to whose throne in[1] Cynthian fires,
     This earthlie Alter endlesse fumes exspires,
Therefore, in fumes of sighes and fires of griefe,
To fearefull chances thou sendst bold reliefe,
Happie, thrise happie, Type, and[2] nurse of death,   5
Who breathlesse, feedes on nothing but our breath,
In whom must vertue and her issue liue,
Or dye for euer; now let humor giue
Seas to mine eyes, that I may quicklie weepe
The shipwracke of the world: or let soft sleepe   10
(Binding my sences) lose my working soule,
That in her highest pitch, she may controule
The court of skill, compact of misterie,
Wanting but franchisement[3] and memorie
To reach all secrets: then in blissfull trance,   15
Raise her (deare Night) to that perseuerance,
That in my torture, she all earths may sing,
And force to tremble in her trumpeting
Heauens christall[4] temples: in her powrs implant
Skill of my griefs, and she can nothing want.   20
    Then like fierce bolts, well rammd with heate & cold
In Ioues Artillerie; my words vnfold,
To breake the labyrinth of euerie eare,   *v*
And make ech frighted soule come forth and heare,
Let them breake harts, as well as yeelding ayre,   25
That all mens bosoms (pierst with no affaires,
But gaine of riches) may be lanced wide,
And with the threates of vertue terrified.
    Sorrowes deare soueraigne, and the queene of rest,
That when vnlightsome, vast, and indigest   30
The formelesse matter of this world did lye,
Fildst euery place with thy Diuinitie,
Why did thy absolute and endlesse sway,
Licence heauens torch, the scepter of the Day,
Distinguisht intercession to thy throne,   35
That long before, all matchlesse rulde alone?
Why letst thou order, orderlesse disperse,
The fighting parents of this vniuerse?
When earth, the ayre, and sea, in fire remaind,
When fire, the sea, and earth, the ayre containd,   40
When ayre, the earth, and fire, the sea enclosde
When sea, fire, ayre, in earth were indisposde,
Nothing, as now, remainde so out of kinde,

All things in grosse, were finer than refinde,
45 Substance was sound within, and had no being,
Now forme giues being; all our essence seeming,
Chaos had soule without a bodie then,
Now bodies liue without the soules of men,
Lumps being digested; monsters, in our pride.
50   And as a wealthie fount, that hils did hide,
Let forth by labor of industrious hands,
Powres out her treasure through the fruitefull strands,
Seemely diuided to a hunderd streames,
Whose bewties shed such profitable beames,
55 And make such Orphean Musicke in their courses,
A₄ᴿ That Cities follow their enchanting forces,
Who running farre, at length ech powres her hart
Into the bosome of the gulfie desart,
As much confounded there, and indigest,
60 As in the chaos of the hills comprest:
So all things now (extract out of the prime)
Are turnd to chaos, and confound the time.
     A stepdame Night of minde about vs clings,
Who broodes beneath her hell obscuring wings,
65 Worlds of confusion, where the soule defamde,
The bodie had bene better neuer framde,
Beneath thy soft, and peace-full couert then,
(Most sacred mother both of Gods and men)
Treasures vnknowne, and more vnprisde did dwell;
70 But in the blind borne shadow of this hell,
This horrid stepdame, blindnesse of the minde,
Nought worth the sight, no sight, but worse then blind,
A Gorgon that with brasse, and snakie brows,
(Most harlot-like) her naked secrets shows:
75 For in th'expansure, and distinct attire,
Of light, and darcknesse, of the sea, and fire,
Of ayre, and earth, and all, all these create,
First set and rulde, in most harmonious state,
Disiunction showes, in all things now amisse,
80 By that first order, what confusion is:
Religious curb, that manadgd men in bounds,
Of publique wellfare; lothing priuate grounds,
(Now cast away, by selfe-lou's paramores)
All are transformd to Calydonian bores,
85 That kill our bleeding vines, displow our fields,
Rend groues in peeces; all things nature yeelds
v Supplanting: tumbling vp in hills of dearth,
The fruitefull disposition of the earth,
Ruine creates men: all to slaughter bent,

Like enuie, fed with others famishment.   90
  And what makes men without the parts of men,
Or in their manhoods, lesse then childeren,
But manlesse natures? all this world was namde
A world of him, for whom it first was framde,
(Who (like a tender Cheurill,) shruncke with fire   95
Of base ambition, and of selfe-desire,
His armes into his shoulders crept for feare
Bountie should vse them; and fierce rape forbeare,
His legges into his greedie belly runne,
The charge of hospitalitie to shunne)   100
In him the world is to a lump reuerst,
That shruncke from forme, that was by forme disperst,
And in nought more then thanklesse auarice,
Not rendring vertue her deserued price.
Kinde Amalthaea was transferd by Ioue,   105
Into his sparckling pauement, for her loue,
Though but a Goate, and giuing him her milke,
Basenesse is flintie; gentrie softe as silke,
In heauens she liues, and rules a liuing signe
In humane bodies: yet not so diuine,   110
That she can worke her kindnesse in our harts.
  The sencelesse Argiue ship, for her deserts,
Bearing to Colchos, and for bringing backe,
The hardie Argonauts, secure of wracke,
The fautor and the God of gratitude,   115
Would not from number of the starres exclude.
A thousand such examples could I cite,
To damne stone-pesants, that like Typhons fight
Against their Maker, and contend to be   [B₁ᴿ]
Of kings, the abiect slaues of drudgerie: 120
Proud of that thraldome: loue the kindest lest,
And hate, not to be hated of the best.
  If then we frame mans figure by his mind,
And that at first, his fashion was assignd,
Erection in such God-like excellence   125
For his soules sake, and her intelligence:
She so degenerate, and growne deprest,
Content to share affections with a beast,
The shape wherewith he should be now indude,
Must beare no signe of mans similitude.   130
Therefore* Promethean Poets with the coles

* He cals them Promethean Poets in this high conceipt, by a figuratiue
comparison betwixt them, that as Pro. with fire fetcht from heauen, made
men: so Poets with the fire of their soules are sayd to create those Harpies,
and Centaures, and thereof he cals their soules Geniale.

Of their most geniale, more-then-humane soules
In liuing verse, created men like these,
With shapes of Centaurs, Harpies, Lapithes,
135 That they in prime of erudition,
When almost sauage vulgar men were growne,
Seeing them selues in those Pierean founts,
Might mend their mindes, asham'd of such accounts.
So when ye heare, the* sweetest Muses sonne,
140 With heauenly rapture of his Musicke, wonne
Rockes, forrests, floods, and winds to leaue their course
In his attendance: it bewrayes the force
His wisedome had, to draw men growne so rude
To ciuill loue of Art, and Fortitude.
145 And not for teaching others[5] insolence,
Had he his date-exceeding excellence
With soueraigne Poets, but for use applyed,
And in his proper actes exemplified;
And that in calming the infernall kinde,
150 To wit, the perturbations of his minde,
v And bringing his Eurydice from hell,
(Which Iustice signifies) is proued well.
But if in rights obseruance any man
Looke backe, with boldnesse lesse then Orphean,
155 Soone falls he to the hell from whence he rose:
The fiction then would temprature dispose,
In all the tender motiues of the minde,
To make man worthie his hel-danting kinde.
The golden chaine of Homers high deuice
160 Ambition is, or cursed auarice,
Which all Gods haling being tyed to Ioue,
Him from his setled height could neuer moue:
Intending this, that though that powrefull chaine
Of most Herculean vigor to constraine
165 Men from true vertue, or their pristine states
Attempt a man that manlesse changes hates,
And is enobled with a deathlesse loue
Of things eternall, dignified aboue:
Nothing shall stirre him from adorning still
170 This shape with vertue, and his powre with will.
    But as rude painters that contend to show
Beasts, foules or fish, all artlesse to bestow
On euery side his natiue counterfet,
Aboue his head, his name had neede to set:
175 So men that will be men, in more then face,
(As in their foreheads) should in actions place

* Calliope
is cald the
sweetest
Muse, her
name being
by significa-
tion, Cantus
suauitas, vel
modulatio.

139 n. Muse] Muses   Cantus] Cautus

More perfect characters, to proue they be
No mockers of their first nobilitie:
Else may they easly passe for beasts or foules:
Soules praise our shapes, and not our shapes our soules.   180
   And as when Chloris paints th'ennamild meads,
A flocke of shepherds to the bagpipe treads
Rude rurall dances with their countrey loues:
Some a farre off obseruing their remoues,   B_{ij}^R
Turnes, and returnes, quicke footing, sodaine stands,   185
Reelings aside, od actions with their hands;
Now backe, now forwards, now lockt arme in arme,
Now hearing musicke, thinke it is a charme,
That like loose froes at Bacchanalean feasts,
Makes them seeme franticke in their barraine iestes;   190
And being clusterd in a shapelesse croude,
With much lesse admiration are allowd.
So our first excellence, so much abusd,
And we (without the harmonie was vsd,
When Saturnes golden scepter stroke the strings   195
Of Ciuill gouernement) make all our doings
Sauour of rudenesse, and obscuritie,
And in our formes shew more deformitie,
Then if we still were wrapt, and smoothered
In that confusion, out of which we fled.   200
   And as when hosts of starres attend thy flight,
(Day of deepe students, most contentfull night)
The morning (mounted on the Muses[6] stead)
Vshers the sonne from[7] Vulcans golden bed,
And then from forth their sundrie roofes of rest,   205
All sorts of men, to sorted taskes addrest,
Spreade this inferiour element: and yeeld
Labour his due: the souldier to the field,
States-men to counsell, Iudges to their pleas,
Merchants to commerce, mariners to seas: 210
All beasts, and birds, the groues and forrests range,
To fill all corners of this round Exchange,
Till thou (deare Night, ô goddesse of most worth)
Letst thy sweet seas of golden humor forth
And Eagle-like dost with thy starrie wings,   215 *v*
[8]Beate in the foules, and beasts to Somnus lodgings,
And haughtie Day to the infernall deepe,
Proclaiming scilence, studie, ease, and sleepe.
All things before thy forces put in rout,
Retiring where the morning fir'd them out.   220
   So to the chaos of our first descent,
(All dayes of honor, and of vertue spent)

We basely make retrait, and are no lesse
Then huge impolisht heapes of filthinesse.
225 Mens faces glitter, and their hearts are blacke,
But thou (great Mistresse of heauens gloomie racke)
Art blacke in face, and glitterst in thy heart.
There is thy glorie, riches, force, and Art;
Opposed earth, beates blacke and blewe thy face,
230 And often doth thy heart it selfe deface,
For spite that to thy vertue-famed traine,
All the choise worthies that did euer raigne
In eldest age, were still preferd by Ioue,
Esteeming that due honor to his loue.
235 There shine they: not to sea-men guides alone,
But sacred presidents to euerie one.
There fixt for euer, where the Day is driuen,
Almost foure hundred times a yeare from heauen.
In hell then let her sit, and neuer rise,
240 Till Morns leaue blushing at her cruelties.
    Meane while, accept, as followers of thy traine,
(Our better parts aspiring to thy raigne)
Vertues obscur'd, and banished the day,
With all the glories of this spongie sway,
245 Prisond in flesh, and that poore flesh in bands
Of stone, and steele, chiefe flowrs of vertues Garlands.
[B~iij~^R] O then most tender fortresse of our woes,
That bleeding lye in vertues ouerthroes,
Hating the whoredome of this painted light:
250 Raise thy chast daughters, ministers of right,
The dreadfull and the iust Eumenides,
And let them wreake the wrongs of our disease,
Drowning the world in bloud, and staine the skies
With their spilt soules, made drunke with tyrannies.
255 Fall Hercules from heauen in tempestes hurld,
And cleanse this beastly stable of the world:
[9]Or bend thy brasen bow against the Sunne,
As in Tartessus, when thou hadst begunne
Thy taske of oxen: heat in more extreames
260 Then thou wouldst suffer, with his enuious beames:
Now make him leaue the world to Night and dreames.
Neuer were vertues labours so enuy'd
As in this light: shoote, shoote, and stoope his pride:
Suffer no more his lustfull rayes to get
265 The Earth with issue: let him still be set
In Somnus thickets: bound about the browes,
With pitchie vapours, and with Ebone bowes.
    [10]Rich-tapird sanctuarie of the blest,

Pallace of Ruth, made all of teares, and rest,
To thy blacke shades and desolation,   270
I consecrate my life; and liuing mone,
Where furies shall for euer fighting be,
And adders hisse the world for hating me,
Foxes shall barke, and Night-rauens belch in grones,
And owles shall hollow my confusions: 275
There will I furnish vp my funerall bed,
Strewd with the bones and relickes of the dead.
Atlas shall let th'Olimpick burthen fall,
To couer my vntombed face withall.   *v*
And when as well, the matter of our kind,   280
As the materiall substance of the mind,
Shall cease their reuolutions, in abode
Of such impure and vgly period,
As the old essence, and insensiue prime:
Then shall the ruines of the fourefold time,   285
Turnd to that lumpe (as rapting Torrents rise)
For euer murmure forth my miseries.
   Ye liuing spirits then, if any liue,
Whom like extreames, do like affections giue,
Shun, shun this cruell light, and end your thrall,   290
In these soft shades of sable funerall:
From whence with ghosts, whom vengeance holds from rest,
Dog-fiends and monsters hanting the distrest,
As men whose parents tyrannie hath slaine,
Whose sisters rape, and bondage do sustaine.   295
But you that ne'er had birth, nor euer prou'd,
How deare a blessing tis to be belou'd,
Whose friends idolatrous desire of gold,
To scorne, and ruine haue your freedome sold:
Whose vertues feele all this, and shew your eyes,   300
Men made of Tartar, and of villanies:
Aspire th'extraction, and the quintessence
Of all the ioyes in earths circumference:
With ghosts, fiends, monsters: as men robd and rackt,
Murtherd in life: from shades with shadowes blackt: 305
Thunder your wrongs, your miseries and hells,
And with the dismall accents of your knells,
Reuiue the dead, and make the liuing dye
In ruth, and terror of your torturie:
Still all the powre of Art into your grones,   310
Scorning your triuiall and remissiue mones,   B(4)R
Compact of fiction, and hyperboles,
(Like wanton mourners, cloyd with too much ease)

296 ne'er] nere

Should leaue the glasses of the hearers eyes
315 Vnbroken, counting all but vanities.
But paint, or else create in serious truth,
A bodie figur'd to your vertues ruth,
That to the sence may shew what damned sinne,
For your extreames this Chaos tumbles in.
320 But wo is wretched me, without a name:
Vertue feeds scorne, and noblest honor, shame:
Pride bathes in teares of poore submission,
And makes his soule, the purple he puts on.
    Kneele then with me, fall worm-like on the ground,
325 And from th'infectious dunghill of this Round,
From mens brasse wits, and golden foolerie,
Weepe, weepe your soules, into felicitie:
Come to this house of mourning, serue the night,
To whom pale day (with whoredome soked quite)
330 Is but a drudge, selling her beauties vse
To rapes, adultries, and to all abuse.
Her labors feast imperiall Night with sports,
Where Loues are Christmast, with all pleasures sorts:
And whom her fugitiue, and far-shot rayes
335 Disioyne, and driue into ten thousand wayes,
Nights glorious mantle wraps in safe abodes,
And frees their neckes from seruile labors lodes:
Her trustie shadowes, succour men dismayd,
Whom Dayes deceiptfull malice hath betrayd:
340 From the silke vapors of her Iueryport,
Sweet Protean dreames she sends of euery sort:
Some taking formes of Princes, to perswade
v Of men deiect, we are their equals made,
Some clad in habit of deceased friends,
345 For whom we mournd, and now haue wisht amends,
And some (deare fauour) Lady-like attyrd,
With pride of Beauties full Meridian fir'd:
Who pitie our contempts, reuiue our harts:
For wisest Ladies loue the inward parts.
350   If these be dreames, euen so are all things else,
That walke this round by heauenly sentinels:
But from Nights port of horne she greets our eyes
With grauer dreames inspir'd with prophesies,
Which oft presage to vs succeeding chances,
355 We proouing that awake, they shew in trances.
If these seeme likewise vaine, or nothing are
Vaine things, or nothing come to vertues share:
For nothing more then dreames, with vs shee findes:
Then since all pleasures vanish like the windes,

And that most serious actions not respecting   360
The second light, are worth but the neglecting,
Since day, or light, in anie qualitie,
For earthly vses do but serue the eye.
And since the eyes most quicke and dangerous vse,
Enflames the heart, and learnes the soule abuse,   365
Since mournings are preferd to banquettings,
And they reach heauen, bred vnder sorrowes wings.
Since Night brings terror to our frailties still,
And shamelesse Day, doth marble vs in ill.
    All you possest with indepressed spirits,   370
Indu'd with nimble, and aspiring wits,
Come consecrate with me, to sacred Night
Your whole endeuours, and detest the light.
Sweete Peaces richest crowne is made of starres,
Most certaine guides of honord Marinars,   375 C(1)R
No pen can any thing eternall wright,
That is not steept in humor of the Night.
    Hence beasts, and birds to caues and bushes then,
And welcome Night, ye noblest heires of men,
Hence Phebus to thy glassie strumpets bed,   380
And neuer more let[11] Themis daughters spred,
Thy golden harnesse on thy rosie horse,
But in close thickets run thy oblique course.
    See now ascends, the glorious Bride of Brides,
Nuptials, and triumphs, glittring by her sides,   385
Iuno and Hymen do her traine adorne,
Ten thousand torches round about them borne:
Dumbe Silence mounted on the Cyprian starre,
With becks, rebukes the winds before his carre,
Where she aduanst; beates downe with cloudie mace,   390
The feeble light to blacke Saturnius pallace:
Behind her, with a brase[12] of siluer Hynds,
In Iuorie chariot, swifter then the winds,
Is great[13] Hyperions horned daughter drawne
Enchantresse-like, deckt in disparent lawne,   395
Circkled with charmes, and incantations,
That ride huge spirits, and outragious passions:
Musicke, and moode, she loues, but loue she hates,
(As curious Ladies do, their publique cates)
This traine, with meteors, comets, lightenings,   400
The dreadfull presence of our Empresse sings:
Which grant for euer (ô eternall Night)
Till vertue flourish in the light of light.

Explicit Hymnus.

381 Note reference supplied.   394 Is] In

Gloss.

¹ He cals these Cynthian fiers of Cynthius or the Sunne. In whose beames the fumes and vapors of the earth are exhald. The earth being as an aulter, and those fumes as sacrificing smokes, because they seeme pleasing to her in resembling her. That the earth is cald an aulter, *Aratus* in *Astronimicis* testifies in these verses:

Α'λλ' ἄρα καὶ περὶ κεῖνο θυτήριον ἀρχαίη νὺξ &c.

Nox antiqua suo curru conuoluitur Aram
Hanc circum, quae signa dedit certissima nautis
Commiserata virûm metuendos vndique casus.

In which verses the substance of the first foure verses is exprest.

² Night is cald the nurse or mother of death by *Hesiodus* in *Theogonia*, in these verses repeating her other issue:

Nox peperit fatumque malum, Parcamque nigrantem
Et mortem & somnum, diuersáque somnia: natos
Hos peperit, nulli dea nox coniuncta marito.

³ *Plato* saith *dicere* is nothing else but *reminisci.*

⁴ The heauenly abodes are often called, celestiall temples by *Homer & alijs.*

⁵ Insolence is here taken for rarenesse or vnwontednesse.

⁶ *Lycophron* in *Alexandra*, affirmes the morning vseth to ride vpon *Pegasus* in his verses:

Aurora montem Phagium aduoluerat
Velocis altum nuper alis Pegasi.

⁷ Vulcan is said by *Natalis Comes* in his *Mythologie*, to haue made a golden bed for the Sunne, wherein he swum sleeping till the morning.

⁸ *Quae lucem pellis sub terras: Orpheus.*

⁹ Here he alludes to the fiction of *Hercules*, that in his labor at *Tartessus* fetching away the oxen, being (more then he liked) heat with the beames of the Sunne, he bent his bow against him, &c. *Vt ait Pherecides in 3.lib. Historiarum.*

¹⁰ This *Periphrasis* of the Night he vseth, because in her the blest, (by whom he intends the vertuous) liuing obscurelie are relieued and quieted, according to those verses before of *Aratus, Commiserata virûm metuendos vndique casus.*

¹¹ *Themis* daughters are the three houres, viz. *Dice, Irene*, and *Eunomia*, begotten by Iupiter. They are said to make ready the horse & chariot of the Sun euery morning. *vt Orph.*

Et Iouis & Themidis Horae de semine natae, &c.

¹² Cynthia or the Moone, is said to be drawne by two white hindes, *vt ait Calimachus:*

Aurea nam domitrix Tityi sunt arma Diana
Cuncta tibi & zona, & fuga quae ceruicibus aurea
Ceruarum imponis currum cum ducis ad aureum.

¹³ *Hesiodus* in *Theogonia* cals her the daughter of *Hyperion*, and *Thya, in his versibus.*

CᵢⱼᴿR

Thia parit Solem magnum, Lunamqûe nitentem
Auroram quaefert lucem mortalibus almam
Coelicolisqûe Deis cunctis, Hyperionis almi
Semine concepit, namque illos Thia decora.

So is she said to weare partie-coloured garments: the rest intimates
her Magick authoritie.

FINIS.

For the rest of his owne inuention, figures and similes, touching
their aptnesse and noueltie he hath not laboured to iustifie them,
because he hopes they wil be proud enough to iustifie themselues,
and proue sufficiently authenticall to such as vnderstand them; for   *v*
the rest, God help them, I can not (do as others), make day seeme a
lighter woman then she is, by painting her.

Thy slender feete, fine slender feete that shame
Thetis sheene feete, which Poets so much fame,
   And heere my latest season I will end.

L E N V O Y.

29

Deare Mistres, if poore wishes heauen would heare,
I would not chuse the empire of the water;
   The empire of the ayre, nor of the earth,
But endlesly my course of life confining
In this fayre Zodiack for euer shining,
   And with thy beauties make me endles mirth.

30

But gracious Loue, if ielous heauen deny
My life this truely-blest varietie,
   Yet will I thee through all the world disperse,
If not in heauen, amongst those brauing fires
Yet heere thy beauties (which the world admires)
   Bright as those flames shall glister in my verse.

HYMNVS IN CYNTHIAM.

NATURES[1] bright eye-sight, and the Nights faire soule,[2]
[3]That with thy triple forehead dost controule
Earth, seas, and hell: and art in dignitie
The greatest, and swiftest Planet in the skie:
5   Peacefull, and warlike, and the[4] powre of fate,
In perfect circle of whose sacred state,
The circles of our hopes are compassed:
All wisedome, beautie, maiestie and dread,
Wrought in the speaking pourtrait of thy face:
10 Great Cynthia, rise out of thy[5] Latmian pallace,
[6]Wash thy bright bodie, in th'Atlanticke streames,
Put on those robes that are most rich in beames:
And in thy All-ill-purging puritie,
(As if the shadie[7] Cytheron did frie
15 In sightfull furie of a solemne fire)
Ascend thy chariot, and make earth admire
Thy old swift changes, made a yong fixt prime,
O let thy beautie scorch the wings of time,
That fluttering he may fall before thine eyes,
20 And beate him selfe to death before he rise.
And as heauens[8] Geniall parts were cut away
By Saturnes hands, with adamantine[9] Harpey,
Onely to shew, that since it was composd
Of vniuersall matter: it enclosd
25 No powre to procreate another heauen:
C$_{iij}$ᴿ So since that adamantine powre is giuen
To thy chast hands, to cut of all desire
Of fleshly sports, and quench to Cupids fire:
Let it approue: no change shall take thee hence,
30 Nor thy throne beare another inference.
For if the enuious forehead of the earth
Lowre on thy age, and claime thee as her birth:
Tapers, nor torches, nor the forrests burning,
Soule-winging musicke, nor teare-stilling mourning,
35 (Vsd of old Romanes and rude Macedons
In thy most sad, and blacke discessions)
We know can nothing further thy recall,
When Nights darke robes (whose obiects blind vs all)
Shall celebrate thy changes funerall.
40 But as in that thrise dreadfull foughten field
Of ruthlesse Cannae, when sweet Rule did yeeld,
Her beauties strongest proofs, and hugest loue:

41 Cannae] Cannas

When men as many as the lamps aboue,
Armd Earth in steele, and made her like the skies,
That two Auroraes did in one day rise;   45
Then with the terror of the trumpets call,
The battels ioynd as if the world did fall:
Continewd long in life-disdaining fight,
Ioues thundring Eagles featherd like the night,
Hou'ring aboue them with indifferent wings,   50
Till Bloods sterne daughter, cruell[10] Tyche flings
The chiefe of one side, to the blushing ground,
And then his men (whom griefs, and feares confound)
Turnd all their cheerfull hopes to grimme despaire,
Some casting of their soules into the aire,   55
Some taken prisners, some extreamely maimd,
And all (as men accurst) on fate exclaimd;
So (gracious Cynthia) in that sable day,   v
When interposed earth takes thee away,
(Our sacred chiefe and soueraigne generall,)   60
As chrimsine a retrait, and steepe a fall
We feare to suffer from this peace, and height,
Whose thancklesse sweet now cloies vs with receipt.
    [11]The Romanes set sweet Musicke to her charmes,
To raise thy stoopings, with her ayrie armes: 65
Vsde loud resoundings with auspicious brasse:
Held torches vp to heauen, and flaming glasse,
Made a whole forrest but a burning eye,
T'admire thy mournefull partings with the skye.
The Macedonians were so stricken dead,   70
With skillesse horrour of thy changes dread:
They wanted harts, to lift vp sounds, or fires,
Or eyes to heauen; but vsd their funerall tyres,
Trembld, and wept; assur'd some mischiefs furie
Would follow that afflicting Augurie.   75
    Nor shall our wisedomes be more arrogant
(O sacred Cynthia) but beleeue thy want
Hath cause to make vs now as much affraid:
Nor shall Democrates who first is said,
To reade in natures browes, thy chaunges cause,   80
Perswade our sorrowes to a vaine applause.
    Times motion, being like the reeling sunnes,
Or as the sea reciprocallie runnes,
Hath brought vs now to their opinions;
As in our garments, ancient fashions   85
Are newlie worne; and as sweet poesie
Will not be clad in her supremacie
With those straunge garments (Romes Hexameters)

47 ioynd] ioyned

As she is English: but in right prefers
C(4)R 90 Our natiue robes, put on with skilfull hands
(English heroicks) to those antick garlands,
Accounting it no meede but mockerie,
When her steepe browes alreadie prop the skie,
To put on startups, and yet let it fall.
95 No otherwise (O Queene celestiall)
Can we beleeue Ephesias state wilbe
But spoile with forreine grace, and change with thee
[12]The purenesse of thy neuer-tainted life,
Scorning the subiect title of a wife,
100 Thy bodie not composed in thy birth,
Of such condensed matter as the earth,
Thy shunning faithlesse mens societie,
Betaking thee to hounds, and Archerie
To deserts, and inaccessible hills,
105 Abhorring pleasure in earths common ills,
Commit most willing rapes on all our harts:
And make vs tremble, lest thy soueraigne parts
(The whole preseruers of our happinesse)
Should yeeld to change, Eclips, or heauinesse.
110 And as thy changes happen by the site,
Neare, or farre distance, of thy* fathers light,
Who (set in absolute remotion) reaues
Thy face of light, and thee all darkned leaues:
So for thy absence, to the shade of death
115 Our soules fly mourning, wingd with our breath.
    Then set thy Christall, and Imperiall throne,
(Girt in thy chast, and neuer-loosing[13] zone)
Gainst Europs Sunne directly opposit,
And giue him darknesse, that doth threat thy light.
120   O how accurst are they thy fauour scorne?[14]
Diseases pine their flockes, tares spoile their corne:
v Old men are blind of issue, and young wiues
Bring forth abortiue frute, that neuer thriues.
    But then how blest are they thy fauour graces,
125 Peace in their hearts, and youth raignes in their faces:
Health strengths their bodies, to subdue the seas,
And dare the Sunne, like Thebane Hercules
To calme the furies, and to quench the fire:
As at thy altars, in thy Persicke Empire,
130 [15]Thy holy women walkt with naked soles
Harmelesse, and confident, on burning coles:
The vertue-temperd mind, euer preserues,
Oyles, and expulsatorie Balme that serues

Eurip. in Phenisses, cals her the daughter not sister of the Sunne, O clarissimi filia Solis Luna aurei circuli lumen: &c.

120 Note reference supplied.

To quench lusts fire, in all things it annoints,
And steeles our feet to march on needles points: 135
And mongst her armes, hath armour to repell
The canon, and the firie darts of hell:
She is the great enchantresse that commands
Spirits of euery region, seas, and lands,
Round heauen it selfe, and all his seuen-fold heights,   140
Are bound to serue the strength of her conceipts:
A perfect type of thy Almightie state,
That holdst the thread, and rul'st the sword of fate.
    Then you that exercise the virgine Court
Of peacefull Thespya, my muse consort,   145
Making her drunken with[16] Gorgonean Dews,
And therewith, all your Extasies infuse,
That she may reach the top-lesse starrie brows
Of steepe Olympus, crownd with freshest bows
Of Daphnean Laurell, and the praises sing   150
Of mightie Cynthia: truely figuring,
(As she is Heccate) her soueraigne kinde,
And in her force, the forces of the mind:
An argument to rauish and refine   D(1)R
An earthly soule, and make it meere diuine.   155
Sing then withall, her Pallace brightnesse bright,
The dasle-sunne perfections of her light,
Circkling her face with glories, sing the walkes,
Where in her heauenly Magicke mood she stalkes,
Her arbours, thickets, and her wondrous game,   160
(A huntresse, being neuer matcht in fame).
Presume not then ye flesh confounded soules,
That cannot beare the full Castalian bowles,
Which seuer mounting spirits from the sences,
To looke in this deepe fount for thy pretenses: 165
The iuice more cleare then day, yet shadows night,
Where humor challengeth no drop of right:
But iudgement shall displaie, to purest eyes
With ease, the bowells of these misteries.
    See then this Planet of our liues discended   170
To rich[17] Ortigia, gloriouslie attended,
Not with her fiftie Ocean Nimphs: nor yet
Hir twentie forresters: but doth beget
By powrefull charmes, delightsome seruitors
Of flowrs, and shadows, mists, and meteors: 175
Her rare Elisian Pallace she did build
With studied wishes, which sweet hope did guild
With sunnie foyle, that lasted but a day:

161 huntresse] huntesse

For night must needs, importune her away.
180   The shapes of euerie wholesome flowre and tree
She gaue those types of hir felicitie.
And Forme her selfe, she mightilie coniurd
Their priselesse values, might not be obscurd,
With disposition baser then diuine,
185   But make that blissfull court of hers to shine
v   With all accomplishment of Architect,
That not the eye of Phebus could detect.
Forme then, twixt two superior pillers framd
This tender building, Pax Imperij nam'd,
190   Which cast a shadow, like a Pyramis
Whose basis, in the plaine or back part is
Of that queint worke: the top so high extended,
That it the region of the Moone transcended:
Without, within it, euerie corner fild
195   By bewtious Forme, as her great mistresse wild.
[18]Here as she sits, the thunder-louing Ioue
In honors past all others showes his loue,
Proclaiming her in compleat Emperie,
Of what soeuer the Olympick skie
200   With tender circumuecture doth embrace,
The chiefest Planet, that doth heauen enchace:
Deare Goddesse, prompt, benigne, and bounteous,
That heares all prayers, from the least of vs
Large riches giues, since she is largely giuen,
205   And all that spring from seede of earth and heauen
She doth commaund: and rules the fates of all,
Old Hesiod sings her thus celestiall:
And now to take the pleasures of the day,
Because her night starre soone will call away,
210   She frames of matter intimate before,
(To wit, a bright, and daseling meteor)
A goodlie Nimph, whose bewtie, bewtie staines
Heau'ns with her iewells; giues all the raines
Oi wished pleasance; frames her golden wings,
215   But them she bindes vp close with purple strings,
Because she now will haue her run alone,
And bid the base, to all affection.
D~ij~^R   And Euthimya is her sacred name,
Since she the cares and toyles of earth must tame:
220   Then straight the flowrs, the shadowes and the mists,
(Fit matter for most pliant humorists)
She hunters makes: and of that substance hounds
Whose mouths deafe heauen, & furrow earth with wounds.

195 Forme] forme

And maruaile not a Nimphe so rich in grace
To hounds rude pursutes should be giuen in chase: 225
For she could turne her selfe to euerie shape
Of swiftest beasts, and at her pleasure scape.
Wealth faunes on fooles; vertues are meate for vices,
Wisedome conformes her selfe to all earths guises,
Good gifts are often giuen to men past good,   230
And Noblesse stoops sometimes beneath his blood.
   The hounds that she created, vast, and fleete
Were grimme Melampus, with th'Ethiops feete,
White Leucon; all eating Pamphagus,
Sharp-sighted Dorceus, wild Oribasus   235
Storme-breathing Lelaps, and the sauage Theron,
Wingd-footed Pterelas, and Hinde-like Ladon,
Greedie Harpyia, and the painted Stycté,
Fierce Tigris, and the thicket-searcher Agre,
The blacke Melaneus, and the bristled Lachne,   240
Leane-lustfull Cyprius, and big chested Alce.
These and such other now the forrest rang'd,
And Euthimya to a Panther changd,
Holds them sweet chase; their mouths they freely spend,
As if the earth in sunder they would rend.   245
Which change of Musick likt the Goddesse so,
That she before her formost Nimphe would go,
And not a huntsman there was eagrer seene
In that sports loue, (yet all were wondrous keene)
Then was their swift, and windie-footed queene.   250 v
And now this spotted game did thicket take,
Where not a hound could hungred passage make:
Such proofe the couert was, all armd in thorne,
With which in their attempts, the doggs were torne,
And fell to howling in their happinesse: 255
As when a flocke of schoole-boys, whom their mistresse
(Held closelie to their bookes) gets leaue to sport,
And then like toyle-freed deare, in headlong sort
With shouts, and shrieks, they hurrey from the schoole.
Some strow the woods, some swimme the siluer poole: 260
All as they list to seuerall pastimes fall,
To feede their famisht wantonnesse with all.
When strait, within the woods some wolfe or beare,
The heedlesse lyms of one doth peecemeale teare,
Affrighteth other, sends some bleeding backe,   265
And some in greedie whirle pitts suffer wracke:
So did the bristled couert check with wounds
The licorous hast of these game greedie hounds.

239 Tigris] Trigris   241 Alce] Aloe   253 couert] couret

In this vast thicket, (whose descriptions task
270 The penns of furies, and of feends would aske:
So more then humane thoughted horrible)
The soules of such as liu'd implausible,
In happie Empire of this Goddesse glories,
And scornd to crowne hir Phanes with sacrifice
275 And ceaselesse walke; exspiring fearefull grones,
Curses, and threats for their confusions.
Her darts, and arrowes, some of them had slaine,
Others hir doggs eate, painting hir disdaine,
After she had transformd them into beasts:
280 Others her monsters carried to their nests,
Rent them in peeces, and their spirits sent
D$_{iij}$^{R} To this blind shade, to waile their banishment.
The huntsmen hearing (since they could not heare)
Their hounds at fault; in eager chase drew neare,
285 Mounted on Lyons, Vnicorns, and Bores,
And saw their hounds lye licking of their sores,
Some yerning at the shroud, as if they chid
Her stinging toungs, that did their chase forbid:
By which they knew the game was that way gone.
290 Then ech man forst the beast he rode vpon,
T'assault the thicket; whose repulsiue thorns
So gald the Lyons, Bores, and Vnicorns,
Dragons, and wolues; that halfe their courages
Were spent in rores, and sounds of heauines:
295 Yet being the Princeliest, and hardiest beasts,
That gaue chiefe fame to those Ortygian forests,
And all their riders furious of their sport,
A fresh assault they gaue, in desperate sort:
And with their falchions made their wayes in wounds:
300 The thicket opend, and let in the hounds.
But from her bosome cast prodigious cries,
Wrapt in her Stigian fumes of miseries:
Which yet the breaths of those couragious steads
Did still drinke vp, and cleerd their ventrous heads:
305 As when the fierie coursers of the sunne,
Vp to the pallace of the morning runne,
And from their nosthrills blow the spitefull day:
So yet those foggie vapors, made them way.
But preasing further, saw such cursed sights,
310 Such Ætnas filld with strange tormented sprites,
That now the vaprous obiect of the eye
Out-pierst the intellect in facultie.
Basenesse was Nobler then Nobilitie:
v For ruth (first shaken from the braine of Loue,

And loue the soule of vertue) now did moue,   315
Not in their soules (spheres meane enough for such)
But in their eyes: and thence did conscience touch
Their harts with pitie: where her proper throne,
Is in the minde, and there should first haue shone:
Eyes should guide bodies, and our soules our eyes,   320
But now the world consistes on contraries:
So sence brought terror; where the mindes presight
Had saft that feare, and done but pittie right,
But seruile feare, now forgd a wood of darts
Within their eyes, and cast them through their harts.   325
Then turnd they bridle, then halfe slaine with feare,
Ech did the other backwardes ouerbeare,
As when th'Italian Duke, a troupe of horse
Sent out in hast against some English force,
From statelie sited sconce-torne Nimigan,   330
Vnder whose walles the[19] Wall most Cynthian,
Stretcheth her siluer limms loded with wealth,
Hearing our horse were marching downe by stealth.
(Who looking for them) warres quicke Artizan
Fame-thriuing Vere, that in those Countries wan   335
More fame then guerdon; ambuscadoes laide
Of certaine foote, and made full well appaide
The hopefull enemie, in sending those
The long-expected subiects of their blowes
To moue their charge; which strait they giue amaine,   340
When we retiring to our strength againe,
The foe pursewes assured of our liues,
And vs within our ambuscado driues,
Who straight with thunder of the drums and shot,
Tempest their wraths on them that wist it not.   345
Then (turning headlong) some escapt vs so,   D(4)R
Some left to ransome, some to ouerthrow,
In such confusion did this troupe retire,
And thought them cursed in that games desire:
Out flew the houndes, that there could nothing finde,   350
Of the slye Panther, that did beard the winde,
Running into it full, to clog the chase,
And tire her followers with too much solace.
And but the superficies of the shade,
Did onely sprinckle with the sent she made,   355
As when the sunne beames on high billowes fall,
And make their shadowes dance vpon a wall,
That is the subiect of his faire reflectings:
Or else; as when a man in summer euenings,

331 19 Wall] 10 wall

360 Something before sunneset, when shadows bee
Rackt with his stooping, to the highest degree,
His shadow clymes the trees, and skales a hill,
While he goes on the beaten passage still,
So sleightlie toucht the Panther with her sent,
365 This irksome couert, and away she went,
Downe to a fruitfull Iland sited by,
Full of all wealth, delight, and Emperie,
Euer with child of curious Architect,
Yet still deliuerd: pau'd with Dames select,
370 On whom rich feete, in fowlest bootes might treade,
And neuer fowle them: for kinde Cupid spreade,
Such perfect colours, on their pleasing faces,
That their reflects clad fowlest weeds with graces,
Bewtie strikes fancie blind; pyed show deceau's vs,
375 Sweet banquets tempt our healths, when temper leaues vs
Inchastitie, is euer prostitute,
Whose trees we loth, when we haue pluckt their fruite.
  v   Hither this Panther fled, now turnd a Bore
More huge then that th'Ætolians plagud so sore,
380 And led the chase through noblest mansions,
Gardens and groues, exempt from Parragons,
In all things ruinous, and slaughtersome,
As was that scourge to the Ætolian kingdome:
After as if a whirlewind draue them one,
385 Full crie, and close, as if they all were one
The hounds pursew, and fright the earth with sound,
Making her tremble; as when windes are bound
In her cold bosome, fighting for euent:
With whose fierce Ague all the world is rent.
390   But dayes arme (tir'd to hold her torch to them)
Now let it fall within the Ocean streame,
The Goddesse blew retraite, and with her blast,
Her morns creation did like vapours wast:
The windes made wing, into the vpper light,
395 And blew abroad the sparckles of the night.
Then (swift as thought) the bright Titanides
Guide and great soueraigne of the marble seas,
With milkwhite Heiffers, mounts into her Sphere,
And leaues vs miserable creatures here.
400   Thus nights, faire dayes: thus griefs do ioyes supplant:
Thus glories grauen in steele and Adamant
Neuer supposd to wast, but grow by wasting,
(Like snow in riuers falne) consume by lasting.
O then thou great[20] Elixer of all treasures,
405 From whom we multiplie our world of pleasures,

Discend againe, ah neuer leaue the earth,
But[21] as thy plenteous humors gaue vs birth,
So let them drowne the world in night, and death
Before this ayre, leaue breaking with thy breath.
Come Goddesse come,[22] the double fatherd sonne,   410 E(1)R
Shall dare no more amongst thy traine to runne,
Nor with poluted handes to touch thy vaile:
His death was darted from the Scorpions taile,
For which her forme to endlesse memorie,
With other lamps, doth lend the heauens an eye,   415
And he that shewd such great presumption,
Is hidden now, beneath a little stone.
    If proude[23] Alpheus offer force againe,
Because he could not once thy loue obtaine,
Thou and thy Nimphs shall stop his mouth with mire,   420
And mocke the fondling, for his mad aspire.
Thy glorious temple[24] (great Lucifera)
That was the studie of all Asia,
Two hunderd twentie sommers to erect,
Built by Chersiphrone thy Architect,   425
In which two hundred, twentie columns stood,
Built by two hunderd twentie kings of blood,
Of curious bewtie, and admired height,
Pictures and statues, of as praysefull sleight,
Conuenient for so chast a Goddesse phane,   430
(Burnt by Herostratus) shall now againe,
Be reexstruct, and this Ephesiabe
Thy countries happie name, come here with thee,
As it was there so shall it now be framde,
And thy faire virgine-chamber euer namde: 435
And as in reconstruction of it there,
There Ladies did no more their iewells weare,
But franckly contribute them all to raise,
A worke of such a chast Religious prayse:
So will our Ladies; for in them it lyes,   440
To spare so much as would that worke suffice:
Our Dames well set their iewels in their myndes,   v
In-sight illustrates; outward brauerie blindes,
The minde hath in her selfe a Deitie,
And in the stretching circle of her eye   445
All things are compast, all things present still,
Will framd to powre, doth make vs what we will,
But keep your iewels, make ye brauer yet,
Elisian Ladies; and (in riches set,
Vpon your foreheads), let vs see your harts: 450
Build Cynthiaes Temple in your vertuous parts,

Let euerie iewell be a vertues glasse:
And no Herostratus shall euer race,
Those holy monuments: but pillers stand,
455 Where euery Grace, and Muse shall hang her garland.
　　The minde in that we like, rules euery limme,
Giues hands to bodies, makes them make them trimme:
Why then in that the body doth dislike,
Should not[25] his sword as great a vennie strike?
460 The bit, and spurre that Monarcke ruleth still,
To further good things, and to curb the ill,
He is the Ganemede, the birde of Ioue,
Rapt to his soueraignes bosome for his loue,
His bewtie was it, not the bodies pride,
465 That made him great Aquarius stellified:
And that minde most is bewtifull and hye,
And nearest comes to a Diuinitie,
That furthest is from spot of earths delight,
Pleasures that lose their substance with their sight,
470 Such one, Saturnius rauisheth to loue,
And fills the cup of all content to Ioue.
　　If wisedome be the mindes true bewtie then,
And that such bewtie shines in vertuous men,
EijR If those sweet Ganemedes shall onely finde,

* 　 * 　 * 　 *

475 Loue of Olimpius, are those wizerds wise,
That nought but gold, and his dyiections prise?
This bewtie hath a fire vpon her brow,
That dimmes the Sunne of base desires in you,
And as the cloudie bosome of the tree,
480 Whose branches will not let the summer see,
His solemne shadows; but do entertaine,
Eternall winter: so thy sacred traine,
Thrise mightie Cynthia should be frozen dead,
To all the lawlesse flames of Cupids Godhead.
485 To this end let thy beames diuinities,
For euer shine vpon their sparckling eyes,
And be as quench to those pestiferent fires,
That through their eyes, impoison their desires,
Thou neuer yet wouldst stoope to base assault,
490 Therefore those Poetes did most highly fault,
That fainde thee[26] fiftie children by Endimion,
And they that write thou hadst but three alone,
Thou neuer any hadst, but didst affect,
Endimion for his studious intellect.
495 Thy soule-chast kisses were for vertues sake,

463 to his] to her

And since his eyes were euermore awake,
To search for knowledge of thy excellence,
And all Astrologie: no negligence,
Or female softnesse fede his learned trance,
Nor was thy vaile once toucht with dalliance,   500
Wise Poetes faine thy Godhead properlie,
The thresholds of mens doores did fortifie,
And therefore built they thankefull alters there,
Seruing thy powre, in most religious feare.
Deare precident for vs to imitate,   505
Whose dores thou guardst against Imperious fate,   v
Keeping our peacefull households safe from sack,
And free'st our ships, when others suffer wracke.
²⁷Thy virgin chamber then that sacred is,
No more let hold, an idle Salmacis,   510
Nor let more sleights, Cydippe iniurie:
Nor let blacke Ioue possest in Scicilie,
Rauish more maids, but maids subdue his might,
With well-steeld lances of thy watchfull sight.
²⁸Then in thy cleare, and Isie Pentacle,   515
Now execute a Magicke miracle:
Slip euerie sort of poisond herbes, and plants,
And bring thy rabid mastiffs to these hants.
Looke with thy fierce aspect, be terror-strong;
Assume thy wondrous shape of halfe a furlong: 520
Put on thy feete of Serpents, viperous hayres,
And act the fearefulst part of thy affaires:
Conuert the violent courses of thy floods,
Remoue whole fields of corne, and hugest woods,
Cast hills into the sea, and make the starrs,.   525
Drop out of heauen, and lose thy Mariners.
    So shall the wonders of thy power be seene,
    And thou for euer liue the Planets Queene.
                                            Explicit Hymnus.
                                            omnis vt vmbra.

¹ He giues her that *Periphrasis, viz.* Natures bright eye sight, be-
cause that by her store of humors, issue is giuen to all birth: and
thereof is she called *Lucina,* and *Ilythyia, quia praeest parturientibus
cum inuocaretur,* and giues them helpe: which *Orpheus* in a Hymne of
her prayse expresseth, and cals her besides *Prothyrea, vt sequitur.*
    Κλῦθί μοι, ὦ πολύσεμνε θεα, &c.
    Audi me veneranda Dea, cui nomina multa:
    Praegnantum adiutrix, parientum dulce leuamen,

499 softnesse] softnsse

Sola puellarum seruatrix, solaque prudens:
Auxilium velox teneris Prothyraea puellis.

And a little after, he shewes her plainlie to be Diana, *Ilythyia*, and
Prothyraea, in these verses:

Solam animi requiem te clamant parturientes.
Sola potes diros partus placare labores
Diana, Ilythyia grauis, sumus & Prothyraea.

² He cals her the soule of the Night, since she is the purest part of
her according to common conceipt.

³ *Orpheus* in these verses, in *Argonauticis* saith she is three headed,
as she is *Heccate*, *Luna*, and *Diana*, *vt sequitur.*

Cumque illis Hecate properans horrenda cucurrit,
Cui trinum caput est, genuit quam Tartarus olim.

The rest aboue will not be denied.

⁴ That she is cald the powre of fate, read *Hesiodus* in *Theogonia*
when he giues her more then this commendation, in these verses:

Iupiter ingentes illi largitur honores,
Muneraque imperium terraeque marisque profundi:
Cunctorumque simul, quae coelum amplectitur altum,
Admittitque preces facilis Dea, prompta, benigna:
Diuitias praebet, quid ei concessa potestas,
Imperat haec cunctis, qui sunt è semine nati:
Et terrae & Coeli, cunctorum fata gubernat.

⁵ In *Latmos* she is supposed to sleepe with *Endymion*, *vt Catullus.*

Vt triuiam furtim sub Latmia saxa relegans,
Dulcis amor Gyro deuocet Aerio.

v   ⁶ Homer with a maruailous Poeticall sweetnesse, saith she washes
her before she apparells her selfe in th'Atlantick sea. And then
shewes her apparell, as in these verses. *In Oceano Lauacri.*

Rursus Atlanteis, in lymphis membra lauata,
Vestibus induta, & nitidis Dea Luna micantes:
Curru iunxit equos celeres, quibus ardua colla.

⁷ Cytheron, as Menander saith was a most faire boy, and beloued
of Tisiphone, who since she could not obtaine his loue, she teares
from her head a Serpent, & threw it at him, which stinging him to
death, the Gods in pittie turned him to a hill of that name, first cald
Asterius, full of woods wherein all Poets haue affirmed wild beasts
liue, and vse it often to expresse their haunts, or store of woods,
whereupon he inuokes Cynthia, to rise in such brightnesse, as if it
were all on fire.

⁸ This is expounded as followeth by Gyraldus Lilius. The applica-
tion most fitly made by this author.

⁹ Harpe should be written thus, not with a y, yet here he vseth it,
lest some, not knowing what it meanes, read it for a Harp, hauing
found this grossenesse in some schollers. It was the sword Perseus
vsed to cut of Medusas head.

¹⁰ Fortune is cald *Tyche*, as witnesseth *Pausanias in Messeniacis,* who affirmes her to be one of the daughters likewise of *Oceanus,* which was playing with *Proserpine,* when *Dis* rauisht her.

> *Vna omnes vario per prata comantia flore,*
> *Candida Leucippe, Phaenoque, Electraque Ianthe.*
> *Melobosisque Tyche, Ocyrhoe praesignis ocellis.*

And *Orpheus* in a Hymne to *Fortuna,* saith she is the daughter of bloud, *vt in his, sanguine prognatam, Vi & inexpugnabile numen.*

¹¹ Plutarch writes thus of the Romanes, and Macedons, in *Paulus Æmilius.*

¹² These are commonly knowne to be the properties of Cynthia.

¹³ This Zone is said to be the girdle of Cynthia. And thereof when maids lost their maidenheads, amongst the Athenians, they vsed to put of their girdles. And after, custome made it a phrase *Zonam*   E⁽₄₎ᴿ *soluere,* to lose their maidenheades, *vt Apolo. lib. I.*

> *Prima soluta mihi est, postremaque Zona quid ipsa,*
> *Inuidit multos natos Lucina misellae.*

¹⁴ These are the verses of *Callimachus* translated to effect.

> *O miseri, quibus ipsa grauem tu concipis iram, &c.*

¹⁵ This Strabo testifieth *Libro duodecimo.*

¹⁶ *Pegasus* is cald *Gorgoneus;* since Poets fayne, that when *Perseus* smote of Medusas head, *Pegasus* flew from the wound: & therefore the Muses fount which he made with his hoofe, is cald *Gorgone.*

¹⁷ *Ortigia* is the countrie where she was brought vp.

¹⁸ These are the verses of *Hesiodus* before.

¹⁹ The Wall is a most excellent riuer, in the Low countries parting with another riuer, cald the Maze, neare a towne in Holland, cald Gurckham, and runnes vp to Guelderland vnder the walls of Nimigen. And these like *Similes,* in my opinion drawne from the honorable deeds of our noble countrimen, clad in comely habit of Poesie, would become a Poeme as well as further-fetcht grounds, if such as be Poets now a dayes would vse them.

²⁰ The Philosophers stone, or *Philosophica Medicina* is cald the great Elixer to which he here alludes.

²¹ This of our birth, is explaned before.

²² The double-fathered sonne is Orion, so cald since he was the sonne of Ioue and Appollo, borne of their seede enclosed in a Bulls hide, which abhorreth not from Philosophie (according to Poets intentions) that one sonne should haue two fathers: for in the generation of elements it is true, since *omnia sint in omnibus.* He offering violence, was stong of a Scorpion to death, for which: the Scorpions figure was made a signe in heauen, as Nicander in *Theriacis* affirmes.

> *Grandine signatum Titanis at inde puella,*
> *Scorpion immisit qui cuspide surgat acuta:*
> *Baeoto vt meditata necem fuit Orioni,*
> *Impuris ausus manibus quia prendere peplum:*

v

Ille Deae est talum percussit Scorpius illi,
Sub paruo lapide occultus vestigia propter.

[23] *Alpheus* taken with the loue of Cynthia, not answered with many repulses, pursued her to her companie of virgins, who mocking him, cast mire in his face, and draue him away. Some affirme him to be a flood, some the sonne of *Parthenia*, some the waggoner of Pelops, &c.

[24] *Lucifera* is her title, and *Ignifera:* giuen by *Euripides*, in *Iphigenia* in *Tauris*.

[25] The bewtie of the minde being signified in *Ganemede*, he here by *Prosopopoeia*, giues a mans shape vnto it.

[26] *Pausanias* in *Eliacis*, affirmes it: others that she had but three, *viz. Paeon*, which Homer cals the Gods Phisition, *Epeus*, and *Ætolus*, *&c*. *Cicero* saith she had none, but onely for his loue to the studie of Astrologie, gaue him chast kisses.

[27] Her temple in *Ephesus* was cald her virgin chamber.

[28] All these are proper to her as she is *Heccate*.

Explicit Coment.

FINIS.

OVIDS BANQVET OF SENCE.

A Coronet for his Mistresse *Philosophie*.

The amorous Zodiack.

The amorous contention of
Phillis and *Flora*.

TO THE TRVLIE
Learned, and my worthy Friende,
Ma. *Mathew Royden.*

SUCH is the wilfull pouertie of iudgements (sweet *Ma:*) wandring like pasportles men, in contempt of the diuine discipline of Poesie, that a man may well feare to frequent their walks: The prophane multitude I hate, & onelie conse-crate my strange Poems to these serching spirits, whom learn-ing hath made noble, and nobilitie sacred; endeuoring that materiall Oration, which you call *Schema;* varying in some rare fiction, from popular custome, euen for the pure sakes of ornament and vtilitie; This of *Euripides* exceeding sweetly
10   relishing with mee; *Lentem coquens ne quicquam olentis addito.*

But that Poesie should be as peruiall as Oratorie, and plainnes her speciall ornament, were the plaine way to bar-barisme: and to make the Asse runne proude of his eares; to take away strength from Lyons, and giue Cammels hornes.

That, *Enargia,* or cleerenes of representation, requird in absolute Poems is not the perspicuous deliuery of a lowe inuention; but high, and harty inuention exprest in most significant, and vnaffected phrase; it serues not a skilfull Painters turne, to draw the figure of a face onely to make
20   knowne who it represents; but hee must lymn, giue luster, shaddow, and heightening; which though ignorants will es-teeme spic'd, and too curious, yet such as haue the iudiciall perspectiue, will see it hath, motion, spirit and life.

There is no confection made to last, but it is admitted more cost and skill then presently to be vsed simples; and in my opinion, that which being with a little endeuour serched, ads a kinde of maiestie to Poesie; is better then that which euery Cobler may sing to his patch.

Obscuritie in affection of words, & indigested concets, is
30   pedanticall and childish; but where it shroudeth it selfe in the hart of his subiect, vtterd with fitnes of figure, and expressiue Epethites; with that darknes wil J still labour to be shad-
v   dowed: rich Minerals are digd out of the bowels of the earth, not found in the superficies and dust of it; charms made of vnlerned characters are not consecrate by the Muses which are diuine artists, but by *Euippes* daughters, that challengd them with meere nature, whose brests J doubt not had beene well worthy commendation, if their comparison had not turnd them into Pyes.

10 *olentis*] *dentis*   12 ornament] ornamrnt

Thus (not affecting glory for mine owne sleight labors,   40
but desirous others should be more worthely glorious, nor
professing sacred Poesie in any degree,) I thought good to
submit to your apt iudgment: acquainted long since with the
true habit of Poesie, and now since your labouring wits en-
deuour heauen-high thoughts of Nature, you haue actual
meanes to sound the philosophical conceits, that my new pen
so seriously courteth. I know, that empty, and dark spirits,
wil complaine of palpable night: but those that before-hand,
haue a radiant, and light-bearing intellect, will say they can
passe through *Corynnas* Garden without the helpe of a   50
Lanterne.

Your owne most worthily
and sincerely affected,
George Chapman.

41 others] other

A₃ᴿ   *Richard Stapleton* to the Author.

Phoebus hath giuen thee both his bow, and Muse;
   With one thou slayst the Artizans of thunder,
   And to thy verse dost such a sound infuse,
   That gatherd storms therewith are blowne in sunder:
The other decks her with her golden wings
   Spred beyond measure, in thy ample verse,
   Where she (as in her bowrs of Lawrell) sings
   Sweet philosophick strains that Feends might pierse,
The soule of brightnes in thy darknes shines
   Most new, and deare: vnstainde with forraine graces,
   And when aspiring sprights shall reach thy lines,
   They will not heare our trebble-termed bases.
With boldnes then thy able Poems vse
Phoebus hath giuen thee both his bow and Muse.

     Tho: Williams of the inner Temple.

Issue of *Semele* that will imbrace
   With fleshly arms the three-wingd wife of thunder:
   Let her sad ruine, such proud thoughts abase
   And view aloofe, this verse in silent wonder,
If neerer your vnhallowed eyes wil pierse,
   Then (with the Satyre) kisse this sacred fire,
   To scorch your lips, that dearely taught thereby
   Your onely soules fit obiects may aspire,
But you high spirrits in thys cloud of gold
   Inioy (like *Ioue*) this bright Saturnian Muse,
   Your eyes can well the dazeling beames behold
   This Pythian lightner freshly doth effuse
To dant the basenes of that bastard traine
Whose twise borne iudgments, formeles still remaine.

v   Another.

Vngratefull Farmers of the Muses land
   That (wanting thrift and iudgment to imploy it)
   Let it manureles and vnfenced stand,
   Till barbarous Cattell enter and destroy it:
Now the true heyre is happily found out
   Who (framing it t'inritch posterities)
   Walles it with spright-fild darknes round about,
   Grass, plants, and sowes; and makes it Paradise.
To which without the *Parcaes* golden bow,
   None can aspire but stick in errors hell;
   A garland to engird a Monarchs brow,

Stapleton to the Author, 3 verse] loose

Then take some paines to ioy so rich a Iewell
Most prize is graspt in labors hardest hand,
And idle soules can nothing rich command.

I. D. of the middle Temple.

Onely that eye which for true loue doth weepe,
   Onely that hart which tender loue doth pierse,
   May read and vnderstand this sacred vierse
For other wits too misticall and deepe:
Betweene these hallowed leaues *Cupid* dooth keepe
   The golden lesson of his second Artist,
   For loue, till now, hath still a Maister mist
Since *Ouids* eyes were closd with iron sleepe;
But now his waking soule in *Chapman* liues,
   Which showes so well the passions of his soule,
   And yet this Muse more cause of wonder giues,
   And doth more Prophet-like loues art enroule:
For Ouids soule, now growne more old and wise,
Poures foorth it selfe in deeper misteries.

Another.

A[₄]ᴿ

Since *Ouid* (loues first gentle Maister) dyed
   She hath a most notorious trueant beene,
   And hath not once in thrice fiue ages seene
That same sweete Muse that was his first sweet guide;
But since *Apollo* who was gratified
   Once with a kisse, hunting on *Cynthus* greene,
   By loues fayre Mother tender Beauties Queene,
This fauor vnto her hath not enuied,
That into whome she will, she may infuse
   For the instruction of her tender sonne,
   The gentle *Ouids* easie supple Muse,
   Which vnto thee (sweet *Chapman*) she hath doone:
Shee makes (in thee) the spirit of *Ouid* moue,
And calles thee second Maister of her loue.

Futurum inuisibile.

Ovids Banquet of
SENCE.

The Argument.

OVID, newly enamoured of *Iulia*, (daughter to *Octauius Augustus Caesar*, after by him called *Corynna*,) secretly conuaid himselfe into a Garden of the Emperors Court: in an Arbor whereof, *Corynna* was bathing; playing vpon her Lute, and singing: which *Ouid* ouer-hearing, was exceedingly pleasde with the sweetnes of her voyce, & to himselfe vttered the comfort he conceiued in his sence of Hearing.   *Auditus.*

Then the odors shee vsde in her bath, breathing a rich sauor, hee expresseth the ioy he felt in his sence of Smelling.   *Olfactus.*

Thus growing more deeplie enamoured, in great contentation with himselfe, he venters to see her in the pride of her nakednesse: which dooing by stealth, he discouered the comfort hee conceiued in Seeing, and the glorie of her beautie.   *Visus.*

Not yet satisfied, hee vseth all his Art to make knowne his being there, without her offence: or (being necessarily offended) to appease her: which done, he entreats a kisse to serue for satisfaction of his Tast, which he obtaines.   *Gustus.*

Then proceedes he to entreaty for the fift sence and there is interrupted.   *Tactus.*

NARRATIO.

The Earth, from heauenly light conceiued heat,
Which mixed all her moyst parts with her dry,
When with right beames the Sun her bosome beat,
And with fit foode her Plants did nutrifie;
    They (which to Earth, as to theyr Mother cling
In forked rootes) now sprinckled plenteously
    With her warme breath; did hasten to the spring,
Gather their proper forces, and extrude
All powre but that, with which they stood indude.

v   2

Then did *Cyrrhus* fill his eyes with fire,
Whose ardor curld the foreheads of the trees,
And made his greene-loue burne in his desire,
When youth, and ease, (Collectors of loues fees)
    Entic'd *Corynna* to a siluer spring,
Enchasing a round Bowre; which with it sees,*
    (As with a Diamant dooth an ameld Ring.)
Into which eye, most pittifully stood
Niobe, shedding teares, that were her blood.

    * *Cyrrhus* is a surname of the Sun, from a towne called *Cyrrha*, where he was honored.
    * By *Prosopopaeia*, he makes ye fountaine ye eye of the round Arbor, as a Diamant seemes to be the eye of a Ring: and therefore sayes, the Arbor sees with the Fountaine.

3

Stone *Niobe*, whose statue to this Fountaine,
In great *Augustus Caesars* grace was brought
From *Sypilus*, the steepe *Mygdonian* Mountaine:
That statue tis, still weepes for former thought,
   Into thys spring *Corynnas* bathing place;
So cunningly to optick reason wrought,
   That a farre of, it shewd a womans face,
Heauie, and weeping; but more neerely viewed,
Nor weeping, heauy, nor a woman shewed.

4

In Sommer onely wrought her exstasie;
And that her story might be still obserued,
Octauius caus'd in curious imagrie,
Her fourteene children should at large be carued,
   Theyr fourteene brests, with fourteene arrowes gored
And set by her, that for her seede so starued
   To a stone Sepulcher herselfe deplored,
In Iuory were they cut; and on each brest,
In golden Elements theyr names imprest.

5

Her sonnes were *Sypilus*, *Agenor*, *Phaedimus*,
Ismenus, *Argus*, and *Damasicthen*,
The seauenth calde like his Grandsire, *Tantalus*.
Her Daughters, were the fayre *Astiochen*,
   Chloris, *Naeera*, and *Pelopie*,
Phaeta, proud *Phthia*, and *Eugigen*,
   All these apposde to violent *Niobe*
Had lookes so deadly sad, so liuely doone,
As if Death liu'd in theyr confusion.

6

Behind theyr Mother two Pyramides
Of freckled Marble, through the Arbor viewed,
On whose sharp brows, *Sol*, and *Tytanides*
In purple and transparent glasse were hewed,
   Through which the Sun-beames on the statues staying,
Made theyr pale bosoms seeme with blood imbrewed,
   Those two sterne Plannets rigors still bewraying
To these dead forms, came liuing beauties essence
Able to make them startle with her presence.

B₂ᴿ

7

In a loose robe of Tynsell foorth she came,
Nothing but it betwixt her nakednes

And enuious light. The downward-burning flame,
Of her rich hayre did threaten new accesse,
  Of ventrous *Phaeton* to scorch the fields:
And thus to bathing came our Poets Goddesse,
  Her handmaides bearing all things pleasure yeelds
To such a seruice; Odors most delighted,
And purest linnen which her lookes had whited.

8

Then cast she off her robe, and stood vpright,
As lightning breakes out of a laboring cloude;
Or as the Morning heauen casts off the Night,
Or as that heauen cast off it selfe, and showde
  Heauens vpper light, to which the brightest day
Is but a black and melancholy shroude:
  Or as when *Venus* striu'd for soueraine sway
Of charmfull beautie, in yong Troyes desire,
So stood *Corynna* vanishing her tire.

9

A soft enflowered banck embrac'd the founte;
Of *Chloris* ensignes, an abstracted field;
Where grew Melanthy, great in Bees account,
Amareus, that precious Balme dooth yeeld,
  Enameld Pansies, vs'd at Nuptials still,
Dianas arrow, *Cupids* crimson shielde,
  Ope-morne, night-shade, and *Venus* nauill,
Solemne Violets, hanging head as shamed,
And verdant Calaminth, for odor famed.

10
v

Sacred Nepenthe, purgatiue of care,
And soueraine Rumex that doth rancor kill,
Sya, and Hyacinth, that Furies weare,
White and red Iessamines, Merry, Melliphill:
  Fayre Crowne-imperiall, Emperor of Flowers,
Immortall Amaranth, white Aphrodill,
  And cup-like Twillpants, stroude in *Bacchus* Bowres,
These cling about this Natures naked Iem,
To taste her sweetes, as Bees doe swarme on them.

11

And now shee vsde the Founte, where *Niobe*,
Toomb'd in her selfe, pourde her lost soule in teares,
Vpon the bosome of this Romaine *Phoebe;*
Who; bathd and Odord; her bright lyms she rears,

And drying her on that disparent grounde;
Her Lute she takes t'enamoure heuenly eares,
    And try if with her voyces vitall sounde,
She could warme life through those cold statues spread,
And cheere the Dame that wept when she was dead.

12

And thus she sung, all naked as she sat,
Laying the happy Lute vpon her thigh,
Not thinking any neere to wonder at
The blisse of her sweet brests diuinitie.

The Song of CORYNNA.

T'is better to contemne then loue,
And to be fayre then wise;
For soules are rulde by eyes:
And Ioues *Bird, ceaz'd by* Cypris *Doue,*
It is our grace and sport to see,
Our beauties sorcerie,
That makes (like destinie)
Men followe vs the more wee flee;
That sets wise Glosses on the foole,
And turns her cheekes to bookes,
Where wisdome sees in lookes
Derision, laughing at his schoole,
    Who (louing) proues, prophanenes, holy;
    Nature, our fate, our wisdome, folly.

13   B₃R

While this was singing, *Ouid* yong in loue
With her perfections, neuer prouing yet
How mercifull a Mistres she would proue,
Boldly embrac'd the power he could not let
    And like a fiery exhalation
Followd the sun, he wisht might neuer set;
    Trusting heerein his constellation
Rul'd by loues beames, which *Iulias* eyes erected,
Whose beauty was the star his life directed.

14

And hauing drencht his anckles in those seas,
He needes would swimme, and car'd not if he drounde:
Loues feete are in his eyes; for if he please
The depth of beauties gulfye floode to sounde,

11. 5 grounde] rounde   14. 4 floode] floodd

He goes vpon his eyes, and vp to them,
At the first steap he is; no shader grounde
   Coulde *Ouid* finde; but in loues holy streame
Was past his eyes, and now did wett his eares,
For his high Soueraignes siluer voice he heares.

15

Whereat his wit, assumed fierye wings,
Soring aboue the temper of his soule,
And he the purifying rapture sings
Of his eares sence, takes full the Thespian boule
   And it carrouseth to his Mistres health,
Whose sprightfull verdure did dull flesh controle,
   And his conceipt he crowneth with the wealth
Of all the Muses in his pleased sences,
When with the eares delight he thus commences:

16

Now Muses come, repayre your broken wings,
(Pluckt, and prophan'd by rusticke Ignorance,)
With feathers of these notes my Mistres sings;
And let quick verse hir drooping head aduance
   From dungeons of contempt to smite the starrs;
In *Iulias* tunes, led forth by furious trance
   A thousand Muses come to bid you warrs,
Diue to your Spring, and hide you from the stroke,
All Poets furies will her tunes inuoke.

v
17

Neuer was any sence so sette on fire
With an immortall ardor, as myne eares;
Her fingers to the strings doth speeche inspire
And numberd laughter; that the descant beares
   To hir sweete voice; whose species through my sence
My spirits to theyr highest function reares;
   To which imprest with ceaseles confluence
It vseth them, as propper to her powre
Marries my soule, and makes it selfe her dowre;

18

Me thinks her tunes flye guilt, like *Attick* Bees
To my eares hiues, with hony tryed to ayre;
My braine is but the combe, the wax, the lees,
My soule the Drone, that liues by their affayre.
   O so it sweets, refines, and rauisheth,

And with what sport they sting in theyr repayre:
   Rise then in swarms, and sting me thus to death
Or turne me into swounde; possesse me whole,
Soule to my life, and essence to my soule.

19

Say gentle Ayre, ô does it not thee good
Thus to be smit with her correcting voyce?
Why daunce ye not, ye daughters of the wood?
Wither for euer, if not now reioyce.
   Rise stones, and build a Cittie with her notes,
And notes infuse with your most Cynthian noyse,
   To all the Trees, sweete flowers, and christall Flotes,
That crowne, and make this cheerefull Garden quick,
Vertue, that every tuch may make such Musick.

20

O that as man is cald a little world
The world might shrink into a little man,
To heare the notes about this Garden hurld,
That skill disperst in tunes so Orphean
   Might not be lost in smiting stocks and trees
That haue no eares; but growne as it began
   Spred theyr renownes, as far as *Phoebus* sees
Through earths dull vaines; that shee like heauen might moue,
In ceaseles Musick, and be fill'd with loue.

21

In precious incense of her holy breath,
My loue doth offer Hecatombs of notes
To all the Gods; who now despise the death
Of Oxen, Heifers, Wethers, Swine, and Goates.
   A Sonnet in her breathing sacrifiz'd,
Delights them more then all beasts bellowing throates,
   As much with heauen, as with my hearing priz'd.
And as guilt Atoms in the sunne appeare,
So greete these sounds the grissells of myne eare,

22

Whose pores doe open wide to theyr regreete,
And my implanted ayre, that ayre embraceth
Which they impresse; I feele theyr nimble feete
Tread my eares Labyrinth; theyr sport amazeth
   They keepe such measure; play themselues and dance.
And now my soule in *Cupids* Furnace blazeth,
   Wrought into furie with theyr daliance:

B₄ᴿ

And as the fire the parched stuble burns,
So fades my flesh, and into spyrit turns.

23

Sweete tunes, braue issue, that from *Iulia* come;
Shooke from her braine, armd like the Queene of Ire;
For first* conceiued in her mentall wombe,
And nourisht with her soules discursiue fire,
   They grew into the power of her thought;
She gaue them dounye plumes from her attire,
   And them to strong imagination brought:
That, to her voice; wherein most mouinglye
Shee (blessing them with kysses) letts them flye.

* In this al-
lusion to the
birth of *Pal-
las;* he shewes
the conceipt
of her Sonnet;
both for mat-
ter and note,
and by Meta-
phor hee ex-

presseth how shee deliuered her words, & tunes, which was by commission of the order,
Philosophers set downe in apprehension of our knoweledge, and by effection of our sences, for
first they affirme, the species of euery obiect propagates it selfe by our spirites to our common
sence, that, deliuers it to the imaginatiue part, that to the Cogitatiue: the Cogitatiue to the
Passiue Intelect; the Passiue Intelect, to that which is called *Dianoia,* or *Discursus;* and that
deliuers it vp to the minde, which order hee obserues in her vtterance.

v
24

Who flye reioysing; but (like noblest mindes)
In giuing others life themselues do dye,
Not able to endure earthes rude vnkindes
Bred in my soueraigns parts too tenderly;
   O that as* Intellects themselues transite
To eache intellegible quallitie,
   My life might passe into my loues conceit,
Thus to be form'd in words, her tunes, and breath,
And with her kysses, sing it selfe to death.

* The Phi-
losopher saith,
*Intellectus in
ipsa intellegi-
bilia transit,*
vpon which
is grounded

thys inuention, that in the same manner his life might passe into hys Mistres conceite, intend-
ing his intellectual life, or soule: which by this Analogie, should bee *Intellectus,* & her conceit,
Intelligibilis.

25

This life were wholy sweete, this onely blisse,
Thus would I liue to dye; Thus sence were feasted,
My life that in my flesh a Chaos is
Should to a Golden worlde be thus dygested;
   Thus should I rule her faces Monarchy,
Whose lookes in seuerall Empires are inuested
   Crown'd now with smiles, and then with modesty,
Thus in her tunes diuision I should raigne,
For her conceipt does all, in euery vaine.

26

My life then turn'd to that, t'each note, and word
Should I consorte her looke; which sweeter sings,
Where songs of solid harmony accord,
Rulde with Loues rule; and prickt with all his stings;
    Thus should I be her notes, before* they be;
While in her blood they sitte with fierye wings
    Not vapord in her voyces stillerie,
Nought are these notes her breast so sweetely frames,
But motions, fled out of her spirits flames.

* This hath reference to the order of her vtterance, exprest before.

27

For as when steele and flint together smit,
With violent action spitt forth sparkes of fire,
And make the tender tynder burne with it;
So my loues soule doth lighten her desire
    Vppon her spyrits in her notes* pretence;
And they conuaye them (for distinckt attire)
    To vse the Wardrobe of the common sence:
From whence in vailes of her rich breath they flye,
And feast the eare with this felicitye.

* So is thys lykewise referd to the order abouesaid, for the more perspicuitie.

28   C(1)R

Me thinks they rayse me from the heauy ground
And moue me swimming in the yeelding ayre:
As Zephirs flowry blasts doe tosse a sounde;
Vpon their wings will I to Heauen repayre,
    And sing them so, Gods shall descend and heare
Ladies must bee ador'd that are but fayre,
    But apt besides with art to tempt the eare
In notes of Nature, is a Goddesse part,
Though oft, mens natures notes, please more then Art.

29

But heere are Art and Nature both confinde,
Art casting Nature in so deepe a trance
That both seeme deade, because they be diuinde,
Buried is Heauen in earthly ignorance,
    Why breake not men then strumpet Follies bounds,
To learne at this pure virgine vtterance?
    No; none but *Ouids* eares can sound these sounds,
Where sing the harts of Loue and Poesie,
Which make my Muse so strong she works too hye.

30

Now in his glowing eares her tunes did sleepe,
And as a siluer Bell, with violent blowe

Of Steele or Iron, when his soundes most deepe,
Doe from his sides and ayres soft bosome flowe,
   A great while after murmures at the stroke,
Letting the hearers eares his hardnes knowe,
   So chid the Ayre to be no longer broke:
And left the accents panting in his eare
Which in this Banquet his first seruice were.

31

Heerewith, as *Ouid* something neerer drew,
Her Odors, odord with her breath and brest,
Into the sensor of his sauor flew,
As if the Phenix hasting to her rest
   Had gatherd all th'Arabian Spicerie
T'enbalme her body in her Tombe, her nest,
   And there lay burning gainst *Apollos* eye,
Whose fiery ayre straight piercing *Ouids* braine
Enflamde his Muse with a more odorouse vaine.

Olfactus.

v

32

And thus he sung, come soueraigne Odors, come
Restore my spirits now in loue consuming,
Wax hotter ayre, make them more sauorsome,
My fainting life with fresh-breath'd soule perfuming,
   The flames of my disease are violent,
And many perish on late helps presuming,
   With which hard fate must I yet stand content,
As Odors put in fire most richly smell,
So men must burne in loue that will excell.

33

And as the ayre is rarefied with heate
But thick and grosse with Summer-killing colde,
So men in loue aspire perfections seate,
When others, slaues to base desire are sold,
   And if that men neere *Ganges* liu'd by sent
Of Flowres, and Trees, more I a thousand fold
   May liue by these pure fumes that doe present
My Mistres quickning, and consuming breath
Where her wish flyes with power of life and death.

34

Me thinks, as in these liberall fumes I burne
My Mistres lips be neere with kisse-entices,
And that which way soeuer I can turne,
She turns withall, and breaths on me her spices,

As if too pure for search of humaine eye
She flewe in ayre disburthening Indian prizes,
    And made each earthly fume to sacrifice.
With her choyse breath fell *Cupid* blowes his fire,
And after, burns himselfe in her desire.

35

Gentle, and noble are theyr tempers framde,
That can be quickned with perfumes and sounds,
And they are cripple-minded, Gowt-wit lamde,
That lye like fire-fit blocks, dead without wounds,
    Stird vp with nought, but hell-descending gaine,
The soule of fooles that all theyr soules confounds,
    The art of Pessants and our Nobles staine,
The bane of vertue and the blisse of sinne.
Which none but fooles and Pessants glorie in.

36   C₂ᴿ

Sweete sounds and Odors, are the heauens, on earth
Where vertues liue, of vertuous men deceast,
Which in such like, receiue theyr second birth
By smell and* hearing endlesly encreast;
    They were meere flesh were not with them delighted,
And euery such is perisht like a beast
    As all they shall that are so foggye sprighted,
Odors feede loue, and loue cleare heauen discouers,
Louers weare sweets then; sweetest mindes, be louers.

* By this
allusion
drawne from
the effects of
sounds and
Odors, he imi-
tates the eter-
nitie of Ver-
tue: saying, the vertues of good men liue in them, because they stir vp pure enclinations to
the like, as if infusde in perfumes & sounds: Besides, he infers, that such as are neyther de-
lighted with sounds (intending by sounds all vtterance of knowledge, as well as musicall af-
fections,) nor with Odors, (which properly drye the braine & delight the instruments of the
soule, making them more capable of her faculties) such saith hee, perrish without memorie.

37

Odor in heate and drynes is concite
Loue then a fire is much thereto affected;
And as ill smells do kill his appetite
With thankful sauors it is still protected;
    Loue liues in spyrits, and our spyrits be
Nourisht with Odors, therefore loue refected;
    And ayre lesse corpulent in quallitie
Then Odors are, doth nourish vitall spyrits
Therefore may they be prou'd of equall merits.

37. 1 concite] consite

38

O soueraigne Odors; not of force to giue
Foode to a thing that liues nor let it dye,
But to ad life to that did neuer liue;
Nor to ad life, but immortallitie.
  Since they pertake her heate that like the fire
Stolne from the wheeles of *Phoebus* waggonrie
  To lumps of earth, can manly lyfe inspire;
Else be these fumes the liues of sweetest dames
That (dead) attend on her for nouell frames.

39

Reioyce blest Clime, thy ayre is so refinde
That while shee liues no hungry pestilence
Can feede her poysoned stomack with thy kynde;
But as the Vnicorns pregredience
  To venomd Pooles, doth purdge them with his horne,
And after him the desarts Residence
  May safely drinke, so in the holesome morne
After her walke, who there attends her eye,
Is sure that day to tast no maladye.

v

40

Thus was his course of Odors sweet and sleight,
Because he long'd to giue his sight assaye,
And as in feruor of the summers height,
The sunne is so ambitious in his sway
  He will not let the Night an howre be plast,
So in this *Cupids* Night (oft seene in day
  Now spred with tender clouds these Odors cast,)
Her sight, his sunne so wrought in his desires,
His sauor vanisht in his visuale fires.

41

So vulture loue on his encreasing liuer,
And fruitfull entrails egerly did feede,
And with the goldnest Arrow in his Quiuer,
Wounds him with longings, that like Torrents bleeds,
  To see the Myne of knowledge that enricht
His minde with pouertie, and desperate neede:
  A sight that with the thought of sight bewitcht,
A sight taught Magick his deepe misterie,
Quicker in danger then* *Dianas* eye.

* Allusion
to the trans-
formation of
Acteon with
the sight of
Diana.

42

Stay therefore *Ouid*, venter not, a sight
May proue thy rudenes, more then shew thee louing,
And make thy Mistres thinke thou think'st her light:
Which thought with lightest Dames is nothing mouing.
   The slender hope of fauor thou hast yet
Should make thee feare, such grosse conclusions prouing:
   Besides, the Thicket *Floras* hands hath set
To hide thy theft, is thinne and hollow harted,
Not meete to haue so high a charge imparted.

43

And should it keepe thy secrets, thine owne eye
Would fill thy thoughts so full of lightenings,
That thou must passe through more extremitie.
Or stand content to burne beneath theyr wings,
   Her honor gainst thy loue, in wager layde,
Thou would'st be prickt with other sences stings,
   To tast, and feele, and yet not there be staide:
These casts, he cast, and more, his wits more quick
Then can be cast, by wits Arithmetick.

44

A simile, expressing the manner of his minds contention in the desire of her sight, and feare of her displeasure.

Forward, and back, and forward went he thus,
Like wanton *Thamysis*, that hastes to greete
The brackish Court of old *Oceanus;*
And as by Londons bosome she doth fleet
   Casts herselfe proudly through the Bridges twists,
Where (as she takes againe her Christall feete:)
   She curls her siluer hayre like Amorists,
Smoothes her bright cheekes, adorns her browes with ships
And Empresse-like along the Coast she trips.

C₃ᴿ

45

Till comming neere the Sea, she heares him rore,
Tumbling her churlish billowes in her face,
Then, more dismaid, then insolent before
Charg'd to rough battaile, for his smooth embrace,
   She crowcheth close within her winding bancks,
And creepes retreate into her peacefull Pallace;
   Yet straite high-flowing in her female prancks
Againe shee will bee wanton, and againe,
By no meanes stayde, nor able to containe.

46

So *Ouid* with his strong affections striuing,
Maskt in a friendly Thicket neere her Bowre
Rubbing his temples, fainting, and reuiuing,
Fitting his garments, praying to the howre,
   Backwards, and forwards went, and durst not venter,
To tempt the tempest of his Mistres lowre,
   Or let his eyes her beauties ocean enter;
At last, with prayer he pierceth *Iunos* eare,
Great Goddesse of audacitie and feare,

47

Great Goddesse of audacitie, and feare,
Queene of Olympus, *Saturns* eldest seede,
That doost the scepter ouer *Samos* beare,
And rul'st all Nuptiale rites with power, and meede,
   Since thou in nature art the meane to mix
Still sulphure humors, and canst therefore speede
   Such as in Cyprian sports theyr pleasures fix,
Venus herselfe, and *Mars* by thee embracing,
Assist my hopes, me and my purpose gracing.

v   48

Make loue within me not too kinde but pleasing,
Exiling Aspen feare out of his forces,
My inward sight, with outward seeing, easing,
And if he please further to stretch his courses,
   Arme me with courage to make good his charges,
Too much desire to please, pleasure diuorces,
   Attemps, and not entreats get Ladies larges,
Wit is with boldnes prompt, with terror danted,
And grace is sooner got of Dames then graunted.

49

This sayde, he charg'd the Arbor with his eye,   *Visus.*
Which pierst it through, and at her brests reflected,
Striking him to the hart with exstasie:
As doe the sun-beames gainst the earth prorected,
   With their reuerberate vigor mount in flames,
And burne much more then where they were directed,
   He saw th'extraction of all fayrest Dames:
The fayre of Beauty, as whole Countries come
And shew theyr riches in a little Roome.

50

Heere *Ouid* sold his freedome for a looke,
And with that looke was ten tymes more enthralde,

He blusht, lookt pale, and like a feuour shooke,
And as a* burning vapor being exhalde
   Promist by *Phoebus* eye to be a star,
Heauens walles denying to be further scalde
   The force dissolues that drewe it vp so far:
And then it lightens gainst his death and fals,
So *Ouids* powre, this powrefull sight appals.

*This simile expres-seth the cause and substance of those ex-halations which vulgar-ly are called falling starres: so *Homer* and *Virgill* calls them, *Stellas cadentes*, *Homer* com-paring the de-scent of *Pal-las* among the Troyans to a falling Starre.

51

This beauties fayre is an enchantment made
By natures witchcraft, tempting men to buy
With endles showes, what endlessly will fade,
   Yet promise chapmen all eternitie:
But like to goods ill got a fate it hath,
Brings men enricht therewith to beggerie
   Vnlesse th'enricher be as rich in fayth,
Enamourd (like good selfe-loue) with her owne,
Seene in another, then tis heauen alone.

52

For sacred beautie, is the fruite of sight,
The curtesie that speakes before the tongue,
The feast of soules, the glory of the light,
   Enuy of age, and euerlasting young,
Pitties Commander, *Cupids* richest throne,
Musick intransed, neuer duely sung,
   The summe and court of all proportion:
And that I may dull speeches best afforde,
All Rethoricks flowers in lesse then in a worde.

$C_{(4)}{}^{R}$

53

Then in the truest wisdome can be thought,
Spight of the publique *Axiom* worldings hold,
That nothing wisdome is, that getteth nought,
   This all-things-nothing, since it is no gold.
Beautie enchasing loue, loue gracing beautie,
To such as constant simpathies enfold,
   To perfect riches dooth a sounder duetie
Then all endeuors, for by all consent
All wealth and wisdome rests in true Content.

54

Contentment is our heauen, and all our deedes
Bend in that circle, seld or neuer closde,
More then the letter in the word preceedes,
And to conduce that compasse is reposde.

More force and art in beautie ioyned with loue,
Then thrones with wisdome, ioyes of them composde
  Are armes more proofe gainst any griefe we proue,
Then all their vertue-scorning miserie
Or iudgments grauen in Stoick grauitie,

55

But as weake colour alwayes is allowde
The proper obiect of a humaine eye,
Though light be with a farre more force endowde
In stirring vp the visuale facultie,
  This colour being but of vertuous light
A feeble Image; and the cause dooth lye
  In th'imperfection of a humaine sight,
So this for loue, and beautie, loues cold fire
May serue for my praise, though it merit higher.

v

56

With this digression, wee will now returne
To *Ouids* prospect in his fancies storme:
Hee thought hee sawe the Arbors bosome burne,
Blaz'd with a fire wrought in a Ladyes forme:
  Where siluer past the least: and Natures vant
Did such a precious miracle performe,
  Shee lay, and seemd a flood of Diamant
Bounded in flesh: as still as *Vespers* hayre,
When not an Aspen leafe is styrred with ayre.

57

Shee lay* at length, like an immortall soule
At endlesse rest in blest *Elisium:*
And then did true felicitie enroule
So fayre a Lady, figure of her kingdome.
  Now *Ouids* Muse as in her tropicke shinde,
And hee (strooke dead) was meere heauen-borne become,
  So his quick verse in equall height was shrinde:
Or els blame mee as his submitted debter,
That neuer Mistresse had to make mee better.

* The amplification of this simile, is taken from the blisfull state of soules in *Elisium*, as *Virgill* faines: and expresseth a regenerate beauty in all life & perfection, not intimating any rest of death. But in peace of that eternall spring, he poynteth to that life of life thys beauty-clad naked Lady.

58

Now as shee lay, attirde in nakednes,
His eye did carue him on that feast of feasts:

[*] He calls
her body (as
it were diuid-
ed with her
breasts,) ye
fields of Para-
dise, and her
armes & legs
the famous
Riuers in it.

Sweet* fields of life which Deaths foote dare not presse,
Flowred with th'vnbroken waues of my Loues brests,
   Vnbroke by depth of those her beauties floods:
See where with bent of Gold curld into Nests
   In her heads Groue, the Spring-bird Lameate broods:
Her body doth present those fields of peace
Where soules are feasted with the soule of ease.

59

To proue which Paradise that nurseth these,
See see the golden Riuers that renowne it:
Rich *Gehon, Tigris, Phison, Euphrates,*
Two from her bright Pelopian shoulders crowne it,
   And two out of her snowye Hills doe glide,
That with a Deluge of delights doe drowne it:
   The highest two, theyr precious streames diuide
To tenne pure floods, that doe the body dutie
Bounding themselues in length, but not in beautie.

60

$D_{(1)}{}^R$

* Hee in-
tends the
office of her
fingers in at-
tyring her,
touching thys
of their
courses, in
theyr inflec-
tion follow-
ing, theyr
playing vpon
an Instru-
ment.

These* winde theyr courses through the painted bowres,
And raise such sounds in theyr inflection,
As ceaseles start from Earth fresh sorts of flowers,
And bound that booke of life with euery section.
   In these the Muses dare not swim for drowning,
Theyr sweetnes poisons with such blest infection,
   And leaues the onely lookers on them swouning,
These forms so decks, and colour makes so shine,
That Gods for them would cease to be diuine.

61

Thus though my loue be no *Elisium*
That cannot moue, from her prefixed place;
Yet haue her feete no powre from thence to come,
For where she is, is all *Elisian* grace:
   And as those happy men are sure of blisse
That can performe so excellent a race
   As that Olympiad where her fauor is,
So shee can meete them; blessing them the rather
And giue her sweetes, as well as let men gather.

62

Ah how should I be so most happy then
T'aspire that place, or make it come to mee?

59. 1 Paradise] Parradise   60.1 n office of her fingers] office her fingers

To gather, or be giuen, the flowre of women?
Elisium must with vertue gotten bee,
  With labors of the soule and continence,
And these can yeeld no ioy with such as she,
  Shee is a sweet *Elisium* for the sence
And Nature dooth not sensuall gifts infuse
But that with sence, shee still intends their vse.

63

The sence is giuen vs to excite the minde,
And that can neuer be by sence excited
But first the sence must her contentment finde,
We therefore must procure the sence delighted,
  That so the soule may vse her facultie;
Mine Eye then to this feast hath her inuited;
  That she might serue the soueraigne of mine Eye,
Shee shall bide Time, and Time so feasted neuer
Shall grow in strength of her renowne for euer.

v ### 64

Betwixt mine Eye and obiect, certayne lynes,
Moue in the figure of a Pyramis,
Whose chapter in mine eyes gray apple shines,
The base within my sacred obiect is:
  On this will I inscribe in golden verse
The meruailes raigning in my soueraigns blisse,
  The arcks of sight, and how her arrowes pierse:
This in the Region of the ayre shall stand
In Fames brasse Court, and all her Trumps commaund.

65

Rich Beautie, that ech Louer labors for,
Tempting as heapes of new-coynd-glowing Gold,
(Rackt of some miserable Treasurer)
Draw his desires, and them in chaynes enfold
  Vrging him still to tell it, and conceale it,
But Beauties treasure neuer can be told:
  None can peculier ioy, yet all must steale it.
O Beautie, this same bloody siedge of thine
Starues me that yeeld, and feedes mee till I pine.

66

And as a Taper burning in the darke
(As if it threatned euery watchfull eye

63. 3 finde] minde

That viewing burns it,) makes that eye his marke,
And hurls guilt Darts at it continually,
   Or as it enuied, any eye but it
Should see in darknes, so my Mistres beautie
   From foorth her secret stand my hart doth hit:
And like the Dart of *Cephalus* dooth kill
Her perfect Louer, though shee meane no ill.

67

Thus, as the innocence of one betraide
Carries an *Argus* with it, though vnknowne,
And Fate, to wreake the trecherie bewraide;
Such vengeance hath my Mistres Beautie showne
   On me the Traitor to her modestie,
So vnassailde, I quite am ouerthrowne,
   And in my tryumph bound in slauerie.
O Beauty, still thy Empire swims in blood,
And in thy peace, Warre stores himselfe with foode.

68

O Beautie, how attractiue is thy powre?
For as the liues heate clings about the hart,
So all Mens hungrie eyes do haunt thy Bowre,
Raigning in Greece, Troy swum to thee in Art;
   Remou'd to Troy, Greece followd thee in feares;
Thy drewst each Syreles sworde, each childles Dart
   And pulld'st the towres of Troy about thine eares:
Shall I then muse that thus thou drawest me?
No, but admire, I stand thus farre from thee.

D₂ᴿ

69

Heerewith shee rose like the Autumnale Starre
Fresh burnisht in the loftie Ocean floode,
That darts his glorious influence more farre
Then any Lampe of bright *Olympus* broode;
   Shee lifts her lightning arms aboue her head,
And stretcheth a Meridian from her blood,
   That slept awake in her *Elisian* bed:
Then knit shee vp, lest loose, her glowing hayre
Should scorch the Center and incense the ayre.

70

Thus when her fayre hart-binding hands had tied
Those liberall Tresses, her high frontier part,
Shee shrunk in curls, and curiously plied

Into the figure of a swelling hart:
  And then with Iewels of deuise, it graced:
One was a Sunne grauen at his Eeuens depart,
  And vnder that a Mans huge shaddow* placed,
Wherein was writ, in sable Charectry,
Decrescente nobilitate, crescunt obscuri.

* At the
Sun going
downe, shad-
owes grow
longest,
whereupon
this Embleme
is deuised.

71

An other was an Eye in Saphire set,
And close vpon it a fresh Lawrell spray,
The skilfull Posie was, *Medio* caret,
To showe not eyes, but meanes must truth display.
  The third was an *Apollo** with his Teme
About a Diall and a worlde in way,
  The Motto was, *Teipsum et orbem,*
Grauen in the Diall; these exceeding rare
And other like accomplements she ware.

* Sight is
one of the
three sences
that hath his
medium ex-
trinsecally,
which now
(supposed
wanting,) lets
the sight by

the close apposition of the Lawrell: the application whereof hath many constructions.
  * The Sun hath as much time to compasse a Diall as the world, & therefore ye world is
placed in the Dyall, expressing the conceite of the Emprese morally which hath a far higher
intention.

v

72

Not *Tygris, Nilus,* nor swift *Euphrates,*
Quoth *Ouid* now, can more subdue my flame,
I must through hell aduenture to displease,
To tast and touch, one kisse may worke the same:
  If more will come, more then much more I will;
Each naturall agent doth his action frame,
  To render that he works on like him styll:
The fire on water working doth induce
Like qualitie vnto his owne in vse.

73

But Heauen in her a sparckling temper blewe
(As loue in mee) and so will soone be wrought,
Good wits will bite at baits most strang and new,
And words well plac'd, moue things were neuer thought;
  What Goddesse is it *Ouids* wits shall dare
And he disgrace them with attempting nought?
  My words shall carry spirits to ensnare,
The subtlest harts affecting sutes importune,
"Best loues are lost for wit when men blame Fortune.

73. 8 subtlest] subtelst

74

Narratio.

[*] *Ouid*
standing be-
hind her, his
face was seene
in the Glasse.

With this, as she was looking in her Glasse,
She saw therein* a mans face looking on her:
Whereat she started from the frighted Grasse,
As if some monstrous Serpent had been shown her:
    Rising as when (the sunne in *Leos* signe)
Auriga with the heauenly Goate vpon her,
    Shows her horn'd forehead with her Kids diuine,
Whose rise, kils Vines, Heauens face with storms disguising;
No man is safe at sea, the Haedy rising.

75

So straight wrapt shee her body in a Clowde,
And threatned tempests for her high disgrace,
Shame from a Bowre of Roses did vnshrowde
And spread her crimson wings vpon her face;
    When running out, poore *Ouid* humbly kneeling
Full in the Arbors mouth, did stay her race
    And saide; faire Nimph, great Goddesse haue some feeling
Of *Ouids* paines; but heare: and your dishonor
Vainely surmisde, shall vanish with my horror.

76   D₃ᴿ

Traytor to Ladies modesties (said shee)
What sauage boldnes hardned thee to this?
Or what base reckoning of my modestie?
What should I thinke thy facts proude reason is?
    Loue (sacred Madam) loue exhaling mee
(Wrapt in his Sulphure,) to this clowde of his
    Made my affections his artillerie,
Shot me at you his proper Cytadell,
And loosing all my forces, heere I fell.

77

This Glosse is common, as thy rudenes strange
Not to forbeare these priuate times, (quoth she)
Whose fixed Rites, none shoulde presume to change
Not where there is adiudg'd inchastitie;
    Our nakednes should be as much conceald
As our accomplishments desire the eye:
    It is a secrete not to be reuealde,
But as Virginitie, and Nuptialls clothed,
And to our honour all to be betrothed.

78

It is a want, where our aboundance lyes,
Giuen a sole dowre t'enrich chast *Hymens* Bed,

A perfect Image of our purities,
And glasse by which our actions should be dressed.
  That tells vs honor is as soone defild
And should be kept as pure, and incompressed,
    But sight attainteth it: for Thought Sights childe
Begetteth sinne; and Nature bides defame,
When light and lawles eyes bewray our shame.

79

Deere Mistresse (answerd *Ouid*,) to direct
Our actions, by the straitest rule that is,
We must in matters Morrall, quite reiect
Vulgar Opinion, euer led amisse
  And let autentique Reason be our guide,
The wife of Truth, and Wisdoms Gouernisse:
    The nature of all actions must be waide,
And as they then appeare, breede loue or loathing,
Vse makes things nothing huge, and huge things nothing.

v

80

As in your sight, how can sight simply beeing
A Sence receiuing essence to his flame
Sent from his obiect, giue it harme by seeing
Whose action* in the Seer hath his frame?
  All excellence of shape is made for sight,
Else, to be like a Beast were no defame;
    Hid Beauties lose theyr ends, and wrong theyr right:
And can kinde loue, (where no harms kinde can be)
Disgrace with seeing that is giuen to see?

* Actio cernendi in homine vel animali, vidente collocanda est. *Aristot.*

81

Tis I (alas) and my hart-burning Eye
Doe all the harme, and feele the harme wee doo:
I am no Basiliske, yet harmles I
Poyson with sight, and mine owne bosome too;
  So am I to my selfe a Sorceresse
Bewitcht with my conceites in her I woo:
    But you vnwrongd, and all dishonorlesse
No ill dares touch, affliction, sorcerie,
One kisse of yours can quickly remedie.

82

I could not times obserue, as others might
Of cold affects, and watry tempers framde,
Yet well assurde the wounder of your sight
Was so farre of from seeing you defamde,

That euer in the Phane of Memorie
Your loue shall shine by it, in mee enflamde.
  Then let your powre be clad in lenitie,
Doe not (as others would) of custome storme,
But proue your wit as pregnant as your forme.

83

Nor is my loue so suddaine, since my hart
Was long loues *Vulcan*, with his pants vnrest,
Ham'ring the shafts bred this delightsome smart:
And as when *Ioue* at once from East and West
  Cast off two Eagles, to discerne the sight
Of this world Center, both his Byrds ioyned brest
  In Cynthian *Delphos*, since *Earths nauill* hight:
So casting off my ceaseles thoughts to see
My harts true Center, all doe meete in thee.

84

* In Cere-
bro est princi-
pium sentien-
di, et inde ne-
rui, qui
instrumenta
sunt motus
voluntarij
oriuntur.
* Natura est
vniuscuiusque
Fatum, vt
Theophr.

Cupid that acts in you, suffers in mee   D(4)²
To make himselfe one tryumph-place of twaine,
Into your tunes and odors turned hee,
And through my sences flew into my braine
  *Where rules the Prince of sence, whose Throne hee takes,
And of my Motions engines framd a chaine
  To leade mee where hee list; and heere hee makes
Nature (my* fate) enforce mee: and resignes
The raines of all, to you, in whom hee shines.

85

For yeelding loue then, doe not hate impart,
Nor let mine Eye, your carefull Harbengere
That hath puruaide your Chamber in my hart,
Be blamde for seeing who it lodged there;
  The freer seruice merrits greater meede,
Princes are seru'd with vnexpected chere,
  And must haue things in store before they neede:
Thus should faire Dames be wise and confident,
Not blushing to be noted excellent.

86

Now, as when Heauen is muffled with the vapors
His long since iust diuorced wife the Earth,
In enuie breath's, to maske his spurrie Tapers
From the vnrich aboundance of her birth,
  When straight the westerne issue of the Ayre

Beates with his flowrie wings those Brats of dearth,
   And giues *Olympus* league to shew his fayre,
So fled th'offended shaddowes of her cheere,
And showd her pleased count'nance full as cleere.

Which for his fourth course made our Poet court her. &c.

v

87

This motion of my soule, my fantasie   *Gustus.*
Created by three sences put in act,
Let iustice nourish with thy simpathie,
Putting my other sences into fact,
   If now thou grant not, now changde that offence;   Alteration-
To suffer change, doth perfect sence compact: em pati est
   Change then, and suffer for the vse of sence,   sentire.
Wee liue not for our selues, the Eare, and Eye,
And euery sence, must serue societie.

88

To furnish then, this Banquet where the tast   * He in-
Is neuer vsde, and yet the cheere diuine,   tends the
The neerest meane deare Mistres that thou hast   common sence
To blesse me with it, is a kysse of thine,   which is *cen-*
   Which grace shall borrow organs of my touch   *trum sensibus*
T'aduance it to that inward* taste of mine   *et speciebus,* &
   Which makes all sence, and shall delight as much   cals it last be-
Then with a kisse (deare life) adorne thy feast   cause it
And let (as Banquets should) the last be best.   dooth, *sapere*
                                                  in effectione
                                                  sensuum.

89

I see vnbidden Guests are boldest still,   *Corynna.*
And well you showe how weake in soule you are
That let rude sence subdue your reasons skill
And feede so spoilefully on sacred fare;
   In temper of such needles feasts as this
We show more bounty still the more we spare,
   Chiefly where birth and state so different is:
Ayre too much rarefied breakes forth in fire,
And fauors too farre vrg'd do end in ire.

90

The difference of our births (imperiall Dame)   *Ouid.*
Is heerein noted with too triuiall eyes
For your rare wits; that should your choices frame
To state of parts, that most doth royalize,
   Not to commend mine owne; but that in yours

Beyond your birth, are perrils soueraignties
　　Which (vrgd) your words had strook with sharper powers;
Tis for mere looke-like Ladies, and for men
To boast of birth that still be childeren,

91

E(1)R

Running to Father straight to helpe theyr needs;
True dignities and rites of reuerence,
Are sowne in mindes, and reapt in liuely deedes,
And onely pollicie makes difference
　　Twixt States, since vertue wants due imperance,
Vertue makes honor, as the soule doth sence,
　　And merit farre exceedes inheritance,
The Graces fill loues cup, his feasts adorning,
Who seekes your seruice now, the Graces scorning.

92

Pure loue (said she) the purest grace pursues,
And there is contact, not by application
Of lips or bodies, but of bodies vertues,
As in our elementale Nation
　　Stars by theyr powers, which are theyr heat and light
Do heauenly works, and that which hath probation
　　By vertuall contact hath the noblest plight,
Both for the lasting and affinitie
It hath with naturall diunitie.

93

Ouid replied; in thys thy vertuall presence
(Most fayre *Corynna*) thou canst not effuse
The true and solid parts of thy pure essence
But doost the superficiall beames produce
　　Of thy rich substance; which because they flow
Rather from forme then from the matters vse
　　Resemblance onely of thy body showe
Whereof they are thy wondrous species,
And t'is thy substance must my longings ease.

94

Speake then sweet ayre, that giu'st our speech euent
And teach my Mistres tractabilitie,
That art to motion most obedient,
And though thy nature, swelling be and high
　　And occupiest so infinite a space,
Yet yeeldst to words, and art condenst thereby

93. 4 the] thy

Past nature prest into a little place
Deare soueraigne then, make ayre thy rule in this,
And me thy worthy seruant with a kisse.

v

95

Ouid (sayd shee) I am well pleasd to yeeld:
Bountie by vertue cannot be abusde:
Nor will I coylie lyft *Mineruas* shielde
Against *Minerua*, honor is not brusde
   With such a tender pressure as a kisse,
Nor yeelding soone to words, though seldome vsde,
   Nicenes in ciuill fauours, folly is:
Long sutes make neuer good a bad detection,
Nor yeelding soone, makes bad, a good affection.

96

To some I know, (and know it for a fault)
Order and reuerence, are repulst in skaling,
When pryde and rudenes, enter with assault,
Consents to fall, are worse to get then falling:
   Willing resistance, takes away the will,
And too much weakenes tis to come with calling:
   Force in these frayes, is better man then skyll
Yet I like skill, and *Ouid* if a kis
May doe thee so much pleasure, heere it is.

97

Her moouing towards him, made *Ouids* eye
Beleeue the Firmament was comming downe
To take him quick to immortalitie,
And that th'Ambrosian kisse set on the Crowne:
   Shee spake in kissing, and her breath infusde
Restoring syrrop to his tast, in swoune:
   And hee imaginde *Hebes* hands had brusde
A banquet of the Gods into his sence,
Which fild him with this furious influence.

98

The motion of the Heauens that did beget
The golden age, and by whose harmonie
Heauen is preserud, in mee on worke is set,
All instruments of deepest melodie
   Set sweet in my desires to my loues liking
With this sweet kisse in mee theyr tunes apply,

As if the best Musitians hands were striking:
This kisse in mee hath endlesse Musicke closed,
Like *Phoebus* Lute, on *Nisus* Towrs imposed.

99

And as a Pible cast into a Spring,
Wee see a sort of trembling cirkles rise,
One forming other in theyr issuing
Till ouer all the Fount they circulize,
  So this perpetuall-motion-making kisse,
Is propagate through all my faculties,
  And makes my breast an endlesse Fount of blisse,
Of which, if Gods could drink, theyr matchlesse fare
Would make them much more blessed then they are.

100

* Qua ra-
tione fiat Ec-
cho.

But* as when sounds doe hollow bodies beate,
Ayre gatherd there, comprest, and thickned,
The selfe same way shee came doth make retreate,
And so effects the sounde reechoed
  Onely in part, because shee weaker is
In that redition, then when first shee fled:
  So I alas, faint eccho of this kisse,
Onely reiterate a slender part
Of that high ioy it worketh in my hart.

101

And thus with feasting, loue is famisht more,
Without my touch are all things turnd to gold,
And till I touch, I cannot ioy my store:
To purchase others, I my selfe haue sold,
  Loue is a wanton famine, rich in foode,
But with a richer appetite controld,
  An argument in figure and in Moode,
Yet hates all arguments: disputing still
For Sence, gainst Reason, with a sencelesse will.

102

Tactus

Then sacred Madam, since my other sences
Haue in your graces tasted such content,
Let wealth not to be spent, feare no expences,
But giue thy bountie true eternizement:
  Making my sences ground-worke, which is, Feeling,
Effect the other, endlesse excellent,
  Their substance with flint-softning softnes steeling:

Then let mee feele, for know sweet beauties Queene,
Dames may be felt, as well as heard or seene.

v

103

For if wee be allowd to serue the Eare
With pleasing tunes, and to delight the Eye
With gracious showes, the Taste with daintie cheere,
The Smell with Odors, ist immodestie
   To serue the sences Emperor, sweet Feeling
With those delights that fit his Emperie?
   Shall Subiects free themselues, and bind theyr King?
Mindes taint no more with bodies touch or tyre,
Then bodies nourish with the mindes desire.

104

The minde then cleere, the body may be vsde,
Which perfectly your touch can spritualize;
As by the great elixer is trans-fusde
Copper to Golde, then grant that deede of prise:
   Such as trans-forme into corrupt effects
What they receaue from Natures purities,
   Should not wrong them that hold her due respects:
To touch your quickning side then giue mee leaue,
Th'abuse of things, must not the vse bereaue.

105

Heere-with, euen glad his arguments to heare,
Worthily willing to haue lawfull grounds
To make the wondrous power of Heauen appeare,
In nothing more then her perfections found,
   Close to her nauill shee her Mantle wrests,
Slacking it vpwards, and the foulds vnwound,
   Showing *Latonas* Twinns, her plenteous brests
The Sunne and *Cynthia* in theyr tryumph-robes
Of Lady-skin; more rich then both theyr Globes.

106

Whereto shee bad, blest *Ouid* put his hand:
Hee, well acknowledging it much too base
For such an action, did a little stand,
Enobling it with tytles full of grace,
   And coniures it with charge of reuerend verse,
To vse with pietie that sacred place,
   And through his Feelings organ to disperse
Worth to his spirits, amply to supply
The porenes of his fleshes facultie.

107

And thus hee sayd: King of the King of Sences,
Engines of all the engines vnder heauen,
To health, and life, defence of all defences,
Bountie by which our nourishment is giuen,
   Beauties bewtifier, kinde acquaintance maker,
Proportions odnes that makes all things euen,
   Wealth of the laborer, wrongs reuengement taker,
Patterne of concord, Lord of exercise,
And figure of that power the world did guise:

108

Deere Hand, most dulie honord in this
And therefore worthy to be well employde:
Yet know, that all that honor nothing is,
Compard with that which now must be enioyd:
   So thinke in all the pleasures these haue showne
(Liken'd to this) thou wert but meere anoyde,
   That all hands merits in thy selfe alone
With this one touch, haue more then recompence,
And therefore feele, with feare and reuerence.

109

See *Cupids* Alps which now thou must goe ouer,
Where snowe that thawes the Sunne doth euer lye:
Where thou maist plaine and feelingly discouer
The worlds fore-past, that flow'd with Milke and Honny:
   Where, (like an Empresse seeing nothing wanting
That may her glorious child-bed bewtifiie)
   Pleasure her selfe lyes big with issue panting:
Euer deliuered, yet with childe still growing,
Full of all blessings, yet all blisse bestowing.

110

This sayd, hee layde his hand vpon her side,
Which made her start like sparckles from a fire,
Or like *Saturnia* from th'Ambrosian pride
Of her morns slumber, frighted with admire
   When *Ioue* layd young *Alcydes* to her brest,
So startled shee, not with a coy retire,
   But with the tender temper shee was blest,
Prouing her sharpe, vnduld with handling yet,
Which keener edge on *Ouids* longings set.

108.6 liken'd] likened

v   111

And feeling still, he sigh'd out this effect;
Alas why lent not heauen the soule a tongue?
Nor language, nor peculier dialect,
To make her high conceits as highly sung,
    But that a fleshlie engine must vnfold
A spirituall notion; birth from Princes sprung
    Pessants must nurse, free vertue waite on gold
And a profest though flattering enemie,
Must pleade my honor, and my libertie.

                                     112

O nature how doost thou defame in this
Our humane honors? yoking men with beasts
And noblest mindes with slaues? thus beauties blisse,
Loue and all vertues that quick spirit feasts
    Surfet on flesh; and thou that banquests mindes,
Most bounteous Mistresse, of thy dull-tongu'd guests
    Reapst not due thanks; thus rude frailetie bindes
What thou giu'st wings; thus ioyes I feele in thee
Hang on thy lips and will not vtterd be.

                                     113

Sweete touch the engine that loues bow doth bend,
The sence wherewith he feeles him deified,
The obiect whereto all his actions tend,
In all his blindenes his most pleasing guide,
    For thy sake will I write the Art of loue,
Since thou doost blow his fire and feede his pride
    Since in thy sphere his health and life doth moue,
For thee I hate who hate societie
And such as self-loue makes his slauerie.

                                     114

In these dog-dayes how this contagion smoothers
The purest bloods with vertues diet fined
Nothing theyr owne, vnlesse they be some others
Spite of themselues, are in themselues confined
    And liue so poore they are of all despised,
Theyr gifts, held down with scorne should be diuined,
    And they like Mummers mask, vnknowne, vnprised:
A thousand meruailes mourne in some such brest
Would make a kinde and worthy Patrone blest.

112.9 vtterd] vttered

115 $E_{(4)}{}^{R}$

To mee (deere Soueraigne) thou art Patronesse,
And I, with that thy graces haue infused,
Will make all fat and foggy braines confesse,
Riches may from a poore verse be deduced:
    And that Golds loue shall leaue them groueling heere,
When thy perfections shall to heauen be Mused,
    Deckt in bright verse, where Angels shall appeare
The praise of vertue, loue, and beauty singing,
Honor to Noblesse, shame to Auarice bringing.

116

Heere *Ouid* interrupted with the view
Of other Dames, who then the Garden painted,
Shrowded himselfe, and did as death eschew
All note by which his loues fame might be tainted:
    And as when mighty *Macedon* had wun
The Monarchie of Earth, yet when hee fainted,
    Grieu'd that no greater action could be doone,
And that there were no more worlds to subdue,
So loues defects, loues Conqueror did rue.

117

But as when expert Painters haue displaid,
To quickest life a Monarchs royall hand
Holding a Scepter, there is yet bewraide
But halfe his fingers; when we vnderstand
    The rest not to be seene; and neuer blame
The Painters Art, in nicest censures skand:
    So in the compasse of this curious frame,
Ouid well knew there was much more intended,
With whose omition none must be offended.
               Intentio, animi actio.
               Explicit conuiuium.

116. 1 interrupted] interupted

Philosophie.

MUSES that sing loues sensuall Emperie,
   And Louers kindling your enraged fires
At *Cupids* bonfires burning in the eye,
   Blowne with the emptie breath of vaine desires,
You that prefer the painted Cabinet
   Before the welthy Iewels it doth store yee,
   That all your ioyes in dying figures set,
   And staine the liuing substance of your glory,
Abiure those ioyes, abhor their memory,
   And let my loue the honord subiect be
   Of loue, and honors compleate historie;
   Your eyes were neuer yet, let in to see
The maiestie and riches of the minde,
But dwell in darknes; for your God is blinde.

2

But dwell in darknes, for your God is blinde,
   Humor poures downe such torrents on his eyes,
   Which (as from Mountaines) fall on his base kind,
   And eate your entrails out with exstasies.
Colour, (whose hands for faintnes are not felt)
   Can binde your waxen thoughts in Adamant,
   And with her painted fires your harts doth melt
   Which beate your soules in peeces with a pant,
But my loue is the cordiall of soules
   Teaching by passion what perfection is,
   In whose fixt beauties shine the sacred scroules,
   And long-lost records of your humane blisse
Spirit to flesh, and soule to spirit giuing,
Loue flowes not from my lyuer, but her liuing.

F(1)R   3

Loue flowes not from my liuer but her liuing,
   From whence all stings to perfect loue are darted
   All powre, and thought of pridefull lust depriuing,
   Her life so pure and she so spotles harted,
In whome sits beautie with so firme a brow
   That age, nor care, nor torment can contract it;
   Heauens glories shining there, doe stuffe alow,
   And vertues constant graces do compact it.

2. 8 peeces] peecs   2. 11 scroules] scroule

83

Her minde (the beame of God) drawes in the fires
    Of her chast eyes, from all earths tempting fewell;
    Which vpward lifts the lookes of her desires
    And makes each precious thought in her a Iewell,
And as huge fires comprest more proudly flame
So her close beauties further blaze her fame.

4

So her close beauties further blaze her fame;
    When from the world, into herselfe reflected
    Shee lets her (shameles) glorie in her shame
    Content for heau'en to be of earth reiected,
Shee thus deprest, knocks at *Olympus* gate,
    And in th'vntainted Temple of her hart
    Doth the diuorceles nuptials celebrate
    Twixt God and her; where loues prophaned dart
Feedes the chast flames of *Hymens* firmament,
    Wherein she sacrificeth, for her part;
    The Robes, lookes, deedes, desires and whole descent
    Of female natures, built in shops of art
Vertue is both the merrit and reward
Of her remou'd, and soule-infusde regard.

5

Of her remou'd, and soule-infusde regard,
    With whose firme species (as with golden Lances)
    She points her liues field, (for all wars prepard)
    And beares one chanceles minde, in all mischances;
Th'inuersed world that goes vpon her head
    And with her wanton heeles doth kyck the sky,
    My loue disdaynes, though she be honored
    And without enuy sees her emperie,
Loaths all her toyes, and thoughts cupidinine,
    Arandging in the army of her face
    All vertues forces, to dismay loose eyne
    That hold no quarter with renowne, or grace,
War to all frailetie; peace of all things pure
Her looke doth promise and her life assure.

6

Her looke doth promise and her life assure;
    A right line, forcing a rebateles point,
    In her high deedes, through euery thing obscure
    To full perfection; not the weake disioint
Of female humors; nor the Protean rages
    Of pied fac'd fashion, that doth shrink and swell,

v

Working poore men like waxen images
And makes them apish strangers where they dwell
Can alter her; titles of primacy,
   Courtship of antick iestures, braineles iests,
   Bloud without soule of false nobilitie,
   Nor any folly that the world infests
Can alter her who with her constant guises
To liuing vertues turns the deadly vices.

F₂ᴿ
7

To liuing vertues turns the deadly vices,
   For couetous shee is, of all good parts,
   Incontinent for still she showes entices
   To consort with them sucking out theyr harts,
Proud, for she scorns prostrate humilitie,
   And gluttonous in store of abstinence,
   Drunk with extractions stild in feruencie
   From contemplation, and true continence,
Burning in wrath, against impatience,
   And sloth it selfe, for she will neuer rise
   From that all-seeing trance (the band of sence)
   Wherein in view of all soules skils she lyes.
No constancie to that her minde doth moue
Nor riches to the vertues of my loue.

8

Nor riches, to the vertues of my loue,
   Nor Empire to her mighty gouernment:
   Which fayre analisde in her beauties groue,
   Showes Lawes for care, and Canons for content:
And as a purple tincture gyuen to Glasse
   By cleere transmission of the Sunne doth taint
   Opposed subiects: so my Mistresse face
   Doth reuerence in her viewers browes depaint,
And like the Pansye, with a little vaile
   Shee giues her inward worke the greater grace;
   Which my lines imitate, though much they faile
   Her gyfts so hie, and tymes conceits so base:
Her vertues then aboue my verse must raise her,
For words want Art, and Art wants words to praise her.

v
9

For words want Art, & Art wants words to praise her,
   Yet shall my actiue and industrious pen,
   Winde his sharpe forheade, through those parts that saise her,
   And register her worth past rarest women.

Her selfe shall be my Muse; that well will knowe
   Her proper inspirations: and aswage
   (With her deere loue) the wrongs my fortunes show,
   Which to my youth, binde hartlesse griefe in age,
Her selfe shall be my comfort and my riches,
   And all my thoughts I will on her conuert,
   Honor, and Error, which the world bewitches,
   Shall still crowne fooles, and tread vpon desert
And neuer shall my friendlesse verse enuie
Muses that Fames loose feathers beautifie.

10

Muses that Fames loose feathers beautifie,
   And such as scorne to tread the Theater,
   As ignorant: the seede of memorie
   Haue most inspirde, and showne theyr glories there
To noblest wits, and men of highest doome,
   That for the kingly Lawrell bent affayre;
   The Theaters of *Athens* and of *Rome*
   Haue beene the Crownes, and not the base empayre.
Farre then be this foule clowdy-browd contempt
   From like-plumde Birds: and let your sacred rymes
   From honors Court theyr seruile feete exempt
   That liue by soothing moods, and seruing tymes:
And let my loue, adorne with modest eyes,
Muses that sing loues sensuall Emperyes.
                            Lucidius olim.

THE AMOROVS ZODIACK.

1

I NEUER see the Sunne, but suddainly
  My soule is mou'd, with spite and ielousie
Of his high blisse in his sweete course discerned:
And am displeasde to see so many signes
As the bright Skye vnworthily diuines,
  Enioy an honor they haue neuer earned.

2

To thinke heauen decks with such a beautious show
A Harpe, a Shyp, a Serpent, and a Crow,
  And such a crew of creatures of no prises,
But to excite in vs th'vnshamefast flames,
With which (long since) *Ioue* wrongd so many Dames,
  Reuiuing in his rule, theyr names and vices.

3

Deare Mistres, whom the Gods bred heere belowe
T'expresse theyr wondrous powre and let vs know
  That before thee they nought did perfect make,
Why may not I (as in those signes the Sunne)
Shine in thy beauties, and as roundly runne,
  To frame (like him) an endlesse Zodiack.

4

With thee Ile furnish both the yeere and Sky,
Running in thee my course of destinie:
  And thou shalt be the rest of all my mouing,
But of thy numberles and perfect graces
(To giue my Moones theyr ful in twelue months spaces)
  I chuse but twelue in guerdon of my louing.

5

Keeping euen way through euery excellence,
Ile make in all, an equall residence
  Of a newe Zodiack: a new *Phoebus* guising,
When (without altering the course of nature)
Ile make the seasons good, and euery creature
  Shall henceforth reckon day, from my first rising.

6

v

To open then the Spring-times golden gate,
And flowre my race with ardor temperate,

87

Ile enter by thy head, and haue for house
In my first month, this heauen-Ram-curled tresse:
Of which, Loue all his charme-chaines doth addresse:
  A Signe fit for a Spring so beautious.

7

Lodgd in that fleece of hayre, yellow, and curld,
Ile take high pleasure to enlight the world,
  And fetter me in gold, thy crisps implies,
Earth (at this Spring spungie and langorsome
With enuie of our ioyes in loue become)
  Shall swarme with flowers, & ayre with painted flies.

8

Thy smooth embowd brow, where all grace I see,
My second month, and second house shall be:
  Which brow, with her cleere beauties shall delight
The Earth (yet sad) and ouerture confer
To herbes, buds, flowers, and verdure gracing Ver,
  Rendring her more then Sommer exquisite.

9

All this fresh Aprill, this sweet month of *Venus*,
I will admire this browe so bounteous:
  This brow, braue Court for loue, and vertue builded,
This brow where Chastitie holds garrison,
This brow that (blushlesse) none can looke vpon,
  This brow with euery grace and honor guilded.

10

Resigning that, to perfect this my yeere
Ile come to see thine eyes: that now I feare:
  Thine eyes, that sparckling like two Twin-borne fires,
(Whose lookes benigne, and shining sweets doe grace
Mays youthfull month with a more pleasing face)
  Iustly the Twinns signe, hold in my desires.

11

F(4)R

Scorcht with the beames these sister-flames eiect,
The liuing sparcks thereof Earth shall effect
  The shock of our ioynd-fires the Sommer starting:
The season by degrees shall change againe
The dayes, theyr longest durance shall retaine,
  The starres their amplest light, and ardor darting.

12

But now I feare, that thronde in such a signe,
Playing with obiects, pleasant and diuine,
　　I should be mou'd to dwell there thirtie dayes:
O no, I could not in so little space,
With ioy admire enough theyr plenteous grace,
　　But euer liue in sun-shine of theyr rayes.

13

Yet this should be in vaine, my forced will
My course designd (begun) shall follow still;
　　So forth I must, when forth this month is wore,
And of the neighbor Signes be borne anew,
Which Signe perhaps may stay mee with the view
　　More to conceiue, and so desire the more.

14

It is thy nose (sterne to thy Barke of loue)
Or which Pyne-like doth crowne a flowrie Groue,
　　Which Nature striud to fashion with her best,
That shee might neuer turne to show more skill:
And that the enuious foole, (vsd to speake ill)
　　Might feele pretended fault chokt in his brest.

15

The violent season in a Signe so bright,
Still more and more, become more proude of light,
　　Should still incense mee in the following Signe:
A signe, whose sight desires a gracious kisse,
And the red confines of thy tongue it is,
　　Where, hotter then before, mine eyes would shine.

16

v

So glow those Corrals, nought but fire respiring
With smiles, or words, or sighs her thoughts attiring
　　Or, be it she a kisse diuinely frameth;
Or that her tongue, shootes forward, and retires,
Doubling like feruent *Syrius*, summers fires
　　In *Leos* month, which all the world enflameth.

17

And now to bid the Boreall signes adew
I come to giue thy virgin-cheekes the view

12. I signe] shine　　16. 4 shootes] shookes　　16. 6 month] mouth

To temper all my fire, and tame my heate,
Which soone will feele it selfe extinct and dead,
In those fayre courts with modestie dispred
    With holy, humble, and chast thoughts repleate.

18

The purple tinct, thy Marble cheekes retaine,
The Marble tinct, thy purple cheeks doth staine
    The Lillies dulie equald with thine eyes,
The tinct that dyes the Morne with deeper red,
Shall hold my course a Month, if (as I dread)
    My fires to issue want not faculties.

19

To ballance now thy more obscured graces
Gainst them the circle of thy head enchaces
    (Twise three Months vsd, to run through twise three houses)
To render in this heauen my labor lasting,
I hast to see the rest, and with one hasting,
    The dripping tyme shall fill the Earth carowses.

20

Then by the necke, my Autumne Ile commence,
Thy necke, that merrits place of excellence
    Such as this is, where with a certaine Sphere
In ballancing the darknes with the light,
It so might wey, with skoles of equall weight
    Thy beauties seene with those doe not appeare.

21   G(1)ᴿ

Now past my month t'admire for built most pure
This Marble piller and her lyneature,
    I come t'inhabit thy most gracious teates,
Teates that feede loue vpon the white riphees,
Teates where he hangs his glory and his trophes
    When victor from the Gods war he retreats.

22

Hid in the vale twixt these two hils confined
This vale the nest of loues, and ioyes diuined
    Shall I inioy mine ease; and fayre be passed
Beneath these parching Alps; and this sweet cold
Is first, thys month, heauen doth to vs vnfold,
    But there shall I still greeue to bee displaced.

23

To sort from this most braue and pompous signe
(Leauing a little my ecliptick lyne
   Lesse superstitious then the other Sunne)
The rest of my Autumnall race Ile end
To see thy hand, (whence I the crowne attend,)
   Since in thy past parts I haue slightly runne.

24

Thy hand, a Lilly gendred of a Rose
That wakes the morning, hid in nights repose:
   And from *Apollos* bed the vaile doth twine,
That each where doth, th'Idalian Minion guide;
That bends his bow; that tyes, and leaues vntyed
   The siluer ribbands of his little Ensigne.

25

In fine, (still drawing to th'Antartick Pole)
The Tropicke signe, Ile runne at for my Gole,
   Which I can scarce expresse with chastitie,
I know in heauen t'is called *Capricorne*
And with the suddaine thought, my case takes horne,
   So (heauen-like,) *Capricorne* the name shall be.

v   26

This (wondrous fit) the wintry *Solstice* seaseth,
Where darknes greater growes and day decreseth,
   Where rather I would be in night then day,
But when I see my iournies doe encrease
Ile straight dispatch me thence, and goe in peace
   To my next house, where I may safer stay.

27

This house alongst thy naked thighs is found,
Naked of spot; made fleshy, firme and round,
   To entertayne loues friends with feeling sport;
These, *Cupids* secret misteries enfold,
And pillers are that *Venus* Phane vphold,
   Of her deare ioyes the glory, and support.

28

Sliding on thy smooth thighs to thys months end;
To thy well fashiond Calues I will descend
   That soone the last house I may apprehend,

Thy slender feete, fine slender feete that shame
Thetis sheene feete, which Poets so much fame,
　And heere my latest season I will end.

LENVOY.

29

Deare Mistres, if poore wishes heauen would heare,
I would not chuse the empire of the water;
　The empire of the ayre, nor of the earth,
But endlesly my course of life confining
In this fayre Zodiack for euer shining,
　And with thy beauties make me endles mirth.

30

But gracious Loue, if ielous heauen deny
My life this truely-blest varietie,
　Yet will I thee through all the world disperse,
If not in heauen, amongst those brauing fires
Yet heere thy beauties (which the world admires)
　Bright as those flames shall glister in my verse.

THE AMOROVS CONTENTION
OF *PHILLIS*

and *Flora*, translated out of a Latine coppie,
written by a Fryer, *Anno*.

1400.

1

IN flowrie season of the yeere,
And when the Firmament was cleere,
When *Tellus* Herbals painted were
With issue of disparant cheere:

2

When th'Vsher to the Morne did rise,
And driue the darknes from the skyes,
Sleepe gaue their visuall liberties,
To *Phillis* and to *Floras* eyes.

3

To walke these Ladies liked best,
(For sleepe reiects the wounded brest,)
Who ioyntly to a Meade addrest
Theyr sportance with the place to feast.

4

Thus made they amorous excesse,
Both Virgins, and both Princesses:
Fayre *Phillis* wore a liberall tresse,
But *Flora*, hers in curls did dresse.

5

Nor in their ornamentall grace,
Nor in behauiour were they base,
Their yeeres and mindes in equall place,
Did youth and his effects embrace.

6

A little yet vnlike they proue,
And somewhat hostilely they stroue.
A Clarke did *Floras* humor moue,
But *Phillis* likt a Souldiours loue.

93

7

For stature and fresh beauties flowrs,
There grew no difference in theyr dowrs:
All things were free to both theyr powrs
Without, and in, theyr courtlie Bowrs.

8

One vowe they made religiously,
And were of one societie:
And onely was theyr imparie
The forme of eythers fantasie.

9

Now did a gentle timely gale,
A little whisper through the Dale,
Where was a place of festiuall,
With verdant grasse adorned all:

10

And in that Meade-proud-making grasse,
A Riuer like to liquid glasse
Did with such soundfull murmure passe,
That with the same it wanton was.

11

Hard by this Brooke, a Pine had seate,
With goodly furniture complete,
To make the place in state more great,
And lessen the inflaming heate,

12

Which was with leaues so beautified
And spred his brest so thick and wide,
That all the Sunnes estranged pride
Sustaind repulse on euery side.

G₃ᴿ

13

Queene *Phillis* by the Foorde did sit,
But *Flora* farre remou'd from it,
The place in all things sweet was fit,
Where th'erbage did their seates admit.

14

Thus while they opposite were set
And could not theyr effects forget,

Loues arrowes and theyr bosoms met,
And both theyr harts did passion-fret.

15

Loue, close, and inward shrowds his fires,
And in faint words, firme sighes expires,
Pale tinctures change theyr cheeks attires,
But modest shame entombes their ires.

16

Phillis dyd *Flora* sighing take,
And *Flora* dyd requitall make:
So both together part the stake,
Till forth the wounds and sicknes brake.

17

In this chang'd speech they long time stayd,
The processe all on loue they layd,
Loue in theyr harts theyr lookes bewraid:
At last, in laughter, *Phillis* sayd:

v

18

Braue Souldier, *Paris*, my harts seisure
In fight, or in his peacefull leysure:
The Souldiers life, is lifes chiefe treasure,
Most worth the Loue-Queenes houshold plesure.

19

While shee her war-friend did prefer,
Flora lookt coy, and laught at her,
And did this aduerse speech auer;
Thou might'st haue said, I loue a Begger.

20

But what doth *Alcibiades*
My Loue: past all in worths excesse:
Whom Nature doth with all gyfts blesse?
O onely Clarks liues, happines.

21

This hard speech, *Phillis* hardly takes,
And thus shee *Floras* patience crakes:
Thou lou'st a Man, pure loue forsakes,
That God, his godlesse belly makes.

22

Rise wretch from this grose exstasie,
A Clarke sole Epicure thinke I:
No elegance can beautifie
A shapelesse lumpe of gluttony.

23

His hart, sweet *Cupids* Tents reiects
That onely meate and drinke affects:
O *Flora*, all mens intelects
Know Souldiers vowes shun those respects.

24   [G₄ᴿ]

Meere helps for neede his minde suffiseth,
Dull sleepe and surfets he despiseth:
Loues Trumpe his temples exerciseth,
Courage and loue, his life compriseth.

25

Who with like band our loues combineth?
Euen natures law thereat repineth,
My Loue, in conquests Palm-wreaths shineth,
Thine feast deforms, mine fight refineth.

26

Flora her modest face enrosed,
Whose second smile, more faire disclosed:
At length, with moouing voyce shee losed
What Art in her stord brest reposed.

27

Phillis, thy fill of speech thou hast,
Thy wit with pointed wings is grast,
Yet vrgest not a truth so vast
That Hemlocks, Lillies haue surpast.

28

Ease-louing Clarks thou holdst for deere,
Seruants to sleepe and belly cheere:
So Enuy, honor would enphere
But giue me eare, Ile giue thee answere.

29

So much inioyes this loue of mine,
He nere enuies, or hirs, or thine,

Household-stuffe, honny, oyle, corne, wine,
Coyne, Iewels, plate, serue his designe.

30

Such pleasing store haue Clarks by-lying
As none can faine their dignifying:
There, Loue claps his glad wings in flying,
Loue euer firme, Loue neuer dying.

31

Loues stings in him are still sustained,
Yet is my Loue nor pynde nor pained,
Ioy hath no part in him restrained
To whom his loue beares thoughts vnfained.

32

Pallid and leane, is thy elected,
Poore, scarce with clothes, or skinne, contected,
His sinewes weake, his breast dyiected,
For nothing causde, makes nought effected.

33

Approching neede is loues meere hell,
Souldiers want gifts to woo loues well:
But Clarks giue much, and still heapes swell,
Theyr rents and ritches so excell.

34

Right well thou knowst (*Phillis* replyde)
What in both arts, and liues abide,
Likely, and clenly thou hast lyde:
But thus our difference is not tryde.

35

When Holy-day the whole world cheeres,
A Clarke a solemne countnance beares,
His crown is shauen, blacke weedes he weares,
And lookes as he would still shed teares.

36

None is so poore of sence or eyne
To whom a Souldier doth not shine,
At ease, like spriteles beasts, liues thine,
Helms and barbd horse do weare out mine.

37

Myne, lowe with Arms makes for-towers lye,
And when on foote, he fight doth trye
While his fayre Squire his horse holdes by
Mine thinks on me, and then they dye.

38

He turns, (fight past, and foes inchased)
And lookes on me with helme vnlaced,
Lifts his strong lyms, and brest straite-graced
And sayes, kisse-blesse me, ô hart-placed.

39

Flora her wrath in pants did spye
And many a Dart at her let flye,
Thou canst not make with heauen-reacht cry
A Cammell pierce a needles eye.

Flora to
Phillis

40

False goes for true, for honny gall,
To make a Clarke, a Souldiers thrall;
Doth loue to Souldiers courage call?
No, but the neede they toyle withall.

41

Good *Phillis*, would thy loue were wise,
No more the truth to contrarise;
Hunger, and thirst, bow Souldiers thyes,
In which deaths path, and *Plutos* lyes.

42

Sharp is the wasting bane of war,
The lot is hard, and straineth far,
The life in stooping doubts doth iar
To get such things as needfull are.

v

43

Knewst thou the guise, thou wouldst not say
Shau'n hayre shamde Clarks, or black array,
Worne higher honors to display,
And that all states they ouer-sway.

44

All things should to my Clarke encline,
Whose croune sustaines th'imperiall signe,

Hee rules, and payes such friends as thine,
And Laye, must stoope to men diuine.

45

Thou sayst, that sloth a Clarke disguiseth,
Who (I confesse) base works despiseth,
But when from cares his free minde riseth,
Heauens course and Natures hee compriseth.

46

Mine Purple decks, thine Maile bedighteth,
Thine liues in warre, mine peace delighteth,
Olde acts of Princes he reciteth,
All of his friend, thinks, seekes, and writeth.

47

What *Venus* can, or Loues-wingd Lord,
First knowes my Clarke, and brings me word,
Musick in cares doth mine afford,
Thine liues by rapine and the sword.

H₂ᴿ

48

Heere speech and strife had both theyr ending,
Phillis askt iudgment, all suspending,
Much stirre they made, yet ceast contending,
And sought a Iudge in homewards wending.

49

With countnances that equall beene,
With equall maiestie beseene,
With equall voyce, and equall spleene
These Ladyes warrd vpon the greene.

50

Phillis, a white robe beautifide,
Flora, wore one of two hews dyde,
Phillis, vpon a Mule did ride,
And *Flora* backt a horse of pride.

51

The Mule was that which beeing create,
Neptune did feede and subiugate:
Which after fayre *Adonis* fate,
Hee *Venus* sent to cheere her state.

52

This, shee, the Queene of Iberine,
(*Phillis* fayre Mother) did resigne
Since shee was giuen to works diuine,
Whence *Phillis* had the Mule in fine.

53

Who of the trappings asks and Bit
The Mule, (though siluer) champing it,
Know, all things were so richly fit,
As *Neptunes* honor might admit.

*54 [56]   v

Then *Phillis*, no decorum wanted,
But rich and beautious, all eyes danted,
Nor *Floras* vertue lesse enchanted,
Who on a welthy Palfrey vanted.

55 [57]

Tamde with his raines, wun heauen for lightnes,
Exceeding faire, and full of witenes:
His breast Art deckt with diuers brightnes
For Ieat black mixt, with Swans pure whitenes.

56 [58]

Young and in daintie shape digested,
His lookes with pride, not rage inuested:
His maine thin hayrd, his neck high-crested,
Small eare, short head, and burly brested.

57 [59]

His broad back stoopt to this Clarks-loued,
Which with his pressure nought was moued,
Straite-leggd, large thighd, and hollow houed,
All Natures skill in him was proued.

58 [60]

An Iuorie seate on him had place,
A hoope of gold did it embrace
Grauen: and the poictrell did enchace
A stone, that starre-like gaue it grace.

---

* Here the numbering of the stanzas, ed. 1595, skips to 56 and so continues. Original numbering noted in square brackets.

59 [61]

Inscription there allurde the eye
With many a wondrous misterie
Of auncient things, made noueltie
That neuer man did yet descry.

60 [62]

The God of Rhetoricks nuptiall Bowre
Adornd with euery heauenly powre,
The contract, and the mariage howre
And all the most vnmeasurd dowre.

61 [63]

No place was there that figurde nought,
That could through all the worke be sought,
But more excesse of meruailes wrought
Then might inceede a humane thought.

62 [64]

The skill of *Mulciber* alone
Engrau'd that admirable throne,
Who looking stedfastly thereon,
Scarce thought his hand such Art had shone.

63 [65]

The trappings wrought he not with ease,
But all his paine employd to please,
And left (to goe in hand with these)
The Targe of great *Aeiacides*.

64 [66]

A styrrop for her feete to presse,
And bridle-bosses he did adresse,
And added raines, in worths excesse
Of his sweet Spouses golden tresse.

65 [67]

Thus on theyr famous Caualrie,
These Prince-borne Damzels seemd to flye
Theyr soft yong cheeke-balls to the eye,
Are of the fresh vermilion Dye.

66 [68]

So Lillies out of Scarlet pere,
So Roses bloomde in Lady Vere,

So shoote two wanton starrs yfere
In the eternall-burning Sphere.

67 [69]

The Chyld-gods gracefull Paradise
They ioyntly purpose to inuise,
And louely emulations rise
In note of one anothers guise.

68 [70]

Phillis to *Flora* laughter led,
And *Flora Phillis* answered:
Phillis, a Merlyn managed,
A Sparhawke, *Flora* carried.

69 [71]

In little time, these Ladyes found
A Groue with euery pleasure crownd,
At whose sweet entrie did resound
A Forde, that flowrd that holy ground.

70 [72]

From thence the sweet-breathd winds conuay
Odors from euery Mirtle spray
And other flowers: to whose aray
A hundred Harps, and Timbrels play.

71 [73]

All pleasures, studie can inuent
The Dames eares instantly present,
Voyces in all sorts different
The foure parts, and the Diapent.

72 [74]   [H₄ᴿ]

To tunes that from those voices flye
With admirable harmonie,
The Tymbrell, Harpe, and Psalterie
Reioyce in rapting symphonie.

73 [75]

There did the Vials voice abounde,
In Musicke Angelike profound,
There did the Phife dispreden round,
His voyce in many a variant sound.

74 [76]

All Birds with tunefull bosoms sing,
The Black-bird makes the woods to ring,
The Thrush, the Iaye, and shee in Spring,
Rues the past rape of *Thraces* King.

75 [77]

Theyr sweet notes to the Musick plying,
Then all the different flowrs descrying,
The Odors in aboundance flying,
Prou'd it the Bowre of Loue soft-lying.

76 [78]

The Virgins some-what entred heere,
And sprinckled with a little feare,
Theyr harts before that held Loue deere,
In Cupids flames encreased were.

77 [79]

And while each winged Forrester
Theyr proper rumors did prefer,
Each Virgins minde made waite on her
Applauses apt and singuler.

78 [80]

Deathles were hee could there repose;
Each path his spicie Odor stroes
Of Mirrh, and Synamon there groes,
And of our blessed Ladyes Rose.

79 [81]

Each tree hath there his seuerall blisse,
In fruits that neuer season misse:
Men may conceiue how sweet Loue is,
By that celestiall Court of his.

80 [82]

The dauncing companies they see
Of young men, and of maydens free,
Whose bodies were as bright in blee,
As starrs illustrate bodies bee.

81 [83]

In which so meruailous a guise
Of vnexpected nouelties,

These Virgins bosoms through theyr eyes,
Are danted with a quicke surprise.

82 [84]

Who stay theyr royall Steeds out-right,
And almost from theyr seats alight,
Forgetting theyr endeuours quite
With that proude rumors sweet affright.

83 [85]

But when sad *Philomen*, did straine
Her rapefull-ruing breast againe,
These Damzels hearing her complaine,
Are re'inflamd in euery vaine.

84 [86]   I₁ᴿ

About the center of the spring
A sacred place is where they sing
And vse theyr supreame worshipping,
Of loues mere-darting fiery King.

85 [87]

There many a two-shapt companie
Of Faunes, Nimphs, Satyres, meete and ply
The Timbrell and the Psalterie
Before Loues sacred maiestie.

86 [88]

There beare they Goblets, big with wine,
And Coronets of flowers combine,
There Nimphs, and Faunes demy-diuine,
Doth *Bacchus* teach to foote it fine.

87 [89]

Who keepe true measure with their feete
That to the instruments doe fleete,
But old *Silenus* playes not sweete
In consort, but indents the streete.

88 [90]

The spring sleepe did his temples lod
As on a long-eard Asse he rod,
Laughters excesse to see him nod
Dissolu'd the bosome of the God.

89 [91]

Fresh cups he euer calles vpon
In sounds of imperfection,
With age and *Bacchus* ouergon,
They stop his voyces Organon.

v

90 [92]

Amongst this gamesome Crew is seene,
The issue of the Cyprian Queene,
Whose head and shoulders feathered beene,
And as the starres his countnance sheene.

91 [93]

In his left hand his Bow hee bare,
And by his side his Quiuer ware:
In power hee sits past all compare,
And with his flames the world doth dare.

92 [94]

A Scepter in his hand he held,
With *Chloris* natiue flowrs, vntild,
And Nectars deathlesse odors stild
From his bright locks the Sun did guild.

93 [95]

The triple Graces there assist,
Sustaining with their brests commist
And knees that Tellus bosome kist
The Challice of this Amorist.

94 [96]

These Vergins now approched neere,
And worshipped, exempt from feare,
Loues God, who was enuirond there
With youth, that honord stiles did beare.

95 [97]

Theyr ioy is super excellent
To see a Court so confluent,
Whom *Cupid* seeing; theyr intent,
He doth with greeting interuent.

I₂ᴿ

96 [98]

He asks the cause for which they came:

94. 4 that] thar

They confidently tell the same,
And he giues prayse to either Dame
That durst so great a war proclame.

97 [99]

To both he spake to make some pause
Vntill theyr honorable cause
Profoundly weighd in euery clause,
Might be expland with all applause.

98 [100]

He was a God, which well they know,
Rehersall needs it not bestow,
They lite, and rest, and plainly show
Where louc striues loue will maister growe.

99 [101]

Loue, Lawes, and Iudges hath in fee,
Nature, and Vse his Iudges be
To whom his whole Courts censures flee
Since past, and things to come they see.

100 [102]

These do the hart of iustice trie
And show the Courts seueritie,
In iudgment, and strong customs eye
The Clarke is fitst for venerie.

101 [103]

Gainst which the Virgines, nothing stroue
Since loues high voyce did it approue,
So both to theyr abods remoue,
But, as at first, rest firme in loue.
                    Explicit Rhithmus Phillidis et Florae.

v CERTAMEN INTER *PHILLIDEM* &
FLORAM.

ANNI parte florida coelo puriore
 Picta terra graminis vario colore
Cum fugaret nubila nuncius aurorae
Liquit sopor oculos Phyllidis & Florae
Placuit virginibus ire spatiatum
Nam soporem reiicit pectus sauciatum
Æquis ergo passibus exeunt in pratum
Vt et locus faciat ludum esse gratum
Eunt ambae vergines & ambae Reginae
Phyllis coma libera Flora compto crine
Nec sunt formae verginum sed formae diuinae
Et respondent facies luci matutinae
Nec stirpe, nec specie, nec ornatu viles
Et annos & animos habent iuueniles
Sed sunt parum impares at parum hostiles
Nam huic placet Clericus & huic placet Miles
Non est differentia corporis aut oris
Sunt vnius voti, sunt vnius moris
Omnia communia sunt intus et foris,
Sola differentia modus est amoris.
Susurrabit modicum ventus tempestiuus
Locus erat viridi gramine festiuus
Et in ipso gramine defluebat riuus
Viuus atque garrulo murmure lasciuus
Ad augmentum decoris et caloris minus
Fuit iuxta riuulum speciosa pinus
Venustata folio late pandens sinus
Nec intrare poterat calor peregrinus
Consedere vergines, herba sedem dedit
Phyllis iuxta riuulum, Flora longe sedit
Et dum sedit vtraque et in sese redit
Amor corda vulnerat et vtramque laedit
Amor est interius latens et occultus
Et breui, certissimos elicit singultus
Pallor genas inficit, alternantur vultus
I₃ᴿ Sed in verecundia furor est sepultus
Phyllis in suspirio Floram deprehendit
Et hanc de consimili Flora reprehendit
Altera sic alteri mutuo rependit
Tandem morbum tetegit et vulnus ostendit
Ille sermo mutuus multum habet more
Et est quaedam series tota de amore
Amor est in animis, amor est in ore
Tandem Phillis incipit et arridit Florae

Miles inquit inclite mea cura Paris,
Vbi modo militas et vbi moraris
O vita militiae vita singularis
Sola digna gaudio Dionaei laris.
Dum puella recolit militem amicum
Flora (ridens) oculos, iacet in obliqum
Et in risu loquitur verbum inimicum
Amo inquit poteras dicere mendicum
Sed quid Alcibiades facit mea cura
Res creata dignior omni creatura
Quem beauit omnibus gratiis natura
O sola faelicia Clericorum iura
Floram Phyllis arguit de sermone duro
Et sermone loquitur Floram commoturo
Nam ecce virgunculam inquit credo puro
Cuius pectus mobile seruit Epicuro
Surge surge misera de furore faedo
Solum esse Clericum Epicurum credo
Nihil elegantiae Clerico concedo
Cuius implet latera moles et pinguedo
A castris Cupidinis cor habet remotum
Qui somnum desiderat et cibum & potum
O puella nobilis omnibus est notum
Quantum distat militis ab hoc voto votum
Solis necessariis Miles est contentus
Somno, cibo, potui, non viuit intentus
Amor illum prohibet ne sit somnolentus
Nam est vita Militis amor et iuuentus
Quis amicos copulit nostros loro pari?   v
Lex, Natura prohibent illos copulari
Meum semper praemium dare tuo dari
Meus nouit ludere, tuus epulari
Haurit flora sanguinem vulta verecundo
Et apparet pulchrior in risu secundo
Et tandem eloquio reserat facundo
Quae corde conceperat artibus faecundo
Satis inquit libere Phyllis es loquuta
Multum es eloquio velox et acuta
Sed non efficaciter verum prosequuta
Vt per te praeualeat lilio cicuta
Dixisti de Clerico qui indulgit sibi
Seruum somni nominas & potus & cibi
Sic solet ab inuido probitas describi
Ecce parem pattere respondebo tibi
Tot et tanta fateor, &c.

FINIS.

HERO AND LEANDER.

TO THE RIGHT WORSHIPFULL, SIR THOMAS WALSINGHAM, KNIGHT.

SIR, wee thinke not our selues discharged of the dutie wee owe to our friend, when wee haue brought the breathlesse bodie to the earth: for albeit the eye there taketh his euer farwell of that beloued obiect, yet the impression of the man, that hath beene deare vnto vs, liuing an after life in our memory, there putteth vs in mind of farther obsequies due vnto the deceased. And namely of the performance of whatsoeuer we may iudge shal make to his liuing credit, and to the effecting of his determinations preuented by the stroke of death. By these meditations (as by an intellectuall will) I suppose my selfe executor to the unhappily deceased author of this Poem, vpon whom knowing that in his life time you bestowed many kind fauors, entertaining the parts of reckoning and woorth which you found in him, with good countenance and liberall affection: I cannot but see so far into the will of him dead, that whatsoeuer issue of his brain should chance to come abroad, that the first breath it should take might be the gentle aire of your liking: for since his selfe had ben accustomed thervnto, it would prooue more agreeable and thriuing to his right children, than any other foster countenance whatsoeuer. At this time seeing that this vnfinished Tragedy happens vnder my hands to be imprinted; of a double duty, the one to your selfe, the other to the deceased, I present the same to your most fauourable allowance, offring my vtmost selfe now and euer to bee readie, At your Worships disposing:

Edward Blunt.

(Ep. Ded.) 1 not *om.* 1629, 1637   3 euer *om.* 1637   6 farther] other 1629, 1637   10 vnhappily 1598¹,², 1600: vnhappie 1606–37   11 that *om.* 1629, 1637   18 thervnto] thereto 1613–37   21 a *om.* 1637   adouble 1629   *Signature* Edward Blunt 1598¹: E. B. 1598² etc.

11,

HERO AND LEANDER.

(The Argument of the First Sestyad.

HEROS description and her Loues,
The Phane of Venus; *where he moues*
His worthie Loue-suite, and attaines;
Whose blisse the wrath of Fates restraines,
For Cupids *grace to* Mercurie,   5
Which tale the Author doth implie.)[1]

On *Hellespont* guiltie of True-loues blood,
In view and opposit two citties stood,
Seaborderers, disioin'd by *Neptunes* might:
The one *Abydos*, the other *Sestos* hight.
At *Sestos*, *Hero* dwelt; *Hero* the faire,   5
Whom young *Apollo* courted for her haire,
And offred as a dower his burning throne,
Where she should sit for men to gaze vpon.
The outside of her garments were of lawne,
The lining purple silke, with guilt starres drawne, 10
Her wide sleeues greene, and bordered with a groue,
Where *Venus* in her naked glory stroue,
To please the carelesse and disdainfull eies
Of proud *Adonis* that before her lies.
Her kirtle blew, whereon was many a staine,   15
Made with the blood of wretched Louers slaine.   ᵥ
Vpon her head she ware a myrtle wreath,
From whence her vaile reacht to the ground beneath.
Her vaile was artificiall flowers and leaues,
Whose workmanship both man and beast deceaues.   20
Many would praise the sweet smell as she past,
When t'was the odour which her breath foorth cast,
And there for honie bees haue sought in vaine,
And beat from thence, haue lighted there againe.
About her necke hung chaines of peble stone,   25
Which lightned by her necke, like Diamonds shone.
She ware no gloues, for neither sunne nor wind
Would burne or parch her hands, but to her mind,
Or warme or coole them, for they tooke delite
To play vpon those hands, they were so white.   30
Buskins of shels all siluered vsed she,
And brancht with blushing corall to the knee;
Where sparrowes pearcht, of hollow pearle and gold,

[1] *Add. 1598²*   3 Seaborders *1598–1613: corr. 1629, 1637*   4 th'other
1629, 1637   9 were] was *Rob.*   10 lining] linnen *1637*   17 wore *1637*

Such as the world would woonder to behold:
35 Those with sweet water oft her handmaid fils,
Which as shee went would cherupe through the bils.
Some say, for her the fairest *Cupid* pyn'd,
And looking in her face, was strooken blind.
But this is true, so like was one the other,
40 As he imagyn'd *Hero* was his mother.
[A₄ᴿ] And oftentimes into her bosome flew,
About her naked necke his bare armes threw,
And laid his childish head vpon her brest,
And with still panting rockt, there tooke his rest.
45 So louely faire was *Hero, Venus* Nun,
As nature wept, thinking she was vndone;
Because she tooke more from her than she left,
And of such wondrous beautie her bereft:
Therefore in signe her treasure suffred wracke,
50 Since *Heroes* time, hath halfe the world beene blacke.
Amorous *Leander*, beautifull and yoong,
(Whose tragedie diuine *Musæus* soong)
Dwelt at *Abidus:* since him dwelt there none,
For whom succeeding times make greater mone.
55 His dangling tresses that were neuer shorne,
Had they beene cut, and vnto *Colchos* borne,
Would haue allur'd the vent'rous youth of *Greece*
To hazard more than for the golden Fleece.
Faire *Cinthia* wisht his armes might be her spheare,
60 Greefe makes her pale, because she mooues not there.
His bodie was as straight as *Circes* wand,
Ioue might haue sipt out *Nectar* from his hand.
Euen as delicious meat is to the tast,
So was his necke in touching, and surpast
65 The white of *Pelops* shoulder. I could tell ye,
How smooth his brest was, & how white his bellie,
v And whose immortall fingars did imprint
That heauenly path, with many a curious dint,
That runs along his backe, but my rude pen
70 Can hardly blazon foorth the loues of men,
Much lesse of powerfull gods: let it suffise,
That my slacke muse sings of *Leanders* eies,
Those orient cheekes and lippes, exceeding his
That leapt into the water for a kis
75 Of his owne shadow, and despising many,
Died ere he could enioy the loue of any.

40 his] her *1613*   44 rockt *1598*¹: rocke *1598*² etc.   54 make *1598, 1637,*
Dyce etc.: may *1600-29, Rob.*   55 dandling *1629, 1637*   72 sings] must
sing *1613-37*   73 Those] These *1613-37*

Had wilde *Hippolitus Leander* seene,
Enamoured of his beautie had he beene,
His presence made the rudest paisant melt,
That in the vast vplandish countrie dwelt,   80
The barbarous *Thratian* soldier moou'd with nought,
Was moou'd with him, and for his fauour sought.
Some swore he was a maid in mans attire,
For in his lookes were all that men desire,
A pleasant smiling cheeke, a speaking eye,   85
A brow for loue to banquet roiallye,
And such as knew he was a man would say,
Leander, thou art made for amorous play:
Why art thou not in loue, and lou'd of all?
Though thou be faire, yet be not thine owne thrall.   90
    The men of wealthie *Sestos*, euerie yeare,
(For his sake whom their goddesse held so deare,
Rose-cheekt *Adonis*) kept a solemne feast.   B₁ᴿ
Thither resorted many a wandring guest,
To meet their loues; such as had none at all,   95
Came louers home from this great festiuall.
For euerie street like to a Firmament
Glistered with breathing stars, who where they went,
Frighted the melancholie earth, which deem'd
Eternall heauen to burne, for so it seem'd,   100
As if another *Phaeton* had got
The guidance of the sunnes rich chariot.
But far aboue the loueliest *Hero* shin'd,
And stole away th'inchaunted gazers mind,
For like Sea-nimphs inueigling harmony,   105
So was her beautie to the standers by.
Nor that night-wandring pale and watrie starre
(When yawning dragons draw her thirling carre
From *Latmus* mount vp to the glomie skie,
Where crown'd with blazing light and maiestie,   110
She proudly sits) more ouer-rules the flood,
Than she the hearts of those that neere her stood.
Euen as, when gawdie Nymphs pursue the chace,
Wretched *Ixions* shaggie footed race,
Incenst with sauage heat, gallop amaine   115
From steepe Pine-bearing mountains to the plaine:
So ran the people foorth to gaze vpon her,
And all that view'd her, were enamour'd on her.
And as in furie of a dreadfull fight,   *v*
Their fellowes being slaine or put to flight,   120

94 wandring] wandered *1606–37*   108 drew *1637*   thirling] whirling *Rob.*
119 in furie of a] in a furie of *1609*

Poore soldiers stand with fear of death dead strooken,
So at her presence all surpris'd and tooken,
Await the sentence of her scornefull eies:
He whom she fauours liues, the other dies.
125 There might you see one sigh, another rage,
And some (their violent passions to asswage)
Compile sharpe satyrs, but alas too late,
For faithfull loue will neuer turne to hate.
And many seeing great princes were denied,
130 Pyn'd as they went, and thinking on her died.
On this feast day, O cursed day and hower,
Went *Hero* thorow *Sestos*, from her tower
To *Venus* temple, w(h)ere vnhappilye,
As after chaunc'd, they did each other spye.
135 So faire a church as this, had *Venus* none,
The wals were of discoloured *Iasper* stone,
Wherein was *Proteus* carued, and o'rehead,
A liuelie vine of greene sea agget spread;
Where by one hand, light headed *Bacchus* hoong,
140 And with the other, wine from grapes out wroong.
Of Christall shining faire the pauement was,
The towne of *Sestos* cal'd it *Venus* glasse.
There might you see the gods in sundrie shapes,
Committing headdie ryots, incest, rapes:
B₂ᴿ 145 For know, that vnderneath this radiant floure
Was *Danaes* statue in a brazen tower,
Ioue slylie stealing from his sisters bed,
To dallie with *Idalian Ganimed*,
And for his loue *Europa* bellowing loud,
150 And tumbling with the Rainbow in a cloud:
Blood-quaffing *Mars* heauing the yron net,
Which limping *Vulcan* and his *Cyclops* set:
Loue kindling fire, to burne such townes as *Troy*,
Syluanus weeping for the louely boy
155 That now is turn'd into a *Cypres* tree,
Vnder whose shade the Wood-gods loue to bee.
And in the midst a siluer altar stood;
There *Hero* sacrificing turtles blood,
Vaild to the ground, vailing her eie-lids close,
160 And modestly they opened as she rose:
Thence flew Loues arrow with the golden head,
And thus *Leander* was enamoured.
Stone still he stood, and euermore he gazed,
Till with the fire that from his count'nance blazed,

137 ouer head *1598²* etc.   159 Vaild *1598¹*, *Dyce* etc.: Taild *1598²–1637*:
Kneel'd *Rob.*

Relenting *Heroes* gentle heart was strooke,   165
Such force and vertue hath an amorous looke.
  It lies not in our power to loue, or hate,
For will in vs is ouer-rul'd by fate.
When two are stript long ere the course begin,
We wish that one should loose, the other win;   170
And one especiallie doe we affect   *v*
Of two gold Ingots like in each respect.
The reason no man knowes, let it suffise,
What we behold is censur'd by our eies.
Where both deliberat, the loue is slight,   175
Who euer lov'd, that lov'd not at first sight?
  He kneel'd, but vnto her deuoutly praid;
Chast *Hero* to her selfe thus softly said:
Were I the saint hee worships, I would heare him,
And as shee spake those words, came somewhat nere him.   180
He started vp, she blusht as one asham'd;
Wherewith *Leander* much more was inflam'd.
He toucht her hand, in touching it she trembled,
Loue deepely grounded, hardly is dissembled.
These louers parled by the touch of hands,   185
True loue is mute, and oft amazed stands.
Thus while dum signs their yeelding harts entangled,
The aire with sparkes of liuing fire was spangled,
And night deepe drencht in mystie *Acheron*

*A periphrasis
of night.*

Heau'd vp her head, and halfe the world vpon   190
Breath'd darkenesse forth (darke night is *Cupids* day).
And now begins *Leander* to display
Loues holy fire, with words, with sighs and teares,
Which like sweet musicke entred *Heroes* eares,
And yet at euerie word shee turn'd aside,   195
And alwaies cut him off as he replide.
At last, like to a bold sharpe Sophister,   B₃ᴿ
With chearefull hope thus he accosted her.
  Faire creature, let me speake without offence,
I would my rude words had the influence,   200
To lead thy thoughts as thy faire lookes doe mine,
Then shouldst thou bee his prisoner who is thine.
Be not vnkind and faire, mishapen stuffe
Are of behauiour boisterous and ruffe.
O shun me not, but heare me ere you goe,   205
God knowes I cannot force loue, as you doe.
My words shall be as spotlesse as my youth,
Full of simplicitie and naked truth.

180 those] these *1637*   somewhat] something *1629, 1637*   184 ground
1637   189-91 *Marginal note om. 1600-37.*   204 behauiours *1613*

This sacrifice (whose sweet perfume descending,
210 From *Venus* altar to your footsteps bending)
Doth testifie that you exceed her farre,
To whom you offer, and whose Nunne you are.
Why should you worship her? her you surpasse,
As much as sparkling Diamonds flaring glasse.
215 A Diamond set in lead his worth retaines,
A heauenly Nimph, belov'd of humane swaines,
Receiues no blemish, but oft-times more grace,
Which makes me hope, although I am but base,
Base in respect of thee, diuine and pure,
220 Dutifull seruice may thy loue procure,
And I in dutie will excell all other,
As thou in beautie doest exceed loues mother.
  v Nor heauen, nor thou, were made to gaze vpon,
As heauen preserues all things, so saue thou one.
225 A stately builded ship, well rig'd and tall,
The Ocean maketh more maiesticall:
Why vowest thou then to liue in *Sestos* here,
Who on Loues seas more glorious wouldst appeare?
Like vntun'd golden strings all women are,
230 Which long time lie vntoucht, will harshly iarre.
Vessels of Brasse oft handled, brightly shine,
What difference betwixt the richest mine
And basest mold, but vse? for both, not vs'de,
Are of like worth. Then treasure is abus'de,
235 When misers keepe it; being put to lone,
In time it will returne vs two for one.
Rich robes themselues and others do adorne,
Neither themselues nor others, if not worne.
Who builds a pallace and rams vp the gate,
240 Shall see it ruinous and desolate.
Ah simple *Hero*, learne thy selfe to cherish,
Lone women like to emptie houses perish.
Lesse sinnes the poore rich man that starues himselfe,
In heaping vp a masse of drossie pelfe,
245 Than such as you: his golden earth remains,
Which after his disceasse, some other gains.
But this faire iem, sweet in the losse alone,
When you fleet hence, can be bequeath'd to none.
[B₄ᴿ] Or if it could, downe from th'enameld skie
250 All heauen would come to claime this legacie,
And with intestine broiles the world destroy,
And quite confound natures sweet harmony.

227 to] no *1606*   232 betwixt] betweene *1637*   242 Lone] Loue *1598²–*
1600   243 sinnes] since *1598²–1606*

Well therefore by the gods decreed it is,
We humane creatures should enjoy that blisse
One is no number, mayds are nothing then,   255
Without the sweet societie of men.
Wilt thou liue single still? one shalt thou bee,
Though neuer-singling *Hymen* couple thee.
Wild sauages, that drinke of running springs,
Thinke water farre excels all earthly things: 260
But they that dayly tast neat wine, despise it.
Virginitie, albeit some highly prise it,
Compar'd with marriage, had you tried them both,
Differs as much as wine and water doth.
Base boullion for the stampes sake we allow,   265
Euen so for mens impression do we you,
By which alone, our reuerend fathers say,
Women receaue perfection euerie way.
This idoll which you terme *Virginitie*,
Is neither essence subiect to the eie,   27c
No, nor to any one exterior sence,
Nor hath it any place of residence,
Nor is't of earth or mold celestiall,
Or capable of any forme at all.
Of that which hath no being doe not boast,   275 *v*
Things that are not at all are neuer lost.
Men foolishly doe call it vertuous,
What vertue is it that is borne with vs?
Much lesse can honour bee ascrib'd thereto,
Honour is purchac'd by the deedes wee do.   280
Beleeue me *Hero*, honour is not wone,
Vntill some honourable deed be done.
Seeke you for chastitie, immortall fame,
And know that some haue wrong'd *Dianas* name?
Whose name is it, if she be false or not,   285
So she be faire, but some vile toongs will blot?
But you are faire (aye me) so wondrous faire,
So yoong, so gentle, and so debonaire,
As *Greece* will thinke, if thus you liue alone,
Some one or other keepes you as his owne.   290
Then *Hero* hate me not, nor from me flie,
To follow swiftly blasting infamie.
Perhaps, thy sacred Priesthood makes thee loath,
Tell me, to whom mad'st thou that heedlesse oath?
    To *Venus*, answered shee, and as shee spake,   295
Foorth from those two tralucent cesternes brake

261 neat] sweet *1637*   266 impressions *1637*   294 mad'st thou] thou
mad'st *1637*

A streame of liquid pearle, which downe her face
Made milk-white paths, wheron the gods might trace
To *Ioues* high court. Hee thus replide: The rites
300 In which Loues beauteous Empresse most delites,
C₁ᴿ Are banquets, Dorick musicke, midnight-reuell,
Plaies, maskes, and all that stern age counteth euill.
Thee as a holy Idiot doth she scorne,
For thou in vowing chastitie hast sworne
305 To rob her name and honour, and thereby
Commit'st a sinne far worse than periurie,
Euen sacrilege against her Deitie,
Through regular and formall puritie.
To expiat which sinne, kisse and shake hands,
310 Such sacrifice as this *Venus* demands.
  Thereat she smild, and did denie him so,
As put thereby, yet might he hope for mo.
Which makes him quickly re-enforce his speech,
And her in humble manner thus beseech.
315 Though neither gods nor men may thee deserue,
Yet for her sake whom you haue vow'd to serue,
Abandon fruitlesse cold Virginitie,
The gentle queene of Loues sole enemie.
Then shall you most resemble *Venus* Nun,
320 When *Venus* sweet rites are perform'd and done.
Flint-brested *Pallas* ioies in single life,
But *Pallas* and your mistresse are at strife.
Loue *Hero* then, and be not tirannous,
But heale the heart, that thou hast wounded thus,
325 Nor staine thy youthfull years with auarice,
Faire fooles delight to be accounted nice.
  v The richest corne dies, if it be not reapt,
Beautie alone is lost, too warily kept.
These arguments he vs'de, and many more,
330 Wherewith she yeelded, that was woon before.
Heroes lookes yeelded, but her words made warre,
Women are woon when they begin to iarre.
Thus hauing swallow'd *Cupids* golden hooke,
The more she striv'd, the deeper was she strooke.
335 Yet euilly faining anger, stroue she still,
And would be thought to graunt against her will.
So hauing paus'd a while, at last shee said:
Who taught thee Rhethoricke to deceiue a maid?
Aye me, such words as these should I abhor,
340 And yet I like them for the Orator.

304 hast] hath *1609*   326 nice] wise *E. P.*   327 richest] ripest *E. P.*
328 warily] early *E. P.*

With that *Leander* stoopt, to haue imbrac'd her,
But from his spreading armes away she cast her,
And thus bespake him: Gentle youth forbeare
To touch the sacred garments which I weare.
Vpon a rocke, and vnderneath a hill,   345
Far from the towne (where all is whist and still,
Saue that the sea playing on yellow sand,
Sends foorth a ratling murmure to the land,
Whose sound allures the golden *Morpheus*
In silence of the night to visite vs.)   350
My turret stands, and there God knowes I play
With *Venus* swannes and sparrowes all the day.
A dwarfish beldame beares me companie,   C₂ᴿ
That hops about the chamber where I lie,
And spends the night (that might be better spent)   355
In vaine discourse, and apish merriment.
Come thither. As she spake this, her toong tript,
For vnawares (*Come thither*) from her slipt,
And sodainly her former colour chang'd,
And here and there her eies through anger rang'd.   360
And like a planet, moouing seuerall waies,
At one selfe instant, she poore soule assaies,
Louing, not to loue at all, and euerie part
Stroue to resist the motions of her hart.
And hands so pure, so innocent, nay such,   365
As might haue made heauen stoope to haue a touch,
Did she vphold to *Venus*, and againe
Vow'd spotlesse chastitie, but all in vaine.
Cupid beats downe her praiers with his wings,
Her vowes aboue the emptie aire he flings: 370
All deepe enrag'd, his sinowie bow he bent,
And shot a shaft that burning from him went,
Wherewith she strooken look'd so dolefully,
As made Loue sigh, to see his tirannie.
And as she wept, her teares to pearle he turn'd,   375
And wound them on his arme, and for her mourn'd.
Then towards the pallace of the destinies,
Laden with languishment and griefe he flies,
And to those sterne nymphs humblie made request,   *v*
Both might enioy ech other, and be blest.   380
But with a ghastly dreadfull countenaunce,
Threatning a thousand deaths at euerie glaunce,
They answered Loue, nor would vouchsafe so much
As one poore word, their hate to him was such.

347 on] upon *1637*   353 beares] keepes *1637*   358 thither] hither *1629*,
1637   370 aboue] about *conj. Dyce¹, Dyce²*   377 toward *1629*

385 Harken a while, and I will tell you why:
Heauens winged herrald, *Ioue-borne Mercury*,
The selfe-same day that he asleepe had layd
Inchaunted Argus, spied a countrie mayd,
Whose carelesse haire, in stead of pearle t'adorne it,
390 Glist'red with deaw, as one that seem'd to skorne it:
Her breath as fragrant as the morning rose,
Her mind pure, and her toong vntaught to glose.
Yet prowd she was, (for loftie pride that dwels
In tow'red courts, is oft in sheapheards cels.)
395 And too too well the faire vermilion knew,
And siluer tincture of her cheekes, that drew
The loue of euerie swaine: On her, this god
Enamoured was, and with his snakie rod,
Did charme her nimble feet, and made her stay,
400 The while vpon a hillocke downe he lay,
And sweetly on his pipe began to play,
And with smooth speech her fancie to assay,
Till in his twining armes he lockt her fast,
And then he woo'd with kisses, and at last,
C₃ᴿ 405 As sheap-heards do, her on the ground hee layd,
And tumbling in the grasse, he often strayd
Beyond the bounds of shame, in being bold
To eie those parts, which no eie should behold.
And like an insolent commaunding louer,
410 Boasting his parentage, would needs discouer
The way to new *Elisium:* but she,
Whose only dower was her chastitie,
Hauing striu'ne in vaine, was now about to crie,
And craue the helpe of sheap-heards that were nie.
415 Herewith he stayd his furie, and began
To giue her leaue to rise: away she ran,
After went *Mercurie*, who vs'd such cunning,
As she to heare his tale, left off her running.
Maids are not woon by brutish force and might,
420 But speeches full of pleasure and delight.
And knowing *Hermes* courted her, was glad
That she such louelinesse and beautie had
As could prouoke his liking, yet was mute,
And neither would denie, nor graunt his sute.
425 Still vowd he loue, she wanting no excuse
To feed him with delaies, as women vse,
Or thirsting after immortalitie,—
All women are ambitious naturallie,—

389 pearles *1637*   400 a] the *1600–37*   406 in] on *1629, 1637*
420 pleasure *1598¹, 1629, 1637, Rob., Dyce:* pleasures *1598²–1613, Cunn., Bull.*

Impos'd vpon her louer such a taske,
As he ought not performe, nor yet she aske.   430
A draught of flowing *Nectar* she requested,   *v*
Wherewith the king of Gods and men is feasted.
He readie to accomplish what she wil'd,
Stole some from *Hebe* (*Hebe Ioues* cup fil'd,)
And gaue it to his simple rustike loue,   435
Which being knowne (as what is hid from *Ioue?*)
He inly storm'd, and waxt more furious
Than for the fire filcht by *Prometheus*,
And thrusts him down from heauen: he wandring here,
In mournfull tearmes, with sad and heauie cheare   440
Complaind to *Cupid*. *Cupid* for his sake,
To be reueng'd on Ioue did vndertake,
And those on whom heauen, earth, and hell relies,
I mean the Adamantine Destinies,
He wounds with loue, and forst them equallie   445
To dote vpon deceitfull *Mercurie*.
They offred him the deadly fatall knife,
That sheares the slender threads of humane life,
At his faire feathered feet the engins layd,
Which th'earth from ougly *Chaos* den vp-wayd: 450
These he regarded not, but did intreat,
That Ioue, vsurper of his fathers seat,
Might presently be banisht into hell,
And aged *Saturne* in *Olympus* dwell.
They granted what he crau'd, and once againe   455
Saturne and *Ops* began their golden raigne.
Murder, rape, warre, lust and trecherie,   [C₄ᴿ]
Were with *Ioue* clos'd in *Stigian* Emprie.
But long this blessed time continued not:
As soone as he his wished purpose got,   460
He recklesse of his promise did despise
The loue of th'euerlasting Destinies.
They seeing it, both Loue and him abhor'd,
And *Iupiter* vnto his place restor'd.
And but that Learning, in despight of Fate,   465
Will mount aloft, and enter heauen gate,
And to the seat of *Ioue* it selfe aduaunce,
Hermes had slept in hell with ignoraunce,
Yet as a punishment they added this,
That he and *Pouertie* should alwaies kis.   470
And to this day is euerie scholler poore,
Grosse gold from them runs headlong to the boore.

447 deadly fatall] fatall deadly *1637*   457 warre, lust] war and lust *Rob.*
etc.   465 but that] that but *1629, 1637*

Likewise the angrie sisters thus deluded,
To venge themselues on *Hermes*, haue concluded
475   That *Midas* brood shall sit in Honors chaire,
To which the *Muses* sonnes are only heire:
And fruitfull wits that in aspiring are,
Shall discontent run into regions farre;
And few great lords in vertuous deeds shall ioy,
480   But be surpris'd with euery garish toy;
And still inrich the loftie seruile clowne,
Who with incroching guile keepes learning downe
v   Then muse not *Cupids* sute no better sped,
Seeing in their loues the Fates were iniured.
(The end of the first Sestyad.

The Argument of the Second Sestyad.

Hero of loue takes deeper sence,
And doth her loue more recompence.
Their first nights meeting, where sweet kisses
Are th' only crownes of both their blisses.
5   *He swims t' Abydus, and returnes;*
Cold Neptune with his beautie burnes,
Whose suite he shuns, and doth aspire
Heros faire towre, and his desire.)[1]

By this, sad *Hero*, with loue vnacquainted,
Viewing *Leanders* face, fell downe and fainted.
He kist her, and breath'd life into her lips,
Wherewith as one displeas'd, away she trips.
5   Yet as she went, full often look'd behind,
And many poore excuses did she find
To linger by the way, and once she stayd,
And would haue turn'd againe, but was afrayd,
D₁ᴿ   In offring parlie, to be counted light.
10   So on she goes, and in her idle flight,
Her painted fanne of curled plumes let fall,
Thinking to traine *Leander* therewithall.
He being a nouice, knew not what she meant,
But stayd, and after her a letter sent,
15   Which ioyfull *Hero* answerd in such sort,
As he had hope to scale the beauteous fort,
Wherein the liberall graces lock'd their wealth,
And therefore to her tower he got by stealth.
Wide open stood the doore, hee need not clime,
20   And she her selfe before the pointed time

477 inaspiring *Dyce etc.*: high-aspiring *conj. Bull.*   ¹ *Add. 1598² etc.*
17 lock *1629, 1637*

Had spread the boord, with roses strowed the roome,
And oft look't out, and mus'd he did not come.
At last he came, O who can tell the greeting
These greedie louers had at their first meeting.
He askt, she gaue, and nothing was denied,   25
Both to each other quickly were affied.
Looke how their hands, so were their hearts vnited,
And what he did she willingly requited.
(Sweet are the kisses, the imbracements sweet,
When like desires and affections meet,   30
For from the earth to heauen is *Cupid* rais'd,
Where fancie is in equall ballance pais'd)
Yet she this rashnesse sodainly repented,
And turn'd aside, and to her selfe lamented,
As if her name and honour had beene wrong'd,   35 v
By being possest of him for whom she long'd:
I, and shee wisht, albeit not from her hart,
That he would leaue her turret and depart.
The mirthfull God of amorous pleasure smil'd,
To see how he this captiue Nymph beguil'd.   40
For hitherto hee did but fan the fire,
And kept it downe that it might mount the hier.
Now waxt she iealous, least his loue abated,
Fearing her owne thoughts made her to be hated.
Therefore vnto him hastily she goes,   45
And like light *Salmacis*, her body throes
Vpon his bosome, where with yeelding eyes
She offers vp her selfe a sacrifice,
To slake his anger if he were displeas'd.
O what god would not therewith be appeas'd?   50
Like *Æsops* cocke, this iewell he enioyed,
And as a brother with his sister toyed,
Supposing nothing else was to be done,
Now he her fauour and good will had wone.
But know you not that creatures wanting sence   55
By nature haue a mutuall appetence,
And wanting organs to aduaunce a step,
Mou'd by Loues force, vnto ech other lep?
Much more in subiects hauing intellect,
Some hidden influence breeds like effect.   60
Albeit *Leander* rude in loue, and raw,   D₂ᴿ
Long dallying with *Hero*, nothing saw
That might delight him more, yet he suspected
Some amorous rites or other were neglected.

30 and] and like *1629, 1637, Rob. to Bull.*   55 you] ye *1613*   58 lep]
leap *1629, 1637, Rob., Cunn.*

65 Therefore vnto his bodie hirs he clung,
   She, fearing on the rushes to be flung,
   Striu'd with redoubled strength: the more she striued,
   The more a gentle pleasing heat reuiued,
   Which taught him all that elder louers know,
70 And now the same gan so to scorch and glow,
   As in plaine termes (yet cunningly) he crau'd it,
   Loue alwaies makes those eloquent that haue it.
   Shee, with a kind of graunting, put him by it,
   And euer as he thought himselfe most nigh it,
75 Like to the tree of *Tantalus* she fled,
   And seeming lauish, sau'de her maydenhead.
   Ne're king more sought to keepe his diademe,
   Than Hero this inestimable gemme.
   Aboue our life we loue a stedfast friend,
80 Yet when a token of great worth we send,
   We often kisse it, often looke thereon,
   And stay the messenger that would be gon:
   No maruell then, though *Hero* would not yeeld
   So soone to part from that she deerely held.
85 Iewels being lost are found againe, this neuer,
   T'is lost but once, and once lost, lost for euer.
 v   Now had the morne espy'de her louers steeds,
   Whereat she starts, puts on her purple weeds,
   And red for anger that he stayd so long,
90 All headlong throwes her selfe the clouds among,
   And now *Leander* fearing to be mist,
   Imbrast her sodainly, tooke leaue, and kist.
   Long was he taking leaue, and loath to go,
   And kist againe, as louers vse to do.
95 Sad *Hero* wroong him by the hand, and wept,
   Saying, let your vowes and promises be kept.
   Then standing at the doore, she turnd about,
   As loath to see *Leander* going out.
   And now the sunne that through th'orizon peepes,
100 As pittying these louers, downeward creepes,
   So that in silence of the cloudie night,
   Though it was morning, did he take his flight.
   But what the secret trustie night conceal'd
   Leanders amorous habit soone reueal'd,
105 With *Cupids* myrtle was his bonet crownd,
   About his armes the purple riband wound,
   Wherewith she wreath'd her largely spreading heare,

68 pleasing] pleasant *1600*   71 he crau'd] he'd crave *Rob.:* he crave
Dyce² etc.   85 being] beene *1613–37*   94 vsde *1600*   100 downwards
1629, 1637   103 what] when *1637*

Nor could the youth abstaine, but he must weare
The sacred ring wherewith she was endow'd,
When first religious chastitie she vow'd: 110
Which made his loue through *Sestos* to bee knowne,
And thence vnto *Abydus* sooner blowne
Than he could saile, for incorporeal Fame,   D₃ᴿ
Whose waight consists in nothing but her name,
Is swifter than the wind, whose tardie plumes   115
Are reeking water and dull earthlie fumes.
Home when he came, he seem'd not to be there,
But like exiled aire thrust from his sphere,
Set in a forren place, and straight from thence,
Alcides like, by mightie violence   120
He would haue chac'd away the swelling maine,
That him from her vniustly did detaine.
Like as the sunne in a Dyameter,
Fires and inflames obiects remooued farre,
And heateth kindly, shining lat'rally;   125
So beautie, sweetly quickens when t'is ny,
But being separated and remooued,
Burnes where it cherisht, murders where it loued.
Therefore euen as an Index to a booke,
So to his mind was yoong *Leanders* looke.   130
O none but gods haue power their loue to hide,
Affection by the count'nance is descride.
The light of hidden fire itselfe discouers,
And loue that is conceal'd, betraies poore louers.
His secret flame apparantly was seene,   135
Leanders Father knew where hee had beene,
And for the same mildly rebuk't his sonne,
Thinking to quench the sparckles new begonne.
But loue resisted once, growes passionate,   *v*
And nothing more than counsaile louers hate.   140
For as a hote prowd horse highly disdaines
To haue his head control'd, but breakes the raines,
Spits foorth the ringled bit, and with his houes
Checkes the submissiue ground: so hee that loues,
The more he is restrain'd, the woorse he fares.   145
What is it now, but mad *Leander* dares?
O *Hero, Hero,* thus he cry'de full oft,
And then he got him to a rocke aloft,
Where hauing spy'de her tower, long star'd he on't,
And pray'd the narrow toyling *Hellespont*   150

113 incorporall *1598²*, *1600*   115 windes *1637*   126 sweetly] quickly
1637   t'is] it's *1609–37*   128 it's cherisht *E. P.*   131 but gods haue
power] haue power but Gods *1613–37*

To part in twaine, that hee might come and go,
But still the rising billowes answered no.
With that hee stript him to the yu'rie skin,
And crying, Loue I come, leapt liuely in.
155   Whereat the saphir visag'd god grew prowd,
And made his capring *Triton* sound alowd,
Imagining that *Ganimed* displeas'd,
Had left the heauens; therefore on him hee seaz'd.
Leander striu'd, the waues about him wound,
160   And puld him to the bottome, where the ground
Was strewd with pearle, and in low corrall groues
Sweet singing Meremaids, sported with their loues
On heapes of heauie gold, and tooke great pleasure
To spurne in carelesse sort the shipwracke treasure.
[D₄ᴿ] 165   For here the stately azure pallace stood,
Where kingly *Neptune* and his traine abode.
The lustie god imbrast him, cald him loue,
And swore he neuer should returne to Ioue.
But when he knew it was not *Ganimed*,
170   For vnder water he was almost dead,
He heau'd him vp, and looking on his face,
Beat downe the bold waues with his triple mace,
Which mounted vp, intending to haue kist him,
And fell in drops like teares, because they mist him.
175   *Leander* being vp, began to swim,
And looking backe, saw *Neptune* follow him,
Whereat agast, the poore soule gan to crie,
O let mee visite *Hero* ere I die.
The god put *Helles* bracelet on his arme,
180   And swore the sea should neuer doe him harme.
He clapt his plumpe cheekes, with his tresses playd,
And smiling wantonly, his loue bewrayd.
He watcht his armes, and as they opend wide,
At euery stroke, betwixt them would he slide,
185   And steale a kisse, and then run out and daunce,
And as he turnd, cast many a lustfull glaunce,—
And threw him gawdie toies to please his eie,—
And diue into the water, and there prie
Vpon his brest, his thighs, and euerie lim,
190   And vp againe, and close beside him swim,
v   And talke of loue: *Leander* made replie,
You are deceau'd, I am no woman I.
Thereat smilde *Neptune*, and then told a tale,
How that a sheapheard sitting in a vale

164 shipwrackt *1629*: shipwreck *Rob., Dyce²* etc.   181 claps *1629, 1637*
187 throw *Dyce* etc.   191 talkt *1600*

Playd with a boy so faire and kind,   195
As for his loue both earth and heauen pyn'd;
That of the cooling riuer durst not drinke,
Least water-nymphs should pull him from the brinke.
And when hee sported in the fragrant lawnes,
Gote-footed Satyrs and vp-staring Fawnes   200
Would steale him thence. Ere halfe this tale was done,
Aye me, *Leander* cryde, th'enamoured sunne,
That now should shine on *Thetis* glassie bower,
Descends vpon my radiant *Heroes* tower.
O that these tardie armes of mine were wings!   205
And as he spake, vpon the waues he springs
Neptune was angrie that hee gaue no eare,
And in his heart reuenging malice bare:
He flung at him his mace, but as it went,
He cald it in, for loue made him repent.   210
The mace returning backe his owne hand hit,
As meaning to be veng'd for darting it.
When this fresh bleeding wound *Leander* viewd,
His colour went and came, as if he rewd
The greefe which *Neptune* felt. In gentle brests,   215
Relenting thoughts, remorse and pittie rests.
And who haue hard hearts, and obdurat minds,   E₁ᴿ
But vicious, harebraind, and illit'rat hinds?
The god seeing him with pittie to be moued,
Thereon concluded that he was beloued.   220
(Loue is too full of faith, too credulous,
With follie and false hope deluding vs.)
Wherefore *Leanders* fancie to surprize,
To the rich *Ocean* for gifts he flies.
'Tis wisedome to giue much, a gift preuailes,   225
When deepe perswading Oratorie failes.
By this *Leander* being nere the land,
Cast downe his wearie feet, and felt the sand.
Breathlesse albeit he were, he rested not,
Till to the solitarie tower he got, .   230
And knockt and cald, at which celestiall noise
The longing heart of *Hero* much more ioies
Then nymphs & sheapheards, when the timbrell rings,
Or crooked Dolphin when the sailer sings;
She stayd not for her robes, but straight arose,   235
And drunke with gladnesse, to the dore she goes,
Where seeing a naked man, she scriecht for feare,
Such sights as this to tender maids are rare,

And ran into the darke herselfe to hide.
240 Rich iewels in the darke are soonest spide.
Vnto her was he led, or rather drawne,
By those white limmes, which sparckled through the lawne.
 v The neerer that he came, the more she fled,
And seeking refuge, slipt into her bed.
245 Whereon *Leander* sitting, thus began,
Through numming cold all feeble, faint and wan:
    If not for loue, yet, loue, for pittie sake,
Me in thy bed and maiden bosome take,
At least vouchsafe these armes some little roome,
250 Who hoping to imbrace thee, cherely swome.
This head was beat with manie a churlish billow,
And therefore let it rest vpon thy pillow.
Herewith afrighted *Hero* shrunke away,
And in her luke-warme place *Leander* lay,
255 Whose liuely heat like fire from heauen fet,
Would animate grosse clay, and higher set
The drooping thoughts of base declining soules,
Then drerie *Mars* carowsing *Nectar* boules.
His hands he cast vpon her like a snare,
260 She ouercome with shame and sallow feare,
Like chast *Diana*, when *Acteon* spyde her,
Being sodainly betraide, dyu'd downe to hide her.
And as her siluer body downeward went,
With both her hands she made the bed a tent,
265 And in her owne mind thought her selfe secure,
O'recast with dim and darksome couerture.
And now she lets him whisper in her eare,
Flatter, intreat, promise, protest and sweare,
E₂ᴿ Yet euer as he greedily assayd
270 To touch those dainties, she the *Harpey* playd,
And euery lim did as a soldier stout,
Defend the fort, and keep the foe-man out.
For though the rising yu'rie mount he scal'd,
Which is with azure circling lines empal'd,
275 Much like a globe, (a globe may I tearme this,
By which loue sailes to regions full of blis,)
Yet there with *Sysiphus* he toyld in vaine,
Till gentle parlie did the truce obtaine.
Wherein *Leander* on her quiuering brest,

246 Through] Though *1598²*, *1600*   257 dropping *1629*, *1637*   260 sallow] shallow *1629*, *1637*   267 now *om. 1637*   269 euer] euer after *1613*
270 daintie *1613*   272 foe-men *1609-37*   279-300 *Owing probably to the displacement of a leaf in Marlowe's lost MS. these lines are given in wrong sequence in all previous editions. The early quartos all insert ll. 279-90 between 300 and 301, which cannot be right. Singer in his edition of 1821 shifted ll. 289,*

Breathlesse spoke some thing, and sigh'd out the rest;   280
Which so preuail'd, as he with small ado
Inclos'd her in his armes and kist her to.
And euerie kisse to her was as a charme,
And to *Leander* as a fresh alarme,
So that the truce was broke, and she alas,   285
(Poore sillie maiden) at his mercie was.
Loue is not ful of pittie (as men say)
But deaffe and cruell, where he meanes to pray.
Euen as a bird, which in our hands we wring,
Foorth plungeth, and oft flutters with her wing,   290
She trembling stroue, this strife of hers (like that
Which made the world) another world begat
Of vnknowne ioy. Treason was in her thought,
And cunningly to yeeld her selfe she sought.
Seeming not woon, yet woon she was at length,   295 *v*
In such warres women vse but halfe their strength.
Leander now like Theban *Hercules*,
Entred the orchard of *Th'esperides*,
Whose fruit none rightly can describe but hee
That puls or shakes it from the golden tree: 300
And now she wisht this night were neuer done,
And sigh'd to thinke vpon th'approching sunne,
For much it greeu'd her that the bright day-light
Should know the pleasure of this blessed night,
And them like *Mars* and *Ericine* display,   305
Both in each others armes chaind as they lay.
Againe she knew not how to frame her looke,
Or speake to him who in a moment tooke
That which so long so charily she kept,
And faine by stealth away she would haue crept,   310
And to some corner secretly haue gone,
Leauing *Leander* in the bed alone.
But as her naked feet were whipping out,
He on the suddaine cling'd her so about,
That Meremaid-like vnto the floore she slid,   315
One halfe appear'd, the other halfe was hid.
Thus neere the bed she blushing stood vpright,
And from her countenance behold ye might
A kind of twilight breake, which through the heare,

290 to a position between 278 and 291, and this order (278, 289–300, 279–88, 301) has been retained by all subsequent editors.   280 some things *1598², 1600*   281 he *om. 1637*   287 pittie] mercy.   304 this] the *1600* 305 them *conj. Broughton, Dyce etc.:* then *Qq* display *Singer etc.:* displayd *Qq*   306 others] other *1600*   lay *Singer etc.:* layd *Qq*   308 who] whom *1600*   316 One] And *1598², 1600*   319 heare] haire *1629, 1637:* air *Singer etc.* hair *is probably meant*

320   As from an orient cloud, glymse here and there.
E₄ᴮ   And round about the chamber this false morne
      Brought foorth the day before the day was borne.
      So *Heroes* ruddie cheeke *Hero* betrayd,
      And her all naked to his sight displayd,
325   Whence his admiring eyes more pleasure tooke
      Than *Dis*, on heapes of gold fixing his looke.
      By this *Apollos* golden harpe began
      To sound foorth musicke to the *Ocean*,
      Which watchfull *Hesperus* no sooner heard,
330   But he the day bright-bearing Car prepar'd,
      And ran before, as Harbenger of light,
      And with his flaring beames mockt ougly night,
      Till she o'recome with anguish, shame, and rage,
      Dang'd downe to hell her loathsome carriage.

Desunt nonnulla.

320 glymse] glimse *1629, 1637*: glimps'd *Singer, etc. The word intended is doubt-less* gleams.   330 day bright-bearing] Day's bright-bearing *conj. Broughton*: bright Day-bearing *Dyce etc.*   334 Dang'd] Hurld *1598², 1600* Desunt nonnulla *1598¹*: *The end of the second Sestyad 1598²–1637. The edition 1598¹ ends here. The rest of the poem, Chapman's work, appeared first in ed. 1598², the text of which is from this point followed.*

TO MY BEST ESTEEMED
AND WORTHELY HONORED

LADY, THE LADY WALSINGHAM,
one of the Ladies of her Maiesties Bed-chamber.

I PRESENT *your Ladiship with the last affections of the first two Louers that euer* Muse *shrinde in the Temple of* Memorie; *being drawne by strange instigation to employ some of my serious time in so trifeling a subiect, which yet made the first Author, diuine* Musæus, *eternall. And were it not that wee must subiect our accounts of these common receiued conceits to seruile custome; it goes much against my hand to signe that for a trifling subiect, on which more worthines of soule hath been shewed, and weight of diuine wit, than can vouchsafe residence in the leaden grauitie of any* Mony-Monger; *in whose profession all serious subiects are concluded. But he that shuns trifles must shun the world; out of whose reuerend heapes of substance and austeritie, I can, and will, ere long, single, or tumble out as brainles and passionate fooleries, as euer panted in the bosome of the most ridiculous Louer. Accept it therfore (good Madam) though as a trifle, yet as a serious argument of my affection: for to bee thought thankefull for all free and honourable fauours, is a great summe of that riches my whole thrift intendeth.*

 Such vncourtly and sillie dispositions as mine, whose contentment hath other obiects than profit or glorie; are as glad, simply for the naked merit of vertue, to honour such as aduance her, as others that are hired to commend with deepeliest politique bountie.

 It hath therefore adioynde much contentment to my desire of your true honour to heare men of desert in Court adde to mine owne knowledge of your noble disposition, how gladly you doe your best to preferre their desires; and haue as absolute respect to their meere good parts, as if they came perfumed and charmed with golden incitements. And this most sweet inclination, that flowes from the truth and eternitie of Nobles, assure your Ladiship doth more suite your other Ornaments, and makes more to the aduancement of your Name, and happines of your proceedings, then if (like others) you displaied Ensignes of state and sowrenes in your forehead; made smooth with nothing but sensualitie and presents.

 This poore Dedication (in figure of the other vnitie betwixt Sir Thomas *and your selfe) hath reioynd you with him, my honoured best friend; whose continuance of ancient kindnes to my still-obscured estate, though it cannot encrease my loue to him, which*

10

[E₄ᴿ]

20

30

v

v

40 *hath euer been entirely circulare; yet shall it encourage my
deserts to their vtmost requitall, and make my hartie grati-
tude speake; to which the vnhappines of my life
hath hetherto been vncomfortable and
painfull dumbnes.*

By your Ladiships vowd in most wished seruice:

George Chapman.

The Argument of the Third Sestyad.   F₁R

Leander *to the enuious light*
Resignes his night-sports with the night,
And swims the Hellespont *againe;*
Thesme *the Deitie soueraigne*
Of Customes and religious rites   5
Appeares, improuing his delites
Since Nuptiall honors he neglected;
Which straight he vowes shall be effected.
Faire Hero *left Deuirginate*
Waies, and with furie wailes her state: 10
But with her loue and womans wit
She argues, and approueth it.

New light giues new directions, Fortunes new
To fashion our indeuours that ensue,
More harsh (at lest more hard) more graue and hie
Our subiect runs, and our sterne *Muse* must flie.
Loues edge is taken off, and that light flame,   5
Those thoughts, ioyes, longings, that before became
High vnexperienst blood, and maids sharpe plights,
Must now grow staid, and censure the delights,   v
That being enioyd aske iudgement; now we praise,
As hauing parted: Euenings crowne the daies.   10
   And now ye wanton loues, and yong desires,
Pied vanitie, the mint of strange Attires;
Ye lisping Flatteries, and obsequious Glances,
Relentfull Musicks, and attractiue Dances,
And you detested Charmes constraining loue,   15
Shun loues stolne sports by that these Louers proue.
   By this the Soueraigne of Heauens golden fires,
And yong *Leander*, Lord of his desires,
Together from their louers armes arose:
Leander into *Hellespontus* throwes   20
His *Hero*-handled bodie, whose delight
Made him disdaine each other Epethite.
And as amidst the enamourd waues he swims,

He cals Phœ-
bus the God of
Gold, since the
vertue of his
beams creates
it.

The God of gold of purpose guilt his lims,
That this word guilt, including double sence,   25
The double guilt of his *Incontinence*,
Might be exprest, that had no stay t'employ
The treasure which the Loue-god let him ioy
In his deare *Hero*, with such sacred thrift,
As had beseemd so sanctified a gift: 30
But like a greedie vulgar Prodigall

Would of the stock dispend, and rudely fall
Before his time, to that vnblessed blessing,
F₂ᴿ Which for lusts plague doth perish with possessing.
35 *Joy grauen in sence, like snow in water wasts;*
Without preserue of vertue nothing lasts.
What man is he that with a welthie eie
Enioyes a beautie richer than the skie,
Through whose white skin, softer then soundest sleep,
40 With damaske eyes, the rubie blood doth peep,
And runs in branches through her azure vaines,
Whose mixture and first fire, his loue attaines;
Whose both hands limit, both Loues deities,
And sweeten humane thoughts like Paradise;
45 Whose disposition silken is and kinde,
Directed with an earth-exempted minde;
Who thinks not heauen with such a loue is giuen?
And who like earth would spend that dower of heauen,
With ranke desire to ioy it all at first?
50 What simply kils our hunger, quencheth thirst,
Clothes but our nakednes, and makes vs liue,
Praise doth not any of her fauours giue:
But what doth plentifully minister
Beautious apparell and delicious cheere,
55 So orderd that it still excites desire,
And still giues pleasure freenes to aspire
The palme of *Bountie*, euer moyst preseruing:
To loues sweet life this is the courtly caruing.
Thus *Time*, and all-states-ordering *Ceremonie*
v 60 Had banisht all offence: *Times* golden *Thie*
Vpholds the flowrie bodie of the earth,
In sacred harmonie, and euery birth
Of men, and actions makes legitimate,
Being vsde aright; *The vse of time is Fate.*
65 Yet did the gentle flood transfer once more
This prize of Loue home to his fathers shore;
Where he vnlades himselfe of that false welth
That makes few rich; treasures composde by stelth;
And to his sister kinde *Hermione*,
70 (Who on the shore kneeld, praying to the sea
For his returne) he all Loues goods did show
In *Hero* seasde for him, in him for *Hero*.
His most kinde sister all his secrets knew,
And to her singing like a shower he flew,
75 Sprinkling the earth, that to their tombs tooke in
Streames dead for loue, to leaue his iuorie skin,

32 of] on

Which yet a snowie fome did leaue aboue,
As soule to the dead water that did loue;
And from thence did the first white Roses spring,
(For loue is sweet and faire in euery thing)   80
And all the sweetned shore as he did goe,
Was crownd with odrous roses white as snow.
Loue-blest *Leander* was with loue so filled,
That loue to all that toucht him he instilled.
And as the colours of all things we see,   85
To our sights powers communicated bee: F,ᴿ
So to all obiects that in compasse came
Of any sence he had; his sences flame
Flowd from his parts, with force so virtuall,
It fir'd with sence things meere insensuall.   90
   Now (with warme baths and odours comforted)
When he lay downe he kindly kist his bed,
As consecrating it to *Heros* right,
And vowd thereafter that what euer sight
Put him in minde of *Hero*, or her blisse,   95
Should be her Altar to prefer a kisse.
   Then laid he forth his late inriched armes,
In whose white circle Loue writ all his charmes,
And made his characters sweet *Heros* lims,
When on his breasts warme sea she sideling swims.   100
And as those armes (held vp in circle) met,
He said: See sister *Heros* Carquenet,
Which she had rather weare about her neck,
Then all the iewels that doth *Juno* deck.
   But as he shooke with passionate desire,   105
To put in flame his other secret fire,
A musick so diuine did pierce his eare,
As neuer yet his rauisht sence did heare:
When suddenly a light of twentie hews
Brake through the roofe, and like the Rainbow views   110
Amazd *Leander;* in whose beames came downe
The Goddesse *Ceremonie*, with a Crowne   *v*
Of all the stars, and heauen with her descended,
Her flaming haire to her bright feete extended,
By which hung all the bench of Deities;   115
And in a chaine, compact of eares and eies,
She led Religion; all her bodie was
Cleere and transparent as the purest glasse:
For she was all presented to the sence;
Deuotion, Order, State, and Reuerence   120
Her shadowes were; Societie, Memorie;
All which her sight made liue; her absence die.

A rich disparent Pentackle she weares,
Drawne full of circles and strange characters:
125 Her face was changeable to euerie eie;
One way lookt ill, another graciouslie;
Which while men viewd, they cheerfull were & holy:
But looking off, vicious and melancholy:
The snakie paths to each obserued law,
130 Did *Policie* in her broad bosome draw:
One hand a Mathematique Christall swayes,
Which gathering in one line a thousand rayes
From her bright eyes, *Confusion* burnes to death,
And all estates of men distinguisheth.
135 By it *Morallitie* and *Comelinesse*
Themselues in all their sightly figures dresse.
Her other hand a lawrell rod applies,
[F₄ᴿ] To beate back *Barbarisme*, and *Auarice*,
That followd eating earth, and excrement
140 And humane lims; and would make proud ascent
To seates of Gods, were *Ceremonie* slaine;
The *Howrs* and *Graces* bore her glorious traine,
And all the sweetes of our societie
Were Spherde, and treasurde in her bountious eie.
145 Thus she appeard, and sharply did reproue
Leanders bluntnes in his violent loue;
Tolde him how poore was substance without rites,
Like bils vnsignd, desires without delites;
Like meates vnseasond; like ranke corne that growes
150 On Cottages, that none or reapes or sowes:
Not being with ciuill forms confirm'd and bounded,
For humane dignities and comforts founded:
But loose and secret all their glories hide,
Feare fils the chamber, darknes decks the Bride.
155 She vanisht, leauing pierst *Leanders* hart
With sence of his vnceremonious part,
In which with plaine neglect of Nuptiall rites,
He close and flatly fell to his delites:
And instantly he vowd to celebrate
160 All rites pertaining to his maried state.
So vp he gets and to his father goes,
To whose glad eares he doth his vowes disclose:
The Nuptials are resolu'd with vtmost powre,
v And he at night would swim to *Heros* towre.
165 From whence he ment to *Sestus* forked Bay
To bring her couertly, where ships must stay,
Sent by his father throughly rigd and mand,

167 his] her

To waft her safely to *Abydus* Strand.
There leaue we him, and with fresh wing pursue
Astonisht *Hero*, whose most wished view   170
I thus long haue forborne, because I left her
So out of countnance, and her spirits bereft her.
To looke on one abasht is impudence,
When of sleight faults he hath too deepe a sence.
Her blushing het her chamber: she lookt out,   175
And all the ayre she purpled round about,
And after it a foule black day befell,
Which euer since a red morne doth foretell:
And still renewes our woes for *Heros* wo,
And foule it prou'd, because it figur'd so   180
The next nights horror, which prepare to heare;
I faile if it prophane your daintiest eare.
    Then thou most strangely-intellectuall fire,
That proper to my soule hast power t'inspire
Her burning faculties, and with the wings   185
Of thy vnspheared flame visitst the springs
Of spirits immortall; Now (as swift as Time
Doth follow Motion) finde th'eternall Clime
Of his free soule, whose liuing subiect stood
Vp to the chin in the Pyerean flood,   190 G₁ᴿ
And drunke to me halfe this Musean storie,
Inscribing it to deathles Memorie:
Confer with it, and make my pledge as deepe,
That neithers draught be consecrate to sleepe.
Tell it how much his late desires I tender,   195
(If yet it know not) and to light surrender
My soules darke ofspring, willing it should die
To loues, to passions, and societie.
    Sweet *Hero* left vpon her bed alone,
Her maidenhead, her vowes, *Leander* gone,   200
And nothing with her but a violent crew
Of new come thoughts that yet she neuer knew,
Euen to her selfe a stranger; was much like
Th'*Iberian* citie that wars hand did strike
By English force in princely *Essex* guide,   205
When peace assur'd her towres hand fortifide;
And golden-fingred *Jndia* had bestowd
Such wealth on her, that strength and Empire flowd
Into her Turrets; and her virgin waste
The wealthie girdle of the Sea embraste: 210
Till our *Leander* that made *Mars* his *Cupid*,

173 on] of *Emended 1629, 37*   183 thou *T. B.*; how *Qg*; now *Rob., Cunn.*;
no *Dyce, Bull.*

For soft loue-sutes, with iron thunders chid:
Swum to her Towers, dissolu'd her virgin zone;
Lead in his power, and made Confusion
215 Run through her streets amazd, that she supposde
 v   She had not been in her owne walls inclosde:
But rapt by wonder to some forraine state,
Seeing all her issue so disconsolate:
And all her peacefull mansions possest
220 With wars iust spoyle, and many a forraine guest
From euery corner driuing an enioyer,
Supplying it with power of a destroyer.
So far'd fayre *Hero* in th'expugned fort
Of her chast bosome, and of euery sort
225 Strange thoughts possest her, ransacking her brest
For that that was not there, her wonted rest.
She was a mother straight and bore with paine,
Thoughts that spake straight and wisht their mother slaine;
She hates their liues, & they their own & hers:
230 Such strife still growes where sin the race prefers.
Loue is a golden bubble full of dreames,
That waking breakes, and fils vs with extreames.
She mus'd how she could looke vpon her Sire,
And not shew that without, that was intire.
235 For as a glasse is an inanimate eie,
And outward formes imbraceth inwardlie:
So is the eye an animate glasse that showes
In-formes without vs. And as *Phœbus* throwes
His beames abroad, though he in clowdes be closde,
240 Still glancing by them till he finde opposde,
A loose and rorid vapour that is fit
G₂ᴿ T'euent his searching beames, and vseth it
To forme a tender twentie-coloured eie,
Cast in a circle round about the skie:
245 So when our firie soule, our bodies starre,
(That euer is in motion circulare)
Conceiues a forme; in seeking to display it
Through all our clowdie parts, it doth conuey it
Forth at the eye, as the most pregnant place,
250 And that reflects it round about the face.
And this euent vncourtly *Hero* thought,
Her inward guilt would in her lookes haue wrought:
For yet the worlds stale cunning she resisted
To beare foule thoughts, yet forge what lookes she listed,
255 And held it for a very sillie sleight,
To make a perfect mettall counterfeit:
Glad to disclaime her selfe, proud of an Art,

That makes the face a Pandar to the hart.
Those be the painted Moones, whose lights prophane
Beauties true Heauen, at full still in their wane.   260
Those be the Lapwing faces that still crie,
Here tis, when that they vow is nothing nie.
Base fooles, when euery moorish fowle can teach
That which men thinke the height of humane reach.
But custome that the Apoplexie is   265
Of beddred nature, and liues led amis,
And takes away all feeling of offence,
Yet brazde not *Heros* brow with impudence;   *v*
And this she thought most hard to bring to pas,
To seeme in countnance other then she was,   270
As if she had two soules; one for the face,
One for the hart; and that they shifted place
As either list to vtter, or conceale
What they conceiu'd: or as one soule did deale
With both affayres at once, keeps and eiects   275
Both at an instant contrarie effects:
Retention and eiection in her powrs
Being acts alike: for this one vice of ours,
That forms the thought, and swaies the countenance,
Rules both our motion and our vtterance.   280
    These and more graue conceits toyld *Heros* spirits:
For though the light of her discoursiue wits,
Perhaps might finde some little hole to pas
Through all these worldly cinctures; yet (alas)
There was a heauenly flame incompast her;   285
Her Goddesse, in whose Phane she did prefer
Her virgin vowes; from whose impulsiue sight
She knew the black shield of the darkest night
Could not defend her, nor wits subtilst art:
This was the point pierst *Hero* to the hart.   290
Who heauie to the death, with a deep sigh
And hand that languisht, tooke a robe was nigh,
Exceeding large, and of black Cypres made,
In which she sate, hid from the day in shade,   G₃ᴿ
Euen ouer head and face downe to her feete;   295
Her left hand made it at her bosome meete;
Her right hand leand on her hart-bowing knee,
Wrapt in vnshapefull foulds: twas death to see:
Her knee stayd that, and that her falling face,
Each limme helpt other to put on disgrace.   300
No forme was seene, where forme held all her sight:
But like an Embrion that saw neuer light:
Or like a scorched statue made a cole

With three-wingd lightning: or a wretched soule
305 Muffled with endles darknes, she did sit:
The night had neuer such a heauie spirit.
Yet might an imitating eye well see,
How fast her cleere teares melted on her knee
Through her black vaile, and turnd as black as it,
310 Mourning to be her teares: then wrought her wit
With her broke vow, her Goddesse wrath, her fame,
All tooles that enginous despayre could frame:
Which made her strow the floore with her torne haire,
And spread her mantle peece-meale in the aire.
315 Like *Ioues* sons club, strong passion strook her downe,
And with a piteous shrieke inforst her swoune:
Her shrieke, made with another shrieke ascend
The frighted Matron that on her did tend:
And as with her owne crie her sence was slaine,
v 320 So with the other it was calde againe.
She rose and to her bed made forced way,
And layd her downe euen where *Leander* lay:
And all this while the red sea of her blood
Ebd with *Leander:* but now turnd the flood,
325 And all her fleete of sprites came swelling in
With childe of saile, and did hot fight begin
With those seuere conceits, she too much markt,
And here *Leanders* beauties were imbarkt.
He came in swimming painted all with ioyes,
330 Such as might sweeten hell: his thought destroyes
All her destroying thoughts: she thought she felt
His heart in hers with her contentions melt,
And chid her soule that it could so much erre,
To check the true ioyes he deseru'd in her.
335 Her fresh heat blood cast figures in her eyes,
And she supposde she saw in *Neptunes* skyes
How her star wandred, washt in smarting brine
For her loues sake, that with immortall wine
Should be embath'd, and swim in more hearts ease,
340 Than there was water in the Sestian seas.
Then said her *Cupid* prompted spirit; Shall I
Sing mones to such delightsome harmony?
Shall slick-tongde fame patcht vp with voyces rude,
The drunken bastard of the multitude,
345 (Begot when father Iudgement is away,
[G₄ᴿ] And gossip-like, sayes because others say,
Takes newes as if it were too hot to eate,
And spits it slauering forth for dog-fees meate)
Make me for forging a phantastique vow,

Presume to beare what makes graue matrons bow?   350
Good vowes are neuer broken with good deedes,
For then good deedes were bad: vowes are but seedes,
And good deeds fruits; euen those good deedes that grow
From other stocks, than from th'obserued vow.
That is a good deede that preuents a bad: 355
Had I not yeelded, slaine my selfe I had.
Hero Leander is, Leander Hero:
Such vertue loue hath to make one of two.
If then *Leander* did my maydenhead git,
Leander being my selfe I still retaine it.   360
We breake chast vowes when we liue loosely euer:
But bound as we are, we liue loosely neuer.
Two constant louers being ioynd in one,
Yeelding to one another, yeeld to none.
We know not how to vow, till loue vnblinde vs,   365
And vowes made ignorantly neuer binde vs.
Too true it is that when t'is gone men hate
The ioyes as vaine they tooke in loues estate:
But that's, since they haue lost, the heauenly light
Should shew them way to iudge of all things right.   370
When life is gone death must implant his terror,
As death is foe to life, so loue to error.   v
Before we loue how range we through this sphere,
Searching the sundrie fancies hunted here:
Now with desire of wealth transported quite   375
Beyond our free humanities delight:
Now with ambition climing falling towrs,
Whose hope to scale our feare to fall deuours:
Now rapt with pastimes, pomp, all ioyes impure;
In things without vs no delight is sure.   380
But loue with all ioyes crownd, within doth sit;
O Goddesse pitie loue and pardon it.
This spake she weeping: but her Goddesse eare
Burnd with too sterne a heat, and would not heare.
Aie me, hath heauens straight fingers no more graces,   385
For such as *Hero*, then for homeliest faces?
Yet she hopte well, and in her sweet conceit
Waying her arguments, she thought them weight:
And that the logick of *Leanders* beautie,
And them together would bring proofes of dutie.   390
And if her soule, that was a skilfull glance
Of Heauens great essence, found such imperance
In her loues beauties; she had confidence
Ioue lou'd him too, and pardond her offence.

383 she *Rob. etc.:* he *Qq*

395 *Beautie in heauen and earth this grace doth win,*
It supples rigor, and it lessens sin.
Thus, her sharpe wit, her loue, her secrecie,
[H₁ᴿ] Trouping together, made her wonder why
She should not leaue her bed, and to the Temple?
400 Her health said she must liue; her sex, dissemble.
She viewd *Leanders* place, and wisht he were
Turnd to his place, so his place were *Leander.*
Aye me (said she) that loues sweet life and sence
Should doe it harme! my loue had not gone hence,
405 Had he been like his place. O blessed place,
Image of Constancie. Thus my loues grace
Parts no where but it leaues some thing behinde
Worth obseruation: he renowmes his kinde.
His motion is like heauens Orbiculer:
410 For where he once is, he is euer there.
This place was mine: *Leander* now t'is thine;
Thou being my selfe, then it is double mine:
Mine, and *Leanders* mine, *Leanders* mine.
O see what wealth it yeelds me, nay yeelds him:
415 For I am in it, he for me doth swim.
Rich, fruitfull loue, that doubling selfe estates
Elixer-like contracts, though separates.
Deare place I kisse thee, and doe welcome thee,
As from *Leander* euer sent to mee.

The end of the third Sestyad.

v The Argument of the Fourth Sestyad.

Hero, *in sacred habit deckt,*
Doth priuate sacrifice effect.
Her Skarfs description wrought by fate,
Ostents that threaten her estate.
5 *The strange, yet Phisicall euents,*
Leanders *counterfeit presents.*
Jn thunder, Ciprides *descends,*
Presaging both the louers ends.
Ecte *the Goddesse of remorce,*
10 *With vocall and articulate force*
Inspires Leucote, Venus *swan,*
T' excuse the beautious Sestian.
Venus, *to wreake her rites abuses,*
Creates the monster Eronusis;

[Er]onusis,
Dissi[mu]la-
tion.

Argument 14–16 The marginal note is partially clipped away in the British
Museum copy of ed. 1598².

Enflaming Heros *Sacrifice,*   15
With lightning darted from her eyes:
And thereof springs the painted beast,
That euer since taints euery breast.

Now from *Leanders* place she rose, and found
Her haire and rent robe scattred on the ground:
Which taking vp, she euery peece did lay   H.ᴿ
Vpon an Altar; where in youth of day
She vsde t'exhibite priuate Sacrifice: 5
Those would she offer to the Deities
Of her faire Goddesse, and her powerfull son,
As relicks of her late-felt passion:
And in that holy sort she vowd to end them,
In hope her violent fancies that did rend them,   10
Would as quite fade in her loues holy fire,
As they should in the flames she ment t'inspire.
Then put she on all her religious weedes,
That deckt her in her secret sacred deedes:
A crowne of Isickles, that sunne nor fire   15
Could euer melt, and figur'd chast desire.
A golden star shinde in her naked breast,
In honour of the Queene-light of the East.
In her right hand she held a siluer wand,
On whose bright top *Peristera* did stand,   20
Who was a Nymph, but now transformd a Doue,
And in her life was deare in *Venus* loue:
And for her sake she euer since that time,
Chusde Doues to draw her Coach through heauens blew clime.
Her plentious haire in curled billowes swims   25
On her bright shoulder: her harmonious lims
Sustainde no more but a most subtile vaile
That hung on them, as it durst not assaile
Their different concord: for the weakest ayre   *v*
Could raise it swelling from her bewties fayre: 30
Nor did it couer, but adumbrate onelie
Her most heart-piercing parts, that a blest eie
Might see (as it did shadow) fearfullie,
All that all-loue-deseruing Paradise:
It was as blew as the most freezing skies,   35
Neere the Seas hew, for thence her Goddesse came:
On it a skarfe she wore of wondrous frame;
In midst whereof she wrought a virgins face,
From whose each cheeke a firie blush did chace
Two crimson flames, that did two waies extend,   40
Spreading the ample skarfe to either end,
Which figur'd the diuision of her minde,

Whiles yet she rested bashfully inclinde,
And stood not resolute to wed *Leander*.
45   This seru'd her white neck for a purple sphere,
And cast it selfe at full breadth downe her back.
There (since the first breath that begun the wrack
Of her free quiet from *Leanders* lips)
She wrought a Sea in one flame full of ships:
50   But that one ship where all her wealth did passe
(Like simple marchants goods) *Leander* was:
For in that Sea she naked figured him;
Her diuing needle taught him how to swim,
And to each thred did such resemblance giue,
H₃ᴿ 55   For ioy to be so like him, it did liue.
    Things senceles liue by art, and rationall die,
     By rude contempt of art and industrie.
Scarce could she work but in her strength of thought,
She feard she prickt *Leander* as she wrought:
60   And oft would shrieke so, that her Guardian frighted,
Would staring haste, as with some mischiefe cited.
    They double life that dead things griefs sustayne:
    They kill that feele not their friends liuing payne.
Sometimes she feard he sought her infamie,
65   And then as she was working of his eie,
She thought to pricke it out to quench her ill:
But as she prickt, it grew more perfect still.
    Trifling attempts no serious acts aduance;
    The fire of loue is blowne by dalliance.
70   In working his fayre neck she did so grace it,
She still was working her owne armes t'imbrace it:
That, and his shoulders, and his hands were seene
Aboue the streame, and with a pure Sea greene
She did so queintly shadow euery lim,
75   All might be seene beneath the waues to swim.
    In this conceited skarfe she wrought beside
A Moone in change, and shooting stars did glide
In number after her with bloodie beames,
Which figur'd her affects in their extreames,
80   Pursuing Nature in her Cynthian bodie,
v   And did her thoughts running on change implie:
For maids take more delights when they prepare
And thinke of wiues states, than when wiues they are.
Beneath all these she wrought a Fisherman,
85   Drawing his nets from forth that Ocean;
Who drew so hard ye might discouer well,
The toughned sinewes in his neck did swell:
His inward straines draue out his blood-shot eyes,

And springs of sweat did in his forehead rise:
Yet was of nought but of a Serpent sped,   90
That in his bosome flew and stung him dead.
And this by fate into her minde was sent,
Not wrought by meere instinct of her intent.
At the skarfs other end her hand did frame,
Neere the forkt point of the deuided flame,   95
A countrie virgin keeping of a Vine,
Who did of hollow bulrushes combine
Snares for the stubble-louing Grashopper,
And by her lay her skrip that nourisht her.
Within a myrtle shade she sate and sung,   100
And tufts of wauing reedes about her sprung:
Where lurkt two Foxes, that while she applide
Her trifling snares, their theeueries did deuide:
One to the vine, another to her skrip,
That she did negligently ouerslip: 105
By which her fruitfull vine and holesome fare,
She suffred spoyld to make a childish snare.   [H₄ᴿ]
These omenous fancies did her soule expresse,
And euery finger made a Prophetesse,
To shew what death was hid in loues disguise,   110
And make her iudgement conquer destinies.
O what sweet formes fayre Ladies soules doe shrowd,
Were they made seene & forced through their blood,
If through their beauties like rich work through lawn,
They would set forth their minds with vertues drawn,   115
In letting graces from their fingers flie,
To still their yeasty thoughts with industrie:
That their plied wits in numbred silks might sing
Passions huge conquest, and their needels leading
Affection prisoner through their own-built citties,   120
Pinniond with stories and Arachnean ditties.
    Proceed we now with *Heros* sacrifice;
She odours burnd, and from their smoke did rise
Vnsauorie fumes, that ayre with plagues inspired,
And then the consecrated sticks she fired,   125
On whose pale flame an angrie spirit flew,
And beate it downe still as it vpward grew.
The virgin Tapers that on th'altar stood,
When she inflam'd them burnd as red as blood:
All sad ostents of that too neere successe,   130
That made such mouing beauties motionlesse.
Then *Hero* wept; but her affrighted eyes
She quickly wrested from the sacrifice: *v*

117 yeasty] yas

Shut them, and inwards for *Leander* lookt,
135 Searcht her soft bosome, and from thence she pluckt
His louely picture: which when she had viewd,
Her beauties were with all loues ioyes renewd.
The odors sweetned, and the fires burnd cleere,
Leanders forme left no ill obiect there.
140 Such was his beautie that the force of light,
Whose knowledge teacheth wonders infinite,
The strength of number and proportion,
Nature had plaste in it to make it knowne
Art was her daughter, and what humane wits
145 For studie lost, intombd in drossie spirits.
After this accident (which for her glorie
Hero could not but make a historie)
Th' inhabitants of *Sestus*, and *Abydus*
Did euerie yeare with feasts propitious,
150 To faire *Leanders* picture sacrifice,
And they were persons of especiall prize
That were allowd it, as an ornament
T' inrich their houses; for the continent
Of the strange vertues all approu'd it held:
155 For euen the very looke of it repeld
All blastings, witchcrafts, and the strifes of nature
In those diseases that no hearbs could cure.
The woolfie sting of Auarice it would pull,
I₁ᴿ And make the rankest miser bountifull.
160 It kild the feare of thunder and of death;
The discords that conceits ingendereth
Twixt man and wife, it for the time would cease:
The flames of loue it quencht, and would increase:
Held in a princes hand it would put out
165 The dreadfulst Comet: it would ease all doubt
Of threatned mischiefes: it would bring asleepe
Such as were mad: it would enforce to weepe
Most barbarous eyes: and many more effects
This picture wrought, and sprung *Leandrian* sects,
170 Of which was *Hero* first: For he whose forme
(Held in her hand) cleerd such a fatall storme,
From hell she thought his person would defend her,
Which night and *Hellespont* would quickly send her.
With this confirmd, she vowd to banish quite
175 All thought of any check to her delite:
And in contempt of sillie bashfulnes,
She would the faith of her desires professe:
Where her Religion should be Policie,
To follow loue with zeale her pietie:

Her chamber her Cathedrall Church should be,   180
And her *Leander* her chiefe Deitie.
For in her loue these did the gods forego;
And though her knowledge did not teach her so,
Yet did it teach her this, that what her hart
Did greatest hold in her selfe greatest part,   185 *v*
That she did make her god; and t'was lesse nought
To leaue gods in profession and in thought,
Than in her loue and life: for therein lies
Most of her duties, and their dignities;
And raile the brain-bald world at what it will,   190
Thats the grand Atheisme that raignes in it still.
Yet singularitie she would vse no more,
For she was singular too much before:
But she would please the world with fayre pretext;
Loue would not leaue her conscience perplext.   195
Great men that will haue lesse doe for them still,
Must beare them out though th'acts be nere so ill.
Meannes must Pandar be to Excellence,
Pleasure attones Falshood and Conscience:
Dissembling was the worst (thought *Hero* then)   200
And that was best now she must liue with men.
O vertuous loue that taught her to doe best,
When she did worst, and when she thought it lest.
Thus would she still proceed in works diuine,
And in her sacred state of priesthood shine,   205
Handling the holy rites with hands as bold,
As if therein she did *Ioues* thunder hold;
And need not feare those menaces of error,
Which she at others threw with greatest terror.
O louely *Hero*, nothing is thy sin,   210
Wayd with those foule faults other Priests are in;   I₂ᴿ
That hauing neither faiths, nor works, nor bewties,
T'engender any scuse for slubberd duties;
With as much countnance fill their holie chayres,
And sweat denouncements gainst prophane affayres,   215
As if their liues were cut out by their places,
And they the only fathers of the Graces.
   Now as with setled minde she did repaire,
Her thoughts to sacrifice, her rauisht haire
And her torne robe which on the altar lay,   220
And only for Religions fire did stay;
She heard a thunder by the Cyclops beaten,
In such a volley as the world did threaten,
Giuen *Venus* as she parted th'ayrie Sphere,

198 Excellence *1629, 37*] Excellencie *1598-1613*

225 Discending now to chide with *Hero* here:
When suddenly the Goddesse waggoners,
The Swans and Turtles that in coupled pheres,
Through all worlds bosoms draw her influence,
Lighted in *Heros* window, and from thence
230 To her fayre shoulders flew the gentle Doues,
Gracefull *Ædone* that sweet pleasure loues,
And ruffoot *Chreste* with the tufted crowne,
Both which did kisse her, though their Goddes frowne.
The Swans did in the solid flood, her glasse,
235 Proyne their fayre plumes; of which the fairest was,
Ioue-lou'd *Leucote*, that pure brightnes is;
v The other bountie-louing *Dapsilis*.
All were in heauen, now they with *Hero* were:
But *Venus* lookes brought wrath, and vrged feare.
240 Her robe was skarlet, black her heads attire,
And through her naked breast shinde streames of fire,
As when the rarefied ayre is driuen
In flashing streames, and opes the darkned heauen.
In her white hand a wreath of yew she bore,
245 And breaking th'icie wreath sweet *Hero* wore,
She forst about her browes her wreath of yew,
And sayd, Now minion to thy fate be trew,
Though not to me, indure what this portends;
Begin where lightnes will, in shame it ends.
250 Loue makes thee cunning; thou art currant now,
By being counterfeit: thy broken vow,
Deceit with her pide garters must reioyne,
And with her stampe thou countnances must coyne:
Coynes, and pure deceits for purities,
255 And still a mayd wilt seeme in cosoned eies,
And haue an antike face to laugh within,
While thy smooth lookes make men digest thy sin.
But since thy lips (lest thought forsworne) forswore,
Be neuer virgins vow worth trusting more.
260 When Beauties dearest did her Goddesse heare,
Breathe such rebukes gainst that she could not cleare;
Dumbe sorrow spake alowd in teares, and blood
I₃ᴿ That from her griefe-burst vaines in piteous flood,
From the sweet conduits of her sauor fell:
265 The gentle Turtles did with moanes make swell
Their shining gorges: the white black-eyde Swans
Did sing as wofull Epicedians,
As they would straightwaies dye: when pities Queene
The Goddesse *Ecte*, that had euer beene

233 frowne *1600–09*] frownd *1598;* frown *1613–37*

Hid in a watrie clowde neere *Heros* cries,   270
Since the first instant of her broken eies,
Gaue bright *Leucote* voyce, and made her speake,
To ease her anguish, whose swolne breast did breake
With anger at her Goddesse, that did touch,
Hero so neere for that she vsde so much.   275
And thrusting her white neck at *Venus*, sayd;
Why may not amorous *Hero* seeme a mayd,
Though she be none, as well as you suppresse
In modest cheekes your inward wantonnesse?
How often haue wee drawne you from aboue,   280
T'exchange with mortals, rites for rites in loue?
Why in your preist then call you that offence
That shines in you, and is your influence?
With this the furies stopt *Leucotes* lips,
Enioynd by *Venus;* who with Rosie whips   285
Beate the kind Bird. Fierce lightning from her eyes
Did set on fire faire *Heros* sacrifice,
Which was her torne robe, and inforced hayre;
And the bright flame became a mayd most faire   *v*

Description and creation of Dissimula-tion.

For her aspect: her tresses were of wire,   290
Knit like a net, where harts all set on fire,
Strugled in pants and could not get release:
Her armes were all with golden pincers drest,
And twentie fashiond knots, pullies, and brakes,
And all her bodie girdled with painted Snakes.   295
Her doune parts in a Scorpions taile combinde,
Freckled with twentie colours; pyed wings shinde
Out of her shoulders; Cloth had neuer die,
Nor sweeter colours neuer viewed eie,
In scorching *Turkie, Cares, Tartarie,*   300
Than shinde about this spirit notorious;
Nor was *Arachnes* web so glorious.
Of lightning and of shreds she was begot;
More hold in base dissemblers is there not.
Her name was *Eronusis. Venus* flew   305
From *Heros* sight, and at her Chariot drew
This wondrous creature to so steepe a height,
That all the world she might command with sleight
Of her gay wings: and then she bad her hast,
Since *Hero* had dissembled, and disgrast   310
Her rites so much, and euery breast infect
With her deceits, she made her Architect
Of all dissimulation, and since then
Neuer was any trust in maides nor men.
                    O it spighted   315 [L₄ᴿ]

Fayre *Venus* hart to see her most delighted.
And one she chusde for temper of her minde,
To be the only ruler of her kinde,
·So soone to let her virgin race be ended;
320 Not simply for the fault a whit offended:
But that in strife for chastnes with the Moone,
Spitefull *Diana* bad her shew but one,
That was her seruant vowd, and liu'd a mayd,
And now she thought to answer that vpbrayd,
325 *Hero* had lost her answer; who knowes not
Venus would seeme as farre from any spot
Of light demeanour, as the very skin
Twixt *Cynthias* browes? Sin is asham'd of Sin.
Vp *Venus* flew, and scarce durst vp for feare
330 Of *Phœbes* laughter, when she past her Sphere:
And so most vgly clowded was the light,
That day was hid in day; night came ere night,
And *Venus* could not through the thick ayre pierce,
Till the daies king, god of vndanted verse,
335 Because she was so plentifull a theame,
To such as wore his Lawrell *Anademe:*
Like to a firie bullet made descent,
And from her passage those fat vapours rent,
That being not throughly rarefide to raine,
340 Melted like pitch as blew as any vaine,
v And scalding tempests made the earth to shrinke
Vnder their feruor, and the world did thinke
In euery drop a torturing Spirit flew,
It pierst so deeply, and it burnd so blew.
345 Betwixt all this and *Hero, Hero* held
Leanders picture as a Persian shield:
And she was free from feare of worst successe;
The more ill threats vs, we suspect the lesse:
As we grow haples, violence subtle growes,
350 Dumb, deafe, & blind, & comes when no man knowes.

The end of the fourth Sestyad.

The Argument of the Fift Sestyad.   K₁ᴿ

Day doubles her accustomd date,
As loth the night, incenst by fate,
Should wrack our louers; Heros *plight,*
Longs for Leander, *and the night:*
Which, ere her thirstie wish recouers,   5
She sends for two betrothed louers,
And marries them, that (with their crew,
Their sports and ceremonies due)
She couertly might celebrate,
With secret ioy her owne estate.   10
She makes a feast, at which appeares
The wilde Nymph Teras, *that still beares*
An Iuory Lute, tels Omenous tales,
And sings at solemne festiuales.

Now was bright *Hero* weary of the day,
Thought an Olympiad in *Leanders* stay.
Sol, and the soft-foote *Howrs* hung on his armes,
And would not let him swim, foreseeing his harmes:
That day *Aurora* double grace obtainde   5
Of her loue *Phœbus;* she his Horses rainde,
Set on his golden knee, and as she list   v
She puld him back; and as she puld, she kist
To haue him turne to bed; he lou'd her more,
To see the loue *Leander Hero* bore.   10
Examples profit much; ten times in one,
In persons full of note, good deedes are done.
   Day was so long, men walking fell asleepe,
The heauie humors that their eyes did steepe,
Made them feare mischiefs. The hard streets were beds   15
For couetous churles, and for ambitious heads,
That spight of Nature would their busines plie.
All thought they had the falling *Epilepsie*,
Men groueld so vpon the smotherd ground,
And pittie did the hart of heauen confound.   20
The Gods, the Graces, and the Muses came
Downe to the Destinies, to stay the frame
Of the true louers deaths, and all worlds teares:
But death before had stopt their cruell eares.
All the Celestials parted mourning then,   25
Pierst with our humane miseries more then men.
Ah, nothing doth the world with mischiefe fill,
But want of feeling one anothers ill.
   With their descent the day grew something fayre,
And cast a brighter robe vpon the ayre.   30

Hero to shorten time with merriment,
For yong *Alcmane*, and bright *Mya* sent,
K₂ᴿ   Two louers that had long crau'd mariage dues
At *Heros* hands: but she did still refuse,
35   For louely *Mya* was her consort vowd
In her maids state, and therefore not allowd
To amorous Nuptials: yet faire *Hero* now
Intended to dispence with her cold vow,
Since hers was broken, and to marrie her:
40   The rites would pleasing matter minister
To her conceits, and shorten tedious day.
They came; sweet Musick vsherd th'odorous way,
And wanton Ayre in twentie sweet forms danst
After her fingers; Beautie and Loue aduanst
45   Their ensignes in the downles rosie faces
Of youths and maids, led after by the Graces.
For all these, *Hero* made a friendly feast,
Welcomd them kindly, did much loue protest,
Winning their harts with all the meanes she might,
50   That when her fault should chance t'abide the light,
Their loues might couer or extenuate it,
And high in her worst fate make pittie sit.
    She married them, and in the banquet came
Borne by the virgins: *Hero* striu'd to frame
55   Her thoughts to mirth. Aye me, but hard it is
To imitate a false and forced blis.
Ill may a sad minde forge a merrie face,
Nor hath constrained laughter any grace.
v   Then layd she wine on cares to make them sinke;
60   *Who feares the threats of fortune, let him drinke.*
    To these quick Nuptials entred suddenly
Admired *Teras* with the Ebon Thye,
A Nymph that haunted the greene *Sestyan* groues,
And would consort soft virgins in their loues,
65   At gaysome Triumphs, and on solemne dayes,
Singing prophetike Elegies and Layes:
And fingring of a siluer Lute she tide,
With black and purple skarfs by her left side.
Apollo gaue it, and her skill withall,
70   And she was term'd his Dwarfe she was so small.
Yet great in vertue, for his beames enclosde
His vertues in her: neuer was proposde
Riddle to her, or Augurie, strange or new,
But she resolu'd it: neuer sleight tale flew
75   From her charmd lips without important sence,
Shewne in some graue succeeding consequence.

This little Siluane with her songs and tales,
Gaue such estate to feasts and Nuptiales,
That though oft times she forewent Tragedies,
Yet for her strangenes still she pleasde their eyes,   80
And for her smalnes they admir'd her so,
They thought her perfect borne and could not grow.
   All eyes were on her: *Hero* did command
An Altar deckt with sacred state should stand,
At the Feasts vpper end close by the Bride,   85 K₃ᴿ
On which the pretie Nymph might sit espide.
Then all were silent; euery one so heares,
As all their sences climbd into their eares:
And first this amorous tale that fitted well,
Fayre *Hero* and the Nuptials she did tell: 90

The tale of Teras.

   Hymen that now is god of Nuptiall rites,
And crownes with honor loue and his delights,
Of *Athens* was a youth so sweet of face,
That many thought him of the femall race:
Such quickning brightnes did his cleere eyes dart,   95
Warme went their beames to his beholders hart.
In such pure leagues his beauties were combinde,
That there your Nuptiall contracts first were signde.
For as proportion, white, and crimsine, meet
In Beauties mixture, all right cleere, and sweet;   100
The eye responsible, the golden haire,
And none is held without the other, faire:
All spring together, all together fade;
Such intermixt affections should inuade
Two perfect louers: which being yet vnseene,   105
Their vertues and their comforts copied beene,
In Beauties concord, subiect to the eie;
And that, in *Hymen*, pleasde so matchleslie,
That louers were esteemde in their full grace,   *v*
Like forme and colour mixt in *Hymens* face;   110
And such sweete concord was thought worthie then
Of torches, musick, feasts, and greatest men:
So *Hymen* lookt, that euen the chastest minde
He mou'd to ioyne in ioyes of sacred kinde:
For onely now his chins first doune consorted   115
His heads rich fleece, in golden curles contorted;
And as he was so lou'd, he lou'd so too,
So should best bewties, bound by Nuptialls doo.
   Bright *Eucharis*, who was by all men saide
The noblest, fayrest, and the richest maide,   120

Of all th' *Athenian* damzels, *Hymen* lou'd
With such transmission, that his heart remou'd
From his white brest to hers, but her estate
In passing his, was so interminate
125 For wealth and honor, that his loue durst feede
On nought but sight and hearing, nor could breede
Hope of requitall, the grand prise of loue;
Nor could he heare or see but he must proue
How his rare bewties musick would agree
130 With maids in consort: therefore robbed he
His chin of those same few first fruits it bore,
And clad in such attire, as Virgins wore,
He kept them companie, and might right well,
For he did all but *Eucharis* excell
[K₄ᴿ] 135 In all the fayre of Beautie: yet he wanted
Vertue to make his owne desires implanted
In his deare *Eucharis;* for women neuer
Loue beautie in their sex, but enuie euer.
His iudgement yet (that durst not suite addresse,
140 Nor past due meanes, presume of due successe)
Reason gat fortune in the end to speede
To his best prayers: but strange it seemd indeede,
That fortune should a chast affection blesse,
Preferment seldome graceth bashfulnesse.
145 Nor grast it *Hymen* yet; but many a dart
And many an amorous thought enthrald his hart,
Ere he obtaind her; and he sick became,
Forst to abstaine her sight, and then the flame
Rag'd in his bosome. O what griefe did fill him:
150 Sight made him sick, and want of sight did kill him.
The virgins wondred where *Diœtia* stayd,
For so did *Hymen* terme himselfe a mayd.
At length with sickly lookes he greeted them:
Tis strange to see gainst what an extreame streame
155 A louer striues; poore *Hymen* lookt so ill,
That as in merit he increased still,
By suffring much, so he in grace decreast.
Women are most wonne when men merit least:
If merit looke not well, loue bids stand by,
160 Loues speciall lesson is to please the eye.
v And *Hymen* soone recouering all he lost,
Deceiuing still these maids, but himselfe most.
His loue and he with many virgin dames,
Noble by birth, noble by beauties flames,
165 Leauing the towne with songs and hallowed lights,

142 prayers *ed. 1821, etc.*] prayes *1598 etc.*

To doe great *Ceres Eleusina* rites
Of zealous Sacrifice; were made a pray
To barbarous Rouers that in ambush lay,
And with rude hands enforst their shining spoyle,
Farre from the darkned Citie, tir'd with toyle.   170
And when the yellow issue of the skie
Came trouping forth, ielous of crueltie,
To their bright fellowes of this vnder heauen,
Into a double night they saw them driuen,
A horride Caue, the theeues black mansion,   175
Where wearie of the iourney they had gon,
Their last nights watch, and drunke with their sweete gains,
Dull *Morpheus* entred, laden with silken chains,
Stronger then iron, and bound the swelling vaines
And tyred sences of these lawles Swaines.   180
But when the virgin lights thus dimly burnd;
O what a hell was heauen in! how they mournd
And wrung their hands, and wound their gentle forms
Into the shapes of sorrow! Golden storms
Fell from their eyes: As when the Sunne appeares,   185
And yet it raines, so shewd their eyes their teares.
And as when funerall dames watch a dead corse,   L₁ᴿ
Weeping about it, telling with remorse
What paines he felt, how long in paine he lay,
How little food he eate, what he would say;   190
And then mixe mournfull tales of others deaths,
Smothering themselues in clowds of their owne breaths;
At length, one cheering other, call for wine,
The golden boale drinks teares out of their eine,
As they drinke wine from it; and round it goes,   195
Each helping other to relieue their woes:
So cast these virgins beauties mutuall raies,
One lights another, face the face displaies;
Lips by reflexion kist, and hands hands shooke,
Euen by the whitenes each of other tooke.   200
    But *Hymen* now vsde friendly *Morpheus* aide,
Slew euery theefe, and rescude euery maide.
And now did his enamourd passion take
Hart from his hartie deede, whose worth did make
His hope of bounteous *Eucharis* more strong;   205
And now came *Loue* with *Proteus*, who had long
Inggl'd the little god with prayers and gifts,
Ran through all shapes, and varied all his shifts,
To win *Loues* stay with him, and make him loue him:
And when he saw no strength of sleight could moue him   210
To make him loue, or stay, he nimbly turnd

Into *Loues* selfe, he so extreamely burnd.

v And thus came *Loue* with *Proteus* and his powre,
T'encounter *Eucharis:* first like the flowre
215 That *Junos* milke did spring, the siluer Lillie,
He fell on *Hymens* hand, who straight did spie
The bounteous Godhead, and with wondrous ioy
Offred it *Eucharis*. She wondrous coy
Drew back her hand: the subtle flowre did woo it,
220 And drawing it neere, mixt so you could not know it.
As two cleere Tapers mixe in one their light,
So did the Lillie and the hand their white:
She viewd it, and her view the forme bestowes
Amongst her spirits: for as colour flowes
225 From superficies of each thing we see,
Euen so with colours formes emitted bee:
And where *Loues* forme is, loue is, loue is forme;
He entred at the eye, his sacred storme
Rose from the hand, loues sweetest instrument:
230 It stird her bloods sea so, that high it went,
And beate in bashfull waues gainst the white shore
Of her diuided cheekes; it rag'd the more,
Because the tide went gainst the haughtie winde
Of her estate and birth: And as we finde
235 In fainting ebs, the flowrie Zephire hurles
The greene-hayrd *Hellespont*, broke in siluer curles
Gainst *Heros* towre: but in his blasts retreate,
The waues obeying him, they after beate,
L₂ᴿ Leauing the chalkie shore a great way pale,
240 Then moyst it freshly with another gale:
So ebd and flowde the blood in *Eucharis* face,
Coynesse and Loue striu'd which had greatest grace,
Virginitie did fight on Coynesse side;
Feare of her parents frownes, and femall pride,
245 Lothing the lower place, more than it loues
The high contents, desert and vertue moues.
With loue fought *Hymens* beautie and his valure,
Which scarce could so much fauour yet allure
To come to strike, but fameles idle stood,
250 *Action is firie valours soueraigne good.*
But Loue once entred, wisht no greater ayde
Then he could find within; thought, thought betrayd,
The bribde, but incorrupted Garrison,
Sung *Jo Hymen;* there those songs begun,
255 And Loue was growne so rich with such a gaine,
And wanton with the ease of his free raigne,
That he would turne into her roughest frownes

To turne them out; and thus he *Hymen* crownes
King of his thoughts, mans greatest Emperie:
This was his first braue step to deitie.   260
   Home to the mourning cittie they repayre,
With newes as holesome as the morning ayre,
To the sad parents of each saued maid:
But *Hymen* and his *Eucharis* had laid
This plat, to make the flame of their delight   265 *v*
Round as the Moone at full, and full as bright.
   Because the parents of chast *Eucharis*
Exceeding *Hymens* so, might crosse their blis;
And as the world rewards deserts, that law
Cannot assist with force: so when they saw   270
Their daughter safe, take vantage of their owne,
Praise *Hymens* valour much, nothing bestowne;
Hymen must leaue the virgins in a Groue
Farre off from *Athens*, and go first to proue
If to restore them all with fame and life,   275
He should enioy his dearest as his wife.
This told to all the maids; the most agree:
The riper sort knowing what t'is to bee
The first mouth of a newes so farre deriu'd,
And that to heare and beare newes braue folks liu'd,   280
As being a carriage speciall hard to beare,
Occurrents, these occurrents being so deare,
They did with grace protest, they were content
T'accost their friends with all their complement,
For *Hymens* good: but to incurre their harme,   285
There he must pardon them. This wit went warme
To *Adoleshes* braine, a Nymph borne hie,
Made all of voyce and fire, that vpwards flie:
Her hart and all her forces neither traine,
Climbd to her tongue, and thither fell her braine,   290
Since it could goe no higher, and it must go,   L_a^R
All powers she had, euen her tongue, did so.
In spirit and quicknes she much ioy did take,
And lou'd her tongue, only for quicknes sake,
And she would hast and tell. The rest all stay,   295
Hymen goes one, the Nymph another way:
And what became of her Ile tell at last:
Yet take her visage now: moyst lipt, long fa'st,
Thin like an iron wedge, so sharpe and tart,
As twere of purpose made to cleaue *Loues* hart.   300
Well were this louely Beautie rid of her,
And *Hymen* did at *Athens* now prefer

296 one *ed. 1821, etc.*] on *Qq*

His welcome suite, which he with ioy aspirde:
A hundred princely youths with him retirde
305 To fetch the Nymphs: Chariots and Musick went,
And home they came: heauen with applauses rent.
The Nuptials straight proceed, whiles all the towne
Fresh in their ioyes might doe them most renowne.
First gold-lockt *Hymen* did to Church repaire,
310 Like a quick offring burnd in flames of haire.
And after, with a virgin firmament,
The Godhead-prouing Bride attended went
Before them all, she lookt in her command,
As if forme-giuing *Cyprias* siluer hand
315 Gripte all their beauties, and crusht out one flame,
She blusht to see how beautie ouercame
v The thoughts of all men. Next before her went
Fiue louely children deckt with ornament
Of her sweet colours, bearing Torches by,
320 For light was held a happie Augurie
Of generation, whose efficient right
Is nothing else but to produce to light.
The od disparent number they did chuse,
To shew the vnion married loues should vse,
325 Since in two equall parts it will not seuer,
But the midst holds one to reioyne it euer,
As common to both parts: men therfore deeme,
That equall number Gods doe not esteeme,
Being authors of sweet peace and vnitie,
330 But pleasing to th'infernall Emperie,
Vnder whose ensignes Wars and Discords fight,
Since an euen number you may disunite
In two parts equall, nought in middle left,
To reunite each part from other reft:
335 And fiue they hold in most especiall prise,
Since t'is the first od number that doth rise
From the two formost numbers vnitie
That od and euen are; which are two, and three,
For one no number is: but thence doth flow
340 The powerfull race of number. Next did go
A noble Matron that did spinning beare
A huswifes rock and spindle, and did weare
[L₄ᴿ] A Weathers skin, with all the snowy fleece,
To intimate that euen the daintiest peece,
345 And noblest borne dame should industrious bee:
That which does good, disgraceth no degree.
   And now to *Junos* Temple they are come,
Where her graue Priest stood in the mariage rome.

On his right arme did hang a skarlet vaile,
And from his shoulders to the ground did traile,   350
On either side, Ribands of white and blew;
With the red vaile he hid the bashfull hew
Of the chast Bride, to shew the modest shame,
In coupling with a man should grace a dame.
Then tooke he the disparent Silks, and tide   355
The Louers by the wasts, and side to side,
In token that thereafter they must binde
In one selfe sacred knot each others minde.
Before them on an Altar he presented
Both fire and water: which was first inuented,   360
Since to ingenerate euery humane creature,
And euery other birth produ'st by Nature,
Moysture and heate must mixe: so man and wife
For humane race must ioyne in Nuptiall life.
Then one of *Junos* Birds, the painted Iay,   365
He sacrifisde, and tooke the gall away.
All which he did behinde the Altar throw,
In signe no bitternes of hate should grow
Twixt maried loues, nor any least disdaine.   *v*
Nothing they spake, for twas esteemd too plaine   370
For the most silken mildnes of a maid,
To let a publique audience heare it said
She boldly tooke the man: and so respected
Was bashfulnes in *Athens:* it erected
To chast *Agneia*, which is Shamefastnesse,   375
A sacred Temple, holding her a Goddesse.
And now to Feasts, Masks, and triumphant showes,
The shining troupes returnd, euen till earths throwes
Brought forth with ioy the thickest part of night,
When the sweet Nuptiall song that vsde to cite   380
All to their rest, was by *Phemonoe* sung,
First *Delphian* Prophetesse, whose graces sprung
Out of the *Muses* well, she sung before
The Bride into her chamber: at which dore
A Matron and a Torch-bearer did stand;   385
A painted box of Confits in her hand
The Matron held, and so did other some
That compast round the honourd Nuptiall rome.
The custome was that euery maid did weare,
During her maidenhead, a silken Sphere   390
About her waste, aboue her inmost weede,
Knit with *Mineruas* knot, and that was freede
By the faire Bridegrome on the mariage night,

381 *Phemonoe*] Phemonoc

With many ceremonies of delight:
M₁ᴿ 395　And yet eternisde *Hymens* tender Bride,
To suffer it dissolu'd so sweetly cride.
The maids that heard, so lou'd, and did adore her,
They wisht with all their hearts to suffer for her.
So had the Matrons, that with Confits stood
400　About the chamber, such affectionate blood,
And so true feeling of her harmeles paines,
That euery one a showre of Confits raines.
For which the Brideyouths scrambling on the ground,
In noyse of that sweet haile her cryes were drownd.
405　And thus blest *Hymen* ioyde his gracious Bride,
And for his ioy was after deifide.
　　The Saffron mirror by which *Phœbus* loue,
Greene *Tellus* decks her, now he held aboue
The clowdy mountaines: and the noble maide,
410　Sharp-visag'd *Adolesche*, that was straide
Out of her way, in hasting with her newes,
Not till this houre th' *Athenian* turrets viewes,
And now brought home by guides, she heard by all
That her long kept occurrents would be stale,
415　And how faire *Hymens* honors did excell
For those rare newes, which she came short to tell.
To heare her deare tongue robd of such a ioy
Made the well-spoken Nymph take such a toy,
That downe she sunke: when lightning from aboue,
420　Shrunk her leane body, and for meere free loue,
　v　Turnd her into the pied-plum'd *Psittacus*,
That now the Parrat is surnam'd by vs,
Who still with counterfeit confusion prates,
Nought but newes common to the commonst mates.
425　This tolde, strange *Teras* toucht her Lute and sung
This dittie, that the Torchie euening sprung.

Epithalamion Teratos.

Come, come deare night, Loues Mart of kisses,
Sweet close of his ambitious line,
The fruitfull summer of his blisses,
430　Loues glorie doth in darknes shine.
O come soft rest of Cares, come night,
Come naked vertues only tire,
The reaped haruest of the light,
Bound vp in sheaues of sacred fire.
435　　*Loue cals to warre,*
　　Sighs his Alarmes,

404 her *Dyce etc.*] their *Qq*　　412 this *1598, Dyce etc.*] his *1600–37*

> *Lips his swords are,*
> *The field his Armes.*

Come Night and lay thy veluet hand
On glorious Dayes outfacing face;   440
And all thy crouned flames command,
For Torches to our Nuptiall grace.

> *Loue cals to warre,*
> *Sighs his Alarmes,*
> *Lips his swords are,*   445 M₂ᴿ
> *The field his Armes.*

No neede haue we of factious Day,
To cast in enuie of thy peace,
Her bals of Discord in thy way:
Here beauties day doth neuer cease,   450
Day is abstracted here,
And varied in a triple sphere.
Hero, Alcmane, Mya, so outshine thee,
Ere thou come here let *Thetis* thrice refine thee.

> *Loue cals to warre,*   455
> *Sighs his Alarmes,*
> *Lips his swords are,*
> *The field his Armes.*

The Euening starre I see:
Rise youths, the Euening starre,   460
Helps Loue to summon warre,
Both now imbracing bee.
Rise youths, loues right claims more then banquets, rise.
Now the bright Marygolds that deck the skies,
Phœbus celestiall flowrs, that (contrarie   465
To his flowers here) ope when he shuts his eie,
And shuts when he doth open, crowne your sports:
Now loue in night, and night in loue exhorts
Courtship and Dances: All your parts employ,
And suite nights rich expansure with your ioy,   470
Loue paints his longings in sweet virgins eyes: *v*
Rise youths, loues right claims more then banquets, rise.
Rise virgins, let fayre Nuptiall loues enfolde
Your fruitles breasts: the maidenheads ye holde
Are not your owne alone, but parted are;   475
Part in disposing them your Parents share,
And that a third part is: so must ye saue
Your loues a third, and you your thirds must haue.
Loue paints his longings in sweet virgins eyes:
Rise youths, loues right claims more then banquets, rise.   480

Herewith the amorous spirit that was so kinde
To *Teras* haire, and combd it downe with winde,

Still as it Comet-like brake from her braine,
Would needes haue *Teras* gone, and did refraine
485   To blow it downe: which staring vp, dismaid
The timorous feast, and she no longer staid:
But bowing to the Bridegrome and the Bride,
Did like a shooting exhalation glide
Out of their sights: the turning of her back
490   Made them all shrieke, it lookt so ghastly black.
O haples *Hero*, that most haples clowde
Thy soone-succeeding Tragedie foreshowde.
Thus all the Nuptiall crew to ioyes depart,
But much-wrongd *Hero*, stood Hels blackest dart:
M₃ᴿ 495   Whose wound because I grieue so to display,
I vse digressions thus t'encrease the day.

The end of the fift Sestyad.

The Argument of the Sixt Sestyad.

Leucote flyes to all the windes,
And from the fates their outrage bindes,
That Hero *and her loue may meete.*
Leander (with Loues *compleate Fleete*
5   *Mand in himselfe) puts forth to Seas,*
When straight the ruthles Destinies,
With Ate *stirre the windes to warre*
Vpon the Hellespont: *Their iarre*
Drownes poore Leander. Heros *eyes*
10   *Wet witnesses of his surprise,*
Her Torch blowne out: Griefe casts her downe
Vpon her loue, and both doth drowne.
In whose iust ruth the God of Seas,
Transformes them to th' Acanthides.

No longer could the day nor Destinies
Delay the night, who now did frowning rise
v   Into her Throne; and at her humorous brests,
Visions and Dreames lay sucking: all mens rests
5   Fell like the mists of death vpon their eyes,
Dayes too long darts so kild their faculties.
The windes yet, like the flowrs to cease began:
For bright *Leucote, Venus* whitest Swan,
That held sweet *Hero* deare, spread her fayre wings,
10   Like to a field of snow, and message brings
From *Venus* to the Fates, t'entreate them lay
Their charge vpon the windes their rage to stay,

That the sterne battaile of the Seas might cease,
And guard *Leander* to his loue in peace.
The Fates consent, (aye me dissembling Fates)   15
They shewd their fauours to conceale their hates,
And draw *Leander* on, least Seas too hie
Should stay his too obsequious destinie:
Who like a fleering slauish Parasite,
In warping profit or a traiterous sleight,   20
Hoopes round his rotten bodie with deuotes,
And pricks his descant face full of false notes,
Praysing with open throte (and othes as fowle
As his false heart) the beautie of an Owle,
Kissing his skipping hand with charmed skips,   25
That cannot leaue, but leapes vpon his lips
Like a cock-sparrow, or a shameles queane
Sharpe at a red-lipt youth, and nought doth meane
Of all his antick shewes, but doth repayre   [M₄ⁿ]
More tender fawnes, and takes a scattred hayre   30
From his tame subiects shoulder; whips, and cals
For euery thing he lacks; creepes gainst the wals
With backward humblesse, to giue needles way:
Thus his false fate did with *Leander* play.
    First to black *Eurus* flies the white *Leucote*,   35
Borne mongst the *Negros* in the *Leuant* Sea,
On whose curld head the glowing Sun doth rise, ⎫
And shewes the soueraigne will of Destinies,   ⎬
To haue him cease his blasts, and downe he lies. ⎭
Next, to the fennie *Notus* course she holds,   40
And found him leaning with his armes in folds
Vpon a rock, his white hayre full of showres,
And him she chargeth by the fatall powres,
To hold in his wet cheekes his clowdie voyce.
To *Zephire* then that doth in flowres reioyce.   45
To snake-foote *Boreas* next she did remoue,
And found him tossing of his rauisht loue,
To heate his frostie bosome hid in snow,
Who with *Leucotes* sight did cease to blow.
Thus all were still to *Heros* harts desire,   50
Who with all speede did consecrate a fire
Of flaming Gummes, and comfortable Spice,
To light her Torch, which in such curious price
She held, being obiect to *Leanders* sight,
That nought but fires perfum'd must giue it light.   55 v
She lou'd it so, she grieu'd to see it burne,
Since it would waste and soone to ashes turne:
Yet if it burnd not, twere not worth her eyes,

What made it nothing, gaue it all the prize.
60   Sweet Torch, true Glasse of our societie;
What man does good, but he consumes thereby?
But thou wert lou'd for good, held high, giuen show:
Poore vertue loth'd for good, obscur'd, held low.
Doe good, be pinde; be deedles good, disgrast:
65   Vnles we feede on men, we let them fast.
Yet *Hero* with these thoughts her Torch did spend.
When Bees makes waxe, Nature doth not intend
It shall be made a Torch: but we that know
The proper vertue of it make it so,
70   And when t'is made we light it: nor did Nature
Propose one life to maids, but each such creature
Makes by her soule the best of her free state,
Which without loue is rude, disconsolate,
And wants loues fire to make it milde and bright,
75   Till when, maids are but Torches wanting light.
Thus gainst our griefe, not cause of griefe we fight,
The right of nought is gleande, but the delight.
Vp went she, but to tell how she descended,
Would God she were not dead, or my verse ended.
80   She was the rule of wishes, summe and end
N₁ᴿ For all the parts that did on loue depend:
Yet cast the Torch his brightnes further forth;
But what shines neerest best, holds truest worth.
Leander did not through such tempests swim
85   To kisse the Torch, although it lighted him:
But all his powres in her desire awaked,
Her loue and vertues cloth'd him richly naked.
Men kisse but fire that only shewes pursue,
Her Torch and *Hero*, figure shew and vertue.
90   Now at opposde *Abydus* nought was heard,
But bleating flocks, and many a bellowing herd,
Slaine for the Nuptials, cracks of falling woods,
Blowes of broad axes, powrings out of floods.
The guiltie *Hellespont* was mixt and stainde
95   With bloodie Torrents, that the shambles raind;
Not arguments of feast, but shewes that bled,
Foretelling that red night that followed.
More blood was spilt, more honors were addrest,
Then could haue graced any happie feast.
100   Rich banquets, triumphs, euery pomp employes
His sumptuous hand: no misers nuptiall ioyes.
Ayre felt continuall thunder with the noyse,
Made in the generall mariage violence:
And no man knew the cause of this expence,

But the two haples Lords, *Leanders* Sire,   105
And poore *Leander*, poorest where the fire
Of credulous loue made him most rich surmisde.
As short was he of that himselfe he prisde,   *v*
As is an emptie Gallant full of forme,
That thinks each looke an act, each drop a storme,   110
That fals from his braue breathings; most brought vp
In our *Metropolis*, and hath his cup
Brought after him to feasts; and much Palme beares,
For his rare iudgement in th'attire he weares,
Hath seene the hot Low Countries, not their heat,   115
Obserues their rampires and their buildings yet.
And for your sweet discourse with mouthes is heard,
Giuing instructions with his very beard.
Hath gone with an Ambassadour, and been
A great mans mate in trauailing, euen to *Rhene*,   120
And then puts all his worth in such a face,
As he saw braue men make, and striues for grace
To get his newes forth; as when you descrie
A ship with all her sayle contends to flie
Out of the narrow Thames with windes vnapt,   125
Now crosseth here, then there, then this way rapt,
And then hath one point reacht; then alters all,
And to another crooked reach doth fall
Of halfe a burdbolts shoote; keeping more coyle,
Then if she danst vpon the Oceans toyle: 130
So serious is his trifling companie,
In all his swelling ship of vacantrie.
And so short of himselfe in his high thought,
Was our *Leander* in his fortunes brought,
And in his fort of loue that he thought won,   135 N₂ᴿ
But otherwise, he skornes comparison.
    O sweet *Leander*, thy large worth I hide
In a short graue; ill fauourd stormes must chide
Thy sacred fauour; I, in floods of inck
Must drowne thy graces, which white papers drink,   140
Euen as thy beauties did the foule black Seas:
I must describe the hell of thy disease,
That heauen did merit: yet I needes must see
Our painted fooles and cockhorse Pessantrie
Still still vsurp, with long liues, loues, and lust,   145
The seates of vertue, cutting short as dust
Her deare bought issue; ill, to worse conuerts,
And tramples in the blood of all deserts.
    Night close and silent now goes fast before
The Captaines and their souldiers to the shore,   150

On whom attended the appointed Fleete
At *Sestus* Bay, that should *Leander* meete,
Who fainde he in another ship would passe:
Which must not be, for no one meane there was
155 To get his loue home, but the course he tooke.
Forth did his beautie for his beautie looke,
And saw her through her Torch, as you beholde
Sometimes within the Sunne a face of golde,
Form'd in strong thoughts, by that traditions force,
160 That saies a God sits there and guides his course.
His sister was with him, to whom he shewd
v His guide by Sea: and sayd, Oft haue you viewd
In one heauen many starres, but neuer yet
In one starre many heauens till now were met.
165 See louely sister, see, now *Hero* shines
No heauen but her appeares: each star repines,
And all are clad in clowdes, as if they mournd,
To be by influence of Earth out-burnd.
Yet doth she shine, and teacheth vertues traine,
170 Still to be constant in Hels blackest raigne;
Though euen the gods themselues do so entreat them
As they did hate, and Earth as she would eate them.
Off went his silken robe, and in he leapt;
Whom the kinde waues so licorously cleapt,
175 Thickning for haste one in another so,
To kisse his skin, that he might almost go
To *Heros* Towre, had that kind minuit lasted.
But now the cruell fates with *Ate* hasted
To all the windes, and made them battaile fight
180 Vpon the *Hellespont*, for eithers right
Pretended to the windie monarchie.
And forth they brake, the Seas mixt with the skie,
And tost distrest *Leander*, being in hell,
As high as heauen; Blisse not in height doth dwell.
185 The Destinies sate dancing on the waues,
To see the glorious windes with mutuall braues
Consume each other: O true glasse to see,
How ruinous ambitious Statists bee
N₃ᴿ To their owne glories! Poore *Leander* cried
190 For help to Sea-borne *Venus;* she denied:
To *Boreas*, that for his *Atthæas* sake,
He would some pittie on his *Hero'* take,
And for his owne loues sake, on his desires:
But Glorie neuer blowes cold Pitties fires.
195 Then calde he *Neptune*, who through all the noise,

162 Oft] oft

Knew with affright his wrackt *Leanders* voice:
And vp he rose, for haste his forehead hit
Gainst heauens hard Christall; his proud waues he smit
With his forkt scepter, that could not obay,
Much greater powers then *Neptunes* gaue them sway,   200
They lou'd *Leander* so, in groanes they brake
When they came neere him; and such space did take
Twixt one another, loth to issue on,
That in their shallow furrowes earth was shone,
And the poore louer tooke a little breath: 205
But the curst Fates sate spinning of his death
On euery waue, and with the seruile windes
Tumbled them on him: And now *Hero* findes
By that she felt her deare *Leanders* state,
She wept and prayed for him to euery fate,   210
And eucry winde that whipt her with her haire
About the face, she kist and spake it faire,
Kneeld to it, gaue it drinke out of her eyes
To quench his thirst: but still their cruelties
Euen her poore Torch enuied, and rudely beate   215
The bating flame from that deare foode it eate: *v*
Deare, for it nourisht her *Leanders* life,
Which with her robe she rescude from their strife:
But silke too soft was, such hard hearts to breake,
And she deare soule, euen as her silke, faint, weake,   220
Could not preserue it: out, O out it went.
Leander still cald *Neptune*, that now rent
His brackish curles, and tore his wrinckled face   ⎫
Where teares in billowes did each other chace,   ⎬
And (burst with ruth) he hurld his marble Mace   ⎭   225
At the sterne Fates, it wounded *Lachèsis*
That drew *Leanders* thread, and could not misse
The thread it selfe, as it her hand did hit,
But smote it full and quite did sunder it.
The more kinde *Neptune* rag'd, the more he raste   230
His loues liues fort, and kild as he embraste.
Anger doth still his owne mishap encrease;
If any comfort liue, it is in peace.
O theeuish Fates, to let Blood, Flesh, and Sence, ⎫
Build two fayre Temples for their Excellence,   ⎬   235
To rob it with a poysoned influence.   ⎭
Though soules gifts starue, the bodies are held dear
In vgliest things; Sence-sport preserues a Beare.
But here nought serues our turnes; O heauen & earth,
How most most wretched is our humane birth?   240
And now did all the tyrannous crew depart,

Knowing there was a storme in *Heros* hart,
[N₄ᴿ] Greater then they could make, & skornd their smart.
She bowd her selfe so low out of her Towre,
245 That wonder twas she fell not ere her howre,
With searching the lamenting waues for him;
Like a poore Snayle, her gentle supple lim
Hung on her Turrets top so most downe right,
As she would diue beneath the darknes quite,
250 To finde her Iewell; Iewell, her *Leander*,
A name of all earths Iewels pleasde not her,
Like his deare name; *Leander*, still my choice,
Come nought but my *Leander;* O my voice
Turne to *Leander:* hence-forth be all sounds,
255 Accents, and phrases that shew all griefes wounds,
Analisde in *Leander*. O black change!
Trumpets doe you with thunder of your clange,
Driue out this changes horror, my voyce faints:
Where all ioy was, now shrieke out all complaints.
260 Thus cryed she, for her mixed soule could tell
Her loue was dead: And when the morning fell
Prostrate vpon the weeping earth for woe,
Blushes that bled out of her cheekes did show,
Leander brought by *Neptune*, brusde and torne,
265 With Cities ruines he to Rocks had worne,
To filthie vsering Rocks that would haue blood,
Though they could get of him no other good.
She saw him, and the sight was much much more,
Then might haue seru'd to kill her; should her store
v 270 Of giant sorrowes speake? O Burst, dye, bleede,
And leaue poore plaints to vs that shall succeede.
She fell on her loues bosome, hugg'd it fast,
And with *Leanders* name she breath'd her last.
Neptune for pittie in his armes did take them,
275 Flung them into the ayre, and did awake them.
Like two sweet birds surnam'd th' *Acanthides*,
Which we call Thistle-warps, that neere no Seas
Dare euer come, but still in couples flie,
And feede on Thistle tops, to testifie
280 The hardnes of their first life in their last:
The first in thornes of loue, and sorrowes past,
And so most beautifull their colours show,
As none (so little) like them: her sad brow
A sable veluet feather couers quite,
285 Euen like the forehead cloths that in the night,
Or when they sorrow, Ladies vse to weare:

270 O] *Added by Dyce.*

Their wings, blew, red and yellow mixt appeare,
Colours, that as we construe colours paint
Their states to life; the yellow shewes their saint,
The deuill *Venus* left them; blew their truth,   290
The red and black, ensignes of death and ruth.
And this true honor from their loue-deaths sprung,
They were the first that euer Poet sung.

FINIS.

EVTHYMIÆ RAPTVS;

or

The Teares of
PEACE.

TO THE HIGH
BORN PRINCE OF MEN,
HENRIE,

THRICE-ROYALL
INHERITOVR TO THE
VNITED KINGDOMS
OF GREAT

Britanne.

THE TEARES
OF PEACE·

INDVCTIO·

NOW that our Soueraign, the great King of Peace,
    Hath (in her grace) outlabour'd *Hercules;*
And, past his Pillars, stretcht her victories;
Since (as he were sole Soule, t'all Royalties)
5 He moues all Kings, in this vast Vniuerse,
To cast chaste Nettes, on th'impious lust of *Mars;*
See, All; and imitate his goodnesse still;
That (hauing cleard so well, warres outward ill)
Hee, God-like, still employes his firme desires,
10 To cast learn'd ynke vpon those inwarde fires,
That kindle worse Warre, in the mindes of men,
Like to incense the outward Warre againe:
Selfe-loue, inflaming so, mens sensuall bloud,
That all good, publique, drownes in priuate good;
15 And that, sinks vnder, his owne ouer-freight;
Mens Reasons, and their Learnings, shipwrackt quite;
And their Religion, that should still be One,
v Takes shapes so many, that most know't in none.
Which, I admiring (since, in each man shinde
20 A light so cleere, that by it, all might finde
(Being well informd) their obiect perfect Peace,
Which keepes the narrow path to Happinesse)
In that discourse; I shund, (as is my vse)
The iarring preace, and all their times abuse;
25 T'enioy least trodden fieldes, and fre'est shades;
Wherein (of all the pleasure that inuades
The life of man, and flies all vulgar feet,
Since silent meditation is most sweet)
I sat to it; discoursing what maine want
30 So ransackt man; that it did quite supplant

The inward Peace I spake of; letting in
(At his loose veines) sad warre, and all his sinne.
When, sodainely, a comfortable light
Brake through the shade; and, after it, the sight
Of a most graue, and goodly person shinde;   35
With eys turnd vpwards, & was outward, blind;
But, inward; past, and future things, he sawe;
And was to both, and present times, their lawe.
His sacred bosome was so full of fire,
That t'was transparent; and made him expire   40
His breath in flames, that did instruct (me thought)
And (as my soule were then at full) they wrought.
At which, I casting downe my humble eyes,
Not daring to attempt their feruencies;
He thus bespake me; Deare minde, do not feare   45
My strange apparance; Now t'is time t'outweare
Thy bashfull disposition, and put on
As confident a countnance, as the Sunne.
For what hast thou to looke on, more diuine,
And horrid, then man is; as hee should shine,   50 A₄ᴿ
And as he doth? what, free'd from this worlds strife;
What he is entring; and what, ending life?
All which, thou onely studiest, and dost knowe;
And, more then which, is onely sought for showe.
Thou must not vnderualue what thou hast,   55
In weighing it with that, which more is grac't;
The worth that weigheth inward, should not long
For outward prices. This should make thee strong
In thy close value; Nought so good can be
As that which lasts good, betwixt God, and thee.   60
Remember thine owne verse—Should Heauen turn Hell,
For deedes well done, I would do euer well.
   This heard, with ioy enough, to breake the twine
Of life and soule, so apt to breake as mine;
I brake into a trance, and then remainde   65
(Like him) an onely soule; and so obtainde
Such bouldnesse, by the sense hee did controule;
That I set looke, to looke; and soule to soule.
I view'd him at his brightest; though, alas,
With all acknowledgement, of what hee was   70
Beyond what I found habited in me;
And thus I spake; O thou that (blinde) dost see
My hart, and soule; what may I reckon thee?
Whose heauenly look showes not; nor voice sounds man?
I am (sayd hee) that spirit *Elysian*,   75
That (in thy natiue ayre; and on the hill

Next *Hitchins* left hand) did thy bosome fill,
With such a flood of soule; that thou wert faine
(With acclamations of her Rapture then)
80 To vent it, to the Echoes of the vale;
v When (meditating of me) a sweet gale
Brought me vpon thee; and thou didst inherit
My true sense (for the time then) in my spirit;
And I, inuisiblie, went prompting thee,
85 To those fayre Greenes, where thou didst english me.
 Scarce he had vttered this, when well I knewe
It was my Princes *Homer;* whose deare viewe
Renew'd my gratefull memorie of the grace
His Highnesse did me for him: which, in face,
90 Me thought the Spirit show'd, was his delight;
And added glory to his heauenly plight:
Who tould me, he brought stay to all my state;
That hee was Angell to me; Starre, and Fate;
Aduancing Colours of good hope to me;
95 And tould me, my retired age should see
Heauens blessing, in a free, and harmelesse life,
Conduct me, through Earths peace-pretending strife,
To that true Peace, whose search I still intend,
And to the calme Shore of a loued ende.
100 But now, as I cast round my rauisht eye,
To see, if this free Soule had companie;
Or that, alone, hee louingly pursude
The hidden places of my Solitude;
He rent a Cloude downe, with his burning hand
105 That at his backe hung, twixt me, and a Land
Neuer inhabited; and sayd; Now, behould
What maine defect it is that doth enfould
The World, in ominous flatteries of a Peace
So full of worse then warre; whose sterne encrease
110 Deuours her issue. With which words, I view'd
A Lady, like a Deitie indew'd;
(But weeping, like a woman) and made way
Out of one Thicket, that sawe neuer day,
B(1)R Towards another; bearing vnderneath
115 Her arme, a Coffine, for some prize of death;
And after her (in funerall forme) did goe
The woddes foure-footed Beasts, by two, and two;
A Male, and Female, matcht, of euerie kinde;
And after them; with like instinct enclinde,
120 The ayrie Nation felt her sorrowes stings;

79 acclamations] So changed by pen from "exclamations" in 17th c handwrit-
ings in nearly all extant copies.

Fell on the earth, kept rancke, and hung their wings.
Which sight I much did pittie, and admire;
And longd to knowe the dame that could inspire
Those Bestials, with such humane Forme, and ruthe;
And how I now should knowe, the hidden Truthe   125
(As *Homer* promist) of that maine defect
That makes men, all their inward Peace reiect
For name of outward: Then hee took my hand;
Led to her; and would make my selfe demand,
(Though he could haue resolv'd me) what shee was?   130
And from what cause, those strange effects had pass?
For whom, She bore that Coffine? and so mournd?
To all which; with all mildnesse, she returnd
Aunswere; that she was Peace; sent down from heauen
With charge, from the Almightie Deitie giuen,   135
T'attend on men; who now had banisht her
From their societies, and made her errc
In that wilde desert; onely Humane loue
(Banisht in like sort) did a long time proue
That life with her; but now, alas, was dead,   140
And lay in that wood to bee buried;
For whom she bore that Coffine, and did mourne;
And that those Beasts were so much humane, borne,
That they, in nature, felt a loue to Peace;
For which, they followd her, when men did cease.   145
This went so neere her heart, it left her tongue;   *v*
And (silent) she gaue time, to note whence sprung
Mens want of Peace, which was from want of loue:
And I observ'd now, what that peace did proue
That men made shift with, & did so much please.   150
For now, the Sunne declining to the Seas,
Made long misshapen shadowes; and true Peace
(Here walking in his Beames) cast such encrease
Of shaddowe from her; that I saw it glide
Through Cities, Courts, and Countryes; and descride,   155
How, in her shadowe only, men there liv'd,
While shee walkt here ith Sunne: and all that thriv'd
Hid in that shade their thrift; nought but her shade
Was Bullwarke gainst all warre that might inuade
Their Countries, or their Consciences; since Loue   160
(That should giue Peace, her substance) now they droue
Into the Deserts; where hee sufferd Fate,
And whose sad Funerals Beasts must celebrate.
With whom, I freely wisht, I had beene nurst;
Because they follow Nature, at their wurst;   165

133 mildnesse] mildensse

And at their best, did teach her. As wee went
I felt a scruple, which I durst not vent,
No not to Peace her selfe, whom it concernd,
For feare to wrong her; So well I haue learnd,
170 To shun iniustice, euen to doues, or flies;
But, to the Diuell, or the Destinies,
Where I am iust, and knowe I honour Truth,
Ile speake my thoughts, in scorne of what ensu'th.
Yet (not resolv'd in th'other) there did shine
175 A Beame of *Homers* fre'er soule, in mine,
That made me see, I might propose my doubt;
Which was; If this were true Peace I found out,
B₂ᴿ That felt such passion? I prov'd her sad part;
And prayd her call, her voice out of her hart
180 (There, kept a wrongfull prisoner to her woe)
To answere, why shee was afflicted so.
Or how, in her, such contraries could fall;
That taught all ioy, and was the life of all?
Shee aunswered; Homer tould me that there are
185 Passions, in which corruption hath no share;
There is a ioy of soule; and why not then
A griefe of soule, that is no skathe to men?
For both are Passions, though not such as raigne
In blood, and humor, that engender paine.
190 Free sufferance for the truth, makes sorrow sing,
And mourning farre more sweet, then banqueting.
Good, that deserueth ioy (receiuing ill)
Doth merit iustly, as much sorrow still:
And is it a corruption to do right?
195 Griefe, that dischargeth Conscience, is delight:
One sets the other off. To stand at gaze
In one position, is a stupide maze,
Fit for a Statue. This resolv'd me well,
That Griefe, in Peace, and Peace in Griefe might dwell.
200 And now fell all things from their naturall Birth:
Passion in Heauen; Stupiditie, in Earth,
Inuerted all; the Muses, Vertues, Graces,
Now sufferd rude, and miserable chaces
From mens societies, to that desert heath;
205 And after them, Religion (chac't by death)
Came weeping, bleeding to the Funerall:
Sought her deare Mother Peace; and downe did fall,
Before her, fainting, on her horned knees;
Turnd horne, with praying for the miseries
v 210 She left the world in; desperate in their sinne;
Marble, her knees pearc't; but heauen could not winne

To stay the weightie ruine of his Glorie
In her sad Exile; all the memorie
Of heauen, and heauenly things, rac't of all hands;
Heauen moues so farre off, that men say it stands;   215
And Earth is turnd the true, and mouing Heauen;
And so tis left; and so is all Truth driuen
From her false bosome; all is left alone,
Till all bee orderd with confusion.
    Thus the poore broode of Peace; driuen, & distrest,   220
Lay brooded all beneath their mothers breast;
Who fell vpon them weeping, as they fell:
All were so pinde, that she containde them well.
And in this Chaos, the digestion
And beautie of the world, lay thrust and throwne.   225
In this deiection, Peace pourd out her Teares,
Worded (with some pause) in my wounded Eares.

JNVOCATIO.

    O ye three-times-thrice sacred Quiristers,
Of Gods great Temple; the small Vniuerse
Of ruinous man: (thus prostrate as ye lye   230
Brooded, and Loded with Calamitie,
Contempt, and shame, in your true mother, Peace)
As you make sad my soule, with your misease:
So make her able fitly to disperse
Your sadnesse, and her owne, in sadder verse.   235
Now (olde, and freely banisht with your selues
From mens societies; as from rockes, and shelues)
Helpe me to sing, and die, on our Thames shore;
And let her lend me, her waues to deplore
(In yours, and your most holy Sisters falls)   240 B₃ᴿ
Heauens fall, and humane Loues, last funeralls.
    And thou, great Prince of men; let thy sweete graces
Shine on these teares; and drie, at length, the faces
Of Peace, and all her heauen-allyed brood;
From whose Doues eyes, is shed the precious blood   245
Of Heauens deare Lamb, that freshly bleeds in them.
Make these no toyes then; gird the Diadem
Of thrice great Britaine, with their Palm and Bayes:
And with thy Eagles feathers, daigne to raise
The heauie body of my humble Muse;   250
That thy great *Homers* spirit in her may vse
Her topless flight, and beare thy Fame aboue
The reach of Mortalls, and their earthly loue;
To that high honour, his *Achilles* wonne,
And make thy glory farre out-shine the Sunne.   255

While this small time gaue Peace (in her kinde Throes)
Vent for the violence of her sodaine woes;
She turnd on her right side, and (leaning on
Her tragique daughters bosome) lookt vpon
260 My heauy lookes, drownd in imploring teares
For her, and that so wrongd deare Race of hers.
At which, euen Peace, exprest a kinde of Spleene;
And, as a carefull Mother, I haue seene
Chide her lov'd Childe, snatcht with som feare from danger:
265 So Peace chid me; and first shed teares of anger.

THE TEARES OF PEACE.

Thou wretched man, whome I discouer, borne   *Peace.*
To want, and sorrowe, and the Vulgars scorne:
v Why haunt'st thou freely, these vnhaunted places,
Emptie of pleasures? empty of all Graces,
270 Fashions, and Riches; by the best pursude
With broken Sleepe, Toyle, Loue, Zeale, Seruitude;
With feare and trembling, with whole liues, and Soules?
While thou break'st sleepes, digst vnder Earth, like moules,
To liue, to seeke me out, whome all men fly:
275 And think'st to finde, light in obscuritie,
Eternitie, in this deepe vale of death:
Look'st euer vpwards, and liu'st still beneath;
Fill'st all thy actions, with strife, what to thinke,
Thy Braine with Ayre, and skatterst it in inke:
280 Of which thou mak'st weeds for thy soule to weare,
As out of fashion, as the bodies are.
I grant their strangenesse, and their too ill grace,   *Interlo*
And too much wretchednesse, to beare the face
Or any likenesse of my soule in them:
285 Whose Instruments, I rue with many a Streame
Of secret Teares for their extream defects,
In vttering her true forms: but their respects
Need not be less'ned, for their being strange,
Or not so vulgar, as the rest that range
290 With headlong Raptures, through the multitude:
Of whom they get grace, for their being rude.
Nought is so shund by Virtue, throwne from Truth,
As that which drawes the vulgar Dames, and Youth.
Truth must confesse it: for where liues there one,   *Pea*
295 That *Truth* or *Vertue*, for themselues alone,
Or seekes, or not contemns? All, all pursue
Wealth, Glory, Greatnesse, Pleasure, Fashions new.
Who studies, studies these: who studies not
And sees that studie, layes the vulgar Plot;

That all the Learning he gets liuing by,   300
Men but for forme, or humour dignifie
(As himselfe studies, but for forme, and showe,
And neuer makes his speciall end, to knowe)
And that an idle, ayrie man of Newes,
A standing Face; a propertie to vse   305 [B₄ᴿ]
In all things vile, makes Booke-wormes, creepe to him:
How scorns he bookes, and booke-worms! O how dim
Burnes a true Soules light, in his Bastard eyes!
And, as a Forrest ouer-grow'n breedes Flyes,
Todes, Adders, Sauadges, that all men shunne;   310
When, on the South-side, in a fresh May Sunne,
In varied Heards, the Beasts lie out, and sleepe,
The busie Gnatts, in swarms a buzzing keepe,
And guild their empty bodies (lift aloft)
In beames, that though they see all, difference nought: 315
So, in mens meerly outward, and false Peace,
Insteade of polisht men, and true encrease,
She brings forth men, with vices ouer-growne:
Women, so light, and like, fewe knowe their owne:
For milde and humane tongues, tongues forkt that sting: 320
And all these (while they may) take Sunne, and spring,

                    *   *   *   *   *   *

To help them sleep, and florish: on whose beames,
And branches, vp they clime, in such extreams
Of proude confusion, from iust Lawes so farre,
That in their Peace, the long Robe sweeps like warre.
Int. That Robe serues great men: why are great so rude?   325
Peac. Since great, and meane, are all but multitude.
For regular Learning, that should difference set
Twixt all mens worths, and make the meane, or great,
As that is meane or great (or chiefe stroke strike)
Serues the Plebeian and the Lord alike.   330
Their obiects, showe their learnings are all one;
Their liues, their obiects; Learning lov'd by none.
Int. You meane, for most part: nor would it displease
That most part, if they heard; since they professe,
Contempt of learning: Nor esteeme it fit,   335
Noblesse should study, see, or count'nance it.
Pea. Can men in blood be Noble, not in soule?
Reason abhorres it; since what doth controule
The rudenesse of the blood, and makes it Noble
(Or hath chiefe meanes, high birth-right to redouble,   340
In making manners soft, and man-like milde,
Not suffering humanes to runne proude, or wilde)   *v*

Is Soule, and learning; (or in loue, or act)
345 In blood where both faile then, lyes Nobless wrackt.
It cannot be denyde: but could you proue,   *Interlo.*
As well, that th'act of learning, or the loue,
(Loue being the act in will) should difference set,
Twixt all mens worths, and make the meane or great,
350 As learning is, or great, or meane in them;
Then cleare, her Right, stood to mans Diadem.
To proue that Learning (the soules actuall frame;   *Pea.*
Without which, tis a blanke; a smoke-hid flame)
Should sit great Arbitresse, of all things donne,
355 And in your soules, (like Gnomons in the Sunne)
Giue Rules to all the circles of your liues;
I proue it, by the Regiment God giues
To man, of all things; to the soule, of man;
To Learning, of the Soule. If then it can
360 Rule, liue; of all things best, is it not best?
O who, what god makes greatest, dares make least?
But, to vse their tearms; Life is Roote and Crest
To all mans Cote of Nobless; his soule is
Field to that Cote; and learning differences
365 All his degrees in honour, being the Cote.
And as a Statuarie, hauing got   *Simi.*
An Alabaster, bigge enough to cut
A humane image in it: till he hath put
His tooles, and art to it; hew'n, formd, left none
370 Of the redundant matter in the Stone;
It beares the image of a man, no more,
Then of a Woolf, a Cammell, or a Boare:
So when the Soule is to the body giuen;
C₁ᴿ (Being substance of Gods Image, sent from heaven)
375 It is not his true Image, till it take
Into the Substance, those fit forms that make
His perfect Image; which are then imprest
By Learning and impulsion; that inuest
Man with Gods forme in liuing Holinesse,
380 By cutting from his Body the excesse
Of Humors, perturbations and Affects;
Which Nature (without Art) no more eiects,
Then without tooles, a naked Artizan
Can, in rude stone, cut th' Image of a man.
385 How then do Ignorants? who, oft, we trie,   *Int.*
Rule perturbations, liue more humanely
Then men held learnd?
Who are not learn'd indeed;   *Pea.*
More then a house fram'd loose, (that still doth neede

The haling vp, and ioyning) is a house:
Nor can you call, men meere Religious,   390
(That haue good wills, to knowledge) Ignorant;
For, virtuous knowledge hath two waies to plant;
By Powre infus'd, and Acquisition;
The first of which, those good men, graft vpon;
For good life is th'effect, of learnings Act;   395
Which th'action of the minde, did first compact
By infusde loue to Learning gainst all ill,
Conquests first step, is to all good, the will.

Int. If *Learning* then, in loue or act must be,
Meane to good life, and true humanitie;   400
Where are our Scarre-crowes now, or men of ragges,
Of Titles meerely, Places, Fortunes, Bragges,
That want and scorne both? Those inuerted men?
Those dungeons; whose soules no more containe
The actuall light of Reason, then darke beasts?   405 *v*
Those Cloudes, driuen still, twixt Gods beame and their brests?
Those Giants, throwing goulden hils gainst heauen?
To no one spice of true humanitie given?

Peace. Of men, there are three sorts, that most foes be
To Learning and her loue; themselues and me: 410
Actiue, *Passiue*, and *Intellectiue* men:
Whose selfe-loues; Learning, and her loue disdaine.
Your Actiue men, consume their whole lifes fire,
In thirst of State-height, higher still and higher,
(Like seeled Pigeons) mounting, to make sport,   415
To lower lookers on; in seeing how short
They come of that they seeke, and with what trouble;
Lamely, and farre from Nature, they redouble
Their paines in flying, more then humbler witts,
To reach death, more direct. For Death that sits,   420
Vpon the fist of Fate, past highest Ayre,
(Since she commands all liues, within that Sphere)
The higher men aduance; the neerer findes
Her seeled Quarries; when, in bitterest windes,
Lightnings, and thunders, and in sharpest hayles   425
Fate casts her off at States; when lower Sayles
Slide calmely to their ends. Your *Passiue* men
(So call'd of onely passing time in vaine)
Passe it, in no good exercise; but are
In meates, and cuppes laborious; and take care   430
To lose without all care their Soule-spent Time;
And since they haue no meanes, nor Spirits to clime,
Like Fowles of Prey, in any high affaire,
See how like Kites they bangle in the Ayre,

435 To stoope at scraps, and garbidge; in respect,
      Of that which men of true peace should select;
C₂ᴿ And how they trot out, in their liues, the Ring;
      With idlely iterating oft one thing,
      A new-fought Combat, an affaire at Sea;
440 A Marriage, or a Progresse, or a Plea.
      No Newes, but fits them, as if made for them,
      Though it be forg'd, but of a womans dreame;
      And stuffe with, such stolne ends, their manlesse breasts,
      (Sticks, rags, and mud) they seem meer Puttock nests:
445 Curious in all mens actions, but their owne;
      All men, and all things censure, though know none.
      Your Intellectiue men, they study hard
      Not to get knowledge, but for meere rewarde.
      And therefore that true knowledge that should be
450 Their studies end, and is in Nature free,
      Will not be made their Broker; hauing powre
      (With her sole selfe) to bring both Bride, and dowre.
      They haue some shadowes of her (as of me,
      Adulterate outward Peace) but neuer see
455 Her true and heauenly face. Yet those shades serue
      (Like errant Knights, that by enchantments swerue,
      From their true Ladyes being; and embrace
      An ougly Witch, with her phantastique face)
      To make them thinke, *Truths* substance in their arms:
460 Which that they haue not, but her shadowes charmes,
      See if my proofes, be like their Arguments
      That leaue *Opinion* still, her free dissents.
      They haue not me with them; that all men knowe
      The highest fruite that doth of knowledge grow;
465 The Bound of all true formes, and onely Act;
      If they be true, they rest; nor can be rackt
      Out of their posture, by *Times* vtmost strength;
      But last the more of force, the more of length;
 v   For they become one substance with the Soule;
470 Which Time with all his adiuncts shall controule.
      But since, men wilfull may beleeue perchance
      (In part of Errors two-folde Ignorance,
      Ill disposition) their skills looke as hie
      And rest in that diuine Securitie;
475 See if their liues make proofe of such a Peace,
      For Learnings Truth makes all lifes vain war cease;
      It making peace with God, and ioines to God;
      Whose information driues her Period
      Through all the Bodies passiue Instruments;
480 And by reflection giues them Soule-contents,

Besides, from perfect Learning you can neuer
Wisedome (with her faire Reigne of Passions) seuer;
For Wisedome is nought else, then Learning fin'd,
And with the vnderstanding Powre combin'd;
That is, a habite of both habits standing;   485
The Bloods vaine humours, euer countermaunding.
But, if these showe, more humour then th'vnlearn'd;
If in them more vaine passion be discern'd;
More mad Ambition; more lust; more deceipt;
More showe of golde, then gold; then drosse, less weight;   490
If Flattery, Auarice haue their soules so giuen,
Headlong, and with such diuelish furies driuen;
That fooles may laugh at their imprudencie,
And Villanes blush at their dishonestie;
Where is true Learning, proov'd to separate these   495
And seate all forms in her Soules height, in peace?
Raging *Euripus*, that (in all their Pride)
Driues Shippes gainst roughest windes, with his fierce Tide,
And ebbes and flowes, seuen times in euerie daie;
Toyles not on Earth with more irregulare swaye,   500
Nor is more turbulent, and mad then they.   C₃ᴿ
And shine; like gould-worms, whom you hardly finde,
By their owne, light; not seene; but heard like winde.
But this is Learning; To haue skill to throwe
Reignes on your bodies powres, that nothing knowe;   505
And fill the soules powers, so with act, and art,
That she can curbe the bodies angrie part;
All perturbations; all affects that stray
From their one obiect; which is to obay
Her Soueraigne Empire; as her selfe should force   510
Their functions onely, to serue her discourse;
And, that; to beat the streight path of one ende
Which is, to make her substance still contend,
To be Gods Image; in informing it,
With knowledge; holy thoughts, and all formes fit   515
For that eternitie, ye seeke in way
Of his sole imitation; and to sway,
Your lifes loue so, that hee may still be Center
To all your pleasures; and you, (here) may enter
The next lifes peace; in gouerning so well   520
Your sensuall parts, that you, as free may dwell
Of vulgare Raptures, here; as when calme death
Dissolues that learned Empire, with your Breath.
To teach, and liue thus, is the onely vse,
And end of Learning, Skill that doth produce   525

508 perturbations] preturbations

But tearmes, and tongues, and Parrating of Arte,
Without that powre to rule the errant part;
Is that which some call, learned ignorance;
A serious trifle; error in a trance.
530   And let a Scholler, all earths volumes carrie,
He will be but a walking dictionarie:
A meere articulate Clocke, that doth but speake
v   By others arts; when wheeles weare, or springs breake,
Or any fault is in him; hee can mend
535   No more then clockes; but at set howres must spend
His mouth, as clocks do; If too fast, speech goe
Hee cannot stay it; nor haste if too slowe.
So that, as Trauaylers, seeke their peace through storms,
In passing many Seas, for many forms,
540   Of forreigne gouernment; indure the paine
Of many faces seeing; and the gaine
That Strangers make, of their strange-louing humors;
Learn tongues; keep note books; all to feed the tumors
Of vaine discourse at home; or serue the course
545   Of State employment, neuer hauing force
T'employ themselues; but idle complements
Must pay their paines, costs, slaueries, all their Rents;
And, though they many men knowe, get few friends:
So couetous Readers; setting many endes
550   To their much skill to talke; studiers of Phrase;
Shifters in Art; to flutter in the Blaze
Of ignorant count'nance; to obtaine degrees
And lye in Learnings bottome, like the Lees,
To be accounted deepe, by shallow men;
555   And carue all Language, in one glorious Pen;
May haue much fame for learning: but th'effect
Proper to perfect Learning; to direct
Reason in such an Art, as that it can
Turne blood to soule, and make both, one calme man;
560   So making peace with God; doth differ farre
From Clearkes that goe with God & man to warre.
But may this Peace, and mans true Empire then,   *Int.*
By learning be obtainde? and taught to men?
Let all men iudge; who is it can denie,   *Pea.*
[C₄ᴿ] 565   That the rich crowne of ould Humanitie,
Is still your birth-right? and was ne're let downe
From heauen, for rule of Beasts liues, but your owne?
You learne the depth of Arts; and (curious) dare
By them (in Natures counterfaits) compare
570   Almost with God; to make perpetually
Motion like heauens; to hang sad Riuers by

The ayre, in ayre; and earth, twixt earth and heauen
By his owne paise. And are these vertues giuen
To powrefull Art, and Vertue's selfe denied?
This proues the other, vaine, and falsified,   575
Wealth, Honour, and the Rule of Realmes doth fall
In lesse then Reasons compasse; yet, what all
Those things are giuen for (which is liuing well)
Wants discipline, and reason to compell.
O foolish men! how many waies ye vex   580
Your liues with pleasing them? and still perplex
Your liberties, with licence? euery way
Casting your eyes, and faculties astray
From their sole obiect? If some few bring forth
(In Nature, freely) something of some worth;   585
Much rude and worthlesse humour runs betwixt;
(Like fruit in deserts) with vile matter mixt.
Nor (since they flatter flesh so) they are bould
(As a most noble spectacle) to behould
Their owne liues; and (like sacred light) to beare   590
There Reason inward: for the Soule (in feare
Of euerie sort of vice, shee there containes)
Flies out; and wanders about other mens;
Feeding, and fatting, her infirmities.
    And as in auntient Citties, t'was the guise   595
To haue some Ports of sad, and haplesse vent,
Through which, all executed men they sent;   *v*
All filth; all offall, cast from what purg'd sinne;
Nought, chaste, or sacred, there going out, or in:
So, through mens refuse eares, will nothing pearse   600
Thats good, or elegant; but the sword; the herse;
And all that doth abhorre, from mans pure vse,
Is each mans onely Siren; only Muse.
And thus, for one God; one fit good; they prise
These idle, foolish, vile varieties.   605
Int. Wretched estate of men, by fortune blest;
That being euer idle, neuer rest;
That haue goods, ere they earne them; and for that,
Want art to vse them. To bee wonderd at
Is Iustice; for Proportion, Ornament;   610
None of the Graces, is so excellent.
Vile things, adorne her: me thought, once I sawe
How, by the Seas shore, she sat giuing lawe
Euen to the streames, and fish (most loose, and wilde)
And was (to my thoughts) wondrous sweet and milde;   615
Yet fire flew from her that dissolued Rocks;
Her lookes, to Pearle turnd pebble; and her locks,

The rough, and sandy bankes, to burnisht gould;
Her white left hand, did goulden bridles holde;
620 And, with her right, she wealthy gifts did giue;
Which with their left hands, men did still receiue;
Vpon a world in her chaste lappe, did lye,
A little Iuory Book, that show'd mine eye,
But one Page onely; that one verse containde,
625 Where all Arts, were contracted, and explainde;
All policies of Princes, all their forces;
Rules for their feares, cares, dangers, pleasures, purses,
All the fayre progresse of their happinesse here,
D,ᴿ Iustice conuerted, and composed there.
630 All which I thought on, when I had exprest
Why great men, of the great states they possest,
Enioyd so little; and I now must note
The large straine of a verse, I long since wrote.
Which (me thought) much ioy, to men poore presented;
635 God hath made none (that all might be) contented.
It might (for the capacitie it beares)   Peace.
Be that concealed and expressiue verse,
That Iustice, in her Iuorie Manuell writ;
Since all Lines to mans Peace, are drawne in it.
640 For great men; though such ample stuffe they haue
To shape contentment; yet, since (like a waue)
It flittes, and takes all formes, retayning none;
(Not fitted to their patterne, which is one)
They may content themselues; God hath not giuen,
645 To men meere earthly, the true Ioyes of heauen;
And so their wilde ambitions either stay;
Or turne their headstrong course, the better way.
For poore men; their cares may be richly easde;
Since rich (with all they haue) liue as displeasde.
650 You teach me to be plaine. But whats the cause,   Int.
That great, and rich, whose stares winne such applause;
With such enforc't, and vile varieties,
Spend time; nor giue their liues glad sacrifice;
But when they eate, and drinke, with tales, iests, sounds;
655 As if (like frantique men, that feele no wounds)
They would expire in laughters? and so erre
From their right way; that like a Trauayler,
(Weariest when neerest to his iourneys ende)
Time best spent euer, with most paine they spend?
660 The cause, is want of Learning; which (being right)   Pea.
ʋ Makes idlenesse a paine; and paine delight.
It makes men knowe, that they (of all things borne
Beneath the siluer Moone, and goulden Morne)

Being onely formes of God; should onely fix
One forme of life to those formes; and not mix   665
With Beastes in formes of their liues. It doth teach,
To giue the soule her Empire; and so reach
To rule of all the bodies mutinous Realme;
In which (once seated) She then takes the Helme,
And gouernes freely; stering to one Port.   670
Then, (like a man in health) the whole consort
Of his tun'd body, sings; which otherwise,
Is like one full of weiward maladies,
Still out of tune; and (like to Spirits raisde
Without a Circle) neuer is appaisde.   675
And then, they haue no strength, but weakens them;
No greatnes, but doth crush them into streame;
No libertie, but turnes into their snare;
Their learnings then, do light them but to erre;
Their ornaments, are burthens; their delights,   680
Are mercinarie, seruile Parasites,
Betraying, laughing; Feends, that raisde in feares,
At parting, shake their Roofes about their eares;
Th'imprison'd thirst, the fortunes of the Free;
The Free, of Rich; Rich, of Nobilitie;   685
Nobilitie, of Kings; and Kings, Gods thrones;
Euen to their lightning flames; and thunder-stones.
O liberall Learning, that well vsde, giues vse
To all things good; how bad is thy abuse!
When, onely thy diuine reflection can   690
(That lights but to thy loue) make good a man;
How can the regular Body of thy light,
Informe, and decke him? the Ills infinite,   D₂ᴿ
That (like beheaded *Hydra's* in that Fen
Of bloud, and flesh, in lewd illiterate men)   695
Aunswere their amputations, with supplyes
That twist their heads, and euer double rise;
Herculean Learning conquers; And O see
How many, and of what fowle formes they be?
Vnquiet, wicked thoughts; vnnumbred passions;   700
Poorenesse of Counsailes; howrely fluctuations;
(In entercourse) of woes, and false delights;
Impotent wils to goodnesse; Appetites
That neuer will bee bridl'd; satisfied;
Nor knowe how, or with what to be supplyed;   705
Feares, and distractions, mixt with greedinesse;
Stupidities of those things ye possesse;
Furies for what ye lose; wrongs done for nonce;
For present, past, and future things, at once

710 Cares vast, and endlesse; miseries, swolne with pride;
Vertues despisde, and vices glorified.
All these, true Learning calmes, and can subdue:
But who turnes learning this way? All pursue
Warre with each other, that exasperates these;
715 For things without; whose ends are inward peace;
And yet those inward Rebels they maintaine.
And as your curious sort of Passiue men,
Thrust their heads through the Roofs of Rich & Poore;
Through all their liues, and fortunes, and explore
720 Forraigne, and home-affayres; their Princes Courts,
Their Counsaile, and Bedchambers for reports;
And (like free-booters) wander out, to win
Matter to feede their mutinous Route within;
(Which are the greedier still) and ouershoote
v 725 Their true-sought inward Peace, for outward boote;
So Learned men, in controuersies spend
(Of tongues, and tearmes, readings, and labours pend)
Their whole liues studies; Glorie, Riches, Place,
In full crie, with the vulgare giuing Chace;
730 And neuer, with their learnings true vse striue
To bridle strifes within them; and to liue
Like men of Peace, whome Art of Peace begat:
But, as their deedes, are most adulterate,
And showe them false Sons, to their Peacefull Mother,
735 In those warres; so their Arts, are prov'd no other.
And let the best of them, a search impose
Vpon his Art: for all the things shee knowes
(All being referd, to all, to her vnknowne)
They will obtaine the same proportion
740 That doth a little brooke that neuer ran
Through Summers Sunne; compar'd with th'Ocean.
But, could he Oracles speake; and wright to charme
A wilde of Sauadges; take Natures Arme,
And plucke into his search, the Circuit
745 Of Earth, and Heauen; the Seas space, and the spirit
Of euerie Starre: the Powers of Herbs, and Stones;
Yet touch not, at his perturbations;
Nor giue them Rule, and temper to obay
Imperiall Reason; in whose Soueraigne sway,
750 Learning is wholly vs'd, and dignified;
To what end serues he? is his learning tryed
That comforting, and that creating Fire
That fashions men? or that which doth inspire
Citties with ciuile conflagrations,
755 Countries, and kingdomes? That Art that attones

	All opposition to good life, is all;	

All opposition to good life, is all;
Liue well ye Learned; and all men ye enthrall.   D₃ᴿ

Interlo. Alas they are discourag'd in their courses;
And (like surpris'd Forts) beaten from their forces.
Bodies, on Rights of Soules did neuer growe   760
With ruder Rage, then barbarous Torrents flowe
Ouer their sacred Pastures; bringing in
Weedes, and all rapine; Temples now begin
To suffer second deluge; Sinne-drownde Beasts,
Making their Altars crack; and the filde Nests   765
Of vulturous Fowles, filling their holy places;
For wonted Ornaments, and Religious graces.

Pea. The chiefe cause is, since they themselues betraie;
Take their Foes baites, for some particular swaie
T'inuert their vniuersall; and this still,   770
Is cause of all ills else; their liuing ill.

Int. Alas! that men should striue for others swaie;
But first to rule themselues: And that being waie
To all mens Bliss; why is it trod by none?
And why are rules so dully lookt vpon   775
That teach that liuely Rule?

Pea. O horrid thing!
Tis Custome powres into your common spring
Such poyson of Example, in things vaine;
That Reason nor Religion can constraine
Mens sights of serious things; and th'onely cause   780
That neither humane nor celestiall lawes
Drawe man more compasse; is his owne slacke bent
T'intend no more his proper Regiment,
Where; if your Actiue men (or men of action)
Their Policie, Auarice, Ambition, Faction,   785
Would turne to making strong, their rule of Passion,
To search, and settle them, in Approbation
Of what they are, and shalbe (which may be   *v*
By Reason, in despight of Policie)
And in one true course, couch their whole Affaires   790
To one true blisse, worth all the spawne of theirs;
If halfe the idle speech, men Passiue spend,
At sensuall meetings, when they recommend
Their sanguine Soules, in laughters, to their Peace,
Were spent in Counsailes how they might decrease   795
That frantique humour of ridiculous blood
(Which addes, they vainely thinke, to their liues flood)
And so conuerted, in true humane mirth,
To speech, what they shall be (dissolv'd from Earth)
In bridling it in flesh; with all the scope   800

Of their owne knowledge here; and future hope:
If (last of all) your Intellectiue men
Would mixe the streames of euery iarring Penne
In one calme Current; that like land flouds, now
805 Make all Zeales bounded Riuers ouer-flowe;
Firme Truth, with question, euery howre pursue;
And yet will have no question, all is true:
Search in that troubled Ocean, for a Ford
That by it selfe runnes; and must beare accord
810 In each mans self; by banishing falshood there,
Wrath, lust, pride, earthy thoughts; before elsewhere.
(For, as in one man, is the world inclosde,
So to forme one, it should be all disposde:)
If all these would concurre to this one end,
815 It would aske all their powres; and all would spend
Life with that reall sweetnesse, which they dreame
Comes in with obiects that are meere extreame:
And make them outward pleasures still apply
Which neuer can come in, but by that key;
[D₄ᴿ] 820 Others aduancements, others Fames desiring;
Thirsting, exploring, praysing, and admiring;
Like lewd adulterers, that their owne wiues scorne,
And other mens, with all their wealth, adorne.
Why, in all outraying, varied ioyes, and courses,
825 That in these errant times, tire all mens forces,
Is this so common wonder of our dayes?
That in poore foretimes, such a fewe could raise
So many wealthy Temples, and these none?
All were deuout then; all deuotions one;
830 And to one end conuerted; and when men
Giue vp themselues to God; all theirs goes then:
A few well-giuen, are worth a world of ill;
And worlds of Powre, not worth one poore good-will.
And what's the cause, that (being but one *Truth*) spreds
835 About the world so manie thousand heads,
Of false Opinions, all self-lov'd as true?
Onely affection, to things more then due:
One Error kist, begetteth infinite.
How can men finde truth, in waies opposite?
840 And with what force, they must take opposite wayes
When all haue opposite obiects? *Truth* displaies
One colourd ensigne; and the world pursues
Ten thousand colours: see (to iudge, who vse
Truth in their Arts;) what light their liues doe giue:
845 For wherefore doe they study, but to liue?
See I Eternities streight milke-white waie,

And One, in this lifes crooked vanities straie;
And, shall I thinke he knowes Truth, following Error?
This; onely this; is the infallible myrror,
To showe, why Ignorants, with learn'd men vaunt,   850
And why your learn'd men, are so ignorant,
Why euery Youth, in one howre will be old   v
In euery knowledge; and why Age doth mould.
Then; As in Rules of true Philosophie
There must be euer due Analogie   855
Betwixt the Powre that knowes, and that is knowne,
So surely ioynde that they are euer one;
The vnderstanding part transcending still
To that it vnderstands, that, to his skill;
All, offering to the Soule, the Soule to God;   860
(By which do all things make their Period
In his high Powre; and make him, All in All;
So, to ascend, the high-heauen-reaching Skale
Of mans true Peace; and make his Art entire,
By calming all his Errors in desire;   865
(Which must preceede, that higher happinesse)
Proportion still, must trauerse her accesse
Betwixt his powre, and will; his Sense and Soule;
And euermore th'exorbitance controule
Of all forms, passing through the bodies Powre,   870
Till in the soule they rest, as in their Towre.

Int.   But; as Earths grosse and elementall fire,
Cannot maintaine it selfe; but doth require
Fresh matter still, to giue it heate, and light;
And, when it is enflam'd; mounts not vpright;   875
But struggles in his lame impure ascent;
Now this waie works, and then is that waie bent,
Not able, straight, t'aspire to his true Sphere
Where burns the fire, eternall, and sincere;
So, best soules here; with heartiest zeales enflam'd   880
In their high flight for heauen; earth-broos'd and lam'd)
Make many faint approches; and are faine,
With much vnworthy matter, to sustaine
Their holiest fire; and with sick feathers, driuen,   E(1)R
And broken Pinions, flutter towards heauen.   885

Peace. The cause is, that you neuer will bestowe
Your best, t'enclose your liues, twixt God, and you;
To count the worlds Loue, Fame, Ioy, Honour, nothing;
But life, (with all your loue to it) betrothing
To his loue; his recomfort; his rewarde;   890
Since no good thought calls to him, but is heard.
Nor neede you, thinke this strange; since he is there,

Present: within you; euer, euerywhere
Where good thoughts are; for Good hath no estate
895 Without him; nor himselfe is, without That:
If then, this Commerce stand twixt you entire;
Trie, if he either, grant not each desire;
Or so conforme it, to his will, in staie;
That you shall finde him, there, in the delaie,
900 As well as th'instant grant; And so prooue, right
How easie, his deare yoke is; and how light
His equall burthen: whether this Commerce
Twixt God and man, be so hard, so peruerse
(In composition); as, the Raritie,
905 Or no-where-patterne of it, doth implie?
Or if, in worthy contemplation
It do not tempt, beyond comparison
Of all things worldly? Sensualitie,
Nothing so easie; all Earths Companie,
910 (Like Rubarb, or the drugges of Thessalie)
Compar'd, in taste with that sweet? O trie then
If, that contradiction (by the God of men)
Of all the lawe, and Prophets, layd vpon
The tempting Lawyer; were a lode, that None
915 Had powre to stand beneath? If Gods deare loue,
Thy Conscience do not, at first sight approue
Deare, aboue all things? And, so passe this shelfe;
To loue (withall) thy Neighbour as thy selfe?
Not, loue as much; but as thy selfe; in this,
920 To let it be as free, as thine owne is;
Without respect of profit, or reward,
Deceipt, or flatterie; politique regard,
Or anie thing, but naked Charitie.
I call, euen God, himselfe; to testifie   *Interlo.*
925 (For men, I know but fewe) that farre aboue
v   All to be here desir'd; I rate his loue.
Thanks to his still-kist-hand, that hath so fram'd
My poore, and abiect life; and so, inflam'd
My soule with his sweete, all-want-seasoning loue;
930 In studying to supply, though not remoue,
My desert fortunes, and vnworthinesse,
With some wisht grace from him; that might expresse
His presence with me; and so dignifie,
My life, to creepe on earth; behold the skie,
935 And giue it meanes enough, for this lowe plight;
Though, hitherto, with no one houres delight,
Heartie or worthie; but in him alone;

906 worthy] worrhy

Who, like a carefull guide, hath hal'd me on;
And (euery minute, sinking) made me swimme,
To this calme Shore; hid, with his Sonne, in him: 940
And here, ay me! (as trembling, I looke back)
I fall againe, and, in my hauen, wracke;
Still being perswaded (by the shamelesse light)
That these are dreames, of my retired Night;
That, all my Reading; Writing; all my paines   945
Are serious trifles; and the idle vaines
Of an vnthriftie Angell, that deludes
My simple fancie; and, by Fate, extendes E_2^R
My Birth-accurst life, from the blisse of men:
And then; my hands I wring; my bosome, then   950
Beate, and could breake ope; fill th'inraged Ayre;
And knock at heauen, with sighs; inuoke Despaire,
At once, to free the tyr'd Earth of my lode;
That these recoiles, (that, Reason doth explode;
Religion damns; and my arm'd Soule defies;   955
Wrastles with Angels; telling Heauen it lies,
If it denie the truth, his Spirit hath writ,
Grauen, in my soule, and there eternisde it)
Should beat me from that rest; and that is this;
That these prodigious Securities   960
That all men snore-in (drowning in vile liues
The Soules of men, because the bodie thriues)
Are Witch-crafts damnable; That all learnings are
Foolish, and false, that with those vile liues square;
That these sowre wizzards, that so grauely scorne   965
Learning with good life; kinde gainst kinde suborne;
And are no more wise, then their shades, are men;
Which (as my finger, can goe to my Penne)
I can demonstrate; that our knowledges,*
(Which we must learne, if euer we professe   970
Knowledge of God; or haue one Notion true)
Are those, which first, and most we should pursue;
That, in their searches, all mens actiue liues,
Are so farre short of their contemplatiues;
As Bodies are of Soules; This life, of Next: 975
And, so much doth the Forme, and whole Context
Of matter, seruing one; exceed the other;
That Heauen, our Father is; as Earth our Mother.
And therefore; in resemblance to approue,
Who are the true bredde; fatherd by his loue;   980 *v*
As Heauen it selfe, doth only, virtually
Mix with the Earth; his Course still keeping hie,

* Knowl-
edge of our
selues.

939 me] we

And Substance, vndisparag'd; (though his Beames
Are dround in many dung-hils; and their Steames,
985 (To vs) obscure him; yet he euer shines:)
So though our soules beames, digge in bodies Mines,
To finde them rich discourses, through their Senses;
And meet with many myddins of offences,
Whose Vapours choke their Organes; yet should they
990 Disperse them by degrees; because their swaie
(In Powre) is absolute; And (in that Powre) shine
As firme as heauen; heauen, nothing so divine.
All this, I holde; and since, that all truth else,
That all else knowe, or can holde; staies and dwelles
995 On these grounds vses; and should all contend
(Knowing our birth here, serues but for this end
To make true meanes, and waies, t'our second life)
To plie those studies; and holde euery strife
To other ends (more then to amplifie,
1000 Adorne, and sweeten these, deseruedly)
As balls cast in our Race; and but grasse knitt
From both sides of our Path; t'ensnare our wit:
And thus, because, the gaudie vulgar light
Burns vp my good.thoughts, form'd in temperate Night,
1005 Rising to see, the good Moone oftentimes
(Like the poore virtues of these vicious times)
Labour as much to lose her light; as when
She fills her waning horns; And how (like men
Raisd to high Places) Exhalations fall
1010 That would be thought Starres; Ile retire from all
The hot glades of Ambition; Companie,
E₂ᴿ That (with their vainenesse) make this vanitie;
And coole to death, in shaddowes of this vale:
To which end, I will cast this Serpents skale;
1015 This loade of life, in life; this fleshie stone;
This bond, and bundle of corruption;
This breathing Sepulcher; this spundge of griefe;
This smiling Enemie; this household-thiefe;
This glasse of ayre; broken with lesse then breath;
1020 This Slaue, bound face to face, to death, till death;
And consecrate my life, to you, and yours:
In which obiection; if that Powre of Powers
That hath reliev'd me thus farre; with a hand
Direct, and most immediate; still will stand
1025 Betwixt me, and the Rapines of the Earth;
And giue my poore paines, but such gratious birth,
As may sustaine me, in my desert Age,
With some powre, to my will; I still will wage

Warre with that false Peace, that exileth you;
And (in my prayd for freedome) euer vow,   1030
Teares in these shades, for your teares; till mine eyes
Poure out my soule in better sacrifise.
Peace. Nor doubt (good friend) but God, to whom I see
Your friendlesse life conuerted; still will be
A rich supply for friends; And still be you   1035
Sure Conuertite to him. This, this way rowe
All to their Countrie. Thinke how hee hath shew'd
You wayes, and by wayes; what to bee pursew'd,
And what auoyded. Still, in his hands be,
If you desire to liue, or safe, or free.   1040
No longer dayes take; Nature doth exact
This resolution of thee, and this fact:
The Foe hayles on thy head; and in thy Face
Insults, and trenches; leaues thee, no worlds grace;   *v*
The walles; in which thou art besieged, shake.   1045
Haue done; Resist no more: but if you take
Firme notice of our speech, and, what you see;
And will adde paines to write all; let it be
Divulged too. Perhappes, of all, some one
May finde some good: But might it touch vpon   1050
Your gratious Princes liking; hee might doe
Good to himselfe, and all his kingdomes too:
So virtuous, a great Example is;
And that, hath thankt, as small a thing as this;
Here being stuffe, and forme, for all true Peace;   1055
And so, of all mens perfect Happinesse.
To which, if hee shall lend his Princely eare,
And giue commandement (from your selfe) to heare
My state; tell him you know me; and that I,
That am the Crowne of Principalitie,   1060
(Though thus cast off by Princes) euer vow
Attendance at his foote; till I may growe
Vp to his bosome; which (being deaw'd in time
With these my Teares) may to my comforts clyme:
Which (when all Pleasures, into Palseys turne,   1065
And Sunne-like Pomp; in his own clowds shal mourne)
Will be acceptiue. Meane space I will pray,
That hee may turne, some toward thought this way;
While the round whirlewindes, of the earths delights
Dust betwixt him and me; and blinde the sights   1070
Of all men rauisht with them; whose encrease
(You well may tell him) fashions not true Peace.
The Peace that they informe; learns but to squat,
While the slye legall foe (that leuels at

1075 Warre, through those false lights) soudainly runs by
[E₄ᴿ] Betwixt you, and your strength; and while you lye,
Couching your eares; and flatting euerie lymme
So close to earth, that you would seeme to him
The Earth it selfe: yet hee knowes who you are;
1080 And, in that vantage, poures on, ready warre.

CONCLVSIO.

Thus, by the way, to humane Loues interring,
These marginall, and secret teares referring
To my disposure (hauing all this howre
Of our vnworldly conference, giuen powre
1085 To her late-fainting issue, to arise)
She raisde her selfe, and them; The Progenies
Of that so ciuile Desert, rising all;
Who fell with her; and to the Funerall
(She bearing still the Coffine) all went on.
1090 And, now giues Time, her states description.
Before her flew Affliction, girt in storms,
Gasht all with gushing wounds; and all the formes
Of bane, and miserie, frowning in her face;
Whom Tyrannie, and Iniustice, had in Chace;
1095 Grimme Persecution, Pouertie, and Shame;
Detraction, Enuie, foule Mishap and lame;
Scruple of Conscience; Feare, Deceipt, Despaire;
Slaunder, and Clamor, that rent all the Ayre;
Hate, Warre, and Massacre; vncrowned Toyle;
1100 And Sickenes (t'all the rest, the Base, and Foile)
Crept after; and his deadly weight, trode downe
Wealth, Beautie, and the glorie of a Crowne.
These vsherd her farre of; as figures giuen,
v To showe, these Crosses borne, make peace with heauen:
1105 But now (made free from them) next her, before;
Peacefull, and young, Herculean silence bore
His craggie Club; which vp, aloft, hee hild;
With which, and his forefingers charme hee stild
All sounds in ayre; and left so free, mine eares,
1110 That I might heare, the musique of the Spheres,
And all the Angels, singing, out of heauen;
Whose tunes were solemne (as to Passion giuen)
For now, that Iustice was the Happinesse there
For all the wrongs to Right, inflicted here.
1115 Such was the Passion that Peace now put on;
And on, all went; when soudainely was gone

1084 vnworldly] vnwordly

All light of heauen before vs; from a wood
Whose sight, fore-seene (now lost) amaz'd wee stood,
The Sunne still gracing vs; when now (the Ayre
Inflam'd with Meteors) we discouerd, fayre,   1120
The skipping Gote; the Horses flaming Mane;
Bearded, and trained Comets; Starres in wane;
The burning sword; the Firebrand, flying Snake;
The Lance; the Torch; the Licking fire; the Drake:
And all else Metors, that did ill abode;   1125
The thunder chid; the lightning leapt abrode;
And yet, when Peace came in, all heauen was cleare;
And then, did all the horrid wood appeare;
Where mortall dangers, more then leaues did growe;
In which wee could not, one free steppe bestowe;   1130
For treading on some murtherd Passenger,
Who thither, was by witchcraft, forc't to erre,
Whose face, the bird hid, that loues Humans best;
That hath the bugle eyes, and Rosie Breast;
And is the yellow Autumns Nightingall.   1135
Peace made vs enter here secure of all;   F(1)R
Where, in a Caue, that through a Rocke did eate
The monster, Murther, held his impious Seat:
A heape of panting Harts, supported him;
On which, he sate, gnawing a reeking lymme,   1140
Of some man newly murtherd. As he eate
His graue-digg'd Browes, like stormy Eaues did sweat;
Which, like incensed Fennes, with mists did smoke;
His hyde was rugged, as an aged Oke
With heathie Leprosies; that still hee fed   1145
With hote, raw lyms, of men late murthered.
His Face was like a Meteor, flashing blood;
His head all bristl'd, like a thornie wood;
His necke cast wrinkles, like a Sea enrag'd;
And, in his vast Armes, was the world engag'd,   1150
Bathing his hands in euerie cruell deed;
Whose Palmes were hell-deepe lakes of boyling lead;
His thighes were mines of poyson, torment, griefe;
In which digg'd Fraude, and Trecherie, for reliefe;
Religions Botcher, Policie; and Pride;   1155
Oppression, Slauerie, Flatterie glorified;
Atheisme, and Tyranny, and gaine vniust;
Franticke Ambition, Enuie, shagge-heard Lust;
Both sorts of Ignorance; and Knowledge swell'd;
And ouer these, the ould wolfe Auarice held   1160
A goulden Scourge, that dropt, with blood and vapor;
With which, he whipt them to their endlesse labor.

From vnder heapes, cast from his fruitfull thyes,
(As ground, to all their damn'd Impieties)
1165   The mourneful Goddesse, drew dead Humane Loue;
Nor could they let her entrie, though they stroue;
And furnac't on her, all their venemous breath;
 v   (For; though all outrage breakes the Peace of death)
She Coffind him; and forth to Funerall
1170   All helpt to beare him: But to sound it all,
My Trumpet fayles; and all my forces shrinke.
Who can enact to life, what kils to thinke?
Nor can the Soules beames bear, through blood & flesh,
Formes of such woe, and height, as now, afresh,
1175   Flow'd from these Obiects: to see Poesie
Prepar'd to doe the speciall obsequie,
And sing the Funerall Oration;
How it did showe, to see her tread vpon
The breast of Death; and on a Furie leane;
1180   How, to her Fist, (as rites of seruice then)
A Cast of Rauens flew; On her shoulders, how
The Foules, that to the Muses Queene we vow,
(The Owle, and Heronshawe) sate, how, for her hayre,
A haplesse Comet, hurld about the Ayre
1185   Her curled Beames: whence sparkes, like falling starres,
Vanisht about her; and with windes aduerse,
Were still blowne back; To which the Phoenix flew;
And (burning on her head) would not renew:
How her diuine Oration did moue,
1190   For th'vnredeemed losse of humane Loue;
Obiect mans future state to reasons eye;
The soules infusion; Immortalitie;
And proue her formes firme, that are here imprest;
How her admirde straines, wrought on euery Beast;
1195   And made the woods cast their Immanitie,
Vp to the Ayre; that did to Citties flye
In Fewell for them: and, in Clowds of smoke,
Euer hang ouer them; cannot be spoke;
Nor how to Humane loue (to Earth now giuen)
F₂ᴿ 1200   A lightening stoop't, and rauisht him to heauen,
And with him Peace, with all her heauenly seede:
Whose outward Rapture, made me inward bleed;
Nor can I therefore, my Intention keepe;
Since Teares want words, & words want teares to weepe.

COROLLARIVM AD *PRINCIPEM*.

1205   Thus shooke I this abortiue from my Braine;
Which, with it, laie in this vnworthy paine:

Yet since your HOMER had his worthy hand
In vent'ring this delaie of your Command,
To end his *Iliades;* deigne (Great Prince of men)
To holde before it your great Shielde; and then   1210
It may, doe seruice, worthy this delaie,
To your more worthy Pleasure; and I maie
Regather the sperst fragments of my spirits,
And march with HOMER through his deathless merits,
To your vndying graces. Nor did he   1215
Vanish with this slight vision; but brought me
Home to my Cabine; and did all the waie
Assure me of your Graces constant staie
To his soules Being, wholly naturalliz'd
And made your Highnesse subiect; which he priz'd,   1220
Past all his honours helde in other Lands;
And that (because a Princes maine state stands
In his owne knowledge, and his powre within)
These works that had chiefe virtue to beginne
Those informations; you would holde most deare;   1225
Since false Ioyes, haue their seasons to appeare
Iust as they are; but these delights were euer   *v*
Perfect and needefull, and would irke you neuer.
    I praying for this happie worke of heauen
In your sweete disposition; the calme Euen   1230
Tooke me to rest; and he with wings of Fire,
To soft Ayres supreame Region did aspire.

By the euer most humbly and truly dedicated
to your most Princely graces,
                                            Geo. Chapman.

PETRARCHS SEVEN

PENITENTIALL PSALMS

With other

Philosophicall
POEMS,
and a

HYMNE TO CHRIST VPON
THE CROSSE.

TO THE RIGHT
WORTHILY HONORD,

graue, and ingenuous Fauorer
of all vertue, Sir *Edw. Phillips*
Knight, Maister of the
Rolles, &c.

SIR, though the name of a Poeme beares too light and vaine
a Character in his forhead, either to answer my most
affectionate desire to do you honour, or deserue your accep-
tance; yet since the subiect & matter is graue and sacred
enough, (how rudely soeuer I haue endeuored to giue it grace
and elocution,) I presumed to preferre to your emptiest leisure
of reading, this poore Dedication. In the substance and soule
of whose humane and diuine obiect, the most wise and religi-
ous that euer writ to these purposes, I haue (for so much as
this little containes) imitated, and celebrated. Good life, and
the true feeling of our humane birth and Being, being the
end of it all: and (as I doubt not your iudiciall and noble ap-
prehension will confesse) the chiefe end of whatsoeuer else,
in all authoritie and principalitie. Notwithstanding (either for
the slendernesse of the volume, or harshnesse of the matter)
I haue not dared to submit it (as the rest of my weake labors)
to my most gracious and sacred Patron, the Prince; reseruing
my thrice humble dutie to his Highnesse, for some much
greater labours, to which it hath pleased him to command me.
And thus most truly thankfull for all your right free and
honorable fauours, I humbly and euer rest

*The most unfained and
constant obseruer of
you and yours,*
Geo. Chapman.

PETRARCHS
SEVEN PENITEN-
TIALL PSALMES.

PSALME I.

Heu mihi Misero.

1

O ME wretch, I haue enrag'd
My Redeemer; and engag'd
  My life, on deaths slow foote presuming:
I haue broke his blessed lawes,
Turning with accursed cause,
  Sauing loue to wrath consuming.

2

Truths straite way, my will forsooke,
And to wretched bywaies tooke,
  Brode, rough, steepe, and full of danger.
Euery way, I labour found,
Anguish, and delights vnsound,
  To my iourneyes end a stranger.

3

Rockes past fowles wings, tooke my flights,
All my dayes spent; all my nights;
  Toyles and streights though still repelling.
One or other beast I met,
Shunning that for which I swet;
  Wild beasts dens were yet my dwelling.

4

Pleasure, that all paine subornes,
Making beds of ease, on thornes,
  Made me found with ruine sleeping.
Rest, in Torments armes I sought,
All good talkt, but all ill thought,
  Laught, at what deseru'd my weeping.

5

What is now then left to do?
What course can I turne me to?
  Danger, such vnscap't toyles pitching.
All my youths faire glosse is gone,

Like a shipwracke each way blowne,
  Yet his pleasures still bewitching.

6

I delay my Hauen to make;
Nor yet safeties true way take;
  On her left hand euer erring:
I a little see my course,
Which in me, the warre makes worse,
  Th'vse of that small sight deferring.

7

Oft I haue attempted flight,
Th'old yoke casting, but his weight
  Thou Nature to my bones impliest.
O that once my necke were easde,
Straight it were; were thy powre pleasd,
  O, of all things high, thou highest.

8

O could I my sinne so hate,
I might loue thee yet, though late;
  But my hope of that is sterued;
Since mine owne hands make my chaines:
Iust, most iust, I grant my paines;
  Labour wrings me most deserued.

9

Mad wretch, how deare haue I bought
Fetters with mine owne hands wrought?
  Freely in deaths ambush falling.
I made; and the foe disposde
Nets that neuer will be losde.
  More I striue, the more enthralling:

10

I look't by, and went secure
In paths slipperie, and impure;
  In my selfe, my sinne still flattering.
I thought youths flowre still would thriue,
Follow'd as his storme did driue,
  With it, all his hemlockes watering:

11

Said; what thinke I of th'extreames
Ere the Meane hath spent his beames?

Each Age hath his proper obiect.
God sees this, and laughs to see.
Pardon soone is got; My knee
　　When I will repent, is subiect.

12

Custome then his slaue doth claime,
Layes on hands that touch and maime;
　　Neuer cour'd repented neuer:
Flight is then, as vaine, as late;
Faith too weake to cast out Fate,
　　Refuge past my reach is euer.

B₃ᴿ

13

I shall perish then in sinne,
If thy aide Lord, makes not in,
　　Mending what doth thus depraue me;
Minde thy word then, Lord, and lend
Thy worke thy hand, crowne my end.
　　From the iawes of Sathan saue me.

14

All glorie to the Father be,
And to the Sonne as great as he:
　　With the coequall sacred Spirit;
Who all beginnings were before,
Are, and shall be euermore.
　　Glorie, all glorie to their merit.

PSALME II.

v

Inuocabo quem offendi.

I will inuoke whom I inflam'd;
Nor will approch, his fierie throne in feare;
I will recall, nor be asham'd
Whom I cast off, and pierce againe his eare.
　　Hope, quite euen lost, I will restore,
　　And dare againe to looke on heauen;
　　The more I fall, inuoke the more;
Prayre once will speed, where eare is euer giuen.

2

In heauen my deare Redeemer dwels,
His eare yet let downe to our lowest sounds;

11. 5 got] gor

His hand can reach the deepest hels;
His hand holds balmes for all our oldest wounds.
 I, in my selfe, do often die;
 But in him, I as oft reuiue;
 My health shines euer in his eye;
That heales in hell, and keepes euen death aliue.

B₄ᴿ

3

Feare all, that would put feare on me;
My sinne most great is, but much more his grace:
Though ill for worse still alterd be:
And I in me, my eagrest foe embrace:
 Yet Truth in this hath euer stood,
 The blackest spots my sinnes let fall,
 One drop of his most precious blood;
Can cleanse and turne, to purest Iuorie all.

4

Strike, Lord, and breake the rockes that grow
In these red seas of thy offence in me:
And cleansing fountaines thence shall flow,
Though of the hardest Adamant they be.
 As cleare as siluer, seas shall rore,
 Descending to that noysome sinke,
 Where euery houre hels horride Bore
Lies plung'd, and drownd, & doth his vomits drinke.

5

Race, Lord, my sinnes inueterate skarres,
And take thy new-built Mansion vp in me:
Though powre failes, see my wils sharpe warres,
And let me please euen while I anger thee.
 Let the remembrance of my sinne,
 With sighs all night ascend thine eare:
 And when the morning light breakes in,
Let health be seene, and all my skies be cleare.

v

6

Thus though I temper ioyes with cares,
Yet keepe thy mercies constant, as my crimes:
Ile cherish, with my faith, my prayres,
And looke still sighing vp for better times.
 My selfe, I euermore will feare,
 But thee, my rest, my hope, still keepe:
 Thy darkest clouds, thy lightnings cleare,
Thy thunders rocke me, that breake others sleepe.

7

My purgatorie O Lord make
My bridall chamber, wedded to thy will:
And let my couch still witnesse take,
In teares still steep't, that I adore thee still.
  My body Ile make pay thee paines,
  Hell iawes shall neuer need to ope.
  Though all loues faile, thine euer raignes,
Thou art my refuge, last, and onely hope.

All glorie to the Father, &c.

PSALME III.   [B₆ᴿ]

Miserere Domine.

1

Stay now, O Lord, my bleeding woes,
  The veine growes low and drie;
O now enough, and too much flowes,
  My sinne is swolne too hie.

2

What rests for the abhorr'd euent?
  Time wasts, but not my woe:
Woes me, poore man, my life is spent
  In asking what to do.

3

Pale Death stands fixt before mine eyes,
  My graue gaspes, and my knell
Rings out in my cold eares the cryes
  And gnashed teeth of hell.

4

How long shall this day mocke my hope,
  With what the next will be?
When shall I once begin to ope,   *v*
  My lockt vp way to thee?

5

Ease Lord, my still-increasing smart,
  Salue not, but cure my wounds:
Direct the counsels of my heart,
  And giue my labours bounds.

3. 4 And] and   teeth] teerh

6

As in me, thou hast skill infusd,
    So will, and action breath:
Lest chidden for thy gifts abusd,
    I weepe and pine to death.

7

See, bound beneath the foe I lie,
    Rapt to his blasted shore:
O claime thy right, nor let me die,
    Let him insult no more.

8

Tell all the ransome I must giue,
    Out of my hourely paines:
See how from all the world I liue,
    To giue griefe all the raines.

[B₆ᴿ]   9

What is behind, in this life aske,
    And in these members sums:
Before the neuer ending taske,
    And bedrid beggerie comes.

10

Shew me thy way, ere thy chiefe light
    Downe to the Ocean diues:
O now tis euening, and the night,
    Is chiefly friend to theeues.

11

Compell me, if thy Call shall faile,
    To make thy straight way, mine:
In any skorn'd state let me wayle,
    So my poore soule be thine.

All glorie to the Father be,
And to the Sonne as great as he,
    With the coequall sacred Spirit:
Who all beginnings were before,
Are, and shall be euermore.
    Glorie, all glorie to their merit.

PSALME IIII.

Recordari libet. *v*

1

Once let me serue, Lord, my desire,
Thy gifts to me recounting, and their prise,
That shame may set my cheekes on fire,
And iust confusion teare in teares mine eyes.
  Since quite forgetting what I am,
  Adorn'd so Godlike with thy grace,
  I yet neglect to praise thy name,
And make thy image in me, poore and base.

2

Thou hast created, euen for me,
The starres, all heauen, and all the turns of time;
For of what vse are these to thee,
Though euery one distinguisht by his clime?
  Thou Sunne and Moone, thou Nights and Dayes,
  Thou Light and Darknesse hast disposd:
  Wrapt earth in waters nimble wayes,
Her vales, hils, plains, with founts, floods, seas enclosd.

3 [B7R]

Her rich wombe thou hast fruitfull made,
With choyce of seeds, that all wayes varied are:
And euery way, our eyes inuade
With formes and graces, in being common, rare.
  In sweete greene herbes thou cloth'st her fields,
  Distinguishest her hils with flowres.
  Her woods thou mak'st her meadowes shields,
Adorn'd with branches, leaues, and odorous bowres.

4

The wearie thou hast rest prepar'd,
The hote refreshest with coole shades of trees,
Which streames melodious enterlar'd,
For sweet retreats, that none but thy eye sees:
  The thirstie, thou giu'st siluer springs;
  The hungrie, berries of all kinds;
  Herbes wholesome, and a world of things,
To nurse our bodies, and informe our mindes.

5

Now let me cast mine eye, and see
With what choice creatures, strangely form'd and faire

All seas, and lands, are fil'd by thee:
v And all the round spread tracts of yeelding aire.
   Whose names or numbers who can reach?
   With all earths powre, yet in thy span:
   All which, thy boundlesse bounties preach,
All laide, O glorie! at the foote of man.

6

Whose body, past all creatures shines,
Such wondrous orders of his parts thou mak'st,
Whose countenance, state, and loue combines:
In him vnmou'd, when all the world thou shak'st.
   Whose soule thou giu'st powre, euen of thee,
   Ordaining it to leaue the earth,
   All heauen, in her discourse to see,
And note how great a wombe, went to her birth.

7

Vnnumberd arts thou add'st in him,
To make his life more queint and more exact:
His eye, eternesse cannot dim.
Whose state he mounts to, with a mind infract:
   Thou shew'st him all the milke-white way,
   Op'st all thy Tabernacles dores
   Learn'st how to praise thee, how to pray,
To shun, and chuse, what likes and what abhorres.

[B₈^R]

8

To keepe him in which hallowed path,
As his companions, and perpetuall guides,
Prayre thou ordainst, thy word and faith,
And loue, that all his foule offences hides.
   And to each step his foote shall take,
   Thy couenants stand like wals of brasse,
   Which, from thy watch towre, good to make,
Thou add'st thine eye for his securer passe.

9

All this deare (Lord) I apprehend,
Thy Spirit euen partially inspiring me:
Which to consort me to my end,
With endlesse thanks, Ile strew my way to thee.
   Confessing falling, thou hast staid:
   Confirm'd me fainting, prostrate raisd,
   With comforts rapt me, quite dismaid,

And dead, hast quickn'd me, to see thee praisd.

All glorie to the Father be,
And to the Sonne, &c.

PSALME V.

Noctes meæ in mærore transeunt.

1

Yet, Lord, vnquiet sinne is stirring,
My long nights, longer grow, like euening shades:
In which woe lost, is all waies erring:
And varied terror euery step inuades.
  Wayes made in teares, shut as they ope,
  My lodestarre I can no way see:
  Lame is my faith, blind loue and hope,
  And, Lord, tis passing ill with me.

2

My sleepe, like glasse, in dreames is broken,
No quiet yeelding, but affright and care,
Signes that my poore life is forspoken:
Lord, courbe the ill, and good in place prepare.
  No more delay my spent desire,
  Tis now full time, for thee to heare:
  Thy loue hath set my soule on fire,
  My heart quite broke twixt hope and feare.

3

$C_{(1)}^R$

No outward light, my life hath graced,
My mind hath euer bene my onely Sunne:
And that so farre hath enuie chaced,
That all in clouds her hated head is runne.
  And while she hides, immortall cares
  Consume the soule, that sense inspires:
  Since outward she sets eyes and eares,
  And other ioyes spend her desires.

4

She musters both without and in me,
Troubles, and tumults: she's my houshold theefe,
Opes all my doores to lust, and enuie,
And all my persecutors lends releefe.
  Bind her, Lord, and my true soule free,
  Preferre the gift thy hand hath giuen:

Thy image in her, crowne in me,
And make vs here free, as in heauen.

All glorie to the Father be,
And to the Sonne, &c.

v

PSALME VI.

Circumuallarunt me inimici.

1

My foes haue girt me in with armes,
  And earthquakes tost vp all my ioynts,
No flesh can answer their alarmes,
  Each speare they manage hath so many points.

2

Death, arm'd in all his horrors, leades:
  Whom more I charge, the lesse he yeelds:
Affections, with an hundred heads,
  Conspire with them, & turne on me their shields.

3

Nor looke I yet, Lord, to the East,
  Nor hope for helpe, where I am will'd:
Nor, as I ought, haue arm'd my breast;
  But rust in sloth, and naked come to field.

4

And therefore hath the host of starres
  Now left me, that before I led:
C₂ᴿ Arm'd Angels tooke my pay in warres,
  From whose height falne, all leaue me here for dead.

5

In falling, I discern'd how sleight,
  My footing was on those blest towres,
I lookt to earth, and her base height,
  And so lost heauen, and all his aidfull powres.

6

Now, broke on earth, my bodie lies,
  Where theeues insult on my sad fall:
Spoyle me of many a daintie prise,
  That farre I fetcht, t'enrich my soule withall.

7

Nor ceasse they, but deforme me too,
  With wounds that make me all engor'd:
And in the desart, leaue me so,
  Halfe dead, all naked, and of all abhorr'd.

8

My head, and bosome, they transfixt,
  But in my torne affections rag'd:
Wounds there, with blood, and matter mixt,
  Corrupt and leaue my very soule engag'd.   *v*

9

There, Lord, my life doth most misgiue,
  There quickly thy white hand bestow:
Thou liu'st, and in thee I may liue.
  Thy fount of life doth euer ouerflow.

10

All this from heauen, thy eyes explore,
  Yet silent sitst, and sufferst all:
Since all I well deserue, and more;
  And must confesse me, wilfull in my fall:

11

And hence tis, that thou letst me bleed,
  Mak'st all men shun, and skorne my life:
That all my workes such enuie breed,
  And my disgrace giues food to all mens strife.

12

But this, since Goodnesse oft doth cause,
  And tis Gods grace to heare his ill:
Since tis a chiefe point in his lawes,
  No thought, without our powre, to make our wil.

13

      C₃ᴿ

Still let the greene seas of their gall,
  Against this rocke with rage be borne:
And from their height, still let me fall:
  Them, stand and laugh, & me lie still and scorne.

14

But, Lord, my fall from thee, ô raise,

12.2 Gods] Goods

And giue my fainting life thy breath:
Sound keepe me euer in thy waies,
   Thou mightie art, and setst downe lawes to death.

15

Driue thou from this my ruines rape,
   These theeues, that make thy *Phane* their den:
And let my innocence escape
   The cunning malice of vngodly men.

All glorie to the Father be,
And to the Sonne as great as he:
   With the coequall sacred Spirit:
Who all beginnings were before,
Are, and shall be euermore.
   Glorie, all glorie to their merit.

v

PSALME VII.

Cogitabam stare.

1

While I was falne, I thought to rise,
And stand, presuming on my thies:
   But thighes, and knees, were too much broken.
My haire stood vp to see such bane
Depresse presumption so prophane:
   I tremble but to heare it spoken.

2

Yet in my strength, my hope was such,
Since I conceiu'd, thou vow'dst as much:
   I fain'd dreames, and reioyc't to faine them:
But weighing awake, thy vowes profound,
Their depth, my lead came short to sound:
   And now, aye me, my teares containe them.

3

For calmes, I into stormes did stere,
And look't through clouds, to see things cleare,
   Thy waies shew'd crook't, like speares in water;
C₄ᴿ   When mine went trauerse, and no Snake
Could winde with that course, I did take:
   No Courtier could so grosly flatter.

4

But which way I soeuer bend,
Thou meet'st me euer in the end:
   Thy finger strikes my ioynts with terrors;
Yet no more strikes, then points the way:
Which, weighing weeping, straight I stay,
   And with my teares cleanse feete and errors.

5

But of my selfe, when I beleeue
To make my steps, thy waies atchieue,
   I turne head, and am treading mazes:
I feele sinnes ambush; and am vext
To be in error so perplext,
   Nor yet can finde rests holy places.

6

I loathe my selfe, and all my deeds,
Like Rubarbe taste, or Colchean weeds:
   I flie them, with their throwes vpon me.
In each new purpose, customes old,   *v*
So checke it, that the stone I rold
   Neuer so oft, againe fals on me.

7

No step in mans trust should be trod,
Vnlesse in mans, as his in God:
   Of which trust, make good life the founder:
Without which, trust no forme, nor art;
Faiths loadstarre is a guiltlesse heart;
   Good life is truths most learn'd expounder.

8

With which, Lord, euer rule my skill;
In which, as I ioyne powre with will,
   So let me trust, my truth in learning,
To such minds, thou all truth setst ope:
The rest are rapt with stormes past hope;
   The lesse, for more deepe arts discerning.

9

Blesse, Lord, who thus their arts employ,
Their sure truth, celebrate with ioy,
   And teare the maskes from others faces;
That make thy Name, a cloake for sinne;   C$_s$^R

Learning but termes to iangle in,
And so disgrace thy best of Graces.

10

Whereof since I haue onely this,
That learnes me what thy true will is,
    Which thou, in comforts still concludest;
My poore Muse still shall sit, and sing,
In that sweete shadow of thy wing,
    Which thou to all earths state obtrudest.

11

As oft as I my fraile foote moue,
From this pure fortresse of thy loue:
    So oft let my glad foes deride me.
I know my weaknesse yet, and feare,
By triall, to build comforts there,
    It doth so like a ruine hide me.

12

My worth is all, but shade, I finde,
And like a fume, before the winde;
    I gaspe with sloth, thy waies applying:
Lie tumbling in corrupted blood;
Loue onely, but can do no good:
    Helpe, Lord, lest I amend not dying.

All glorie to the Father be,
And to the Sonne as great as he,
    With the coequall sacred Spirit:
Who all beginnings were before:
Are, and shall be euermore.
    Glorie, all glorie to their merit.

*The end of Petrarchs seuen
Penitentiall Psalmes.*

[C₆ᴿ]

THE I. PSALME

more strictly translated.

1

O me accurst, since I haue set on me
    (Incenst so sternely) my so meeke Redeemer;
And haue bene proud in prides supreme degree;
    Of his so serious law, a sleight esteemer.

I left the narrow right way with my will,
  In bywaies brode, and farre about transferred:
And euery way found toyle, and euery ill,
  Yet still in tracts more rough, and steepe I erred.

3

Where one or other of the brutish heard
  My feete encounterd, yet more brute affected:
Euen to the dens of sauage beasts I err'd,
  And there my manlesse mansion house erected.

4

I haunted pleasure still, where sorrow mournd,
  My couch of ease, in sharpest brambles making: *v*
I hop't for rest, where restlesse torment burnd,
  In ruines bosome, sleepes securely taking.

5

Now then, aye me, what resteth to be done,
  Where shall I turne me, where such dangers tremble?
My youths faire flowres, are altogether gone,
  And now a wretched shipwracke I resemble.

6

That (all the merchandise, and venture lost,)
Swims naked forth, with seas and tempests tost.

7

Farre from my hauen, I roue, touch at no streme
  That any course to my saluation tenders:
But waies sinister, rauish me with them:
  I see a little; which more grieuous renders.

8

My inward conflict; since my charges passe
  Vpon my selfe; and my sad soule endanger:
Anger with sinne striues; but so huge a masse
  Of cruell miseries oppresse mine anger,

9   [C₇ᴿ]

That it confounds me, nor leaues place for breath.
  Oft I attempt to flie, and meditation
Contends to shake off my old yoke of death,
  But to my bones cleaues the vncur'd vexation.

10

O that at length, my necke his yoke could cleare,
  Which would be straite, wouldst thou ô highest will it:
O that so angrie with my sinne I were,
  That I could loue thee, though thus late fulfill it.

11

But much I feare it, since my freedome is
  So with mine owne hands out of heart, & sterued:
And I must yeeld, my torment iust in this,
  Sorrow, and labor, wring me most deserued.

12

Mad wretch, what haue I to my selfe procured?
Mine owne hands forg'd, the chains I haue endur'd.

13

In deaths blacke ambush, with my will I fell,
  And wheresoeuer vulgar brode waies traine me:
Nets are disposde for me, by him of hell.
  When more retir'd, more narrow paths containe me.

v

14

There meete my feete with fitted snares as sure,
  I (wretch) looke downeward, and of one side euer;
And euerie slipperie way I walke secure,
  My sins forget their traitrous flatteries neuer.

15

I thought the grace of youth could neuer erre,
  And follow'd where his boundles force wold driue me,
Said to my selfe; Why should th'extremes deterre,
  Before youths season, of the meane depriue me?

16

Each age is bounded in his proper ends;
  God, I know, sees this, but he laughs and sees it:
Pardon, at any time, or prayre attends;
  Repentance still weeps when thy wish decrees it.

17

Then vilest custome challengeth his slaue,
  And laies on hand, that all defence denies me;
And then no place reseru'd for flight I haue:
  Subdu'd I am, and farre my refuge flies me.

[C₈ᴿ]

18

Die in my sinne I shall, vnlesse my aide
   Stoopes from aloft, of which deserts depriue me.
Yet haue thou mercie, Lord, helpe one dismaide,
   Thy word retain, & from hell mouth retriue me.

All glorie to the Father be,
And to the Sonne as great as he:
   With the coequall sacred Spirit;
Who all beginnings were before,
Are, and shall be euermore.
   Glorie, all glorie to their merit.

A HYMNE TO OVR

Sauiour on the Crosse.

Haile great Redeemer, man, and God, all haile,
Whose feruent agonie, tore the temples vaile,
Let sacrifices out, darke Prophesies
And miracles: and let in, for all these,
*A simple pietie, a naked heart,   5
And humble spirit, that no lesse impart,
And proue thy Godhead to vs, being as rare,
And in all sacred powre, as circulare.
Water and blood mixt, were not swet from thee
With deadlier hardnesse: more diuinitie   10
Of supportation, then through flesh and blood,
Good doctrine is diffusde, and life as good.
O open to me then, (like thy spread armes
That East & West reach) all those misticke charmes
That hold vs in thy life and discipline: 15
Thy merits in thy loue so thrice diuine;
It made thee, being our God, assume our man;
And like our Champion Olympian,
Come to the field gainst Sathan, and our sinne:
Wrastle with torments, and the garland winne   20 D₁ᴿ
From death & hell; which cannot crown our browes
¹But blood must follow: thornes mixe with thy bowes
Of conquering Lawrell, fast naild to thy Crosse,
Are all the glories we can here engrosse.
Proue then to those, that in vaine glories place   25
Their happinesse here: they hold not by thy grace,
To those whose powres, proudly oppose thy lawes,
Oppressing Vertue, giuing Vice applause:

** Simplici-
tie of pietie,
and good life,
answerable to
such doctrine
in men; now
as rare as mir-
acles in other
times: and re-
quire as much
diuinitie of
supportation.*

*¹ As our
Sauiours
browes bled
with his
crowne of
thorns.*

26 they] thy

v

They neuer manage iust authoritie,

30 But thee in thy deare members crucifie.

Thou couldst haue come in glorie past them all,
With powre to force thy pleasure, and empale
Thy Church with brasse, & Adamant, that no swine,
Nor theeues, nor hypocrites, nor fiends[2] diuine

35 Could haue broke in, or rooted, or put on
Vestments of Pietie, when their hearts had none:
Or rapt to ruine with pretext, to saue:
Would[3] pompe, and radiance, rather not out braue
Thy naked truth, then cloath, or countnance it

v 40 With grace, and such sincerenesse as is fit:
But since true pietie weares her pearles within,
And outward paintings onely pranke vp sinne:
Since bodies strengthned, soules go to the wall;
Since God we cannot serue and Beliall;

45 Therefore thou putst on, earths most abiect plight,
Hid'st thee in humblesse, vnderwentst despight,
Mockerie, detraction, shame, blowes, vilest death.
These, thou, thy[4] souldiers taughtst to fight beneath:
Mad'st a commanding President of these,

50 Perfect, perpetuall: bearing all the keyes
To holinesse, and heauen. To these, such lawes
Thou in thy blood writst: that were no more cause
[5]T'enflame our loues, and feruent faiths in thee,
Then in them, truths diuine simplicitie,

55 Twere full enough; for therein we may well
See thy white finger furrowing blackest hell,
In turning vp the errors that our sence
And sensuall powres, incurre by negligence
Of our eternall truth-exploring soule.

D₂ᴿ 60 All Churches powres, thy writ word doth controule;
And mixt it with the fabulous Alchoran,
A man might boult it out, as floure from branne;
Easily discerning it, a heauenly birth,
Brake it but now out, and but crept on earth.

65 Yet (as if God lackt mans election,
And shadowes were creators of the Sunne)
Men must authorise it: antiquities
Must be explor'd, to spirit, and giue it thies,
And[6] controuersies, thicke as flies at Spring,

70 Must be maintain'd about th'ingenuous meaning;
When no stile can expresse it selfe so cleare,
Nor holds so euen, and firme a character.
Those mysteries that are not to be reacht,
Still to be striu'd with, make them more impeacht:

*2 Such as
are Diuines in
profession;
and in fact,
diuels, or
Wolues in
sheepes cloth-
ing.*

*3 Pompe
and outward
glorie, rather
outface truth
then counte-
nance it.*

*4 Christ
taught all his
militant soul-
diers to fight
vnder the en-
signes of
Shame and
Death.*

*5 We need
no other exci-
tation to our
faith in God,
and good life,
but the Scrip-
tures, and vse
of their
meanes pre-
scribed.*

*6 τα μὲν
πάρεργα ὣς
ἔργα: τα δὲ
ἔργα ὣς
πάρεργα. In
these contro-
uersies men
make the By
the Maine:
the Maine the
By.*

*Simile.

7 Men seeke
heauen, with
vsing the en-
emies to it;
Money and
Auarice.

8 Alciones
nest described
in part, out
of Plut. to
which the
Church is
compared.

9 If the bird
be lesse, the
sea will get in;
by which
meanes though
she may get in,
she could not
preserue it.

1 Altars of
the Church for
her holiest
places vnder-
stood

*And as the Mill fares with an ill pickt grist,   75
When any stone, the stones is got betwist,
Rumbling together, fill the graine with grit;
Offends the eare, sets teeth an edge with it:
Blunts the pict quarrie so, twill grinde no more,
Spoyles bread, and scants the Millars custom'd store.   80
So in the Church, when controuersie fals,   v
It marres her musicke, shakes her batterd wals,
Grates tender consciences, and weakens faith;
The bread of life taints, & makes worke for Death;
Darkens truths light, with her perplext Abysmes,   85
And dustlike grinds men into sects and schismes.
And what's the cause? the words deficiencie?
In volume, matter, perspecuitie?
Ambition, lust, and damned auarice,
Peruert, and each the sacred word applies   90
To his prophane ends; all to profite giuen,
7And pursnets lay to catch the ioyes of heauen.
    Since truth, and reall worth, men seldome sease,
    Impostors most, and sleightest learnings please.
And, where the true Church, like the nest should be   95
Of chast, and prouident8 Alcione:
(To which is onely one straight orifice,
Which is so strictly fitted to her sise,
9That no bird bigger then her selfe, or lesse,
Can pierce and keepe it, or discerne th'accesse: 100 D3R
Nor which the sea it selfe, on which tis made,
Can euer ouerflow, or once inuade;)
1Now wayes so many to her Altars are,
So easie, so prophane, and populare:
That torrents charg'd with weeds, and sin-drownd beasts, 105
Breake in, lode, cracke them: sensuall ioyes and feasts
Corrupt their pure fumes: and the slendrest flash
Of lust, or profite, makes a standing plash
Of sinne about them, which men will not passe.
Looke (Lord) vpon them, build them wals of brasse,   110
To keepe prophane feete off: do not thou
In wounds and anguish euer ouerflow,
And suffer such in ease, and sensualitie,
Dare to reiect thy rules of humble life:
The minds true peace, & turne their zeales to strife,   115
For obiects earthly, and corporeall.
A tricke of humblesse now they practise all,
Confesse their no deserts, habilities none:
Professe all frailties, and amend not one:

80 custom'd] cutom'd   88 perspecuitie] perspecutitie

120 As if a priuiledge they meant to claime
In sinning by acknowledging the maime
Sinne gaue in Adam: Nor the surplussage
v Of thy redemption, seeme to put in gage
For his transgression: that thy vertuous paines
125 (Deare Lord) haue eat out all their former staines;
That thy most mightie innocence had powre
To cleanse their guilts: that the vnualued dowre
Thou mad'st the Church thy spouse, in pietie,
And (to endure paines impious) constancie,
130 Will and alacritie (if they inuoke)
To beare the sweete lode, and the easie yoke
Of thy iniunctions, in diffusing these
(In thy perfection) through her faculties:
In euery fiuer, suffering to her vse,
135 And perfecting the forme thou didst infuse
[2]In mans creation: made him cleare as then
Of all the frailties, since defiling men.
[3]And as a runner at th'Olympian games,
With all the luggage he can lay on, frames
140 His whole powres to ye race, bags, pockets, greaues
Stuft full of sand he weares, which when he leaues,
And doth his other weightie weeds vncouer,
With which halfe smotherd, he is wrapt all ouer:
D₄ᴿ Then seemes he light, and fresh as morning aire;
145 Guirds him with silkes, swaddles with roulers faire
His lightsome body: and away he scoures
So swift, and light, he scarce treads down the flowrs:
So to our game proposde, of endlesse ioy
(Before thy deare death) when we did employ,
150 Our tainted powres; we felt them clogd and chain'd
With sinne and bondage, which did rust, and raign'd
In our most mortall bodies: but when thou
Strip'dst vs of these bands, and from foote to brow
Guirt, rold, and trimd vs vp in thy deserts:
155 Free were our feete, and hands; and spritely hearts
Leapt in our bosoms; and (ascribing still
All to thy merits: both our powre and will
To euery thought of goodnesse, wrought by thee;
[4]That diuine scarlet, in which thou didst die
160 Our cleansd consistence; lasting still in powre
T'enable acts in vs, as the next howre
To thy most sauing, glorious sufferance)
We may make all our manly powres aduance
Vp to thy Image; and these formes of earth,

160 consistence] consistens

[2] *Vbi abundauit delictum, superabundauit gratia.* Rom. 5. ver. 20.
[3] *A simile, to life expressing mans estate, before our Sauiours descension.*

[4] *Our Sauiours blood, now and euer, as fresh, and vertuous as in the howre it was shed for vs.*

Beauties and mockeries, matcht in beastly birth: 165
We may despise, with still aspiring spirits   v
To thy high graces, in thy still fresh merits:
Not touching at this base and spongie mould,
For any springs of lust, or mines of gold.
   For else (milde Sauiour, pardon me to speake)   170
How did thy foote, the Serpents forhead breake?
How hath the Nectar of thy vertuous blood,
The sinke of Adams forfeit ouerflow'd?
How doth it set vs free, if we still stand

⁵ *Our Sau-*
iour suffered
nothing for
himselfe, his
owne better-
nesse, or com-
fort: but for
vs and ours.

⁵(For all thy sufferings) bound both foote and hand   175
Vassals to Sathan? Didst thou onely die,
Thine owne diuine deserts to glorifie,
And shew thou couldst do this? O were not those
Giuen to our vse in powre? If we shall lose
By damn'd relapse, grace to enact that powre: 180
And basely giue vp our redemptions towre,
Before we trie our strengths, built all on thine,

⁶ *It is false*
humilitie to
lay necessar-
ily (all our
Sauiours grace
vnderstood)
the victorie of
our bodies, on
our soules.

⁶And with a humblesse, false, and Asinine,
Flattering our senses, lay vpon our soules
The burthens of their conquests, and like Moules   185 [D₅ᴿ]
Grouell in earth still, being aduanc't to heauen:
(Cowes that we are) in heards how are we driuen
To Sathans shambles? Wherein stand we for
Thy heauenly image, Hels great Conqueror?
Didst thou not offer, to restore our fall   190
Thy sacrifice, full, once, and one for all?
If we be still downe, how then can we rise
Againe with thee, and seeke crownes in the skies?
But we excuse this; saying, We are but men,
And must erre, must fall: what thou didst sustaine   195
To free our beastly frailties, neuer can

⁷ *Man is a*
liuing soule.
Gen. 2.
⁸ *We do not*
like men when
we sin, (for as
we are true
and worthie
men, we are
Gods images:)
but like brut-
ish creatures,
slauishly and
wilfully con-
quered with the
powers of
flesh.

With all thy grace, by any powre in man
Make good thy Rise to vs: O blasphemie
In hypocriticall humilitie!
⁷As we are men, we death and hell controule,   200
Since thou createdst man a liuing soule:
⁸As euerie houre we sinne, we do like beasts:
Heedlesse, and wilfull, murthering in our breasts
Thy saued image, out of which, one cals
Our humane soules, mortall celestialls: 205 v
When casting off a good lifes godlike grace,
We fall from God; and then make good our place
When we returne to him: and so are said
To liue: when life like his true forme we leade,

165 matcht] match   203 Heedlesse] Needlesse

210 And die (as much as can immortall creature:)
    [1]Not that we vtterly can ceasse to be,
    But that we fall from life's best qualitie.
       But we are tost out of our humane Throne
    By pied and Protean opinion;
215 We vouch thee onely, for pretext and fashion,
    And are not inward with thy death and passion.
    We slauishly renounce thy royaltie
    With which thou crownst vs in thy victorie:
    Spend all our manhood in the fiends defence,
220 And drowne thy right, in beastly negligence.
       God neuer is deceiu'd so, to respect,
    His shade in Angels beauties, to neglect
    His owne most cleare and rapting louelinesse:
    Nor Angels dote so on the species
225 And grace giuen to our soule (which is their shade)
[D₆ᴿ] That therefore they will let their owne formes fade.
    And yet our soule (which most deserues our woe,
    And that from which our whole mishap doth flow)
    So softn'd is, and rapt (as with a storme)
230 With flatteries of our base corporeall forme,
    (Which is her shadow) that she quite forsakes
    Her proper noblesse, and for nothing takes
    The beauties that for her loue, thou putst on;
    In torments rarefied farre past the Sunne.
235   Hence came the cruell fate that Orpheus
    Sings of Narcissus: who being amorous
    Of his shade in the water (which denotes
    Beautie in bodies, that like water flotes)
    Despisd himselfe, his soule, and so let fade
240 His substance for a neuer-purchast shade.
    Since soules of their vse, ignorant are still,
    With this vile bodies vse, men neuer fill.
       And, as the Suns light, in streames ne're so faire
    Is but a shadow, to his light in aire,
245 His splendor that in aire we so admire,
    [2]Is but a shadow to his beames in fire:
    In fire his brightnesse, but a shadow is
    To radiance fir'd, in that pure brest of his:
v   So as the subiect on which thy grace shines,
250 Is thicke, or cleare; to earth or heauen inclines;
    So that truths light showes; so thy passion takes;
    With which, who inward is, and thy breast makes
    Bulwarke to his breast, against all the darts

[1] οὐ τῇ εἶς, τὸ μὴ εἶναι ἐκβάσει ἀλλὰ τῇ τοῦ εὖ εἶναι ἀποπτώσει. Hier. in Carm. Pythag. Non quod existere desinat, sed quod vitae praestantia exciderit.

[2] Simile.

210 can] an   246 footnote number 2]3

The foe stil shoots more, more his late blow smarts,
And sea-like raues most, where tis most withstood.   255
He tasts the strength and vertue of thy blood:
He knows that when flesh is most sooth'd, & grac't,
Admir'd and magnified, ador'd, and plac't
In height of all the blouds Idolatry,
And fed with all the spirits of Luxury,   260
³One thought of ioy, in any soule that knowes
Her owne true strength, and thereon doth repose;
Bringing her bodies organs to attend
Chiefly her powres, to her eternall end;
Makes all things outward; and the sweetest sin,   265
That rauisheth the beastly flesh within;
All but a fiend, prankt in an Angels plume:
A shade, a fraud, before the wind a fume.
  Hayle then diuine Redeemer, still all haile,
All glorie, gratitude, and all auaile,   270
Be giuen thy all-deseruing agonie;   [D₇ᴿ]
Whose vineger thou Nectar mak'st in me,
Whose goodnesse freely all my ill turnes good:
Since thou being crusht, & straind throgh flesh & blood:
Each nerue and artire needs must tast of thee.   275
What odour burn'd in ayres that noisome be,
Leaues not his sent there? O then how much more
Must thou, whose sweetnesse swet eternall odour,
Stick where it breath'd, & for whom thy sweet breath,
Thou freely gau'st vp, to reuiue his death?   280
Let those that shrink then as their conscience lodes,
That fight in Sathans right, and faint in Gods,
Still count them slaues to Sathan. I am none:
Thy fight hath freed me, thine thou mak'st mine owne.

*O then (my sweetest and my ,onely life)   285
Confirme this comfort, purchast with thy griefe,
And my despisde soule of the world, loue thou:
No thought to any other ioy I vow.
Order these last steps of my abiect state,
Straite on the marke a man should leuell at: 290
And grant that while I striue to forme in me,
Thy sacred image, no aduersitie
May make me draw one limme, or line amisse: v
Let no vile fashion wrest my faculties
From what becomes that Image. Quiet so   295
My bodies powres, that neither weale nor wo,

³ *The minds ioy farre aboue the bodies, to those few, whom God hath inspird with the soules true vse.*

* *Inuocatio.*

256 tasts] rasts   261 Footnote number supplied, both for text and note.

May stirre one thought vp, gainst thy freest will.
Grant, that in me, my mindes waues may be still:
The world for no extreme may vse her voice;
300   Nor Fortune treading reeds, make any noise.

                                        Amen.

Complaine not whatsoeuer Need inuades,
But heauiest fortunes beare as lightest shades.
v   Ἀνέχου καὶ Ἀπέχου.

[D₈ᴿ]   VIRGILS EPIGRAM

                    of a good man.

¹A good and wise man (such as hardly one   ¹ *The Sunne*
Of millions, could be found out by the Sun)   *vsurpt for*
Is Iudge himselfe, of what stuffe he is wrought, *Apollo; whose*
                                                  Oracle being
And doth explore his whole man to a thought.   *askt for such a*
5   What ere great men do; what their sawcie bawdes; *man, found*
What vulgar censure barks at, or applauds   *onely Socrates.*
His carriage still is chearfull and secure;
He, in himselfe, worldlike, full, round, and sure.
    ²Lest, through his polisht parts, the slendrest staine   ² *Externae*
10 Of things without, in him should sit, and raigne;   *nequid labis*
                                                             per læuia
sidat. This verse Ascensius ioynes with the next before; which is nothing so; the sence being vtterly
repugnant, as any impartiall and iudiciall conferrer (I suppose) will confirme.

To whatsoeuer length, the fierie Sunne,
Burning in Cancer, doth the day light runne;
How faire soeuer Night shall stretch her shades,
When Phoebus gloomie Capricorne inuades;
15 He studies still; and with the equal beame,
v   ³His ballance turnes; himselfe weighs to th'extreme.   ³ *Cogitat.*
    Lest any crannie gaspe, or angle swell   *& iusto truti-*
Through his strict forme: and that he may compell   *nae se exam-*
His equall parts to meete in such a sphere,   *ine pensat.*
20 That with a *compasse tried, it shall not erre: *This verse is*
                                                             likewise mis-
What *euer subiect is, is solide still: *ioyned in the*
Wound him, and with your* violent fingers feele   *order of As-*
                                                             censcius,which
                                                             makes the
period to those before.
    * *I here needlessly take a little licence: for the word is* Amussis, *the mind of the Author being as*
well exprest in A compasse. Sit solidum quodcunque subest, nec inania subtus. Subest *and*
subtus *Ascens. confounds in his sence; which the presnesse and matter of this Poem allowes not:*
it being in a Translator sooner and better seen then a Commentor. He would turne digitis pellenti-
bus, *to* digitis palantibus. *To which place, the true order is hard to hit. And that truth in my conuer-*
sion (how opposite soeuer any may stand) with any conference, I make no doubt I shall perswade.

All parts within him, you shall neuer find
An emptie corner, or an abiect mind.
   He neuer lets his watchfull lights descend,   25
To those sweet sleepes that all iust men attend,
Till all the acts the long day doth beget,
With thought on thought laid, he doth oft repeate:
Examines what hath past him, as forgot:
What deed or word was vsde in time, what not.   30 E(1)R
Why this deed of Decorum felt defect?
Of reason, that? What left I by neglect?
Why set I this opinion downe for true,
That had bene better chang'd? Why did I* rue
Need in one poore so, that I felt my mind   35

* Miseratus
egentem, cur
aliquem frac-
ta persensi
mento dolorem. *Ascens. very iudicially makes this good man in this dittie opposite to a good
Christian, since Christ (the president of all good men) enioynes vs, vt supra omnia misericordes
simus. But his meaning here is, that a good and wise man should not so pitie the want of any, that
he should want manly patience himselfe to sustaine it. And his reason Seruius alledgeth for him
is this, saying, In quem cadit vna mentis perturbatio, posse in eum omnes cadere: sicut potest
omni virtute pollere cui virtus vna contigerit.*

(To breach of her free powres) with griefe declin'd?
Why will'd I what was better not to will?
Why (wicked that I was) preferr'd I still
Profite to honestie? Why any one
Gaue I a foule word? or but lookt vpon,   40
With count'nance churlish? Why should nature draw
More my affects, then manly reasons law?
   Through all these thoughts, words works, thus making way,
And all reuoluing, from the Euen till day:
Angrie, with what amisse, abusde the light,   45 *v*
Palme and reward he giues to what was right.

A great Man.

[1] A great & politike man, such as is, or may be op-posed, to good or wise.

[1]A great and politicke man (which I oppose
To good and wise) is neuer as he showes.
Neuer explores himselfe to find his faults:
But cloaking them, before his conscience halts,
Flatters himselfe, and others flatteries buyes,   5
Seemes made of truth, and is a forge of lies,
Breeds bawdes and sycophants, and traitors makes
To betray traitors; playes, and keepes the stakes,
Is iudge and iuror, goes on life and death:
And damns before the fault hath any breath.   10
Weighs faith in falsehoods ballance; iustice does

43 these] this

To cloake oppression; taile-down downward groes:
Earth his whole end is: heauen he mockes, and hell:
²And thinkes that is not, that in him doth dwell.

15 Good, with Gods right hand giuen, his left takes t'euil:
E₂ᴿ When holy most he seemes, he most is euill.
Ill vpon ill he layes: th'embroderie
Wrought on his state, is like a leprosie,
The whiter, still the fouler. What his like,
20 What ill in all the bodie politike
Thriues in, and most is curst: his most blisse fires:
And of two ils, still to the worst aspires.
When his thrift feeds, iustice and mercie feare him:
And (*Wolf-like fed) he gnars at all men nere him.

*² The priua-
tion of a good
life, and there-
in the ioyes of
heauen, is hell
in this world.*

* *As Wolues
and Tigers
horribly*

*gnarre, in their feeding: so these zealous, and giuen-ouer great ones to their own lusts and ambi-
tions: in aspiring to them, and their ends, fare, to all that come nere them in competencie: or that
resist their deuouring.*

25 Neuer is chearefull, but when flatterie trailes
On* squatting profite; or when Policie vailes

* *This allu-
deth to hounds*

*vpon the traile of a squat Hare, and making a chearefull crie about her, is applyed to the forced
cheare or flatterie this great man sheweth, when he hunts for his profite.*

Some vile corruption: that lookes red with anguish
Like wauing reeds, his windshook comforts languish.
Paies neuer debt, but what he should not ow;
30 Is sure and swift to hurt, yet thinks him slow.
His bountie is most rare, but when it comes,
Tis most superfluous, and with strook-vp drums.
v Lest any true good pierce him, with such good
As ill breeds in him, Mortar, made with blood
35 Heapes stone-wals in his heart, to keepe it out.
His sensuall faith, his soules truth keepes in doubt,
And like a rude, *vnlearn'd Plebeian,
Without him seekes his whole insulting man.
¹Nor can endure, as a most deare prospect,
40 To looke into his own life, and reflect
Reason vpon it, like a Sunne still shining,
To giue it comfort, ripening, and refining:
But his blacke soule, being so deformd with sinne,
He still abhorres; with all things hid within:
45 And forth he wanders, with the outward fashion,
Feeding, and fatting vp his reprobation.
Disorderly he sets foorth euerie deed,
Good neuer doing, but where is no need.
If any *ill he does, (and hunts through blood,

* *Plebij
status & nota
est nunquam
à seipso vel
damnum ex-
pectare, vel
vtilitatem,
sed à rebus
externis.*

¹ *How a
good great
man should
employ his
greatnesse.*

* *The most
vnchristian
disposition of
a great and ill
man, in fol-
lowing any
that withstand
his ill.*

For shame, ruth, right, religion) be withstood,   50
The markt withstander, his race, kin, least friend,   E₃ᴿ
That neuer did, in least degree offend,
He prosecutes, with hir'd intelligence
To fate, defying God and conscience,
And to the vtmost mite, he rauisheth   55
All they can yeeld him, rackt past life and death.
In all his acts, he this doth verifie,
The greater man, the lesse humanitie.

* This hath
reference (as
most of the rest
hath) to the
good man be-
fore, being this
mans opposite.

    While *Phebus runs his course through all the signes,
He neuer studies; but he vndermines,   60
Blowes vp, and ruines, with pretext to saue:
Plots treason, and lies hid in th'actors graue.
Vast crannies gaspe in him, as wide as hell,
And angles, gibbet-like, about him swell:
Yet seemes he smooth and polisht, but no more   65
Solide within, then is a Medlars core.
The kings frown fels him, like a gun-strooke fowle:
When downe he lies, and casts the calfe his soule.
He neuer sleepes but being tir'd with lust:
Examines what past, not enough vniust;   70
Not bringing wealth enough, not state, not grace:
Not shewing miserie bedrid in his face:
Not skorning vertue, not deprauing her,
Whose ruth so flies him, that her Bane's his cheare.   v
In short, exploring all that passe his guards,   75
Each good he plagues, and euerie ill rewards.

A sleight man.

A sleight, and mixt man (set as twere the meane
Twixt both the first) from both their heapes doth gleane:
Is neither good, wise, great, nor politick,
Yet tastes of all these with a naturall tricke.
Nature and Art, sometimes meet in his parts: 5
Sometimes deuided are: the austere arts,
Splint him together, set him in a brake
Of forme and reading. Nor is let partake

¹ *Intending
in his writing.
&c.*

With iudgement, wit, or¹ sweetnesse: but as time,
Terms, language, and degrees, haue let him clime,   10
To learn'd opinion; so he there doth stand,
Starke as a statue; stirres nor foote nor hand.
Nor any truth knowes: knowledge is a meane
To make him ignorant, and rapts him cleane,

² *Quo ma-
gis alantur, eo
magis ea
laedi.*

In stormes from truth. For what Hippocrates   15
Says of foule² bodies (what most nourishes,
That most annoies them) is more true of mindes: E₄ᴿ

For there, their first inherent prauitie blinds
Their powres preiudicate: and all things true
20   Proposd to them, corrupts, and doth eschue:
Some, as too full of toyle; of preiudice some:
Some fruitlesse, or past powre to ouercome:
With which, it so augments, that he will seeme
With[3] iudgement, what he should hold, to contemne
25   And is incurable. And this is he
Whose learning formes not lifes integritie.
     This the mere Artist; the mixt naturalist,
With foole-quicke memorie, makes his hand a fist,
And catcheth Flies, and Nifles: and retaines
30   With heartie studie, and vnthriftie paines,
What your composd man shuns. With these his pen
And prompt tongue tickles th'eares of vulgar men:
Sometimes takes matter too, and vtters it
With an admir'd and heauenly straine of wit:
35   Yet with all this, hath humors more then can
Be thrust into a foole, or to a woman.
v   As nature made him, reason came by chance,
Held her torch to him, cast him in a trance;
And makes him vtter things that (being awake
40   In life and manners) he doth quite forsake.
He will be graue, and yet is light as aire;
He will be proude, yet poore euen to despaire.
Neuer sat Truth in a tribunall fit,
But in a modest, staid, and humble wit.
45   *I rather wish to be a naturall bred,*
Then these great wits with madnesse leauened.
     He's bold, and frontlesse, passionate, and mad,
Drunken, adulterous, good at all things bad.
Yet for one good, he quotes the best in pride,
50   And is enstil'd a man well qualifide.
     These delicate shadowes of things vertuous then
Cast on these vitious, pleasing, patcht vp men,
Are but the diuels cousenages to blind
Mens sensuall eyes, and choke the enuied mind.
55   And where the truly *learnd is euermore
Gods simple Image, and true imitator:
[E₅R]   These sophisters are emulators still
(Cousening, ambitious) of men true in skill.
Their imperfections yet are hid in sleight,
60   Of the felt darknesse, breath'd out by deceipt,
The truly learn'd, is likewise hid, and failes
To pierce eyes vulgar, but with other vailes.
And they are the diuine beames, truth casts round

[3] *To be therefore instructed in the truth of knowledge, or aspire to any egregious vertue; not stiffe & vnioínted Art serues: but he must be helpt besides, benigniore nascendi hora. According to this of Iuuenal.*—plus etenim fati valet hora benigni, Quam si te Veneris commendet epistola Marti.

* *The truly learned imitateth God, the sophister emulateth man. His imperfections are hid in the mists imposture breathes: the others perfections are vnseene by the brightnesse truth casts about his temples, that dazle ignorant and corrupt beholders, or apprehenders.*

About his beauties, that do quite confound
Sensuall beholders. Scuse these rare seene then,   65
And take more heede of common sleighted men.

A good woman.

A woman good, and faire (which no dame can
Esteeme much easier found then a good man)
Sets not her selfe to shew, nor found would be:
Rather her vertues flie abroad then she.
Dreames not on fashions, loues no gossips feasts,   5
Affects no newes, no tales, no guests, no ieasts:
Her worke, and reading writs of worthiest men:
Her husbands pleasure, well taught childeren:
Her housholds fit prouision to see spent,
As fits her husbands will, and his consent: 10
Spends pleasingly her time, delighting still,
To her iust dutie, to adapt her will.   v
Vertue she loues, rewards and honors it,
And hates all scoffing, bold and idle wit:
Pious and wise she is, and treads vpon   15
This foolish and this false opinion,
That learning fits not women; since it may
Her naturall cunning helpe, and make more way
To light, and close affects: for so it can
Courbe and compose them too, as in a man: 20
And, being noble, is the noblest meane,
To spend her time: thoughts idle and vncleane,
Preuenting and suppressing: to which end
She entertaines it: and doth more commend
Time spent in that, then houswiferies low kindes,   25
As short of that, as bodies are of minds.
If it may hurt, is powre of good lesse great,
Since food may lust excite, shall she not eate?
    She is not Moon-like, that the Sunne, her spouse
Being furthest off, is cleare and glorious: 30
And being neare, growes pallid and obscure:
But in her husbands presence, is most pure,
In all chast ornaments, bright still with him,
And in his absence, all retir'd and dim:
With him still kind and pleasing, still the same;   35
Yet with her weeds, not putting off her shame:
But when for bed-rites her attire is gone,   [E₆ᴿ]
In place thereof her modest shame goes on.
Not with her husband lies, but he with her:
And in their loue-ioyes doth so much prefer   40
Modest example, that she will not kisse

Her husband, when her daughter present is.
When a iust husbands right he would enioy,
She neither flies him, nor with moods is coy.
45   One, of the light dame sauours, th'other showes
Pride, nor from loues ingenuous humor flowes.
And as *Geometricians approue,
That lines, nor superficies, do moue
Themselues, but by their bodies motions go:
50   So your good woman neuer striues to grow
Strong in her owne affections and delights,
But to her husbands equall appetites,
Earnests and ieasts, and lookes austerities,
Her selfe in all her subiect powres applies.
55   Since lifes chiefe cares on him are euer laid,
*In cares she euer comforts, vndismaid,
v   Though her heart grieues, her lookes yet makes it sleight,
Dissembling euermore, without deceit.
*And as the twins of learn'd Hippocrates,
60   If one were sicke, the other felt disease:
If one reioyc't; ioy th'others spirits fed:
If one were grieu'd, the other sorrowed:
*So fares she with her husband; euery thought
(Weightie in him) still watcht in her, and wrought.
65   *And as those that in Elephants delight,
Neuer come neare them in weeds rich and bright;
Nor Buls approch in scarlet; since those hewes,
Through both those beasts, enrag'd affects diffuse:
And as from Tygres, men the Timbrels sound
70   And Cimbals keepe away; since they abound
Thereby in furie, and their owne flesh teare:
So when t'a good wife, it is made appeare,
That rich attire, and curiositie
In wires, tires, shadowes, do displease the eye
75   Of her lou'd husband; musicke, dancing, breeds
Offence in him; she layes by all those weeds,
Leaues dancing, musicke; and at euery part
Studies to please; and does it from her heart.
[E,R]   *As greatnesse in a Steede; so dignitie*
80   *Needs in a woman, courbe, and bit, and eie,*
If once she weds, shee's two for one before:
Single againe, she neuer doubles more.

marginal notes:

* Geome-
trae dicunt,
lineas & su-
perficies, non
seipsis mou-
eri, sed motus
corporum
comitari.

* *A good
wife in most
cares, should
euer vndis-
maid comfort
her husband.*

* *Simile.*

* *A good
wife watcheth
her husbands
serious
thoughts in his
lookes, and
applies her
owne to them.*

* *Simile.*

VIRGILS EPIGRAM

of Play.

Despise base gaine; mad Auarice hurts the mind:
Ye wise, shun fraud; beleeue the learn'd, ye blind.
At play put passions downe, as monies are.
He playes secure, whose trunks hold crowns to spare:
Who brings all with him, shall go out with none: 5
A greedie gamester euer ends vndone.
Peace holy is to men of honest minds;
If ye will play, then courbe your warring splenes:
No man wins alwayes. It shames mans true worth,
Of but three Furies, to fare like a fourth.   10
Correct your earnest spirits, and play indeed:
At staid years be not mou'd: nere play for need.

VIRGILS EPIGRAM   *v*

of wine and women.

Be not enthrall'd with wine, nor womens loue,
For both by one meanes hurt: as women proue
Meanes to effeminate, and mens powres decline:
So doth the too much indulgence of wine,
Staggers the vpright steps a man should take,   5
Dissolues his nerues, and makes his goers weake.
Blind loue makes many all their thoughts expresse,
Whose like effect hath brainlesse drunkennesse.
Wilde Cupid oft beates vp warres sterne alarmes,
As oft fierce Bacchus cals our hands to armes.   10
Dishonest Venus made Mars Ilion sease:
And Bacchus lost with warre the Lapithes.
Lastly, when both make mad misgouern'd minds,
Feare, shame, all vertues vanish with the winds.
With Giues make Venus hold her legs together,   15
And bind Liaeus in his iuie with her.
Let wine quench thirst, sweet Venus children beare,
Whose bounds once broke, ye buy their pleasures deare.

VIRGILS EPIGRAM   [E₈ᴿ]

of this letter Y.

This letter of Pythagoras, that beares
This forkt distinction, to conceit prefers
The forme mans life beares. Vertues hard way takes
Vpon the right hand path: which entrie makes

5   (To sensuall eyes) with difficult affaire:
But when ye once haue climb'd the highest staire,
The beautie and the sweetnesse it containes,
Giue rest and comfort, farre past all your paines.
The broad-way in a brauery paints ye forth
10 (In th'entrie) softnesse, and much shade of worth:
But when ye reach the top, the taken Ones
It headlong hurles downe, torne at sharpest stones.
He then, whom vertues loue, shall victor crowne,
Of hardest fortunes, praise wins and renowne:
15 But he that sloth and fruitlesse luxurie
Pursues, and doth with foolish warinesse flie
Opposed paines, (that all best acts befall)
Liues poore and vile, and dies despisde of all.

v   A FRAGMENT OF

the Teares of peace.

O that some sacred labour would let in
The ocean through my womb, to clense my sin;
I, that belou'd of Heauen, as his true wife,
Was wont to bring forth a delightsome life
5 To all his creatures: and had vertues hand
To my deliuerance, decking euery land
(Where warre was banisht) with religious Temples,
Cloisters and monuments in admir'd examples
Of Christian pietie, and respect of soules,
10 Now drunke with Auarice and th'adulterous boules
Of the light Cyprian, and by Dis deflowr'd,
I bring forth seed, by which I am deuour'd:
Infectuous darknesse from my intrails flies,
That blasts Religion, breeds black heresies,
15 Strikes vertue bedrid, fame dumb, knowledge blind,
And for free bounties (like an Easterne wind)
Knits nets of Caterpillers, that all fruites
Of planting peace, catch with contentious suites.
And see (O heauen) a warre that inward breeds
20 Worse farre then Ciuill, where in brazen steeds,
Armes are let in vnseene, and fire and sword
F(1)R Wound and consume men with the rauenous hord
Of priuate riches, like prickt pictures charm'd,
And hid in dunghils, where some one is arm'd
25 With armes of thousands; and in such small time,
(Euen out of nakednesse) that the dismall crime
Stickes in his blasing forehead like a starre,

9 respect] repect

Signall of rapine and spoile worse then warre,
These warres giue such slie poison for the spleene,
That men affect and studie for their teene,⁣ 30
That it recures the wolfe in auarice,
And makes him freely spend his golden thies:
Yet no one thought spends on poore Vertues peace.
Warres, that as peace abounds, do still increase.
Warres where in endlesse rout the kingdome erres,⁣ 35
Where misers mightie grow the mightie misers,
Where partiall Lucre Iustice sword doth draw:
Where Eris turnes into Eunomia,
And makes Mars weare the long robe, to performe
A fight more blacke and cruell, with lesse storme,⁣ 40
To make for stratageme, a policie driuen
Euen to the conquest, ere th'alarme be giuen.
And for set battels where the quarrell dies,
Warres that make lanes through whole posteritics,
Arachne wins from Pallas all good parts,⁣ 45
To take her part, and euery part conuerts⁣ v
His honie into poison: abusde Peace
Is turn'd to fruitlesse and impostum'd ease,
For whom the dwarfe Contraction is at worke
In all professions; and makes heauen lurke⁣ 50
In corner pleasures: learning in the braine
Of a dull linguist, and all tight in gaine,
All rule in onely powre, all true zeale
In trustlesse auarice: all the commonweale
In few mens purses. Volumes fild with fame⁣ 55
Of deathlesse soules, in signing a large name;
Loue of all good in selfe loue: all deserts
In sole desert of hate. Thus Ease inuerts

*Ease and Securitie described.

*My fruitfull labours, and swolne blind with lust,
Creepes from her selfe, trauailes in yeelding dust;⁣ 60
Euen reeking in her neuershifted bed:
Where with benumbd securitie she is fed:
Held vp in Ignorance, and Ambitions armes,
Lighted by Comets, sung to by blind charmes.
Behind whom Danger waites, subiection, spoyle,⁣ 65
Disease, and massacre, and vncrowned Toyle:
Earth sinkes beneath her, heauen fals: yet she deafe
Heares not their thundring ruines: nor one leafe
Of all her Aspen pleasures, euer stirres;⁣ F₂ᴿ
In such dead calmes her starke presumption erres.⁣ 70

For good men.

A good man want? will God so much deny
His lawes, his witnesses, his ministrie?

Which onely for examples he maintaines
Against th'vnlearnd, to proue, he is, and raignes:
5 And all things gouerns iustly: nor neglects
Things humane, but at euery part protects
A good man so, that if he liues or dies,
All things sort well with him? If he denies
A plenteous life to me, and sees it fit
10 I should liue poorely; What, alas, is it?
But that (refusing to endanger me
In the forlorne hope of men rich and hie,)
Like a most carefull Captaine, he doth sound
Retraite to me; makes me come backe, giue ground
15 To any, that hath least delight to be
A scuffler in mans warre for vanitie?
And I obey, I follow, and I praise
My good Commander. All the cloudie daies
Of my darke life, my enuied Muse shall sing
𝄢 20 His secret loue to goodnesse: I will bring
Glad tidings to the obscure few he keepes:
Tell his high deeds, his wonders, which the deepes,
Of pouertie, and humblesse, most expresse,
And weepe out (for kinde ioy) his holinesse.

Pleasd with thy place.

God hath the whole world perfect made, & free;
His parts to th'vse of all. Men then, that be
Parts of that all, must as the generall sway
Of that importeth, willingly obay
5 In euerie thing, without their powres to change.
He that (vnpleasd to hold his place) will range,
Can in no other be containd, thats fit:
And so resisting all, is crusht with it.
But he that knowing how diuine a frame
10 The whole world is, and of it all can name
(Without selfe flatterie) no part so diuine
As he himselfe, and therefore will confine
Freely, his whole powres, in his proper part:
Goes on most god-like. He that striues t'inuert
15 The vniuersall course, with his poore way:
Not onely, dustlike, shiuers with the sway;
[F₈ᴿ] But (crossing God in his great worke) all earth
Beares not so cursed, and so damn'd a birth.
This then the vniuersall discipline
20 Of manners comprehends: a man to ioyne
Himselfe with th'vniuerse, and wish to be

Title, Pleasd] Please

Made all with it, and go on, round as he.
Not plucking from the whole his wretched part,
And into streights, or into nought reuert:
Wishing the complete vniuerse might be   25
Subiect to such a ragge of it, as he.
But to consider great necessitie,
All things, as well refract, as voluntarie
Reduceth to the high celestiall cause:
Which he that yeelds to, with a mans applause,   30
And cheeke by cheeke goes, crossing it, no breath,
But like Gods image followes to the death:
That man is perfect wise, and euerie thing,
(Each cause and euerie part distinguishing)
In nature, with enough Art vnderstands,   35
And that full glorie merits at all hands,
That doth the whole world, at all parts adorne,
And appertaines to one celestiall borne.

Of sodaine Death.   v

What action wouldst thou wish to haue in hand,
If sodain death shold come for his command?
I would be doing good to most good men
That most did need, or to their childeren,
And in aduice (to make them their true heires)   5
I would be giuing vp my soule to theirs.
To which effect if Death should find me giuen,
I would with both my hands held vp to heauen,
Make these my last words to my deitie:
Those faculties thou hast bestowd on me   10
To vnderstand thy gouernment and will
I haue, in all fit actions offerd still
To thy diuine acceptance, and as farre
As I had influence from thy bounties starre,
I haue made good thy forme infusde in me: 15
Th'anticipations giuen me naturally,
I haue with all my studie, art, and prayre
Fitted to euerie obiect, and affaire
My life presented, and my knowledge taught.
My poore saile, as it hath bene euer fraught   20
With thy free goodnesse, hath bene ballast to
With all my gratitude. What is to do,
Supply it sacred Sauiour: thy high grace   [F₄ᴿ]
In my poore gifts, receiue againe, and place
Where it shall please thee: thy gifts neuer die   25
But, hauing brought one to felicitie,
Descend againe, and helpe another vp, &c.

Height in Humilitie.

Why should I speak imperious courtiers faire?
Lest they exclude thee, at thy Court repaire.
If they shall see me enter willingly,
Let them exclude me. If necessitie
5   Driue me amongst them, and they shut the dore,
I do my best, and they can do no more.
Gods will, and mine, then weigh'd: I his preferre,
Being his vow'd lackey, and poore sufferer:
I trie what his will is, and will with it:
10   No gate is shut to me; that shame must fit
Shamelesse intruders. Why feare I disgrace
To beare ill censure by a man of face?
Will any thinke that impudence can be
An equal demonstration of me?
15   Tis kingly, Cyrus (said Antisthenes)
When thou doest well, to heare this ill of these.
v   But many pitie thy defects in thee.
I mocke them euer that so pittie me.
Strangers they are, and know not what I am;
20   Where I place good and ill, nor euer came
Where my course lies: but theirs the world may know:
They lay it out, onely to name and show.
If comfort follow truth of knowledge still,
They meete with little truth; for if their skill
25   Get not applause, their comfort comes to nought.
I studie still to be, they to be thought.
Are they lesse frustrate of their ends then I?
Or fall they lesse into the ils they flie?
Are they industrious more? lesse passionate?
30   Lesse faltring in their course? more celebrate
Truth in their comforts? But they get before
Much in opinion. True, they seeke it more.

For stay in competence.

Thou that enioyst onely enough to liue,
Why grieu'st thou that the giuer does not giue
Foode with the fullest, when as much as thou
He thinkes him emptie? Tis a state so low
5   That I am fearefull euerie howre to sinke.
E₅ᴿ   Well said. Vnthankfull fearefull, eate and drinke,
And feare to sterue still. Knowst thou not who sings
Before the theefe? The penurie of things
Whither conferres it? Drawes it not one breath
10   With great satietie? End not both in death?

Thy entrailes, with thy want, together shrinke;
He bursts with cruditie, and too much drinke.
Will not thy want then with a chearefull eye
Make thee expect death? whom sterne tyrannie,
Empire, and all the glut of thirstie store,   15
Shun with pale cheekes affrighted euermore?
Earth is a whore, and brings vp all her brats
With her insatiate gadflie: euen her flats
High as her hils looke; lusting, lusting still,
No earthly pleasure euer hath her fill.   20
Turne a new leafe then: thirst for things past death;
And thou shalt neuer thinke of things beneath.
How should I thirst so, hauing no such heate?
Fast, pray, to haue it: better neuer eate,
Then still the more thou eatst the more desire.   25
But wilt thou quench this ouerneedie fire?
Canst thou not write, nor reade, nor keepe a gate,
Teach children, be a porter? That poore state
Were base and hatefull. Is that base to thee,
That is not thy worke? That necessitie   30 v
Inflicts vpon thee? that inuades thee to
Onely as head-aches and agues do?
That the great Ordrer of th'vniuerse sees
So good, he puts it in his master peece?
But men will scorn me. Let them then go by,   35
They will not touch thee: he that shifts his eye
To others eye-browes, must himselfe be blind.
Leau'st thou thy selfe for others? tis the mind
Of all that God and euery good forsakes.
If he goes thy way, follow: if he takes   40
An opposite course, canst thou still go along,
And end thy course? Go right, though all else wrong.
    But you are learn'd, and know Philosophie
To be a shift to salue necessitie:
Loue syllogismes, figures, and to make   45
All men admire how excellent you spake.
Your caution is to keepe a studious eye,
Lest you be caught with carpes of sophistrie:
To be a man of reading, when alas,
All these are caught in a Plebeians case.   50
None such poore fooles, incontinent, couetous,
Atheisticall, deceitfull, villanous.
Shew me thy studies end, and what may be
Those weights and measures, that are vsde by thee,   [F₆ᴿ]
To mete these ashes barreld vp in man.   55
Is not the wreath his, that most truly can

Make a man happie? And (in short) is that
Any way wrought more, then in teaching what
Will make a man most ioyfully embrace
60 The course his end holds, and his proper place?
Not suffering his affections to disperse,
But fit the maine sway of the vniuerse.

Of the Will.

The empire of the Will is euer sau'd,
Except lost by it selfe, when tis deprau'd.

Of Man.

Man is so soueraigne and diuine a state,
That not contracted and elaborate,
The world he beares about with him alone,
But euen the Maker makes his breast his throne.

v   ### Of a Philosopher.

Does a Philosopher inuite, or pray
Any to heare him? or not make his way,
As meate and drinke doth? or the Sunne excite
Onely by vertue of his heate and light?

Of Ambition.

Who, others loues and honors goes about,
Would haue things outward, not to be without.

Of Friendship.

Now I am old, my old friends loues I wish,
As I am good, & more old, grow more fresh.
Friends constant, not like lakes are standing euer,
But like sweet streames, euer the same, yet neuer
5 Still, profiting themselues, and perfecting.
And as a riuer furthest from his spring,
Takes vertue of his course, and all the way
Greater and greater growes, till with the sea
He combats for his empire, and gets in,
10 Curling his billowes, till his stile he win:
[F₇ᴿ] So worthy men should make good to their ends,
Increase of goodness; such men make thy friends.
Such nobler are, the poorer was their source;
And though with crooks & turns, yet keep their course,
15 Though still their strength, they did some weaknesse show,
(All thankes to God yet) now it is not so.

Will is the garden first, then Knowledge plants;
Who knowes and wils well, neuer vertue wants:
Though oft he faile in good, he nought neglects;
The affect, not the effect, God respects.   20
But as the Academickes euer rate
A man for learning, with that estimate
They made of him, when in the schooles he liu'd;
And how so ere he scatter'd since, or thriu'd,
Still they esteeme him as they held him then: 25
So fares it with the doomes of vulgar men;
If once they knew a man defectiue, still
The staine stickes by him; better he his skill,
His life and parts, till quite refin'd from him
He was at first; good drownes, ill still doth swim: 30
Best men are long in making: he that soone
Sparkles and flourishes, as soone is gone.
A wretched thing it is, when nature giues
A man good gifts, that still the more he liues,
The more they die. And where the complete man   35 v
(Much lesse esteem'd) is long before he can
The passage cleare, betwixt his soule and sense,
And of his body gaine such eminence,
That all his organs open are, and fit
To serue their Empresse; th'other man of wit,   40
At first is seru'd with all those instruments:
Open they are, and full, and free euents
All he can thinke obtaines, and forth there flies
Flashes from him, thicke as the Meteord skies,
Like which he lookes, and vp drawes all mens eies,   45
Euen to amaze: yet like those Meteors,
(Onely in ayre imprest) away he soares,
His organs shut: and twixt his life and soule,
Sue a diuorce aliue. Such ne're enroule
In thy brasse booke of Friendship: such are made   50
To please light spirits, not to grow but fade.
Nor friends for old acquaintance chuse, but faith,
Discretion, good life, and contempt of death:
That foes wrongs beare with Christian patience,
Against which fighting, Reason hath no fence: 55
That lay their fingers on their lips the more,
The more their wrong'd simplicities deplore,
And stop their mouthes to euery enemies ill,
With th'ill he does them. Thus good men do still,   [F₈ᴿ]
And onely good men friends are: make no friend   60
Of fleshie-beast-men, friendships of the mind.

Of plentie and freedome in goodnesse.

Not to haue want, what riches doth exceed?
Not to be subiect, what superior thing?
He that to nought aspires, doth nothing need: *Resp.*
Who breakes no law, is subiect to no King.

Of Attention.

When for the least time, thou lett'st fall thine eare
From still attending, things still fit to heare,
And giu'st thy mind way to thy bodies will:
Imagine not thou hold'st the raines so still,
5 That at thy pleasure thou canst turne her in:
But be assur'd that one dayes soothed sinne,
Will aske thee many to amend and mourne:
And make thy mind so willing to adiourne
That instant-due amendment, that twill breed
10 A custome to do ill; and that will need
v A new birth to reforme. What? May I then
(By any diligence, or powre in men)
Auoid transgression? No, tis past thy powre:
But this thou maist do; euery day and houre,
15 In that be labouring still, that lets transgression:
And worth my counsell tis, that this impression
Fixt in thy mind, and all meanes vsde in man,
He may transgresse as little as he can.
    If still thou saist, To morrow I will win
20 My mind to this attention: therein
Thou saist as much, as this day I will be
Abiect and impudent: it shall be free
This day for others to liue Lords of me,
To leade and rule me: this day I will giue
25 Reines to my passions, I will enuious liue,
Wrathfull and lustfull: I will leaue the state
Man holds in me, and turne adulterate,
Vulgar and beastly. See to how much ill
Thou stand'st indulgent. But all this thy will
30 Shall mend to morrow: how much better twere
This day thou shouldst mans godlike scepter beare:
For if to morrow, in thy strengths neglect,
Much more to day, while tis vncounter-checkt.

G(1)ᴿ   *To liue with little.*

When thou seest any honour'd by the king,
Oppose thou this, thou thirsts for no such thing.
When thou seest any rich, see what in sted

Of those his riches thou hast purchased.
If nothing, nothing fits such idle wretches.   5
If thou hast that, that makes thee need no riches,
Know thou hast more, and of a greater price,
And that which is to God a sacrifice.
When thou seest one linkt with a louely wife,
Thou canst containe, and leade a single life.   10
Seeme these things smal to thee? O how much more
Do euen those great ones, and those men of store
Desire those small things, then their greatest owne:
That they could scorn their states so bladder-blown,
Their riches, and euen those delicious Dames,   15
That feast their blood with such enchanted flames?
For haue not yet thy wits the difference found,
Betwixt a feu'rie mans thirst, and one sound?
He hauing drunke is pleasd: the other lies
Fretting and lothing, vomits out his eyes: 20
His drinke to choler turnes, and ten parts more
His vicious heate inflames him, then before.
So while the long fit of his drie desire   v
Lasts in a rich man, such insatiate fire
He feeles within him. While the like fit lasts   25
In one ambitious, so he thirsts, and wasts.
While the fit lasts, and lust hath any fewell;
So fares the fond venerean with his iewell,
There being linkt to euery one of these
Feares, emulations, sleeplesse Ielosies,   30
Foule cogitations, foule words, fouler deeds.
Enough be that then, that may serue thy needs,
What thou canst keepe in thy free powre alone,
Others affect, and thou reiect'st thine owne.
Both will not draw in one yoke: one release   35
And th'other vse, or neither keepe in peace
Twixt both distracted. Things within thee prise:
Onely within, thy helpe and ruine lies.
What wall so fencefull? what possession
So constant, and so properly our owne?   40
What dignitie so expert of deceipts?
All trade-like beggarly, and full of sleights.
On which who sets his mind, is sure to grieue,
Feed on faint hopes, neuer his ends atcheeue,
Fall into that he shuns, and neuer rest,   45
But bad esteeme his state, when tis at best.
Serue but thy minde with obiects fit for her,   [G₂ᴿ]
And for things outward thou shalt neuer care.
Obtaine but her true, and particular vse

50 And obtaine all things. Nor let doubt, abuse
Thy will to winne her, as being coy enclind,
Nought is so pliant as a humane mind.
 And what shall I obtaine, obtaining her,
 Not wishing all, but some particular?
55 What wouldst thou wish for her dowre more then these?
To make thee pleasant, of one hard to please?
To make thee modest, of one impudent;
Temperate, and chast, of one incontinent:
Faithfull, being faithlesse. Fit not these thy will?
60 Affect'st thou greater? What thou dost, do still:
I giue thee ouer, doing all I can,
Th'art past recure, with all that God giues man.

To yong imaginaries in knowledge.

Neuer for common signes, dispraise or praise,
Nor art, nor want of art, for what he saies
Ascribe to any. Men may both waies make
v In forme, & speech, a mans quicke doome mistake.
5 All then that stand in any ranke of Art,
Certaine decrees haue, how they shall impart
That which is in them: which decrees, because
They are within men, making there the lawes
To all their actions, hardly shew without:
10 And till their ensignes are displaid, make doubt
To go against or with them: nor will they
So well in words, as in their deeds display.
Decrees are not degrees. If thou shalt giue
Titles of learning, to such men as liue
15 Like rude Plebeians, since they haue degrees,
Thou shalt do like Plebeians. He that sees
A man held learn'd do rudely, rather may
Take for that deed, his learned name away,
Then giu't him for his name. True learnings act,
20 And speciall obiect is, so to compact
The will, and euery actiue powre in man,
That more then men illiterate, he can
Keepe all his actions in the narrow way
To God and goodnesse, and there force their stay
25 As in charm'd circles. Termes, tongs, reading, all
That can within a man, cald learned, fall;
Whose life is led yet like an ignorant mans:
G₃ᴿ Are but as tooles to goutie Artizans,
That cannot vse them; or like childrens arts,
30 That out of habite, and by rootes of hearts,
Construe and perce their lessons, yet discerne

Nought of the matter, whose good words they learn:
Or like our Chimicke Magi, that can call
All termes of Art out, but no gold at all:
And so are learn'd like them, of whom, none knows   35
His Arts cleare truth, but are meere Ciniflos.
   But sacred learning, men so much prophane,
That when they see a learn'd-accounted man
Liues like a brute man; they will neuer take
His learn'd name from him, for opinions sake: 40
But on the false ground brutishly conclude,
That learning profites not. You beastly rude,
Know, it more profites, being exact and true,
Then all earths high waies chokt with herds of you.
   But must degrees, & termes, and time in schooles,   45
Needs make men learn'd, in life being worse then fooles?
What other Art liues in so happy aire,
That onely for his habite, and his haire,
His false professors worth you will commend?
Are there not precepts, matter, and an end   50
To euery science? which, not kept, nor showne
By vnderstanding; vnderstanding knowne   v
By fact; the end, by things to th'end directed,
What hap, or hope haue they to be protected?
Yet find such, greatest friends: and such professe   55
Most learning, and will preasse for most accesse
Into her presence, and her priuiest state,
When they haue hardly knockt yet at her gate.
Externall circumscription neuer serues
To proue vs men: blood, flesh, nor bones nor nerues,   60
But that which all these vseth, and doth guide:
Gods image in a soule eternifide,
Which he that shewes not in such acts as tend
To that eternesse, making that their end:
In this world nothing knowes, nor after can,   65
But is more any creature then a man.
This rather were the way, if thou wouldst be,
A true proficient in philosophie:
Dissemble what thou studiest, till alone
By thy impartiall contention   70
Thou prou'st thee fit, to do as to professe.
And if thou still professe it not, what lesse
Is thy philosophie, if in thy deeds
Rather then signes, and shadowes, it proceedes?
Shew with what temper thou dost drinke, and eate: 75
How farre from wrong thy deeds are, angers heate;   G₄ᴿ

41 ground] gound   65 nor] uor

How thou sustainst, and abstainst; how farre gone
In appetite and auersation:
To what account thou doest affections call,
80   Both naturall, and aduentitiall:
That thou art faithfull, pious, humble, kind,
Enemie to enuie: of a chearefull mind,
Constant, and dantlesse. All this when men see
Done with the learnedst, then let censure thee;
85   But if so dull, and blind of soule they are,
Not to acknowledge heauenly Mulciber,
To be a famous Artist by his deeds,
But they must see him in his working weeds:
What ill is it, if thou art neuer knowne
90   To men so poore of apprehension?
Are they within thee, or so much with thee
As thou thy selfe art? Can their dull eyes see
Thy thoughts at worke? Or how like one thats sworn
To thy destruction, all thy powres are borne
95   T'entrap thy selfe? whom thou dost hardlier please
Then thou canst them? Arme then thy mind with these:
I haue decrees set downe twixt me and God;
I know his precepts, I will beare his lode,
But what men throw vpon me, I reiect:
v 100   No man shall let the freedome I elect;
I haue an owner that will challenge me,
Strong to defend, enough to satisfie:
The rod of Mercurie, will charme all these,
And make them neither strange, nor hard to please.
105   And these decrees, in houses constitute
Friendship, and loue: in fields cause store of fruite:
In cities, riches; and in temples zeale:
And all the world would make one commonweale.
Shun braggart glorie, seeke no place, no name:
110   No shewes, no company, no laughing game,
No fashion: nor no champion of thy praise,
As children sweete meates loue, and holidaies:
Be knowing shamefastnesse, thy grace, and guard,
As others are with dores, wals, porters bard.
115   Liue close awhile; so fruits grow, so their seed
Must in the earth a little time lie hid;
Spring by degrees, and so be ripe at last.
But if the Eare, be to the blades top past
Before the ioynt amidst the blade, be knit,
120   The corne is lanke, and no Sunne ripens it.
Like which art thou yong Nouice; florishing
Before thy time, winter shall burne thy spring.

The husbandman dislikes his fields faire birth,
When timelesse heate beates on vnreadie earth,   [G₅ᴿ]
Grieues lest his fruits with aire should be too bold,   125
And not endure the likely-coming cold.
Comfort the roote then first, then let appeare
The blades ioynt knit, and then produce the Eare:
So Natures selfe, thou shalt constraine, and be
Blest with a wealthy crop in spite of thee.   130

Of Constancie in goodnesse.

Who feares disgrace for things wel done, that knows it?
Wrong euer does most harme to him that does it.
Who more ioy takes, that men his good aduance,
Then in the good it selfe, does it by chance:
That being the worke of others; this his owne.   5
In all these actions therefore that are common,
Men neuer should for praise or dispraise care,
But looke to the Decrees, from whence they are.

Of Learning.

Learning, the Art is of good life: they then
That leade not good liues, are not learned men.

For ill successe.   v

If thou sustainst in any sort an ill,
Beare some good with thee to change for it still.

Of negligence.

When thou letst loose thy mind to obiects vain
Tis not in thee to call her backe againe:
And therefore when thy pleasure in her good
Droopes, and would downe in melancholy blood,
Feed her alacritie with any thought   5
Or word, that euer her recomfort wrought.

Of iniurie.

When thou art wrong'd, see if the wrong proceed
From fault within thy iudgement, word or deed:
If not, let him beware that iniures thee,
And all that sooth him; and be thy state free.

Of Attire.

In habite, nor in any ill to th'eie,
Affright the vulgar from Philosophie:
But as in lookes, words, workes, men witnesse thee

Comely and checklesse, so in habite be.
[G₆ᴿ] 5 For if a man shall shew me one commended
For wit, skill, iudgement, neuer so extended,
That goes fantastically, and doth fit
The vulgar fashion; neuer thinke his wit
Is of a sound peece, but hath bracks in it.
10 If slouenly and nastily in weeds
Thou keep'st thy body, such must be thy deeds.
Hence, to the desart, which thou well deseru'st,
And now no more for mans societie seru'st.
Externall want to this height doth expresse
15 Both inward negligence, and rottennesse.

FRAGMENTS.

Of Circumspection.

In hope to scape the law, do nought amisse,
The penance euer in the action is.

Of Sufferance.

It argues more powre willingly to yeeld
To what by no repulse can be repeld,
Then to be victor of the greatest state,
We can with any fortune subiugate.

v ### Of the Soule.

The Soule serues with her functions to excite,
Abhorre, prepare, and order appetite,
Cause auersation, and susception:
In all which, all her will is built vpon
5 Ill receiu'd iudgements; which reforme with good;
And as with ill she yeelded to thy blood,
And made thy pleasures, God and man displease,
She will as well set both their powres at peace,
With righteous habits, and delight thee more
10 With doing good now, then with ill before.

Of great men.

When Homer made Achilles passionate,
Wrathfull, reuengefull, and insatiate
In his affections; what man will denie
He did compose all that of industrie?
5 To let men see, that men of most renowne,
Strong'st, noblest, fairest, if they set not downe
Decrees within them, for disposing these,

Of iudgement, resolution, vprightnesse,
And vertuous knowledge of their vse and ends,
Mishaps and miserie, no lesse extends   10
To their destruction, with all that they prisde,   [G₇ᴿ]
Then to the poorest, and the most despisde.

Of learned men.

Who knows not truth, knows nothing; who what's best
Knowes not, not¹ truth knowes. Who (alone profest
In that which best is) liues bad: Best not knowes,
Since with that Best and Truth, such ioy still goes,
That he that finds them, cannot but dispose   5
His whole life to them. Seruile Auarice can
Prophane no liberall-knowledge-coueting man.
Such hypocrites, opinions onely haue;
Without the minds² vse: which doth more depraue
Their knowing powres, then if they³ nought did know. 10
For if with all the sciences they flow,
Not hauing that, that such ioy brings withall,
As cannot in vnlearn'd mens courses fall:
As with a⁴ tempest they are rapt past hope
Of knowing Truth, because they thinke his scope   15
Is in their tongues, much reading, speech profuse,
Since they are meanes to Truth in their true vse:
⁵But tis a fashion for the damned crue,   *v*
One thing to praise, another to pursue:
As those learn'd men do, that in words preferre   20
Heauen and good life, yet in their liues so erre,
That all heauen is not broade enough for them
To hit or aime at, but the vulgar streame
Hurries them headlong with it: and no more
They know or shall know, then the rudest Bore.   25

FINIS.

¹ Si absit scientia optimi, nihil scitur.
² Qui opinioni absque mente, consenserint.
³ Prodest multis non nosse quicquam.
⁴ Nonne meritó, multa tempestate iactabitur?
⁵ Absurdam alia laudare, alia sequi.

AN EPICEDE OR

FVNERALL SONG:

On the most disastrous Death, of the
High-borne *Prince* of Men, HENRY
Prince of WALES, &c.

TO MY AFFECTIO-
NATE, AND TRVE

Friend, Mr. *Henry Jones.*

My truest Friend:

THE most vnualuable and dismaifull loss of my most deare
and Heroicall Patrone, Prince HENRY, hath so stricken
all my spirits to the earth, that I will neuer more dare, to looke
vp to any greatnesse; but resoluing the little rest of my poore
life to obscuritie, and the shadow of his death; prepare euer
hereafter, for the light of heauen.

So absolute, constant, and noble, your loue hath beene to
mee; that if I should not as effectually, by all my best ex-
pressions, acknowledge it; I could neither satisfie mine owne
affection, nor deserue yours.

Accept therefore, as freely as I acknowledge, this vnprofit-
able signe of my loue; till God blessing my future labours, I
may adde a full end, to whatsoeuer is begunne in your assur-
ance of my requitall. A little, blest, makes a great feast (my
best friend) and therefore despaire not, but that, out of that
little, our loues alwayes made euen, may make you say, you
haue rather beene happy in your kindnesse, then in the least
degree, hurt. There may fauours passe betwixt poore friends,
which euen the richest, and greatest may enuy. And GOD
that yet neuer let me liue, I know will neuer let me die an
empaire to any friend. If any good, more then requitall suc-
ceede, it is all yours as freely, as euer yours was mine; in
which noble freedome and alacritie of doing; you haue thrice
done, all I acknowledge. And thus knowing, I giue you little
contentment, in this so farre vnexpected publication of my
gratitude; I rest satisfied with the ingenuous discharge of
mine owne office. Your extraordinary and noble loue and
sorrow, borne to our most sweet PRINCE, entitles you
worthily to this Dedication: which (with my generall Loue,
vnfainedly protested to your whole Name and Family) I con-
clude you as desertfull of, at my hands, as our Noblest Earles;
and so euer remaine

Your most true poore Friend,

Geo: Chapman.

1 loss] hope. Shepherd's emendation.

AN EPICED,

or

Funerall Song:

On the most disastrous Death, of the
High-borne *Prince* of Men, *HENRY*
Prince of WALES, &c.

IF euer aduerse Influence enui'd
　The glory of our Lands, or tooke a pride
To trample on our height; or in the Eye
Strooke all the pomp of Principalitie,
Now it hath done so; Oh, if euer Heauen　　　　　5
Made with the earth his angry reckening euen,
Now it hath done so. Euer, euer be
Admir'd, and fear'd, that Triple Maiestie
Whose finger could so easily sticke a Fate,
Twixt least Felicity, and greatest state;　　　　10
Such, as should melt our shore into a Sea,　　　　v
And dry our Ocean with Calamitie.
Heauen open'd, and but show'd him to our eies,
Then shut againe, and show'd our Miseries.

Expostula-
tio à perturba-
tione.
　　　O God, to what end are thy Graces giuen?　　　15
Onely to show the world, Men fit for Heauen,
Then rauish them, as if too good for Earth?
We know, the most, exempt in wealth, power, Birth,
Or any other blessing; should employ
(As to their chiefe end) all things they enioy,　　　20
To make them fit for Heauen; and not pursue
With hearty appetite, the damned crue
Of meerely sensuall and earthly pleasures:
But when one hath done so; shal strait the tresures
Digg'd to, in those deeps, be consum'd by death?　　　25
Shall not the rest, that error swalloweth,
Be, by the Patterne of that Master-peece,
Help't to instruct their erring faculties;
When, without cleare example; euen the best

Potentia ex-
pers sapientiae
quo maior est,
eo perniciosi-
or: sapientia
procul à poten-
tia manca
videtur.
Plat.
(That cannot put by knowledge to the Test　　　30
What they are taught) serue like the worst in field?
Is power to force, who will not freely yield,
(Being great assistant, to diuine example)
As vaine a Pillar to thy Manly Temple?
When (without perfect knowledge, which scarce one　35 B₂R
Of many kingdoms reach) no other stone
Man hath to build one corner of thy Phane,

Saue one of these? But when the desperate wane
Of power, and of example to all good,
40　So spent is, that one cannot turne the flood,
Of goodnes, gainst her ebbe; but both must plie,
And be at full to; or her streame will drie;
Where shall they meete againe, now he is gone
Where both went foot by foot; & both were one?
45　　One that in hope, tooke vp to toplesse height
All his great Ancestors; his one saile, freight
With all, all Princes treasures; he like one
Of no importance; no way built vpon,
Vanisht without the end; for which he had
50　Such matchlesse vertues, & was God-like made?
Haue thy best workes no better cause t'expresse
Themselues like men, and thy true Images?
To toile in vertues study, to sustaine
(With comfort for her) want, & shame, & paine;
55　No nobler end in this life, then a death
Timeles, and wretched, wrought with lesse then breath?
And nothing solide, worthy of our soules?
Nothing that Reason, more then Sense extols?
v　Nothing that may in perfect iudgement be
60　A fit foote for our Crowne eternitie?
All which, thou seem'st to tell vs, in this one
Killing discomfort; apt to make our mone
Conclude gainst all things, serious and good;
Our selues, not thy forms, but Chymaeras brood.
65　　Now Princes, dare ye boast your vig'rous states
That Fortunes breath thus builds and ruinates?
Exalt your spirits? trust in flowry youth?
Giue reynes to pleasure? all your humors sooth?
Licence in rapine? Powers exempt from lawes?
70　Contempt of all things, but your own applause?
And think your swindge to any tyranny giuen,
Will stretch as broad, & last as long as heauen;
When he that curb'd with vertues hand his powre,
His youth with continence; his sweet with sowre,
75　Boldnes with pious feare; his pallats height
Applied to health, and not to appetite;
Felt timeles sicknes charge; state, power to flie,
And glutted Death with all his crueltie?
　　Partiall deuourer euer of the best,
80　With headlong rapture, sparing long the rest
Could not the precious teares his Father shed,
(That are with Kingdomes to be ransomed?)
B₃ᴿ　His Bleeding prayer, vpon his knees t'implore,

Chymaera,
a monster,
hauing his
head and
brest like a
Lyon; his
belly like a
Gote; and
taile like a
Dragon.

To Death.

The Prayer
of the King
in the Princes
sicknes.

That if for any sinne of his, Heauen tore
From his most Royall body that chiefe Limme,   85
It might be ransom'd, for the rest of Him?
    Could not the sacred eies thou didst prophane
In his great Mothers teares? The spightful bane
Thou pour'dst vpon the cheeks of al the Graces
In his more gracious Sisters? The defaces   90
(With all the Furies ouer-flowing Galles)
Cursedly fronting her neere Nuptials?
Could not, O could not, the Almighty ruth
Of all these force thee to forbeare the youth
Of our Incomparable Prince of Men?   95
Whose Age had made thy Iron Forcke his Pen,
T'eternise what it now doth murder meerely;
And shal haue from my soule, my curses yerely.
    Tyrant, what knew'st thou, but the barbarous wound
Thou gau'st the son, the Father might confound?   100
Both liu'd so mixtly, and were ioyntly One,
Spirit to spirit cleft. The Humor bred
In one heart, straight was with the other fed;
The bloud of one, the others heart did fire;
The heart and humour, were the Sonne & Sire;   105
The heart yet, void of humors slender'st part,   v
May easier liue, then humour without heart;
The Riuer needes the helpfull fountaine euer,
More then the Fountaine, the supplyed Riuer.

Simil.
As th'Iron then, when it hath once put on   110
The Magnets qualitie, to the vertuous Stone
Is euer drawne, and not the stone to it:

Apodesis.
So may the heauens, the sonnes Fate, not admit
To draw the Fathers, till a hundred yeeres
Haue drown'd that Issue to him in our teares.   115

Reditio ad
Principem.
    Blest yet, and sacred shall thy memory be,
O-nothing-lesse-then-mortall Deitie.
Thy Graces, like the Sunne, to all men giuing;
Fatall to thee in death, but kill me liuing.
Now, as inuerted, like th'*Antipodes*,   120
The world (in all things of desert to please)
Is falne on vs, with thee: thy ruines lye
On our burst bosomes, as if from the skye
The *Day-star*, greater then the world were driuen
Suncke to the Earth, and left a hole in Heauen;   125
Throgh which, a second deluge now poures down
On our poore Earth; in which are ouer-flowne
The seeds of all the sacred Vertues, set
In his Spring-Court; where all the prime spirits met

[B₄ᴿ] 130 Of all our Kingdomes; as if from the death,
That in men liuing; basenes and rapine sheath,
Where they before liu'd; they vnwares were come
Into a free, and fresh *Elisium;*
Casting regenerate, and refined eyes
135 On him that rais'd them from their graues of vice,
Digg'd in their old grounds, to spring fresh on those
That his diuine Ideas did propose,
First to himselfe; & then would forme in them.
Who did not thirst to plant his sonne neer him
140 As neer the *Thames* their houses? what one worth
Was there in all our world, that set not forth
All his deserts, to pilgrime to his fauors,
With all deuotion, offering all his labors?
And how the wilde Bore, Barbarisme, now
145 Will roote these Quick-sets vp? What hearb shall grow,
That is not sown in his inhumane tracts?
No thought of good shall spring, but many acts
Will crop, or blast, or blow it vp: and see
How left to this, the mournfull Familie,
150 Muffled in black clouds, full of teares are driuen
With stormes about the relickes of this Heauen;
Retiring from the world, like Corses, herst,
v Home to their graues, a hundred waies disperst.
O that this court-schoole; this *Olimpus* meerly,
155 Where two-fold Man was practisde; should so early
Dissolue the celebration purpos'd there,
Of all *Heroique* parts, when farre and neere,
All were resolu'd t'admire, None to contend,
When, in the place of all, one wretched end
160 Will take vp all endeauours; Harpye Gaine,
Pandar to Gote, Ambition; goulden Chaine
To true mans freedome; not from heau'n let fal
To draw men vp; But shot from Hell to hale
All men, as bondslaues, to his Turckish den,
165 For Toades, and Adders, far more fit then men.
His house had well his surname from a *Saint,*
All things so sacred, did so liuely paint
Their pious figures in it: And as well
His other house, did in his Name fore-tell
170 What it should harbour; a rich world of parts
Bonfire-like kindling, the still-feasted Arts,
Which now on bridles bite, and puft Contempt
Spurres to Despaire, from all fit food exempt.
O what a frame of Good, in all hopes rais'd
175 Came tumbling downe with him! as when was seisde

Those that came to the Princes seruice seem'd (compared with the places they liu'd in before) to rise from death to the fields of life, intending the best part of yong and noble Gentlemen.

The parting of the Princes Seruants.

The Princes house an Olimpus, where all contention of vertues were practised.

Non Homeri Aurea Restis.

Saint *Iames* his house.

Richmond.

By Grecian furie, famous *Jlion*,
Whose fall, still rings out his Confusion.
What *Triumphs*, scattered at his feete, lye smoking! $G_{(sio)} = C_1^R$
Banquets that will not downe; their cherers choking,
Fields fought, and hidden now, with future slaughter,   180
Furies sit frowning, where late sat sweet laughter,
The actiue lying maim'd, the healthfull crasde,
All round about his Herse! And how amaz'd
The change of things stands! how astonisht ioy
Wonders he euer was! yet euery Toy   185
Quits this graue losse: Rainbowes no sooner taint
Thinne dewye vapors, which oppos'd beames paint
Round in an instant, (at which children stare
And slight the Sunne, that makes them circular
And so disparent) then mere gawds pierce men,   190
Slighting the graue, like fooles, and children;
So courtly nere plagues, sooth and stupefie.
And with such paine, men leaue selfe flatterie

The Prince
not to be
wrought on
by flattery.

Of which, to see him free (who stood no lesse
Then a full siege of such) who can expresse   195
His most direct infusion from aboue,
Farre from the humorous seede of mortal loue?

His knowl-
edge and wis-
dome.

    He knew, that Iustice simply vsd, was best,
Made princes most secure, most lou'd, most blest;
No Artezan; No Scholler; could pretend,   200
No Statesman; No Diuine; for his owne end
Any thing to him, but he would descend   *v*
The depth of any right belong'd to it,
Where they could merit, or himselfe should quit.
    He would not trust, with what himselfe concern'd,   205
Any in any kinde; but euer learn'd

Any man is
capable of his
own fit
course and of-
fice in any
thing.

The grounds of what he built on: Nothing lies
In mans fit course, that his own knowledge flies,
Eyther direct, or circumstantiall.
O what are Princes then, that neuer call   210
Their actions to account, but flatterers trust
To make their triall, if vniust or iust?
Flatterers are houshold theeues, traitors by law,
That rob kings honors, & their soules-bloud draw;

Apostrophe.
Men grow so
vgly by trust-
ing flattery
with their in-
formations,
that when

Diseases, that keep nourishment from their food.   215
And as to know himselfe, is mans chiefe good,
So that which intercepts that supreame skill,
(Which Flattery is) is the supreamest ill:

they see themselues truely, by casting their eyes inward, they cast themselues away with
their owne lothing.

Whose lookes will breede the Basilisk in kings eyes,
220 That by reflexion of his sight, dyes.
*And as a Nurse lab'ring a wayward Childe,   *Simil.*
Day, and night watching it, like an offspring wilde;
Talkes infinitely idly to it still;
Sings with a standing throate, to worse from ill;
C₂ᴿ 225 Lord-blesses it; beares with his pewks and cryes;
And to giue it a long lifes miseries,
Sweetens his food, rocks, kisses, sings againe;
Plyes it with rattles, and all obiects vaine:
So Flatterers, with as seruile childish things,
230 Obserue, & sooth the waiward moods of kings;
So kings, that flatterers loue, had neede to haue
As nurse-like councellors, & contemn the graue;
Themselues as wayward, and as noisome too;
Full as vntuneable in all they doe,
235 As poore sicke Infants; euer breeding Teeth
In all their humours, that be worse then Death.
How wise then was our Prince that hated these,
And wold with nought but truth his humor plese
Nor would he giue a place, but where hee saw
240 One that could vse it; and become a Law
Both to his fortunes, and his Princes Honor.
Who would giue *fortune* noght she took vpon her,
Not giue but to desert; nor take a chance,
That might not iustly, his wisht ends aduance.
245 His Good he ioyn'd with Equitie and Truth;
Wisedome in yeeres, crown'd his ripe head in youth;
His heart wore all the folds of Policie,
Yet went as naked as Simplicitie.
v Knew good and ill; but onely good did loue;
250 In him the Serpent did embrace the Doue.
Hee was not curious to sound all the streame
Of others acts, yet kept his owne from them:
"He whose most darke deeds dare not stand the light,
"Begot was of imposture and the night.
255 "Who surer then a Man, doth ends secure;
"Eyther a God is, or a Diuell sure.
The President of men; whom (as men can)
All men should imitate, was God and Man.
In these cleere deepes our Prince fish't: troubl'd streams
260 Of bloud & vantage challenge diadems.
In summe, (knot-like) hee was together put,
That no man could dissolue, and so was cut.
But we shal see our foule-mouth'd factions spite
(Markt, witch-like, with one blacke eie, th'other white)

Ope, & oppose against this spotlesse sun; 265
Such, heauen strike blinder then th'eclipsed moon
Twixt whom and noblesse, or humanities truth,
As much dull earth lies, and as little ruth,
(Should all things sacred perish) as there lyes
Twixt *Phaebe*, and the Light-fount of the skies, 270
In her most darke delinquence: vermine right,
That prey in darknesse, and abhorre the light;
Liue by the spoile of vertue; are not well C₃ᴿ
But when they heare news, from their father hell
Of some blacke mischiefe; neuer do good deed, 275
But where it does much harme, or hath no need.
What shall become of vertues far-short traine,
When thou their head art reacht, high Prince of men?
O that thy life could haue disperst deaths stormes,
To giue faire act to those Heroique formes, 280
With which al good rules had enricht thy mind,
Preparing for affayres of euery kinde;
Peace being but a pause to breathe fierce warre;
No warrant dormant, to neglect his Starre;
The licence sence hath, is t'informe the soule; 285
Not to suppresse her; and our lusts extoll;
This life in all things, to enioy the next;
Of which lawes, thy youth, both contain'd the text
And the contents; ah, that thy grey-ripe yeeres
Had made of all, *Caesarean* Commentares, 290
(More then can now be thogt) in fact t'enroule;
And make blacke Faction blush away her soule.

Simil.   That, as a Temple, built when Pietie
Did to diuine ends offer specially,
What men enioy'd; that wondrous state exprest, 295
Strange Art, strange cost; yet who had interest
In all the frame of it; and saw those dayes,
Admir'd but little; and as little praise *v*
Gaue to the goodly Fabricke: but when men,
That liue whole Ages after, view it, then, 300
They gaze, and wonder; and the longer time
It stands, the more it glorifies his prime;
Growes fresh in honor, and the age doth shame
That in such Monuments neglect such fame;
So had thy sacred Frame beene rais'd to height, 305
Forme, fulnesse, ornament: the more the light
Had giuen it view, the more had Men admir'd;
And tho men now are scarce to warmnesse fir'd
With loue of thee; but rather colde and dead
To all sense of the grace they forfeited 310

In thy neglect, and losse; yet after-ages
Would be inflam'd, and put on holy rages
With thy inspiring vertues; cursing those
Whose breaths dare blast thus, in the bud, the Rose.
315 But thou (woe's me) art blown vp before blowne,
And as the ruines of some famous Towne,
Show here a Temple stood; a Pallace, here;
A Cytadell, an Amphitheater;
Of which (ahlas) some broken Arches, still
320 (Pillars, or Columns rac't; which Art did fill
[C₄ᴿ] With all her riches and Diuinitie)
Retaine their great, and worthy memory:
So of our Princes state, I nought rehearse
But show his ruines, bleeding in my verse.
325 What poison'd Ast'risme, may his death accuse?
Tell thy astonisht Prophet (deathles Muse)
And make my starres therein, the more aduerse,
The more aduance, with sacred rage my Verse,
And so adorne my dearest Fautors Herse,
330 That all the wits prophane, of these bold times
May feare to spend the spawne of their rancke rymes
On any touch of him, that shold be sung
To eares diuine, and aske an Angels tongue.
With this it thundred; and a lightning show'd
335 Where she sate writing in a sable cloud;
A Penne so hard and sharpe exprest her plight,
It bit through Flint; and did in Diamant write;
Her words, she sung, and laid out such a brest,
As melted Heauen, and vext the very blest.
340 In which she cal'd all worlds to her complaints,
And how our losse grew, thus with teares shee paints:
Hear earth & heauen (& you that haue no eares)
Hell, and the hearts of tyrants, heare my teares:
v Thus Brittaine *Henry* tooke his timelesse end;
345 When his great Father did so far transcend
All other Kings; and that he had a Sonne
In all his Fathers gifts, so farre begunne,
As added to *Fames* Pynions, double wings;
And (as braue riuers, broken from their springs,
350 The further off, grow greater, and disdaine
To spread a narrower current then the Maine)
Had drawne in all deserts such ample Spheares,
As Hope yet neuer turn'd about his yeeres.
All other Princes with his parts comparing;
355 Like all Heauens pettie Luminaries faring,
To radiant *Lucifer* (the dayes first borne)

*Musae la-
chrimae.* The
cause and
manner of the
Princes
death.

Rhamnusia
(Goddesse of
reuenge, and
taken for
Fortune) in
enuy of our
Prince, excit-
ed *Feuer*
against him.

It hurld a fire red as a threatning Morne
On fiery *Rhamnusias* sere, and sulphurous spight,
Who turn'd the sterne orbs of her ghastly sight,
About each corner of her vaste Command,   360
And (in the turning of her bloudy hand)
Sought how to ruine endlessly our Hope,
And set to all mishap all entries ope.
And see how ready meanes to mischiefe are;

The *Feuer*
the Prince
died on (by
Prosopopeia)
described by
her effects &
circum-
stances.

She saw, fast by, the bloud-affecting *Feuer*,   365
(Euen when th'Autumnal-starre began t'expire)
Gathering in vapours thinne, Ethereall fire:
Of which, her venomde finger did jmpart   D$_{(1)}$R
To our braue Princes fount of heat, the heart;
A praeternaturall heat; which through the vaines   370
And Arteries, by th'blood and spirits meanes
Diffus'd about the body, and jnflam'd,
Begat a Feuor to be neuer nam'd.
And now this loather of the louely Light,
(Begot of *Erebus*, and vglie Night)   375
Mounted in hast, her new, and noysefull Carre,

The Fever
the Prince
dyed off, is
observ'd by
our Moderne
Phisitions to
bee begun in
Hungarie.

Whose wheeles had beam-spokes from th'Hungarian star;
And all the other frame, and freight; from thence
Deriu'd their rude and ruthlesse jnfluence.
Vp to her left side, lept jnfernall Death   380
His head hid in a cloud of sensuall breath;
By her sat furious *Anguish, Pale Despight;*
Murmure, and *Sorrow,* and possest *Affright;*
Yellow Corruption, Marow-eating Care;
Languor, chill Trembling, fits Irregulare;   385
Inconstant Collor, *feeble voyc't Complaint;*
Relentles Rigor, and *Confusion* faint;

Out of the
property of
the Hare that
never shuts
her eyes
sleeping.

Frantick Distemper; & Hare-eyd vnrest;
And short-breath'd *Thirst,* with th'euer-burning breast;
A wreath of Adders bound her trenched Browes,   390
Where *Torment* Ambusht lay with all her throws.
Marmarian Lyons, frindg'd with flaming *Manes,*   v

*Marmaricae
Leones, of
Marmarica* a
Region in *Af-
frica* where

Drew this grym furie, and her brood of *Banes,*
Their hearts of glowing *Coles,* murmurd, & ror'd,
To beare her crook't yokes, and her *Banes* abhord,   395
To their deare *Prince,* that bore them in his *Armes,*

the fiercest Lyons are bred; with which Feuer is supposd to bee drawn, for their excesse of heat
& violence, part of the effects of this Feuer. The properties of the Feuer in these effects.

And should not suffer, for his *Good,* their *Harmes;*
Then from Hels burning whirlepit vp she hallde,

391 *Torment* italicized.

The horrid *Monster* fierce *Echidna* calde;
400 That from her *Stigian Iawes*, doth vomit ever,
Quitture, and *Venome*, yet is empty neuer:
Then burnt her bloodshot eyes, her *Temples* yet
Were cold as Ice, her *Necke* all drownd in swet:
Palenes spred all her breast, her lifes heat stung:
405 The Minds *Interpreter*, her scorched tongue,
Flow'd with blew poison: from her yawning *Mouth*
Rhumes fell like spouts fild from the stormy *South:*
Which being corrupt, the hewe of *Saffron* tooke;
A feruent Vapor, all her body shooke:
410 From whence, her *Vexed Spirits*, a noysome smell,
Expyr'd in fumes that lookt as blacke as *Hell.*
A ceaseles Torrent did her *Nosthrils* steepe,
Her witherd *Entrailes* tooke no rest, *No sleepe:*
Her swoln throte ratl'd, warmd with lifes last spark
415 And in her salt jawes, painfull Coughs did barke:
D₂ᴿ Her teeth were staind with Rust, her sluttish hand
Shee held out reeeking like a *New-quench-Brand:*
Arm'd with crook'd *Tallons* like the horned *Moone,*
All *Cheere*, all *Ease*, all *Hope* with her was gone:
420 In her left hand a quenchles fire did glow,
And in her *Right Palme* freez'd *Sithonian* Snow:
The ancient *Romanes* did a *Temple* build
To her, as whome a Deitie they held:
So hyd, and farre from cure of *Man* shee flyes,
425 In whose *Lifes Power* she mates the Deities.
When fell *Rhamnusia* saw this Monster nere,
(Her steele *Heart* sharpning) thus she spake to her:
Seest thou this Prince (great *Maid* & seed of *Night*)
Whose brows cast beams about them, like the *Light:*
430 Who ioyes securely in all present *State,*
Nor dreams what *Fortune* is, or future *Fate:*
At whome, with fingers, and with fixed eyes
All Kingdomes *Point*, and *Looke*, and *Sacrifice:*
Could be content to giue him: *Temples* rayse
435 To his *Expectance*, and *Vnbounded Praise:*
His *Now-ripe Spirits*, and *Valor* doth despise,
Sicknesse, and *Sword*, that giue our *Godheads* Prise:
His worth contracts the worlds, in his sole *Hope,*
Religion, Vertue, Conquest haue no scope:
v 440 But his Indowments; At him, at him, flie;
More swift, and timelesse, more the Deitie;
His Sommer, Winter with the jellid flakes;
His pure Life, poyson, sting out with thy Snakes;
This is a worke will Fame thy Maidenhead:

Rhamnusi-
as excitation
of feuer.

Rham:
durst no
longer indure
her, beeing
stirred into
furie.

With this, her speach and she together fledde;   445
Nor durst she more endure her dreadfull eyes;
Who stung with goads, her roaring Lyons thyes;
And brandisht, round about, her Snak-curld head
With her left hand; the Torch it managed.

And now Heavens Smith, kindl'd his Forge & blew;   450
And throgh the round Pole, thick the sparkls flew

The starry
Euening de-
scrib'd by

When great Prince *Henrie*, the delight of fame;

Vulcans setting to worke at that time. The Night being ever chiefely consecrate to the Works
of the Gods, and out of this Deities fires, the Starres are suppos'd to flye; as sparkles of them.

Darkn'd the Pallace, of his Fathers Name;
And hid his white lyms, in his downie Bed;
Then Heaven wept falling Stars that summoned   455
(With soft, and silent Motion) sleepe to breath
On his bright Temples, th'Ominous forme of death;
Which now the cruel Goddes did permit,
That she might enter so, her Mayden fit.

When the good Angell, his kind Guardian,   460
Her wither'd foot, saw neare this spring of Man;
He shrik't and said; what, what are thy rude ends;

The good
Angell of the
Prince to the
Fever, as shee
approacht.

Cannot, in him alone, all vertues friends,
(Melted into his all-vpholding Neru's;   D₂ᴿ
For whose Assistance, euery Deity serues)   465
Mooue thee to proue thy Godhead, blessing him
With long long life, whose light extinckt, wil dim,
All heavenly graces? all this, moou'd her nought;
But on, & in his, all our rujnes wrought.

She toucht the Thresholds, and the thresholds shooke;   470
The dore-posts, *Palenes* pierst with her faint look:
The dores brake open, and the fatall Bed
Rudely sh'aproacht, & thus her fell mouth said;
Henrie, why tak'st thou thus thy rest secure?

Feuer to
the prince;
who is

Nought doubting what Fortune & fates assure;   475
Thou neuer yet felt'st my red right hands maims,
That I to thee, and fate to me proclaimes;

thought by a
friend of mine to speake too mildly; not being *satis compos mentis Portice*, in this. Her counsell
or perswasion, shewing onlie how the Prince was perswaded & resolu'd in his deadlyest suf-
ferance of her which shee is made to speake in spight of her selfe, since he at her worst was so
sacredly resolute.

Thy fate stands jdle; spinns no more thy thread;
Die thou must (great Prince) sigh not; beare thy head
In all things free, even with necessity.   480

450 n chiefely] chiefesly
475 n thought] thougght   477 to thee] co thee

If sweet it be to liue; tis sweet to dye:
This said shee shooke at him her Torche, and cast
A fire in him, that all his breast embrac't,
Then darting through his heart a deadly cold,
485 And as much venome as his vaines could hold.
Death, Death, O Death, jnserting, thrusting in,
Shut his faire eyes, and op't our vglie sinne.
v This scene resolu'd on, by her selfe and fate;
Was there a sight so pale, and desperate,
490 Euer before seene, in a thrust-through State?
The poore *Verginian*, miserable sayle,
A long-long-Night-turnd-Day, that liu'd in Hell
Neuer so portrayd, where the Billowes stroue
(Blackt like so many Devils) which should proue
495 The damned Victor; all their furies heighting;
Their Drum, the thunder; & their Colours lightning,
Both souldiers in the battel; one contending
To drown the waues in Noyse; the other spending
His Hel-hot sulphurous flames to drink them dry:
500 When heaven was lost, when not a teare-wrackt eye
Could tell in all that dead time, if they were,
Sincking or sayling; till a quickning cleere
Gaue light to saue them by the ruth of Rocks
At the *Bermudas;* where the tearing shocks
505 And all the miseries before, more felt
Then here halfe told; All, All this did not melt
Those desperate few, still dying more in teares,
Then this Death, all men, to the Marrow weares:
All that are Men; the rest, those drudging Beasts,
510 That onely beare of Men, the Coates, and Crests;
And for their Slaue, sick, that can earne them pence,
[D₄ʳ] More mourne (O Monsters) then for such a Prince;
Whose soules do ebbe & flow still with their gain,
Whom nothing moues but pelf, & their own pain;
515 Let such (great Heauen) be onely borne to beare,
All that can follow this meere Massacre.
　　Lost is our poore Prince; all his sad jndurers;
The busie Art of those that should be Curers;
The sacred vowes made by the zealous King,
520 His God-like Syre; his often visiting;
Nor thy graue prayers and presence (holy Man)
This Realms thrice Reverend Metropolitan,
That was the worthy Father to his soule:
Th'jnsulting Feuer could one fit controule.

488 scene] seene　　　499 to] the　　　522 Realms] Realme

Description of the tempest that cast Sir Th. Gates on the Bermudas, & the state of his Ship and Men, to this Kingdomes Plight applyd in the Princes death.

The Archbishop of Canterbury passing pyous in care of the Prince.

S. *Ed: Phil-*
lips Master of
the Rols and
the Princes
Chancelor, a
chiefe sor-
rower for him.

Nor let me here forget on farre, and neare;   525
And in his lifes loue, Passing deepe and deare;
That doth his sacred *Memorie* adore,
Virtues true favtor his graue *Chancellor,*
Whose worth in all workes should a *Place* enioie,
Where his fit *Fame* her *Trumpet* shall jmploie,   530
Whose *Cares,* and *Prayers,* were euer vsde to ease
His feu'rous Warre, & send him healthfull peace.
Yet sicke our *Prince* is still; who though the steps
Of bitter *Death,* he saw bring in by heaps
Clouds to his *Luster,* and poore rest of light;   535

The prince
heroical his
bearing his
sicknes at the
Kings com-
ming to see
him, carefull
not to dis-
comfort him.

And felt his last Day suffering lasting Night;   *v*
His true-bred-braue soule, shrunck yet at no part,
Downe kept he all sighs, with his powers al-Hart;
Cler'd euen his dying browes: and (in an Eye
Manly dissembling) hid his Misery: 540
And all to spare the Royall heat so spent
In his sad Father, fearefull of th'event.
       And now did *Phoebus* with his Twelfth Lampe show
The world his haples light: and in his Brow

The Twelfth
Day after his
beginning to
bee sicke, his
sicknes was
held   incura-
ble.

A Torch of Pitch stuck, lighting halfe t'half skies,   545
When lifes last error prest the broken eyes
Of this heart-breaking Prince; his forc't look fled;
Fled was all Colour from his cheekes; yet fed
His spirit, his sight: with dying now, he cast
On his kind King, and Father: on whome, fast   550
He fixt his fading beames: and with his view
A little did their empty Orbs renew:
His Mind saw him, come from the deeps of Death,

The prince
dying to the
King.

To whome he said, O Author of my Breath:
Soule to my life, and essence to my Soule,   555
Why grieue you so, that should al griefe controule?
Death's sweet to me, that you are stil lifes creature,
I now haue finisht the great worke of Nature.
I see you pay a perfect Fathers debt
And in a feastfull Peace your Empire kept;   560 E(1)R
If your true Sonnes last words haue any right
In your most righteous Bosome, doe not fright
Your hearkning kingdoms to your cariage now;

The sor-
rowes and be-
mones of the
King Queene,
Prince and
most Princely
Sister, for the
Princes
death.

All yours, in mee, I here resigne to you,
My youth (J pray to God with my last powres)   565
Substract from me may adde to you and yours.
       Thus vanisht he, this swift, thus instantly;
Ah now I see, euen heauenly powres must dye.
       Now shift the *King* and *Queene* from court to court
But no way can shift off their cares resort,   570

That which we hate the more we flie, pursues,
That which we loue, the more we seek, eschewes:
Now weepes his Princely *Brother;* Now alas
His Cynthian *Sister,* (our sole earthly Grace)
575 Like *Hebes* fount still ouerflowes her bounds,
And in her cold lips, stick astonisht sounds,
Sh'oppresseth her sweet kinde; In her soft brest
Care can no vent finde, it is so comprest.
    And see how the Promethean Liuer growes
580 As vulture Griefe deuoures it: see fresh showes
Reuiue woes sence, and multiply her soule;
And worthely; for who would teares controle
On such a springing ground? Tis dearely fit,
To pay all tribute, Thought can poure on it:
v 585 For why were Funerals first vs'd but for these,
Presag'd and cast in their Natiuities?
The streames were checkt a while: so Torrents staid
Enrage the more; but are (left free) allaid.
    Now our grim waues march altogether; Now
590 Our blacke seas runne so high, they ouerflow
The clouds they nourish; now the gloomy herse
Puts on the Sunne: Reuiue, reuiue (dead verse)
Death hath slain death; there ther the person lies
Whose death should buy out all mortalities.
595   But let the world be now a heape of death,
Lifes ioy lyes dead in him, and challengeth
No lesse a reason: If all motion stoode
Benumb'd and stupefied, with his frozen blood;
And like a Tombe-stone, fixt, lay all the seas;
600 There were fit pillers for our Hercules
To bound the world with: Men had better dye
Then out-liue free times; slaues to Policie.
    On on sad Traine, as from a crannid rocke
Bee-swarmes rob'd of their honey, ceasles flock.
605 Mourne, mourne, dissected now his cold lims lie,
Ah, knit so late with flame, and Maiestie.
Where's now his gracious smile, his sparkling eie
His Iudgement, Valour, Magnanimitie?
O God, what doth not one short hour snatch vp
E_b^R 610 Of all mans glosse? still ouer-flowes the cup
Of his burst cares; put with no nerues together,
And lighter, then the shadow of a feather.
    On: make earth pomp as frequent as ye can,
'Twill still leaue black, the fairest flower of man;
615 Yee well may lay all cost on miserie,

The funer-
all described.

592 verse] vierse

Tis all can boast, the proud'st humanitie.
   If yong *Marcellus* had to grace his fall,
Sixe hundred Herses at his Funerall;
Sylla sixe thousand, let Prince *Henry* haue
Sixe Millions bring him to his greedy graue.   620
And now the States of earth, thus mourn below;
Behold in Heauen, *Loue* with his broken Bow,
His quiuer downwards turn'd, his brands put out
Hanging his wings; with sighes all black about.
   Nor lesse, our losse, his Mothers heart infests,   625
Her melting palmes, beating her snowy brests;
As much confus'd, as when the Calidon Bore
The thigh of her diuine *Adonis* tore:
Her vowes all vaine, resolu'd to blesse his yeeres
With Issue Royall, and exempt from freres;   630
Who now dyed fruitlesse; and preuented then
The blest of women, of the best of men.
   Mourne all ye Arts, ye are not of the earth;
Fall, fall with him; rise with his second birth.
Lastly, with gifts enrich the sable Phane,   635 *v*
And odorous lights eternally maintaine;
Sing Priests, O sing now, his eternall rest,
His lights eternall; and his soules free brest
As ioyes eternall; so of those the best;
And this short verse be on his Tomb imprest.   640

EPITAPHIVM.

So flits, ahlas, an euerlasting Riuer,
As our losse in him, past, will last for euer.
The golden Age, Star-like, shot through our Skye;
Aim'd at his pompe renew'd, and stucke in's eye.
And (like the sacred knot, together put)
Since no man could dissolue him, he was cut.

Aliud EPITAPH.

Whom all the vast frame of the fixed Earth
Shrunk vnder; now, a weake Herse stands beneath;
His Fate, he past in fact; in hope, his Birth;
His youth, in good life; and in spirit, his death.

Aliud EPITAPH.

Blest be his great Begetter; blest the Wombe
That gaue him birth, though much too neare his Tombe.
In them was hee, and they in him were blest:
What their most gracious powers gaue him, was his least.
His Person grac't the Earth; and of the Skies,
His blessed Spirit, the praise is, and the prise.

FINIS.

EVGENIA.

TO THE MOST
WORTHY, AND RE-
LIGIOVSLY-NOBLE, Fran-
cis, Lord Russell, Baron
of Thornehaugh, &c.

BECAUSE (my most worthy Lord) worthiest Men, and
the due estimations of their worthinesse; were seldome,
or neuer contemporaries; The world hauing alwaies an Epi-
methean, and after wit, for the fit respect of all lasting good-
nesse; As a little excitement to their late considerations; I
haue endeuord to set these weake watches, by the Memories
of your most worthy Lord and Father; Wherein, whatsoeuer
is presently defectiue; The Anniuersaries that (for as many
yeares as God shall please to giue me life and facultie) I con-
stantly resolue to performe to his Noblest Name and Vertues;
shall, I hope be furnisht with supplies, amendfull, and accept-
able. And if the preseru'd Memories of good men, haue beene
euer good meanes to informe good men; These Paper me-
morials that haue euer out-lasted, Brasse, and Marble; And
worne out all the barbarous rages, both of sword and fire;
Neede not, appeare to the world so superfluous and vaine as
they seeme: Nor present men with such irksome obiects as
most vulgarly they doe. Howsoeuer, nothing (God willing)
shall discourage my resolution, to what (with his assistance)
I haue aduisedly vowed; Religious contemplation being the
whole scopes, and setters vp of my poore lifes rest; what better
retreat can I make from the Communes of the world; then
to the most due memories of his rare Pieties. In the meane
space, let me beseech your best Lo: that for whatsoeuer hath
now failed of the Honor I intended; My seruiceable and in-
fallible loue may stand accepted suretie, for all worthy supple-
ment; which submitting thrise humbly to your most in-
genuous and iudicious disposition;

I euer abide

The most vnfained vowd Tributorie to
your good LL. vertues, merits,
and familie.

Geo. Chapman.

EVGENIA.

Or

True Nobilities Trance, for death

of the most religiously noble William
Lord Russell, &c.

Inductio.

Eugenia or true Noblesse.	EVGENIA, seeing true Noblesse of no price,
	Nought noble now, but seruile *Auarice*,
	Lothing the basenes, high states euen professe,
	And loded with an ominous heauinesse:
	She flew for comfort to her sister *Fame;* 5
	Of whose most auncient house, the brasen frame
	In middst of all the vniuerse doth shine,
The house of Fame.	Twixt Earth, the Seas, and all those tracts diuine,
	That are the Confines of the triple world;
	Through whose still open gates are ceaselesse hurl'd, 10
	The sounds of all things, breaking aire in earth;
	Where all mens acts are seene, each death, and birth.
	Eugenia, here arriu'd; her sister gaue
	All entertainement she could wish to haue;
	Through all her pallace led her, hand in hand: 15
	Shew'd her chiefe roomes to her, and bad commaund
	The best of those chiefe, and would haue her chuse:
	Ech chiefe, had diuers, fit for different vse,
	All with inscriptions of diuine deuise *v*
	In euery chambers curious frontespice. 20
	Besides the names of euery famely,
	Enobled for effects of Pietie.
	Vertue and valour; none that purchase't name,
	By any base course toucht at t'house of *Fame;*
	Nor those that toucht there, stai'd there, if they lost 25
	The worth first in them, though they kept their bost:
	Such vanish like the seas inflated waues,
	Ech chase out other, and their fome's their graues.
	Amongst the solid then, that there indur'd;
	Eugenia (euen by subtile fate alur'd) 30
	Chus'd an inscription, that did highly please
The russe-lides registred in the house of Fame.	Seeing in fine gould grauen, the *Russelides:*
	Fame prais'd her choice, and said, the name was giuen
	By sacred purpose and presage of heauen,
	Expressing in the birth, th'Antiquitie 35
	Of that most virtue season'd Famelie,

The word importing an effect of age,
And long liu'd Labor; prouing the presage,
That foresaw actions, which should *Labors* be,
40 Wrinckl'd with time, and aged industrie.
She here repos'd, and from the base world gone,
To cheere her earthly desolation,
The Heraulds, and the Registers of fame,
Of life and death, and all things worth the name,
45 (Th'ingenuous *Muses*) follow'd, and with them
The cheerefull *Graces:* and of each extreame,
The parting vertues: of all which, not one
Would stay, when she, that grac't them all was gone.
Religion flew before, for she being ground
50 And roote to all acts, noble and renown'd,
B₂ᴿ Their vaines bleede neuer, but hers, first haue vent,
Shee's their plaine forme, and they her ornament.
All these together now in Fames old house,
Which (though of brasse) is yet most ruinouse,
55 They saw the sun looke pale, and cast through aire,
Discoullor'd beames; nor could he paint so faire,
Heauens bow in dewie vapors, but he left
The greater part vnform'd; the circle cleft,
And like a buls necke shortned; no hews seene,
60 But onely one, and that was watrish greene:
His heate was chok't vp, as in ouens comprest
Halfe stifeling men; heauens drooping face was drest
In gloomy thunderstrocks: earth, seas, arrai'd
In all presage of storme: The Bittours plaid
65 And met in flocks; the Herons set clamours gone,
That ratteled vp aires triple Region.
The Cormorants to drie land did addresse,
And cried away, all foules that vs'd the seas.
The wanton Swallows Iirckt the standing springs
70 Met in dull lakes; and flew so close, their wings
Shau'd the top waters: Frogs crokt; the Swart crow
Measur'd the sea-sands, with pace passing slow,
And often souc't her ominous heat of blood
Quite ouer head and shoulders in the flood,
75 Still scoulding at the Raines so slow accesse:
The trumpet throated, the *Naupliades*,
Their clangers threw about, and summond vp
All cloudes to crowne imperious tempests cup:
The erring *Dolphin* puft the fomie maine
80 Hither and thither, and did vpwards raine:

ρυσσαλεος
Signifies rugo-
sus.

*Tempesta-
tis Praesagia.*

The water
gal de-
scribed.

Beasts,
Foules &
Fish presag-
ing Tempests.
Bittours.
Herons. Cor-
morands.
Swallowes.
Frogs.
Crowes.

Cranes
cald the
Naupliades of
Nauplius
King of
Euboeai
turnd to a
Crane.

The Dol-
phin.

63 thunderstrocks] thunderstocks   63 n Cormorands.]   Cormorand
71 Swart] Fwart   76 n Euboeai] Euborai   turnd to a crane] turnc
to Graue   77 clangers] claugers

The Rauen.

The Rauen sat belching out his funerall din,
Venting his voice, with sucking of it in.

The Ant.

The patient of all labours, the poore Ant   *v*
Her egges to caues brought: Molehils proofe did want
To keepe such teares out, as heau'n now would weepe.   85

The Can-
ker-worme.
The Crab.

The hundred-footed Canker-wormes did creepe
Thicke on the wet wals. The slow Crab did take
Pibbles into her mouth, and ballas make
Of grauell, for her stay, against the Gales,

Whales.

Close clinging to the shore. Sea-Giant whales   90
The watrie mountaines darted at the skie.

The Flie.

And (no lesse ominous) the petulant Flie
Bit bitterly for blood, as then most sweete.

The Dog.

The louing Dog dig'd earth vp with his feete,

The Asse.

The Asse (as weather wise) confirm'd these feares,   95
And neuer left shaking his flaggie eares.

The Bee.

Th'ingenious Bee wrought euer neere her hiue.
The Cloddie Ashes, kept coales long aliue,
And Dead Coales quickn'd; both transparent cleere:

*Pluma
nastans.*
Leaues.
Thistle
Downe.
Lambes.

The Riuers crownd with Swimming feathers were.   100
The Trees greene fleeces flew about the aire
And Aged thistles lost their downie haire,
Cattaile would run from out their sheds vndriuen,
To th'ample pastures: Lambes were sprightly giuen,
And all in iumpes about the short leas borne: 105

Rams.

Rammes fiercely butted, locking horne in horne.
The storme now neere: those cattell that abroade
Vndriuen ranne from their shelter; vndriuen, trod

The Oxe.

Homewards as fast: the large bond Oxen lookt
Oft on the broad Heauen, and the soft aire suckt,   110
Smelling it in; their reeking nostrils still
Sucking the cleere dew from the Daffadill:
Bow'd to their sides their broad heads, and their haire
Lickt smooth at all parts; lou'd their night tide laire:
And late in night, did bellow from the stall,   115 B₈ᴿ
As thence the tempest would his blasts exhale.

The Swine.

The Swine, her neuer made bed now did plie
And with her Snowt strow'd euery way her stie,

The Wolfe.

The wolfe hould in her den; Th'insatiate beast,
Now fearing no man, met him brest to brest,   120
And like a murtherous begger, him allur'd;
Haunting the home-groues husbandmen manur'd.

Falling
Starres.
Gloworms.

Then night her circle closd; and shut in day,
Her siluer spangles shedding euery way
And earths poore starres (the Glowormes) lay abroad   125

110 broad] btoad   114 night tide] rightside

As thicke as Heau'ns; that now no twinckle showd,
Sodainstly plucking in their guilty heads.
And forth the Windes brake, from their brasen beds
That strooke the mountaines so, they cried quite out.
130 The Thunder chid; the lightning leapt about;
And cloudes so gusht, as *Iris* nere were showne
But in fresh deluge, Heau'n it selfe came downe:
Yet all this was not, halfe due ominous state
To lead so great and consequent a fate,
135 As tooke from vs, this rare religious Lord;
Since his example, euen th'Almighty word
Strength'end with men; now Faith so faint is growne,
Cold, and feeles feuers of confusion:
And if we note that true Religion
140 Crownes all our worth; without which we haue none;
And that her truth is in so few exprest
By life that answers, her true loue profest,
That verball pleadings onely, make her thought
A word, no Thing; example that is wrought
145 Out of her being beleeu'd, and proues to be
Both her, and her diuine sincerity.
  v Who can enough grace? or see magnified
His fame in whom it liu'd, who in it di'd?
Forth then: this tempest past: *Eugenia* bled
150 As it had raign'd blood, and so seconded,
The watry Cataracts, that feare on feare
Shooke the poor Guests of *Fame:* and then newes were
Of this Lords death: At which all gaue a shricke
That would haue drownd the tempest: it did strike
155 *Eugenia* so: She fell into a traunce
Whose deepe deiection, none could readuance:
Fame in her eare, did such a blast inspire,
Of her loues liuing vertues, as got fire
In frosen Death, and he came stalking in,
160 Proclaiming lowd, the victorie of sinne.
The virtues spake, the cheerefull muses sung,
The graces held her eies ope, yet her tongue
Denied her function: till at last, their crie
Cal'd downe, Religion, to her extasie,
165 Who halfe intraunc't her selfe was; all the part   Religion
She had of humaines pinde euen to her heart: described.
And made her forme, as if transformd she were,
Into a leane, and lisping Grashopper:
As small and faintly spake she; her strength's losse,
170 Made her goe lame, and leaning on the crosse,
Stooping, and crooked, and her ioints did cracke,

As all the weight of earth were on her backe:
Her lookes were like the pictures that are made,
To th'optike reason; one way like a shade,
Another monster like, and euery way   175
To passers by, and such as made no stay,
To view her in a right line, face to face,
She seem'd a serious trifle; all her grace,
Show'd in her fixt inspection; and then   B₄ᴿ
She was the onely grace of dames and men: 180
All hid in cobwebbs came she forth, like these
Poore country churches, chappels cald of ease
For so of worldly ends, men zealous were.
None (hundred handed) would lend one to her:
Nor had they one, to doe so good a deede: 185
None will doe good, but where there is no neede.
All full of spiders was her homespun weede,
Where soules like flies hung, of which, some would striue
To breake the net, their bodies yet aliue,
Some (all their bodies eate) the spiders thighes   190
Left hanging like the onely wings of flies.
She cheerd *Eugenia*, and would haue her speake,
But she with her late blood lost, was so weake,
She could not moue a sound, beleeuing then,
That she no more should liue in Noblemen.   195
Religion said she err'd, where none would come,
And that griefe made her misse her way at home,
He had a Sonne, so fitting for his place
As left not through it all, the slendrest space:
One that in pietie, and all parts of kinde   200
His fathers person imag'd, and his minde,
Op't his death's wound, powr'd fresh iuice through ech vaine,
Refin'd his age, and made him liue againe.
This since Religion whisper'd in her eare,
(Though with her faint voice) yet it did more cheere   205
Her daunted powers, then that shrill blast of Fame,
With which Death wak't, & quicke amongst them came.
Then her soules motion, her soft phantasie,
(That sence in act put, doth create) did plie
Her spirits so, she felt her speeches powre   210
A little retriu'd; euen that night and houre   v
He died on   She lost her loue: that night, that doth forerun
a Munday   The labouring weeke in rest, and of the Moone
night.   Retaines her Surname; when (though still halfe dead)
Her Noblesse forc't her griefe to let her head   215
Rise from her Pillow, and for that night giue

201 imag'd] manag'd. Shepherd's emendation.   211 that] thar

Way to her speech, in which she much did striue
To iustifie the greatnes of her griefe
Euen to her traunce, that from her tooke her life.

VIGILIA PRIMA.

220 And worthely; for who can liue and see
A death so worth life? t'is impiety
Not to pay griefe, as much to vertue gone
As comfort to her deare fruition:
Those Pores and Passes, that our pleasures lend,
225 Let in our miseries, euen in natures end;
Nay where she takes in ioie, at entries few
Griefe enters all parts; euen the places due
By health to pleasure: euery slendrest griefe
From all our greatest ioies; takes th'edge and life.
230 Must we to pleasures vow deuotions euer?
Those indigent repletions, that will neuer,
Fill though they burst? and then least satiate are
When Surfet serues in their idolatrous Fare?
Griefes, *Sighes*, and Teares, and Eiulations to,
235 Consumptions, Traunces; all the bane of woe
We should susteine; since loue of euery good
In one all goodnesse; buies it with his blood,
And you, Religion, whom the world hath pin'd
To whose deiections, Spiders are more kinde
C(1)R 240 Then Wolfe like Humanes; Those fain'd peruerse *Bees*
That poisons suck from your sincerities;
And clothe you only but to make them nests
And nets to catch them liuings; what now rests?
For your recomfort, no man liuing now
245 Will any true care take of me or you.
How then will this poore remnant of your powres
This cut vp quick *Anatomie* of yours,
This *Ghost* and shadow of you be preseru'd?
Good life, that only feedes you, is so steru'd,
250 That you must perish; T'is not Noble now
To be religious; T'is for men of vow
Giuen, and (indeede) cast out from this worlds ship
To Whales and Monsters of earth's couetous deepe.
They that get liuings by Religion,
255 Must be religious; And who liues vpon
Any demeanes, that eates not out their heart?
If liuing be the end of lifes desert;
Life future is a dreame; but of a thought;
A Spiders web, that's out of nothing wrought:

Eugenia.

A paire of *Tarriers* to set Fooles aworke,   260
And lighter then the shadow of a corke:
And then are all things nothing to a man
Of any reason; Life is not a spanne;
All's fiction; all haue writ, beleeu'd, susteyn'd;
Earth and great Heau'ne made, for a Good mere fayn'd.   265
Ambitious Bubbles, holding nought within
But only Gawdes, and properties for sin;
And doe by no necessitie contayne
Iudgement, and obiect; lifes ioy, ills payne;
Proportionable to our good or ill;   270
All is an *Animall*, that hath no will
To order all his parts, nor no respects;   v
But hath peculiar actions, and effects,
That from the whole doe no excitements take,
Nor his impulsion their prime motion make: 275
This 'gainst the common Notions Nature giues
Our rarest Artists vtter in their liues:
Of them, Great men hold, that must ignorant be;
Skils superficiall, fit Nobilitie.
By those graue *Magnets*, at the fountaines head   280
Our Countrie states (the crooked streames) are led
By them, the Rabble; and from hence doth rise
Their errours maze: Each sees with others eyes:
Euen Artists (borne with the traditionall streame,)
Others of their coate trust, as others them: 285
Not knowledge, but opinion, being their Guide;
Not truth, nor loue of Truth; but lust and pride;
Truth lothes to prostitute her selfe to men
That doe but court, and studie Name and gaine,
And if they doe not only, and past all,   290
Entirely loue her; Shee will neuer fall,
Within a kenning of the deepliest learn'd;
Nay, least of all, shee is by them discern'd;
For, they presuming on meere termes, tongues, fame,
Much reading (which are noblest breathes t'inflame   295
Her quenchles fire;) But shee being still in calme
And her lampe nourisht, with so rich a Balme,
As at the heartie will, loue; Thought takes fire,
That seeke her first, and last; all base desire
Of name, gold, honor, counted clay to her;   300
Yet nought the slower come; if men prefer
Her to the first place; and with such delight
And such a sacred rage of Appetite;
That sweetest sins to her, more bitter be,   C₂ᴿ

260 to] so   265 mere] more.   Shepherd's emendation.

305 Then *Rubarb*, or the drugs of *Thessalie:*
Without which Tests, to trie her perfect gold,
All tongues flie vp in fume. All such as hold
Their skils of those Lordes, haue to Truth no right;
But are with Tempests rauisht from her sight.

310 A rout of things they know, but know them ill;
Which Truthes loue, and Good-lifes want, argue still.
Wise men, and Iust they are, that only know
All duties that to Men and God we owe:
Such was at all parts our most Noble friend,

315 Both place, and practise from his Birth t'his end,
Renowming him, with all things fit to be
The Presidents of all Nobilitie.
His Birth and Noble breeding, who needes show?
Me thinks euen the *Antipodes* should know,

320 Noble, and Pietie passe, where nought hath past,
And as they pierst past all things, stick as fast.
How farre his worth they carried (when the arts
Had laid their ground-worke) into forreigne parts,
France, and infectious *Italie*, can tell;

325 Through which he yet made way; and neuer fell
(In *Antick* affectation of their guises,
Nor (for their owne ends) impious deuices,)
From the Religious Integritie
His Birth, and admiration did implie

330 In his vnchang'd powrs; But did arme the more
His solid vertues; and their sleights abhore.
    Cold *Rhenus*, and *Danubius* streames he past
Through *Hungarie*, and *Germanie* the vast;
In quest of action; and the discipline

335 Of brightly armes; In which, with grace diuine
 v His goodly Person shone; And valour strooke
Sparkles from steele, that fire at wonder tooke.
    In *Belgia*, The Nurce and Schoole of Warre,
Through Sieges, Battailes, he made circulare

340 His militarie skill; where, our great Queene
(That with her little Kingdome, curb'd the spleene
Of *Spaine*, and *France;* And with her mightie hand
Made euen that most diuided Kingdome stand,)
Gaue him her Empires pledge for his Command;

345 And, in her owne Dominions, a Crowne
Set on his Temples; in the high Renowne
Of that full Gouernement, his vertues swaide;
Which, wood-housde, wilde Rebellion obaide.
    Thus, as a Riuer, that the more his force

350 Runs from his fount, takes vertue of his course,

*Pessimum
est multarum
rerum peritia
acquisita
male, φρόνιμοι
καὶ, δίκαιοι,
&c. Plat. Al-
cib. 2.*

He was
Lord Gouer-
nour of
Vlyssing.

He was
three yeares
Lord Deputie
of Ireland.

And growes more great and strong still; Nor doth stay,
Till it mixe streames with his Great Sire, the Sea;
So, till he matcht his greatest Ancetor,
He neuer ceast to amplifie his store.
    His Fathers parts, all Fathers dues indu'd,   355
As he did, all Sonnes offices include
Of the good Earle of *Bedford*, the Sire gainde
The surname; and the Good, the Sonne maintaynde.
Heauen, in them Both, the *Graces* gifts emploide;
What they consum'd, encreast; What gaue, enioyd.   360
The vse; not the possession of things
Commends their worth, and their encreases springs,
And that vse must haue Influence from his ground
Religion; with which, all his Acts were crownd.
Nor could a man, distinguish twixt his deedes,   365
And saie; This Act, from Fortitude proceedes,
This from Humanitie; This from Continence.
But each, from all the vertues influence   C₃ᴿ
Had their composure; prouing the decree
The Stoiques made; and we may iustifie;   370

Quicquid agit, sapiens, omnibus virtutibus agit.
    Each action, that a wise man makes his fruit,
    He doth with all the vertues execute.
Some one, the ground-worke laying; All the rest
Flow in as fellowes, with their interest.
What man, not imitating him, can be   375
Noble, or pious, in the best degree?
Religion seasons all Nobilitie.
Take that euen from the Greatest; you shall see
How lanck he showes in his felicitie;

Faith, Hope, Charitie, the summe of Religion.
For his Incharitie, he winnes no loue: 380
For his Faiths want, to him none faithfull proue:
For his felt ill, he cannot hope for good,
But feare strikes euery shadow through his blood.
    What such men want, content with pieties shade,
With that, and her heart, was this Lord, all made.   385
In Noble being, and making good his place,
Stooping for height, to nothing that was base.
Nobles example haue, and Gentrie may
Affect no Nobles, met with, in that way.
Ignobles (if his worth he will apply,)   390
May, (though most base) outreach Nobilitie.
    Obserue then, after all his high'st command
How equall, and vnchangeable a hand
He bore in thought of it, with things most low, .

364 Acts] Arts. Shepherd's emendation.   366 saie] said   Act]
Art   390 apply] appay. Shepherd's emendation.

395 For that he might, to all example show:
He made not height his end, nor happinesse here,
But, as more high, more good he might appere,
(Height simply, holding no good, much lesse all)
He willingly from all his tops did fall,
v 400 And, for Retreat, a Personage made his home;
Where, (neare the Church) he nearer God, did come;
Each weeke day doing his deuotion
With some few Beads-folke; To whom, still was showne
His secret *Bedfords* hand; Nor would he stay
405 The Needie asking; but preuent their way
And goe to them, t'enquire, how they could liue,
And, to auoid, euen thanks, where he did giue;
He would their hardly-nourisht liues supply
With shew of lending; yet, (That industrie
410 Might not in them be lesned, to relieue
Their states themselues,) He would haue some one giue
His word for the repayment; which (sweet Lord)
He neuer tooke; nor askt a thankefull word.
And therein, truly imitated God,
415 Who giues vs Lawes to keepe; The Period
Of whose iniunction, points not at his good;
But, knowing, that when they are vnderstood,
Their vnderstanding, by obseruing prou'd,
Would make vs see; that in that Circle mou'd
420 Our taught felicitie; Nor can we ad
With all our obseruations; what may glad
His still at full state, in the best degree,
Other then this; That as Philosophie
Saies there is euermore proportion
425 Betwixt the knowing part, and what is knowne
So joynd, that both, are absolutely one;
So when we know God, in things here below,
And truly keepe th'abstracted good we know;
(God being all goodnesse) we with him combine,
430 And therein shew, the all in all, doth shine:
This briefly, for the life of my blest loue,
[C₄ᴿ] Which now combinde is, with the life aboue;
His death (to name which, I abhor to liue,)
O sister, doe you, with your trump achieue.
435   As Fame addrest to this; The morning came
And burn'd vp all things sacred, with her flame.
When now some Night-birds of the day began
To call, and crie, and gibber, Man to Man;

*Oportet esse
Analogiam in-
ter potentiam
cognoscentem,
& hoc quod
cognoscitur,
&c. Intellec-
tus, in ipsa in-
telligibilia
transit. Cul.
ex Arist.*

429 we] which. Shepherd's emendation   434 achieue] admire.   Shep-
herd's emendation.   438 gibber] gibbet

Swolne fordges puft abroad their windie Ire,
Aire, Earth, and water turnd, and all to Fire;   440
And in their strife for Chymicall euents
Made transmutation of the Elements.
They blew, and Hammers beat, and euery noise
Was emptying tumult, out of men, and boies.
Bursting the aire with it; and deafning *Th'Eare:*   445
The black fumes of whose breaths did all besmeare
And choake the *Muses*, and such rude Clouds reare,
As all the World, a Dyers furnace were.
Gainst which, Fames Guests, their dores & windows closde;
As their poore labours were in earth opposde.   450

Explicit Vigilia Prima.

VIGILIAE SECUNDAE.

Inductio,

Now to the Nestfull woods, the Broode of Flight
Had on their black wings brought, the zealous Night,
When Fames friends, op't the windowes they shut in,
To barre Daies worldly light; and Mens rude Din;
In Tumults raisd about their fierce affairs,   455 *v*
That deafen heauen to their distracted prairs,
With all the vertues; Graue Religion
That slept with them all day, to ope begun
Her Eares, and Red Eyes; hearing euery way
The clocks, and knells of Cities, and the Bay   460
Of Countrie Dogs, that mock mens daily Carck,
And after them, all night, at shadowes barke.
   Though all Fames brazen Gates, and windowes stoode
Ope day and night, yet had her tenderd broode
Close in their priuate chambers, their owne fashion,   465
Silence, and Night, doe best fit Contemplation.
And as Fame said of old, that peacefull night
The Gods chiefe day was, since their chiefe delight
In fixt calme stood; Themselues in quiet still,
Earths cares to pursue, to skale their high hill;   470

Men of true knowledge, vertue, and religion, (which are figured in the *Muses*, vertues, &c.) make their chiefe gaine, in prouiding for the second life; and therefore thriue not in this; so much as false and worldly Professors. Nor can those men therefore thriue so much in true knowledge, and pietie.

So these poor labourers for the second life
(Diuine powres imitating) all their strife

439 Ire] Ice   469 calme] callure. Shepherd's emendation.

Spend for hereafter, and thereafter thriue.
This vantage yet; These haue of men aliue,
475 (These liuing dead to this life,) That as they
Studying this world in chiefe, on this world prey
When they haue praid; more then these fed with prayrs;
So these that studie here, to be heauens heyrs,
(Vertue and skill pursuing, in chiefe end)
480 More thriftie therein are; and their oiles spend
More chearfully; and finde Truth more with ease;
For these are in the way: The couetous Prease
Of Truths Professors, (in by-waies perplext)
March like those marginall Notes that spoile the Text.
485 These thirsting Fames report of this Lords death,
The curious Dame, that weighs and locks vp breath,
D(1)R Formd in fit words (as God doth euen our thoughts
That nothing of good men, may come to noughts)
Addrest her to be ecchoe to his words
490 Which (though not many) yet may teach all Lords;

* * * * * * * * * * * * * *

And neither strange, nor eloquent, nor new,
Doctrine that toucheth soules, or saues, or kils,
A good man dying, vtters Oracles.
And now was Fame, aduanc't past sight vpon
A hill of brasse, that farre the sunne outshone;
Day, and night shining; neuer going downe:
495 Her browes encompast, with a triple crowne:
Each chac't with Iewels, vallewd past mens liues.
Her trumpet then she sounded, that reuiues
Men long since buried: to whose clanges sing
All the afflicted virtues, conquering
500 All their afflicters, her triumphe brauer bore
The arts (for armes) of all mens worth before;
Disparag'd worths, shew'd there, the perfect things;
And beggers worthy arts were blasd with kings:
Desert findes meanes to vtter: Fame to holde
505 Both arts, and words, most secret, and most olde:
Nor doe they euer their existence leaue
Nor any that their virtues loue, deceaue.
Fame hauing summond fit attention:
And all her guests into expectance blowne:
510 Like the morne's trumpe: when day is neere inflam'd:
She clapt her goulden wings, and thus proclaimd.

The Cock.

498 chac't] ac't. Shepherd: "Enchased".

VIGILIA SECVNDA.

Fames re-
port of the
Lord Russell
dying.

When by diuine presage, this god-like Lord
Felt health decline: and knew she gaue the word,   515
Through all his powrs; to make a guard, for death,   v
Frends helthfull (sleighting still what followeth)
Nobly perswaded (as themselues would be
Toucht with the like effects of maladie,)
That his conceipt of weakenesse was too strong.   520
He askt them, why they wisht him to prolong
His needefull resolution to die;
As if t'were fit to feare felicitie;
Or that he doubted it; And all the chere
The hearty Scriptures did inuite to, were   525
Serud vp in painted dishes; and to make
(Onely for fashion) sicke men, sit, and take,
And seeme to eate to; though but as their banes,
Onely to die accounted Christians.
Hungry, to heauens feast come, and cheerefully   530
Eate what you wish; Ile teach ye all to die:
If ye beleeue, expresse it in your liues

Who would
not did re-
sist, Nature
and necessi-
tie.
*Qui muta-
tur, idem non
est; si idem
non est, ne est
quidem. Pl.*

That best appeare in death; gainst whom who striues
Would, faithlesse, and most reasonlesse denie
All lawes of Nature, and Necessitie.   535
No fraile thing, simply is; No Flesh nor blood
Pertakes with Essence; All the flitting flood
Of natures mortall; Birth and death doe tosse
Vpwards and downewards, euer at a losse;
Humaine Births euer are, and neuer stay,   540
Still in mutation; we die euery day:
Ridiculous are we then, in one death flying,
That dead so often are; and euer dying.
Ye feare your owne shades; they are fooles that make
Deaths forme so ougelie, and remembrance take   545
Of their dissoluing by so foule a sight,
When death presents the faire of heauenly light.
The ghostly forme, that in this world we leaue.   D₂ᴿ
When death dissolues vs; wise men should conceiue
Showes well, what life is; farre from figuring death: 550
Am I this truncke? It is my painted sheath:
As braue young men, thinke they are, what they weare;
So these, encourage men, with what they feare.
    Make death an Angell, skaling, of a heauen

Death dis-
cribed by his
true effects.

And croune him with the Asterisme of seauen;   555
To show he is the death of deadly sinnes:
A rich spring make his Robe, since he begins
Our endlesse Summer: let his shoulders spring

Both the sweete Cupids, for his either wing,
560 Since loue, and ioy in death, to heauen vs bring:
Hang on the Iuorie Brawne of his right arme,
A bunch of goulden keis; his left a swarme
Of thriftie Bees, in token we haue done
The yeare, our lifes toile, and our fruites haue shone
565 In hoonnie of our good workes, labord here:
Before his flaming bosome, let him weare
A shining Christall; since through him we see
The louely forms of our felicitie.
His thighes make, both the heauen-supporting Poles,
570 Since he sustaines heauen, storing it, with soules.
His left hand, let a plenties horne extend:
His right, a booke to contemplate our end:
 This forme, conceaue death beares, since truely this
In his effects, informes vs, what he is.
575 Who, in life, flies not, to inheritance giuen?
And, why not then, in death, t'inherit heauen?
Wrastlers for games, know they shall neuer be,
(Till their strife end, and they haue victorie)
Cround with their garlands, nor receiue their game,
v 580 And in our heauens strife, know not we the same?
Why striue we; not being certaine to obtaine
If we doe conquer? and because we gaine
Conquest in faith, why faint we? since therein
We lose both strife, and conquest? who will winne
585 Must lose in this strife; in deaths easie lists
Who yelds, subdues, he's conquerd, that resists.
 Each morning, setting forth to your affaires,
These things commend ye, to our God in praiers:
Direct me, God, in all this daies expence
590 As thy necessitie of prouidence
Thinks fit for me: what euer way you leade
And point out for me; I will gladly tread;
So being, thy sonne, and pious; sticke, and goe
Compeld as slaue, and my impietie slow.
595 And how most wretchedly shall those that beare
Authority, and swimme in riches here,
(Resisting death for them) be forc't in feare
To goe with him; when all they can oppose,
They insolent, and impotently lose?
600 None of those men, that most spent oile and blood,
With studie for ioies fullest tast in good
In this life, euer could their longings fill,
Their reasons strayning through their bodies stil

592 tread] dread   599 They] The. Shepherd's emendation.

Cupid and Ioculous supporting them the true and heauenly Cupids; as the other are earthly.

Achellous horne.

His praier.

Watrish and troubl'd; as through clouds and mists;
And wrestler like, rusht euer on their lists;   605
Too streight; and choak't with prease to comprehend
The strugling contemplation of their end.
    He that with God did wrestle, all in night;
Figurd our strife with truth here, for his light;
Which seene, through death, being but a touch ith thigh   610
Blessing both vs and our posteritie,
Who would not wish death? touching feare to die   D₃ᴿ
For my estates disposure (whose cares lie
Heauie on some mens hearts) my sure hope is
My sonne will make, my disposition, his: 615
Acquiting me of any cause to feare.
And (sonne) what of my constant hopes you heare
Make spurs to proue; that what I hope, you are,
I shall leaue something worthy of your care:
Nor wast, nor labor the encrease too much,   620
Nor let your pleasure in their vse be such,
As at their most, their too much ioy may breede:
For you must suffer, the same naturall neede
Of parting from them, that you now beholde
Makes all my ioy in them, so deadly colde.   625
Let nothing seeme to you so full of merit,
As may inflame you with the greater spirit,
Nor no aduerse chance, stoope their height a haire,
But in the height and depth of ech affaire,
Be still the same, and hold your owne entire,   630
Like heauen, in cloudes, or finest gould, in fire.
To rise and fall, for water is, and winde:
A man, all Center is, all stay, all minde,
The bodie onely, made her instrument:
And to her ends, in all acts must consent,   635
Without which order, all this life hath none,
But breeds the other lifes confusion.
Respect to things without vs, hinder this
Inward consent of our soules faculties.
Things outward therefore, thinke no further yours   640
Then they yeelde homage, to your inward powers,
In their obedience to your reasons vse,
Which for their order, deitie did infuse.
For when the happiest outside man, on earth   *v*
Weighs all his haps together, such a dearth   645
He shall finde in their plenty, euery way,
That if with solid iudgement he suruay
Their goodliest presence, he will one thought call

The Angell
toucht Iacob
in the hollow
of his thigh;
& blest him;
though he
made him
halt; which
figurd the
necessite of
death in the
best; without
which touch,
he could not
be blest
with eterni-
tie.

The Lord
Russell, to
you now most
worthy Lord,
his Sonne.

619 leaue] laue   644 happiest] hadpiest   645 together] to ether

Of God, and a good conscience worth it all.
650 Nor doth th'imagind good, of ill so please
As that the best, and sweetest Images
Faind to himselfe thereof: he can make end
In any true ioy, but doe euer tend
To ioy, and grieue at once: what most doth please
655 Ends in sence bodilie, or mindes disease.
Why then should ill, be chusd by policie,
When no where, he can finde vacuitie
Of cares, or labors? no where rests content
With his meere selfe? at no time findes vnbent,
660 No, nor, vndrawne, euen compasse, his rackt minde,
His bloody arrowes to, in euery kinde
Tugg'd to the head, and ceaselesse shot away,
At flying obiects, that make flight their stay?
Horde gould, heape honors vp, build towers to heauen,
665 Get Capps, and knees, make your obseruance euen
With and aboue Gods (as most great ones doe)
Vnlesse you settle, your affections to,
And to insatiate appetite impose
A glutted end, your selfe, from feares, and woes
670 Manfully freeing, as to men that pine
And burne with feuers, you fill cups of wine,
The cholerique, honie giue, and fulsome meate
On sicke men force, that at the daintiest sweate.
Who yet, their hurtfull tempers turnd to good,
675 Milde spirits generate, and gentle blood,
D₄ᴿ With restitution of their naturall heate;
Euen cheese and water cresses they will eate
With tast enough: so make but strong your minde,
With her fit rule; and cates of humblest kinde
680 You tast with height of pleasure, turning all
Perticular to the pleasure generall.
Learne to loue truely, good, and honest things,
And you shall finde there, wealth, and honors springs
Enabling you a priuate path to treade,
685 As well as life, in prease of Empire leade.
Those deedes become, one greatly Noble best,
That doe most good, and pinch his greatnesse lest,
That sore not high, nor yet their fethers pull;
Neuer superfluous, euer yet at full,
690 That to eternall ends, in chiefe aspire,
And nothing fit, without themselues require.
But these are neuer taught, till they be lou'd,
And we must teach their loue to; both being mou'd
With one impulsion; and a third to these

(Which is good life) doth from one doctrine rise.   695
    Liberall, and seruile, we may teach all arts
Whose whole; some cut, into sixhundred parts,
Which I admire, since th'art of good life lies
By none profest, and good mens fames that rise
From that arts doctrine, are as rarely seene   700
As Centaures, or sicilian Giants bene.

The soule
(which is
Gods only in-
fusion) hath
as much
meanes to in-
flame her
proper forme,
as the body
the loue be-
longing to it.

For Gods loue and good life yet, as too true
We proue, our bodies, meanes haue to imbrue
Their powers with carnall loue; will any say
That God doth not as powerfull meanes conuay   705
For his works loue, into it as doth man
Into the body? the soule neuer can
In no propriety, loue her contrarie: v
Life loues not death, nor death eternity:
Nor she that deathlesse is, what death doth claime: 710
If she then (by Gods grace) at Gods loue aime:
May she not meanes claime by his liberall word
(That promiseth his mercie will afford
His loue to all that loue him) to obtaine

Homeri,
Aurea Restis
afflatu diuino
Resurrectionis
prefiguratio.

That which she seeks therein, and hould the chaine   715
Of his infusion, that let downe from heauen
Can draw vp, euen the earth? the flesh is geuen
A liuer that formes loue; And hath not she
In all her powrs, one Christ-blest Facultie
To be her liuer, to informe his loue?   720
In all chiefe parts, that in the great world moue
Proportion and similitude, haue place,

Analogia
Mundi &
Corporis
Principum
partium.

With this our little world. The great worlds face
Inserted Starres hath, as lucifluent eies:
The sunne, doth with the heart analogise.   725
And through the world, his heate and light disperse:
As doth the heart through mans small vniuerse.
The two vast lineaments, the sea and earth
Are to the world, as to a humaine birth
The ventricle, and bladder, and the Moone,   730
Being interposd, betwixt the Earth, and Sunne:
Is as the liuer, plac't betwixt the heart
And ventricle: if these then we conuert
To a resemblance, with our bodies powres:
Shall not our bodies Queene, this soule of ours,   735
For her vse finde, as seruiceable parts
In her commaund with vse of all her Arts?
All which are liuers to inflame desire:
And Eagles eyes to take in three forck't fire,

731 Earth] Earrh

E(1)ᴿ 740 (That doth the dazeling Trinitie intend)
T'enflame her loue thereof; In sacred end
Her selfe being th'Eagle; And the Queene of Kings,
That of our Kings King, beares beneath her wings
The dreadfull Thunder, the Almightie word;
745 All which (called fiction) with sure Truth accord.
    But if men may, teach all arts else but this
Art of good life; (that all their subiect is,
And obiect to in this life; And for which
Both Earth and Heauen, so faire are and so rich;
750 Yet this must needes want forme and discipline,
Reason, and stay: and only fortune shine
In her composure,) O want wise men eyes
To see in what suds, all their learning lyes?
Not such as learne not: but as teach not right
755 Are chiefly blamefull. Good life takes her light
From her owne flame: He that will teach an art,
Must first performe himselfe the leading part.
Who kindles fire without fire? He that striues
Without his owne good life, to forme good liues;
760 Motions that all the sacred Booke affords
But Conjurations makes, with holy words;
That of the Tempter sauour, more then God:
Temptations; Not perswasions brings abrode;
With Tempests, thinks to conjure quick, dead coales,
765 Torments, not Comforts, sick, and dying Soules.
And as the windes, all met at wofull fires
Kindl'd in Cities; stuffe with all their Ires
Their puft-vp cheekes; Tosse flames from house to house;
And neuer leaue till their drie Rage Carouse
770 A whole Townes life-bloud, in a generall flame;
Yet Tapers, Torches, all the lights men frame
_v_ For needefull vses, put directly out;
So, at the conflagration, that the rout
Of proude, and couetous zeales, hath so enrag'd,
775 In Gods deare Citie; Tempests still engag'd
In spleenefull controuersies, daily rise;
Cheekes euer puft with hollow pieties,
The wilde flames feeding, yet extinguisht quite,
Of needefull good life; both the heat and light.
780 Gods loue, that both inflames, giuen all offence,
And heauens chaste Kingdome suffering violence.
Which they incense, and plie with batteries,
To point at it; and shew men where it is.
When he, his sparkling forehead euer showes
785 Where peace is crownd, and where no vapour blowes;

The soule,
Mythologisd
is the Eagle
which is said
to beare the
thunder vn-
der her wings;
Th[e] light-
ning, (which
is ca[l]led
Trisulcus
figuring the
thrice sacred
Trinitie) in
he[r] eyes.
The word, in-
tended by the
Thunder;
which diuine
Scripture
call[s] _Gods
voice._

Simil.

Where patience, milde humilitie, and loue;
Faith, and good workes, with douelike paces moue
Vnder the shadow of his starrie wings;
Proue all they owe him; Not with words, but things,
Contention, cleane puts out zeales quiet flame: 790
Truths doctrine rather should be taught with shame,
Then such proude honors, as her manners change:
Contempt, and pouertie, her battailes range;
Plaine, simple life, more propagate her birth,
Then all the policie, and pompe of earth.   795
There is a sweet in good life, that must goe
Arme in arme with it, which men should teach to.
The end that should in euery Teacher meet,

Docere, vt   With his beginning; is to make good, sweet:
honesta fiant Who with meere arte, and place, good life doth plie,   800
suauia; Lac.   Attempts with pride to teach humilitie.
Humilitie, Truths salt; and supple Spirit
That workes, and seasons all men borne t'inherit,
The Kingdome, on whose blest shore my foot now   E₂ᴿ
Is gladly fixt; Let that then season you;   805
It makes, and crownes true Nobles, and commends
Euen to felicitie, our births, and ends.

The Morn-   Now threw the busie day, through humorous blood
ing.   Her sensuall stings, and strooke the heart from good.
Things outward, with the Mother of their Grace,   810
(The gawdie light) things inward quite out-face,
To this Pied worlds, austere, and woluish care,
All things meere trifles seeme, but those that are.
Eugenia, that from Fame might comfort take,
Let Trance still shut her eyes, and would not wake, 815
But heard all speech, like this worlds counsaile cares:
As if shee heard not, and betwixt her eares.
Twixt life, and death, shee lay still; This sowre sweet
That pietie ministers, doth neuer meet
With fit secretion, and refining here: 820
Being like hard fruit, whose true taste ends the yeere.
The most enforciue bare Relation
Of pious offices, is held but fashion: •
Proude flesh, holds out, her customarie will
And yeelds, resisting; Moues without a will   825
To comforts promist, and no bond but faith
For the performance, and her suretie death.
And this, euen in the weede *Eugenia* wore,

Alluding to   Of humane flesh, cleft like the shirt of gore
Alcides; of   That figurde this lifes, Offall for the graue   830
whose shirt   And makes the Noblest that indues it, raue.
this is the
Mythologie.   *Explicit Vigilia Secunda.*

v

VIGILÆ TERTIÆ.

Inductio.

By this, the Babell of confused sounds,
(The clamorous game-giuen world) his mouthlike wounds
Felt leaue their raging; The sweet Euen had dropt

835   Her silent Balms in, and their gaping stopt.
Mineruas Birds, whoop't at him as he drew
His many heads home. Sleepes wing'd Vshers flew
Off from their Flitches; and about Mens noses
Plaid buzz. The Beetle, that his whole life loses

840   In gathering Muck, still wallowing there, did raise
With his Irate wings, his most vnwieldie paise;
And, with his knellike humming, gaue the Dor
Of Death to Men, as all they labourd for.

[T]he
Mouths [of]
worldlings,
[from] their
still [cr]ying
out and
[lon]ging for
[ri]ches &
Ho[no]urs,
without
[sat]isfaction,
or [ea]se, may

more [w]orthily bee [ca]lled their [w]ounds; Both [from] their re[se]mblance to [wo]unds, and [als]o since the [m]ines of their [wo]rldly thirsts, [ar]e chiefly vt[ter]ed by them. [Ba]tts, calld [th]e Vshers of [Sl]epe, since [th]ey make [th]eir flights [be]fore his time [of] binding our [sen]ses. Their [da]y spent most [in] feeding on [ba]con flitches. [Be]etles, called [Do]rs.

The golden backt, and siluer-bellied Snaile

845   His moist Mines melted, creeping from his shell,
And made crook't Mazes of his glittering slime,
To shew in what paths, worldlings spend their time.
All these, The Euening only, make their morne,
And thus employ it, as men mock-dayes borne.

850   Abroade then crept, the world-scar'd broode of Peace,
To greet *Eugenia;* whose Trance still did sease
Her griefe rackt Powrs, which since her loue did make
Iust ioy* to her; Religion would not make.
    In midst of all her sable Chamber, lay

855   *Eugenia* corselike. The despisde of day,
(The Muses, Graces, Vertues, Poesie
But then arriu'd there) on the Pauement by
Sate round: Religion (as of that rich Ring
The precious stone) did th'ends together bring

[E₃ᴿ] 860   Of their Celestiall circle: All so plac't,
As they her Armes were; And shee them embrac't.
All then, wisht Fame, to giue her Trump the rest,
(Euen to the deaths word) of the liuing blest.
    Fame (like the Lyon-frighting Bird, in chere

865   Proude to report parts, that so sacred were,)
Her rosie Throte stretcht, and did thus extend
To his last motion, his proceeding end.

Snailes.

* τεταρπώ-
με[σθα] γόοιο.

[De]lectati
fueri[mu]s
luctu. [Ho]m.
ψ.v.10.

833 mouthlike] monthlike   gloss (l. 2) Mouths] Moneths   835 Balms]
Bala'ms

VIGILIA TERTIA.

Still looking, neuer stooping to his death,

Simil.
Like some great Combattant, that though giuen breath,

Fame of the Lord *Russels* death. Hee neuer lay [a] day from his first daies sicknes to his last[,] nor wore so much as a night cap.
Yet eyes his Foe still; No glance cast aside,   870
To giue aduantage of a touch vnspied:
So, those twice seuen daies, that his lifes Foe gaue
His sicknes breath (though in his sight, his graue
Gaspt for his dutie, in deaths instant deede)
He neuer lay, nor wore a sickly weede.   875

The Scripture. The weapon he gaue Death against him, out of *S. Paul* since it shewe[d] a little his distraction, was a Text, as followeth.
  If Death of him gat; He of Death, got more;
And fortified himselfe still with the store
The sacred Magazine yeelded: Where he found
Weapons that grew; and made each word a wound,
Of which he gaue his ghastly Enimie one   880
To be his Trophey when the fight was done.
Which was a frailtie in him that would faine
Haue proued a fainting; But who growes againe
Vp to his strength, is stronger far then hee,
Whose forces neuer felt infirmitie.   885

The Text hee chusde was out of *S. Pau[l]* to the *Phillip[pians]* the first chap[.] and 23 verse. *Coarctor autem è duobus, &c.*
He chusde his Funerall Text, that shewd him strooke
With some distraction; yet the forme he tooke
From the most learn'd Apostle; chearde him so
That deaths aduantage, prou'd his ouerthrow.
The Prophet that was rauisht quick to heauen,   890 *v*
And neuer fought with Death; Nor those foule seuen
His vgly Ministers, in that extreme,
Triumphs in so rich a Diademe,
As he in heauen weares. The more wrestling here
(The Garland won) the more our price is there.   895
But in our worldly ends, so fraile we are,
That we the Garland giue to euery care
That doth assaile vs; each particular misse,
Of that for which the body carefull is;
Our other plenties, prouing meerly wants,   900
And all that the celestiall prouidence plants
Still in our reach; is to our vse despisde:
And, only what we can not compasse prisde.
  When this fault sence proues true, as Reason saies;
Why let we Sense still interpose delaies   905
To our true Reasons comforts? Ruling so
That either we must rage still in our woe,
Or beare it with so false a patience,
As showes no more our ease then our offence;
Exprest in grudging at our penance still: 910

---

878 Magazine] Morgazine

Our grudging showne, in our no more curb'd will,
To our most iust Imposers; then to leaue
Moodie, and muddie, our apt powrs to grieue:
Not, that we may not beare a suffering show
915 In our afflictions, weighing grauely how
We may dispose them to our best amends;
But, not take so much sorrow as transcends
Our healths; or shewes, we let griefe further goe,
Then our Content, that God will haue it so;
920 Remayning in such plight; as if we thought
That this our phisique of affliction wrought
[E₄ᴿ] More painefully, then with a healthfull neede;
When our all-skil'd Phisition doth proceede
So strictly in his obiect of our ease,
925 (So may he mend vs to and soundly please)
That not a scruple, nor the slendrest graine
Of any Corasiue, shall rack our paine
Past his full point of our most needfull cure;
Weight, measure, number, all Gods workes assure.
930 Which, not because infallible Scripture saies,
We only may beleeue (though that cause weies
More then enough to strengthen any Faith:)
But God to euery sound beliefe conuaith
A Regular knowledge; to informe vs how
935 We may sustaine his burthens, though we bow
Vnder their sad weight; which when once we proue;
It will annexe to our beliefe such loue,
That (as the Sunne, mists) quite shall cleare our care,
And make our generall peace so circulare;
940 That Faith and Hope, at either end shall pull
And make it come: Round as the Moone at full.
   And this, doe many know, though (as t'is said
By that most comforable Truth, our head,
After his Prophet) with the arte of th'eare;
945 Yet, nothing vnderstanding yee shall heare;
Yee, looking on; shall see, and not perceiue,
As often our diuerted thoughts bereaue
The vse of both those senses, though we be
In reach of sights, and sounds; and heare and see.
950   For as the eye discernes not black from white,   *Simil.*
Colour, from sound; till with a noble light
The soule casts on it, it is made descrie;
So, till the soules blanck Intellectuall eye:
v   The worlds soule rinseth in his actiue raies,
955 And her Rac't table fills with formes; it staies
Blanck to all Notions that informe vs how

To make our cares with in our comforts grow:
Our fainting, in the free reach of our faith,
And, in our lifes fixt peace, all feare of death.
Which true light to this Lords soule, shining came   960
And fixt him Rock-like, till his Faith did flame.
    His conflict past, he to the comfort went,
That makes those Thornes, Crownes; The blest *Sacrament*,
Of which, The powrefull consecrated bread;
(That cheares the liuing, and reuiues the dead,   965
Receiud, with feare, and faith; that one yoke beare;
Feare, that awes Faith; and Faith that tempers feare,)
Assum'd by him: This witnesse he did giue
Of what he tooke: I constantly belieue;
That as I take, hold, and by grace shall eate   970
This sacred bread; So that flesh that did sweat
Water and bloud, in my deare Sauiours side;
I shall in this bread, all exhibified,
In my Eternall safeties full effect,
Take, hold, and eate, as his most sure Elect.   975
    To this effect; Effectually the Wine,
(Turnd the true bloud, of the eternall Vine
His most lou'd Sauiour,) Then, as fresh in powre
As in the very instant of that howre,
In which 'twas shed for him; he did belieue   980
To his saluation; he did then receiue.
    Thus held he combat, till his latest day,
Walking, and after; Conquerd, as he lay,
Spake to his latest howre; And when no more
He could by speach impart, th'amazing store   985
Of his assurd ioies, that as surely last;   F(1)R
His diligent diuine, desird a tast
Of his still strong assurance by some signe;
When both his hands, euen then wrought in the mine
Of his exhaustles faith; that cround his Euen,   990
And cast such treasure vp, as purchast heauen,
Thus his most christian combat did conclude,
He conquering most, when most he was subdude.
    Yet, not to leaue him here; his funerall
Deserues in part, to be obseru'd of all.   995
In which, his sonne; his owne kinde zealous spirit
Did with his honors, and his lands inherit;
Whose pious nature, paying manly teares,
(Which stony ioies stoppe in most other heires)
To his departure: whose attending close   1000
(Through dust, and heate) the bodie in repose;

For all that wants of fit Illustration to this most religious and worthy Lord; I referre the reader to the learned and godly sermon of Mr. Walker made at his funerall.

957 in our comforts] in comforts. Shepherd's emendation.

Next Euen; and the whole way to his home:
Whose there, fresh deawing with kinde Balmes his tombe;
Whose liberall hand, to nere two thousand pore;
1005 Whose laying vp, as his most prised store
His fathers life-bought counsailes; all, as nought
I will not touch here: None giues these a thought;
But how his teares led others; all the Phane
Flowing with such brine; seasoning parts humane
1010 Offerd to pietie, which kinde, dead to, now
Yet here so plenteous; me thinks should not show
Lesse then a wonder; and may argue well
That from some sacred fount, these riuers fell:
O why wept, mans great Patterne for his friend,
1015 But these affections, grauely to commend?
     But these things now are nothing; the proud Morne   The Morn-
Now on her typtoes, view'd this stuffe, with skorne.   ing[.]
 v   Scripture examples; parts of manlie kinde;
The most vpright flames of the godlike minde;
1020 Like winter lightnings are; that doe portend
Wretched euents, to all men they commend;
All things inuerted are; nought brookes the light
But what may well make blush the blackest night.

Explicit Vigilia Tertia.

VIGILIÆ QUARTÆ & VLTIMÆ.

Inductio.

The tast of all ioies in societie   The Eue-
1025 The sicke world felt a little satisfie: ning.
The garland, and the Iuie-twisted lance,
Put on, and tost were, by the God of dance.
Vulcan guilt houses, th'Elutherian feast
Of all the liberals: now paid Rites to rest.
1030 Songs, Hymeneals, all the cares of day
Tumults, and quarrels, turnd to peace and play.
Representation, that the Chymists part
Plaies in her pastimes, now turnd with her Art
This Iron world into the goulden age,
1035 Earths antient worthes, showing on her stage:
Where those sweete swarmes that tast no crabbed lacks
Hang thicke, with all their honnie on their backs,
Imbrac't with musicke, and the pride of wit:
Silence much more in solemne state doth sit
1040 In that faire concourse, with an Actors voice,

1007 here] her   1017 with] which   1030 Hymeneals] Hymenrals

Then where Rich Law insults, still vext with noise,   F₂ᴿ
And where nine Herolds could not crowne her peace,
One Prologue here, puts on her wreath with ease.
Loue ioies began to burne; and all did rise
To giue the thriftlesse euening sacrifice.   1045
   Then went the muses, virtues, graces on,
The Herse, and Toombe, the croune to set vpon
Of this most endlesse noble Lord deceast,
And to his soules ioy, and his bodies rest
A Hymne aduance, which to the Trumpe of Fame,   1050
Poore Poesie sung; Her euery other dame
(Th'ingenuous Muses) ringing out, the Chore;
Fame sounded; Poesie, sung the part before:

Hymnus ad D. Russelium defunctum:

Poes.   Rising and setting, let the sunne
              Grace whom we honor;   1055
          And euer at her full, the Moone
              Assume vpon her,
          The forme his Noblesse did put on;
          In whose Orb, all the vertues shone,
              With beames decreasing neuer;   1060
          Till faith, in her firme Rocke reposde;
          Religion, his lifes Circle closd,
              And opened life for euer.
Mus. Cho.   Earth, seas, the Aire, and Heauen, O heare
          These Rites of ours, that euery yeare,   1065
              We vow thy Herse,
          And breath the flames of soules entire,
          Thrice het, with heauens creating fire,
              In deathlesse verse.

2   v

Poes.   Russell, Lord Russell, while we pay   1070
              Thy name our numbers:
          Directed by the eye of day
              That neuer slumbers:
          May all Heauens Quire of Angels sing,
          And glorifie in thee, their king   1075
              That death with death subdueth;
          While we strike Earths sounds dumbe, and deafe,
          And Croune thee with a feastfull leafe
              Whose verdure still reneweth.
Mus. Cho.   Earth, Seas, the Aire, and Heauen, O heare,   1080
          These Rites of ours, that euery yeare

     1068 het] Het

We vow his Herse;
And breath the flames of soules entire,
Thrice het, with heauens creating fire
1085   In deathles vierse.

3

Euer O euer may this Eue   Poes.
    That we keepe holy,
Thy name encreasing honors giue,
    That serue it solely.
1090 And second with diuine encrease
Thy progenies religious peace,
    Zeales Altars euer smoking;
And their true Pieties excite
With full draughts of celestiall light,
1095   Thy vertues still inuoking.
Earth, Seas, the Aire, and Heauen O heare   Mus. Cho.
These Rites of ours, that euery yeare
    We vow his Herse, &c.

F₃ᴿ   4

Requests that Iustice would fulfill   Poes.
1100   Great Giuer giue them,
Vniust moodes, make them bridle still
    And here, out liue them.
Directly let their zealous praiers
Her eyen ope in their blest affaires,
1105   And of their Noblest Father;
Enable them to fill the Place;
And euery one; proofes of his Race
    From his Example gather.
Earth, Seas, the Aire, and Heauen, O heare   Mus. Cho.
1110 These rites of ours that euery yeare
    We vow his Herse, &c.

5

Honors, that vertues keepe in height   Poes.
    With fires deceased;
All know, make vp their Comforts weight,
1115   And them more blessed.
And therefore in thus wishing thine,
We wish the more, thy worth may shine,
    Great Grace of all men Noble;
From whose life, faith, and zeale did flow,
1120 In whose death, they shall freshly grow,

1104 eyen] euen

And thy blest Race redouble.

Mus. Cho. Earth, Seas, the Aire, and Heauen, &c.

6

Poes. Monsters, for Nobles, let the Earth,
　　　Bring forth to brand her;
And their Adulterate Beastly Birth　　　　　　　1125
　　　At swindge commaund her.
Yet slaues made to their Lusts, and Hell
They shall but here, like Giants dwell,　　　　　*v*
　　　And breede but flames, and Thunder
To beate them vnder their owne Hils,　　　　　1130
Their sweetes turnd Torments, their Goods, ils,
　　　Thy Race, their Enuies wonder.

Mus. Cho. Earth, Seas, the Aire, &c.

7

Poes. Exult, and triumph then in all
　　　Thy thoughts intended,　　　　　　　　1135
Which heauen did into Ioies exhall
　　　For thee, ascended.
If not a haire, Much lesse a thought
Shall *losse* claime, of what Goodnesse ought,
　　　But shine in heauen together;　　　　　1140
Whose ioies (to truely-studied soules)
Shall shine euen here, like ashe-kept Coles,
　　　Laid open gainst the weather.

Mus. Cho. Earth, Seas, the Aire, &c.

8

Poes. Knowledge, not fashiond here to feele　　　1145
　　　Heauens promist pleasure;
In lifes sea, is a turnd-vp Keele
　　　With all her Treasure:
Not One, return'd from Death, to tell
The Ioies of Heauen, the paines of Hell,　　　　1150
　　　Can ad to that relation;
Which (possible impulsions vs'd)
The Soule knowes here: and spirits infus'd,
　　　Farre past her first creation.

Mus. Cho. Earth, Seas, the Aire, &c.　　　　　　1155

9

Poes. Infuse this into his deare kinde,
　　　Truth's free vnfolder:　　　　　　　　[F₄ᴿ]

With Fire that first informd the minde,
   Now nothing coulder.
1160   For which the Thrice Almighty One:
The *Spirit*, Sire, and *word* still done:
   Praise giue, that gifts transcendeth.
Despisd soules, Comfort with thy loue:
In whom, with thy first motion moue,
1165   Till in fixt truth it endeth:
Earth, Seas, the Aire, and Heauen, O heare,   Mus. Cho.
These Rites of ours, that euery yeare,
   We vow thy Herse:
And breath the flames of soules intire,
1170   Thrice het with heauens creating Fire,
      In deathlesse verse,

Explicit Hymnus.

With this, *Eugenia*, from her Trance arose   Peror.
And in her loues assur'd Ioies did repose,
Her Noble Sorrowes, being assur'd with al
1175   That no effect did memorably fall,
From his Renown'd Example, but was found
In his true Sonne, and would in him resound.
   Then left she straight Fames loftie region:
Stoop't Earth, and vowd to dwell with him, or None,
1180   Whom since the Muses, Vertues, Graces now,
Of force must follow (sweete Lord) be not you
Carelesse of them, that she esteemd so deare:
For howsoeuer they to Earth appeare,
Where in their Truth they are, and are not prisd,
1185   In them, is true Religion despisd.
Remember your Religious Father then,
And after him: Be you the man of men.
v   To these, the Night, thus short sem'd, and thus bare   The Morn-
Was euery clamorous worldling, at his care,   ing.
1190   Care cried in Cities, and in Countries ror'd:
Now was the soule, a Toie: Her gifts abhor'd,
All Ornament, but brauery, was a staine:
Nought now akinne to wit, but Cosening Gaine.
Crafts, and Deceipts enricht, made Arts so poore:
1195   Which Artists seeing: Rich apparraile wore   Artists pro-
And bore out Art, Light's onely made for show   fest onely.
And show for lightnesse; Grauest Booke Men now
Most rich in show bee, for their approbation,
And neuer swagger, but in sacred Fashion.
1200   Looke blancke on good life: and point-blancke on Thrift:

1195 wore] were

He that is richest, hath the wholiest gift.
In Night Men dreame: Day best showes what is fit;
Learning was made for Gaine, Not Gaine, for it.
Now bellies deafned eares, in euery streete,
And backs bore more then heads, heads more then feete.   1205

Explicit Eugeniae Ecstasis
Musa quae Inuidia?

FINIS.

ANDROMEDA
LIBERATA.

TO THE PREIVDICATE AND
PEREMPTORY READER.

I AM still in your hands; but was first in his, that (being our great sustainer of Sincerity, and Jnnocence) will, J hope, defend mee from falling. J thinke you know not him J intend, more then you know me, nor can you know mee, since your knowledge is imagined so much aboue mine, that it must needes ouersee. He that lies on the ground can fall no lower. By such as backebite the highest, the lowest must looke to be deuor'd, Forth with your curious Scrutinie, and finde my Rush as knotty as you lust, and your owne Crab-tree, as smooth. Twillbe most ridiculous and pleasing, to sit in a corner, and spend your teeth to the stumps, in mumbling an ould Sparrow, till your lips bleed, and your eyes water: when all the faults you can finde are first in your selues, t'is no *Herculean* labor to cracke what you breed. Ahlas who knowes not your uttermost dimensions? Or loues not the best things
v   you would seeme to loue, in deed, and better? *Truth* was neuer the Fount of *Faction*. In whose Sphere since your purest thoughts moue, their motion must of force be oblique and angulare. But whatsoeuer your disease bee, I know it incurable, because your vrine will neuer shew it. At aduenture, at no hand be let blood for it, but rather sooth your ranke bloods and rub one another.

You yet, ingenuous and iudicious Reader: that (as you are your selfe) retaine in a sound bodie, as sounde a soule: if your gentle tractability, haue vnwares let the common surfet surprize you: abstaine, take Phisique heere, and recouer. Since you reade to learne, teach: Since you desire to bee reform'd, reforme freely. Such shall be rich Balmes to it, comfort, and strengthen the braine it beares, and make it healthfully neese out, whatsoeuer anoies it. *Vale.*

The Argument.   A₂ᴿ

Andromeda, Daughter of *Cepheus*, King of *Æthiopia;* and
Cassiope (a virgine exempted from comparison in all the
vertues & beauties, both of minde and bodie) for the enuie of
Iuno to her Mother; being compar'd with her for beauty
and wisedome; (or as others write, maligned by the *Nereides*,
for the eminent Graces of her selfe) moued so much the *Deities*
displeasures; that they procur'd *Neptune* to send into the
Region of *Cepheus*, a whale so monstrously vaste and dread-
full: that all the fields he spoild and wasted; all the noblest
edifices tumbling to ruine; the strongest citties of the king-
dome, not forcible enough to withstand his inuasions. Of
which so vnsufferable a plague *Cepheus* consulting with an
Oracle; and asking both the cause, and remedie; after ac-
customed sacrifices, the Oracle gaue answer, that the calamity
would neuer cease, till his onely daughter *Andromeda*, was
exposed to the Monster. *Cepheus* returnd, and with Iron
chaines bound his daughter to a rocke, before a cittie of the
kingdome called *Ioppe*. At which cittie, the same time,
Perseus arriued with the head of *Medusa* &c. who pittying
so matchles a virgines exposure to so miserable an euent;
dissolu'd her chaines and tooke her from the Rock. Both   *v*
sitting together to expect the monster, & he rauenously hast-
ing to deuoure her, *Perseus*, turnd part of him into stone,
& through the rest made way with his sword to his vtter
slaughter. When (holding it wreath enough for so renownd a
victory) He took *Andromeda* to wife, & had by her one
daughter called *Perse*, another *Erythraea*, of whom, the sea in
those parts is called *Mare Erythraeum;* since she both liued
and died there: and one sonne called after himselfe, another
Electrion, a third *Sthenelus:* and after liued Princely and
happily with his wife and his owne Mother to his death. Then
faind for their vertues to be made Constellations in Heauen.

TO THE RIGHT
WORTHILY HONORED,
Robert Earle of Sommerset, &c.

AND

HJS MOST NOBLE LADY
the Ladie FRANCES.

¶₃ᴿ

A S nothing vnder heauen is more remou'd
From Truth & virtue, then *Opinions* prou'd
By vulgar *Voices*: So is nought more true
Nor soundly virtuous then things held by few:
Whom *Knowledge* (entred by the sacred line,
And gouernd euermore by grace diuine,)
Keepes in the narrow path to spacious heauen,
And therefore, should no knowing spirit be driuen
From fact, nor purpose; for the spleens prophane
Of humours errant, and *Plebeian;*
But, Famelike, gather force as he goes forth,
The *Crowne* of all *Acts* ends in onely worth.
  Nor will I feare to prostrate this poore Rage
Of forespoke *Poesie*, to your patronage,
(Thrice worthy Earle), & your vnequald grace
(Most Noble Countesse) for the one-ear'd Race
Of set-eyd vulgars, that will no waie see
But that their stiffe necks driue them headlongy,
Stung with the Gadflie of misgouernd zeale:
Nor heare but one tale and that euer ill.
These I contemne, as no Rubs fit for me
To checke at, in my way t'*Jntegritie.*
Nor will ye be incenst that such a Toie
Should put on the presumption to enioie
Your grauer eare, my Lord, and your faire eye
(Illustrous Ladie) since poore *Poesie*
Hath beene a Iewell in the richest eare
Of all the Nuptiall States, that euer were.
  For as the Bodies pulse (in Phisique) is
A little thing; yet therein th'Arteries
Bewray their motion, and disclose, to Art
The strength, or weakenesse, of the vitall part;
Perpetually moouing, like a watch
Put in our Bodies: So this three mens catch,

13 prostrate] postrate

305

This little Soules Pulse, *Poesie*, panting still   35
Like to a dancing pease vpon a Quill,
Made with a childes breath, vp and downe to fly,
(Is no more manly thought); And yet thereby
Euen in the corps of all the world we can
Discouer all the good and bad of man,   40
Anatomise his nakednesse, and be
To his chiefe Ornament, a Maiestie:
Erect him past his human Period
And heighten his transition into God.
    Thus Sun-like, did the learnd and most diuine   45
Of all the golden world, make *Poesie* shine;
That now, but like a glow worm, gleams by night
Like Teachers, scarce found, by their proper light.
But this (my Lord) and all poore virtues else
Expos'd, ahlas, like perdu Sentinels   50
To warne the world of what must needs be nie,   *v*
For pride, and auarice, glas'd by *Sanctitie*,
Must be distinguisht, and decided by
Your cleere, ingenuous, and most quiet eye
Exempt from passionate, and duskie fumes,   55
That blinde our Reason: and in which consumes
The Soule, halfe choakt, with stomacke casting mists
Bred in the purest, turnd mere humorists.
And where with douelike sweet humility
They all things should authorise or deny,   60
The vulgar heate and pride of splene and blood
Blaze their opinions, which cannot be good.
For as the Bodies Shadow, neuer can
Shew the distinct, and exact Forme of Man;
So nor the bodies passionate affects   65
Can euer teach well what the Soule respects.
For how can mortall things, immortall shew?
Or that which false is, represent the trew?
The peacefull mixture then that meetes in yow
(Most temperat Earl) that nought to rule doth ow: 70
In which, as in a thorough kindled Fire,   ¶¶₍₁₎ᴿ
Light and *Heat* marrie *Judgement* and *Desire*,
Reason is still in quiet, and extends
All things t'aduantage of your honored Ends,
May well authorise all your Acts of Note,   75
Since all Acts vicious, are of *Passion* got:
Through dead Calms, of our Perturbations euer
Truths Voice (to soules eares set) we heare or neuer.
The meerely animate Man, doth nothing see

64 exact] expact

That tends to heauen: It must be onely He
That is mere soule: Her separable powers
The scepter giuing heere: That then discourse
Of Motions that in sence doe neuer fall,
Yet know them too, and can distinguish all
With such a freedome, that our earthly parts
Sincke all to earth: And then th'ingenuous arts
Doe their true office, Then true Policie
Windes like a serpent, through all Empery,
Her folds on both sides bounded, like a flood
With high-shores listed, making great and good
Whom she instructeth, to which, you (my Lord)
May lay all claimes that Temper can afford;
Nought gathering ere t'is ripe: and so must taste
Kindely and sweetely, and the longer last.
All fruits, in youth, ripe in you; and must so
Imply a facultie to euer growe.
   And as the morning that is calme and gray,
Deckt all with curld clowds, that the Sunne doth lay
With varied coullours; All aloft exhall'd
As they t'adorn euen heauen it selfe were call'd,
And could not fall in slendrest deawes till Night,
But keepe daies Beauty firme and exquisite;
More for delight fit, and doth more adorne
Euen th' Euen with *Graces*, then the youthful morn:
So you (sweete Earle) stay youth in aged bounds
Euen absolute now, in all lifes grauest grounds,
Like Aire, fill euery corner of your place,
Your grace, your virtue heightening: virtue, grace,
And keeping all clowds high, aire calme, & cleer
And in your selfe all that their height should rere,
Your life and light will proue a still full Moone,
And all your night time nobler then your noone.
The Sunne is in his rising, height, and set
Still (in himselfe) alike, at all parts great,
His light, heat, greatnes, coullors that are showne
To vs, as his charge, meerely is our owne:
So let your charge, my Lord, in others be,
But in your selfe hold Sun-like constancie.
For as men skild in Natures study, say,
The world was not the world, nor did conuay
To coupling bodies Natures common forme,
But (all confus'd, like waues struck with a storme)
Some small were, and (in no set being, staid)
All comprehension, and connexion fled;
The greater, and the more compact disturb'd

With ceaseles warre, and by no order curb'd,
Till earth receiuing her set magnitude
Was fixt her selfe, and all her Birth indu'd
With staie and law: so this small world of ours
Is but a *Chaos* of corporeall powers,   130
Nor yeelds his mixt parts, forms that may become   v
A human Nature; But at randome rome
Past brutish fashions, and so neuer can
Be cald the ciuill bodie of a man;
But in it, and against it selfe still fights,   135
In competence of Cares, Ioyes, Appetites:
The more great in command, made seruile more,
Glutted, not satisfied: in plenty, poore:
Till vp the Soule mounts, and the Scepter swaies
Th'admired Fabricke of her world suruaies,   140
And as it hath a magnitude confinde,
So all the powers therein, she sees combinde
In fit Acts for one end, which is t'obay
Reason, her *Regent; Nature* giuing way:
Peace, Concord, Order, Stay proclaim'd, and *Law*   145
And none commanding, if not all in Awe,
Passion, and *Anger*, made to vnder lie,   ⎞
And heere concludes, mans mortall Monarchie   ⎬
In which, your Lordships milde Soule sits so hie   ⎠
Yet cares so little to be seene, or heard,   150
That in the good thereof, her scope is Sphear'd.   ¶¶ₛᴿ
The *Theban Ruler*, paralleling Right,
Who, thirst of glory turnd to appetite
Of inward *Goodnesse*, was of speech so spare,
To heare, and learne, so couetous, and yare,   155
That (of his yeares) none, things so many knew:
Nor in his speeches, ventured on so few:
Forth then (my Lord) & these things euer thirst
Till *Scandall* pine, and *'Bane-fed* enuie burst.
    And you, (most noble) Lady as in blood   160
In minde be Noblest, make our factious brood
Whose forked tongs, wold fain your honor sting
Conuert their venomd points into their spring:
Whose owne harts guilty, of faults faind in yours
Wold fain be posting off: but, arme your powers   165
With such a siege of vertues, that no vice
Of all your Foes, *Aduantage* may entice
To sally forth, and charge you with offence,
But sterue within, for very conscience
Of that Integritie, they see exprest   170

131 become] becom

In your cleere life: Of which, th'examples Rest,
May be so blamelesse; that all past must be
(Being Fount to th'other) most vndoubtedly
Confest vntouch't; and *Curiositie*
175 The beame picke rather from her own squint eie,
Then ramp stil at the motes shade, faind in yours,
Nought doth so shame this chimick serch of ours
As when we prie long for assur'd huge prise,
Our glasses broke, all vp in vapor flies.
180   And as, the Royall Beast, whose image you
Beare in your armes, and aires great Eagle too;
Still as they goe, are said to keepe in close
Their seres, & Tallons, lest their points shold lose
Their vseful sharpnes, when they serue no vse:
185 So this our sharp-eyd search that we abuse
In others brests, we should keepe in, t'explore
Our owne fowle bosomes, and quit them before
We ransacke others: but (great Ladie) leaue
These Rules to them they touch; do you receaue
190 Those free ioies in your honour, and your Loue
[¶¶ᶜᴿ] That you can say are yours; and euer moue
Where your command, as soon is seru'd as known,
Joyes plac't without you, neuer are your owne.

Your Honours euer most humbly
and faithfully vowd.

Geo. Chapman.

182 Still] Sill   192 known] kown

AWAY, vngodly Vulgars, far away,
   Flie ye prophane, that dare not view the day,
Nor speake to men but shadowes, nor would heare
Of any newes, but what seditious were,
Hatefull and harmefull euer to the best,   5
Whispering their scandals, glorifying the rest,
Jmpious, and yet gainst all ills but your owne,
The hotest sweaters of religion;
Whose poysons all things to your spleenes peruert,
And all streames measure by the Fount your Heart,   10
That are in nought but misrule regulare,
To whose eyes all seeme ill, but those that are,
That hate yee know not why, nor with more cause,   v
Giue whom yee most loue your prophane applause,
That when Kings and their Peeres, whose piercing eies   15
Broke through their broken sleepes and policies,
Mens inmost Cabinets disclose and hearts;
Whose hands *Ioues* ballance (weighing all desarts)
Haue let downe to them; which graue conscience,
Charg'd with the blood and soule of Jnnocence,   20
Holds with her white hand, (when her either skole,
Apt to be sway'd with euery graine of Soule,
Her selfe swaies vp or downe, to heauen or hell,
Approue an action) you must yet conceale
A deeper insight, and retaine a taint   25
To cast vpon the pure soule of a Saint.
   Away, in our milde Sphere doth nothing moue,
But all-creating, all preseruing *Loue*,
At whose flames, vertues, lighted euen to starres,
All vicious Enuies, and seditious Iars,   30
Bane-spitting Murmures and detracting Spels,
Bannish with curses to the blackest hels:
Defence of *Beauty* and of *Innocence*,   B(2)R
And taking off the chaines of *Insolence*,
From their prophan'd and godlike Lineaments,   35
Actions heroique, and diuine descents,
All the sweet *Graces*, euen from death reuiu'd,
All sacred fruites, from barren Rockes deriu'd,
Th'Immortall Subiects of our Nuptials are:
Thee then (iust scourge of factious populare;   40
Fautor of peace, and all the powers that moue
In sacred Circle of religious Loue;
Fountaine of royall learning, and the rich

Treasure of Counsailes, and mellifluous speech:)
45 Let me inuoke, that one drop of thy spring
May spirit my aged Muse, and make her sing,
As if th'inspir'd brest, of eternall youth
Had lent her Accents, and all-mouing truth.
The Kingdome that the gods so much did loue,
50 And often feasted all the Powers aboue:
At whose prime beauties the enamour'd Sunne,
His Morning beames lights, and doth ouerrunne
v The world with Ardor (*Æthiopia*)
Bore in her throne diuine *Andromeda*,
55 To *Cepheus* and *Cassiope* his Queene:
Whose boundlesse beauties, made ore'flow the spleene
Of euery *Neirid*, for surpassing them:
The Sun to her, resign'd his Diadem:
And all the *Deities*, admiring stood,
60 Affirming nothing mou'd, like flesh and blood:
Thunder would court her with words sweetly phraz'd,
And lightning stucke 'twixt heau'n and earth amaz'd.
This matchlesse virgin had a mother too,
That did for beautie, and for wisdome goe
65 Before the formost Ladies of her time:
To whom of super-excellence the crime
Was likewise lai'd by *Iuno*, and from hence
Pin'd Enuie suckt, the poison of offence.
No truth of excellence, was euer seene,
70 *But bore the venome of the Vulgares spleene.*
 And now the much enrag'd *Neireides*
Obtain'd of him that moues the marble seas
B₃ᴿ (To wreake the vertue, they cal'd Jnsolence)
A whale so monstrous, and so past defence,
75 That all the royall Region he laid wast,
And all the noblest edifices rac't:
Nor from his plague, were strongest Cities free,
His bodies vast heape rag'd so heauily.
With noblest names and bloods is still embrewd
80 *The monstrous beast, the rauenous Multitude.*
 This plague thus preying vpon all the land,
With so incomprehensible a hand:
The pious virgin of the father sought,
By Oracles to know, what cause had brought
85 Such banefull outrage ouer all his State,
And what might reconcile the Deities hate.
His orisons and sacrifices past,
The Oracle gaue answere, that the waste
His Country suffered, neuer would conclude,

Till his *Andromeda* he did extrude,   90
To rapine of the Monster, he (good man,)
Resolu'd to satiate the *Leuiathan:*
With her, before his Country, though he lou'd   *v*
Her past himselfe, and bore a spirit mou'd
To rescue Innocence in any one   95
That was to him, or his, but kindly knowne,
To grace, or profite; doe them any good
That lay in swift streame of his noblest blood,
Constant to all, yet to his deerest seed,
(For rights sake) flitting: thinking true indeed,   100
The generall vprore, that t'was sinne in her,
That made men so exclaime, and gods conferre
Their approbation: saying the Kingdomes bale
Must end by her exposure to the Whale:
With whom the Whale-like vulgare did agree,   105
And their foule spleenes, thought her impiety;
Her most wise mother yet, the sterne intent,
Vow'd with her best endeauour to preuent;
And tolde her what her father did addresse.
Shee (fearefull) fled into the wildernesse: 110
And to th'instinct of sauage beasts would yeeld,
Before a father that would cease to shield
A daughter, so diuine and Jnnocent: B₄ᴿ
Her feet were wing'd, and all the search out went,
That after her was ordered: but shee flew,   115
And burst the winds that did incenst pursue,
And with enamoured sighes, her parts assaile,
Plaide with her haire, and held her by the vaile:
From whom shee brake, and did to woods repaire:
Still where shee went, her beauties dide the ayre,   120
And with her warme blood, made proud *Flora* blush:
But seeking shelter in each shadie bush:
Beauty like fire, comprest, more strength receiues
And shee was still seene shining through the leaues.
Hunted from thence, the Sunne euen turn'd to see,   125
So more then Sunne-like a *Diuinity,*
Blinded her eyes, and all inuasion seekes
To dance vpon the mixture of her cheekes,
Which show'd to all, that follow'd after far,
As vnderneath the roundure of a starre,   130
The euening skie is purple'd with his beames:
Her lookes fir'd all things with her loues extreames.
Her necke a chaine of orient pearle did decke,   *v*
The pearles were faire, but fairer was her necke:
Her breasts (laid out) show'd all enflamed sights   135

Loue, lie a sunning, twixt two *Crysolites:*
Her naked wrists showde, as if through the skie,
A hand were thrust, to signe the Deitie.
Her hands, the confines, and digestions were
140 Of Beauties world; Loue fixt his pillars there.
　　Her eyes that others caught, now made her caught,
Who to her father, for the whale was brought,
Bound to a barraine Rocke, and death expected;
But heau'n hath still such Innocence protected:
145 Beauty needs feare no Monsters, for the sea,
(Mother of Monsters) sent *Alcyone,*
To warrant her, not onely gainst the waues,
But all the deathes hid in her watrie graues.
The louing birds flight made about her still,
150 (Still good presaging) shew'd heau'ns sauing will:
Which cheering her, did comfort all the shore
That mourn'd in shade of her sad eyes before:
C(1)R Her lookes to perle turn'd peble, and her locks
To burnisht gold transform'd the burning Rocks.
155 　　And now came roring to the tied, the Tide,
All the *Neireides* deckt in all their pride
Mounted on Dolphins, roade to see their wreake
The waues fom'd with their enuies; that did speake
In mutest fishes, with their leapes aloft
160 For brutish ioy of the reuenge they sought.
The people greedie of disastrous sights
And newes, (the food of idle appetites)
From the kings Chamber, straight knew his intent,
And almost his resolu'd thoughts did preuent
165 In drie waues beating thicke about the Shore
And then came on the prodegie, that bore
In one masse mixt their Image; that still spread
A thousand bodies vnder one sole head
Of one minde still to ill all ill men are
170 *Strange sights and mischiefes fit the Populare.*
　　Vpon the Monster red *Rhamnusia* rode,
The Sauage leapt beneath his bloody load
v Mad of his prey, giu'n ouer now by all:
When any high, haue any meanes to fall,
175 *Their greatest louers proue false props to proue it*
And for the mischiefe onely, praise and loue it.
There is no good they will not then commend,
Nor no Religion but they will pretend
A mighty title to, when both are vs'd,
180 *To warrant Innouation, or see brus'd*
The friendlesse Reed, that vnder all feet lies:

The sound parts euermore, they passe like flies,
And dwell vpon the sores, ill in themselues,
They clearely saile with ouer rockes and shelues,
But good in others ship wracke in the Deepes: 185
Much more vniust is he that truely keepes
Laws for more shew, his owne ends vnderstood
Then he that breakes them for anothers good.
And 'tis the height of all malignity,
To tender good so, that yee ill implie: 190
To treade on Pride but with a greater pride.
When where no ill, but in ill thoughts is tri'd,
To speake well is a charity diuine: C₂ᴿ
The rest retaine the poyson serpentine
Vnder their lips, that sacred liues condemne,   195
And wee may worthily apply to them,
This tragicke execration: perish hee
That sifts too far humane infirmity.

But as your cupping glasses still exhale
The humour that is euer worst of all   200
Jn all the flesh: So these spic't conscienc't men
The worst of things explore still, and retaine.
Or rather, as in certaine Cities were
Some ports through which all rites piaculare,
All Executed men, all filth were brought,   205
Of all things chast, or pure, or sacred, nought
Entring or issuing there: so curious men,
Nought manly, elegant, or not vncleane,
Embrace, or bray out: Acts of staine are still
Their Syrens, and their Muses: Any ill   210
Js to their appetites, their supreme good,
And sweeter then their necessary food.
All men almost in all things they apply   v
The *By* the *Maine* make, and the *Maine* the *By*.

Thus this sweete Ladies sad exposure was   215
Of all these moodes in men, the only glasse:
But now the man that next to Ioue comptrold
The triple world; got with a shoure of gold:
(Armed with *Medusa's* head, and *Enyos* eye:
The Adamantine sword of *Mercury*   220
The helme of *Pluto*, and *Minerua's Mirror*,
That from the *Gorgus* made his passe with Terror)
Came to the rescue of this enuied mayd:
Drew neere, and first, in admiration stay'd
That for the common ill of all the land,   225
She the particular obloquie should stand:
And that a beauty, no lesse then diuine

Should men and women finde so serpentine
As but to thinke her any such euent:
230 Much lesse that eies and hands should giue consent
To such a danger and to such a death.
But though the whole Realme laboured vnderneath
C₃ᴿ So foule an error, yet since *Ioue* and he
Tendred her beauty, and integretie,
235 In spight of all; the more he set vp spirrit
To doe her right; the more all wrong'd her merit,
He that both vertue had, and beauty too
Equall with her; to both knew what to doe:
The Ruthles still go laught at to the Graue
240 *Those that no good will doe, no goodnesse haue:*
The minde a spirit is, and cal'd the glasse
In which we see God; and corporeall grace
The mirror is, in which we see the minde.
Amongst the fairest women you could finde
245 Then *Perseus*, none more faire; mongst worthiest men,
No one more manly: *This the glasse is then*
To shew where our complexion is combinde;
A womans beauty, and a manly minde:
Such was the halfe-diuine-borne Troian Terror
250 Where both Sex graces, met as in their Mirror.
Perseus of Loues owne forme, those fiue parts had
Which some giue man, that is the loueliest made:
v Or rather that is loueliest enclin'd,
And beares (with shape) the beauty of the mind:
255 Young was he, yet not youthfull, since mid-yeeres,
The golden meane holds in mens loues and feares:
Aptly composde, and soft (or delicate)
Flexible (or tender) calme (or temperate)
Of these fiue, three, make most exactly knowne,
260 The Bodies temperate complexion:
The other two, the order doe expresse,
The measure and whole Trim of comelinesse.
A temperate corporature (learn'd Nature saith)
A smooth, a soft, a solid flesh bewrayeth:
265 Which state of body shewes th'affections State
Jn all the humours, to be moderate;
For which cause, soft or delicate they call
Our conquering *Perseus*, and but yong withall,
Since time or yeeres in men too much reuolu'd,
270 The subtiler parts of humour being resolu'd,
More thicke parts rest, of fire and aire the want,
Makes earth and water more predominant:
[C₄ᴿ] Flexible they calde him, since his quicke conceit,

And pliant disposition, at the height
Tooke each occasion, and to Acts approu'd,   275
As soone as he was full inform'd, he mou'd,
Not flexible, as of inconstant state, ⎫
Nor soft, as if too much effeminate, ⎬
For these to a complexion moderate ⎭
(Which we before affirme in him) imply,   280
A most vnequall contrariety.
Composure fit for *Ioues* sonne *Perseus* had,
And to his forme, his mind fit answere made:
"As to be lou'd, the fairest fittest are;
"To loue so to, most apt are the most faire,   285
"Light like it selfe, transparent bodies makes,
"At ones act, th'other ioint impression takes.
"*Perseus*, (as if transparent) at first sight,
"Was shot quite thorough with her beauties light:
"Beauty breedes loue, loue consummates a man.   290
"For loue, being true, and *Eleutherean*,
"No Jniurie nor contumelie beares;
"That his beloued, eyther feeles or feares,   v
"All good-wils enterchange it doth conclude
"And mans whole summe holds, which is gratitude: 295
"No wisdome, noblesse, force of armes, nor lawes,
"Without loue, wins man, his compleat applause:
"Loue, makes him valiant, past all else desires ⎫
"For *Mars*, that is, of all heau'ns erring fires ⎬
"Most full of fortitude (since he inspires ⎭   300
"Men with most valour) *Cytherǫa* tames:
"For when in heau'ns blunt Angels shine his flames,
"Or he, his second or eight house ascends
"Of rul'd Natiuities; and then portends
"Ill to the then-borne: *Venus* in aspect   305
"*Sextile*, or *Trine* doth (being conioyn'd) correct
"His most malignitie: And when his starre
"The birth of any gouernes (fit for warre
"The Jssue making much to wrath enclin'd
"And to the ventrous greatnesse of the minde)   310
"Jf *Venus* neere him shine; she doth not let
"His magnanimity, but in order set
"The vice of Anger making *Mars* more milde   D₍₁₎ᴿ
"And gets the mastry of him in the childe:
"*Mars* neuer masters her; but if she guide   315
"She loue inclines: and *Mars* set by her side
"Her fires more ardent render, with his heat:
"So that if he at any birth be set
"In th'house of *Venus*, *Libra*, or the *Bull*,

320 "The then-borne burnes, and loues flames feels at full.
"Besides, *Mars* still doth after *Venus* moue
"*Venus* not after *Mars*: because, of Loue
"Boldnesse is hand-maid, Loue not so of her:
"For not because men, bold affections beare
325 "Loues golden nets doth their affects enfold;
"But since men loue, they therefore are more bold
"And made to dare, euen *Death*, for their belou'd,
"And finally, Loues Fortitude is prou'd
"Past all, most cleerely; for this cause alone
330 "All things submit to Loue, but loue to none.
"Celestials, Animals, all Corporeall things,
"Wisemen, and Strong, Slaue-rich, and Free-borne Kings
v "Are loues contributories; no guifts can buy,
"No threats can loue constraine, or terrifie
335 "For loue is Free, and his Jmpulsions still
"Spring from his owne free, and ingenious will.
"Not God himselfe, would willing loue enforce
"But did at first decree, his liberall course:
"Such is his liberty, that all affects
340 "All arts and Acts, the minde besides directs
"To some wish't recompence, but loue aspires
"To no possessions, but his owne desires:
"As if his wish in his owne sphere did moue,
"And no reward were worthy Loue but Loue.
345 Thus *Perseus* stood affected, in a Time
When all loue, but of riches was a crime
A fancy and a follie. And this fact
To adde to loues deseruings, did detract;
For twas a Monster and a monstrous thing
350 Whence he should combat out, his nuptiall ring,
The monster vulgar thought, and conquerd gaue
The combatant already, the foule graue
D₂ᴿ Of their fore-speakings, gaping for him stood
And cast out fumes as from the Stigian flood
355 Gainst his great enterprise, which was so fit
For *Ioues* cheefe *Minion*, that *Plebeian* wit
Could not conceiue it: Acts that are too hie
For Fames crackt voice, resound all Jnfamie:
O poore of vnderstanding: if there were
360 Of all your Acts, one onely that did beare
Mans worthie Image, euen of all your best
Which truth could not discouer, to be drest
In your owne ends, which Truths selfe not compels,
But couers in your bottoms, sinckes and hels,
365 Whose opening would abhor the sunne to see

(So ye stood sure of safe deliuerie
Being great with gaine or propagating lust)
A man might feare your hubbubs; and some trust
Giue that most false *Epiphonem,* that giues
Your voice, the praise of gods: but view your liues   370
With eyes impartiall, and ye may abhorre
To censure high acts, when your owne taste more
Of damned danger: *Perseus* scorn'd to feare   *v*
The ill of good Acts, though hel-mouth gap't there:
Came to *Andromeda;* sat by, and cheerd: 375
But she that lou'd, through all the death she fear'd,
At first sight, like her Louer: for his sake
Resolu'd to die, ere he should vndertake
A combat with a Monster so past man
To tame or vanquish, though of *Ioue* he wanne   380
A power past all men els, for man should still
Aduance his powers to rescue good from ill,
Where meanes of rescue seru'd: and neuer where
Ventures of rescue, so impossible were
That would encrease the danger: two for one   385
Expose to Ruine: Therefore she alone
Would stand the Monsters Fury and the Shame
Of those harsh bands: for if he ouercame
The monstrous world would take the monsters part
So much the more: and say some sorcerouse art   390
Not his pure valour, nor his Jnnocence
Preuail'd in her deliuerance, her offence
Would still the same be counted, for whose ill   D,ᴿ
The Land was threatned by the Oracle.
The poisoned Murmures of the multitude   395
Rise more, the more, desert or power obtrude:
Against their most (sayd he) come J the more:
Vertue, in constant sufferance we adore.
Nor could death fright him, for he dies that loues:
And so all bitternesse from death remoues.   400
He dies that loues, because his euery thought,
(Himselfe forgot) in his belou'd is wrought.
Jf of himselfe his thoughts are not imploy'd
Nor in himselfe they are by him enioy'd.
And since not in himselfe, his minde hath Act   405
(The mindes act chiefly being of thought compact)
Who workes not in himselfe, himselfe not is:
For, these two are in man ioynt properties,
To worke, and Be; for *Being* can be neuer
But *Operation,* is combined euer.   410
Nor *Operation, Being* doth exceed,

Nor workes man where he is not: still his deed
v His being, consorting, no true Louers minde
He in himselfe can therefore euer finde
415 Since in himselfe it workes not, if he giues
Being from himselfe, not in himselfe he liues:
And he that liues not, dead is, Truth then said
That whosoeuer is in loue, is dead.
Jf death the Monster brought then, he had laid
420 A second life vp, in the loued Mayd:
And had she died, his third life Fame decreed,
Since death is conquer'd in each liuing deed:
Then came the Monster on, who being showne
His charmed sheild, his halfe he turn'd to stone
425 And through the other with his sword made way:
Till like a ruin'd Cittie, dead he lay
Before his loue: The *Neirids* with a shrieke
And *Syrens* (fearefull to sustaine the like)
And euen the ruthlesse and the sencelesse Tide
430 Before his howre, ran roring terrifi'd,
Backe to their strength: wonders and monsters both,
With constant magnanimitie, like froth
[D₄ᴿ] Sodainely vanish, smother'd with their prease;
No wonder lasts but vertue: which no lesse
435 We may esteeme, since t'is as seldome found
Firme & sincere, and when no vulgar ground
Or flourish on it, fits the vulgar eye
Who views it not but as a prodegie?
Plebeian admiration, needes must signe
440 All true-borne Acts, or like false fires they shine:
Jf *Perseus* for such warrant had contain'd
His high exploit, what honour had he gain'd?
Who would haue set his hand to his designe
But in his skorne? skorne censures things diuine:
445 True worth (like truth) sits in a groundlesse pit
And none but true eyes see the depth of it.
Perseus had *Enyos* eye, and saw within
That grace, which out-lookes, held a desperate sin:
He, for it selfe, with his owne end went on,
450 And with his louely rescu'd *Paragon*
Long'd of his Conquest, for the latest shocke:
Dissolu'd her chaines, and tooke her from the rocke
v Now woing for his life that fled to her
As hers in him lay: Loue did both confer
455 To one in both: himselfe in her he found,
She with her selfe, in onely him was crownd:
While thee J loue (sayd he) you louing mee

In you J finde my selfe: thought on by thee,
And I (lost in my selfe by thee neglected)
In thee recouer'd am, by thee affected: 460
The same in me you worke, miraculous strange
Twixt two true Louers is this enterchange,
For after J haue lost my selfe, if I
Redeeme my selfe by thee, by thee supply
I of my selfe haue, if by thee I saue   465
My selfe so lost, thee more then me I haue.
And neerer to thee, then my selfe I am
Since to my selfe no otherwise I came
Then by thee being the meane: In mutuall loue
One onely death and two reuiualls moue: 470
For he that loues, when he himselfe neglects
Dies in himselfe once, In her he affects
Straight he renewes, when she with equall fire   E_{(1)}^{R}
Embraceth him, as he did her desire:
Againe he liues too, when he surely seeth   475
Himselfe in her made him: O blessed death
Which two liues follow: O Commerce most strange
Where, who himselfe doth for another change,
Nor hath himselfe, nor ceaseth still to haue:
O gaine, beyond which no desire can craue,   480
When two are so made one, that either is
For one made two, and doubled as in this:
Who one life had: one interuenient death
Makes him distinctly draw a two fold breath:
Jn mutuall Loue the wreake most iust is found,   485
When each so kill that each cure others wound;
But Churlish *Homicides*, must death sustaine,
For who belou'd, not yeelding loue againe
And so the life doth from his loue deuide
Denies himselfe to be a *Homicide?*   490
For he no lesse a *Homicide* is held,
That man to be borne lets: then he that kild
A man that is borne: He is bolder farre   *v*
That present life reaues: but he crueller
That to the to-be borne, enuies the light   495
And puts their eyes out, ere they haue their sight.
All good things euer we desire to haue,
And not to haue alone, but still to saue:
All mortall good, defectiue is, and fraile;
Vnlesse in place of things, on point to faile,   500
We daily new beget. That things innate
May last, the languishing we re'create:
Jn generation, re'creation is,

And from the prosecution of this
505   Man his instinct of generation takes.
Since generation, in continuance, makes
Mortals, similitudes, of powers diuine,
Diuine worth doth in generation shine.
Thus *Perseus* sayd, and not because he sau'd
510   Her life alone, he her in marriage crau'd:
But with her life, the life of likely Race
Was chiefe end of his action, in whose grace
E₂R   Her royall father brought him to his Court
With all the then assembled glad resort
515   Of Kings and Princes: where were solemniz'd
Th'admired Nuptialls: which great Heau'n so priz'd
That *Ioue* againe stoopt in a goulden showre
T'enrich the Nuptiall; as the Natall howre
Of happy *Perseus*: white-armd *Iuno* to:
520   Depos'd her greatnesse, and what she could do
To grace the *Bride & Bride-groome*, was vouchsaft.
All Subiect-deities stoopt to: and the Shaft
Golden and mutuall, with which loue comprest
Both th'enuied Louers: offerd to, and kist.
525   All answerablie feasted to their States:
In all the Starres beames, stoopt the reuerend Fates:
And the rere banquet, that fore ranne the Bed
With his presage shut vp, and seconded:
And sayd they sung verse, that Posteritie
530   Jn no age should reproue, for *Perfidie.*

PARCARVM EPITHALAMION.

v

O you this kingdomes glory that shall be
Parents to so renownd a Progenie
As earth shall enuie, and heauen glory in,
Accept of their liues threds, which Fates shal spin
535   Their true spoke oracle, and liue to see
Your sonnes sonnes enter such a *Progenie*,
As to the last times of the world shall last:
Haste you that guide the web, haste spindles haste.

See *Hesperus*, with nuptiall wishes crownd,
540   Take and enioy; In all ye wish abound,
Abound, for who should Wish crowne with her store
But you that slew what barren made the shore?
You that in winter, make your spring to come
Your Summer needs must be *Elisium:*

541 Wish] wish

A race of mere soules springing, that shall cast   545
Their bodies off in cares, and all ioyes taste.
Haste then that sacred web, haste spindles haste.

Ioue loues not many, therefore let those few   E₃ᴿ
That his guifts grace, affect still to renew:
For none can last the same; that proper is   550
To onely more then *Semideities:*
To last yet by renewing, all that haue
More merit then to make their birth their graue,
As in themselues life, life in others saue:
First to be great seeke, then lou'd, then to last: 555
Haste you that guide the web, haste spindles haste.

She comes, ô Bridegroom, shew thy selfe enflam'd
And of what tender tinder Loue is flam'd:
Catch with ech sparke, her beauties hurle about:
Nay with ech thoght of her be rapt throughout;   560
Melt let thy liuer, pant thy startled heart:
Mount Loue on earthquakes in thy euery part:
A thousand hewes on thine, let her lookes cast;
Dissolue thy selfe to be by her embrac't,
Haste ye that guide the web, haste spindles haste.   565

As in each bodie, there is ebbe and flood   *v*
Of blood in euery vaine, of spirits in blood;
Of Ioyes in spirits, of the Soule in Ioyes,
And nature through your liues, this change imploies
To make her constant: so each minde retaines   570
Manners and customs, where vicicitude reignes:
Opinions, pleasures, which such change enchains.
And in this enterchange all man doth last,
Haste then who guide the web, haste spindles haste.

Who bodie loues best, feedes on dantiest meats,   575
Who fairest seed seekes, fairest women gets:
Who loues the minde, with loueliest disciplines
Loues to enforme her, in which verity shines.
Her beauty yet, we see not, since not her:
But bodies (being her formes) who faire formes beare   580
We view, and chiefely seeke her beauties there.
The fairest then, for faire birth, see embrac't,
Haste ye that guide the web, haste spindles haste.

Starres ye are now, and ouershine the earth: E₄ᴿ
Starres shall ye be heereafter, and your birth   585
In bodies rule heere, as your selues in heau'n,
What heer *Detraction* steals, shall there be giuen:

The bound that heer you freed shal triumph there⎫
The chaine that touch't her wrists shal be a starre ⎬
590   Your beauties few can view, so bright they are: ⎭
Like you shalbe your birth, with grace disgrac't,
Haste ye that rule the web, haste spindles haste.

Thus by diuine instinct, the fates enrag'd,
Of *Perseus* and *Andromeda* presag'd
595   Who, (when the worthy nuptial State was done
And that act past, which only two makes one,
Flesh of each flesh and bone of eithers bone)
Left *Cepheus* Court; both freed and honoured.
The louing Victor, and blest *Bride-groome* led
600   Home to the Seriphins, his rescu'd Bride;
Who (after issue highly magnifi'd)
v   Both rapt to heau'n, did constellations reigne,
And to an Asterisme was turn'd the chaine
That onely touch't his grace of flesh & blood,
605   In all which stands the Fates kinde *Omen* good.

F$_{(1)}$^{R} APODOSIS.

Thus through the Fount of stormes (the cruell seas)
Her Monsters and malignant deities,
Great *Perseus* made high and triumphant way
To his starre crownd deed, and bright Nuptiall day.
610   And thus doe you, that *Perseus* place supply
In our *Ioues* loue, get *Persean* victorie
Of our Land Whale, foule Barbarisme, and all
His brood of pride, and liues Atheisticall:
That more their pallats, and their purses prise
615   Then propagating *Persean* victories:
Take Monsters parts, not aucthor manly parts:
For Monsters kill the Man-informing Arts:
And like a lothed prodegie despise
The rapture that the Arts doth naturalise,
620   Creating and immortalising men:
Who scornes in her the Godheads vertue then,
The Godheads selfe hath boldnesse to despise,
And hate not her, but their Eternities:
v   Seeke vertues loue, and vicious flatteries hate,
625   Heere is no true sweete, but in knowing State.
Who *Honor* hurts, neglecting vertues loue,
Commits but Rapes on pleasures; for not *Ioue*
His power in thunder hath, or downeright flames,
But his chiefe Rule, his Loue and Wisedome frames.
630   You then, that in loues strife haue ouercome

The greatest Subiect blood of Christendome,
The greatest subiect minde take, and in Both
Be absolute man: and giue that end your oth.
So shall my sad astonisht *Muse* arriue
At her chiefe obiect: which is, to reuiue   635
By quickning honor, in the absolute best:
And since none are, but in Eternitie, blest,
He that in paper can register things
That Brasse and Marble shall denie euen Kings:
Should not be trod on by ech present flash: 640
The Monster slaine then, with your cleere Seas, wash
From spots of Earth, Heauens beauty in the minde
In which, through death, hath all true Noblesse shinde.

FINIS.

A FREE AND OFFENCELES
IVSTIFICATION
OF
ANDROMEDA LIBERATA.

A FREE AND OF-
FENCELES IVSTIFI-
cation: Of a lately publisht and most

*maliciously misinterpreted
Poeme; Entituled.*

Andromeda liberata.

AS *Learning*, hath delighted from her Cradle, to hide her
selfe from the base and prophane *Vulgare*, her ancient
Enemy; vnder diuers vailes of *Hieroglyphickes*, Fables, and
the like; So hath she pleased her selfe with no disguise more;
then in misteries and allegoricall fictions of *Poesie*. These haue
in that kinde, beene of speciall reputation; as taking place of
the rest, both for priority of time, and precedence of vse;
being borne in the ould world, long before *Hieroglyphicks* or
Fabels were conceiued: And deliuered from the Fathers to
10 the Sonnes of Art; without any Aucthor but *Antiquity*. Yet
v euer held in high Reuerence and Aucthority; as supposed to
conceale, within the vtter barke (as their Eternities approue)
some sappe of hidden Truth: As either some dimme and ob-
scure prints of diuinity, and the sacred history; Or the
grounds of naturall, or rules of morall Philosophie, for the
recommending of some vertue, or curing some vice in generall
(For howsoeuer Phisitions alledge; that their medecins, re-
spect *non Hominem, sed Socratem;* not euery, but such a
speciall body: Yet *Poets* professe the contrary, that their
20 phisique intends *non Socratem sed Hominem*, not the in-
diuiduall but the vniuersall) Or else recording some memor-
able Examples for the vse of policie and state: euer (I say)
enclosing within the Rinde, some fruit of knowledge howso-
euer darkened; and (by reason of the obscurity) of ambiguous
and different construction. Εστι τε φύσει ποιητικὴ ἡ συμπᾶσα
αἰνιγματώδης &c. *Est enim ipsa Natura vniuersa Poesis*   *Plat. in*
aenigmatum plena, nec quiuis eam dignoscit: This Ambiguity   *Alcib. 2.*
in the sence, hath giuen scope to the varietie of expositions;
while Poets in al ages (challenging, as their Birth-rights, the
30 vse and application of these fictions) haue euer beene allowed
to fashion both, *pro & contra*, to their owne offencelesse, and
iudicious occasions. And borrowing so farre the priuiledg'd
licence of their professions; haue enlarged, or altred the
Allegory, with inuentions and dispositions of their owne, to
extend it to their present doctrinall and illustrous purposes.
₃ᴿ By which aucthority, my selfe (resoluing amongst others, to
offer up my poore mite, to the honour of the late Nuptials;

betwixt the two most Noble personages, whose honored
names renown the front of my Poeme) singled out (as in some
parts harmelessly, and gracefully applicable to the occasion)   40
The Nuptials of *Perseus* and *Andromeda*, an innocent and
spotlesse virgine, rescu'd from the polluted throate of a
monster; which I in this place applied to the sauage multi-
tude; peruerting her most lawfully-sought propagation, both
of blood and blessing, to their owne most lawlesse and las-
ciuious intentions: from which in all right she was legally and
formally deliuered. Nor did I euer imagine till now so farre-
fetcht a thought in malice (such was my simplicitie) That
the fiction being as ancient as the first world, was originally
intended to the dishonor of any person now liuing: but pre-   50
sum'd, that the application being free, I might *pro meo iure*
dispose it (innocently) to mine owne obiect: if at least, in
mine owne wrighting, I might be reasonablie & conscionablie
master of mine owne meaning. And to this sense, I confinde
the allegory throughout my Poeme; as euery word thereof,
(concerning that point) doth cleerely and necessarilie demon-
strate: without the least intendment (I vow to God) against
any noble personages free state, or honor. Nor make I any
noble (whose meere shadowes herein, the vulgar perhaps may
imitate) any thought the more mixt with the grosse substance   60
of the vulgar: but present the vulgare onely in their vnseuerd   v
herde; as euer in antient tradition of all autenticall Aucthours
they haue been resembled: To whom they were neuer behold-
ing for any fairer Titles; then the base, ignoble, barbarous,
giddie multitude; The Monster with many heads (which the
Caligula   Emperor, in his displeasure, wisht to haue sprung from one
necke; that all at one blow, he might haue vntrunckt them)
cui lumen ademptum; without an Eye; or, at most, seeing all
by one sight (like the Lamiae, who had but one eie to serue
all their directions, which, as anie one of them went abroad,   70
she put on, and put off when she came home) giuing vp their
vnderstandings to their affections, and taking vp their
Canes igno-   affections on other mens credits, neuer examining the causes
tis allatrant,   of their Loues or hates, but (like curres) alwaies barking at
notis blandi-   all they know not; whose most honored deseruings (were
untur Sen.   they knowen to them as to others of neerer and truer observa-
tion) might impresse in them as much reuerence as their
ignorance doth rudenesse: Euermore baying lowdest at the
most eminent Reputations, & with whom (as in the kingdom of
Frogges) the most lowd Crier, is the loftiest Ruler: No reason   80
nor aucthority able to stoope them; though neuer so iudicially
& religiously vrdging them: whose impartiall and cleere

52 innocently] innocenly

truth, not their owne bold blindnesse can denie; vnlesse they
will dare to mutter with the Oratour touching the Delphicke
Oracles, and say our Oracles of *Truth*, did likewise φιλιππείζειν,   *Demosthenes.*
encline to Philip: putting no difference betwixt *Illusion* and
Truth, the consciences of learned religious men, and the cun-
nings of prophane. And then how may my poore endeauours,
in dutie to *Truth*, and my most deare Conscience (for Reputa-
tion, since it stands, for the most part, on beasts feete, and
Deserts hand is nothing to warrant it, let it goe with the
beastly) reforme or escape their vnrelenting detractions?
The Loues of the right vertuous and truly noble, I haue
euer as much esteemed, as despised the rest: finding euer of
the first sort, in all degrees, as worthy as any of my rancke,
till (hauing enough to doe, in mine owne necessary ends,
hating to insinuate and labour their confirmation, and en-
crease of opinion, further then their owne free iudgements
would excite and direct them) I still met with vndermining
laborers for themselues, who (esteeming all worth their own,
which they detract from others) deminisht me much in some
changeable estimations (*Amicus enim Animal facile mutabile*)
whose supplies yet farre better haue still brought me vn-
sought: and till this most vnequall impression opprest me,
I stood firme vp with many, now onely, with God and my
selfe. For the violent hoobub, setting my song to their owne
tunes, haue made it yeeld so harsh and distastefull a sound to
my best friends, that my Integritie, euen they hold, affected
with the shrill eccho thereof, by reflexion; receiuing it from
the mouthes of others. And thus (to omit, as strooke dumbe
with the disdaine of it, their most vnmanly lie both of my
baffling and wounding, saying, Take this for your *Andromeda*,
not being so much as toucht, I witnesse God, nor one sillable
suffering) I will descend to a conclusion with this; that in all
this my seede time, sowing others honours, *Inuidus supersemi-
nauit Zizania &c*. Whiles I slept in mine innocencie, the
enuious man hath beene heere, who like a venomous spider,
drawing this subtle thred out of himselfe, cunningly spred
it into the eares of the manie (who as they see all with one
eye, so heare all with one eare, and that alwaies the left)
where multiplying and getting strength it was spred into an
Artificiall webbe, to entangle my poore poeticall flie; being
otherwise (God knowes) far enough from all venome, saue
what hath been forc'st into her, by her poisonous enemy to
sting her to death. But the allusion (you will say) may be ex-
tended so farre; but *qui nimium emulget elicet sanguinem;*
a malicious reader by straining the Allegorie past his inten-

102 *Amicus enim*] *Amicuse nim*

tionall limits, may make it giue blood, where it yeeldes
naturally milke, and ouercurious wits may discouer a sting in
a flie: But as a guiltlesse prisoner at the barre sayd to a   130
Lawyer thundring against his life, *Num quia tu disertus es, ego
peribo?* because malice is witty, must Innocence be con-
demned? Or if some other, not sufficiently examining what
I haue written, shall by mistaking the title, suppose it carrie   **$_{(1)}$R
such an vnderstanding; doth any Law therfore cast that
meaning vpon me? Or doth any rule of reason make it good,
that let the writer meane what he list, his writing notwith-
standing must be construed *in mentem Legentis?* to the intend-
ment of the Reader? If then, for the mistaking of an enuious
or vnskilfull Reader, who commonly bring *praeiudicia pro*   140
iudicijs, I shal be exposed to the hate of the better sort, or
taken forciblie into any powrefull displeasure, I shall esteeme
it an acte as cruell and tyranous, as that of the Emperour,
who put a Consul to death for the errour of a publique Crier;
misnaming him Emperour in stead of Consul. For my selfe
I may iustly say thus much, that if my whole life were layd
on the racke, it could neuer accuse me for a *Satyrist* or
Libeller, to play with worthie mens reputations; or if my
vaine were so addicted, yet could I so farre be giuen ouer,
as without cause or end, to aduenture on personages of re-   150
nownd nobilitie? hauing infallible reason to assure my selfe,
that euen those most honoured personages, to whose graces
I chiefly intended these labors, might they but in the least
degree haue suspected any such allusion by me purposed,
as is now most iniuriously surmised against me, they would
haue abhorred me and banisht me their sight. To conclude
Hic Rhodus, hic saltus; as I said of my life, so of my lines;
heere is the Poeme; let euerie sillable of it be tortured by
any how partiall and preiudicate soeuer (for as the case hath   *v*
beene carried: I can now looke for no difference) and if the   160
least particle thereof, can be brought, necessarilie or iustly to
confesse, any harmefull intention of mine to the height
imagined, hauing already past the test of some of the most
Iudiciall and Noble of this Kingdome: if *Malice* will still make
vnanswerably mine, what her selfe hath meerely inuented,
and say with Phisitians, that the fault of the first concoction
cannot be corrected in the second, (my meat supposed
Harpy-like rauisht at first, into her vicious stomacke) And
that as *Herodotus* is vniustly said to praise onlie the *Athenians*,
that all *Grecians* else he might the more freelie depraue, so   170
Malice will as licentiouslie affirme, that my Poeme hath some-
thing honourablie applicable, that the rest might the more

153 least] laest

safely discouer my malignance: And lastelie, If my Iudges
(being preiudicd with my accusation, haue no eare left to
heare my defence) will therefore powerfullie continue their
hostilitie both against my life & reputation, then *Collum
securi*, I must endure at how inhumane hands soeuer (at
least) my poore credits amputation: humblie retiring my
selfe within the Castle of my Innocence, & there in patience
180   possessing my Soule, quietlie abide their vttermost outrage:
defending my selfe, as I maie, from the better sort, by a
cleere conscience, from the baser, by an eternall contempt.

*Pereas, qui calamitates hominum
colligis*. E u r :

**₂R   The worst of the greatest Act.
Æ t n a q u e n c h t .

D i s t : *Two Plants in one soile fruitlesse;
Both transplanted:*

*(V n t o u c h t) f i n d e f i t m e a n e s f o r
posterity granted.*

The worst of the least.
The spleenelesse Flie.

D i s t : *The Innocent deliuerd, her destroier
Her trophe is: Her Sauer, Her Enioyer.*

Tamen haec fremit Plebs, L i v :

Yet further opposd; admit a little further answer.

181 defending] dedefending

DIALOGUS.

The Persons *Pheme* and *Theodines*.

PHE. Ho! you! *Theodines* you must not dreame
Y'are thus dismist in Peace, seas too extreame
Your song hath stird vp, to be calmd so soone:
Nay, in your hauen you shipwracke, y'are vndone,   *v*
Your *Perseus* is displeasd, and sleighteth now   5
Your worke, as idle, and as seruile, yow.
The Peoples god-voice, hath exclamd away
Your mistie cloudes, and he sees cleere as day
Y'aue made him scandald for anothers wrong,
Wishing vnpublisht your vnpopular song.   10

Theo. O thou with peoples breaths and bubbles fild,
Euer deliuered, euermore with childe:
How Court and Citty burnish with thy breede
Of newes and nifles? seasoning all their feede
With nothing, but what onely (drest like thee)   15
Of surfet tasts and superfluitie?
Let all thy bladder-blowers still inspire
And make embroderd foote-bals for the mire
With thy suggestions: On the clouen feete
Of thy *Chymaera* tost from streete to streete;   20
Our *Perseus* skornes to skuffle with the prease ⎫
Or like th'inconstant Moone be, that like these ⎬
Makes her selfe readie by her glasse the seas ⎭
The common *Rendes vous* of all rude streames:
And fed in some part, with our common *Thames*   25
As that is hourely seru'd with sewers and sinckes,
Strengthening and cleansing our sweet meats and drinkes,
Our *Perseus* by *Mineruaes* perfect *Mirror*
Informes his beauties: that reformed from th'error
Which *Change* and *Fashion* in most others finde,   30
Like his fair bodie, he may make his minde,
Decke that with knowing ornaments, and then
Effuse his radiance, vpon knowing *Men*,
Which can no more faile then the sunne to show
By his in-light, his outward ouerflow.   35
Perseus? (that when *Minerua* in her spring
Which renders deathlesse, euery noble thing   **₃R
Clarified in it, thrice washt hath his foode)
Take from a Sow, that washeth in her floode
(The common kennell) euery gut she feedes?   40
His food then thinking cleaner? And but then

332

Take it for manly, when vnfit for Men?
Can I seeme seruile to him, when ahlas
My whole *Lifes freedome*, shewes I neuer was?
45   If I be rude in speech, or not expresse
My *Plaine Minde*, with affected Courtlines
His *Insight* can into the *Fountaine* reach,
And knowes, sound *meaning* nere vsde *glosing* speach.

Phem. Well, be he as you hope, but this beleeue,
50   All friends haue left you, all that knew you grieue
(For faire condition in you) that your *Thrall*,
To one Mans humour, should so lose them all:

Theo. One may be worth all, and they *thus implie*
Themselues are all bad, that one *Good* enuie.
55   *Goodnesse* and *Truth they are* (the *All-good* knowes)
To whom my free Soule all her labours vowes.
If friends for this forsake me, let them flie;
And know that no more their inconstancie
Grieues, or disheartens my resolu'd endeauours
60   Then I had shaken off so many feauers.
My faire condition moues them: Euen right thus
Far'd the Phisition, *Aristoxenus*
With still poore *Socrates;* who terming rude,
Lustfull, vnlearnd, and with no wit indude
65   The most wise Man, did adde yet, he is iust;
And with that praise, would giue his dispraise trust.
For as a man, whom Arte hath flattery taught,
v   And is at all parts, master of his Craft;
With long and varied praises, doth sometimes
70   Mixe by the way, some sleight and peruiall crimes
As sawce; to giue his flatteries taste and scope,
So that Malignitie, may giue her hope
Of faults beleeu'd effect, she likewise laies
In her strowd passage, some light flowers of praise.
75   But tis not me ahlas, they thus pursue
With such vnprofiting, Cunning, nor embrue
Their bitter spent mouthes, with such bloud-mixt fome,
In chace of any action that can come
From my poore forme, but from the foot they tread
80   Those passages, that thence affect the head.
And why? who knowes? not that next spirit that is
Organe to all their knowing faculties,
Or else, I know I oft haue read of one   *Linceus.*
So sharpe-eyd, he could see through Oke and Stone,
85   Another that high set in *Sicilie*
As farre as *Carthage* numbred with his eye,

The Nauie vnder saile, which was dissite
A night and daies saile; with windes most fore-right;

Callicrates.
Mirmecides.

And others, that such curious chariots made
As with a flies wing, they hid all in shade,   90
And in a Sesamine (small Indian graine)
Engrau'd a page of *Homers* verses plaine.
These farre-seene meruailes, I could neuer see
Being made of downe right, flat simplicitie,
How neere our curious Craftsmen come to these   95
They must demonstrate, ere they winne the wise:

Phe. But who are those you reckon *Homicides*
In your rackt Poeme? I sweare, that diuides
Your wondering Reader, far from your applause.

Theo. I ioie in that, for weighing with this cause   100 **⋆R
Their other Reason, men may cleerely see,
How sharpe and pregnant their constructions be.
I proue by Argument, that he that loues
Is deade, and onely in his louer moues.
His Louer as t'were taking life from him: 105
And praising that kinde slaughter I condemne
As churlish *Homicides*, who will denie

*See my rea-
sons in their
places.*

In loue twixt two, the possibility
To propagate their liues into descent
Needefull and lawfull, and that argument   110

*Quippe non
minus homi-
cida consendus*

Is *Platoes*, to a word, which much commends
The two great personages, who wanting th'ends

*est qui hominem praecipit nasciturum; quam qui natum tellite medio. Audacior autem, qui pre-
sentem abrumpit vitam, crudelior, qui lucem inuidet nascituro, & nondum natos filios suos enecat.
Plat. in Sympo.*

Of wedlocke, as they were; with one consent
Sought cleere disiunction, which (with blest euent)
May ioine both otherwise, with such encrease   115
Of worthy Ofspring, that posterities
May blesse their fautors, and their fauoures now:
Whom now such bans and poisons ouerflow.

Phem. Bound to a barraine rocke, and death expected,
See that with all your skill then cleane dissected.   120
That (barraine) cleere your edge of, if you can.

Theo. As if that could applied be to a Man?
O barraine Malice! was it euer sayd
A man was barraine? or the burthen layd
Of bearing fruite on Man? if not, nor this   125
Epithete barraine, can be construed his

In least proprietie: but that such a one
As was *Andromeda;* in whose parts shone
All beauties, both of bodie and of minde ⎫
130   The sea dame to a barraine rock should binde ⎬
In enuie least some other of her kinde ⎭
v   Should challenge them for beauty any more;
Encreast the cause of making all deplore
So deare an innocent, with all desert
135   No more then (for Humanities shame) peruert
For of your whole huge reckonings heere's the sum,
O saeclum insipiens, & insicetum.

Quod dignis adimit, transit
ad Impios.

Virgo sanè
egregia, & om-
nibus animi &
corporis doti-
bus ornatissi-
ma Natal: Co:
de Andro-
meda.

PRO VERE,
AVTVMNI LACHRYMAE.

TO
THE MOST
WORTHILY HONORED
and Iudicially-Noble Louer and
Fautor of all Goodnesse and Vertue,
ROBERT, Earle of SO-
MERSET, &c.

*A*LL lest *Good,* That but onely aymes at *Great,*
   I know (best *Earle*) may boldly make retreat
To your *Retreat,* from this Worlds open *Ill.*
Of *Goodnesse* therefore, The *Prime* part (the *Will*)
Enflam'd my *Pow'rs,* to celebrate as farre
As their force reacht, This *Thunderbolt of Warre.*
His wisht *Good,* and the true Note of his *Worth,*
(Yet neuer, to his full *Desert,* set forth)
Being *Root,* and *Top,* to this his *Plant of Fame,*
Which cannot furnish with an *Anagram*
Of iust *Offence,* and Desire to wrest
All the *free* Letters here; by such a *Test*
To any *Blame:* for equall *Heauen* auert,
It should returne *Reproach,* to prayse *Desert;*
How haplesse, and peruerse, soeuer bee
The *Enuies,* and *Infortunes* following Mee:
Whose true, and simple-onely-ayme at *Merit,*
Makes your acceptiue, and still-bettering *Spirit*
My *Wane* view, as at *Full* still; and sustaine
A *Life,* that other subtler *Lords* disdaine:
Being *Suttlers* more, to *Braggart-written Men,*
(Though still deceiu'd) then any truest *Pen.*
Yet Hee's as wise, that to *Impostors* giues,
As *Children,* that hang *Counters* on their sleeues:
Or (to pare all his *Wisdome* to the *Quick*)
That, for th'*Elixar,* hugges the Dust of *Brick.*
Goe then your owne *Way* still; and *God* with you
Will goe, till his state all your steppes auow.
The *World* still in such impious *Error* strayes,
That all wayes fearefull are, but *Pious* wayes.

Your best Lordships
euer most worthily
bounden,
      Geo: Chapman.

339

PRO VERE,
AVTVMNI
LACHRYMAE.

ALL my yeeres comforts, fall in Showres of Teares,
That this full Spring of Man, This VERE of VERES,

* * * * * * * *

Famine should barre my Fruites, whose Bountie breedes them,
The faithlesse World loue to deuoure who feedes them.
Now can th'Exempt Ile from the World, no more   5 v
(With all her arm'd Fires) such a Spring restore.
The dull Earth thinkes not This; Though should I summe
The Master-Martiall Spirits of Christendome,
In his few Nerues; My Summe (t'a thought) were true.
But who liues now, that giues true Worth his due?   10
'Tis so diuine a Sparke, and loues to liue
So close in Men; that hardly it will giue
The Owner notice of his Pow'r or Being.
Nought glories to be seene, that's worth the seeing.
God, and all good Spirits, shunne all Earthy sight,   15 B₍₁₎ᴿ
And all true Worth, abhorres the guilty Light,
Infus'de to few, to make it choice and deare,
And yet how cheape the Chiefe of all is VERE?
As if his want, wee could with Ease supply.
When should from Heauen fall His Illustrious Eye,   20
We might a Bon-Fire thinke would fill his Sphere,
As well as any other, make vp VERE.
Too much this: why? All know, that some one Houre
Hath sent a Soule downe, with a richer Dowre
Then many Ages after, had the Graces,   25 v
To Equall in the Reach of all their Races.
As when the Sunne in his *Æqualor* shines,
Creating Gold, and precious Minerall Mines
In some one Soyle of Earth, and chosen Veine;
When, not 'twixt *Gades* and *Ganges*, Hee againe   30
Will daine t'enrich so, any other Mould.
Nor did great Heauens free Finger, (That extold
The Race of bright ELIZA's blessed Raigne,
Past all fore-Races, for all sorts of Men,
Schollers, and Souldiers, Courtiers, Counsellors)   35 B₂ᴿ
Of all Those, chuse but Three (as Successors)
Eyther to other, in the Rule of Warre;

Whose Each, was All, his three-Forckt-Fire and Starre:

Their last, This VERE; being no lesse Circular

40   In guard of our engag'd Ile (were he here)

Then *Neptunes* Marble Rampier: But (being There

Circled with Danger) Danger to vs All;

As Round, as Wrackfull, and Reciprocall.

Must all our Hopes in Warre then! Safeties All;

v 45   In Thee (O VERE) confound their Spring and Fall?

And thy Spirit (Fetcht off, Not to be confinde

In lesse Bounds, then the broad wings of the Winde)

In a Dutch Cytadell, dye pinn'd, and pin'de?

O England, Let not thy old constant Tye

50   To Vertue, and thy English Valour lye

Ballanc't (like Fortunes faithlesse Leuitie)

Twixt two light wings: Nor leaue Eternall VERE

In this vndue plight. But much rather beare

Armes in his Rescue, And resemble her,

B₈ᴿ 55   Whom long time thou hast seru'd (The PAPHIAN Queene)

When (all asham'd of her still-giglet Spleene)

She cast away her Glasses, and her Fannes,

And Habites of th'Effeminate *Persians*,

Her *Ceston*, and her paintings; and in grace

60   Of great LYCVRGVS, tooke to her Embrace,

Cask, Launce, and Shield, and swum the *Spartan* Flood

(EVROTAS) to his ayde, to saue the blood

Of so much Iustice, as in him had feare

To wracke his Kingdome. Be (I say) like her,

v 65   In what is chaste, and vertuous, as well

As what is loose, and wanton; and repell

This Plague of Famine, from thy fullest Man:

For, to thy Fame, 'twill be a lasting Ban,

To let him perish, Battailes haue beene lay'd

70   In Ballance oft, with Kingdomes; and hee weigh'd,

With Victorie, in Battailes. Muster then

(Onely for him vp) all thy Arm'd Men,

And in thy well-rigg'd Nymphs Maritimall,

Ship them, and plough vp all the Seas of *Gall*,

[B₄ᴿ] 75   Of all thy Enemies, in their Armed Prease;

And (past Remission) flye to his Release.

'Tis done, as sure as counsail'd: For who can

Resist God, in the Right of such a Man?

And, with such Men, to be his Instruments,

80   As hee hath made to liue in Forts and Tents,

And not in soft SARDANAPALIAN Sties

Of Swinish Ease, and Goatish Venneries.

And know (Great Queene of Iles) That Men that are

Lord *Norris.*

Sir *Francis Vere.*

Sir *Horatio Vere.*

In Heauens Endowments, so Diuinely rare,
No Earthy Powre should too securely dare   85 *v*
To hazard with Neglect, since as much 'tis,

Genitalia   As if the Worlds begetting Faculties
Corpora.   Should suffer ruine; with whose losse would lye
The World it selfe, and all Posteritie.
For worthy men the breeders are of Worth,   90
And Heauens broode in them (cast as Offall forth)
Will quite discourage Heauen to yeeld vs more:
Worths onely want, makes all Earths plenty, poore.
But thou hast now a kind and Pious King,
That will not suffer his immortall Spring   95 C(1)ᴿ
To die vntimely; if in him it lye,
To lend him Rescue: Nor will therefore I
Let one Teare fall more from my Muses Eye,
That else has vow'd to pine with him, and dye.
But neuer was (in best Times most Abuses)   100
A Peace so wretched, as to sterue the Muses.

FINIS.

99 has] ha's

A IVSTIFICATION OF
A STRANGE
ACTION OF NERO

In burying
One of the cast HAYRES of
his Mistresse
POPPAEA.

TO THE RIGHT
VIRTVOVS AND WOR-
thily honoured Gentleman RI-
CHARD HVBERT,
Esquire.

SIR, Greate workes get little regard; little and light are most affected with height: *Omne leve sursum; grave deorsum;* you know; For which, and because Custome or Fashion, is another Nature, and that it is now the fashion to iustifie Strange Actions; I (vtterly against mine owne fashion)
v followed the vulgar, and assaid what might bee said, for iustification of a Strange Action of *Nero;* in burying with a solemne Funerall one of the cast hayres of his Mistresse *Poppea.* And not to make little labours altogether vnworthy
10 the sight of the great; I say with the great defender of little labours, *Jn tenui labor est, at tenuis non gloria.* Howsoeuer; As Seamen seeing the aproches of Whales cast out empty vessells, to serue their harmefull pleasures, and diuert them from euerting their maine aduenture; (for in the vast and immane power of any thing, no thing is distinguisht; great and precious things, basest and vilest serue alike their wild and vnwildy swinges) so my selfe hauing yet once more some worthier worke then this Oration, and following Translation,
A₃ᴿ to passe this sea of the land; expose to the land and vulgar
20 Leuiathan, these slight aduentures. The rather, because the Translation containing in two or three instances, a prepara-tion to the iustification of my ensuing intended Translations, lest some should account them, as they haue my former con-uersions in some places; licenses, bold ones, and utterly re-dundant. Though your iudiciall selfe (as I haue heard) hath taken those liberal redundances, rather as the necessary ouer-flowings of *Nilus;* then rude or harmefull torrents swolne with headstrong showers. To whose iudgement and merit, submits these and all his other seruices,

George Chapman.

THE
FVNERALL ORATION
made at the buriall of one of POP-
PAEAS *hayres.*

THIS solemne Pageant graced with so glorious a Presence
as your Highnesse selfe, and others, as you see, that
mourne in their gowns and laugh in their sleeues; may perhaps
breed a wonder in those that know not the cause, and laughter
in those that know it. To see the mighty Emperor of *Rome*
march in a mourning habit, and after him all the state of the
Empire either present or presented; The Peeres in person
though with drie eyes, yet God knowes their hearts; Others in
their Rankes; One representing the state of a Courticr (as I
iudge by his legge;) another of a Citizen (as I iudge by his
head;) another of a Souldier, (as I iudge by his looke;) an-
other the state Poeticall (as I iudge by his clothes;) for the
state Physicall, it hath no place heere; for who euer saw a
Physitian follow a Funerall? To see, I say, all this Assemblie
masking in this Funerall pomp; could hee that saw it imagine
any lesse Funerall subiect would follow, then the Herse of
your deare Mother *Agrippina?* or your beloued wife *Octauia?*
or else of her whom you preferre to them both, your diuine
Poppaea? At least who would imagine, that a poore hayre
broken loose from his fellowes; or shaken off, like a windfall
from the golden tree before his time; should haue the honour
of this Imperiall solemnitie: And bee able to glory like the flie
in the Cart; good heauen what a troope of fooles haue I
gathered together?

It is fatall to all honourable actions to fall vnder the scourge
of detracting tongues, and for the most part to bee condemn'd
before they come to triall. In regard whereof, I will borrow so
much of your patience, as that I may in a word or two examine
the whole ground of this spectacle: Not doubting but that I
shall make it appeare to all vpright eares, that it is an action
most worthy your wisedome (my gracious Soveraigne) and
that this silly, this base, this contemptible hayre on this
Herse supported, receiues no thought of honour, but what it
well deserueth. *Etiam capillus unus habet umbram suam,* was
the saying of your master *Seneca;* and may not your Highnesse
goe one step further, and say, *Etiam capillus unus habet urnam
suam?* To enter into the common place of womens hayre, I
list not; though it would afford scope enough for my pen to
play in; that Theame hath beene already canvast, and worne

346

40 halfe threedbare by Poets and their fellowes. My meaning
is not to exceede the compasse of this hayre, which we haue
here in hand. This sacred beame falne from that sunne of
beauty *Poppaea;* whose very name is able to giue it honour,

v though otherwise base. And albeit hayre were of it selfe the
most abiect excrement that were, yet should *Poppaeas* hayre
be reputed honourable. I am not ignorant that hayre is noted
by many as an excrement, a fleeting commodity, subiect to
spring, and fall; & he whose whole head last day was not worth
one hayre, it shall bee in as good estate the next day as it was

50 euer before: And such as last yeare had as faire a crop of haire
as euer fruitfull head afforded; if there come but a hot sum-
mer; it shall bee so smooth that a man may slur a Dye on't.
An excrement, it is, I deny not; and yet are not all excrements
to be vilified as things of no value: for Muske, Ciuet, Amber,
are they not all excrements? yet what more pleasing to the
daintiest sense wee haue? Nature giues many things with the
left hand, which Art receiues with the right: Sublimate and
other drugges are by nature poyson: yet Art turnes them to
wholsome medicines; so hayre though by nature giuen vs as an

60 excrement, yet by Art it is made our capitall ornament. For
whereas the head is accounted the chiefe member of the body,

B,R hayre is giuen vs as the chiefe ornament of the head; I meane
of womens heads; for men haue other ornaments belonging to
their heads, as shall hereafter appeare more largely. And how-
soeuer hayre fals within the name of excrement; yet it is
euermore the argument of a rancke or rich soyle where it
growes, and of a barren where it failes; for I dare bouldly
pronounce in despight of all paltry prouerbs, that a mans wit
is euer rankest, when his hayre is at the fullest. I say not his

70 wit is best, but ranckest; for I am not ignorant, that the
ranckest flesh is not alwayes the soundest, as the ranckest
breath is not alwaies the sweetest. And thus much more I will
adde for the generall commendation of hayre, that nature in
no part hath exprest such curious and subtill skill as in this
(as wee terme it) excrement; for what more excellent point of
Art can there be, then to indurate and harden a thinne vapor
into a dry and solid substance? And this whole bush of hayre,
hath both his being and his nourishment from those sweet

v vapors, which breathe and steame from the quintessence of

80 the braine, through those subtill pores of the head in which
they are fashioned and spunne by natures finger into so
slender and delicate a thred; as if she intended to doe like
the painter that came to see *Apelles*, drew that subtill lyne
for a masterpeece of his workmanship. And besides the
highest place giuen to the hayre, and singularity of workman-

ship exprest in it, Nature hath endowed it with this speciall
priuiledge, and left therein so great an impression of her selfe,
as it is the most certaine marke by which we may ayme at
the complexion and condition of euery man; as red hayre on
a man is a signe of trechery, what tis in a woman, let the sweet   90
musique of rime inspire vs; a soft hayre chicken-hearted; a
harsh hayre churlish natur'd; a flaxen hayre foolish brain'd;
what a black-hayr'd man is aske the prouerbe; if ye beleeue
not that, aske your wiues; if they will not tell you, looke in
your glasses, and ye shall see it written on your foreheads.
So that nature hauing honoured hayre with so great a priui-
ledge of her fauour, why should wee not thinke it worthy all   B(4)R
honour in it selfe without any addition of other circumstance.
And if Nature hath grac't the whole Garland with this
honour, may not euery flower challenge his part? If any   100
hayre, then this hayre (the argument of our present mourn-
ing) more then any: But wee must not thinke (Princes and
Senators) that the vndanted heart of our Emperor, which
neuer was knowne to shrinke at the butchering of his owne
mother *Agrippina;* and could without any touch of remorse,
heare (if not behold) the murther of his most deare wife
Octavia after her diuorce; wee must not thinke (I say) this
Adamantine heart of his could resolue into softnesse, for the
losse of a common or ordinary hayre. But this was (alas why
is it not) a hayre of such rare and matchlesse perfection,   110
whether yee take it by the colour or by the substance, as it
is impossible for nature in her whole shop to patterne it: So
subtill and slender as it can scarce be seene, much lesse felt;
and yet so strong as it is able to binde *Hercules* hand and foot;   v
and make it another of his labors to extricate himselfe. In a
word it is such a flowre as growes in no garden but *Poppaeas;*
borne to the wonder of men, the enuie of women, the glory of
the Gods, &c. A hayre of such matchlesse perfection, that if
any where it should be found by chance, the most ignorant
would esteeme it of infinite value, as certaynely some hayres   120
haue beene. The purple hayre of *Nisus,* whereon his kingdome
and life depended, may serue for an instance. And how many
yong gallants doe I know my selfe, euery hayre of whose chin,
is worth a thousand crowns; and others (but simple forni-
cators) that haue neuer a hayre on their crownes, but is worth
a Kings ransome? At how much higher rate then shall we
value this hayre, which if it were not *Poppaeas,* yet being
such as it is, it deseru'd high estimation; but being *Poppaeas*
(if it were not such) it can bee worth no lesse. When therefore
a hayre of this excellence is fallen like an Apple from the   130
golden Tree, can the losse bee light? And can such losse doe

C(1)ᴿ lesse then beget a iust and vnfayned griefe, not proceeding
from humour in our Emperour, nor flattery in vs, but out of
true iudgement in vs all? Albeit I must adde this for the
qualifying of your griefe (most sacred Emperour) that this
diuine hayre is not vtterly lost; It is but sent as a Harbenger
before, the rest must follow it: And in the meane time this
remaines in blessed estate; it is at rest; it is free from the
trouble and incombrance which her miserable fellowes that
140 suruiue are dayly enforc't to endure. The cruell combe shall
no more fasten his teeth vpon it; it shall no more bee tortured
with curling bodkins, tied vp each night in knots, wearied
with tyres, and by all meanes barr'd of that naturall freedome
in which it was borne: And, which is a torment aboue tor-
ments, subiect to the fearefull tincture of Age, and to change
his amber hew into witherd and mortified gray. From all this
feare and trouble this happie hayre is freed; it rests quietly in
his Vrne, straight to bee consecrated as a relique vpon this
altar of *Venus*, there to bee kept as her treasure, till it hath
v 150 fetcht to it a fayre number more; and then to be employed
by *Venus*, eyther as a bracelet for her paramour *Mars*, or else
(which I rather beleeue) for a Periwig for her selfe; all his
fellowes and his Mistresse, hauing from it taken the infection
of the falling sicknesse. *Dixi*.

COMMENDATORY
AND OCCASIONAL
VERSES.

(To the Author of *Nennio*.)

G. Chapman to the Author.

ACCEPT thrice Noble *Nennio* at his hand
That cannot bid himselfe welcome at home,
A thrice due welcome to our natiue strand,
Italian, *French*, and *English* now become.
Thrice Noble, not in that vsde Epethite,
But Noble first, to know whence Noblesse sprung,
Then in thy labour bringing it to light,
Thirdly, in being adorned with our tung.
And since so (like it selfe) thy Land affoords
The right of Noblesse to all noble parts,
I wish our friend, giuing thee English words,
With much desert of Loue in English harts,
    As he hath made one strange an Englishman,
    May make our mindes in this, *Italian*.

Ex tenebris.

De Guiana, Carmen Epicum.

What worke of honour and eternall name,
For all the worlde t'enuie and vs t'atchieue,
Filles me with furie, and giues armed handes
To my heartes peace, that els would gladlie turne
5   My limmes and euery sence into my thoughtes
Rapt with the thirsted action of my mind?
O *Clio, Honors Muse*, sing in my voyce,
Tell the attempt, and prophecie th'exploit
Of his *Eliza*-consecrated sworde,
10   That in this peacefull charme of *Englands* sleepe,
Opens most tenderlie her aged throte,
Offring to poure fresh youth through all her vaines,
That flesh of brasse, and ribs of steele retaines.

Riches, and *Conquest*, and *Renowme* I sing,
15   *Riches* with honour, *Conquest* without bloud,
Enough to seat the Monarchie of earth,
Like to *Ioues* Eagle, on *Elizas* hand.
Guiana, whose rich feet are mines of golde,
Whose forehead knockes against the roofe of Starres,
20   Stands on her tip-toes at faire *England* looking,
Kissing her hand, bowing her mightie breast,
And euery signe of all submission making,
To be her sister, and the daughter both

Of our most sacred Maide: whose barrennesse
Is the true fruite of vertue, that may get,   25
Beare and bring foorth anew in all perfection,
What heretofore sauage corruption held
In barbarous *Chaos;* and in this affaire
Become her father, mother, and her heire.

Then most admired Soueraigne, let your breath   30
Goe foorth vpon the waters, and create
A golden worlde in this our yron age,
And be the prosperous forewind to a Fleet,
That seconding your last, may goe before it
In all successe of profite and renowme: 35
Doubt not but your election was diuine,
(As well by *Fate* as your high iudgement ordred)
To raise him with choise Bounties, that could adde
Height to his height; and like a liberall vine,
Not onelie beare his vertuous fruit aloft,   40
Free from the Presse of squint-eyd *Enuies* feet,
But decke his gracious Proppe with golden bunches,
And shroude it with broad leaues of *Rule* oregrowne
From all blacke tempestes of inuasion.

Those Conquests that like generall earthquakes shooke   45
The solid world, and made it fall before them,
Built all their braue attemptes on weaker groundes,
And lesse persuasiue likelihoods then this;
Nor was there euer princelie Fount so long
Powr'd foorth a sea of Rule with so free course,   50
And such ascending Maiestie as you:
Then be not like a rough and violent wind,
That in the morning rends the Forrestes downe,
Shoues vp the seas to heauen, makes earth to tremble,
And toombes his wastfull brauerie in the Euen: 55
But as a riuer from a mountaine running,
The further he extends, the greater growes,
And by his thriftie race strengthens his streame,
Euen to ioyne battale with th'imperious sea
Disdaining his repulse, and in despight   60
Of his proud furie, mixeth with his maine,
Taking on him his titles and commandes:
So let thy soueraigne Empire be encreast,
And with *Iberian Neptune* part the stake,
Whose *Trident* he the triple worlde would make.   65
You then that would be wise in Wisdomes spight,
Directing with discredite of direction,
And hunt for honour, hunting him to death,

With whome before you will inherite gold,
70   You will loose golde, for which you loose your soules;
      You that choose nought for right, but certaintie,
      And feare that value will get onlie blowes,
      Placing your faith in *Incredulitie;*
      Sit till you see a woonder, *Vertue* rich:
75   Till *Honour* hauing golde, rob golde of honour;
      Till as men hate desert that getteth nought,
      They loath all getting that deserues not ought,
      And vse you gold-made men, as dregges of men;
      And till your poysoned soules, like Spiders lurking
80   In sluttish chinckes, in mystes of Cobwebs hide
      Your foggie bodies, and your dunghill pride.

      O *Incredulitie,* the wit of Fooles,
      That slouenlie will spit on all thinges faire,
      The *Cowards castle,* and the *Sluggards cradle,*
85   How easie t'is to be an Infidell?

      But you *Patrician* Spirites that refine
      Your flesh to fire, and issue like a flame
      On braue endeuours, knowing that in them
      The tract of heauen in morne-like glorie opens,
90   That know you cannot be the Kinges of earth,
      (Claiming the Rightes of your creation)
      And let the Mynes of earth be Kinges of you;
      That are so farre from doubting likelie driftes,
      That in things hardest y'are most confident;
95   You that know death liues, where power liues vnusde,
      Ioying to shine in waues that burie you,
      And so make way for life euen through your graues;
      That will not be content like horse to hold
      A thread-bare beaten waie to home affaires:
100   But where the sea in enuie of your raigne,
      Closeth her wombe, as fast as tis disclosde,
      That she like *Auarice* might swallowe all,
      And let none find right passage through her rage:
      There your wise soules as swift as *Eurus* lead
105   Your Bodies through, to profit and renowne,
      And skorne to let your bodies chooke your soules,
      In the rude breath and prisoned life of beastes:
      You that heerein renounce the course of earth,
      And lift your eies for guidance to the starres,
110   That liue not for your selues, but to possesse
      Your honour'd countrey of a generall store;
      In pitie of the spoyle rude self-loue makes,
      Of them whose liues and yours one aire doth feede,

One soile doeth nourish, and one strength combine;
You that are blest with sence of all things noble   115
In this attempt your compleat woorthes redouble.

But how is *Nature* at her heart corrupted,
(I meane euen in her most ennobled birth?)
How in excesse of Sence is Sence bereft her?
That her most lightening-like effectes of lust   120
Wound through her flesh, her soule, her flesh vnwounded;
And she must neede incitements to her good,
Euen from that part she hurtes. O how most like
Art thou (heroike Author of this Act)
To this wrong'd soule of *Nature:* that sustainst   125
Paine, charge, and perill for thy countreys good,
And she much like a bodie numb'd with surfets,
Feeles not thy gentle applications
For the health, vse, & honor of her powers.
Yet shall my verse through all her ease-lockt eares   130
Trumpet the Noblesse of thy high intent,
And if it cannot into act proceed,
The fault and bitter pennance of the fault
Make red some others eyes with penitence,
For thine are cleare; and what more nimble spirites   135
Apter to byte at such vnhooked baytes,
Gaine by our losse; that must we needs confesse
Thy princelie valure would haue purchast vs.
Which shall be fame eternall to thy name,
Though thy contentment in thy graue desires,   140
Of our aduancement, faile deseru'd effect,
O how I feare thy glorie which I loue,
Least it should dearelie growe by our decrease.
Natures that stick in golden-graueld springs,
In mucke-pits cannot scape their swallowings.   145

But we shall foorth I know; Golde is our Fate,
Which all our actes doeth fashion and create.

Then in the *Thespiads* bright Propheticke Fount,
Me thinkes I see our Liege rise from her throne,
Her eares and thoughtes in steepe amaze erected,   150
At the most rare endeuour of her power.
And now she blesseth with her woonted Graces
Th'industrious Knight, the soule of this exploit,
Dismissing him to conuoy of his starres.
And now for loue and honour of his woorth,   155
Our twise-borne Nobles bring him Bridegroome-like,
That is espousde for vertue to his loue

With feastes and musicke, rauishing the aire,
  To his *Argolian* Fleet, where round about
160 His bating Colours English valure swarmes
  In haste, as if *Guianian Orenoque*
  With his Fell waters fell vpon our shore.
  And now a wind as forward as their spirits,
  Sets their glad feet on smooth *Guianas* breast,
165 Where (as if ech man were an *Orpheus*)
  A world of Sauadges fall tame before them,
  Storing their theft-free treasuries with golde,
  And there doth plentie crowne their wealthie fieldes,
  There *Learning* eates no more his thriftlesse books,
170 Nor *Valure* Estridge-like his yron armes.
  There *Beautie* is no strumpet for her wantes,
  Nor *Gallique* humours putrifie her bloud:
  But all our Youth take *Hymens* lightes in hand,
  And fill each roofe with honor'd progenie.
175 There makes *Societie* Adamantine chaines,
  And ioins their harts with wealth, whom wealth disioyn'd.
  There healthfull Recreations strowe their meades,
  And make their mansions daunce with neighborhood,
  That here were drown'd in churlish *Auarice*.
180 And there do Pallaces and temples rise
  Out of the earth, and kisse th'enamored skies,
  Where new *Britania*, humblie kneeles to heauen,
  The world to her, and both at her blest feete,
  In whom the Circles of all Empire meet.

G C.

Peristeros: or the male Turtle.

Not like that loose and partie-liuer'd Sect
  Of idle Louers, that (as different Lights,
On colour'd subiects, different hewes reflect;)
  Change their Affections with their Mistris Sights,
5 That with her Praise, or Dispraise, drowne, or flote,
  And must be fed with fresh Conceits, and Fashions;
Neuer waxe cold, but die: loue not, but dote:
  "(Loues fires, staid Iudgements blow, not humorous Passions,)
Whose Loues vpon their Louers pomp depend,
10 And quench as fast as her Eyes sparkle twinkles,
"(Nought lasts that doth to outward worth contend,
  "Al Loue in smooth browes born is tomb'd in wrinkles.)
But like the consecrated *Bird of loue,   * The
  Whose whole lifes hap to his *sole-mate alluded,   *Turtle.*
                                                        * The
15 Whome no prowd flockes of other Foules could moue,   *Phoenix.*

But in her selfe all companie concluded.
She was to him th'*Analisde* World of Pleasure,
  Her firmenesse cloth'd him in varietie;
Excesse of all things, he ioyd in her measure,
  Mourn'd when she mourn'd, and dieth when she dies,   20
Like him I bound th'instinct of all my powres,
  In her that bounds the Empire of desert,
And Time nor Change (that all things elsc deuoures,
  But truth eterniz'd in a constant heart)
Can change me more from her, then her from merit,   25
That is my forme, and giues my being, spirit.

George Chapman.

(Sonnet to Walsingham: *All Fools.*)

To My Long Lou'd and
Honourable *Friend Sir Thomas
Walsingham Knight.*

Should I expose to euery common eye,
  The least allow'd birth of my shaken braine;
And not entitle it perticulerly
  To your acceptance, I were wurse then vaine.
And though I am most loth to passe your sight
  with any such light marke of vanitie,
Being markt with Age for Aimes of greater weight,
  and drownd in darke Death-vshering melancholy,   •
Yet least by others stealth it be imprest,
  without my passport, patcht with others wit,
Of two enforst ills I elect the least;
  and so desire your loue will censure it;
    Though my old fortune keepe me still obscure,
    The light shall still bewray my ould'loue sure.

IN SEIANVM
BEN. IONSONI
Et Musis, et sibi

in Delicijs.

So brings the wealth-contracting Ieweller
  Pearles and deare Stones, from richest shores & streames,
As thy accomplisht Trauaile doth confer
  From skill-inriched soules, their wealthier Gems;
So doth his hand enchase in ammeld Gould,   5
  Cut, and adornd beyond their Natiue Merits,

His solid Flames, as thine hath here inrould
    In more then Goulden Verse, those betterd spirits;
So he entreasures *Princes* Cabinets,
10   As thy Wealth will their wished Libraries;
So, on the throate of the rude Sea, he sets
    His ventrous foote, for his illustrous Prise;
And through wilde Desarts, armd with wilder Beasts,
    As thou aduenturst on the Multitude,
15 Vpon the boggy, and engulfed brests
    Of Hyrelings, sworne to finde most Right, most rude:
And he, in stormes at Sea, doth not endure,
    Nor in vast Desarts, amongst Woolues, more danger;
Then we, that would with *Vertue* liue secure,
20   Sustaine for her in euery *Vices* anger.
Nor is this *Allegorie* vniustly rackt,
    To this strange length; Onely that Iewels are,
In estimation meerely, so exact:
    And thy worke, in it selfe, is deare and Rare.
25 Wherein *Minerua* had beene vanquished,
    Had she, by it, her sacred Loomes aduanc't,
And through thy subiect wouen her graphicke Thread,
    Contending therein, to be more entranc't;
For, though thy hand was scarce addrest to drawe
30   The Semi-circle of *Seianus* life,
Thy *Muse* yet makes it the whole Sphaere, and Lawe
    To all State Liues: and bounds Ambitions strife.
And as a little Brooke creepes from his Spring,
    With shallow tremblings, through the lowest Vales,
35 As if he feard his streame abroad to bring,
    Least prophane Feete should wrong it, and rude Gales;
But finding happy Channels, and supplies
    Of other Fordes mixe with his modest course,
He growes a goodly Riuer, and descries
40   The strength, that mannd him, since he left his Source;
Then takes he in delightsome Meades, and Groues,
    And, with his two-edg'd waters, flourishes
Before great Palaces, and all Mens Loues
    Build by his shores, to greete his Passages:
45 So thy chaste *Muse*, by vertuous selfe-mistrust,
    Which is a true Marke of the truest Merit,
In Virgin feare of Mens illiterate Lust,
    Shut her soft wings, and durst not showe her spirit;
Till, nobly cherisht, now thou lett'st her flie,
50   Singing the sable *Orgies* of the *Muses*,
And in the highest Pitche of *Tragedie*,

22 To] to

Mak'st her command, al things thy Ground produces.
But, as it is a Signe of Loues first firing,
   Not Pleasure by a louely Presence taken,
And Bouldnesse to attempt; but close Retiring,   55
   To places desolate, and Feuer-shaken;
So, when the loue of Knowledge first affects vs,
   Our Tongues doe falter, and the Flame doth roue
Through our thinne spirits, and of feare detects vs
   T'attaine her Truth, whom we so truely loue.   60
Nor can (saith *Æschilus*) a faire young Dame,
   Kept long without a Husband, more containe
Her amorous eye, from breaking forth in flame,
   When she beholds a Youth that fits her vaine;
Then any mans first taste of Knowledge truly   65
   Can bridle the affection she inspireth:
But let it flie on Men, that most vnduly
   Haunt her with hate, and all the Loues she fireth.
If our Teeth, Head, or but our Finger ake,
   We straight seeke the Phisitian; If a Feuer,   70
Or any curefull maladie we take,
   The graue Phisitian is desired euer:
But if proud Melancholie, Lunacie,
   Or direct Madnesse ouer-heate our braines,
We Rage, Beate out, or the Phisitian flie,   75
   Loosing with vehemence, euen the sense of Paines.
So of Offenders, they are past recure,
   That with a tyranous spleene, their stings extend
Gainst their Reprouers; They that will endure
   All discreete Discipline, are not said t'offend.   80
Though Others qualified, then, with Naturall skill,
   (More sweete mouthd, and affecting shrewder wits)
Blanche Coles, call Illnesse, good, and Goodnesse ill,
   Breath thou the fire, that true-spoke Knowledge fits.
Thou canst not then be Great? yes. Who is he,   85
   (Said the good *Spartane* King) greater then I,
That is not likewise iuster? No degree
   Can boast of emminence, or Emperie,
(As the great *Stagerite* held) in any One
   Beyond Another, whose Soule farther sees,   90
And in whose Life the Gods are better knowne:
   Degrees of Knowledge difference all Degrees.
Thy *Poëme*, therefore, hath this due respect,
   That it lets passe nothing, without obseruing,
Worthy Instruction; or that might correct   95
   Rude manners, and renowme the well deseruing:

88 Can] can

Performing such a liuely Euidence
In thy Narrations, that thy Hearers still
Thou turnst to thy Spectators; and the sense
100   That thy Spectators haue of good or ill,
Thou iniect'st ioyntly to thy Readers soules.
    So deare is held, so deckt thy numerous Taske,
As thou putt'st handles to the *Thespian* Boules,
    Or stuckst rich Plumes in the *Palladian* Caske.
105 All thy worth, yet, thy selfe must Patronise,
    By quaffing more of the *Castalian* Head;
In expiscation of whose Mysteries,
    Our Netts must still be clogd, with heauy Lead,
To make them sincke, and catche: For cheerefull Gould,
110   Was neuer found in the *Pierian* Streames,
But Wants, and Scornes, and Shames for siluer sould.
    What, what shall we elect in these extreames?
Now by the Shafts of the great CYRRHAN *Poet*,
    That beare all light, that is, about the world;
115 I would haue all dull *Poet*-Haters know it,
    They shall be soule-bound, and in darknesse hurld,
A thousand yeares, (as *Sathan* was, their Syre)
    Ere Any worthy, the *Poetique* Name,
(Might I, that warme but, at the *Muses* fire,
120   Presume to guard it) should let Deathlesse *Fame*
Light halfe a beame of all her hundred Eyes,
    At his dimme Taper, in their memories.
Flie, flie, you are to neare; so odorous Flowers
    Being held too neere the Sensor of our Sense,
125 Render not pure, nor so sincere their powers,
    As being held a little distance thence;
Because much troubled Earthy parts improue them:
    Which mixed with the Odors we exhall,
Do vitiate what we drawe in. But remooue them
130   A little space, the Earthy parts do fall,
And what is pure, and hote by his tenuitye,
    Is to our powers of Sauor purely borne.
But flie, or staie; Vse thou the assiduitie,
    Fit for a true Contemner of their scorne.
135 Our *Phoebus* may, with his exampling Beames,
    Burne out the webs from their *Arachnean* eyes,
Whose Knowledge (Day-star to all Diadems,)
    Should banish knowledge-hating Policies:
So others, great in the Scientiall grace,
140   His *Chancelor*, fautor of all humane *Skils;*
His *Treasurer*, taking thèm into his Place,

98 In] in   124 Being] being   132 Is] is

Northumber, that, with thèm, his *Crescent* fils,
Graue *Worc'ster*, in whose Nerues they guard their fire,
Northampton, that to all his height in bloud,
Heightens his soule, with thèm, And *Deuonshire*,   145
    In whom their Streams, ebd to their Spring, are Floud,
Oraculous *Salisburie*, whose inspired voice,
    In State proportions, sings their misteries,
And (though last Namd) first, in whom They reioyce,
    To whose true worth, They vow most obsequies,   150
Most Noble *Suffolke*, who by Nature Noble,
    And iudgement vertuous, cannot fall by Fortune,
Who when our Hearde, came not to drinke, but trouble
    The *Muses* waters, did a Wall importune,
(Midst of assaults) about their sacred Riuer;   155
    In whose behalfes, my poore Soule, (consecrate
To poorest Vertue) to the longest Liuer,
    His Name, in spight of Death, shall propagate.
O could the World but feele how sweete a touch
    A good Deed hath in one in loue with Goodnesse,   160
(If *Poesie* were not rauished so much,
    And her composde Rage, held the simplest Woodnesse,
Though of all heates, that temper humane braines,
    Hers euer was most subtle, high, and holy,
First binding sauadge Liues, in ciuile Chaines: 165
    Solely religious, and adored solely,)
If men felt this, they would not thinke a Loue,
    That giues it selfe, in her, did vanities giue;
Who is (in Earth, though lowe) in Worth aboue,
    Most able t'honour Life, though least to liue.   170
        And so *good Friend*, safe passage to thy Freight,
            To thee a long Peace, through a vertuous strife,
        In which, lets both contend to *Vertues* height,
            Not making *Fame* our Obiect, but *good life*.

Come forth SEIANVS, fall before this Booke,
    And of thy *Falles Reuiuer*, aske forgiuenesse,
That thy lowe Birth and Merits, durst to looke
    A Fortune in the face, of such vneuennesse;
For so his feruent loue to *Vertue*, hates,
    That her pluckt plumes should wing *Vice* to such calling,
That he presents thee to all marking *States*,
    As if thou hadst beene all this while in falling.
His strong Arme plucking, from the *Midle-world*,
    Fames Brazen House, and layes her Towre as lowe,
As HOMERS *Barathrum;* that, from Heauen hurld,
    Thou might'st fall on it: and thy Ruines growe

To all Posterities, from his worke, the Ground,
And vnder Heau'n, nought but his *Song* might sound.

Hæc Commentatus est

Georgius Chapmannus.

To his deare Friend,
Beniamin Ionson
his
VOLPONE.

Come, yet, more forth, VOLPONE, and thy chase
 Performe to al length, for thy breath wil serue thee;
The Vsurer shal, neuer, weare thy case:
 Men do not hunt to kill, but to preserue thee.
Before the bést houndes, thou dost, still, but play;
 And, for our whelpes, alasse, they yelp in vaine:
Thou hast no earth; thou hunt'st the *Milke-white way;*
 And, through th'*Elisian* feilds, dost make thy traine.
And as the *Symbole* of lifes Guard, the HARE,
 That, sleeping, wakes; and, for her feare, was saf't:
So, thou shalt be aduanc'd, and made a *Starre*,
 Pole to all witts, beleeu'd in, for thy craft.
In which, the *Scenes* both Marke, and Mystery
 Is hit, and sounded, to please best, and worst;
To all which, since thou mak'st so sweete a cry,
 Take all thy *best fare*, and be nothing *curst.*

G. C.

To his louing friend M. *Jo. Flet-*
cher concerning his Pastorall, being
both a Poeme and a play:

There are no sureties (good friend) Will be taken
For workes that vulgar-good-name hath forsaken:
A Poeme and a play too! why tis like
A scholler that's a Poet: their names strike
5 Their pestilence inward, when they take the aire;
And kill out right: one cannot both fates beare.
But, as a Poet thats no scholler, makes
Vulgarity his whiffler, and so takes
Passage with ease, & state through both sides prease

1 sureties *2 ed. ff*] suerties *1 ed.*

Of Pageant seers: or as schollers please   10
That are no Poets; more then Poets learnd;
Since their art solely, is by soules discernd;
The others fals within the common sence
And sheds (like common light) her influence:
So, were your play no Poeme, but a thing   15
That euery Cobler to his patch might sing:
A rout of nifles (like the multitude)
With no one limme of any art indude:
Like would to like, and praise you: but because,
Your poeme onely hath by vs applause,   20
Renews the golden world; and holds through all
The holy lawes of homely pastorall;
Where flowers, and founts, and Nimphs, & semi-Gods,
And all the Graces finde their old abods:
Where forrests flourish but in endlesse verse;   25
And meddowes, nothing fit for purchasers:
This Iron age that eates it selfe, will neuer
Bite at your golden world; that others, euer
Lou'd as it selfe: then like your Booke do you
Liue in ould peace: and that for praise allow.   30

G Chapman.

(To Byrd, Bull, and Gibbons on *Parthenia*.)

MR: GEO: CHAPMAN
In worthye loue of this new worck,
and the most Autenticall Aucthors.

By theis choice lessons of theise Musique Masters;
  Ancient, and heightn'd with the Arts full Bowles,
Let all our moderne, mere Phantastique Tasters,
  (Whose Art but forreigne Noueltie extolls)
Rule and confine theyr fancies; and prefer
  The constant right, & depthe Art should produce;
To all lite flashes, by whose light they err;
  This wittie Age, hath wisedome least in use;
The World, ould growing, Ould, with it, grow Men;
  Theyr skylls decaying, like theyr bodies strengthe;
Yonge Men, to oulde are now but Childeren:
  First Rules of Art, encrease still with theyr lengthe.
Which see in this new worcke, yet neuer seene:
Art, the more oulde, growes euer the more greene.

TO HIS LOVED SONNE,
NAT. FIELD, AND HIS WE-
ther-cocke Woman.

To many formes, as well as many waies,
  Thy Actiue Muse, turnes like thy Acted woman:
In which, disprais'd inconstancie, turnes praise;
  Th' Addition being, and grace of *Homers* Sea-man,
In this life's rough Seas tost, yet still the same:
  So turns thy wit, Inconstancy to stay,
And stay t'Inconstancy: And as swift Fame
  Growes as she goes, in Fame so thriue thy Play,
And thus to standing, turne thy womans fall,
Wit turn'd to euerie thing, prooues stay in all.

George Chapman.

A HYMNE TO HYMEN FOR THE
MOST TIME-FITTED NVPTIALLS
of our thrice gratious
Princesse Elizabeth, &c.

Sing, Sing a Rapture to all Nuptiall eares,
Bright *Hymens* torches, drunke vp *Parcaes* teares:
Sweet *Hymen; Hymen*, Mightiest of Gods,
Attoning of all-taming blood the odds;
5   Two into One, contracting; One to Two
Dilating; which no other God can doe.
Mak'st sure, with change, and lett'st the married try,
Of Man and woman, the Variety.
And as a flower, halfe scorcht with daies long heate   Simil.
10 Thirsts for refreshing, with Nights cooling sweate,
The wings of *Zephire*, fanning still her face,
No chere can ad to her heart-thirsty grace;
Yet weares she gainst those fires that make her fade,
Her thicke hayrs proofe, all hyd, in Mid-nights shade;
15 Her Helth, is all in dews; Hope, all in showres,
Whose want bewailde, she pines in all her powres:
So Loue-scorch't Virgines, nourish quenchles fires;
The Fathers cares; the Mothers kind desires.
Their Gould, and Garments, of the newest guise,
20 Can nothing comfort their scorcht Phantasies,
But, taken rauish't vp, in *Hymens* armes,
His Circkle holds, for all their anguish, charms:
Then, as a glad Graft, in the spring Sunne shines,   Simil. ad
That all the helps, of Earth, and Heauen combines   eandem expli-
                                                          cat.
25 In Her sweet grouth: Puts in the Morning on

Her cheerefull ayres; the Sunnes rich fires, at Noone:
At Euen the sweete deaws, and at Night with starrs,
In all their vertuous influences shares;
So, in the Bridegroomes sweet embrace; the Bride,
All varied Ioies tasts, in their naked pride: 30
To which the richest weedes; are weedes, to flowres;
Come *Hymen* then; come close these Nuptiall howres
With all yeares comforts. Come; each virgin keepes
Her odorous kisses for thee; Goulden sleepes
Will, in their humors, neuer steepe an eie,   35
Till thou inuit'st them with thy Harmony.
Why staiest thou? see each Virgin doth prepare
Embraces for thee; Her white brests laies bare
To tempt thy soft hand; let's such glances flie
As make starres shoote, to imitate her eye.   40
Puts Arts attires on, that put Natures dounc:
Singes, Dances, sets on euery foote a Crowne,
Sighes, in her songs, and dances; kisseth Ayre
Till Rites, and words past, thou in deedes repaire;
The whole court Io sings: Io the Ayre: 45
Io, the flouds, and fields: Io, most faire,
Most sweet, most happy *Hymen;* Come: away;
With all thy Comforts come; old Matrons pray,
With young Maides Languors; Birds bill, build, and breed
To teach thee thy kinde, euery flowre & weed   50
Looks vp to gratulate thy long'd for fruites;
Thrice giuen, are free, and timely-granted suites:
There is a seed by thee now to be sowne,
In whose fruit Earth, shall see her glories show'n,
At all parts perfect; and must therefore loose   55
No minutes time; from times vse all fruite flowes;

Simil.   And as the tender Hyacinth, that growes
Where *Phoebus* most his golden beames bestowes,
Is propt with care; is water'd euery howre;
The sweet windes adding their encreasing powre,   60
The scattered drops of Nights refreshing dew,
Hasting the full grace, of his glorious hew,
Which once disclosing, must be gatherd straight,
Or hew, and Odor both, will lose their height;
So, of a Virgine, high, and richly kept,   65
The grace and sweetnes full growne must be reap't,
Or, forth her spirits fly, in empty Ayre;
The sooner fading; the more sweete and faire.
Gentle, O Gentle *Hymen*, be not then
Cruell, That kindest art to Maids, and Men;   70

70 art] arts

These two, One Twyn are; and their mutuall blisse,
Not in thy beames, but in thy Bosome is.
Nor can their hands fast, their harts ioyes make sweet;
Their harts, in brests are; and their Brests must meete.
75   Let, there be Peace, yet Murmur: and that noise,
Beget of peace, the Nuptiall battailes ioyes.
Let Peace grow cruell, and take wrake of all,
The warres delay brought thy full Festiuall.
Harke, harke, O now the sweete Twyn murmur sounds;
80   *Hymen* is come, and all his heate abounds;
Shut all Dores; None, but *Hymens* lights aduance;
No sound styr, let, dumb Ioy, enioy a trance.
Sing, sing a Rapture to all Nuptiall eares,
Bright *Hymens* Torches drunke vp *Parcaes* teares.

FINIS.

(To Christopher Brooke on his *Ghost of Richard the Third*.)

To his Ingenuous, and much
lou'd Friend, *the Author*.

You now amids our Muses Smithfield are
To sell your *Pegasus*, where Hackney ware
(Rid by the swish swash Rippiers of the Time,
Pamper'd and fronted with a Ribband Ryme)
5   Though but some halfe Houre soundly try'd, they tyre,
Yet sell, as quicknd with Eternall Fire.
All things are made for sale; sell man and all
For sale, to Hell: There is no Soule, to sale.
Your flippant sence-delighter, smooth, and fine,
10   Fyr'd with his Bush Muse, and his sharpe Hedge Wine,
Will sell like good old Gascoine. What does then
Thy Purple in graine, with these Red-Oker men?
Swarth Chimney sweepe, that to his Horne doth sing,
More Custome gets; then in the *Thespian* Spring,
15   The thrice bath'd Singer to the *Delphian* Lyre,
Though all must needs be rid heere; yet t'aspire
To common sale, with all turne-seruing Iades,
Fits Pandars, and the strong voic't Fish-wife Trades.
Affect not that then, and come welcome forth,
20   Though to some few, whose welcom's somthing worth:
Not one, not one (sayes *Perseus*) will reade mine;
Or two, or none; 'Tis Pageant Orsadine
That goes for gold in your Barbarian Rate,
You must be pleas'd then to change gold for that.

5 Houre] House

Might I be Patterne to the meanest few   25
Euen now when hayres of Women-hated-hew
Are wither'd on me; I delight to see
My Lines thus desolately liue like me,
Not any thing I doe, but is like Nuts
At th'ends of Meales left; when each Appetite gluts.   30
Some Poet yet can leuell you a Verse
At the Receipt of Custome; that shall Pierce
A sale Assister; as if with one Eye   ⎫
He went a Burding; strikes Fowles as they fly, ⎬
And has the very Art of Foulerie.   ⎭   35
Which Art you must not enuie; be you pleas'd
To hit Desert; fly others, as diseas'd,
Whose being pierst, is but to be infected;
And as bold Puritans (esteem'd elected)
Keep from no common Plague, which so encreases;   40
So these feed all Poeticall Diseases.
Best Ayre, lest dwellers hath; yet thinke not I
Fore-speake the sale of thy sound Poesie;
But would in one so worth encouragement
The care of what is counted worst, preuent;   45
　　And with thy cheerefull going forth with this;
　　Thy Muse in first Ranke of our Muses is.
　　　　Non datur ad Musas currere lata via.
　　　　　　　　　　　　　　Geor: Chapman.

(To Grimestone on his translation of Coeffetau's *Table of Humaine Passions.*)

To his long-lou'd and worthy *friend*, Mr. Edward Grimeston, Sergeant at Armes; of his vnwea-*ried and honored labors.*

Such is the vnequall, and inhumane vice
Of these vile *Times*, that each man sets his price
On others Labors; And the lasiest *Drone*
That neuer drop of honey, of his owne
Brought to the publique *Hiue*, distasts all ours   5
And (in the worlds wit) feeds far worthier Powers.   .
Tis Noble to be idle; Base to be
Of any Art, Good Mind, or Industry.
Another sort of dull Opinionists,
Consume their stupid liues in learned mists;   10
Yet would be seene (poore soules) beyond the Sun;
But that like *Dolon*, in the darke they run,
Other *Explorers* fearing. And these men

Like *Cheaters*, foyst in false dice to their *Den*,
15 To win mens thoughts of th'onely truly learnd,
And feede on that conceit, before tis earnd.
To strengthen which, their Markets are the Marts
Where sounds and Names of *Artsmen*, & all *Arts*
They stuffe their windy memories withall;
20 And then when ere their Creditors shall call
They pay them, with these *Tokens*, all they owe;
Then, Honest men they are, then all things know.
When all employd in priuate conference;
They count all rude that are of open braines
25 Feare to be fooles in print, though in their *Cels*
(In Learn'd mens vizards) they are little else.
They that for feare of being cald fooles, hide, ⎫
Like hid men more they stir the more are spied, ⎬
Whose learnings are as ignorantly applied, ⎭
30 As those illiterate Peripaticke soules,
That all their liues, do nought but measure *Poules;*
Yet neuer know how short or long it is,
More then their liues, or all their idle blisse.
  In short, All men that least deseruings haue,
35 Men of most merit euer most depraue.
How euer (friend) tis in vs must assure
Our outward Acts; and signe their passe secure.
Nor feare to find your Noble paines impeacht,
But write as long as *Foxe*, or *Nowell* preacht:
40 For when all wizards haue their bolts let fly,
There's no such proofe of worth, as *Industry*.
  E merito solers Industria reddat honorem.

George Chapman.

(On the Tragic History of *Hipolito and Isabella*.)

To the Volume

By sale of all things, humane and diuine,
Since all sorts liue; what selles lifes sacred line,
And with that life, the soule puts vnder Presse;
Me thinkes should render rich Men, *Midasses:*
Here then th'Immortall soule is sold, with life
Of two, by Loue made one, in Man and Wife.
Loue breedes Opinion, and Opinion, Loue,
In whose Orbs, all the liberall Sciences mooue:
  All which contracted in one Tragedy,
  Sell (great *Octauius;*) and *Augustus* be,
  In all worth, for thy sale commoditie.

G. C.

VERSES
FROM
ENGLAND'S PARNASSVS
and from
MANUSCRIPT.

UNTRACED QUOTATIONS IN
ENGLAND'S PARNASSVS, 1600.

777   Many vse temples to set godly faces
On impious hearts; those sinnes vse most excesse,
That seeke their shrowdes in fained holinesse.

G. Chapman.   *Vide. Dissimulation.*

1842 ——— The gentle humorous night,
Implyes her middle course, and the sharpe east,
Breathes on my spirit with his fierie steedes.

G. Chapman.

2054 See where she issues in her beauties pompe,
As *Flora* to salute the morning sunne:
Who when she shakes her tresses in the ayre,
Raines on the earth dissolued pearle in showres,
Which with his beames the sunne exhales to heauen:
She holdes the spring and sommer in her armes,
And euery plant puts on his freshest robes
To daunce attendance on her princely steps,
Springing and fading as she comes and goes.

G. Chapman.

2055 Her hayre was loose, & bout her shoulders hung,
Vpon her browes did *Venus* naked lye,
And in her eyes did all the Graces swim.
Her cheekes that showd the temper of the mind,
Were beauties mornings where she euer rose,
Her lyps were loues rich altars where she makes
Her hart a neuer-ceasing sacrifice:
Her teeth stoode like a ranke of *Dians* maydes
When naked in a secrete bower they bathe;
Her long round necke was *Cupids* quiuer calld,
And her sweet words that flew from her, his shafts,
Her soft round brests were his sole trauaild Alpes,
Where snow that thawed with sunne did euer lye,
Her fingers bounds to her rich deitie.

Idem.

EPICVRES FRVGALLITIE:

Frugallitie is no philosophie
That is not gelte of pride and miserie,
That hang hym like A nastie bore behynde,

373

And grunt hym out of all the human kynd;
That dares assume to free A man of god
Without whome he's A rogue past periode,
A spawne of lust, Jn sacke and Johnson sodd.

Ge: Chapman.

AN JNVECTIVE WRIGHTEN BY MR. GEORGE CHAPMAN AGAINST MR. BEN: JOHNSON.

Greate-Learned wittie-Ben: be pleasd to light
The world with that three-forked fire; Nor fright
All vs thy sublearn'd with Luciferous Boast
That thou art most-greate-most-learn'd-wittie most
Of all the kingdome; nay of all the earth,   5
As being a thing betwixtt a humane birth
And an Jnfernall; No humanitye
Of the deuine soule shewing Man Jn the,
Being all of pride Composde and surcudrie.
   Thus ytt might Argue; yf thy petulant will   10
May Flieblowe all men with thy great swans Quill,
Jf itt Cann wright noe playes; yf thy plaies faile,
All the Earnests of our kingdome straight must vaile
To thy wilde furie; that, as yf a feinde
Had sleipte his Cirkell; showste thy brest is splend,   15
Frisking so madly that gaynst Towne and Courte
Thou plant'st thy battrie Jn most hedious Sorte.
Jf thy pied humours suffer least empaire,
And any vapour vex thy virulent Aire,
The Dunkerkes keepe not our Cole ships Jn Awe   20
More then thy Moods are thy Admires Law—
All eles, as well the graffters of thy pawes
With panicke Terrors flie bedrid of cause,
And lett the swinish Jtche of thy fell wreake
Rub gainst the presence Royall without Checke.   25
How must state vse the yf thy vaines thus leake?
   Thou must bee Muzzelde Ringd and lett Jn Chaines,
Lest dames with childe a bide vntymely paynes
And Children perrish: didst thou not put out
A boies Right eye that Croste thy mankind poute?   30
If all this yett find perdone Fee and grace,
The happiest outlaw th'art that euer was.
Goodnes to virtue is a godlike thinge,
And man with god Joynes in a good doing kinge.
But to giue vice hur Name; and on all his   35
(As her puer Merritts) to confer all this,

Who will not argue itt redounds? what euer
Vice is sustaynd withall, turnes pestilent feuer.
What norishes vertue, euer more Conuerts
40 To blood and sperritts of nothing but deserts.
And shall a viper hanging on hur hand
By his owne poyson his full swindge Commande?
How shall graue virtue sperritt her honord fame,
Yf Mottlye mockerye maie dispose her shame
45 Neuer soe dully? nor with such a dust }
And Clouted Choller? tis the foulest lust
That euer yett did violate actions Just.
But yf this weighd, proud vile and saucie sperritt,
Depraueing euerye exemplarye merritt,
50 May itt nought lesse all his fatt hopes Jnherritt.
    When men turne Harpies, theire bloods standing lakes,
Greene bellied Serpents, and blacke freckled Snakes
Crawling Jn their vnwelldye Clottered waues,
Their tongues growne forked, and thair sorcerous pens
55 Like pickturs prickt, and hid Jn smoaking dunghills
Vext with the Sunn, tis tyme J thinke to banish
And Cast out such vnhallowedly disloyall
From bloods thrice Sacred and deuinely Royall.
    Thers an Jnuention Mountibancke enough
60 To make petars to blow vpp men's good names,
Virties and Dignities for vices pleasure;
Take but an Jdle and Rediculous Crew
Of base back biters that ytt neuer knew
Virtue or worth to manage; great flesh flies
65 Slight all the Clere and sound partes whear thay pass
And dwell vppon the soares; and Call to them
The Common learned, gatherer of poysons
For enuied Merritts that hee Cannott aequall,
And lett hym gleane from Malice and foule mouthes
70 Deuices long since donn and sett them downe
With splene stupide and dead as bruitish restes,
Transforming all most wrathfull fumes to Jests,
Letting the king his Royall eare allowe;
And thers a reputation, broke as smale }
75 And with as maygtye Arguments lett fall
As the Greeke Mans' pure bodies Genitall.
    So that yf scandalls false beare free their sprite,
All guiltles formes, are forc't with rape and flight.
And shall all other Raisers of their names
80 T'aires highest Region, buy such short-wingd fames,
Hould not their titles, and whole states like tenures?
May wee not humblest things with highest rate

And least with greatest, whear right must Moderate?
  Now to your parts Calde good; your sacred deske
(The wooden fountayne of the Mightye Muses)   85
(Alas) is burned; and ther all their wealth faylde
(That neuer Cann with all tyme be retaylde
Why then as good not name them) yes, O yes,
Tenn tymes repeated will all braue things please,
Not with theire Titles yett, and pore selfe prayses.   90
Hee liues yett (heauen be praysed) that Can wright
Jn his ripe yeares much better, and new borne
Jn spight of Vulcan, whome all true pens scorne.
Yett lett me name them in meane tyme to Chere
His greddie followers with a prickt vpp eare;   95
Jtt does him selfe ease and why them no good?
Come serue ytt in then giue hime goulden food.
Noe Bodie (hee dares saie) yet haue sound parts
Of profound search and Mastrie Jn the artes;
And perfect then his English Grammare too   100
To teach some what thayr nurses could not doe,
The puritie of Language, and Amonge
The rest; his Journye Jnto Scotland songe,
And twice twelue years storde vpp humanitie,
With humble gleanings Jn Deuenytye,   105
After the fathers and those wiser guides
That faction had not drawne to steddie sides.
Canst thou lose theise by fire; and liue yet able
To wright past Joues wrath, fier and Ayre things stable,
Yet Curse as thou wert lost for euerye bable?   110
  Some pore thinge wright new; a Riche Caskett Ben
All of riche Jems t'adorne most learned men,
Or a Reclaime of most Jacete supposes
To teach full habited-men to blowe their noses,
Make the king merrie; would'st thou now be knowne   115
The Deuill and the Vice, and both Jn one?
Thow doest things backwards, are men thought to knowe
Mastries in th'arts with saying thay doe soe,
And criing fire out Jn a dreame to kings.
Burne things vnborne, and that way generate things?   120
Wright some new Lactean way to thy highe presence,
And make not euer thy strong fancie essence
To all thou wouldst be thought on all worlds worth;
Or eles like Hercules Furens breaking forth,
Biting the grene-clothe, as a doge a stone,   125
And for ridiculous shaddow of the bone
Hazard the substance; will thy fortune still

113 MS. ~~Reproues~~ supposes

(Spight of all learning) backe the witt thy will,
Though thy playe genius, hange his broken wings
130 Full of sicke feathers, and with forced things
Jmp thy scaenes, Labord and Vnnaturall?
And nothing good Comes with thy thrice vext Call
Comes thou not yet: nor yet? O no, Nor yett,
Yet are thy learnd Admires soe deep sett
135 Jn thy preferment aboue all that Cite
The sunn in challendge for the heate and light
Of bothe heauens Jnfluences which of you two knewe ⎱
And haue most power Jn them; Greate Ben tis you. ⎰
Examine hime some truely Judging sperritt,
140 That pride nor fortune hath to blind his merritt.
Hee matcht with all booke-fiers hee euer read;
His Deske poore Candle Rents; his owne fat head
With all the learnd worlds; Alexanders flame
That Caesars Conquest Cowd, and stript his fame,
145 He shames Not to giue reckoning Jn with his:
As yf the king perdoning his petulencies
Should paie his huge loss to in such a skore
As all earths learned fiers hee gather'd for.
What thinkest thow (Just frind) equalde not this pride
150 All yet that euer, Hell or heauen defied?
And yet for all this, this Clube will Jnflict
His faultfull paine, and him enough Conuicte.
Hee onlye reading showed; Learning, nor witt;
Onlye Dame Gilians fier his Deske will fitt.
155 But for his shift by fier to saue the Lose
Of his vast Learning; this may proue ytt grose:
True Muses euer, vent breathes mixt with fier,
Which, formed Jn Numbers, they Jn flames expire,
Not onlye flames kindl'd with thayr owne blest breath
160 That giue the vnborne Life; and eternise death.
Great Ben: J knowe that this is Jn thy hand,
And how thou fixt on heauens fixt starre dost stand
Jn all mens Admirations and Comande.
For all that can be scribled gainst the sortes
165 Of thy drad Repurcussions and Reportes,
The Kingdome yeldes not such another man:
Wounder of men hee is; the player Cann
And bookeseller proue true; yf thay could knowe
Onlye on dropp, that driues Jn such A flowe.
170 Are thay not learned beasts, the better farr
Theire drossie exhalations, A starr
Theire brainles Admirations may render.
For Learning Jn the wise sort is but Lender

Of mens Prime Notions Doctrine; theire owne way
Of all skills preciptible formes A key   175
Forging to wealth, and Honor soothed sence,
Neuer exploring truth or Consequence,
Jnforming any vertue or good Life,
And therfore Plaier, Bookseller, or wife
Of eyther, (needing no such curiouse key)   180
All men and things, may knowe their owne rude way;
Jmagination and our appetite
Forming our speach no easier then thay lighte
All letterles Companions; t'all thay know
Here or here after that like earths sonns plowe   185
All vnderworlds and euer downewards growe.
   Nor lett your learnings thinck egredious Ben:
Thes letterles Companions are not men
With all the Arts and sciences Jndued,
Jf of mans true and worthiest knowledge rude,   190
Which is to knowe and be, one Compleat man,
And that not all the swelling Ocean
Of Artes and sciences, cann poure both Jn;
Jf that braue skill, then when thou didst begine
To studdye letters, thy great witt had plide   195
Freelye and onlye thy Disease of pride
Jn vulgar praise, had neuer bound thy, . . .

More then this neuer came to my
hands, but lost in his sickenes.

POEMS
PREFATORY AND
DEDICATORY

to the

ILIADS,

ODYSSEYS,

and

HYMNS of HOMER.

(To *M. Harriots*, accompanying *Achilles Shield*.)

TO MY ADMIRED AND SOVLE-LOVED FRIEND

Mayster of all essentiall and true knowledge,
M. Harriots.

T O you whose depth of soule measures the height,
And all dimensions of all workes of weight,
Reason being ground, structure and ornament,
To all inuentions, graue and permanent,
5 And your cleare eyes the Spheres where *Reason* moues;
This Artizan, this God of rationall loues
Blind *Homer;* in this shield, and in the rest
Of his seuen bookes, which my hard hand hath drest,
In rough integuments I send for censure,
10 That my long time and labours deepe extensure
Spent to conduct him to our enuious light,
In your allowance may receiue some right
To their endeuours; and take vertuous heart
From your applause, crownd with their owne desert.
15 Such crownes suffice the free and royall mind,
But these subiected hangbyes of our kind,
These children that will neuer stand alone,
But must be nourisht with corruption,
Which are our bodies; that are traitors borne,
20 To their owne crownes their soules: betraid to scorne,
To gaudie insolence and ignorance:
By their base fleshes frailties, that must daunce,
Prophane attendance at their states and birth,
That are meere seruants to this seruile earth,
25 These must haue other crownes for meedes then merits,
Or sterue themselues, and quench their fierie spirits.
Thus as the soule vpon the flesh depends,
Vertue must wait on wealth; we must make friends,
Of the vnrighteous Mammon, and our sleights,
30 Must beare the formes of fooles or Parasites.
Rich mine of knowledge, ô that my strange muse
Without this bodies nourishment could vse,
Her zealous faculties, onely t'aspire,
Instructiue light from your whole Sphere of fire:
35 But woe is me, what zeale or power soeuer
My free soule hath, my body will be neuer
Able t'attend: neuer shal I enioy,
Th'end of my happles birth: neuer employ

That smotherd feruour that in lothed embers,
Lyes swept from light, and no cleare howre remembers.   40
O had your perfect eye Organs to pierce
Into that Chaos whence this stiffled verse
By violence breakes: where Gloweworme like doth shine
In nights of sorrow, this hid soule of mine:
And how her genuine formes struggle for birth,   45
Vnder the clawes of this fowle Panther earth;
Then vnder all those formes you should discerne
My loue to you, in my desire to learne.
Skill and the loue of skill do euer kisse:
No band of loue so stronge as knowledge is;   50
Which who is he that may not learne of you,
Whom learning doth with his lights throne endow?
What learned fields pay not their flowers t'adorne
Your odorous wreathe? compact, put on and worne,
By apt and Adamantine industrie,   55
Proposing still demonstrate veritie,
For your great obiect, farre from plodding gaine,
Or thirst of glorie; when absurd and vayne,
Most students in their whole instruction are,
But in traditions meere particular: 60
Leaning like rotten howses, on out beames,
And with true light fade in themselues like dreames.
True learning hath a body absolute,
That in apparant sence it selfe can suite,
Not hid in ayrie termes as if it were   65
Like spirits fantastike that put men in feare,
And are but bugs form'd in their fowle conceites,
Nor made for sale glas'd with sophistique sleights;
But wrought for all times proofe, strong to bide prease,
And shiuer ignorants like *Hercules*,   70
On their owne dunghils; but our formall Clearkes
Blowne for profession, spend their soules in sparkes,
Fram'de of dismembred parts that make most show,
And like to broken limmes of knowledge goe.
When thy true wisedome by thy learning wonne   75
Shall honour learning while there shines a Sunne;
And thine owne name in merite; farre aboue,
Their Timpanies of state that armes of loue,
Fortune or blood shall lift to dignitie;
Whome though you reuerence, and your emperie   80
Of spirit and soule, be seruitude they thinke
And but a beame of light broke through a chink
To all their watrish splendor: and much more
To the great Sunne, and all thinges they adore,

85 In staring ignorance: yet your selfe shall shine
Aboue all this in knowledge most diuine,
And all shall homage to your true-worth owe,
You comprehending all, that all, not you.
    And when thy writings that now errors Night
90 Chokes earth with mistes, breake forth like easterne light,
Showing to euery comprehensiue eye,
High fectious brawles becalmde by vnitie,
Nature made all transparent, and her hart
Gripte in thy hand, crushing digested Art
95 In flames vnmeasurde, measurde out of it,
On whose head for her crowne thy soule shall sitte,
Crownd with Heauens inward brightnes shewing cleare
What true man is, and how like gnats appeare:
O fortune-glossed Pompists, and proud Misers,
100 That are of Arts such impudent despisers;
Then past anticipating doomes and skornes,
Which for selfe grace ech ignorant subornes,
Their glowing and amazed eyes shall see
How short of thy soules strength my weake words be,
105 And that I do not like our Poets preferre
For profit, praise, and keepe a squeaking stirre
With cald on muses to vnchilde their braines
Of winde and vapor: lying still in paynes,
Of worthy issue; but as one profest
110 In nought but truthes deare loue the soules true rest.
    Continue then your sweet iudiciall kindnesse,
To your true friend, that though this lumpe of blindnes,
This skornefull, this despisde, inuerted world,
Whose head is furie-like with Adders curlde,
115 And all her bulke a poysoned Porcupine,
Her stings and quilles darting at worthes deuine,
Keepe vnder my estate with all contempt,
And make me liue euen from my selfe exempt,
Yet if you see some gleames of wrastling fire,
120 Breake from my spirits oppression, shewing desire
To become worthy to pertake your skill,
(Since vertues first and chiefe steppe is to will)
Comfort me with it and proue you affect me,
Though all the rotten spawne of earth reiect me.
125 For though I now consume in poesie,
Yet *Homer* being my roote I can not die.
But lest to vse all Poesie in the sight,
Of graue philosophie shew braines too light
To comprehend her depth of misterie,
130 I vow t'is onely strong necessitie

Gouernes my paines herein, which yet may vse
A mans whole life without the least abuse.
And though to rime and giue a verse smooth feet,
Vttering to vulgar pallattes passions sweet
Chaunce often in such weake capriccious spirits,   135
As in nought else haue tollerable merits,
Yet where high *Poesies* natiue habite shines,
From whose reflections flow eternall lines:
Philosophy retirde to darkest caues
She can discouer: and the proud worldes braues   140
Answere in any thing but impudence,
With circle of her general excellence.
For ample instance *Homer* more then serueth,
And what his graue and learned Muse deserueth,
Since it is made a Courtly question now,   145
His competent and partles iudge be you;
If these vaine lines and his deserts arise
To the high serches of your serious eyes
As he is English: and I could not chuse
But to your Name this short inscription vse,   150
As well assurde you would approue my payne
In my traduction; and besides this vayne
Excuse my thoughts as bent to others ames:
Might my will rule me, and when any flames
Of my prest soule break forth to their own show,   155
Thinke they must hold engrauen regard of you.
Of you in whom the worth of all the Graces,
Due to the mindes giftes, might embrew the faces
Of such as skorne them, and with tiranous eye
Contemne the sweat of vertuous industrie.   160
But as ill lines new fild with incke vndryed,
An empty Pen with their owne stuffe applied
Can blot them out: so shall their wealth-burst wombes
Be made with emptie Penne their honours tombes.

FINIS.

(Epistle Dedicatory: *The Iliads.*)

TO THE HIGH
BORNE PRINCE OF
MEN, *HENRIE* THRICE

Royall inheritor to the vnited kingdoms
of Great Brittaine, &c.

SINCE perfect happinesse, by Princes sought,
 Is not with birth, borne, nor Exchequers bought;
Nor followes in great Traines; nor is possest
With any outward State; but makes him blest
5 That gouernes inward; and beholdeth theare,
All his affections stand about him bare;
That by his power can send to Towre, and death,
All traitrous passions; marshalling beneath
His iustice, his meere will; and in his minde
10 Holds such a scepter, as can keepe confinde
His whole lifes actions in the royall bounds
Of Vertue and Religion; and their grounds
Takes in, to sow his honours, his delights,
And complete empire: you should learne these rights
15 (Great Prince of men) by Princely presidents;
Which here, in all kinds, my true zeale presents
To furnish your youths groundworke, and first State;
And let you see, one Godlike man create
All sorts of worthiest men; to be contriu'd
20 In your worth onely; giuing him reuiu'd,
For whose life, *Alexander* would haue giuen
One of his kingdomes: who (as sent from heauen,
And thinking well, that so diuine a creature
Would neuer more enrich the race of Nature)
25 Kept as his Crowne his workes; and thought them still
His Angels; in all power, to rule his will;
And would affirme that *Homers* poesie
Did more aduance his Asian victorie,
Then all his Armies. O! tis wondrous much
30 (Though nothing prisde) that the right vertuous touch
Of a well written soule, to vertue moues.
Nor haue we soules to purpose, if their loues
Of fitting obiects be not so inflam'd.
How much then, were this kingdomes maine soule maim'd,
35 To want this great inflamer of all powers
That moue in humane soules? All Realmes but yours,
Are honor'd with him; and hold blest that State
That haue his workes to reade and contemplate.
In which, Humanitie to her height is raisde;

Which all the world (yet, none enough) hath praisde.   40
Seas, earth, and heauen, he did in verse comprise;
Out-sung the Muses, and did equalise
Their king *Apollo;* being so farre from cause
Of Princes light thoughts, that their grauest lawes
May finde stuffe to be fashioned by his lines.   45
Through all the pompe of kingdomes still he shines,
And graceth all his gracers. Then let lie
Your Lutes, and Viols, and more loftily
Make the Heroiques of your *Homer* sung,
To Drums and Trumpets set his Angels tongue: 50
And with the Princely sport of Haukes you vse,
Behold the kingly flight of his high Muse:
And see how like the Phoenix she renues
Her age, and starrie feathers in your sunne;
Thousands of yeares attending; euerie onc   55
Blowing the holy fire, and throwing in
Their seasons, kingdomes, nations that haue bin
Subuerted in them; lawes, religions, all
Offerd to Change, and greedie Funerall;
Yet still your *Homer* lasting, liuing, raigning;   60
And proues, how firme Truth builds in Poets faining.

     A Princes statue, or in Marble caru'd,
Or steele, or gold, and shrin'd (to be preseru'd)
Aloft on Pillars, or Pyramides;
Time into lowest ruines may depresse: 65
But, drawne with all his vertues in learn'd verse,
Fame shall resound them on Obliuions herse,
Till graues gaspe with her blasts, and dead men rise.
No gold can follow, where true Poesie flies.

     Then let not this Diuinitie in earth   70
(Deare Prince) be sleighted, as she were the birth
Of idle Fancie; since she workes so hie:
Nor let her poore disposer (Learning) lie
Stil bed-rid. Both which, being in men defac't;
In men (with them) is Gods bright image rac't.   75
For, as the Sunne, and Moone, are figures giuen
Of his refulgent Deitie in Heauen:
So, Learning, and her Lightner, Poesie,
In earth present his fierie Maiestie.
Nor are Kings like him, since their Diademes   80
Thunder, and lighten, and proiect braue beames;
But since they his cleare vertues emulate;
In Truth and Iustice, imaging his State;
In Bountie, and Humanitie since they shine;
Then which, is nothing (like him) more diuine: 85

Not Fire, not Light; the Sunnes admired course;
The Rise, nor Set of Starres; nor all their force
In vs, and all this Cope beneath the Skie;
Nor great *Existence*, term'd his Treasurie;
90 Since not, for being greatest, he is blest;
But being Iust, and in all vertues best.
    What sets his Iustice, and his Truth, best forth,
(Best Prince) then vse best; which is Poesies worth.
For, as great Princes, well inform'd and deckt
95 With gracious vertue, giue more sure effect
To her perswasions, pleasures, reall worth,
Then all th'inferiour subiects she sets forth;
Since there, she shines at full; hath birth, wealth, state,
Power, fortune, honor, fit to eleuate
100 Her heauenly merits; and so fit they are
Since she was made for them, and they for her:
So, Truth, with Poesie grac't, is fairer farre,
More proper, mouing, chaste, and regular,
Then when she runnes away with vntruss't Prose;
105 Proportion, that doth orderly dispose
Her vertuous treasure, and is Queene of Graces;
In Poesie, decking her with choicest Phrases,
Figures and numbers: when loose Prose puts on
Plaine letter-habits; makes her trot, vpon
110 Dull earthly businesse (she being meere diuine:)
Holds her to homely Cates, and harsh hedge-wine,
That should drinke Poesies Nectar; euerie way
One made for other, as the Sunne and Day,
Princes and vertues. And, as in a spring,
115 The plyant water, mou'd with any thing
Let fall into it, puts her motion out
In perfect circles, that moue round about
The gentle fountaine, one another, raising:
So Truth, and Poesie worke; so Poesie blazing,
120 All subiects falne in her exhaustlesse fount,
Works most exactly; makes a true account
Of all things to her high discharges giuen,
Till all be circular, and round as heauen.
    And lastly, great Prince, marke and pardon me;
125 As in a flourishing, and ripe fruit Tree,
Nature hath made the barke to saue the Bole;
The Bole, the sappe; the sappe, to decke the whole
With leaues and branches; they to beare and shield
The vsefull fruite; the fruite it selfe to yeeld
130 Guard to the kernell, and for that all those
(Since out of that againe, the whole Tree growes:)

So, in our Tree of man, whose neruie Roote
Springs in his top; from thence euen to his foote,
There runnes a mutuall aide, through all his parts,
The soule.   All ioyn'd in one to serue his Queene of Arts.   135
In which, doth Poesie, like the kernell lie
Obscur'd; though her Promethean facultie
Can create men, and make euen death to liue;
For which she should liue honor'd; Kings should giue
Comfort and helpe to her, that she might still   140
Hold vp their spirits in vertue; make the will,
That gouernes in them, to the power conform'd;
The power to iustice; that the scandals, storm'd
Against the poore Dame, clear'd by your faire Grace,
Your Grace may shine the clearer. Her low place,   145
Not shewing her, the highest leaues obscure.
Who raise her, raise themselues: and he sits sure,
Whom her wing'd hand aduanceth; since on it
Eternitie doth (crowning Vertue) sit.
All whose poore seed, like violets in their beds,   150
Now grow with bosome-hung, and hidden heads:
For whom I must speake (though their Fate conuinces
Me, worst of Poets) to you, best of Princes.

By the most humble and faithfull implorer for
all the graces to your highnesse eterni-
sed by your Diuine Homer.

Geo. Chapman.

137 Obscur'd] Oscur'd

(Memorial Verses to Prince Henry: *Whole Works of Homer.*)

TO THE IMORTALL MEMORIE, OF
THE INCOMPARABLE HEROE,
HENRYE PRINCE OF WALES.

Thy Toomb, Arms, Statue; All things fitt to fall
At foote of Deathe; And worship Funerall
Forme hath bestow'd: for Forme, is nought too deare:
Thy solid Virtues yet; eternis'd here;
My bloode, and wasted spirritts haue onely founde
Commanded Cost: And broke so riche a grounde,
(Not to interr; But make thee euer springe)
As Arms, Toombs, Statues; euerye Earthy Thinge,
Shall fade and vanishe into fume before:
What lasts; thriues lest: yet; welth of soule is poore;
And so tis kept: Not thy thrice sacred will

Sign'd with thy Deathe; moues any to fullfill
Thy Just bequests to me:·Thow, dead . then; J
Liue deade, for giuing thee Eternitie:·
             Ad Famam
To all Tymes future, This Tymes Marck extend;
Homer, no Patrone founde; Nor Chapman freind:
            Ignotus nimis omnibus;
            Sat notus, moritur sibi:·

(An Anagram on Henry: *The Iliads*.)

AN ANAGRAM OF THE NAME

OF OVR DRAD PRINCE, MY MOST

Gracious and sacred *Mæcænas;*

HENRYE PRINCE OF WALES
OVR SUNN, HEYR, PEACE, LIFE.

Be to vs as thy great Name doth import,
    (Prince of the people;) nor suppose it vaine,
That in this secret, and prophetique sort,
    Thy Name and Noblest Title doth containe
So much right to vs; and as great a good.
    Nature doth nothing vainly; much lesse Art
Perfecting Nature. No spirit in our blood,
    But in our soules discourses beares a part.
What Nature giues at random in the one,
    In th'other, orderd, our diuine part serues.
Thou art not HEYR then, to our state alone;
    But SVNN, PEACE, LIFE. And what thy powre deserues
Of vs, and our good, in thy vtmost strife;
    Shall make thee to thy selfe, HEYR, SVNN, PEACE, LIFE.

TO THE SACRED FOVNTAINE

OF PRINCES; SOLE EMPRESSE OF
BEAVTIE AND VERTUE; *ANNE,*

Queene of England, &c.

With whatsoeuer Honour we adorne
    Your Royall issue; we must gratulate yow
Imperiall Soueraigne. Who of you is borne,
    Is you; One Tree, make both the Bole, and Bow.
If it be honour then to ioyne you both
    To such a powerfull worke, as shall defend
Both from foule *Death*, and *Ages* ougly Moth;

This is an Honor, that shall neuer end.
They know not vertue then, that know not what
  The vertue of defending vertue is:
It comprehends the guard of all your State,
  And ioynes your Greatnesse to as great a Blisse.
Shield vertue, and aduance her then, Great Queene;
  And make this Booke your Glasse, to make it seene.

Your Maiesties in all subiection most
humbly consecrate,

Geo. Chapman.

(*Iliads.*)

TO THE READER.

Lest with foule hands you touch these holy Rites;
  And with preiudicacies too prophane,
Passe Homer, *in your other Poets sleights;*
  Wash here. In this Porch to his numerous Phane,
Heare ancient Oracles speake, and tell you whom
  You haue to censure. First then Silius *heare,*
Who thrice was Consull in renowned Rome;
  Whose verse (saith Martiall) *nothing shall out-weare.*

Silius Italicus. Lib. 13.

He, in *Elysium*, hauing cast his eye
  Vpon the figure of a Youth, whose haire
With purple Ribands braided curiously,
  Hung on his shoulders wondrous bright and faire;
Said, Virgine, What is he whose heauenly face   5
  Shines past all others, as the Morne the Night;
Whom many maruelling soules, from place to place,
  Pursue, and haunt, with sounds of such delight?
Whose countenance (wer't not in the Stygian shade)
  Would make me, questionlesse, beleeue he were   10
A verie God. The learned Virgine made
  This answer: If thou shouldst beleeue it here,
Thou shouldst not erre: he well deseru'd to be
  Esteem'd a God; nor held his so-much breast
A little presence of the Deitie: 15
  His verse comprisde earth, seas, starres, soules at rest:
In song, the Muses he did equalise;
  In honor, *Phoebus:* he was onely soule;
Saw all things spher'd in Nature, without eyes,
  And raisde your *Troy* vp to the starrie Pole.   20
Glad *Scipio*, viewing well this Prince of Ghosts,

Said, O if Fates would giue this Poet leaue,
  To sing the acts done by the Romane Hoasts;
  How much beyond, would future times receiue
25 The same facts, made by any other knowne?
  O blest *Æacides!* to haue the grace
  That out of such a mouth, thou shouldst be showne
  To wondring Nations, as enricht the race
  Of all times future, with what he did know:
30   Thy vertue, with his verse, shall euer grow.

Now heare an Angell sing our Poets Fame;
Whom Fate, for his diuine song, gaue that name.

Angelus Politianus, in Nutricia.

More liuing, then in old *Demodocus,*
  Fame glories to waxe yong in *Homers* verse.
And as when bright *Hyperion* holds to vs
  His golden Torch; we see the starres disperse
5 And euery way flie heauen; the pallid Moone
  Euen almost vanishing before his sight:
So with the dazling beames of *Homers* Sunne,
  All other ancient Poets lose their light.
Whom when *Apollo* heard, out of his starre,
10   Singing the godlike Acts of honor'd men;
And equalling the actuall rage of warre,
  With onely the diuine straines of his pen;
He stood amaz'd, and freely did confesse
  Himselfe was equall'd in *Maeonides.*

Next, heare the graue and learned Plinie *vse*
His censure of our sacred poets Muse.
            Plin. Nat. hist. lib. 7. Cap 29.
  Turnd into verse; that no Prose may come neare *Homer.*

Whom shall we choose the glorie of all wits,
  Held through so many sorts of discipline,
And such varietie of workes, and spirits;
  But Grecian *Homer?* like whom none did shine,
5 For forme of worke and matter. And because
  Our proud doome of him may stand iustified
By noblest iudgements; and receiue applause
  In spite of enuie, and illiterate pride;
Great *Macedon,* amongst his matchlesse spoiles,
10   Tooke from rich *Persia* (on his Fortunes cast)
A Casket finding (full of precious oyles)
  Form'd all of gold, with wealthy stones enchac't:
He tooke the oyles out; and his nearest friends

Askt, in what better guard it might be vsde?
All giuing their conceipts, to seuerall ends;   15
   He answerd; His affections rather chusde
An vse quite opposite to all their kinds:
   And *Homers* bookes should with that guard be seru'd;
That the most precious worke of all mens minds,
   In the most precious place, might be preseru'd.   20

Idem. lib. The Fount of wit was *Homer;* Learnings Syre,
17. cap. 5.   And gaue Antiquitie, her liuing fire.
Idem. lib.
25. cap. 3. Volumes of like praise, I could heape on this,
   Of men more ancient, and more learn'd then these:
But since true Vertue, enough louely is
   With her owne beauties; all the suffrages
Of others I omit; and would more faine   5
   That *Homer,* for himselfe, should be belou'd
Who euerie sort of loue-worth did containe.
   Which now I haue in my conuersion prou'd,
I must confesse, I hardly dare referre
   To reading iudgements; since, so generally,   10
Custome hath made euen th'ablest Agents erre
   In these translations; all so much apply

Of Transla- Their paines and cunnings, word for word to render
tion, and the   Their patient Authors; when they may as well,
naturall dif- Make fish with fowle, Camels with Whales engender;   15
ference of Di-   Or their tongues speech, in other mouths compell.
alects, neces- For, euen as different a production
sarily to be ob-   Aske Greeke and English; since as they in sounds,
serued in it. And letters, shunne one forme, and vnison;
   So haue their sense, and elegancie bounds   20
In their distinguisht natures, and require
   Onely a iudgement to make both consent,
In sense and elocution; and aspire
   As well to reach the spirit that was spent
In his example; as with arte to pierce   25
   His Grammar, and etymologie of words.

Ironice. But, as great Clerkes, can write no English verse;
   Because (alas! great Clerks) English affords
(Say they) no height, nor copie; a rude toung,
   (Since tis their Natiue): but in Greeke or Latine   30
Their wits are rare; for thence true Poesie sprong:
   Though them (Truth knowes) they haue but skil to chat-in,
Compar'd with that they might say in their owne;
   Since thither th'others full soule cannot make
The ample transmigration to be showne   35

25 example *1609*] exanple

In Nature-louing Poesie: So the brake
That those Translators sticke in, that affect
　　Their word-for-word traductions (where they lose
　The free grace of their naturall Dialect
40　　　And shame their Authors, with a forced Glose)
　I laugh to see; and yet as much abhorre
　　More licence from the words, then may expresse
　Their full compression, and make cleare the Author.
　　From whose truth, if you thinke my feet digresse,
45　Because I vse needfull Periphrases;
　　Reade *Valla*, *Hessus*, that in Latine Prose,
　And Verse conuert him; reade the *Messines*,
　　That into Tuscan turns him; and the Glose
　Graue *Salel* makes in French, as he translates:
50　　Which (for th'aforesaide reasons) all must doo;
　And see that my conuersion much abates
　　The licence they take, and more showes him too:
　Whose right, not all those great learn'd men haue done
　　(In some maine parts), that were his Commentars:
55　But (as the illustration of the Sunne
　　Should be attempted by the erring starres)
　They fail'd to search his deepe, and treasurous hart.
　　The cause was, since they wanted the fit key
　Of Nature, in their down-right strength of Art;
60　　With Poesie, to open Poesie.
　Which in my Poeme of the mysteries
　　Reueal'd in *Homer*, I will clearely proue;
　Till whose neere birth, suspend your Calumnies,
　　And farre-wide imputations of selfe loue.
65　Tis further from me, then the worst that reades;
　　Professing me the worst of all that wright:
　Yet what, in following one, that brauely leades,
　　The worst may show, let this proofe hold the light.
　But grant it cleere: yet hath detraction got
70　　My blinde side, in the forme, my verse puts on;
　Much like a dung-hill Mastife, that dares not
　　Assault the man he barkes at; but the stone
　He throwes at him, takes in his eager iawes,
　　And spoyles his teeth because they cannot spoyle.
75　The long verse hath by proofe receiu'd applause
　　Beyond each number: and the foile,
　That squint-ey'd Enuie takes, is censur'd plaine.
　　For, this long Poeme askes this length of verse,
　Which I my selfe ingenuously maintaine
80　　Too long, our shorter Authors to reherse.
　And, for our tongue, that still is so empayr'd

*Our English
language,
aboue all
others, for
Rhythmicall
Poesie.*

By trauailing linguists; I can proue it cleare,
That no tongue hath the Muses vtterance heyr'd
  For verse, and that sweet Musique to the eare
Strooke out of rime, so naturally as this;   85
  Our Monosyllables, so kindly fall
And meete, opposde in rime, as they did kisse:
  French and Italian, most immetricall;
Their many syllables, in harsh Collision,
  Fall as they brake their necks; their bastard Rimes,   90
Saluting as they iustl'd in transition,
  And set our teeth on edge; nor tunes, nor times
Kept in their falles. And me thinkes, their long words
  Shew in short verse, as in a narrow place,
Two opposites should meet, with two-hand swords   95
  Vnweildily, without or vse or grace.
Thus hauing rid the rubs, and strow'd these flowers
  In our thrice sacred *Homers* English way;
What rests to make him, yet more worthy yours?
  To cite more prayse of him, were meere delay   100
To your glad searches, for what those men found,
  That gaue his praise, past all, so high a place:
Whose vertues were so many, and so cround,
  By all consents, Diuine; that not to grace,
Or adde increase to them, the world doth need   105
  Another *Homer;* but euen to rehearse
And number them: they did so much exceed;
  Men thought him not a man; but that his verse
Some meere celestiall nature did adorne.
  And that all may well conclude, it could not be,   110
That for the place where any man was borne,
  So long, and mortally, could disagree
So many Nations, as for *Homer* striu'd,
  Vnlesse his spurre in them, had bene diuine.
Then end their strife, and loue him (thus reuiu'd)   115
  As borne in *England:* see him ouer-shine
All other-Countrie Poets; and trust this,
  That whose-soeuer Muse dares vse her wing
When his Muse flies, she will be truss't by his;
  And show as if a Bernacle should spring   120
Beneath an Eagle. In none since was seene
  A soule so full of heauen as earth's in him.
O! if our moderne Poesie had beene
  As louely as the Ladie he did lymne,
What barbarous worldling, groueling after gaine,   125
  Could vse her louely parts, with such rude hate,
As now she suffers vnder euery swaine?

Since then tis nought but her abuse and Fate,
That thus empaires her; what is this to her
130 As she is reall? or in naturall right?
But since in true Religion men should erre
As much as Poesie, should th'abuse excite
The like contempt of her Diuinitie?
And that her truth, and right saint sacred Merites,
135 In most liues, breed but reuerence formally;
What wonder is't if Poesie inherits
Much less obseruance; being but Agent for her,
And singer of her lawes, that others say?
Forth then ye Mowles, sonnes of the earth abhorre her;
140 Keepe still on in the durty vulgar way,
Till durt receiue your soules, to which ye vow;
And with your poison'd spirits bewitch our thrifts.
Ye cannot so despise vs as we you.
Not one of you, aboue his Mowlehill lifts
145 His earthy Minde; but, as a sort of beasts,
Kept by their Guardians, neuer care to heare
Their manly voices; but when, in their fists,
They breathe wild whistles; and the beasts rude eare
Heares their Curres barking; then by heapes they flie,
150 Headlong together: So men, beastly giuen,
The manly soules voice (sacred Poesie,
Whose Hymnes the Angels euer sing in heauen)
Contemne, and heare not: but when brutish noises
(For Gaine, Lust, Honour, in litigious Prose)
155 Are bellow'd-out, and cracke the barbarous voices
Of Turkish Stentors; O! ye leane to those,
Like itching Horse, to blockes, or high May-poles;
And breake nought but the wind of wealth, wealth, All
In all your Documents; your Asinine soules
160 (Proud of their burthens) feele not how they gall.
But as an Asse, that in a field of weeds
Affects a thistle, and falles fiercely to it;
That pricks, and gals him; yet he feeds, and bleeds;
Forbeares a while, and licks; but cannot woo it
165 To leaue the sharpnes; when (to wreake his smart)
He beates it with his foote; then backward kickes,
Because the Thistle gald his forward part;
Nor leaues till all be eate, for all the prickes;
Then falles to others with as hote a strife;
170 And in that honourable warre doth waste
The tall heate of his stomacke, and his life:
So, in this world of weeds, you worldlings taste
Your most-lou'd dainties; with such warre, buy peace;

Hunger for torments; vertue kicke for vice;
Cares, for your states, do with your states increase: 175
And though ye dreame ye feast in Paradise,
Yet Reasons Day-light, shewes ye at your meate
Asses at Thistles, bleeding as ye eate.

TO THE RIGHT GRACIOVS

and worthy, the Duke of LENNOX.

Amongst th'Heroes of the Worlds prime years,
    Stand here, great Duke, & see them shine about you:
Informe your princely minde and spirit by theirs,
    And then, like them, liue euer; looke without you;
For subiects fit to vse your place, and grace:
    Which throw about you, as the Sunne, his Raies;
In quickning, with their power, the dying Race
    Of friendlesse *Vertue;* since they thus can raise
Their honor'd Raisers, to *Eternitie.*
    None euer liu'd by *Selfe-loue:* Others good
Is th'obiect of our owne. They (liuing) die,
    That burie in themselues their fortunes brood.
    To this soule, then, your gracious count'nance giue;
    That gaue, to such as you, such meanes to liue.

TO THE MOST GRAVE AND

honored Temperer of Law, and Equitie, the Lord CHANCELOR, &c.

That Poesie is not so remou'd a thing
    From graue administry of publike weales,
As these times take it; heare this Poet sing,
    Most iudging Lord: and see how he reueales
The mysteries of Rule, and rules to guide
    The life of Man, through all his choicest waies.
Nor be your timely paines the lesse applyed
    For Poesies idle name; because her Raies
Haue shin'd through greatest Counsellors, and Kings.
    Heare Royall *Hermes* sing th'Egyptian Lawes;
How *Solon, Draco, Zoroastes* sings
    Their Lawes in verse: and let their iust applause
(By all the world giuen) yours (by vs) allow;
    That, since you grace all vertue, honour you.

TO THE MOST WORTHIE

Earle, Lord Treasurer, and Treasure of our
Countrey, the Earle of SALISBVRY, &c.

Vouchsafe, Great Treasurer, to turne your eye,
　And see the opening of a Grecian Mine;
Which, Wisedome long since made her Treasury;
　And now her title doth to you resigne.
Wherein as th'Ocean walks not, with such waues,
　The Round of this Realme, as your Wisedomes seas;
Nor, with his great eye, sees; his Marble, saues
　Our State, like your Vlyssian policies:
So, none like HOMER hath the World enspher'd;
　Earth, Seas, & heauen, fixt in his verse, and mouing;
Whom all times wisest Men, haue held vnper'de;
　And therfore would conclude with your approuing.
Then grace his spirit, that all wise men hath grac't,
And made things euer flitting, euer last.

An Anagram.
Robert Cecyl, Earle of Salisburye.
Curb foes; thy care, is all our erly Be.

TO THE MOST HONOR'D RE-

storer of ancient Nobilitie, both in blood and
vertue, the Earle of SVFFOLKE, &c.

Ioine, Noblest Earle, in giuing worthy grace,
　To this great gracer of Nobilitie:
See here what sort of men, your honor'd place
　Doth properly command; if Poesie
(Profest by them) were worthily exprest.
　The grauest, wisest, greatest, need not, then,
Account that part of your command the least;
　Nor them such idle, needlesse, worthlesse Men.
Who can be worthier Men in publique weales,
　Then those (at all parts) that prescrib'd the best?
That stird vp noblest vertues, holiest zeales;
　And euermore haue liu'd as they profest?
A world of worthiest Men, see one create,
　(Great Earle); whom no man since could imitate.

TO THE MOST NOBLE AND

learned Earle, the Earle of NORTHAMTON, &c.

To you, most learned Earle, whose learning can
    Reiect vnlearned Custome, and Embrace
The reall vertues of a worthie Man,
    I prostrate this great *Worthie*, for your grace;
And pray that Poesies well-deseru'd ill Name
    (Being such, as many moderne Poets make her)
May nought eclipse her cleare essentiall flame:
    But as she shines here, so refuse or take her.
Nor do I hope; but euen your high affaires
    May suffer intermixture with her view;
Where *Wisedome* sits her for the highest chaires;
    And mindes, growne old, with cares of State, renew:
You then (great Earle) that in his owne tongue know
    This king of Poets; see his English show.

TO THE MOST NOBLE, MY

singular good Lord, the Earle of Arundell.

Stand by your noblest stocke; and euer grow
    In loue, and grace of vertue most admir'd;
And we will pay the sacrifice we owe
    Of prayre and honour, with all good desir'd
To your diuine soule; that shall euer liue
    In height of all blisse prepar'd here beneath,
In that ingenuous and free grace you giue
    To knowledge; onely Bulwarke against Death.
Whose rare sustainers here, her powres sustaine
    Hereafter. Such reciprocall effects
Meet in her vertues. Where the loue doth raigne,
    The Act of knowledge crownes our intellects.
    Where th'Act, nor Loue is, there, like beasts men die:
    Not Life, but Time is their Eternitie.

TO THE LEARNED AND

most noble Patrone of learning the Earle of
PEMBROOKE, &c.

Aboue all others may your Honor shine;
    As, past all others, your ingenuous beames
Exhale into your grace the forme diuine
    Of godlike *Learning;* whose exiled streames
Runne to your succour, charg'd with all the wracke
    Of sacred Vertue. Now the barbarous witch

(Foule *Ignorance*) sits charming of them backe
    To their first Fountaine, in the great and rich;
Though our great Soueraigne counter-checke her charmes
    (Who in all learning, reignes so past example)
Yet (with her) *Turkish Policie* puts on armes,
    To raze all knowledge in mans Christian Temple.
(You following yet our king) your guard redouble:
    Pure are those streames, that these times cannot trouble.

TO THE RIGHT GRACIOVS

Illustrator of vertue, and worthy of the fauour
Royall, the Earle of MONTGOMRIE.

There runs a blood, faire Earle, through your cleare vains
    That well entitles you to all things Noble;
Which still the liuing Sydnian soule maintaines,
    And your Names ancient Noblesse doth redouble:
For which I must needs tender to your Graces
    This noblest worke of Man; as made your Right.
And though *Ignoblesse*, all such workes defaces
    As tend to *Learning*, and the soules delight:
Yet since the sacred Penne doth testifie,
    That *Wisedome* (which is *Learnings* naturall birth)
Is the cleare Mirror of Gods Maiestie,
    And *Image* of his goodnesse here in earth;
If you the *Daughter* wish, respect the *Mother:*
    One cannot be obtain'd, without the other.

TO THE MOST LEARNED

and Noble Concluder of the Warres Arte,
and the Muses, the Lord LISLE, &c.

Nor let my paines herein (long honor'd Lord)
    Faile of your ancient Nobly-good respects;
Though obscure *Fortune* neuer would afford
    My seruice show, till these thus late effects.
And though my poore deserts weigh'd neuer more
    Then might keepe downe their worthlesse memorie
From your high thoughts (enrich with better store)
    Yet yours, in me, are fixt eternally;
Which all my fit occasions well shall proue.
    Meane space (with your most Noble Nephewes) daine
To shew your free and honorable loue
    To this Greeke Poet, in his English vaine.
You cannot more the point of death controule;
    Then to stand close by such a liuing soule.

TO THE GREAT AND VER-

tuous, the Countesse of MONTGOMRIE.

Your Fame (great Lady) is so lowd resounded,
  By your free Trumpet, my right worthy frend;
That, with it, all my forces stand confounded,
  Arm'd, and disarm'd at once, to one iust end;
To honor and describe the blest consent
  Twixt your high blood and soule, in vertues rare.
Of which, my friends praise is so eminent,
  That I shall hardly like his *Echo* fare,
To render onely th'ends of his shrill Verse.
  Besides; my Bounds are short; and I must, meerely,
My will to honour your rare parts, rehearse;
  With more time, singing your renowme more clearely.
Mean-time, take *Homer* for my wants supply:
  To whom adioyn'd, your Name shall neuer die.

TO THE HAPPY STARRE, DI-

*scouered in our Sydneian Asterisme; comfort of
learning, Sphere of all the vertues, the Lady* WROTHE.

When all our other Starres set (in their skies)
  To Vertue, and all honor of her kind;
That you (rare Lady) should so clearely rise,
  Makes all the vertuous glorifie your mind.
And let true Reason, and Religion trie,
  If it be Fancie, not iudiciall Right,
In you t'oppose the times Apostasie,
  To take the soules part, and her sauing Light,
While others blinde and burie both in Sense;
  When, tis the onely end, for which all liue.
And, could those soules, in whom it dies, dispense
  As much with their Religion; they would giue
That as small grace. Then shun their course, faire Starre;
  And still keepe your way, pure, and circular.

TO THE RIGHT NOBLE PA-

*tronesse and Grace of Vertue, the Countesse
of* BEDFORD.

To you, faire Patronesse, and Muse to Learning;
  The Fount of learning and the Muses sends
This Cordiall for your vertues; and forewarning
  To leaue no good, for th'ill the world commends.

Custome seduceth but the vulgar sort:
  With whom, when *Noblesse* mixeth, she is vulgare;
The truly-Noble, still repaire their Fort,
  With gracing good excitements, and gifts rare;
In which the narrow path, to Happinesse,
  Is onely beaten. *Vulgar pleasure* sets
Nets for her selfe, in swinge of her excesse;
  And beates her selfe there dead, ere free she gets.
Since pleasure then with pleasure still doth waste;
  Still please with vertue Madame: That will last.

TO THE RIGHT VALOROVS

and virtuous Lord, the Earle of
SOVTH-HAMTON, &c.

In Choice of all our Countries Noblest spirits
  (Borne slauisher barbarisme to conuince)
I could not but inuoke your honor'd Merits,
  To follow the swift vertue of our Prince.
The cries of *Vertue*, and her *Fortresse, Learning,*
  Brake earth, and to *Elysium* did descend,
To call vp *Homer:* who therein discerning
  That his excitements, to their good, had end
(As being a Grecian) puts-on English armes;
  And to the hardie Natures in these climes
Strikes-vp his high and spiritfull alarmes,
  That they may cleare earth of those impious Crimes
Whose conquest (though most faintly all apply)
  You know (learn'd Earle) all liue for, and should die.

11 Strikes *1609*] Stikes

TO MY EXCEEDING GOOD

Lord, the Earle of SVSSEX: *with duty alwaies
remembred to his honor'd Countesse.*

You that haue made, in our great Princes Name
  (At his high birth) his holy Christian vowes;
May witnesse now (to his eternall Fame)
  How he performes them thus far: & stil growes
Aboue his birth in vertue; past his yeares,
  In strength of Bountie, and great Fortitude.
Amongst this traine, then, of our choicest Peeres,
  That follow him in chace of vices rude,
Summon'd by his great Herald *Homers* voice;
  March you; and euer let your Familie

(In your vowes made for such a Prince) reioyce.
  Your seruice to his State shall neuer die.
And, for my true obseruance, let this show,
  No meanes escapes when I may honour you.

TO THE RIGHT NOBLE AND

Heroicall, my singular good Lord, the Lord
of WALDEN, &c.

Nor let the vulgar sway *Opinion* beares
  (Rare Lord) that Poesies fauor shewes men vaine,
Ranke you amongst her sterne disfauourers;
  She all things worthy fauour doth maintaine.
Vertue, in all things else, at best she betters;
  Honour she heightens, and giues Life in Death;
She is the ornament, and soule of letters:
  The worlds deceipt before her vanisheth.
Simple she is as Doues, like Serpents wise;
  Sharpe, graue, and sacred: nought but things diuine,
And things diuining, fit her faculties;
  (Accepting her as she is genuine.)
  If she be vaine then, all things else are vile;
  If vertuous, still be Patrone of her stile.

TO THE MOST TRVLY-NO-

ble and Vertue-gracing Knight Sir
Thomas HOWARD.

The true, and nothing-lesse-then sacred spirit
  That moues your feete so farre from the prophane;
In skorne of Price, and grace of humblest merit,
  Shall fill your Names sphere; neuer seeing it wane.
It is so rare, in blood so high as yours
  To entertaine the humble skill of Truth;
And put a vertuous end to all your powres;
  That th'honor Age askes, we giue you in youth.
Your Youth hath wonne the maistrie of your Mind;
  As *Homer* sings of his *Antilochus*,
The parallell of you in euery kind,
  Valiant, and milde, and most ingenious.
  Go on in Vertue, after Death and grow,
  And shine like *Ledas* twins; my Lord and you.

Euer most humbly and faithfully deuoted to you,
and all the rare Patrons of diuine HOMER.
                                    Geo. Chapman.

TO THE RIGHT NOBLE AND

most toward Lord in all the Heroicall vertues,
Vicount CRANBORNE, &c.

Neuer may honor'd expedition
  In grace of *Wisedome* (first in this booke arm'd
With *Ioues* bright shield) be Nobly set vpon
  By any other; but your spirit charm'd
In birth with *Wisedomes* vertues; may set downe
  Foote with the formost. To which honor'd end
(Deare Lord) I could not but your name renowne
  Amongst our other Worthies; and commend
The grace of him that all things good hath grac't
  To your faire countn'ance. You shall neuer see
Valour, and vertue in such Tropicks plac't,
  And mouing vp to immortalitie,
  As in this worke. What then, fits you so fairely,
  As to see rarest deeds, and so as rarely?

TO THE MOST HONORD, AND

Judiciall honorer of retired vertue, Vicount
ROCHESTER, *&c.*

You that in so great eminence, liue retir'd
  (Rare Lord) approue your greatnesse cannot call
Your iudgement from the inward state requir'd
  To blaze the outward; which doth neuer fall
In men by chance raisd, but by merit still.
  He seekes not state, that curbs it being found:
Who seekes it not, neuer comes by it ill;
  Nor ill can vse it. Spring then from this ground,
And let thy fruits be fauours done to Good,
  As thy Good is adorn'd with royall fauours;
So shall pale Enuie famish with her food;
  And thou spread further by thy vaine deprauours.
  True Greatnesse cares not to be seene but thus;
  And thus, aboue our selues, you honour vs.

TO THE RIGHT GRAVE AND

noble Patrone of all the Vertues, Sir Edward
Philips, maister of the ROLES, *&c.*

The Lord not by the house must haue his grace;
  But by the Lord the house: Nor is a man
Any thing betterd by his eminent place;
  But his place, by his Merits. Neither can

Your last place here, make you lesse first in honor,
  Then if you stood first. Perfect Honor euer
Vertue distinguishes; and takes vpon her
  Not place but worth; which place abaseth neuer.
So much you know of this; so much you show,
  In constant gracing, for it selfe, each Good,
That all Forme, but the matter which I owe
  To your deserts, I still leaue vnderstood.
  And if this first of workes, your grace you giue,
  It shall not be the last shall make you liue.

(*1609*)

To our English Athenia, Chaste Arbitresse of vertue and
learning, the Ladie ARBELLA; reuiu'd HOMER *submits
cause of renewing her former conference with his original
spirit; and prayes her iudiciall grace to his English Conuer-
sion.*

What to the learn'd *Athenia* can be giuen
  (As offering) fitter, then this Fount of Learning?
Of Wisedome, Fortitude; all gifts of Heauen?
  That by them, both the height, bredth, depth discerning
Of this diuine soule, when of old he liv'd;
  (Like his great Pallas, leading through his wars)
Her faire hand, through his spirit thus reuiv'd,
  May lead the Reader; showe his Commentars;
All that haue turnd him into any tongue:
  And iudge if ours reueale not Mysteries,
That others neuer knew, since neuer sung;
  Not in opinion; but that satisfies.
  Grace then (great Lady) his so gracious Muse,
  And to his whole worke his whole spirit infuse.

To the right Noble, and (by the great eternizer of Vertue, Sir
P. SYDNEY) long since, eterniz'd, Right vertuous, *the
accomplisht Lord* WOTTON, &c.

Your friend (great SYDNEY) my long honor'd Lord,
  (Since friendship is the bond of two, in one)
Tels vs, that you (his quicke part) doe afforde
  Our Land the liuing minde that in him shone.
To whom there neuer came a richer gift
  Then the Soules riches; from men ne're so poore:
And that makes me, the soule of *Homer* lift
  To your acceptance; since one minde both bore.
Our Prince vouchsafes it: and of his high Traine
  I wish you, with the Noblest of our Time.

See here, if Poesie be so slight and vaine
   As men esteeme her in our moderne Rime.
The great'st, and wisest men that euer were,
   Haue giuen her grace: and (I hope) you will, here.

(*Odysseys.*)

TO THE MOST
WORTHILY HONO-
RED, MY SINGVLAR
GOOD LORD, ROBERT,
Earle of SOMERSET,
Lord Chamber-
laine, &c.

I haue aduentured (Right Noble Earle) out of my vtmost,
and euer-vowed seruice to your Vertues, to entitle their
Merits to the Patronage of *Homers* English life: whose wisht
naturall life, the great MACEDON would haue protected, as
the spirit of his Empire,

   That he to his vnmeasur'd mightie Acts,
   Might adde a Fame as vast; and their extracts,
   In fires as bright, and endlesse as the starres,
   His breast might breathe; and thunder out his warres.
5   But that great Monarks loue of fame and praise,
   Receiues an enuious Cloud in our foule daies:
   For since our Great ones, ceasse themselues to do
   Deeds worth their praise; they hold it folly too,
   To feed their praise in others. But what can
10 (Of all the gifts that are) be giuen to man,
   More precious then *Eternitie* and *Glorie*,
   Singing their praises, in vnsilenc't storie?
   Which No blacke Day, No nation, nor no Age;
   No change of Time or Fortune, Force, nor Rage,
15 Shall euer race? All which, the Monarch knew,
   Where *Homer* liu'd entitl'd, would ensew:
              _____ *Cuius de gurgite viuo*
Combibit arcanos vatum omnis turba furores, &c.
   From whose deepe Fount of life, the thirstie rout
   Of Thespian Prophets, haue lien sucking out
   Their sacred rages. And as th'influent stone
20 Of Father *Ioues* great and laborious Sonne,
   Lifts high the heauie Iron; and farre implies

Ex Angeli
Politiani
Ambra.

The wide Orbs; that the Needle rectifies,
In vertuous guide of euery sea-driuen course,
To all aspiring, his one boundlesse force:
So from one *Homer*, all the holy fire,   25
That euer did the hidden heate inspire
In each true Muse, came cleerly sparkling downe,
And must for him, compose one flaming Crowne.
    He, at *Ioues* Table set, fils out to vs,
Cups that repaire Age, sad and ruinous;   30
And giues it Built, of an eternall stand,
With his all-sinewie Odyssæan hand.
Shifts Time, and Fate; puts Death in Lifes free state;
And Life doth into Ages propagate.
He doth in Men, the Gods affects inflame;   35
His fuell Vertue, blowne by *Praise* and *Fame*:
And with the high soules, first impulsions driuen,
Breakes through rude Chaos, Earth, the Seas, and Heauen.
The Nerues of all things hid in Nature, lie
Naked before him; all their Harmonie   40
Tun'd to his Accents; that in Beasts breathe Minds.
What Fowles, what Floods, what Earth, what Aire, what Winds,
What fires Æthereall; what the Gods conclude
In all their Counsels, his Muse makes indude
With varied voices, that euen rockes haue mou'd.   45
And yet for all this, (naked Vertue lou'd)
Honors without her, he, as abiect, prises;
And foolish Fame, deriu'd from thence, despises.
When from the vulgar, taking glorious bound,
Vp to the Mountaine, where the Muse is crownd;   50
He sits and laughs, to see the iaded Rabble,
Toile to his hard heights, t'all accesse vnable, &c.

Thus far Angel. Politi-anus, for the most part translated.

And that your Lordship may in his Face, take view of his
Mind: the first word of his Iliads, is μηνιν, *wrath*: the first
word of his Odysses, ανδρα, *Man*: contracting in either word,
his each workes Proposition. In one, *Predominant Perturba-
tion;* in the other, *ouer-ruling Wisedome:* in one, the Bodies
feruour and fashion of outward Fortitude, to all possible
height of Heroicall Action; in the other, the Minds inward,
constant, and vnconquerd Empire; vnbroken, vnalterd, with
any most insolent, and tyrannous infliction. To many most
soueraigne praises is this Poeme entitled; but to that *Grace*   10
in chiefe, which sets on the Crowne, both of Poets and Ora-
tors; το τα μικρα, μεγαλως; και τα κοινα καινως: that is, *Parua
magnè dicere; peruulgata nouè, ieiuna plenè:* To speake things
litle, greatly; things commune, rarely; things barren and

emptie, fruitfully and fully. The returne of a man into his
Countrie, is his whole scope and obiect; which, in it selfe,
your Lordship may well say, is ieiune and fruitlesse enough;
affoording nothing feastfull, nothing magnificent. And yet
euen this, doth the diuine inspiration, render vast, illustrous,
20   and of miraculous composure. And for this (my Lord) is this
Poeme preferred to his *Iliads:* for therein much magnificence,
both of person and action, giues great aide to his industrie;
but in this, are these helpes, exceeding sparing, or nothing;
and yet is the Structure so elaborate, and pompous, that the
poore plaine Groundworke (considered together) may seeme
the naturally rich wombe to it, and produce it needfully.
Much wondered at therefore, is the Censure of *Dionysius
Longinus* (a man otherwise affirmed, graue, and of elegant
iudgement) comparing *Homer* in his *Iliads*, to the Sunne
30   rising; in his *Odysses*, to his descent or setting. Or to the
Ocean robd of his aesture; many tributorie flouds and riuers
of excellent ornament, withheld from their obseruance. When
this his worke so farre exceeds the *Ocean*, with all his Court
and concourse; that all his Sea, is onely a seruiceable streame
to it. Nor can it be compared to any One power to be named
in nature; being an entirely wel-sorted and digested Con-
fluence of all. Where the most solide and graue, is made as
nimble and fluent, as the most airie and firie; the nimble and
fluent, as firme and well bounded as the most graue and solid.
40   And (taking all together) of so tender impression, and of such
Command to the voice of the *Muse;* that they knocke heauen
with her breath, and discouer their foundations as low as hell.
Nor is this all-comprising *Poesie*, phantastique, or meere
fictiue; but the most material, and doctrinall illations of
Truth; both for all manly information of Manners in the
yong; all prescription of Iustice, and euen Christian pietie,
in the most graue and high-gouernd. To illustrate both
which, in both kinds, with all height of expression, the Poet
creates both a Bodie and a Soule in them. Wherein, if the
50   Bodie (being the letter, or historie) seemes fictiue, and beyond
Possibilitie to bring into Act: the sence then and Allegorie
(which is the soule) is to be sought: which intends a more
eminent expressure of *Vertue*, for her louelinesse; and of *Vice*
for her vglinesse, in their seuerall effects; going beyond the
life, then any Art within life, can possibly delineate. Why
then is *Fiction*, to this end, so hatefull to our true Ignorants?
Or why should a poore Chronicler of a Lord Maiors naked
Truth, (that peraduenture will last his yeare) include more
worth with our moderne wizerds, then *Homer* for his naked

28 Longinus] Longimus

Vlysses, clad in eternall Fiction? But this Prozer *Dionysius,*   60
and the rest of these graue, and reputatiuely learned, (that
dare vndertake for their grauities, the headstrong censure of
all things; and challenge the vnderstanding of these Toyes in
their childhoods: when euen these childish vanities, retaine
deepe and most necessarie learning enough in them, to make
them children in their ages, and teach them while they liue)
are not in these absolutely diuine Infusions, allowd either
voice or relish: for, *Qui Poeticas ad fores accedit. &c.* (sayes
the Diuine Philosopher) he that knocks at the Gates of the
Muses; sine Musarum furore, is neither to be admitted entrie,   70
nor a touch at their Thresholds: his opinion of entrie, ridicu-
lous, and his presumption impious. Nor must Poets them-
selues (might I a litle insist on these contempts; not tempting
too farre your Lordships *Vlyssean* patience) presume to these
doores, without the truly genuine, and peculiar induction:
There being in *Poesie* a twofold rapture, (or alienation of
soule, as the abouesaid Teacher termes it) one *Insania,* a dis-
ease of the mind, and a meere madnesse, by which the in-
fected is thrust beneath all the degrees of humanitie: *& ex
homine, Brutum quodammodo redditur:* (for which, poore   80
Poesie, in this diseasd and impostorous age, is so barbarously
vilified) the other is, *Diuinus furor;* by which the sound and
diuinely healthfull, *supra hominis naturam erigitur, & in
Deum transit.* One a perfection directly infused from God:
the other an infection, obliquely and degenerately proceeding
from man. Of the diuine *Furie* (my Lord) your *Homer* hath
euer bene, both first and last *Instance;* being pronounced ab-
solutely, τον σοφωτατον, και τεν θειοτατον ποιητην; the most
wise and most diuine Poet. Against whom, whosoeuer shall
open his prophane mouth, may worthily receiue answer, with   90
this of his diuine defender; (*Empedocles, Heraclitus, Prota-
goras, Epichar: &c.* being of *Homers* part) τις ουν, &c. who
against such an Armie, and the Generall *Homer* dares at-
tempt the assault, but he must be reputed ridiculous? And
yet against this hoast, and this inuincible Commander, shall
we haue every *Besogne* and foole a Leader. The common herd
(I assure my self) readie to receiue it on their hornes. Their
infected Leaders,

> Such men, as sideling ride the ambling *Muse;*
> Whose saddle is as frequent as the stuse;
> Whose Raptures are in euery Pageant seene,
> In euery Wassall rime, and Dancing greene:
> When he that writes by any beame of Truth,   5
> Must diue as deepe as he; past shallow youth.

Truth dwels in Gulphs, whose Deepes hide shades so rich,
That *Night* sits muffl'd there, in clouds of pitch:
More Darke then Nature made her; and requires
10 (To cleare her tough mists) Heauens great fire of fires;
To whom, the Sunne it selfe is but a Beame.
For sicke soules then (but rapt in foolish Dreame)
To wrestle with these Heau'n-strong mysteries;
What madnesse is it? when their light, serues eies
15 That are not worldly, in their least aspect;
But truly pure; and aime at Heauen, direct.
Yet these, none like; but what the brazen head
Blatters abroad; no sooner borne, but dead.

Holding then in eternal contempt (my Lord) those short-
liued Bubbles; eternize your vertue and iudgement with the
Grecian Monark; esteeming, not as the least of your New-
yeares Presents,

Homer (three thousand yeares dead) now reuiu'd,
20 Euen from that dull Death, that in life he liu'd;
When none conceited him; none vnderstood,
That so much life, in so much death as blood
Conueys about it, could mixe. But when Death
Drunke vp the bloudie Mist, that humane breath
25 Pour'd round about him (Pouertie and Spight,
Thickning the haplesse vapor) then Truths light
Glimmerd about his Poeme: the pincht soule,
(Amidst the Mysteries it did enroule)
Brake powrefully abroad. And as we see
30 The Sunne all hid in clouds, at length'got free,
Through some forc't couert, ouer all the wayes,
Neare and beneath him, shootes his vented rayes
Farre off, and stickes them in some litle Glade;
All woods, fields, riuers, left besides in shade:
35 So your *Apollo*, from that world of light,
Closde in his Poems bodie; shot to sight
Some few forc't Beames; which neare him, were not seene,
(As in his life or countrie) Fate and Spleene,
Clouding their radiance; which when Death had clear'd;
40 To farre off Regions, his free beames appear'd:
In which, all stood and wonderd; striuing which,
His Birth and Rapture, should in right enrich.
Twelue *Labours* of your *Thespian Hercules*,
I now present your Lordship; Do but please
45 To lend Life meanes, till th'other Twelue receaue

20 from] ftom

Equall atchieuement; and let Death then reaue
My life now lost in our Patrician Loues,
That knocke heads with the herd: in whom there moues
One blood, one soule: both drownd in one set height
Of stupid Enuie, and meere popular Spight.   50
Whose loues, with no good, did my least veine fill;
And from their hates, I feare as little ill.
Their Bounties nourish not, when most they feed,
But where there is no Merit, or no Need:
Raine into riuers still; and are such showres,   55
As bubbles spring, and ouerflow the flowres.
Their worse parts, and worst men, their Best subornes,
Like winter Cowes, whose milke runnes to their hornes.
And as litigious Clients bookes of Law,
Cost infinitely; taste of all the Awe,   60
Bencht in our kingdomes Policie, Pietie, State;
Earne all their deepe explorings; satiate
All sorts there thrust together by the heart,
With thirst of wisedome, spent on either part:
Horrid examples made of Life and Death,   65
From their fine stuffe wouen: yet when once the breath
Of sentence leaues them, all their worth is drawne
As drie as dust; and weares like Cobweb Lawne:
So these men set a price vpon their worth,
That no man giues, but those that trot it forth,   70
Through *Needs* foule wayes; feed *Humors*, with all cost,
Though *Iudgement* sterues in them: *Rout: State* engrost
(At all Tabacco benches, solemne Tables,
Where all that crosse their Enuies, are their fables)
In their ranke faction: Shame, and Death approu'd   75
Fit Penance for their Opposites: none lou'd
But those that rub them: not a Reason heard,
That doth not sooth and glorifie their preferd
Bitter Opinions. When, would *Truth* resume
The cause to his hands; all would flie in fume   80
Before his sentence; since the innocent mind,
Iust God makes good; to whom their worst is wind.
For, that I freely all my Thoughts expresse,
My Conscience is my Thousand witnesses:
And to this stay, my constant Comforts vow;   85
You for the world I haue, or God for you.

CERTAINE ANCIENT GREEKE EPIGRAMMES
Translated.

All starres are drunke vp by the firie Sunne;
And in so much a flame, lies shrunke the Moone::
Homers all-liu'd Name, all Names leaues in Death;
Whose splendor onely, Muses Bosomes breath.

Another.

Heau'ns fires shall first fall darkn'd from his Sphere;
Graue Night, the light weed of the Day shall weare:
Fresh streames shall chace the Sea; tough Plowes shall teare
Her fishie bottomes: Men, in long date dead,
Shall rise, and liue; before Obliuion shed
Those still-greene leaues, that crowne great *Homers* head.

Another.

The great *Maeonides* doth onely write;
And to him dictates, the great God of Light.

Another.

Seuen kingdomes stroue, in which should swell the wombe
That bore great *Homer;* whom Fame freed from Tombe:
Argos, Chius, Pylos, Smyrna, Colophone;
The learn'd *Athenian*, and *Vlyssean* Throne.

Another.

Art thou of *Chius*? No. Of *Salamine*?
As little. Was the *Smyrnean* Countrie thine?
Nor so. Which then? Was *Cumas*? *Colophone*?
Nor one, nor other. Art thou then of none,
That Fame proclames thee? None. Thy Reason call:
If I confesse of one, I anger all.

(Epilogue to the *Odysses*.)

So wrought diuine *Vlysses* through his woes:
So, croun'd the Light with him; His Mothers Throes;
As through his great Renowner, I haue wrought;
And my safe saile, to sacred Anchor brought.
5   Nor did the *Argiue* ship, more burthen feele,
That bore the Care of all men, in her Keele;
Then my aduenturous Barke: The *Colchean* Fleece,
Not halfe so precious, as this soule of *Greece*,
In whose songs I haue made our shores reioyce,
10   And *Greeke* it selfe veile, to our *English* voyce.
Yet this inestimable Pearle, wil all

Our Dunghil *Chanticheres*, but obuious call;
Each Moderne scraper, this Gem scratching by;
His Oate preferring far. Let such, let ly:
So scorne the stars the clouds; as true-soul'd men   15
Despise Deceiuers. For, as Clouds would faine
Obscure the Stars yet (Regions left below
With all their enuies) bar them but of show;
For they shine euer, and wil shine, when they
Dissolue in sinckes, make Mire, and temper Clay: 20
So puft Impostors (our *Muse-vapours*) striue,
With their selfe-blowne additions, to depriue
Men solid, of their full; though infinite short
They come in their compare; and false report
Of leuelling, or touching, at their light,   25
That still retaine their radiance, and cleere right;
And shal shine euer When, alas, one blast
Of least disgrace, teares down th'Impostors Mast;
His Tops, and Tacklings; His whole Freight, and He
Confiscate to the Fishy Monarchy;   30
His trash, by foolish Fame bought now, from hence,
Giuen to serue *Mackarell* forth, and *Frankincence*.
  Such then, and any; too soft-ey'd to see
Through workes so solid, any worth, so free
Of all the learn'd professions, as is fit   35
To praise at such price; let him thinke his wit
Too weake to rate it; rather then oppose
With his poore pow'rs, Ages, and Hosts of Foes.

To the Ruines of Troy,

and Greece.

Troy rac't; *Greece* wrackt: who mournes? Ye both may bost;
Else th'*Ilyads*, and *Odysses*, had bene lost.

Ad Deum.

The onely true God, (betwixt whom and Me,
I onely bound my comforts; and agree
With all my actions) onely truly knowes,
And can iudge truly me, with all that goes
To all my Faculties. In whose free grace   5
And inspiration, I onely place
All meanes to know (with my meanes; Study, praire,
In, & from his word taken) staire by staire,
In all continual contentation, rising
To knowledge of his Truth; and practising   10
His wil in it, with my sole Sauiours aide,

Guide, and enlightning: Nothing done, nor saide,
Nor thought that good is; but acknowledg'd by
His inclination, skill, and faculty.
15 By which, to finde the way out to his loue
Past all the worlds; the sphere is, where doth moue
My studies, prai'rs, and pow'rs: No pleasure taken
But sign'd by his: for which, my blood forsaken,
My soule I cleaue to: and what (in his blood
20 That hath redeem'd, cleansd, taught her) fits her good.

Deo opt. Max. gloria.

(*Hymns of Homer.*)
TO MY EVER
MOST-WORTHIE-TO-BE-MOST
HONOR'D LORD,
THE EARLE OF SOMERSET, &c.

Not forc't by fortune; but since your free minde ⎫
(Made by affliction) rests in choice resign'd ⎬
To calme Retreate; laid quite beneath the winde ⎭
Of Grace, and Glory: I well know, my Lord,
5 You would not be entitl'd to a word
That might a thought remoue from your Repose, ⎫
To thunder and spit Flames, as Greatnesse does; ⎬
For all the Trumps, that still tell where he goes. ⎭
Of which Trumps, *Dedication* being One,
10 Me thinks I see you start to heare it blowne.
      But this is no such Trump as summons Lords,
Gainst Enuies steele, to draw their leaden swords,
Or gainst Hare-lipt *Detraction, Contempt,*
All which, from all Resistance stand exempt,
15 It being as hard to seuer *Wrong* from *Merit,*
As meate-indude, from blood; or blood from spirit.
Nor in the spirits Chariot rides the soule
In bodies chaste, with more diuine controule;
Nor virtue shines more in a louely Face;
20 Then true desert, is stuck off with Disgrace.
And therefore truth it selfe that had to blesse
The merit of it all, Almightinesse;
Would not protect it, from the Bane and Ban
Of all Moodes most distraught, and *Stygian;*
25 As counting it the Crowne of all Desert,
Borne to All Heauen, to take of Earth, no part

26 All Heauen] Heauen.   Following Chapman's own correction.

Of false Ioy here, for Ioyes-there-endlesse troth,
Nor sell his Birthright for a messe of Broth.
But stay and still sustaine, and his Blisse bring,
Like to the hatching of the Black-thornes spring,   30
With bitter frosts, and smarting haile-stormes forth;
Fates loue Bces labors; onely *Paine* crownes *Worth.*
This *Dedication* calls no Greatnes then,
To patrone this Greatnes-creating Penn;
Nor you to add to your dead calme a breath;   }   35
For those arm'd Angells, that in spight of death
Inspir'd those flowrs that wrought this *poets* wreath}
Shall keepe it euer, Poesies steepest Starr,
As, in Earths flaming wals, Heauens seuenfold Carr,
(From all the wildes of *Neptunes* watrie sphere)   40
For euer guards the *Erymanthian Beare.*
    Since then your Lordship, settles in your shade
A life retir'd; and no Retreate is made
But to some strength; (for else, tis no Retreate,
But rudely running from your Battailes heate)   45
I giue this, as your strength: your strength, my Lord,
In Counsailes and Examples, that afford
More Guard, then whole Hosts of corporeal powre,
And more deliuerance, teach the fatall *Howre.*
    Turne not your medcine then, to your disease,}   50
By your too set, and sleight repulse of these,
The Adiuncts of your matchlesse *Odysses;*
Since on that wisest minde of Man, relies
Refuge from all Liues Infelicities.
    Nor sing these, such diuision from them;   55
But that these spinn the thred of the same streame,
From one selfe Distaffs stuff: for Poesies Pen
(Through al theames) is t'informe the liues of Men:
All whose Retreates, neede strengths of all degrees;
Without which; (had you euen *Herculean* knees;)   60
Your foes fresh Charges, would, at length preuaile,
To leaue your Noblest suff'rance, no least saile.
Strength then, the Obiect is of all Retreates;
Strength needes no friends trust; strength, your foes defeates.
Retire to strength then, of eternall things,   65
And y'are eternall; for our knowing Spring's
Flow into those things that we truely know;
Which (being Eternall) we are render'd so.
And though your high-fixt Light passe infinite farr
Th' aduicefull Guide, of my still-trembling Starr;   70
Yet heare what my dischardg'd Peece must foretell,
Standing your Poore, and Perdue Sentinell.

Kings may perhaps wish, euen your Beggars Voice
To their Eternities; how skorn'd a choice
75   Soeuer, now it lies; And (dead I) may
Extend your life to lights extreamest Raie.
If not; your *Homer* yet, past doubt shall make,
Immortall, like himselfe, your Bounties stake
Put in my hands, to propagate your Fame,
80   Such virtue reigns in such vnited Name.
     Retire to him then for aduice, and skill
To know, things call'd worst, Best; and Best most ill;
Which knowne; truths best chuse; and retire to still.
And as our *English Generall*, (whose Name
85   Shall equall interest finde in T'House of Fame,
With all Earths great'st Commanders) in Retreate
To *Belgian Gant*, stood all *Spaines* Armies heate,
By *Parma* led; though but one thousand strong:
Three miles together thrusting through the throng
90   Of Th'Enimies Horse, (still pouring on their Fall
Twixt him & home) & thunderd through them al:
The *Gallick* Monsiour standing on the wall,
And wondring at his dreadfull Discipline;
Fir'd with a Valor, that spit spirit Diuine:
95   In fiue Battaillons randging all his Men;
Bristl'd with Pikes, and flanck't with Flanckers ten;
Gaue fire still in his Rere; retir'd and wrought,
Downe to his fixt strength still: retir'd and fought;
All the Battaillons of the Enemies Horse
100   Storming vpon him still, their fieriest Force;
Charge vpon Charge laid fresh: he fresh as day
Repulsing all; and forcing glorious way
Into the Gates; the gaspt (as swounes for Ayre)
And tooke their life in, with vntoucht Repaire:
105   So fight out (sweet Earle) your Retreate in Peace;
No ope-warr equalls that, where priuie Prease
Of neuer-numberd odds of Enimie
Arm'd all by Enuie, in blinde Ambush lie,
To rush out, like an open threatning skie,
110   Broke al in Meteors round about your eares.
Gainst which, (though far from hence) through al your Reres
Haue fires prepar'd; wisdome, with wisdome flanck,
And all your forces randge in present ranck;
Retiring as you now fought in your strength,
115   From all the Force laid, in times vtmost length,
To charge, and basely, come on you behind.
The Doctrine of all which, you here shall finde,
And, in the true Glasse of a humane Minde,

A simile il-
lustrating the
most renownd
seruice Of
Generall
Noris in his
Retreate be-
fore *Gant*,
neuer before
made sacred
to *Memorie*.

Your *Odysses;* the Body letting see:
All his life past, through Infelicitie,   120
And manage of it all. In which to friend,
The full Muse brings you both the prime and end
Of all Arts ambient in the Orbe of Man;
Which neuer darknesse most Cimmerian
Can giue Eclipse; since (blinde) He all things sawe,   125
And to all, euer since, liu'd Lord, and Lawe.
And though our mere-learn'd men; & Modern wise⎫
Taste not poore Poesies Ingenuities,   ⎬
Being crusted with their couetous Leprosies;   ⎭
But hold her paines, worse then the spiders worke,   130
And lighter then the shadowe of a Corke:
Yet th'ancient learn'd, heat with celestiall fire,
Affirmes her flames so sacred and entire;

Vt non sine   That, not without Gods greatest grace she can
Maximo   Fall in the wid'st Capacitie of Man.   135
fauore Dei   If yet, the vile Soule of this Verminous time;   ⎫
comparari   Loue more the Sale-Muse; and the Squirrels chime,   ⎬
queat. Pla. in Then this full sphere of Poesies sweetest Prime;   ⎭
Ione.   Giue them vnenuied, their vaine veine, and vent;
And rest your wings, in his approu'd Ascent   140
That yet was neuer reacht; nor euer fell
Into affections bought with things that sell,
Being the *Sunns Flowre;* and wrapt so in his skie,
He cannot yeeld to euery Candles eye.

> *Whose most worthy Discoueries, to your*
> *Lordships Iudiciall Perspectiue in most*
> *subdude Humilitie submitteth,*

George Chapman.

(Epilogue to the *Hymns.*)

The Worke that I was borne to doe, is done.
Glory to him, that the Conclusion
Makes the beginning of my life: and Neuer
Let me be said to liue; till I liue Euer.
    Where's the outliuing of my Fortunes then,   5
Ye errant vapors of Fames Lernean Fenn?
That (like possest stormes) blast all; not in Herde
With your abhorr'd heads: who, because casher'de
By Men, for Monsters; thinck Men, Monsters All,
That are not of your pyed Hood, and your Hall.   10
When you are nothing but the scumm of things, ⎫
And must be cast off: Drones, that haue no stings, ⎬
Nor any more soule, then a stone hath wings.   ⎭

Auant ye *Haggs;* your Hates, and Scandalls are,⎫
15 The Crownes, and Comforts of a good Mans Care;⎬
By whose impartiall Perpendiculare;   ⎭
All is extuberance, and Tumor All,
That you your Ornaments, and glories call.
Your wrie Mouthes censure right? your blister'd Tongues,
20 That licke but itches? and whose vlcerous Lungs
Come vp at all things permanent, and sound?
O you (like flies in Dreggs) in Humors droun'd;
Your loues, like *Atoms*, lost in gloomie Ayre;
J would not retriue with a wither'd Haire.
25 Hate, and cast still your stings then; for your kisses
Betray but *Truth;* and your Applaud's, are Hisses.
    To see our supercilious wizerds frowne;
Their faces falne like Froggs; and coming downe,
Stincking the Sunn out; make me shine the more:
30 And like a checkt flood, bear aboue the shore,
That their prophane Opinions faine would set,
To what they see not; know not; nor can let.
Yet then, our learn'd Men, with their Torrents come
Roring from their forc't Hills, all crown'd with fome,
35 That one not taught like them, should learne to know
Their Greeke rootes, & from thence the Groues that grow,
Casting such rich shades, from great *Homers* wings:
That first, and last, command the Muses springs.
Though he's best Scholler, that through paines and vows;
40 Made his owne Master onely; all things know's.
Nor pleades my poor skill; forme; or learned Place;
But dantlesse labor, constant Prayer, and Grace.
And what's all their skill, but vast varied reading?
As if brode-beaten High-waies had the leading
45 To Truths abstract, and narrow Path, and Pit?
Found in no walke, of any worldly wit.
And without Truth; all's onely sleight of hand,
Or our Law-learning, in a Forraine Land;
Embroderie spent on Cobwebs; Braggart show
50 Of Men that all things learne; and nothing know.
For Ostentation, humble Truth still flies,
And all confederate fashionists, defies.
And as some sharpe-browd Doctor, (English borne;)
Jn much learn'd Latine Jdioms can adorne
55 A verse with rare Attractions; yet become
His English Muse, like an Arachnean Loome,
Wrought spight of *Pallas;* and therein bewraies
More tongue then truth; beggs, and adopts his Bayes;

17 Tumor] excretion.   Following Chapman's own correction.

So *Ostentation,* bee hee neuer so
Larded with labour, to suborne his showe;   60
Shall soothe within him, but a bastard soule,
No more Heauen heyring, then Earths sonne the Moule.
But as in dead Calmes, emptiest smokes arise
Vncheckt and free; vp, strait into the skies;
So drousie Peace, that in her humor steepes   65
All she affects, lets such rise while she sleepes.
Many, and most Men, haue of wealth least store,
But None the gracious shame that fits the Pore;
So most learn'd Men, enough are Jgnorant;
But few the grace haue, to confesse their want,   70
Till Liues, and Learnings, come concomitant.
For from Mens knowledges; their Liues-Acts flowe;
Vaineglorious Acts then, vaine proue all they know.
As Night, thc life-enclining starrs, best showes;
So liues obscure, the starriest soules disclose.   75
  For me; let iust Men iudge by what J show
In Acts expos'd, how much I erre, or knowe;
And let not *Enuie,* make all worse then nought
With her meere headstrong, and quite braineles thought:
Others, for doing nothing; giuing All;   80
And bounding all worth in her bursten Gall.
  God and my deare Redeemer, rescue Me
From Mens immane, and mad Impietie;
And by my life and soule, (sole knowne to them)
Make me of *Palme,* or *Yew,* an Anadem.   85
And so, my sole God, the thrice sacred Trine,
Beare all th'Ascription, of all Me and Mine.

Supplico tibi Domine, Pater et Dux rationis nostrae; vt Nostrae Nobilitatis recordemur, qua tu nos ornasti; et vt tu nobis prestò sis, vt jis qui per sese mouentur; vt et à Corporis contagio, Brutorumque affectuum repurgemur; eosque superemus, atque regamus; et, sicut decet; pro instrumentis jis vtamur. Deinde, vt nobis Adiumento sis; ad accuratam rationis nostrae correctionem; et coniunctionem cum jis qui verè sunt, per lucem veritatis. Et tertiùm, Saluatori supplex oro; vt ab oculis animorum nostrorum, caliginem prorsus abstergas; vt norimus bene, qui Deus, aut Mortalis habendus, *Amen.*

Sine honore viuam, Nulloque Numero ero.

Prose 6 Adiumento] Adiuneto.   Following Chapman's own correction.

NOTES.

NOTES

Two explanations are necessary to help the reader about points of reference in these notes. Wherever the word *gloss* is used, the reference is to an annotation made by Chapman himself, whereas the word *note* refers to an annotation by the editor. On points of diction where the reference is to "Loane," the reader is referred to George G. Loane, "A Thousand and One Notes on 'A New English Dictionary' " (1920) and "A Thousand and Two Notes on 'A New English Dictionary,' " *Philological Society's Transactions* (1925–30).

Σκία νυκτός. / THE SHADOW / OF NIGHT: CONTAINING / TWO POETICALL HYMNES, / Deuised by *G. C. Gent.* / *Versus mei habebunt aliquantum Noctis.* / *Antilo.* / (*device:* Anchora Spei.) / *AT LONDON,* / Printed by *R.F.* for *William Ponsonby.* / 1594

A-E⁴. 4to.

Contents: (A₁ʳ) Title; A₂ "To My Deare and most Worthy Friend Master Mathew Roydon;" A₃ʳ–C₁ʳ Hymnus in Noctem; C₁ᵛ–C₂ʳ Gloss; C₂ᵛ–E₂ᵛ Hymnus in Cynthiam; E₃ʳ–E₄ᵛ Gloss.

Entered: 31 de. 1593

Copies Used: British Museum C.39.d.62   Bodleian   Malone 299 (6)   Victoria and Albert Dyce 2025   Harvard College 14424. 14. 50*   Huntington Library. Checked by Miss Marianne Gateson   Dr. Rosenbach's copy. Checked by Miss Marianne Gateson.

Punctuation Revised.

Hymnus in Noctem. 95 Parenthesis deleted at end of line   104 Final period instead of colon   120 Final colon instead of period   144 Final period instead of comma   148 Final semicolon instead of period   149 No new paragraph   190 Final semicolon instead of period   260 Final colon instead of period   301 Final colon instead of period   Gloss 13 Period added after Latin quotation

Hymnus in Cynthiam. 9 Final colon instead of period   20 Final period instead of colon   25 Final colon instead of period   30 Final period instead of colon   32 Final colon instead of period   45 Final colon instead of period   57 Final semicolon instead of period   60 Final parenthesis added   90–91 Beginning of parenthesis placed before *English* instead of before *put*   159 Final comma instead of period   161 Final period added   200 Final comma added   223 Final period instead of comma   227 Final period instead of comma   266 Final comma instead of period   325 Final period instead of colon   Gloss 15 Final period instead of semicolon

This book, Chapman's first published poetry, provides the chief evidence used to identify Chapman as the exponent of the School of Night, a literary and metaphysical school which is thought to be ridiculed by Shakespeare in *Love's Labour's Lost.* The idea of this "School" was first suggested by Arthur Acheson in *Shakespeare and the Rival Poet* (1903). The idea is supported by Dover Wilson and Quiller-Couch in the Cambridge edition of *L.L.L.* The story which has accumulated around it is succinctly told in the first chapter of Miss M. C. Bradbrook's book, *The School of Night* (1936). The latest full length commentator on *L.L.L.,* Miss Frances A. Yates, makes the suggestion that in the epistle dedicatory Chapman is defending the cause of serious artists and students against the views of John Eliot incorporated by Gabriel Harvey in his *Pierces Supererogation* (1593). See *A Study of Love's Labour's Lost* (1936), Chapter IV.

Epistle Dedicatory.

"Master Mathew Roydon" (fl.1580–1622) was a minor poet chiefly noted for having been one of the company, which included Sir Walter Raleigh and the poet Warner, implicated in the charges of blasphemy made against Christopher Marlowe. Roydon's poem on Sidney, *Elegie, or Friends passion for his Astrophill*, appeared in the *Phoenix Nest* (1593). Little is known about him, but judging by the praise of Nashe and the deference with which Chapman addresses him, he must have been a person of considerable consequence in the literary circles of his day.

4–8 Franck L. Schoell, in his *Etudes sur l'Humanisme Continental en Angleterre à la Fin de la Renaissance*, p. 179, compares this passage to one in the *Mythologiae* of Natalis Comes, Bk. VII, Ch. 11. This work of Comes, as Schoell has amply demonstrated, is the chief source of both the hymns which constitute *The Shadow of Night*. Comes' compendium of classical mythology, first published in 1551 and often reprinted, was an immensely popular book; Schoell gives a partial list of the editions on p. 27n of his *Etudes*. Since there is no telling which one Chapman had by him, references in these notes will be made to book and chapter only, not to page.

16–17 *supererogation . . . pierst*) See F. A. Yates, *A Study of Love's Labour's Lost*, p. 83 seq. She argues that this is a reference to Harvey's *Pierces Supererogation*.

20 *heauenly familiar*) This is the phrase that, taken in conjunction with the title of these poems, gives rise to the supposition that Chapman was the rival poet of Shakespeare's sonnets. See the argument in the New Variorum edition of the sonnets on sonnet 86,

> " . . . that affable familiar ghost
> Which nightly gulls him with intelligence."

21 *Intonsi Catones*) Horace's phrase in *Odes*, ii. 15, 11.

30 *Darbie*) Ferdinando Stanley, 5th Earl of Derby (1559?–94). Called "ingenious" doubtless because he composed verses, some of which appeared in Bodenham's *Belvedere* (1600). He was the Amyntas of Spenser's *Colin Clouts Come Home Againe*, and was highly esteemed by Greene and Nashe. (See *D.N.B.*) The date of his death, 16 April, 1594, fixes the publication of *The Shadow of Night* in the early part of the year 1594.

30 *Northumberland*) Henry Percy, 9th Earl of Northumberland (1564–1632). Northumberland is known chiefly as a scholar and mathematician, though both he and Derby were interested in the more occult study of alchemy. In 1605 he was suspected of being party to the Gunpowder Plot and was imprisoned, with Raleigh, in the Tower. Chapman refers to him again, *In Seianum*, 142, and it is interesting to know that during the long term of the Earl's imprisonment Chapman's *Homer* was one of the three English books which he had with him.

31 *heire of Hunsdon*) George Carey, 2nd Lord Hunsdon (1547–1603). He succeeded to the peerage in 1596. There is no evidence that he was a scholar, hence no reason for his being classed with the other two noblemen. He was the Governor of the Isle of Wight, and the only written works of his which are known are various manuscripts on state matters affecting the island. As Lord Chamberlain (March 1596/7) he was patron of Shakespeare's company.

35 *darknesse*) The theory that a certain degree of "darkness" is advisable in works of profound content is not as peculiar to Chapman as has sometimes been indicated, but appears fairly frequently in Renaissance criticism. Compare, for instance, Sir Fredericke's argument in Castiglione's *Courtier* (Hoby's translation, 1561, Everyman ed., p. 51). And Sir Philip Sidney, though he believed that poetry should instruct by pleasing and bring home the lessons of philosophy to the minds and hearts of its readers, made the qualification that "there are many mysteries contained in poetry which of purpose were written darkly, lest by profane wits it should be abused." Chapman elaborates this theory in the last two paragraphs of his Epistle to Roydon prefixed to *Ouids Banquet of Sence.*

Hymnus in Noctem.

1 *seq.* and gloss 1. Schoell (p. 182) compares the *Mythologiae* of Comes, III, 12, "De Nocte."

5 and gloss 2. *Idem.*

13 *court of skill*) Miss Bradbrook equates this phrase with the School of Night. (*The School of Night*, p. 130.)

14 and gloss 3. As in the *Phaedo*, 72e–76, obviously picked up from some Latin commentator. The Socratic thesis that "our learning is nothing but recollection," which learning needs but to be released, *enfranchised*, from its hold in memory to become part of our conscious mental equipment.

19 *christall*) Here is identical with "celestial," or the "crystalline sphere," as proved by the accompanying gloss. Cf. *Byron's Conspiracy*, IV. i. 40, and T. M. Parrott's note thereon.

21–22 The previous editor of the poems, R. H. Shepherd, compares *Bussy*, IV. ii. 37, and *Caesar and Pompey*, II. v. 4.

29–49 Since these lines embody a concept which is central to Chapman's thought and is retained in much of his later work, the lineage of the passage is worth tracing. The conception of Chaos as the general parent of the universe, whose offspring were Erebus and Night, goes back as far as Hesiod's *Theogony*, but it first assumes the proportion of a physical theory in Ovid's *Metamorphoses* (i. 5–31), a passage which Chapman certainly knew. The image of Chaos "indigest" (30 and 59–60), "Chaos, rudis, indigestaque moles" (*Met.*, i. 7), is repeated with variations both in his poems and plays. Cf. *O.B. of S.*, st. 25; *T. of P.*, 224–225; *Humourous Day's Mirth*, Sc. VII. 209–211; *Bussy*, IV. i. 163–164; *Revenge of Bussy*, V. i. 1–3; *Caesar and Pompey*, II. v. 7–11, and v. ii. 80–81. For lines 39–46 Chapman leans heavily on Joshua Sylvester's translation of the *Divine Weeks* of Du Bartas (first ed. 1590 or 1591). The parallel passage comes in the First Day of the First Week, and is here copied from the folio of 1608, sig. C4v.

> That first World (yet) was a most formless *Form*,
> A confus'd Heap, a *Chaos* most deform,
> A Gulf of Gulfs, a Body ill compact,
> An ugly medly, where all difference lackt:
> Where th'Elements lay iumbled al together,
> Where hot and colde were iarring each with either;
> The blunt and sharp, the dank against the drie,
> The hard with soft, the base against the high;
> Bitter with sweet: and while this brawl did last,
> The Earth in Heav'n, the Heav'n in Earth was plac't;
> Earth, Aire, and Fire were with the water mixt;
> Water, Earth, Aire within the Fire were fixt;
> Fire, Water, Earth, did in the Aire abide;
> Aire, Fire, and Water, in the Earth did hide.

It is obvious that Chapman had Sylvester's book open before him. Note also the similarity in their use of the word "*Form*," a key word in Chapman's metaphysical utterances, where it is often repeated in the sense given it by scholastic philosophy: "The essential determinant principle of a thing; that which makes anything (matter) a determinate species or kind of being; the essential creative quality." *N.E.D.* The concept of "infinite shapes of creatures" bred in "an huge eternal *Chaos*" from which they emerge to take on "forme" for their borrowed matter is elaborately displayed by Spenser: *Faerie Queene*, III. vi. 35–38.

In Chapman, cf. *H. in N.*, 101–104; *H. in C.*, 182, 188; *O.B. of S.*, st. 93; *To Reader—Iliads* (in translating Pliny), 5; *Sonnet to Arundel—Iliads*, 1609, 6–8; *Eug.*, 536–553; 702 *seq.* gloss; *Epic.*, 280; *And. Lib.*, 580.

63–74 Since this striking figure is the nearest thing one can point to as the theme of the poem, it is worth quoting the Latin of Comes from which it is derived: *Myth.*, III, 12, "De Nocte." (Schoell, p. 180): "Verum de ijs, quae fabulose de Nocte dici solent, satis.

Ex illa nuper commemoratae pestes natae esse dicuntur, quoniam inscitia & malitia mortalium, quae Nox est mentis, omnium prope calamitatum, quae humanum genus inuadunt, parens est & altrix." Compare Spenser, *Faerie Queene*, III. iv. 55–60, and Shakespeare, *The Rape of Lucrece*, 764 *seq.*

84 *Calydonian bores*) These boars were sent by Diana as a curse to the kingdom of Calydon. The episode is first related in the *Iliad*, IX, 536 *seq.*, but Chapman may have picked up the reference from Comes, *Myth.*, VII, 3, "De Apro Calydonio." At any rate, he uses it again: cf. *Widow's Tears*, II. iv. 204–205, and *Epic.*, 627–628, where he adds an image to the verse of Politianus which he is translating.

93 *manlesse natures*) See note to *T. of P.*, 443–444.

105–111 Schoell (p. 180) compares Comes, *Myth.*, VI, 11, "De Capra Caelesti." By the "liuing signe" Chapman is referring to the zodiacal sign of the goat, *Capra*. Jove had placed the goat Amalthea among the stars in gratitude for her having fed him her milk when he was an infant on the island of Crete.

112–116 Schoell (p. 181) compares Comes, *Myth.*, VI, 10, "De Argonaui."

117–122 The argument is elliptical here. Chapman says that he could cite a thousand examples of Jove gratefully creating stars as he had from the goat and the ship. His theme is that man need not think that he is cast in the highest shape. He carries out the analogy of the Maker and Jove by comparing worldlings to the primitive monster Typhon, a hundred-headed beast, who fought against Jove and was subdued by a thunder-bolt.

132 and gloss. Chapman here is using the prime meaning of *genial:* "pertaining to generation, generative." L. *genialis*, used chiefly in the phrase, *lectus genialis*. The precise way in which Chapman uses it for a creative deity is not paralleled in the *N.E.D.* till the mid-seventeenth century. Cf. *Paradise Lost*, IV, 712.

139–170 Schoell (p. 35n) compares Comes, *Myth.*, VII, 14, "*De Orpheo*," and II, 4, "De Iunone."

159 Though this reference to the golden chain of Homer comes straight from Comes' "De Iunone," Chapman was later to come upon it at first hand when translating the *Iliads*, VIII, 16 *seq.*, and used it again in *Epic.*, 161–164 & gloss, and *Eug.*, 715 & gloss. Chapman's reiterated use of the golden chain as a symbol of man's being linked to the divine is, of course, non-Homeric. Macrobius made a similar mistaken identification. See A. O. Lovejoy, *The Great Chain of Being* (1936), p. 63. Since Homer's description of the chain was of such interest to Chapman, it is interesting to refer to his own version of the lines. Jove is telling the Gods not to engage in war:

> Indanger it the whiles and see: let downe our golden chaine;
> And, at it, let all Deities, their vtmost strengths constraine,
> To draw me to the earth from heauen: you neuer shall preuaile,
> Though with your most contention, ye dare my state assaile:
> But when my will shall be disposd, to draw you all to me;
> Euen with the earth it selfe, and seas, ye shall enforced be.
> Then will I to Olympus top, our vertuous engine bind,
> And by it euerie thing shall hang, by my command inclind:
> So much I am supreme to Gods; to men supreme as much.

Cf. *Faerie Queene*, II. vii. 46.

194–196 Saturn's reign was supposed to have been the golden age of Italy, and he was celebrated as an ample provider.

205–220 and accompanying glosses 6, 7, & 8. Schoell (pp. 182–183) traces the references to Comes, *Myth.*: 6 from VI, 2, "De Aurora;" 7 from V, 17, "De Sole;" 8 from III, 12, "De Nocte."

232–235 Refers back to the passage about the stars, 105–122.

255–259 and gloss 9. Schoell (p. 183) compares Comes, *Myth.*, VII, 1, "De Hercule."

260 *his*) The masculine pronoun in this line and throughout the passage refers to the "Sunne."

268 and gloss 10. Schoell (p. 183) compares the passage from Aratus cited in Comes, *Myth.*, III, 12, "De Nocte." See Chapman's gloss 1.

289 *affections*) See note to *H. in C.*, 217.

314 *glasses of the hearers eyes*) A figure derived from the popular renaissance concept that eyes are the mirror of the soul: see, for instance, Bembo's discourse on love in the fourth book of the *Courtier*. Compare Chapman's image with Donne's *Canonization*, 41, and Shakespeare's *Richard II*, I. iii. 208–209.

333 *Christmast*) The earliest example in the *N.E.D.* of this colloquial verb.

340 *Iueryport*) Sleep has two gates, those of ivory and those of horn, here transferred to Night. See *Od.* XIX, 562, and *Aen.* VI, 893–896. The gate of horn is mentioned in l. 352.

369 *marble*) This particular use of the verb in the sense that Loane defines as "make insensitive" is not found in the *N.E.D.*

376–377 This couplet is notable as having provided certain scholars with their chief reason for calling Chapman the poet of the School of Night. (See introductory note p. 421.)

381–382 and gloss 11. Schoell (p. 184) compares Comes, *Myth.*, IV, 16, "De Horis."

392–393 and gloss 12. Schoell (p. 184) compares Comes, *Myth.*, III, 18, "De Diana."

394–396 and gloss 13. Schoell (p. 185) compares Comes, *Myth.*, VI, 2, "De Aurora."

Hymnus in Cynthiam.

1 and gloss 1. Schoell (p. 193) compares Comes, *Myth.*, III, 18, "De Diana," and IV, 1, "De Lucina."

2 and gloss 3. Schoell (p. 193) compares Comes, *Myth.*, III, 15, "De Hecate."

5 and gloss 4. *Idem.*

6–9 Chapman frequently describes the perfect or complete life as circular and calls on a variety of celestial or natural phenomena to further his conception. Here he likens the complete life to the full moon, as later in *Eug.*, 938–941, and 1056–63. The platonic conception of the circle as the perfect form is common in Renaissance criticism and poetry and derives often from the exposition of Plotinus. Castiglione gives simple explanations of the doctrine in his *Courtier* (Hoby's translation, 1561, Everyman ed., pp. 308 and 321). John Donne argues frequently from the concept that "of all forms the circle is the perfectest," and there is a particularly interesting adumbration of the theory in Spenser's *Faerie Queene*, II. ix. 22. See also Chapman's note to *Virgil's Epigram of a Good Man*, 8.

10 and gloss 5. Schoell (p. 193) compares Comes, *Myth.*, III, 17, "De Luna."

11 and gloss 6. *Idem.*

14 and gloss 7. Schoell (p. 193) compares Comes, *Myth.*, III, 10, "De Eumenidibus."

21–25 and gloss 8. Schoell, pp. 193 and 25n. Although Chapman takes his interpretation of this myth straight from Comes, *Myth.*, II, 1, "De Ioue," "Huic partes genitales abscidit Jupiter, quia nullo tempore alius mundus generabitur, cum hic constet ex universa materia," he refers to another writer, Lilius Gregorius Gyraldus (1479–1552), the author of several compilations of which *De Deis Gentium* was the most widely known.

22 and gloss 9. Schoell (p. 193) compares Comes, *Myth.*, IV, 22, "De Typhone."

31–39 Schoell (p. 186) compares Comes, *Myth.*, III, 17, "De Luna."

36 *discessions*) Eclipses. Not given in the *N.E.D.*

40–41 Hannibal's annihilating defeat of the Romans, B. C. 216, during the Second Punic War.

51 and gloss 10. Schoell (p. 193) compares Comes, *Myth.*, IV, 9, "De Fortuna."

64–75 and gloss 11. Schoell (pp. 186 and 193) compares Comes, *Myth.*, III. 17, "De Luna."

79 Democrates is mentioned in Comes, *Myth.*, III, 17, "De Luna," but not exactly in this context. He was the Greek philosopher of Abdera (b. B. C. 460?), popularly called "the laughing philosopher," whose studies of the cosmological system are known only through fragments.

86–94 Chapman was to defend a long line of verse, the English fourteener, for poems of long scope in his epistle "To the Understander," *Achilles Shield* (1598), and his epistle "To the Reader," *Iliads* (1609–1611). See lines 75–80 of that poem, and note.

111 and marginal gloss. Schoell (p. 187) compares Comes, *Myth.*, III, 17, "De Luna."

116–119 The compliment to Queen Elizabeth which is implied throughout this long invocation is here made explicit.

117 and gloss 13. Schoell (p. 193) compares Comes, *Myth.*, III, 18, "De Diana."

120–123 and gloss 14. *Idem.*

129–131 and gloss 15. Schoell, p. 187. The description of the Persian women and the reference to Strabo both come from Comes, *Myth.*, III, 18, "De Diana." Parrott compares *Byron's Conspiracy*, III, ii, 227–228.

140 That is, the spheres of the seven planets.

146 and gloss 16. Schoell (p. 193) compares Comes, *Myth.*, VII, 11, "De Medusa."

152–154 *Heccate . . . the forces of the mind*) Hecate, unknown to Homer, is found in Hesiod; see the *Theogony*, 411–452, a passage sometimes called the Hymn to Hecate. She was a goddess who stood high in the regard of Zeus, and was sometimes identified with Artemis, sometimes with Persephone. " . . . she appears as a personification of the divine power, and is the instrument through which the gods affect their will, though themselves far away." *Dictionary of Classical Antiquities.*

154 *An argument*) Hereby stating the theme of the rest of the poem.

162–165 These lines have been taken as a rebuke to Shakespeare for his erotic *Venus and Adonis*. The reference would then be to the Ovidian motto prefixed to that poem:

> Vilia miretur vulgus; mihi flavus Apollo
> Pocula Castalia plena ministret aqua.

182–207 and gloss 18. The suggestion comes from Comes, *Myth.*, III, 17, "De Luna," (Schoell, p. 188), but Chapman much extends it. Schoell (p. 193) also compares Comes, *Myth.*, III, 15, "De Hecate." Note the extraordinary personification of Form, which along with its counterpart, substance, appears as one of Chapman's favorite abstract philosophical ideas.

186 *Architect*) Architecture. Cf. 368 and note.

210 *intimate*) Essential. The first example of this meaning in the *N.E.D.* is 1632. (Loane)

217 *bid the base*) means "challenge," originally from the game of "Prisoner's Base." Cf. *The Shepheardes Calendar, October*, 5; and *Venus and Adonis*, 303.
Affection) Miss Bradbrook says that this word signifies " 'desire,' Chapman's usual sense," (p. 140). But this is scarcely the regular meaning in Chapman's writing where the word recurs with some frequency in the sense of natural dispositions (not limited to desire), following, in the mediæval sense, the παθήματα of Plato and Aristotle. Cf. *H. in C.*, 289, and *O.B. of S.*, 38n.
In this passage, however, he is using the word in the other mediæval meaning, still current in his day, of passion as opposed to reason. This meaning he expounds very clearly in his note to the *Georgicks of Hesiod*, I, n. 29: "For Mans corporeall part; which is figur'd in Epimetheus; signifying the inconsiderate and headlong force of affections; not obeying his reasonable part, or soule; nor vsing foresight fit for the preuention of ill; which is figur'd in Prometheus; . . . " The line therefore means that the nymph's wings are bound up before she starts her hunt to challenge all corporeal passions. Another clear and interesting use of the word in this second sense is found in *Eugenia*, 667–670:

> Vnlesse you settle, your *affections* to,
> And to insatiate appetite impose
> A glutted end, your selfe, from feares, and woes
> Manfully freeing, . . .

Here the word is derived straight from Xylander's Plutarch: "nisi animi *affectus* sedaueris, & inexpletae cupidati finem imposueris, teque ipsum metu & solicitudinibus liberaueris" (*De Virtute & Vitio*, 101).

218 *Euthimya*) A name of Chapman's own invention from the Greek εὐθυμία or Cheerfulness. Hence the symbol of the binding up of her gay wings before she starts the chase against the passions. The concept is one of contentment or joy of the mind: cf. the title to his poem, *Euthymiae Raptus*.

221 *humorists*) The use here seems to be peculiar to Chapman. It is not found in the *N.E.D.*, but evidently derives from the prime meaning of humor: moisture. "Pliant Humorists" would be those who are made out of such natural objects as he has just mentioned, particularly out of the "mists." They are men who are dominated by their passions.

230–231 Acheson found in this couplet a reference to Shakespeare and Southampton. See his *Shakespeare's Sonnet Story*, p. 269.

232–241 The description of the hounds created by Cynthia (their names and epithets) comes from Comes, *Myth.*, VI, 24, "De Actaeone." See Schoell, p. 190. Comes gets them from Ovid, *Met.*, iii, 206–225; they are Actaeon's hounds who chase him after Diana has turned him into a stag because he has seen her naked. For various interpretations of this passage, see Janet Spens, *Chapman's Ethical Thought, Essays and Studies . . . of the English Association*, Vol. XI, p. 166; M. C. Bradbrook, *The School of Night*, p. 139 *seq.*; Douglas Bush, *Mythology and the Renaissance Tradition*, p. 202, n. 11.

243 *seq.* Miss Bradbrook, *op. cit.*, pp. 139–140, identifies the Panther into which Euthimya turns herself with Pride, and the Boar with Lust, but the symbols are scarcely so limited as this. Cf. dedicatory poem *To M. Harriots* (*Achilles Shield*), 46, where Chapman identifies the foulness of Earth with the Panther.

244 *their mouths they freely spend*) A favorite idiom of Chapman's. Cf. *T. of P.*, 535–536; *Justif. of And. Lib., Dial.*, 77; *Hymn to Hermes*, 273–274.

267 *bristled*) Set as with bristles. Earlier than the first example in the *N.E.D.* (Loane)

272 *implausible*) Refusing praise. There is no example of the word in this active sense in the *N.E.D.* (Loane)

282–283 The meaning of these lines is that the huntsmen knew that the hounds had lost their scent (were "at fault"), since they could no longer hear them baying in the chase.

296 *Ortygian*) Ortygia, ancient name of Delos: birthplace of Diana. Cf. gloss 17.

305–307 Schoell (p. 190) compares Comes, *Myth.*, V, 17, "De Sole." Also compare *Tamburlaine*, II, IV. iv. 6–9 for the same image.

328 *seq.* Chapman's use of the first person in this elaborate simile and his lively knowledge of the engagement have led to a general supposition that he had fought in the Wars of the Netherlands. We know now for sure that he had been on the continent, evidence for his sojourn having been found by Professor Mark Eccles in a document in the Public Record Office, C 2 Jas. 1, C 25/65.

328 *th'Italian Duke*) The Duke of Parma.

330 *sconce-torne Nimigan*) I cannot find any reference to a fort (sconce) in Nymeghen having been "torne." The phrase probably means that the town was shot at past the sconce which Prince Maurice built on the River Wall, in defiance of an Ordinance of Nymeghen. This was the Knodsenborgh sconce, built by the Estates in the spring and summer of 1590, and is consistently called a sconce in Grimestone. For whole account, see Grimestone, *A Generall Historie of the Netherlands* (ed. 1627), p. 916. The description of the harassment of the town thus concludes: "It was victualled and furnished of all things for six moneths, wherein there were foure or fiue hundred men placed, vnder *Gerrard* of Youth, after that, he lay in the Betuwe, and made the River Wahall his defence, meaning in time by continually shooting to tire them of Nymeghen: and to that end, from Bomell to the Tolehouse or Schencks sconce he placed souldiers, and by the ayde of some ships of warre, kept the Riuer of Wahall to stop the enemies passage, for that the Earle of Mansfeldt lying in Cuick, and dayly growing stronger, made a shew as if he would passe the Riuer of Wahall, they of Nymeghen importuning him thereunto, who otherwise by reason of the sconce were very much distressed."

335–336 *Vere*) Sir Francis Vere, who won "more fame then guerdon," because Elizabeth refused to make him a peer. See Markham, *The Fighting Veres*, pp. 362–363. Sir Francis Vere's own description of this engagement is found in his *Commentaries* (Wm. Dillingham, 1657, pp. 20–23), but I quote the shorter account of Grimestone (*op. cit.*, p. 929). The engagement took place in 1591. "Prince Maurice, hearing that the Spaniard was come into the Betuwe, leauing Groning he went thether, going downe at Arnhen in Guelderland, he past the Rhine there, vpon a bridge which he caused to be made with all speed, meaning to doe the Spaniard an affront. Hauing layd an ambush of horse and foot not farre from the Rhine vnder the conduct of the Earle of Solms, and of Sir *Francis Vere*, Generall of the English: he sent two Cornets to view the Dukes campe, who being discouered, were charged by six companies of horse, amongst the which the Dukes was one, who at the first made some shew of resistance, but turning their backes suddenly they fled, the Spaniards following them vntill they had past their ambush; they they that fled turning head againe they were compassed in of all sides, and charged so furiously, as in a short time they were all defeated or put to rout; many were slaine, or prisoners, . . . The Duke of Parma beeing in a high place, within Nymeghen, did with his owne eyes see this defeate of his men." Whereupon they retired precipitately, accompanied by jeers from the citizens of Nymeghen.

345 *Tempest*) Trans. verb: "send forth as a storm."

361 *Rackt*) Increased in length.

368 This line still refers to the island which is said to be ever-productive of curious architectural devices and achievements, such as the pavement made of select Dames. "Architect" in the sense of "Architecture" is not given in the *N.E.D.*, but compare Browne's *Brit. Past.*, I. 4. 405: Loane. This concept of being still with child yet still delivered is repeated in *O.B. of S.*, 109, 7-8, and the *Justif. of And. Lib., Dial.*, 12.

376-377 This couplet appears as No. 908 in *England's Parnassus*.

388 *euent*) The "way out," or "issue."

403 Note that this is the same image as in the famous lines in Burns' *Tam o' Shanter*, 61-62. Chapman uses it again in *H. and L.*, III, 35-36.

407 and gloss 21. See gloss 1.

410-417 and gloss 22. Schoell (p. 191) compares Comes, *Myth.*, VIII, 12, "De Orione."

418-421 and gloss 23. Schoell (p. 191) compares Comes, *Myth.*, III, 18, "De Diana."

422 and gloss 24. *Idem.*

422-442 See Schoell, pp. 35-36. Chapman is here mythologizing the description of the temple found in *Myth.*, III, 18, "De Diana."

432 *reexstruct*) Rebuilt. This is the only example of the word in the *N.E.D.*

460-476 Schoell (p. 191) compares Comes, *Myth.*, IX, 13, "De Ganymede."

474-475 Asterisks have been supplied; a line has evidently been left out.

489-500 and gloss 26. Schoell (p. 192) compares Comes, *Myth.*, IV, 8, "De Endymione."

510 *an idle Salmacis*) Salmacis who loved Hermaphroditus, a son of Hermes and Aphrodite. She was a nymph of the fountain in which he bathed, but he turned a deaf ear to her amorous entreaties. She embraced him and prayed the gods to make their bodies one, which prayer was granted. See Ovid, *Met.*, iv. 306 *seq.* "Idle" because Hermaphroditus would not embrace her.

511 *Cydippe*) A heroine of a popular Greek love-story whose lover Acontius trapped her into marrying him by a clever trick which he performed during a festival in the temple of Diana.

512 *black Ioue*) Pluto. Loane compares Drummond, Song I to Pan; and Seneca, *Herc. Oet.*, 1705, "Maesta nigri regna Iovis."

Ouids Banquet of / SENCE. / A Coronet for his Mistresse Phi- / losophie, and his amorous / *Zodiacke.* / With a translation of a Latine coppie, written / by a Fryer, Anno Dom. 1400. / *Quis leget haec? Nemo Hercule Nemo, / vel duo vel nemo:* Persius. / (*device:* SIBI CONSCIA RECTI.) / *AT LONDON,* / Printed by I. R. for Richard Smith. / *Anno Dom. 1595.* /

A-I⁴. 4to.

Contents: (A₁ʳ) Title; (A₁ᵛ) blank; A₂ "To . . . Ma. Mathew Royden;" A₃ʳ "Richard Stapleton to the Author;" and "Tho: Williams of the inner Temple;" A₃ᵛ "Another," and "I. D. of the middle Temple;" (A₄ʳ) "Another;" (A₄ᵛ) blank; B₁ʳ-(E₄ʳ) "Ouids Banquet of Sence;" (E₄ᵛ)-F₂ᵛ "A Coronet for his Mistresse *Philosophie;*" F₃ʳ-G₁ᵛ "The amorous Zodiack;" G₂ʳ-I₂ʳ "The amorous contention . . . ;" I₂ᵛ-I₃ᵛ "Certamen inter *Phillidem & Floram*." I₃ᵛ Device: initialed R. S. Time, a satyr, with scythe and hour glass bringing naked woman out of a cave. "Tempore Patet Occulta Veritas;" (I₄ blank).

Not Entered.

Copies Used: British Museum C.56.c.6.   Bodleian   Malone 210 (5)   Victoria and Albert   Dyce 2026   Harvard College 14424. 14. 38*

Textual Notes.

The copies are extraordinarily similar, printing rather crowded and somewhat careless. On sig. H₂ᵛ, top of page, numbering of *Phillis and Flora* stanzas skips from 53 to 56.— *Variants: Coronet*, F₂ᵛ Sonnet 10. 3. *ignorant:*) Mal. 210 (5), Dyce 2026; ignorant) B.M. C.56.c.6, Harvard College 14424. 14. 38.
A second edition was published after Chapman's death, in 1639, which omits *Phillis and Flora*, and attributes all three of the other poems to Ovid, without any reference to Chapman. The printing is poor.

OUID'S / BANQUET / of / Sence. / With / A Coronet for his Mistresse / Philosophy; / and / His Amorous Zodiacke. / Quis leget haec? Nemo Hercule Nemo, / vel duo vel nemo: Persius. / London. / Printed by B. A. and T. F. and are to be / sold by R. Horseman, at his shop in the Strand / neere unto Yorke House, 1639. /

A-D8. 8vo.

Entered to W. Ward, 6 no. 1598.

Contents: A₁ blank; A₂ʳ Title; A₂ᵛ blank; pp. 1–44, "Ovid's Banquet of Sence;" pp. 45–50 "Ovid's Coronet for his Mistresse Philosophie;" pp. 51–58 "Ovid's Amorous Zodiacke;" D₈ blank.

Note changes in titles of poems.

Variants in printing, *Ouids Banquet of Sence*. (i—1st ed; ii—2nd)

I	II	I	II
24.2 do dye	to dye	80.6 were	where
48.7 attemps	attempts	84.2 of twain	in twain
54.3 word	world	92.1 Pure	Lure
60.11 office her fingers	office of her fingers	100.1 sounds	sounde
66.7 stand	sound	104.2 spritualize	sp'ritualize

Punctuation Revised.

Period added to last line of second sonnet by I. D.

Ouids Banquet of Sence. 12.4 Final period instead of comma   18.6 Final colon instead of question mark   21.9 Final comma instead of period   34.4 Final comma added   37.9 Final period instead of semicolon   38.9 Final period instead of semicolon   41.6 Final colon added   46.7 Final semicolon instead of comma   47.7 Final comma added   51.3 Final comma added   65.6 Final colon added   65.7 Final period instead of comma   73.7 Final comma added   83.2 Final comma added   90.9 Final comma instead of period   91.5 Final comma added   91.9 Final semicolon instead of comma   105.9 Final period added   112.5 Final comma added

A Coronet for his Mistresse Philosophie. 1.9 Final comma instead of period   6.9 *her;* instead of *her,*   Final comma added   6.10 *iestures,* instead of *iestures;* Final comma added   6.11 Final comma added   9.8 Final parenthesis deleted   10.6 Final semicolon instead of comma   10.8 Final period instead of colon

The Amorous Zodiack. 3.3 Final comma added   10.6 Final period instead of comma   12.6 Final period instead of colon   22.5 Final comma added

Phillis and Flora. 52.2 Parenthesis completed   84.4 Final period added   98.4 Final period added

Epistle Dedicatory.

For Roydon, see note to epistle dedicatory, *S. of N.*

6–9 *endeuoring that materiall Oration . . . vtilitie*) From Plutarch's essay, *De Homero*, Xylander's translation. From this point on throughout most of the poems we find Chapman making frequent use of Plutarch's *Moralia*. Schoell has shown, in Ch. IV and Appendix II of *Etudes sur l'Humanisme Continental en Angleterre*, that Chapman, together with most of his contemporaries, knew Plutarch's essays through the Latin translation of Gulielmus Xylander (Wilhelm Holtzman), used by Estienne in his great Greco-Latin edition of Plutarch (1572). Parrott first noticed in his study of the plays that Chapman had used a Latin Plutarch, and Schoell has pointed out many of the parallels in the poems.

9–10 *This of Euripides . . . Lentem coquens ne quicquam olentis addito*) "Of" means "about." *Olentis* is an emendation from *dentis*, following the suggestion made by George Loane in *T.L.S.*, Feb. 21, 1935. Schoell points out (p. 46) that Chapman may have taken this adage from Erasmus who got it from Aristotle's *De Sensu*, 443 b. It is there quoted as a jibe at Euripides' over-refinement of style. In Erasmus the form is "Ubi lenticula coquitur, non oportet unguentum infundere."

11 *peruiall*) This adjective meaning "easily seen through," and the adverb "pervially" are favorite words in Chapman's vocabulary. There are no illustrations of them in the *N.E.D.* from any other writer. Cf. *Ded. to Seauen Books of Il.* 1598; *Com. to Il.* II, 71; *Com. to Il.* XIII, 556; *Com. to Il.* XIV, 343; *Justif. of And. Lib., Dial.*, 70.

14 *and giue Cammels hornes*) See Parrott's note to *Rev. of Bussy*, II. i. 176–181, a passage in which Chapman makes an extended simile out of a version of the fable of Aesop which relates how the camel begged hornes from Jove.

27–28 *which euery Cobler may sing to his patch*) Cf. *To Fletcher*, 16.

29 *Obscuritie in affection of words . . . et seq.*) See note to l. 35 of the Epistle to Roydon, *S. of N.*, and George Williamson, *The Donne Tradition*, p. 60 seq.

36–39 *Euippes daughters*) The Pierides. See Ovid, *Met.*, v. 294 *seq.* The nine daughters of Evippe challenged the Muses to a contest in song, and were later metamorphosed into magpies "which can imitate any sound they please."

50 *Corynnas Garden*) The garden of Ovid's fictitious mistress in which the action of the poem takes place.

Complimentary Sonnets.

Richard Stapleton. Richard Stapleton was a personal friend of Chapman, as we know from the Preface to the Reader, *Iliads* (1611). He also wrote commendatory verses to Greene's *Never Too Late*. Rollins argues for his being the editor of *The Phoenix Nest* (1593). See the introduction to his edition of that anthology.

Tho: Williams of the Inner Temple. There are only two Thomas Williamses recorded as entered in the Inner Temple in the record of 1547–1660. 1) T. W. of Stowforde, near Ivybridge, Devon, second son of Thomas Williams M. P. Born 1542, died 1620. 2) T. W. of Wollaston, Salop. Eldest son of Reginald Williams, Sheriff of Montgomeryshire, 1574.

I.D. of the Middle Temple. He is Sir John Davies, whose well known epigrams were written about this year, 1595. He had become a member of the Middle Temple in 1588.

Ouid's Banquet of Sence.

The Argument. Douglas Bush points to the most likely source for the main theme of this argument: "Ficino's discussion of 'Ratio, Visus, Auditus, Olfactus, Gustus, & Tactus,' in *Comm. in Convivium* (*Omnia Divini Platonis Opera*, Lyons, 1548), v. 2." (*Mythology and the Renaissance Tradition*, p. 204n.) A manuscript note of Schoell points to a parallel of the idea of this poem in Lemaire de Belges' *Illustration de Gaule*, from which it had been copied by Boiardo, Ariosto, etc. He also points out the same idea in a song by Jonson, *Poetaster*, IV. v. 198 *seq.*, and calls attention to a dialogue in Pontanus' *De amore conjugali*, III, between Corinna and Ovid.

stanza 3 This stanza is adapted from Pausanias, as quoted in Comes, *Myth.*, VI, 13, "De Niobe." See Schoell, p. 39. For Chapman's use of Comes' *Mythologiae*, see notes to *S. of N.*

3.6 *optick reason*) Translated straight from Comes' *ad opticam rationem*, and remembered by Chapman in his very similar descriptions of perspective pictures: *Chabot*, I. i. 68, and *Eugenia*, 174. See note to *Eug.*, 173–178.

5 The sons of Niobe were enumerated in Comes, *Myth.*, VI, 13, "De Niobe." See Schoell, p. 194.

7.5 *Phaeton*) See Ovid's *Met.*, ii. 272 *seq.* for his story.

11.5 *that disparent grounde*) "Grounde" emended from "rounde," since the phrase evidently refers to the "enflowred banck" surrounding the fountain on which she stands as she dries herself. "Disparent" means "diverse, of various appearance," and refers to the variety of flowers just named. The only illustration of this word with this meaning in the *N.E.D.* is taken from Chapman, Com. to *Il.* II, 355. It is also used by R. S. (if the ascription of the poem is correct) in *Phillis and Flora*, I. 4, and Chapman in *H. & L.*, III. 123, and v. 355; and *Epic.*, 190.

13.8 *Julia*) Alternate name for Corinna. See "Argument."

14.3 *Loues feete are in his eyes*) Miss Holmes, in her *Aspects of Elizabethan Imagery*, p. 97, uses this metaphysical conceit as illustrative of Chapman's "questing habit of mind which makes him like a less swift and passionate Donne. 'Love's feet are in his eyes' is only a more wilful way of saying that love is engendered in the eyes and fed with gazing." (*Merchant of Venice*, III. ii. 67–68)

14.6 *shader*) Shadier.

15–30 Leslie H. Rutledge gives a full explanation of the psychology and imagery in these stanzas in his doctoral dissertation, *George Chapman's Theory of the Soul and of Poetry*, pp. 24–28, Harvard University, 1938.

17.5 *species*) The emanation from the voice which constitutes the direct object of cognition for his sense of hearing. Cf. 93.8, and *Coronet*, 5.2.

19.7 *Flotes*) Waves.

21.8 *as guilt Atoms in the sunne appeare*) Cf. Donne, *Elegy* XIII.

9 *grissells of myne eare*) The ear was usually referred to as gristly in current physiology. Cf. Vicary's *Anatomie*, Ch. V.

22.1 *regreete*) Return of the greeting in the line above.

23.3 Probably stems from Aristotle, *De Anima*, Bk. III, but derivation untraced. Chapman also refers to the "common sence" in 27.7 gloss, 88.7 gloss, and in *To Fletcher*, 13.

24.5 gloss. "The Philosopher" is Aristotle, and the saying a favorite of Chapman's. Cf. *Eug.*, 423–426 and gloss, and also his note to l. 343 of the *Iliads* XIV: "And, indeed, where a man is understood, there is ever a proportion betwixt the writer's wit and the writee's (that I may speak with authority) according to my old lesson in Philosophy: *Intellectus in ipsa intelligibilia transit.*"

25.3–4 *Chaos . . . dygested*) See note to *H. in N.*, 29–49.

31.3 *sensor of his sauor*) The nose. The noun "sensor" as the organ which does the sensing does not appear in the *N.E.D.* and seems to be of Chapman's invention; cf. *In Seianum*, 124. "Sauor" here means "smell;" cf. *H. & L.*, IV. 264.

32.8 In a manuscript note Schoell compares Theophrastus, "De odoribus."

37.1 and gloss to 36. See Aristotle, *De Anima*, 422 a, and *De Sensu*, 443 b, for the argument that odor comes from what is dry and is excited by heat.
concite) Concited; excited. A participial form invented by Chapman for the purpose of rhyme.

39.4 *pregredience*) "A going before," the only example of this noun in the *N.E.D.* The unicorn goes before the inhabitants.

6 *Residence*) Residents: other beasts of the desert.

41.9 gloss. Ovid, *Met.*, iii. 138 *seq.*

44–45 See *De Guiana*, 56–62 and note.

47 Taken from Comes, *Myth.*, II, 4, "De Iunone," including the *sulphureis humoribus.* See Schoell, p. 194.

49.4 *prorected*) Chapman's invention, not in the *N.E.D.* (ad. L. *pro*, forth+*rect-us*, straight)

  9 *And shew theyr riches in a little Roome*) John Bakeless traces the history of this image in his *Christopher Marlowe*, pp. 172–173. Chapman's line seems to echo one from *The Jew of Malta*, I. 72, (1589–90), "Infinite riches in a little roome," an image which Marlowe, in turn, had borrowed from Harrison's *Description of England* (1577), "Great commoditie in a little room." The famous line is later recaptured by Jonson in his *Sad Shepherd*, I. i. 13, "The sacred treasure in this blessed room."

50.4 and gloss. Chapman was very fond of this image of "falling stars" or "falling exhalations." Cf. *T. of P.*, 1009–10, 1185; *Eug.*, 123–124 & gloss; *Ep. to Somerset, H. of H.*, 109–110; *Byron's Consp.*, Prol., 12–15; *Byron's Trag.*, IV. ii. 292; *Bussy*, V. iv. 144–145.

54.1–4 For Chapman's reiterated belief in the theory of the circle as the perfect form, see note to *H. in C.*, 6. In these lines he seems to mean that the Circle of man's Contentment is not fully closed any more than is the letter C which "preceedes" in the words Contentment and Circle and suggests the complete circle of the compass.

57.9 This sounds autobiographical, but it is also reminiscent of Ovid. See *Amores*, I. i.

58.7 *the Spring-bird Lameate*) All efforts to discover a bird of this name have failed. The most hopeful emendation suggested is "laureate," used as an adjective, but the picture thereby suggested is not entirely satisfactory.

59.4 *Pelopian shoulders*) Ivory shoulders. After being killed and served to the gods by Tantalus, Pelops was restored to life and his missing shoulder which had been eaten by Ceres was replaced by one of ivory that had curative properties.

59.8 *tenne pure floods*) Her fingers.

63.3 The emendation of "minde" to "finde" was suggested by Douglas Bush, *Mythology*, p. 204n; "minde" is a misprint caused by the occurrence of the same word at the end of l. 1.

64.1–4 Schoell (p. 224) compares Plutarch's *Symposiacon*, lib. 1, 625 e. Chapman's word *Pyramis* is *Conus*, however, in Xylander's Latin; *Pyramide* is the word of Amyot's French translation.

65.7 *peculier*) A verb of Chapman's invention, not in the *N.E.D.*, meaning "appropriate to one's own private use."

66.8–9 Cephalus killed by accident his loving but jealous wife, Procris, one day when he was out hunting.

68.4 *Troy swum to thee in Art*) A reference to Helen and the *Iliad:* the phraseology forecasts Chapman's translation of the famous scene where Helen appears at the Scaean Gates:

> she took a pride
> To set her thoughts at gaze, and see, in her clear beauty's flood,
> What choice of glory *swum* to her yet tender womanhood. III. 148-150.

And Priam tells her:

> do not think I lay the wars, endur'd by us, on thee,
> The Gods have sent them, and the tears in which they *swum* to me.
>   III. 181–182.

69.1 *Autumnale Starre*) Sirius.

69.6 *And Stretcheth a Meridian from her blood*) That is, she stretched her arms to their highest possible extent. Having reached this position of mid-day brightness, her hair must carry the heat back to the center of her body.

71.5 gloss. *Emprese*) Empress or Impress, a motto or significant device.

74.6 *Auriga*) Constellation: the Waggoner.

  the heauenly Goate) The star Capella.

74.9 *Haedy*) Haedi, a small double star in the hand of the Waggoner (Auriga). Cf. "pluviales Haedi," Virgil, *Aen.*, IX. 668.

78.6 *incompressed*) Chapman uses the verb *compress* as equivalent to "embrace;" sometimes with an implied, sometimes with a definite meaning of "to rape." Cf. *And. Lib.*, 523, his essay, "Of Homer," where the verb is taken straight from Divus' Latin in Spondanus, and *Byron's Consp.*, I. ii. 37–38.

84.5 gloss. Leslie Rutledge, *op. cit.*, p. 32, compares *The Blind Beggar of Alexandria*, Sc. vi. 73 *seq.* on the "Prince of Sence . . . my brain." The exact source of the Latin is untraced, but it is a commonplace of physiology.

86.3 *breath's*) Verb: breathes.
Spurrie Tapers) Sharp beams of light. "Spurry," radiating like the points of a spur-rowel, is an adjective which seems to have been invented by Chapman. Cf. his *Il.*, XIX. 368, (1611), the first example of the word given in the *N.E.D.*

90–91 These two stanzas summarize the theme of *Nennio* for which Chapman wrote commendatory verses in the same year as this poem, 1595. See note to that poem.

91.5 *imperance*) Commanding quality. This line and *H. & L.*, III. 392, furnish the only examples of this noun in the *N.E.D.*

93.8 *species*) Cf. use in 17.5 and *Coronet*, 5.2.

98.9 For the story of Nisus, King of Megara, see Ovid, *Met.*, viii. Apollo's lyre, which had been placed in his tower, made the tower itself resound.

99.1–4 Chapman repeats this image of the spreading circles in water in his epistle to Prince Henry, *Iliads* (1609–11), lines 114–117. Schoell, referring to Du Bartas in a footnote of his article, "Une Source Nouvelle de Chapman," *Revue Germanique* (1913), p. 429, writes: "En relisant les 'Colonies' (2ᵉ semaine, 2ᵉ jour), nous croyons avoir trouvé l'original d'une image favorite de Chapman, celle de l'onde circulaire qui, provoquée par le jet d'un caillou dans une source, va s'enlargissant jusqu'aux bords (Comparez 'Colonies,' v. 283 *seq.* avec Chapman . . .)." Cf. Donne's *Love's Growth*, John Davies' *Of the Soule of Man*, and Jonson's poem to Thomas Palmer's *The Sprite of Trees & Herbes* (Newdigate ed., pp. 247–248)—a poem that sounds much more like Chapman than Jonson.

100.1–4 Cf. Aristotle's *De Anima*, 419 b.

102.5 *My sences ground-worke, which is, Feeling*)⎫
103.5 *the sences Emperor, sweet Feeling*)⎬
Leslie Rutledge, *op. cit.*, p. 36, points out that the theory that Feeling is the chief of the senses derives from *De Anima*, II. ii, and compares *Chabot*, IV. i. 190 *seq.*

104.3 *great elixer*) Otherwise called "the Philosopher's Stone," or *Philosophica Medicina*. See *H. in C.*, 404 and gloss 20; also *H. & L.*, III. 417; and compare *B.B. of Alex.*, Sc. ii. 62–63, and 68.

109.7–8 The same conceit was used in describing the architecture of the beautiful island in *H. in C.*, 368–369. See also *Justif. of And. Lib., Dial.*, 12.

110.1–6 Schoell compares Comes, *Myth.*, III. 4, "De Iunone." *Saturnia*) Juno. *Alcydes*) Hercules.

115.6 *Mused*) Ponder over, contemplate.

116.5–9 See Plutarch's *De anima tranquillitate*, 466 d, Schoell, p. 225.

A Coronet for his Mistresse Philosophie.

These ten sonnets have been used as a strong part of the evidence linking Chapman to Shakespeare in bands of rivalry. Arthur Acheson, in his *Shakespeare's Sonnet Story*, p. 277 *seq.* set forth the thesis that Shakespeare is addressed in sonnet I as a loose and sensual poet, that VI. 9–14 is intended as a slur on his social condition, that IX. 13–14 refers to *Venus and Adonis* and *Lucrece*, and that X. 10–14 links Shakespeare as a writer for the stage with Shakespeare seeking by his dedications the patronage of Southampton whose favor Chapman is supposed to have sought in vain. Percy Allen, in *Anne Cecil*, p. 246, points to VI. 4–6 as an attack on Lord Oxford, whom he supposes to have written Shakespeare's works.

2.14 and 3.1 *lyuer*) The vital organ which was anciently supposed to be the seat of passionate love.

5.2 *species*) Cf. *O.B. of S.*, 17.5 and note.

5.5 *Inuersed*) Compare epistle *To Harriots, Achilles Shield*, 113, where Chapman repeats this image; *Epic.*, 120–121, where it is inverted like the Antipodes; *Bussy*, I. i. 2, where "Reward goes backwards, Honour on his head;" and *T. of P.*, 403, where it is men who are inverted.

5.9 *cupidinine*) Cupidinous, lustful. Not in *N.E.D.*

9.3 *forheade*) Point. A favorite word of Chapman, here rather strangely used. Cf. *H. in N.*, 176; *H. in C.*, 2, 31, 450; *De Guiana*, 19.

10 The construction of this sonnet is particularly difficult, but it is an important one to understand for its critical as well as its possible autobiographical interest. Chapman defends the art of drama on the grounds of its great classic tradition, at the same time that he condemns his own fellow-dramatists who write plays solely with an eye to the favor of their patrons.

  1 *Muses that Fames loose feathers beautifie*) It is the Muses who are beautified by Fame's loose feathers; see the last two lines of the sonnet where Chapman wants instead to beautify them with "modest eyes" (so that they will become more demure and sing of his Mistress Philosophy instead of sensual love).

  3 *As ignorant:*) The colon after "ignorant" is kept in accordance with Bod. Mal. 210 (5), and Dyce 2026, as well as the second edition of the poem, 1639. It does not occur in the Harvard College Library copy nor B.M. C.56.c.6. The colon marks the end of the apostrophe to 'The Muses who are beautified by specious Fame and those people "as ignorant" as said Muses who scorn dramatic art.' The colon is a strong mark of punctuation in Chapman's writing, not necessarily used to introduce a subordinate clause.

  4 *theyr*) Antecedent: the "seede of memory," "seede" plural.

  6 *affayre;*) The final semicolon has been added in place of a comma. The word is taken in the 5th meaning given in the *N.E.D.*, "doing, action, performance," a meaning which is illustrated from Chapman's *Il.*, v. 503.

  8 *empayre.*) The final period has been added in place of a colon, which, although a strong mark of punctuation in Chapman, does not make the break after the 8th line as decisive as it should be for the sense. "Empayre" means "impairment, injury."

  10 *like-plumde Birds:*) Genuine dramatists who are like the deservedly famous ones of ancient Athens and Rome.

  11 *theyr*) Antecedent: those dramatists in the next line who live by soothing moods and time-serving.
    exempt) Remove.

  13 *my love*) Philosophy.

Lucidius Olim) An implied promise that all this will be made 'clearer in the future.' Chapman, however, did not publish another poem to his Mistress Philosophy.

The amorous Zodiack.

This poem is a translation, without acknowledgement, of a French poem by Gilles Durant. See Sidney Lee, *French Renaissance in England*, p. 231, and Appendix II. The poem, entitled "Le zodiac amoureux," was published anonymously in 1587, 1588, and under his own name in 1594 in "Les Œuvres poetiques du Sieur de la Bergerie, avec les imitations tirées du Latin de J. Bonnefons." Professor Parrott suggests that there is no evidence that this translation is by Chapman. That is true. If the poem comes from another hand, it is obvious to suppose that it may be the work of "R. S." who wrote the following translation, *Phillis and Flora*. See note to that poem.

  12.1 *sign*) The original reading is "thronde in such a shine." For "shine," Shepherd reads "shrine," and Sidney Lee (*op. cit.*, p. 422) reads "sign," the correct emendation since it follows the French, "ce Signe."

  14.1–2   C'est ce beau Nez traitis, qui dedans ton visage
                 Paroist ainsi qu'un Pin au milieu d'un bocage.

    6 *month*) Following Lee's emendation. The original reading is "mouth."

  21.4 *riphees*) Word invented from Riphean Mountains. "Tetons qu'Amour poistrist da(ns) les neige Riphées."

  25.6 *my case takes horne*) "mon cas prit corne."

The amorous contention of Phillis and Flora.

This poem would seem to be almost certainly not of Chapman's composition, and was probably included in the volume as a courtesy to his friend Richard Stapleton who wrote a commendatory sonnet for the book. The poem was reprinted separately in 1598 with the following title-page:

Phillis and Flora. / The sweete and / ciuill contention of / two amorous Ladyes. /Translated out of Latine: by / R. S. Esquire. / Aut Marti vel Mercurio. / Imprinted at London by W. W. / for Richarde Iohnes. / 1598.

There are a good many revisions in this 1598 version, but since the poem is not Chapman's, they are not given here. The 1598 volume does not include the specimen of the Latin original.

For arguments linking the author "R. S." with Richard Stapleton, see Sidney Lee, "Chapman's Amorous Zodiacke," *Mod. Phil.*, III (1905); *French Renaissance in England;* and Prof. Rollins' introduction to his edition of *The Phoenix Nest.*

Sidney Lee gives the following description of the translation: "The English writer is here translating with some literalness a mediæval Latin poem, which was at one time wrongly attributed to Walter Mapes. The English verse is followed by ninety-five Latin verses, extracted from a Latin poem entitled 'Certamen inter Phillidem & Floram.' The Latin poem probably dates from the twelfth century; it is far earlier than the year 1400, to which the superscription assigns it. . . . The rhyming metre of the Latin is carefully followed in the English version in Chapman's volume."

The poem is included in this edition of Chapman's poems only for the purpose of reproducing the 1595 edition of *Ouids Banquet of Sence*, and appears without editorial revision, except for the correction of the numbering of the stanzas, beginning stanza 54. The original numbers from that point appear in square brackets.

HERO AND / LEANDER: / Begun by *Christopher Marloe;* and / *finished by* George Chapman. / *Ut Nectar, Jngenium.* / (*device*) / *At London* / Printed by *Felix Kingston,* for *Paule Linley,* and / are to be solde in Paules Church-yard, at the signe of the Blacke-beare. / 1598. /

A–N⁴. 4to.

Contents: (A₁ʳ) Title; A₂ E. B.'s epistle dedicatory to Sir Thomas Walsingham; A₃ʳ–E₃ʳ first and second Sestiads by Marlowe; E₃ᵛ–(E₄ᵛ) Chapman's epistle dedicatory to the Lady Walsingham; F₁ʳ–(N₄ᵛ) third, fourth, fifth, and sixth Sestiads by Chapman.

The above title-page is that of the second edition of *Hero and Leander,* the first to include Chapman's continuation. Earlier in 1598 Edward Blount had printed, in quarto, Marlowe's two sestiads. On March 2, 1597/8 he assigned the book over to Paul Linley.

The schedule of subsequent editions is as follows.

Copies used.		*Copies used.*
1600 Bodleian Library, Malone 133	1622	
1606 British Museum, C 71. b. 32	1629	British Museum, C 57. i. 44
1609 Victoria and Albert, Dyce 6214		Victoria and Albert, Dyce 6215
1613 British Museum, C 57. i. 45	1637	British Museum, C 57. i. 43; G. 11472
1617		Victoria and Albert, Dyce 6216

Tucker Brooke adds a possible third edition in 1598 and one in 1616, but John Bakeless finds no trace of either. See his *Christopher Marlowe* (1937), p. 350.

There is little textual value to the reprints made of the poem from 1600 to 1637. From 1606 on, the punctuation is changed liberally, and seldom bettered. Ignoring the vast variety

in spelling and punctuation where these variations bear no significance, the principal
textual variants in Chapman's sestiads are given in the following schedule. The editions of
1617 and 1622 are not referred to. They are to be found in the Huntington Library, but the
editor has not had the opportunity of collating them.

Textual Notes.

Dedication to Lady Walsingham omitted after 1598.

Third Sestyad. Arg. 11 womens 1637
    7 maids) made 1613, 1629; make 1637   24 *Marginal note omitted*, 1600–37   a
purpose 1637   30 to sanctifie 1637   37 that) who 1637   48 dower)
power 1613–37   71 good 1629, 37   85 colour 1629, 37   96 her) the
1629, 37   104 doe 1629, 37   119 For as she was presented 1629, 37
134 extinguisheth: 1637   173 of 1598–1613; on 1629, 37   196 it) I 1629, 37
light) delight 1613–37   206 Whence 1606, 09   213 Towers), townes, 1600–
37   virgins 1613–37   226 For that which 1629, 37   259 the) his 1609–37
263 fowle) foole 1600–37   294 hid) had 1600–37   295 her) the 1629, 37
298 twas) was 1613–37   319 her sence) the sence 1629, 37   325 spirits 1600–
37   334 he) she 1629, 37   the) that 1637   342 delightfull 1637   343 slick't
tongue 1637   347 Take 1613–37   380 thing 1629, 37   383 Thus 1629,
37   386 For such *Hero*, 1606–13; For such a *Hero*, 1629, 37   403 loues sweet)
sweet loue 1609–37   404 had) hath 1613

Fourth Sestyad. Arg. 14 *Marginal note omitted*, 1600–37
    1 arose, 1600–09   16 chast) strange 1629, 37   27 most) more 1637
30 bewties) beauties 1600–09; beauteous 1613–37   36 for) from 1613–37
62 They) Thy 1613–37   griefe 1613–37   82 delight 1629, 37   85 that) the
1629, 37   86 ye) yet 1629, 37   88 draue) drue 1629, 37   91 stung)
flung 1613   95 forke 1613–37   101 wauering 1613–37   118 might) must
1629, 37   129 them burnd as bloud: 1606, 09; them, burn'd as blood, 1613; them,
then they burn'd as blood, 1629, 37   137 love 1637   161 conceit 1629, 37
165 ease) end 1629, 37   169 *Leanders* 1629, 37   180 should) shall 1637
198 Excellence, 1629, 37   213 scuse) sauce 1613–37   215 denouncement
1629, 37   223 valley 1613–37   232 the) a 1637   233 frownd. 1598;
frowne. 1600–09; frown 1613–29; frown; 1637   235 Proine their plumes, 1613;
Proine vp their plumes, 1629, 37   239 looke 1629, 37   253–254 ... coine /
Coyne, and impure deceits for purities, 1629, 37   255 will 1629, 37
259 worth) with 1600–37   264 sauor) fauour 1629, 37   265 moane 1637
270 a) the 1629, 37   283 is) in 1629, 37   290 *Marginal note omitted*, 1606–37
295 girdled) girt 1629, 37   314 nor) or 1629, 37   317 temper) tempter 1629,
37   321 in) for 1637

Fift Sestyad.) Fifth 1600–09; fift 1613; fifth 1629, 37   36 maide 1606; maid 1609–37
    80 their) her 1629, 37   86 might) may 1637   101 eyes 1637   104 affec-
tion 1629, 37   129 would) will 1637   158 when merit least: 1609; least, 1613
173 this) the 1637   178 silke 1629, 37   197 mutuall) mortall 1629, 37
207 Iuggl'd 1606–37   220 you) she 1637   233 the tide) their tide 1629, 37
241 and flood in *Eucharis* face 1600–13; and flowed in *Eucharis* face 1629, 37
248 fauour) valure 1629, 37   289 neither 1598–1629; nether 1637   313 Be-
fore them, she 1629, 37   335 prise,) price 1629, 37   338 which two 1629, 37
349 arme) hand 1613–37   357 hereafter 1629, 37   358 other 1600–09
365 Then) The 1613–37   368 no hate of bitternesse 1613–37   378 earth
1600–37   383 *Muses*, well she 1609–37   391 about her inmost 1629, 37
411 her newes) the newes 1637   412 this) his 1600–37   414 would) should
1637   421 Turnd into 1600–13   428 his) this 1637   433 The) That
1629, 37   reapest 1613–37   449 Herbals 1629, 37   the way, 1637   450 Here)
her 1609–37   464 deckt 1600–09   474 ye) you 1629, 37   476 share,) are,

1629, 37   485 starting vp 1629, 37   The end of the fift Sestyad.) fifth
1600–37
Sixt Sestyad.) Sisth 1600–37 Arg. 2 blindes, 1600–37   7 Arte 1606–37   With Art
doe stir 1629, 37   wars 1637   8 iarres 1613–37   9 Drowne 1629, 37
19 fleeting 1609–37   32 against 1609–37   33 humblenesse, 1613–37
36 amongst 1600–13   67 make 1613–37   68 It should be 1609, 13; I should
be 1629, 37   72 free) true 1600–37   95 torrent, 1600–37   104 this) his
1629, 37   108 himselfe he surprisde, 1609; 13; himselfe surpris'd: 1629, 37
109 is) in 1609–37   141 beauty 1637   150 and souldiers 1600–13; and the
souldiers 1629, 37   151 attend 1637   166 hers 1629, 37   173 silke 1629,
37   200 power 1637   204 shone,) shewne, 1600–37   221 it out, O out
1613–37   240 How most wretched 1637   271 plaints) plants 1600–37
275 into) in the 1613–37   281 and) that 1600   286 vsde 1600–37
290 The daintie Venus left them blew, their truth, 1600–37   291 The) Their
1613–37   292 this) thus 1609–37   loue death 1600, 06; loue-death 1609–37

Punctuation Revised.

III   4 Final period instead of comma   244 Final colon instead of period   257 Com-
ma instead of semicolon after *selfe*   267 Final comma instead of colon   270 Fi-
nal comma instead of period   298 Final colon added   299 Final comma
added   332 Colon delected after *hers*   397 Comma added after *loue*
IV   33 Final comma added   125 Final comma instead of period   189 Final semi-
colon instead of comma   190 Final comma instead of semicolon   230 Final
comma instead of period (*Q.* 1613)   234 Comma added after *flood*   300 Com-
ma added after *Cares*   328 Question mark instead of semicolon after *browes*
Final period added
V   Arg. 7 Final comma added
11 Semicolon added after *much*   121 Final semicolon deleted   192 Final
semicolon instead of period   215 Comma added after *spring*   272 Final
semicolon instead of period   291 Comma instead of colon after *higher*
345 Final colon instead of comma   381 Final comma instead of colon
427 Comma added after *Come* (*Qq.* 1613–39)   460 Comma added after *youths*
VI   Arg. 10 Final comma added
40 Comma deleted after *Notus*   64 *Doe good, be pinde;* instead of *Doe good be pinde,*
89 Commas deleted after *figure* and *shew*   107 Final period instead of comma
134 Final comma instead of period   152 Final comma instead of period

It is impossible to give an exact date to the composition of Chapman's continuation of
Marlowe's *Hero and Leander*, though he is likely to have written his sestiads early in 1598
when the rights of the poem were transferred to Linley and a republication was in sight.
There is no reason to accept the far-fetched interpretation made by some critics of the
passage in the Third Sestyad, 183–198, that Marlowe had asked Chapman to finish his
poem. Such a possibility is ruled out by Marlowe's sudden violent death. In 1598 also,
another poet, Henry Petowe, made an attempt at completing the poem; his feeble effort
was published by Andrew Harris.
Marlowe's initial two sestiads are here reprinted, without annotation, from the version
provided by Tucker Brooke, based on the first edition of 1598.* L. C. Martin in his edition

* Key to Tucker Brooke's textual notes.
1598 {*1598*[1]—Blount's quarto edition of that year, containing only Marlowe's part.
{*1598*[2]—Linley's quarto edition of that year (Brit. Mus. C.40.e.68).
1600—Quarto edition of that year.
1606—Quarto edition of that year.
1609—Quarto edition of that year.
1613—Quarto edition of that year.
1616—Edition of that year.

of Marlowe's *Poems*, Vol. IV of *The Works and Life of Christopher Marlowe* (London, 1931), furnished many critical notes for Chapman's sestiads as well as Marlowe's. Selected borrowings from his notes are here acknowledged with the initials, *L. C. M.* Other editors referred to are:

Ed. 1821—Select English Poets, No. VIII. Tucker Brooke and others refer to this editor as "S. W. Singer," but there is a note in the preface (p. lxiv) to the effect that Singer had appointed "a journeyman" to do the work of the eighth volume.
Dyce—Dyce's edition of Marlowe, 1850, 1858, etc.
Cunningham—Cunningham's edition of Marlowe, 1870, etc.
T. B.—Tucker Brooke's edition of Marlowe, 1910.

Epistle Dedicatory.

Chapman dedicates his four sestiads to *Lady Walsingham*, wife of Sir Thomas Walsingham, to whom the printer, Edward Blount, had dedicated Marlowe's fragment. The Walsinghams had been interested patrons of Marlowe, and useful ones—for Sir Thomas was a second cousin of the Secretary of State in charge of the government secret service, Sir Francis Walsingham, and thus procured lucrative employment for the poet. In 1608 Chapman dedicated *The Conspiracy and Tragedy of Byron* to Sir Thomas Walsingham, explaining that he had hitherto refrained from dedicating works to him because he knows Walsingham ever to have "stood little affected to these unprofitable rites of Dedication." See also the sonnet, p. 358, which is conjecturally prefixed to *All Fools*, and the note to that sonnet.

5 *Musaeus*) A semi-mythical Greek Poet to whom the comparatively late Greek poem, *Hero and Leander*, has always been attributed. In 1616 Chapman's translation of Musaeus' poem was published. He translated from the Latin of Marcus Musurus (first ed. 1494–95), and most of the assembled lore about Musaeus is repeated in his short prefatory essay, "Of Musaeus."
40 *circulare*) See *H. in C.*, 6–9 note.

Third Sestyad.

Sestyad) "Derived from Sestos. Σηστιάς is one name for the poem by Musaeus; and the word *sestiad* is here used as a name for each division of the English poem; compare the use of 'Iliad' to mean one book of the whole work; Chapman translates the 'Iliads of Homer.' But since *Hero and Leander* is divided into six books, 'sestiad' has sometimes been employed subsequently to mean one of the six parts of any poem so divided." *L.C.M.*, p. 27.

Argument 4 *Thesme*) A name coined from the Greek θεσμός, rite.
6 *improuing*) Censuring. (ad. L. *improbaro*) Dyce and subsequent editors emended this now obsolete verb to "reprouing."
32 *dispend*) Spend (wastefully).
35–36 Cf. *H. in C.*, 403 and note.
50–58 Cf. Xylander's Plutarch, *Amatorius*, 756 e. (Schoell, p. 225). For Chapman's use of Xylander's Latin Plutarch, see *Ep. to Roydon, O.B. of S.*, 6–7 note.

1617—Edition of that year.
1622—Quarto edition of that year.
1629—Quarto edition of that year.
1637—Quarto edition of that year.
Singer—*Select English Poets*, ed. S. W. Singer, No. VIII, 1821.
Rob.—Robinson's edition of Marlowe, 1826.
Dyce { *Dyce¹*—Dyce's first edition of Marlowe, 1850.
{ *Dyce²*—Dyce's revised edition of Marlowe, 1858, etc.
Cunn.—Cunningham's edition of Marlowe, 1870, etc.
Bull.—Bullen's edition of Marlowe, 1885.
T. B.—The present editor.
Broughton—Conjectures of J. B. in copy of *Rob.* (Brit. Mus. 11771 d).
E. P.—Quotations from *Hero and Leander* in *England's Parnassus*, 1600.

60–63 The image seems to mean that out of a union of Time and the flowery Earth are born men and actions, which births are legitimate because the union is sacred.

90 *meere*) *T.B.* emends to "weere," contrary to the readings of *Qq*, *Dyce*, etc., but "meere" is used as an adverb modifying "insensuall," and means "absolutely." The usage is characteristic of Chapman: cf. *T. of P.*, 390 and note. He means that Leander's senses were so inflamed they fired even things that lacked senses.

105 E. Malone, according to a note in his copy of the poem, Q 1637 (B.M. C.57.i.43), believed that Chapman's contribution starts with this line, but he had not seen the edition of 1598 which carries the dedication before the third sestiad.

110 *Rainbow views*) Should be read together as a compound noun.

115 *all the bench of Deities*) The word "bench" is applied collectively to persons who occupy official seats. Chapman uses the same phrase, "the other bench of gods," in *Il.*, VI. 513.

123 *disparent*) Diversely colored. See note to *O.B. of S.*, 11.5.

183–198 Compare this passage in which Chapman sends his "strangely-intellectual fire" to commune with Marlowe's soul, and calls his poem his "soules darke offspring," to the poem, *To Harriots*, 31–48.

187–188 *as swift as Time Doth follow Motion*) "Motion is *in* time, conditioned by it, so that Time may be regarded as coincident with it. The phrase means immediately, quick as a flash." *L.C.M.*

189 *subiect*) Substance.

204 *Iberian citie*) Cadiz, taken by Essex in June, 1596.

234 *intire*) Interior; inward.

238 *In-formes*) A compound invented by Chapman. The eye reveals the "formes" that are within us, a common renaissance concept. Compare the use of the prefix with Chapman's *Il.*, v. 76, "underneath the in-muscles and the bone."

238–250 Taken largely from Xylander's Plutarch, *Amatorius*, 765 e. (Schoell, p. 226).

241 *rorid*) Suggested by Xylander's *roridae*.

246 *circulare*) See note to *H. in C.*, 6–9.

261 *Lapwing*) Deceitful. Earlier than any example of the word as an attribute in the *N.E.D.* (Loane.)

263 *moorish fowle*) Picks up the image of the "Lapwing faces." Those men are fools who are deceived by false expressions, and every fowl of the moors can teach them all they think there is to learn. Cunningham suggests a pun on "fool" and "fowle" in this line.

389 *logick*) Transf., "a means of convincing;" earlier than the first example in the *N.E.D.* (Loane.)

392 *imperance*) Commandingness. Cf. *O.B. of S.*, 91.5 and note.

410 *Orbiculer*) Circular. In spite of the capital letter, this is an adjective.

417 Although the property of the elixir, or quintessence, is usually spoken of as a binding one, Miss E. Holmes points out that it also has the opposite property. See Böhme, *Three Principles*, English translation (1648), p. 105: "The Tincture is a thing that separateth, and bringeth the pure and cleere, from the impure." (*L.C.M.*)

Fourth Sestyad.

Argument 9 *Ecte*) Probably invented from οἶκτος, pity. See l. 268 seq.

11 *Leucote*) From λευκότης, whiteness. See l. 236 and l. 272 seq.

14 *Eronusis*) "A compound, probably from Ἔρως & νόσος, or νοῦσος." *Ed. 1821.*

31 *adumbrate*) Verb: shade. Earlier than the first example in the *N.E.D.*

49–51 An adaptation of one of Chapman's favorite adages from Erasmus: "Ne uni navi facultates," *Ad.*, IV. iv. 6. Cf. *Charlemagne*, I. i. 413–414; *Rev. of Bussy*, v. v. 183–189; *Widow's Tears*, III. ii. 71–73. (Schoell, p. 47.)

59 Dyce notes: "This conceit was suggested to Chapman by a passage in Skelton's *Phyllyp Sparowe;*

> But whan I saw sowing his beke,
> Methought, my sparow did speke,
> And opened his pretty byll,
> Saynge, 'Mayd, ye are in wyll

> Agayne me for to kyll,
> Ye prycke me in the head'.

81–82 Martin compares *Bussy*, IV. i. 9–21.

84 *seq.* Dyce points out that "this description of the fisherman as well as the picture which follows it, are borrowed (with alterations) from the first *Idyl* of Theocritus."

97–98 *combine Snares*) "Combine" in this sense of "construct" is not given in the *N.E.D.*

117 *yeasty*) Emended from "yas," which is undoubtedly a misprint. Most editors follow the editor of 1821 in reading "eyas," a young hawk, for which usage they derive support from Spenser, *An Hymne of Heavenly Love*, 24. This emendation, however, is far-fetched and creates a confused image. Mrs. Kathleen Tillotson has made the plausible suggestion to me that the "yas" might quite easily be a printer's error for "yasty" (yeasty), the *ty* being skipped because of its resemblance to the initial *th* of the following word. "Yeasty" is an adjective used by Chapman in his Homeric translations.

121 *Arachnean*) For the story of Arachne, the Lydian maiden who was turned into a spider, see Ovid, *Met.*, vi. Chapman uses her name as an adjective to imply something fine and elaborate like her weaving. Cf. later in this same sestyad, l. 302; *Frag. of the Teares of Peace*, 45 note; and *In Seianum*, 136.

169 *sprung*) Earlier than the first example in the *N.E.D.* of "spring" in sense of "set going." (Loane.)

227 *pheres*) Feres, mates.

231 *Ædone*) From ἡδονή, pleasure.

232 *Chreste*) Probably a fusion of χρηστός, good, and "crista," a tuft. (*L.C.M.*)

236 *Leucote*) See Argument 11, note.

237 *Dapsilis*) From δαψιλής, abundant; or, of persons, liberal, bounteous. (*L.C.M.*)

264 *conduits of her sauor*) The word "sauour" was emended to "favour" in *Qq* 1629, 1637, and this reading is followed by *Ed. 1821*, Dyce, T.B. However, the phrase has a close parallel in *O.B. of S.*, 31.3 where Chapman speaks of the nose as the "sensor of his sauor." In support of this reading, one can also compare a passage in Sylvester's translation of Du Bartas, "Sixt Day of first Weeke," (ed. 1608, p. 167):

> The Nose, no less for vse then beautie makes:
> For, as a Conduit, it both giues and takes
> Our liuing breath: . . .

267 *Epicedians*) Epicediums. This is the first example of this form of the word given in the *N.E.D.*

269 *Ecte*) See Argument 9, and note.

288 *inforced*) Having been subjected to force (enforced); here meaning, "pulled out."

305 See Argument 14 with marginal gloss, and note.

Fift Sestyad.

2 *Olympiad*) Period of four years, from one Olympic games to another. Chapman had used this term in a conceit, *O.B. of S.*, 61. 7.

43–46 Cf. Shakespeare, *Romeo and Juliet*, v. iii. 94–96.

62 *Teras*) From τέρας, a sign, or portent.

79 *forewent*) Went before.

101 *responsible*) There is no active sense of this adjective in the *N.E.D.* (Loane.)

119 *Eucharis*) From εὔχαρις, pleasing.

207 *Inggl'd*) Coaxed.

287 *Adoleshe*) From ἀδολέσχης, a talker.

289 *neither*) Nether.

298 *fa'st*) Faced.

317–340 Cf. Xylander's Plutarch, *Quaestiones Romanae*, 263 f, 264 a. (Schoell, p. 226).

337–340 L. C. Martin notes on these lines Chapman's probable indebtedness to Aristotle. The references, provided him by Miss E. Holmes, are the *Metaphysics*, XIV. 1, and the

Physics, IV. 12. See Marlowe's sestiad, I. 255, "One is no number." Martin also compares Sir. T. Browne, *Garden of Cyrus*, V: "the Conjugal Number, which ancient Numerists made out by two and three, the first parity and imparity;" and Shakespeare, Sonnet 136. 8: "Among a number one is reckoned none."

359–364 Cf. Xylander's Plutarch, *Quaestiones Romanae*, 263 c, e. (Schoell, p. 227).

365–369 *Ibid.*, *Coniugalia Praecepta*, 141 e.

426 *Torchie*) Earlier than the first example of this word in the *N.E.D.* (Loane.)

428 *ambitious*) Circling, an extension of the original sense, not given in the *N.E.D.* Cf. *Chabot.* I. i. 189–190. (Loane.)

449 *bals of Discord*) Reference to the golden apples of Atalanta's race. Cf. *T. of P.*, 1001.

470 *expansure*) Expanse. The only examples of this word in the *N.E.D.* are from Chapman. Cf. *Sir Giles Goosecappe*, IV. iii. 10, and *Il.*, XVII. 320.

Sixt Sestyad.

Argument 14 *Acanthides*) See note to l. 276.

7 Cf. Wordsworth, Sonnet, "The world is too much with us," 6–7.

21 *deuotes*) Devotions. The line seems to mean that he holds himself together by various allegiances, all of them false, as the next lines show.

25–26 "Hand" is the subject of the verbs, "leaue" and "leapes." However charming his gesture of throwing a kiss, the hand does not follow through, but leaps to his own lips, remaining there.

30 *fawnes*) Acts of fawning.

47 *his rauisht loue*) "Orithyia, daughter of Erectheus, who was carried off by Boreas." (*L.C.M.*)

115 Implies that the Gallant had not fought in the War of the Netherlands, though he had travelled there.

118 *with his very beard*) Evidently means "aggressively, rudely." There is no exact equivalent of the idiom in the *N.E.D.*

120 *Rhene*) Rhine.

132 *vacantrie*) Vacancy, idleness. This is the only example of the word in the *N.E.D.*

144 *cockhorse*) Sb. used as modifer. The phrase, "cockhorse Pessantrie," means people in exalted positions who are really no better than peasants.

191 *Atthaea*) "Formed by Chapman from Αττθίς, Attica." (*Ed. 1821.*) The reference is to Orithyia; cf. l. 47 and note. Dyce refers to Musaeus, *Hero and Leander*, 322.

237–238 Even though spiritual talents are let starve, bodies are usually preserved, even ugly ones like that of the bear which is preserved for the game of bear baiting.

256 *Analisde in Leander*) Reduced to their elements in Leander. Cf. *Peristeros*, 17, the only example of this use in the *N.E.D.*

276 *Acanthides*) Derived from ἀκανθίς, gold-finch; and ἄκανθα, thistle; see l. 279.

285 *forehead cloths*) Cloths used to prevent wrinkles. (*Ed. 1821.*)

EVTHYMIÆ / *RAPTVS;* / OR / The Teares of PEACE: / *With* / Interlocutions. / *By* GEO. CHAPMAN. / AT LONDON, / Printed by H. L. for *Rich. Bonian*, and / H. *Walley:* and are to be solde at the / spread-eagle, neere the great / North-door of S. *Pauls* /Church. 1609.

A–E⁴; F². 4to.

Contents: (A₁ʳ) Title; (A₂ʳ) Inscription to the Prince; A₃ʳ–B₂ᵛ Indvctio; B₂ᵛ–B₃ʳ Inuocatio; B₃ʳ–(E₄ʳ) "The Teares of Peace;" (E₄ʳ)–F₂ʳ Conclusio; F₂ʳ⁻ᵛ Corollarium ad Principem.

Entered: 4 my

Copies Used: British Museum c.30.e.3   Victoria and Albert   Dyce 2038   Harvard College 14424. 14. 35*

Textual Notes.

There are no variations in the B.M., Harvard, and Dyce copies. One correction is made in all three copies in what looks like a seventeenth century hand. It occurs on A₄ʳ (l. 79) where the word "exclamations" is changed to "acclamations." The revision is retained in this edition. "Acclamations" is a common word in Chapman (see *Iliads*), and the identical revision in three copies of the poem makes it seem likely that it was originally an author's correction. The printing of the book is careless.

Punctuation Revised.

262 Final semicolon instead of period   325 Final period instead of semicolon 326 Final question mark instead of comma   327 Final period instead of question mark   345 Final period instead of comma   351 Final period instead of comma   669 Parenthesis instead of comma after *seated*   803 Final period deleted   851 Final comma instead of period   981 Parenthesis deleted at beginning of line   1000 Comma added after *these* instead of parenthesis 1132 Final comma instead of period   1135 Final period instead of semicolon.

1–6 These lines refer to the respite of the War in the Netherlands by a twelve-year truce which had been concluded in the spring of 1609. The treaty had been brought to a conclusion by the mediation of King Henry of France and King James of England.
2 *her*) Peace.
74 *sounds*) Have a suggestion of. Loane compares Virgil "nec vox hominem sonat." (*Aen.* I. 328.)
77 seq. *Hitchin*) Chapman's birthplace. According to this passage, Chapman claims to have been directly inspired at least twice by the spirit of Homer: once some time before 1598 when he brought out the first installment of his translation, the second time on this occasion of his being shown a vision of Peace. The question which has naturally been asked, then, is whether Homer was the "affable familiar ghost" of Shakespeare's rival-poet sonnet, 86. Miss Janet Spens, in *Chapman's Ethical Thought, Essays and Studies . . . of the English Association*, XI, 150, finds Chapman's relation to Homer reminiscent of Dante's to Virgil.

83 *My true sense (for the time then) in my spirit;*) Meaning that when Homer's spirit visited Chapman it brought with it the true meaning of Homer's poetry, at least for the time Chapman was doing the translating.
132 The coffin proves to be that of Love. See ll. 138–142.
184–185 In reference to these lines, Dr. Rutledge has called my attention to the marginal gloss to *Eugenia*, 853. Chapman there quotes from the *Iliad* XXIII, 10, which he wordily translates in his own version as,

> When with our friend's kind's woe our hearts have felt delight to do
> A virtuous soul right.

The passage in which this phrase occurs describes the mourning for Patroclus, and it seems likely that Chapman is thinking of the same passage when he here says that,

> Homer tould me that there are
> Passions, in which corruption hath no share,

and goes on to say that grief can be not only pure but also a positive pleasure when it "dischargeth Conscience."
224–225 See *H. in N.*, 29–49, and note, on Chapman's juxtaposition of chaos and digestion.
Invocatio. Spoken by the poet, though from the last lines of the *Inductio* one expects Peace to begin. But she has had to pause for grief (227) and "this small time" (256) is taken up with the *Invocatio.*
238 The scene of the vision here shifts from Hitchin to London.
251–252 *Her*) In both lines is his Muse.

259 *Her tragique daughter*) Religion. See l. 205.

287 *Forms*) The essential principles.

301 ⎫
302 ⎬ *forme*) Outward appearance.

321–322 The row of asterisks has been inserted. Between these two lines there must be at least one couplet omitted. The "them" and "whose" of l. 322 have, as it stands, no antecedent in the application of the simile.

325 *the long Robe*) Garb of Lawyers. In their false peace the long robe of the law is like war.

327 *all but multitude*) i.e. The great and mean men are all part of a mixed and undistinguished crowd.

328 *seq*. For this stoical discussion of Learning, compare the poem, *To Yong Imaginaries in Knowledge*. Miss Janet Spens (*op. cit.*, p. 168) sums up Chapman's concept thus: "Learning, therefore, appears to be intense, original thought. Its purpose is to arrive at the knowledge of the individual ideal, 'the weed of the soul,' and through this at the knowledge of God."

330 *or chiefe stroke strike*) i.e. Worth determined on the ground that whoever strikes the chief stroke is the one who does the best deed.

346–351 Chapman means that if you could prove that the act of Learning or the love of it should be the distinguishing mark which sets off great men from the little ones, then Learning would have a clear right to receive man's crown.

355 *Gnomons*) The pillars or rods which cast the shadows on sun-dials.

362–365 Heraldic figure of speech. Life is the "Roote" or lineage which entitles man to his coat of arms and the "Crest" which in the "coat" is borne above the shield and helmet. The soul is the "field," or the surface of the shield itself.

390–391 Nor can you call men who are only religious . . . ignorant.

411 *Intellectiue*) Applied, after Aristotle, to one of the parts of the soul.

415 *seeled Pigeons*) Pigeons with their eyes stitched closed, the "quarries," or prey, of l. 424.

434 *Bangle*) Beat about loosely, not swooping on prey. Earlier than the first example in the *N.E.D.*

443–444 Janet Spens (*op. cit.*, p. 153) writes: "Chapman seems to have coined the word 'manless' to express utter worthlessness, lacking in the essential humane qualities. By that he means, in the first place, and in common with all the writers of his time, lacking in that which distinguishes man from the brutes, namely reason or judgment. But his second meaning, although derived from Cicero, is rather peculiar to himself. By 'manless' he means chiefly 'lacking in a consistent and unique personality.' These two lines are descriptive of this second kind of man."
Cf. *H. in N.*, 93; *Petrarch's First Psalme more strictly translated*, 3. 4.
puttock) Bird of prey, the kite.

595–603 Chapman takes this figure from Plutarch, *De curiositate*, 518 b. See Schoell, p. 230. He uses it again in *And. Lib.*, 203–207. Compare also Spenser, *F.Q.*, II. ix. 32, and Nashe, *The Terrors of Night* (ed. McKerrow, I. 357).

655 Parrott compares *Gentleman Usher*, IV. iii. 55–56.

674–675 Shepherd compares *Bussy*, III. ii. 367.

727 *pend*) Penned, written.

872–879 Shepherd compares *Caesar and Pompey*, III. ii. 22–26.

910 *the drugges of Thessalie*) The province of Thessaly was known throughout the ancient world as the home of sorcery and superstition. Lucan (*Pharsalia*, vi. 438 *seq*.) says that the foul practice of poisoning with *"herbae nocentes"* came into Rome from Thessaly. Marlowe also refers to these drugs: *Tamburlaine*, I, v. ii. 70.

942 *in my hauen, wracke*) Schoell points out (p. 46) that this phrase reproduces a popular adage found in Erasmus, "*In Portu Impingere*," used here for the sake of its familiarity. Cf. *Bussy*, I. i. 33; *Mons. d'Olive*, I. i. 174–5; and *Justif. of And. Lib., Dial.*, 4.

988 *myddins*) Dung-hills.

1001 *balls cast in our Race*) Obstacles. Cf. *H. & L.*, v. 449 and note.

1020 The same line appears in *Byron's Tragedy*, v. iv. 38.

1022 *obiection*) Though this word may possibly be taken in one of its regular meanings as a "placing," it seems more likely that Chapman uses it for "object," or "end:" i.e. of consecrating his life to Peace. Chapman has simply added the suffix for the sake of rhythm.

1043–44 The foe hales insults on thy head and trenches (wrinkles) in thy face.

1067 *acceptiue*) Passive: "fit or suitable for acceptance." Chapman's *Il.*, VII. 85 (1598) affords the first illustration of this use in the *N.E.D.*

1081 *humane Loues interring*) Referring back to the funeral of Love to which Peace was setting forth with a coffin in the *Inductio*, 115. Her "teares," in the language of the period, are her observations and lamentations made on the occasion and have formed the central part of the poem. They are "marginall" because they serve to gloss the main text of the death of Love.

Corollarium ad Principem

1205–15 This passage refers to the *Twelve Books of Homer's Iliads*, n.d., published earlier in the same year as *The Teares of Peace* (1609). This was the first of Chapman's Homeric publications to be dedicated to Prince Henry who, it is evident from this passage, had then ordered him to finish the translation.

1215 *he*) Throughout the rest of the passage "he" is the Spirit of Homer who had appeared to Chapman at the beginning of the poem and had revealed to him the vision of Peace setting forth to Love's funerals.

PETRARCHS / SEVEN PENI- / TENTIALL PSALMS, / PARAPHRASTICALLY / TRANSLATED: / *With other* / Philosophicall POEMS, and a HYMNE / to Christ vpon the Crosse. / *Written by* GEORGE CHAPMAN. / *Arri. Epict.* /

Progressus sum in medium, & pacem
Omnibus hominibus proclamo.

At mihi quod viuo detraxerit inuida turba,
Post obitum duplici foenore reddet honos.

/ LONDON, / Imprinted for MATTHEW SELMAN, / dwelling in Fleete-streete neare / Chancerie lane. / 1612. /

A⁴; B–G⁸. 8vo.

Contents: A₁ blank; A₂ʳ Title; A₃ʳ–A₄ᵛ Dedication to Phillips; B₁ʳ–C₅ᵛ, pp. 1–26, "Petrarchs seuen Penitentiall Psalmes;" C₆ʳ–C₈ʳ, pp. 27–31, "The I Psalme more strictly translated;" C₄ᵛ–D₇ᵛ, pp. 32–46, "A Hymne to our Sauiour on the Crosse;" D₈ʳ–G₇ᵛ, pp. 47–94, "Poems;" G₈ blank.

Entered: 13 ja.

Copy Used: Bodleian 8⁰ G. 67. Th.

Punctuation Revised.

Psalm I. 4.1 Final comma added
Psalm IIII. 2.8 Final period added   7.7 Comma added after *thee*
The I. Psalme more strictly translated. 14.2 Parenthesis added after *wretch*
Hymn to Sauiour. 44 Final semicolon instead of period   94 Final period instead of
    colon   102 Final semicolon and parenthesis instead of period
A Great Man. 4 Final comma instead of period
A Sleight Man. 3 Final comma instead of period   50 Final period instead of colon
Fragment of the Teares of Peace. 56 Final semicolon added
For stay in competence. 27 Final comma instead of question mark   28 Question mark
    after *porter* instead of period

Of Friendship. 5 Comma added after *Still*   40 *Empresse; th'other* instead of *Empresse.*
Th'*other*
To liue with little. 28 Final comma added   50 Period added after *things*
To yong imaginaries in knowledge. 60 Final comma added

Title-page.

The first two Latin lines are versified from Wolfius' translation of Arrian's *Discourses of Epictetus*, IV, v. With this quotation, Chapman announces his intention of effecting a consolidation between the stoicism of Epictetus and the pure Christianity of Petrarch's Psalms. (See comment in Schoell, *Etudes sur l'Humanisme Continental . . .*, p. 104.) The second pair of Latin verses are from Propertius, III. i. 21–22. (Schoell, p. 104n.) They are used again on the engraved title-page of the *Odysseys.*

Epistle Dedicatory.

Sir Edward Phillips) In the following year, 1613, Chapman dedicated the *Masque of the Middle Temple* to Phillips from whose house the procession started, and in 1611 he had added an extra sonnet to the *Iliads* in his honor; see notes to the sonnets. The fact that he had addressed three dedications to this gentleman of the Prince's household makes it seem probable that Phillips, unlike most of the gentry to whom Chapman dedicated poems, had made some acknowledgement of the compliment.
17 *reseruing my thrice humble . . . seq.*) That is, the completion of his Homeric translation which Prince Henry did not live to accept.

Petrarchs Psalmes.

Petrarch's psalms were composed c.1355 and appeared in collected editions of his work in 1496, 1501, 1554, and 1581. In the edition of 1581, which Chapman may well have used, they appear in Vol. II, p. 369. Chapman's versions are free paraphrases, and the Latin phrases which precede each psalm are the first words of Petrarch's prose psalm. This is not Chapman's only connection with Petrarch. See Schoell, "Une Source Nouvelle de Chapman," *Revue Germanique* (1913), for the identification of a passage in the "De contemptu mundi, sive Secretum meum" as the source of the first scene of Act III in *Monsieur d'Olive* (1606).

Psalme I.
12.3 *cour'd*) Covered, in the sense of "recovered" from the "maime" which Custome's hands have laid on him.
Psalme IIII.
1.4 *And iust confusion teare in teares mine eyes.*) A typical Chapmanesque turn in translating, of which there are manifold examples, particularly in the *Odysseys.* The Latin is "ut sit mihi confusio ante oculos."
3.4 This line is added to the original by way of explanation.
4.3 *enterlar'd*) Interlarded, in sense of "intermixed."
Psalme VII.
6.2 *Colchean weeds*) Meadow-saffron, used in a medicine for gout and rheumatism. Not mentioned in Petrarch.
12.2 This image is repeated in *Hymne to our Saviour*, 268. Petrarch: "fumus ante impetum uentorum."
The I. Psalme more strictly translated.
3.4 *manlesse*) See note to *T. of P.*, 443–444.

A Hymne to our Sauiour on the Crosse.

8 *circulare*) The highest sense in which Chapman uses one of his favorite words: moral and spiritual perfection.
64 *Brake it but now out*) The construction is difficult here. I take it to be elliptical and to mean: 'if it would only break out now.' The meaning of the passage is 'The holy writ needs only the slightest chance to reveal itself, and does not need to stalk abroad to be

perceived; though, as it is, it is submerged with scholastic and ecclesiastical controversy.'

68 *thies*) The word "thighs" in this figurative use is not given in the *N.E.D.*

69 gloss. Cf. *And. Lib.*, 213–214.

74 *impeacht*) Hindered.

78 *an edge*) Variant of "on edge." Cf. Shakespeare, *I Henry IV*, III. i. 133.

79 *Blunts the pict quarrie so, twill grinde no more*) I can find no other illustration of the use of the word "quarrie" for "millstone," which it must clearly mean in this passage. The surface of the millstones of the time were furrowed or grooved, possibly with a "pick," which would explain Chapman's participle, "pict." When a stone had got between the ridges of the millstone they would be blunted and could "grinde no more."

92 *And pursnets lay to catch the ioyes of heauen*.) Pursnet, a bag-shaped net. Compare the figure with that in Wyatt's "Whoso list to hunt . . . ," l. 8, "Since in a net I seek to hold the wind." Proverbial.

95–102 and glosses 8 & 9. From Xylander's Plutarch, *De amore prolis*, 494 b, and *De Solertia animalium*, 983 d. See Schoell, pp. 231–232.

97 *straight*) Strait.

108–109 A common enough Elizabethan figure: the standing pool of venomous odor and horrid breeding, but particularly well liked by Chapman. Cf. *Caesar and Pompey*, I. i. 18–23, and *Inv. against Johnson*, 51–54. The figure appears most elaborately worked out by Sylvester in his Du Bartas, "The Vocation," (ed. 1608, p. 437).

134 *fiuer*) Fibre.

145 *roulers*) Rollers, or long bandages.

159 *die*) Dye.

160 *consistence*) Would seem to mean something like "material coherence of form," or, in other words, our bodies which are cleansed by partaking of the Lord's blood. But it is an odd use of the word, and there is no precedent for the original spelling, *consistens*.

165 Dr. Rutledge suggested to me the possibility of emending this line. I have changed the original "match in beastly birth" to "matcht in beastly birth." The "beastly birth" carries the same meaning as in *O.B. of S.*, 112.2–3: *manly*, meaning the spiritual essence that partakes of divinity; *beastly*, the physical substance which we share with the animals. See later in the poem, 194 *seq.* and gloss 8.

203 *Heedlesse*) Following George G. Loane's emendation from "Needlesse."

204 *saued*) Shepherd emended to "sacred," but Chapman is fond of the past participle in an active sense, and here means "saving."

210 can) Following Loane's emendation from "an."

210–211 A verse is needed between these two lines to complete the couplet, but, inasmuch as the sense is clear without it, the omission may have been an oversight on the part of the poet rather than of the printer.

211 gloss. Hierocles of Alexandria (fl. c. 415–450), a pupil of Plutarch of Athens, wrote a commentary on the verses of Pythagoras. The quotation which Chapman here gives in a note and translates in his poem comes from *Carmen Pythagoricum*, 40–44. (Schoell, p. 106.) It was one of Epictetus' favorite quotations. See *Discourses*, III, 10 and IV, 6. The Greek follows the corrected version provided by Loane who has checked the original of Hierocles on the first Golden Verse of Pythagoras in an edition of Hierocles, 1583 (Paris). (*N. & Q.*, vol. 174, Feb. 12, 1938.) The Greek as printed in Chapman's gloss is hopelessly confused.

216 *inward with*) There is no parallel in the *N.E.D.* for this unusual prepositional phrase, but its meaning is clear.

221–248 This passage is adapted from Ficino, *In Convivium Platonis de Amore, Commentarium*, Sexta Oratio, cap. 17: *Quae Comparatio inter pulchritudines Dei, Angeli, Animae, Corporis.* (See Schoell, pp. 7–8.) For the full extent of Chapman's indebtedness to the Italian scholar Marsilius Ficinus, consult the first chapter of Schoell's *Etudes sur l'Humanisme Continental.* Ficino (1433–1499) translated Plato at the command of Cosimo de Medici, adding voluminous commentaries to his translation. His work was reprinted in the Greco-Latin edition of Firmin-Didot which Chapman used. Schoell takes his citations from the Basle edition of this work, 1576. As has already been pointed out, Chapman was at work on the translation of the *Odysseys* at the time this

Hymne, etc. were printed, and traces of Ficino are also to be found in the *Odysseys:* see the Epistle to Somerset, and the note to l. 116 of the 12th book. But his most extensive borrowings from Ficino are in the *Andromeda Liberata;* see notes to that poem.

268 *before the wind a fume)* Cf. Psalm, VII., 12.2. And Parrott compares *Bussy*, I. i. 18. The Greek phrase, Ἀνέχου καὶ Ἀπέχου, with which Chapman ends his poem is Epictetus' rule of life: "Bear and forebear." See Wolfius' *Vita*.

Virgils Epigram of a good man.

From his notes, we know that Chapman translated the Virgilian epigrams from the edition annotated by Iodocus Badius Ascensius. The edition containing Ascensius' commentaries nearest in date to Chapman of any of the editions in the B.M. is that of Venice, 1566, and is here used. *Virgilii Maronis, Poeta Mantuani, Universum Poema: cum Absoluta Servii Honorati Mauri, Grammatici, & Badij Ascensij interpretatione. . . .* Venetiis, Apud Ioannem Mariam Bonellum M.D. LXVI. Chapman's notes on the *Epigramma de Viro Bono* are taken from pp. 397–400 of this edition. There are 26 lines in the Latin poem, and 12 columns of Ascensius' comment.

8 The good man is "in himselfe, worldlike, full, round, and sure." Since frequent mention has been made of Chapman's concept of the circle as the perfect moral form (see particularly notes to *H. in C.*, 6), it is interesting to read Ascensius' comment on this point, ed. 1566, p. 399. "Teres atque rotundus, Teres dicitur longus & rotundus, qualis interdum hasta, rotunda figura, est orbicularis, & sphaerica, qualis pilae qua ludimus. Est ergo vir fortis, vndique plenus, habens omnes dimensiones solidas qui n. rotundus est, illi nil deest, nec ab ante, nec à retro, nec à dextera, nec à sinistra, Quod vero teretem habet formam, illi nihil deest inter sursum & deorsum oblongum n. est. Ideo aūt, teres, atque rotundus est."

9 gloss. In the edition of 1566 the two lines Chapman argues about are separated by a comma.

Securus, mundi instar habens, teres atque rotundus,
Externe ne quid labis per laeuia sidat.

16 gloss. In the same edition, the line quoted ends with a colon. The tone of Chapman's critical comments on Ascensius is very reminiscent of that which he habitually employs in writing about the translators and commentators of Homer.

20 gloss. *Amussis)* Is a carpenter's line.

21 *Subiect)* Use of this word explained by the Latin *subest* in the note.

21 gloss. *presnesse)* Conciseness. The only parallel in the *N.E.D.* occurs in 1728. Compare Chapman's essay, *Of Hesiodus*, prefixed to his translation of Hesiod's *Georgics:* "one of the purest and pressest writers."

22 gloss. The divergence of opinion rests with *pello*, strike, and *palor*, stray.

25 *lights)* Eyes.

34 gloss. Ascensius here refers to Servius, whose comments on the *Aeneid* are included with Ascensius' own, ed. 1566.

43 *these)* Emended from *this*. The line summarizes what has gone before: these thoughts, words, and acts which the good man "revolves," turns over in his mind, before going to sleep. He spends the night on this review.

45 *abusde the light)* He is angry with such bad deeds and words of his as had 'abused the day;' whereas, in the following line, he praises what was done well.

A great Man.

37 gloss. From Hieronymus Wolfius' translation of Epictetus, *Enchiridion*, LXXI. This quotation may be used to introduce a book from which a great many of the following poems are taken: the Latin version of Epictetus by Hieronymus Wolfius (1516–80). For the identification of this text as the one Chapman used, see Schoell, Ch. v. Although the book was first printed in 1563, Chapman probably used the edition of 1595. Wolfius' book contains the Manual (or *Enchiridion*), the discourses collected by Arrian, the sayings gathered from Stobaeus, and the commentaries of Simplicius. It will be noticed that the stoical poems in this 1612 volume of poems are often taken straight

from the Latin of Wolfius, as also are many passages in *The Revenge of Bussy d'Ambois*. It was Chapman's most important reading in the years 1611–12.

48 Cf. *Eug.*, 186; *Widow's Tears*, v. iii. 297–298; *Bussy*, I. i. 97.

68 *and casts the calfe his soule.*) The line means that he lies dead and expires his animal soul.

A sleight man.

Sleight) Here meaning *unimportant* and *worthless*, though it is sometimes turned to its other meaning of *crafty*, as, explicitly, in l. 59. The spelling is possible though unusual; compare *A good woman*, 57.

1–4 That is, he is half between the Good Man (good and wise) and the Great Man (great and politic).

7–8 *a brake Of forme and reading.*) *Forme* probably in the sense of "manner and method." The arts teach him methods of writing, but these are never fused with judgment and he has to get along with set conventions.

13–26 including notes, from Simplicius' commentary on Ch. VI of the *Enchiridion*. See note to *A great Man*, 37 gloss, and Schoell, p. 248.

27 Goes back to his division between Art and Nature, l. 5. Lines 6–26 have described the sleight, or mixed, man as Artist (i.e. how he takes his learning and how it affects what he writes or says); 27–50 go on to describe him as Naturalist (i.e. what he is by nature and how accidental even reason is in his discourses).

29 *Nifles*) Trifles.

55 gloss, and 61–65. Referring again to Chapman's view that Truth is shrouded in darknes' not to be penetrated by the idle beholder. See notes to epistle dedicatory of *The Shadow of Night*.

65–66 He ends on a pun, urging his reader to pay more attention to those truly wise men who are commonly slighted.

A good woman.

29–end. From Plutarch's *Conjugalia praecepta, passim;* Schoell, p. 233.

36 Plutarch quotes this saying from Herodotus. Compare *Rev. of Bussy*, III. ii. 163, and see Parrott's note.

47–54 Chapman later recast these lines for *Rev. of Bussy*, I. ii. 53–61.

47 gloss. Quoted from Plutarch, *op. cit.*

59 *And as the twins of learn'd Hippocrates*,) Shepherd pointed out that this simile occurs twice in Chapman's plays: *Gen. Usher*, IV. iii. 17, and *Masque of Middle Temple*, 320–327. Parrott refers to Lyly (*Works*, II, 77), St. Augustine (*De Civitate Dei*, v. 2), and Cicero's *De Fato*, a lost work. Hippocrates' twins are not mentioned in Plutarch's *Conjugalia praecepta*, the source of the poem. They appear in Robert Cawdray's *Treasurie of Similies* (1600), p. 851. Hippocrates was supposed to have pronounced a pair of brothers twins because they sickened at the same time, and the course of their disease was the same. See also *Hymen*, 71.

65–66 Cf. *Byron's Consp.*, II. ii. 40.

Virgils Epigram of Play.

See note to *Virgils Epigram of a good man*. This epigram, "De Ludo contra, auritam, & iram lepidum epigramma," appears on p. 400R of the edition containing Ascensius' comments which is here used.

Virgils Epigram of wine and women.

See note to *Virgils . . . good man*. This epigram, "De Venere, & vino, contra luxuriam & ebrietatem," appears on p. 402R.

12 *Warre*) Shepherd emended to "wine," but Chapman means "war;" see l. 10. The Centaurs, being drunk, were defeated by the Lapithes; hence Bacchus "lost." See Ovid, *Met.*, xii. 210 *seq.;* and *Od.*, xxi. 295 *seq.*

16 *Liaeus*) Bacchus. See Chapman's note on the name Ληναιος, Hesiod II, gloss 23, "Bacchus being called Ληναιος, *quoniam torcularibus et vini expressione praeest.*"

Virgils Epigram of this letter Y.

See note to *Virgils . . . good man.* The epigram appears on p. 403R.

5 *affaire*) See note to *Coronet*, 10.6.

A Fragment of the Teares of peace.

For the poem, from a draft of which this passage was salvaged, see *Euthymiae Raptus; or The Teares of Peace.* The speaker is Peace.

23–24 *prickt pictures . . . dunghils*) This image seems to refer to some sorcerous practice of pricking a picture of a person and then hiding it in offal, a process of magic calculated to kill one's enemy. Cf. *Inv. against Jonson*, 55.

30 *their teene*) Their own injury.

45 *Arachne*) The Lydian maiden who might be said to have "won" from Athena, because she challenged the goddess to compete with her weaving, and then produced a piece of cloth which Athena found faultless. But the competition had a sad ending, for Athena tore the cloth, and Arachne hanged herself. Athena turned her into a spider, and the rope into a spider's web. Chapman uses Arachne's victory as another symbol for a world that is topsy-turvy: Eris becomes Eunomia, and Mars wears the long robe.

47 *His honie*) Its honey; i.e. the honey of every good part of Pallas.

For good men.

This entire poem is taken from Epictetus, *Discourses*, III, xxvi, "Ad eos qui inopiam timent." See note to *A great Man*, 37 gloss, and Schoell, p. 249.

Pleasd with thy place.

Pleasd) Emended from *Please.* Cf. l. 6. The misprinting of *e* for *d* is a common error. This poem was omitted by Shepherd in his edition of Chapman's Poems.

1–18 As Parrot points out, these lines were later used in *Rev. of Bussy*, III. iv. 58–75. They are an elaboration of a passage in Epictetus, *Discourses*, IV, vii. 6–11. See note to *A great Man*, 37 gloss.

19–38 The second half of this poem was also used in the *Rev. of Bussy*, IV. i. 137–157.

20–23 See note to *H. in C.*, 6.

28 *refract*) Verb: "reflect."

In remodeling this poem into two speeches of Clermont (*Rev. of Bussy*), Chapman makes a few revisions:

Compare *Rev. of Bussy*, III. iv. 58–75:

2 and 8 all) th'All.

5 powres) power.

15 vniuersall) Universal's.

Compare *Rev. of Bussy*, IV. i. 137–157:

19–23 He starts out to cast the passage into blank verse, but ends by falling back into the original couplets (23–38).

29 high) prime.

33 perfect) truly.

(Readings from Parrott's edition.)

Of sodaine Death.

This whole poem is expanded from a passage in Epictetus, *Discourses*, IV, x. See note to *A great Man*, 37 gloss, and Schoell, p. 250.

5 *their*) Antecedent: the "good men," l. 3.

6 *theirs*) Antecedent: "their children," l. 4.

Height in Humilitie.

This poem is composed from two passages in Epictetus: "De timoris vacuitate," *Discourses*, IV, vii, and "Ad eos qui dolent se esse miserabilis," IV, vi. See note to *A great Man*, 37 gloss

and Schoell, pp. 251–252. An interlocutory technique is used in lines 2 and 31–32.
15 *Cyrus*) Persian prince, d. 401.
   Antisthenes) Founder of the Cynic sect of philosophy, from which Stoicism sprang.

For stay in competence.

Almost the entire poem (1–19, 24–62) is taken from Epictetus, *Discourses*, III, xxvi, "Ad eos qui inopiam timent." See Schoell, pp. 252–254. Like the preceding poem, it is a dialogue. The second speaker comes in midway in l. 4 through l. 5, l. 23, in last half of l. 28 and first half of l. 29, and in l. 35.
7–8 Shepherd adds the gloss, "Cantabit vacuus coram latrone viator," a quotation from Juvenal, x. 22.
18 *gadflie*) Used figuratively for an irresistible impulse. From the late Latin use (Juvenal) of *oestrus* for "frenzy, enthusiasm."

Of Man.

Since man's state partakes of divinity, it is neither a microcosm, "contracted," nor made by art, "elaborate;" on the contrary, having been made by God, his breast is sufficiently divine to be God's throne.

Of Friendship.

3 Cf. *Hymne to Sauiour*, 108–109 and note.
6–10 Cf. *De Guiana*, 56–62 and note.
20 *The affect, not the effect*) The mental disposition, not the achieved result.
44 *Meteord*) Not given in the *N.E.D.* (Loane.)

Of plentie and freedome in goodnesse.

These verses were omitted by Shepherd in his edition of the Poems. They were used later by Chapman in the *Rev. of Bussy*, IV. v. 22–25. See Parrott.
3 gloss. *Resp.*) Responsio. The rest of the poem answers the questions in ll. 1–2.

Of Attention.

This poem is made from a passage in the *Discourses* of Epictetus, IV, xii, "De Attentione." See Schoell, p. 255. As in *Height in Humilitie* and *For stay in competence*, an interlocutor speaks from the second half of l. 11 through the first half of l. 13.

To liue with little.

Except for ll. 47–50, this whole poem is composed from three passages in the *Discourses* of Epictetus: two from IV, ix, "Ad eum qui impudens esse coeperat;" and one, the basis of ll. 39–42, from IV, v, "Ad pugnaces & immanes." See Schoell, p. 257.
53–54 The interlocutory technique is used again.

To yong imaginaries in knowledge.

This poem is based almost entirely on various passages in Epictetus' *Discourses*, IV, viii, IV, v, and IV, vii. Schoell gives the correspondences in full, pp. 259–261. Linking lines of Chapman's own invention are 13–16, 19–25, 29–36, 42–46, 51–58, 81–84, 91–104, 109–114. Compare the long passage on learning in *T. of P.*, 328 *seq.*
3 *Ascribe to any*) i.e. Ascribe characteristics to any person. Latin, "tribueritis."
13 *degrees*) Academic degrees.
30 *by rootes of hearts*) "Learning by heart," mere memory work. The regular phrase is "by rote of heart," but "heart" is here turned into the plural for the sake of rhyme.
31 *perce*) An unusual spelling, or perhaps misprint, of the word "pearce," meaning "parse."
36 *Ciniflos*) An English plural for the Latin "ciniflo," a slave who aided in the dressing of a lady's hair. Superficial servants of the arts.
77–80 The latinate words in these lines so closely reflect the original passage, it is worth

quoting: "quomodo tolerem, quomodo *abstineam,* quomodo rem geram, quomodo *appetitione* utar, quomodo *aversatione,* quomodo *affectiones* & *naturales* & accersitas tuear, . . . "
aversation) Aversion.
aduentitiall) Adventitious, accidental.

Of Attire.

4 *checklesse*) Without reproach.

Of the Soule.

3 *Cause auersation and susception*) Aversation; see *Yong imaginaries,* 78: "aversion." The first illustration of this definition in the *N.E.D.* is from Chapman's *Bussy.* Susception: susceptibility or acceptance, in contrast to "aversation." This use of the word seems to be original with Chapman.

Of great men.

This poem was omitted by Shepherd in his edition of the Poems. As Parrott notes, the lines appear later in the *Rev. of Bussy,* III. iv. 14–25. Shepherd's omission of three poems from this volume (*Pleasd with thy Place, Of plenty and freedome in goodnesse,* and *Of great men*), which at first consideration seems an inexplicable lapse, evidently can be accounted for by the fact that he had discovered that Chapman used them all again for speeches in the *Rev. of Bussy.* He probably felt like protecting his poet from the possible charge of artistic thriftiness. In fitting the poem into Clermont's speech, Chapman made two revisions:
4 all that) it all.
9 vertuous) certain.

Of learned men.

18 *the damned crew*) An idiom of the day used as a title for a particular band of ruffians. Chapman uses it for any "licentious band of worldlings." Cf. *Epic.,* 22, and *Od.,* XVI. 38 and note.
18 gloss. Schoell finds (p. 117n) that Chapman took this note from an annotation to the Latin translation of the Plutarchan "libellus," *Gryllus,* which was reprinted in the volume of Simplicius' commentaries on Epictetus (ed. Cologne, 1595).

AN / EPICEDE / OR / *Funerall Song:* / On the most disastrous Death, of the / High-borne *Prince* of Men, HENRY / Prince of WALES, &c. / *With* / The Funeralls, and Representation of / the Herse of the same High and mighty Prince; / Prince of *Wales,* Duke of *Cornewaile* and *Rothsay,* / Count Palatine of *Chester,* Earle of *Carick,* / and late Knight of the most Noble / Order of the Garter. /

Which Noble *Prince* deceased at St. / *James,* the sixt day of *Nouember,* 1612. / and was most Princely interred the seuenth / day of *December* following, within the / Abbey of *Westminister,* in the Eigh- / teenth yeere of his Age. /

LONDON: / Printed by *T.S.* for *Iohn Budge,* and are to bee / sould at his shop at the great south dore of / *Paules,* and at Brittanes Bursse. 1612. /

Entered: 11 de. 1612.

Epicede: A², B–D⁴, E². 4to.

The *Funerals* has a separate title page, dated 1613. It is a prose tract describing the funeral The complete volume (see Grenville copy, B.M.) also contains a folded engraving which pictures the hearse and effigy of the Prince, with Latin verses below by Hugo Holland and English verses by Chapman. In addition to this rare folded plate, the complete volume of the *Epicede* and *Funerals* contains an extra leaf stamped in solid black which bears the crest of the Prince of Wales. In the Dyce copy 2041 (Victoria and Albert Museum) there is a version of the engraving of Henry's hearse taken from a smaller plate. It bears the same verses by Holland and Chapman, but with certain variations in spelling and punctuation, as necessitated by the smaller amount of space.

Signature C misprinted G.

In sheet D the running title which is elsewhere "*Epicedium, or, a Funerall Song.*" changes to "*Epicedium or, Funerall Song.*" Reverts in E to original form.

Textual Notes.

Sheet B has been revised in the course of printing. The only other variants are found on D$_4^r$. The nine copies which have been used for the compilation of the list of variants are as follows:

British Museum G.11,258	designated	A	Yale University	designated	Y
C.30.e.4		B	Harvard College 14424. 14. 31*		P
Victoria and Albert Dyce 2040		D1	(William Penn's copy.)		
Dyce 2041		D2	14424. 14. 30*		F
Bodleian Malone 713 (3)		M	(Buxton Forman's copy.)		
Wood 319		W			

UNCORRECTED			CORRECTED
B$_1^r$ Title,	*Song.* A, Y		*Song:* B, D1, D2, M, W, P, F
B$_1^v$ (l. 23)	pleasures: A, Y, P		pleasures? B, D1, D2, M, W, F
(l. 28)	faculties; A, Y, P		faculties? B, D1. D2 M, W, F
B$_2^r$ (l. 49)	Vanish A, Y, P		Vanisht B, D1, D2, M, W, F
(l. 58)	extols? A, Y, P		extols! B, D1, D2, M, W, F
B$_3^r$ (l. 93)	new paragraph A, Y		no new paragraph B, D1, D2, M, W, P, F
(l. 101)	one, A, Y		One, B, D1, D2, M, W, P, F
B$_3^v$ (l. 107)	without a heart; A, Y, P		without heart; B, D1, D2, M, W, F
(l. 110n)	*Simile.* A, Y, P		*Simil.* B, D1, D2, M, W, F
(l. 116n)	*Redicio* A, Y, P		*Reditio* B, D1, D2, M, W, F
(l. 122)	fallen A, Y, P		falne B, D1, D2, M, W, F
B$_4^r$ (l. 152)	Corses A, Y, P		Corses, B, D1, D2, M, W, F
B$_4^v$ (l. 172)	bridels A, Y		bridles B, D1, D2, M, W, P, F
D$_4^r$ (l. 526)	loue. B, D1, D2		loue, A, M, W, Y, P, F
(l. 532)	feurous B, D1, D2		feu'rous A, M, W, Y, P, F

In lines 23 and 28 we should naturally prefer the punctuation of A, as did the compositor, but the revised punctuation is evidently that of Chapman's copy. In composing long questions, he often uses the question mark several times in the course of the sentence, probably to keep the voice pitched to a note of enquiry. In this poem see ll. 45–50 and 65–70, and compare *For stay in competence*, 29–34, and *Height in Humilitie*, 27–31. But according to this line of argument, the reviser has made the error in l. 59.

The printer was very short on upper case W's and uses every device to get around his difficulty, even the small *vv*. These are all corrected in the present edition.

Punctuation Revised.

73 Final comma added   74 Final comma added   78 Final question mark instead of period   182 Final comma instead of question mark   183 *Herse!* instead of *Herse?*   185 *was!* instead of *was?*   191 Final semicolon instead of period   192 Final period added   193 Final period deleted   199 Final semicolon added   208 Final comma added   229 No new paragraph   259 Colon added after *fish't*   329 Final comma instead of period   389 Final semicolon added   390 Final comma instead of semicolon   391 Final period added   408 Final semicolon instead of comma   459 Final period instead of semicolon

469 Final period instead of colon   485 Final period added   532 Final period instead of comma   578 Final period instead of colon   599 Final semicolon added   605 Final comma added   621 Final semicolon added   622 Final comma instead of semicolon   Epitaphium No. 1. 6. *cut.* instead of *cut.*)

Epistle Dedicatory.

Nothing is known of the identity of this Mr. Henry Jones, but Chapman had presented a copy of the *Iliads* to him with the autograph inscription: "In witness of his best love so borne to his best deserving friende Mr. Henrye Jones: George Chapman gives him theise fruites of his best labors, and desires love betwixt us as long-lived as Homer." (See Hooper's ed. of Chapman's *Iliads*, I, LV.)

22 *damned crue*) See note to *Of learned men*, 18.

90 *Sisters*) Sing. poss. Sister's cheeks. The Princess Elizabeth who was about to marry Prince Frederick. See *Hymn to Hymen*.

99–115 This passage is directly derived from the commentary of Ficino on Plato, *In Convivium, Oratio* VII, cap. iv. See Schoell, p. 11.

120–121 For image of the inverted world, see *Coronet*, 5.5–6 and note.

142 *pilgrime*) Is a verb; hence the original capital letter has been deleted.

161–164 and gloss. For the golden chain, see *H. in N.*, 159 and note.

164 *his*) Antecedent: Ambition, the "one wretched end," (159).

185–191 The construction of the sentence is "no sooner taint . . . then mere gawds pierce." For *disparent* (190) see *O.B. of S.*, 11.5 and note. The *pierce* (190) means "penetrate," as the colors of the rainbow do the vapors.

213–218 This digression on Flatterers is taken from Xylander's Latin Plutarch, *De adul. & amici discrim.*, 49 a. See Schoell, p. 234.

259–260 The sense of this couplet is saved by punctuating after the word *fish't*. There is originally no punctuation in the couplet. The image goes back to 251–252. The Prince was secure because he followed God (fished in clear streams) rather than following men (whose streams are troubled and hence a menace to the crown).

290 *Caesarean Commentares*) Caesar's Commentaries on the Gallic War, i.e. the reflections of ripe age on the achievements of youth. Clement Edmondes had dedicated his edition of this book to Prince Henry, (1609?). It had been part of the course of education recommended by his father.

325 *poison'd Ast'risme*) The first example in the *N.E.D.* of the word *Asterism*, "a cluster of stars," is from Chapman, *B.B. of Alex.*, Sc. 5, 53 (1598).

330–333 The "wits profane" were not scared off. Practically every poet of the time wrote an elegy on the death of Prince Henry, among them: Heywood, Webster, Tourneur, Donne, Wither, Campion, Herbert, Drummond of Hawthornden, and Sylvester. But this passage shows Chapman to have been among the first.

334 *With this*) That is, his invocation to his Muse, l. 326.

335 *she*) The Muse.

338 *laid out such a brest*) Made such a cry. Cf. Chapman's *Batrachomyomachia*, 118. The phrase is used for Dragons by Topsell.

349–351 See *De Guiana*, 56–62 and note.

354 *seq.* From this point on, with only a few digressions, Chapman's poem follows closely the Latin elegy of Angelus Politianus, "Elegia sive Epicedion In *Albierae Albitiae immaturum exitum*," *Opera* (Lyons, 1546), Tom. II, 259 *seq.* This fact was first mentioned by Sidney Lee in a note to his *French Renaissance in England* (1910), p. 466, but was made the main subject of an article by Schoell, *Mod. Phil.*, Vol. XIII. In this article one will find a summary of Politianus' elegy on the 15 year old girl, with a detailed study of Chapman's adaptation of the Latin; hence only a few of the most striking correspondences will be mentioned here. The only considerable passages having no equivalent in the Latin elegy are the description of Sir Thomas Gates' shipwreck, the description of visitors to the Prince's bedside, and the allusions to the Archbishop and Sir Edward Phillips.

358 *Rhamnusia*) The goddess Nemesis worshipped at Rhamnus.

365 *seq.* The Prince's illness lasted all autumn, the crisis setting in on Oct. 25th. The per-
plexity of his many physicians and their failure to come to any diagnosis are set forth
in every account of the Prince's life and death. For full history, with reference to ap-
propriate documents, see Thomas Birch, *The Life of Henry Prince of Wales* (1760).
The symptoms of his disease were so obscure, there lingered a persistent rumor that
he had been poisoned.

366 *th' Autumnal-starre*) Sirius.

377 and gloss. This seems to be the only known reference to the fever's being "Hungarian."
Quoted by Birch, p. 333n.

388 and gloss. *Hare-eyd unrest*) The phrase in Politianus is "Trepidaeque Insomnia men-
tis."

390 *trenched*) Earlier than the first example of this figurative use given in the *N.E.D.*
(Loane.)

392–395 From Politianus,

> Marmaricique trahunt dominae juga curva leones,
> Ignea queis rabido murmure corda fremunt.
> (105–106)

Chapman enlarges the metaphor, making it more of a picture. Having once found the
Marmarian lions in Politianus, he had looked up their properties in some book of ref-
erence and gives the information in a gloss.

398–401 *Echidna*) The mother of Cerberus is read into the lines of Politianus through a mis-
translation. The "Echidnas" of the original meant the vipers that crowned the head
of Fever. Nor was the "whirlepit" present, for the word "Vertice" in Politianus meant
"head." See Schoell, *Mod. Phil.*, Vol. XIII, 35.

> Vertice Diva feras ardenti attollit Echidnas,
> Quae saniem Stygio semper ab ore vomunt.
> (107–108)

401 *Quitture*) Quitter. Pus; suppurating matter.

421–423 The Sithonian snow and the Roman Temple are both in Politianus, 121–124.

428 *seed of Night*) See l. 375.

450–451 This image was only suggested, not fulfilled, in the Latin.

> Interea humentum noctis variantia pallam
> Hesperus in rutilo sparserat astra polo.
> (141–142)

459 *her Mayden fit*) The frenzy of Fever, just spoken of as "th'Ominous forme of Death."
Fever is a maiden, as we learn in l. 443.

461 *Her*) Fever's

this spring of Man) The same phrase is used of Vere: *De Vere*, 2.

491 *seq.* This storm occurred 20 July, 1609. The expedition had sailed May, 1609, with nine
ships to colonize Virginia. The flag ship, carrying 150 men, was separated from the
others by the storm and cast on the shore of the Bermudas. A report of the storm and
consequent discovery of the islands was published in a short pamphlet, 1610, "A Dis-
covery of the Bermudas, otherwise called the Ile of Divels: By Sir Thomas Gates,
Sir George Sommers, and Captayne Newport . . . Sil. Iourdan. London, Printed by
Iohn Windet." It is the same storm which is supposed to have inspired *The Tempest*.

522 *Metropolitan*) In its prime meaning of the bishop who has the oversight of the other
bishops in his province, and whose see was known as the metropolis of the province.
The Archbishop of Canterbury was Dr. George Abbot.

525–532 and gloss. Sir Edward Phillips, a man genuinely admired by Chapman, and hence
especially named even though he was only one of a number of officers in the Prince's
household. See the epistle dedicatory to *P.S.P.P.*, and the sonnet added to the *Iliads*.

559–563 Referring to King James' influence in bringing about the truce in the War in the
Netherlands, 1609. See opening of *T. of P.*

612 Cf. *Eug.*, 261.
625 *his mother*) That is, Cupid's mother, Venus.
627–628 This image is not in the Latin. Compare *H. in N.*, 84 and note, and *Widow's Tears*, II. iv. 204–205.
The second epitaph is the one which was engraved below the representation of the hearse. See bibliographical note.

EVGENIA: / OR / TRVE NOBILITIES / TRANCE; FOR THE MOST / MEMORABLE DEATH, OF / THE THRICE NOBLE AND / RELIGIOUS; / WILLIAM Lord / RVSSEL, &c. / Diuided into foure Vigils of / the Night. / By GEO. CHAPMAN. / Anno Domini, 1614: /

A²; B–F⁴. 4to.

Contents: (A₁ʳ) Title; A² "Epistle Dedicatorie" to Frances, Lord Russell; B₁ʳ–B₄ᵛ "Inductio;" B₄ᵛ–C₄ʳ "Vigilia prima;" C₄ʳ–D₁ʳ "Vigiliae Secundae. Inductio;" D₁ʳ–E₂ʳ "Vigilia secunda;" E₂ᵛ–E₃ʳ "Vigiliae Tertiae. Inductio;" E₃ʳ–F₁ᵛ "Vigilia Tertia;" F₁ᵛ–F₂ʳ "Vigiliae Quartae & vltimae. Inductio;" F₂ʳ–F₄ʳ "Hymnus ad D. Russelium defunctum;" F₄ "Peror."

Not Entered.

Copies Used: Duke of Bedford's, Woburn Abbey, Woburn, Bletchley.   University of Edinburgh, Drummond Collection.

Textual Note.

The private printer of this quarto did a careless job. Words are omitted or twisted more frequently than is common with commercially published books of the period. Corrections of misprints are noted at the bottom of the page, as well as emendations accepted from Shepherd or made by the present editor.

Punctuation Revised.

Ep. Ded. 6 *that* (*for* instead of (*that for*   Periods added to the marginal glosses to lines 67, 69, 97, and 537
48 Final period instead of comma   52 Final period added   90 Final period deleted   140 Final semicolon instead of period   142 Final comma instead of period   186 Final period added   207 Final period added   211 Final period deleted   298 Commas deleted after *heartie* and after *Thought*   307 Parenthesis deleted after *fume*   454 Final semicolon instead of period   472 Final period deleted   473 Final period instead of colon   478 Final comma instead of period   497 Final colon instead of period   498 Final period instead of colon   512 Final colon instead of period   519 End of parenthesis supplied   611 Final comma added   726 Final colon instead of period   727 Final period instead of colon   752 Final period deleted   806 Final period deleted   815 Final comma instead of period   949 Final period instead of colon   1031 Final period added   1042 No new paragraph   1046 Final comma added   1094 Final comma instead of period   1095 Final period instead of comma   1109 Comma added after *Aire*   1152 End of parenthesis supplied   1202 Final semicolon added   1203 *Not Gaine*, instead of *Not Gaine;*

Words capitalized in accordance with the general practice in the text: 159 & 207 Death   164 Religion   435 & 494 Fame

Epistle Dedicatory.

The principal points of interest in the life of William, Lord Russell, whose death is the occasion for this poem, are found in the notes to ll. 323–348. His son Francis, Lord Russell,

Baron of Thornhaugh, succeeded to the title Baron of Thornhaugh in 1613, the year before this poem was printed. In 1627 he became fourth Earl of Bedford. It is interesting to note, as a matter of subsequent family history relating him to Chapman's most infamous patron, that in 1637 his second son, William, fifth Earl and first Duke of Bedford, married Anne, daughter of Robert Carr, Earl of Somerset.

3 *Epimethean*) Chapman explains this symbol in his 29th note to *Hesiod* I., "For Mans corporeall part; which is figur'd in Epimetheus; signifying the inconsiderate and head-long force of affections; not obeying his reasonable part, or soule; nor vsing foresight fit for the preuention of ill; which is figur'd in Prometheus; He is deceiued with a false show of pleasure; for the substantiall, and true delight, fit to be embrac't." The word "Epimethean" is used again in *Bussy*, IV. ii. 31.

6 *watches*) Vigils.

8-11 *The Anniuersaries . . . shall . . . be furnisht with supplies*) Chapman never, so far as we know, further commemorated William, Lord Russell. In writing this poem, he probably, as so often in his career, had hoped for financial assistance and perhaps even a permanent patron, in which hopes he was disappointed.

Eugenia.

9 *triple world*) Earth, sea, and hell. See *H. in C.*, 2-3.

47 *parting vertues*) This use of the ppl.a. in the sense of "departing" is a forecast of Milton's "parting Genius" (*Nativity*, xx, 6), and "parting Angel" (*P.L.* IX, 276).

48 *she*) Is still Eugenia.

49-52 *she*) Is Religion.

55-127 I feel fairly sure that this passage, with its accompanying notes, has a Latin source, but I have not been able to locate it.

58 gloss *water-gal*) The water-gall is an old expression for a secondary or imperfectly-formed rainbow.

75 gloss. I cannot find that King Nauplius ever had any traffic with Cranes! If this is a pure fabrication of Chapman's, it might possibly be explained on the hypothesis that "Cranes" was a misprint for "Dames" in some book he had seen. Nauplius was cred-ited with having "changed" the fidelity of certain Greek wives in spite during their husbands' absence at Troy. Naupliades (i.e. the son of Nauplius) was Palamedes.

100 *Swimming feathers*) *Pluma nastans*, from the various birds who had been so active in the lines above.

135 *this rare religious Lord*) Russell, whose death, which the storm had been presaging, is now mentioned for the first time.

158 *her loues*) i.e. Lord Russell's.

159 *Death*) Is here personified and enters on the scene. Not capitalized in the original text. Reference to his waking comes in l. 207.

173-178 The kind of picture here described was known at the time as a "perspective pic-ture." Chapman had already made use of them for figurative purposes in *All Fools*, I. i. 47-48, had made indirect reference to them in *H. & L.*, III. 125-126, and was again to use them figuratively in *Chabot*, I. i. 68-72. They must have reminded him of Pausanias' description of the statue of Niobe, as found in Comes' *Mythologiae* and recast by him in *O.B. of S.*, stanza 3. In that stanza he first uses the phrase "optick reason," which he takes straight from Comes and retains in this simile in *Eugenia*, as well as in *Chabot*, I. i. 68.

The most illuminating reference to the way such pictures were made is one given by Parrott in a note to the lines in *All Fools*. There he quotes Collier's reference to Tollet's note on *Twelfth Night*, v. i. 244 in Johnson and Steevens' edition of Shakespeare. "It is a pretty art that in a pleated paper and Table furrowed and indented men make one picture to represent several faces—that being viewed from one place or standing did show the head of a Spaniard, and from another the head of an ass."

These pictures certainly took the fancy of writers at that time. Shakespeare refers to them in *Twelfth Night*, v. i. 219, and *Richard II*, II. ii. 18; Jonson in the *Alchemist*, III. iv. 88-100; Drayton in *Mortianeriados*, 2332-38 (reference kindly given by Kathleen Tillotson); and Burton in Democritus' Address to the Reader, *The Anatomy of Melancholy*, (Bohn ed. I, p. 132).

186 See note to *A great Man*, 48.

208 *phantasie*) Defined according to scholastic psychology as "the mental apprehension of an object of perception," or as "the image impressed on the mind by an object of sense." The sense here is auditory: Eugenia is revived by the apprehension of Russell's qualities created ("That sence in act put") by what Religion whispered to her. Leslie Rutledge in his doctoral dissertation, *George Chapman's Theory of the Soul and of Poetry* (Harvard, 1938), points out that Ficino discusses *phantasia* as one of the three lower powers of the soul: *Theol. Plat.*, XVI, v.

212 and gloss. 9 March, 1613.

257–265 Accepting Shepherd's emendation of "mere" for "more" in l. 265, these lines mean that if living is the only end of life, then the after-life is the most tenuous dream and there is nothing left of importance to a reasonable man; life is no longer just a bridge spanning birth and death to immortality, and all that has been written and believed about Earth and Heaven being made for a good end is merely feigned.

260 *A paire of Tarriers to set Fooles aworke*,) "To" emended from "so." "Tarriers" was another word for "tiring-irons," see *N.E.D.*, 1601. "The very frame . . . resembleth fitlie a paire of tarriours, or tyring yrons." These tarriers were a mechanical puzzle: a number of rings fastened on to a wire loop and attached to a thin piece of metal. The puzzle was to take all the rings thus fettered off the loop. This line, then, is specially to be compared with Drayton, *Elegies, to W. Jeffries*, 100, "A Tarrying-iron for fooles to labour at."

261 and gloss. *And lighter then the shadow of a corke*:) Proverbial: Cf. Strabo I. ὡς τὸ κουφότερον εἶναι φελλοῦ σκιᾶς. He repeats the line *verbatim* in his *Ep. to Somerset, H. of H.*, 131, and there is a variant of the proverb, *Epic.*, 612.

265 *fayn'd*) In the sense of *fashioned*. The grammatical structure of this couplet is involved. It means that everyone has written and believed that earth and heaven were fashioned for some good purpose rather than to harbor such an ephemeral sort of irreligious living as has just been described.

298–299 These lines are a puzzle. They were originally punctuated as follows:

As at the heartie, will, loue; Thought, takes fire,
That seeke her first, and last; all base desire

Making it somewhat plainer by dropping the commas after "heartie" and "Thought," the sense is probably: 'as love is nourished at the hearty will; the thought of those who seek her first and last takes fire.'

305 Cf. *T. of P.*, 910 and note.

320 *Noble*) Although one would expect an abstract noun here to match "Pietie," "Noble" must mean "Nobleman." Cf. 386–391.

323–337 Russell spent several years as a young man in traveling through the countries here named. He returned from this tour about 1579, then made his first campaign in the Low Countries during which he was knighted.

335 *brightly*) The adverbial form used as an adjective for the sake of metre, though Shepherd's emendation to "knightly" is a smooth one. The original word is plausible considering what follows.

338–344 Russell had long service in the Netherlands. He returned there with the Earl of Leicester in 1585 and supported Leicester in his quarrel with the Estates. On the death of Sidney he succeeded him as Governor of Flushing. In 1588 he was relieved, at his own request, of the duties which he seems to have performed very successfully.

339 *circulare*) Perfect, complete. For other illustrations of this use of the word, as distinct from its moral meaning, see *H. & L.*, Ded. to Lady Walsingham, 40; *Hesiod*, Ded.; *Eug.*, 939, *Hymn to Hermes*, 874; *Batrachomyomachia*, 184; and several places in the *Odysseys*.

345–348 The crown set on Russell's head by Queen Elizabeth for governing within her domains was his appointment as Lord-Deputy of Ireland in place of Sir Wm. Fitzwilliam, May 1594. Exactly three years after his appointment, a detachment sent out by him was successful in capturing Fiagh MacHugh O'Byrne who had been causing the English much trouble ever since 1580 when Russell had first been sent to Ireland in command of a company of recruits to hold him in check along the Wicklow frontier. Fiagh's country was notoriously wild and inaccessible, as Chapman here explains in his compound epithet *wood-housde*. Wild rebellion, housed in the woods, obeyed the sway of Russell's vertues.

349–354 See note to *De Guiana*, 56–62.

355–358 Wm. Lord Russell's father was Francis Russell, second Earl of Bedford, 1527?–1585. When the Earl's father, John Russell, was created Earl of Bedford in 1550, Francis was styled Lord Russell. This title is what Chapman means by his *surname*.

361 seq. It is evident that the book which Chapman had before him while composing the next few hundred lines of *Eugenia* was the Latin translation of Plutarch's essays by Gulielmus Xylander (Wilhelm Holtzman, 1532–76), the translation made in 1570 and used by Estienne in his Greco-Latin edition of Plutarch in 1572. For the extent and nature of Chapman's indebtedness to this Latin text, see Schoell's *Etudes sur l'Humanisme Continental* . . . , Ch. IV, and Appendix II. Parallel passages will be referred to in the present notes without citations since they can be found in Schoell.

361–374 Cf. Xylander's Plutarch, *De Alexandri fortuna vel virtute*, Oratio II, 337 c, and Oratio I, 332 c. Marginal note from the latter. (Schoell, pp. 240 and 73.)

423–426 and gloss. Cf. *O.B. of S.*, 24.5 gloss and note. The significance of *"Cul. ex Arist."* [otle] remains a mystery; however, for the family history of the idea, see Rutledge, *op. cit.*, p. 147, n. 3.

429 *which*) Refers to "things," l. 427.

435 *As Fame addrest to this;*) Fame not capitalized in the original. Eugenia has finished her long speech and has told Fame to celebrate Russell with her Trumpet.

437–438 The night-birds began to "call off" the day by raising a dark storm.

471 gloss. *Professors*) Not academic, but simply any people who openly profess their worldly interests.

480 *their oiles spend*) "Burning the midnight oil." Cf. l. 600 where oil is spent in study of mortal joys.

482 *For these are in the way;*) For these are on the direct path, in distinction to Truth's Professors in the next line who take the by-ways.

485 *These*) Must refer back to the "poor labourers for the second life" (471) who are "thirsting" for the true knowledge they will derive from hearing about Russell's death.

490–491 Asterisks added where a line has been omitted by the printer.

497 *triple crown*) Has reference to the three-fold papal tiara, which was considered the touchstone on which all other crowns were tried. The three crowns which encircled the dome-shaped diadem, orb, and cross were symbolic of triple dignity and were "usually richly wrought with jewels." In the *Faerie Queene*, I. vii. 16.4, Duessa appropriately wears a "triple crown."

503 The line would be clearer without the parenthesis. Fame is armed with the arts of good men.

530 Russell begins to speak and continues through l. 807.

532–543 and gloss. Compare Xylander's Plutarch, *Ei apud Delphos*, 392 a, b, c, d. (Schoell, p. 240.) The marginal note is abbreviated from two sentences in 392 d. PL is Plutarch.

542 *in one death flying*) i.e. In flying from one final death.

555 *Asterisme of seauen*) The Pleiades. See note to *Epic.*, 325.

559 gloss. *Ioculous*) Seems to be a "cupid" of Chapman's own invention.

571 gloss. *Achellous horn*) Ovid, *Met.*, ix. 87. The Naiads changed the horn which Hercules took from the river god Achelous, when he was fighting in the shape of a bull, into the horn of plenty.

577–580 Cf. Xylander's Plutarch, *Non posse suauiter vivi sec*, *Ep.*, 1105 c. (Schoell, p. 241.)

608–611 and gloss. *Genesis*, 32.

630–631 Cf. Xylander's Plutarch, *De consolatione ad Apollonium*, 102 f. (Schoell, p. 241.)

654–685 Cf. Xylander's Plutarch, *De virtute & vitio*, 101 a, b, c, d. (Schoell, p. 242.)

660 *euen compasse*) The phrase means "measure, proper proportion, or regularity," and is here used as an adverbial modifier.

665 *Get Capps, and knees*) Current expression for "bare-headed, and bowing or kneeling." Russell tells his son how easy it is to "get" this kind of false salutation. Cf. *Chabot,* II. ii. 46.

667 *affections*) See note to *H. in C.,* 217.

715 and gloss. See *H. in N.,* 159 and note, and *Epic.,* 161. The interpretation in Chapman's gloss that the chain is "diuino Resurrectionis prefiguratio," is not found among Spondanus' interpretations of the passage.

721–733 Cf. Xylander's Plutarch, *De facie in orbe lunae,* 928 b. (Schoell, p. 243.)

724 *lucifluent*) A word of Chapman's own invention; not found in the *N.E.D.* The Latin is "Luciferi oculi."

725 *analogise*) The first illustration in the *N.E.D.* of the verb used in this way, "To show itself analogous," is in 1733.

732–733 See Plutarch, *op. cit.,* "Luna Soli & terrae interposita, sicvt iecur inter cor & ventriculum, aut aliud molle viscus insitum: . . . "

739–740 and gloss. Jove's lightning called *Trisulcus,* three-shafted, by Ovid.

746–755 Cf. Xylander's Plutarch, *Virtutem doceri posse,* 439 b, d. (Schoell, p. 243.)

766–779 Based on one sentence in Plutarch, but much amplified. Xylander's Plutarch, *Symposiacon,* lib. II, 633 e. (Schoell, p. 244.)

796–799 and gloss. Cf. Xylander's Plutarch, *Virtutem doceri posse,* 439 e. (Schoell, p. 244.) "Et Laco interrogatus quid vtilitatis adferret pueris quos instituebat: facio, respondit, vt honesta eis fiant suauia." Estienne uses Laco's translation of this essay in his edition of Plutarch.

807 Russell's words, as repeated by Fame, end with this line.

823–831 and gloss. *Alcides*) Hercules. Hercules' wife, Deianira, soaked the shirt in the blood of the dying centaur, Nessus, not knowing that his blood had been poisoned, but thinking only that it had magic properties to preserve Hercules' love for her.

832 *seq.* gloss. The margins of both extant copies are most unfortunately cut very deep at this point. Suggested readings are supplied in square brackets.

833 reads "monthlike wounds," probably a misprint for "mouthlike," an error which the printer repeats in setting up the note. It is confusing to have the subject of the sentence, "world," tucked into a parenthesis.

836 *he*) Still the "world."
Mineruas Birds) Owls.

837 *Sleepes wing'd Ushers*) Bats; see gloss.

848 All these (birds, beetles, and snails) make the evening their only morning.

853 gloss. Restored by Dr. Rutledge.

886 and glosses. The Reverend William Walker, who preached his funeral sermon, tells about the choice of the text. "Phil. l. 23. *I am in a strait betweene two, hauing a desire to be loosed and a desire to be with Christ.* "Which words I do not casually select for my Text, but am almost necessarily enioyned to vse; both for that this Noble Lord, did in his health and sicknesse often repeate them, and reapt much comfort by them: And also, chiefely because I haue heard him desire in time of his health, that these Words might be the Theame of his Funerall Sermon."—p. 5 of "A Sermon Preached at the Funerals of the Right Honourable, William, Lord Russell, Baron of Thornhaugh, at Thornhaugh, in Northampton-Shire, the 16. of September. 1613. . . . By William Walker, Batchelour of Diuinitie, and Preacher of the word of God at Cheswicke in Middlesex. . . . London: Printed for Iohn Hodgets. 1614." (8)+62 pp. 4to. This sermon evidently lay before Chapman as he wrote.

891–892 The seven foul ministers of Death: doubtless, the seven Deadly Sins.

939 See note to *H. in C.,* 6 *seq.*

950–952 Aristotelian echo. See *De Anima,* 418 b–419 a.

969–975 Paraphrasing the words of Russell as reported by William Walker who administered the sacrament to him three days before his death. *Sermon . . .* p. 52, see above, 886n.

973 *exhibified*) There is no such word in the *N.E.D.* Chapman invented the form for the purpose of rhyme.

982–993 Walker reports that Russell was subjected to trial and temptation between the time of his taking the Communion and his death, but that he emerged from this spiritual trial victorious.

994 gloss. See note to 886 above. The article on William, Lord Russell, in the *D.N.B.* seems to be at fault in giving the date of his death as March 9, and of his interment as March 16. Miss Gladys Scott-Thomson, archivist to the late Duke of Bedford, writes that, though there is no entry of his death in the register of Thornhaugh nor on his tomb there, the official date given at the College of Arms is August 9th, "and their entry is practically certain to be absolutely accurate as it was necessary for them to keep a careful record in all cases of deaths of peers." Hence the date given on the title-page of Walker's Sermon stating that the funeral was held on Sept. 16 is probably correct.

1014 Jesus "who wept for Lazarus." See Chapman's commentary to Book I of the *Iliads*, note on l. 360, in defence of Achilles' weeping.

1028 Eleutheria, the feast of liberty, celebrated by the Greeks, after the battle of Plataea (479 B.C.), in honour of Zeus Eleutherius (the deliverer). No slave could minister on this occasion. Chapman's "liberals" hence means "free men," a use of the word as a substantive which does not appear in the *N.E.D.* His use of "Elutherian" is also earlier than the first example in the *N.E.D.*: cf. *And. Lib.*, 291.

1046 *on*) Goes with "went." No final comma in the original.

1051 *euery other dame*) All other women: i.e. the Muses.

1052 *Chore*) Chorus.

1056–63 The perfect life compared to the circle of the full moon. See note to *H. in C.*, 6 *seq.*

ANDROMEDA / LIBERATA. / OR / THE NVPTIALS OF / PERSEVS and ANDRO-MEDA. / By GEORGE CHAPMAN. / *Nihil a veritate nec virtute remotius quam vulgaris opinio.* Pet. / (*Device:* "Mihi conscia recti.") / LONDON, / Printed for LAVRENCE L'ISLE and are to be sold / *at his shop in St, Paules-Church-yard, at the signe of* / the Tigers-head. 1614. /

(*1); A⁴; ¶ ¶⁴; B–E⁴; F¹. 4to.

Contents: (*1ʳ) Title; A₁ "To the preiudicate . . . Reader;" A₂ "The Argument;" (A₃ʳ) ¶₃ʳ– (¶ ¶₄ʳ) The Epistle Dedicatory; B₁ʳ–E₄ᵛ "Andromeda Liberata;" F "Apodosis."
9 leaves of prefatory matter: signatures run as follows: 1) no sig., 2) A, 3) A₂, 4) ¶₃, 5) no sig., 6) ¶ ¶, 7) ¶ ¶₂, 8) ¶ ¶₃, 9) no sig.

Entered: 16 mr.

Textual Notes.

There are several minor variations, particularly in foldings E and F which show signs of having been revised for punctuation. In noting these revisions, the following symbols are used:

British Museum C.34.f.18	A	British Museum	Grenville copy G.11,259	G
Bodleian 4⁰ L.71 Art.	B	Harvard College 14424.14.25*		H
Victoria and Albert	Dyce 2046 D	Morgan Library 42 A		M

B₂ʳ (l. 33)	Innocence, A, G, B, H, M		Innocnce; D
C₂ʳ (l. 194)	serpentine G, D, B, H, M		serpentine, A
E₁ᵛ (l. 494)	reaues: G, B	reaues, A, D, H, M	
(l. 496)	sight. G, B	sight: A, D, H, M	
(l. 501)	beget. That G, B	beget: That A, D, H, M	
(l. 502)	re'create G, B	recreate A, D, H, M	
(l. 503)	re'creation G, B	recreation A, D, H, M	

	(l. 505)	takes. G, B	takes: A, D, H, M
	(l. 508)	shine. G, B	shine: A, D, H, M
E₂ʳ	(l. 519)	*Perseus.* G, B	*Perseus:* A, D, H, M
	(l. 521)	vouchsaft. G, B	vouchsaft: A, D, H, M
	(l. 522)	stoopt to: G, B	stoopt to, A, D, H, M
E₃ᵛ	(l. 570)	constant: G, B	constant, A, D, H, M
	(l. 578)	shines. G, B	shines: A, D, H, M
	(l. 581)	there. G, B	there: A, D, H, M
E₄ʳ	(l. 587)	*Detraction* G, B	detraction A, D, H, M
	(l. 589)	shal G, B	shall A, D, H, M
	(l. 591)	with grace G, B	which grace A, D, H, M
	(ll. 595–597)	(when the worthy . . . eithers bone) G, B	
		No parenthesis A, D, H, M	
	(l. 598)	honoured. G, B	honoured, A, D, H, M
F₁ʳ	(l. 620)	men: G, A, B, H, M	men, D
	(l. 621)	Who scornes G, A, B, H, M	Who scornes, D
F₁ᵛ	(l. 631)	Christendome, G, M	Crhistendome, A, D, B, H

It is clear that the Grenville copy and the Bodleian copy contain the corrected version of sheet E, and that the Grenville copy is the only one of the six to include all the other corrections; hence, the Grenville copy is followed in the present text. Line 589 is no exception as at first sight might appear. The shorter spelling has been adopted to make the long line look better with the bracket.

Punctuation Revised.

Epistle Dedicatory. 37 *breath,* instead of *breath;*   38 Semicolon supplied after *thought)*; 51 Final comma added   72 Final comma instead of period   77–91 Inverted commas removed from the beginnings of the lines   88 Final comma instead of period   94 Final period instead of comma   108 Final comma added 110 Final comma added   112 Final period instead of comma   116 Final colon instead of period   129 *law:* instead of *law,*   Final colon deleted   130 Final comma instead of colon

Andromeda Liberata. 8 Final semicolon instead of period   15 Parenthesis deleted before *whose*   20 Final comma instead of period   24 Final comma deleted 106 Final semicolon instead of comma   108 Final semicolon instead of period 109 Final period instead of semicolon   155 Final comma added   336–344 Inverted commas continued at beginning of lines   364 Final comma instead of period   395 Final period deleted   446 Final period added   502 Final colon added   524 Final period instead of colon   591 Final comma added   601 Parenthesis completed

The occasion for the composition of this poem was the marriage of the Lady Frances, daughter of Thomas Howard, Earl of Suffolk, and former wife of the Earl of Essex, to Robert Earl of Somerset. The tale of the marriage here celebrated is a famous one. Robert Carr, a conspicuous favorite of King James, had accompanied him from Scotland as a page, and had been knighted on Dec. 23, 1607. In 1609 he had been presented with Sherborne, Raleigh's estate; on March 25, 1611, he had been created Viscount Rochester and promoted to a seat in the House of Lords, the first Scot put there by James. In 1612, on Salisbury's death, he conducted James' correspondence with the title of Secretary. In the same year began his intrigue with the Countess of Essex. She asked for an annulment of her marriage on the grounds that Essex was impotent, a charge hotly denied by him, and after a prolonged and most unsavory legal and ecclesiastical struggle, her marriage was nullified on Sept. 25, 1613, so that she could marry Carr. Ten days before had occurred the murder of Sir Thomas Overbury, the character writer. He had been a great friend of Carr, had run errands between him and Lady Frances and written love letters for him, but when he realized that the lady's relatives were members of the Spanish party (her great-uncle was the Earl of Northampton, leader of the political Catholics), his enthusiasm for the couple cooled, and he incurred the anger of Lady Essex. Obviously he was a potentially dangerous enemy to them, and on a trumped-up reason Rochester succeeded in getting him into the Tower, 26 April, 1613. There he died of an injection administered by the boy of an apothecary who was later proved to have been employed by Lady Frances. Rochester's fortunes, however, continued to flourish for a while in spite of his growing unpopularity at court. On Nov. 3, he was created Earl of Somerset; On Dec. 23, Treasurer of Scotland, and three days later was married to Lady Frances. In 1614, the year of Chapman's poem, he was made Lord Chamberlain and Keeper of the Privy Seal after the death of Northampton. But the end was approaching: in 1615, though Somerset continued to enjoy James' confidence, the new favorite, George Villiers, was rising in the king's estimation, and there was a mounting tension in Somerset's relations with James. In the autumn of that year the facts about Overbury's murder began to come to light, and the Earl and Countess of Somerset were put in confinement. They were tried for the Overbury murder in May, 1616, with Bacon conducting the prosecution for the state. Though the Countess confessed to the crime whereas the Earl pleaded innocent, they were both judged guilty. James pardoned Lady Frances and spared Somerset's life. They were kept in the Tower until 1622.

Norma Dobie Solve in her *Stuart Politics in Chapman's Tragedy of Chabot* (University of Michigan, 1928) has done a good deal to explain Chapman's enlistment in such an unpopular cause as the Somerset couple. (See particularly pp. 36–40.) There exists considerable doubt as to Somerset's guilt: the evidence used against him was entirely circumstantial and none of it connected him specifically with his wife's activities. His self-defence was noted at the time for its manliness and candor. Since Chapman knew and liked him, he may well have been among those who felt that the king and Bacon were using his wife's guilt as a convenient means of disposing of him. The fact that the couple whose marriage had been so hazardously won chose to stay together after such terrible events (for the Countess voluntarily stayed with Somerset in the Tower) would probably have so appealed to Chapman that he continued to include the Countess in his loyal feelings for the Earl. At any rate, he remained permanently loyal to them: see the dedications to the *Odysseys*, *De Vere*, and the *Hymns of Homer*. The *Andromeda Liberata* was, however, the first work which he dedicated to Somerset, and it was not well received, as we know from the following *Justification of Andromeda Liberata*. Ben Jonson also celebrated the marriage, but in verses privately printed for Somerset (*Poems*, Newdigate ed., p. 286).

The Argument. This narrative is an exact translation of passages in Comes' *Mythologiae*: from VIII, 25, "De Andromeda," and VII, 18, "De Perseo." See Schoell, p. 195.

Epistle Dedicatory.

29–38 The suggestion comes from Plutarch's *De Socratis genio*, 581 e, but the figurative treatment is different. See Schoell, p. 234. For Chapman's use of Xylander's Latin Plutarch, see note to *Ep. to Roydon, O.B. of S.*, 6–9.

34 *this three mens catch*) Not in Plutarch. A song in which one man catches up the words of another: poetry considered light and ludicrous.

36 Not in Plutarch. Compare Hoby's translation of the *Courtier* (Everyman ed., p. 122), "Therefore (in mine opinion) they deserve none other praise or rewarde, than the great Alexander gave unto him, that standing a far off, did so well broch Chiche peason upon a needle."

63–68 This doctrine is stated by Ficino in his *Convivium Platonis de Amore Commentarium*, II, ii and II, iv. For Ficino, see note to *A Hymn to our Sauiour*, 221–248.

75 *May well authorise*) The subject is "The peacefull mixture" (69). Lines 71–74 are parenthetical.

152–157 From Xylander's Plutarch, *De Socratis genio*, 592 f. See Schoell, p. 234.

160–179 This paragraph refers to the gossip and curiosity concerning Lady Frances' contention that she was still a virgin at the time of the dissolution of her marriage with

Essex. She was married to Somerset with her hair flowing loose, the sign of a virgin bride.

174–175 It is usually Envy that is endowed with the "squint-eye." See note to *De Guiana*, 41.

180–188 From Plutarch, *De curiositate*, 520 f. See Schoell, p. 235.

Andromeda Liberata.

40 *populare*) A substantive: the "common people." Cf. l. 170.

53–92 This statement of the fable is taken from Comes, at the beginning of *Myth.*, VIII, 25, "De Andromeda." See Schoell, p. 196.

143 This is one of the lines which landed Chapman in trouble. See the conclusion to his *Justification*, where he tries to get out of his difficulty by asking whether the adjective, "barren," can ever be applied to a man. The reference, if taken personally, must have seemed applicable to the Earl of Essex, whom the Lady Frances in her divorce proceedings had accused of impotency.

171 *Rhamnusia*) Nemesis; see note to *Epic.*, 358.

196–198 Chapman is here using a favorite quotation of Plutarch's. The saying is from Euripides (see the *Justification* where it is quoted), but Chapman got it from Plutarch. Schoell (p. 235) quotes from *De curiositate*, 520 b, and *De Herodoti malignitate*, 855 c.

213–214 See the gloss to l. 69 of *A Hymn to our Sauiour*, where Chapman quotes the Greek phrase he is here translating.

216 *the only glasse*) i.e. Cupping-glass (199) to draw off the concentrated evil humors of men.

218 *triple world*) Earth, sea, hell. See *H. in C.*, 2–3.

219 *Enyo*) The goddess of war.

291 *Eleutherean*) Free. See note to *Eug.*, 1028.

321–344 Translated from Ficino, *In Convivium, Oratio* v, cap. viii. Schoell quotes the second half of this passage (p. 15).

369 *Epiphonem*) A rhetorical term for a striking reflection that sums up the sense of a discourse.

401–418 From Ficino, *In Convivium, Oratio* II, cap. viii. See Schoell, p. 16.

451 *Long'd of his Conquests, for the latest shocke:*) Longed for his conquest, for the ultimate encounter.

487–497 From Ficino, *In Convivium, Oratio* II, cap. viii and VI, xiv. See Schoell, p. 17. This was to prove an unfortunate passage for Chapman; see *Justification, Dial.*, 97 *seq.* If Chapman is making any personal allusion in this passage, it is to the Earl of Essex, whom Lady Frances had charged with impotency. He might be considered a "Homicide," because he had not begotten a child (491–492). The whole speech of Perseus on Generation is certainly an *apologia* for Somerset's taking over Essex's wife.

519 *to*) Too.

523 *comprest*) See note to *O.B. of S.*, 78.6.

527 *rere banquet*) A sumptuous banquet; see the analogous term: rere-supper. It makes an antithesis with "fore ranne."

603 *Asterisme*) See note to *Epic.*, 325.

A FREE AND / OFFENCELES / Iustification, / OF / A LATELY PVBLISHT / and most maliciously misinter- / *preted Poeme:* / ENTITVLED / Andromeda liberata. / *Veritatem qui amat, emat.* / (*Device:* "VERITAS * FILIA * TEMPORIS *") / LONDON, / Printed for LAVRENCE L'ISLE and are to be sold / at his shop in *Pauls* church-yard at the signe / of the *Tigers-head*. 1614. /

*–***⁴. 4to.

Contents: (*₁ʳ) Title; *₂ʳ–**₁ᵛ, "A Free . . . Iustification" (prose); **₂ʳ–(**₄ᵛ) "Dialogus" (verse).

Not entered.

Copies Used: Victoria and Albert   Dyce 2047   Bodleian   Art 4⁰ A 36

Punctuation Revised.

Dialogus. 65 Final semicolon instead of period   87 *saile,* instead of *saile.*

The occasion for the composition of this tract and poem in defence of *Andromeda Liberata* is amply described in the work itself. That poem had not only disgraced the poet with the Essex faction, but presumedly had displeased Somerset himself. This Chapman indicates in lines 5–10 of the Dialogus, or poem, which follows the prose *Justification:* the lines which have Rumor say flatly, "Your *Perseus* is displeasd. . . ." In this sequel to *Andromeda Liberata* Chapman tries to defend specifically the passages which had given offence. Evidently he succeeded in mollifying Somerset, if indeed that gentleman had ever been seriously offended, for at the end of the same year, 1614, we find him dedicating to the Earl as a New Year's gift the first twelve books of the *Odysseys.*

Justification.

51–54 Of the Lamiae: from Plutarch's *De curiositate,* 515 f., Xylander's Latin translation. See Schoell, p. 236.

78–79 *Amicus enim Animal facile mutabile*) Schoell (p. 73) refers to Plutarch's version of this saying from Plato in *De animi tranquillitate,* 474 e.

89–94 Of the spider: Schoell draws attention (p. 53) both to the discussion of the adage, "Ex se fingit velut Araneus," in Erasmus, and (p. 236) to its source in Plutarch's *De Iside & Osiride,* 358 f. He also compares this passage with *Rev. of Bussy,* II. i. 142 seq.

96–97 *qui nimium emulget elicet sanguinem*) Adaptation of a Hebrew proverb found in the *Adages* of Erasmus. See Schoell, pp. 45–46.

119 *Hic Rhodus, hic saltus*) An adage to be found in Erasmus; see Schoell, p. 44. Of a young man who was supposed to have made tremendous leaps while he was at Rhodes: here is Rhodes, here leap. Chapman says, "Here is my poem, all you have to do is read it."

Pereas, qui calamitates hominum colligis. Eur:) Quoted by Plutarch in *De Herodoti malignitate,* 855 c. Schoell, p. 73.

Dialogus.

Pheme is Rumor; Theodines is Chapman himself, divinely-inspired.

4 From the adage, "In portu impingere," found in Erasmus. See Schoell, p. 46, and compare *Bussy,* I. i. 33, *Mons. d'Olive,* I. i. 174–175, and *T. of P.,* 942.

5 *your Perseus*) Somerset.

12 Cf. *H. in C.,* 368, and *O.B. of S.,* 109.7–8.

43–44 In other words, Chapman had not yet secured Somerset as his Homeric patron.

61–74 Adapted from Plutarch's *De Herodoti malignitate,* 856 c. See Schoell, p. 237.

70 *peruiall*) See note to *Ep. to Roydon, O.B. of S.,* II.

83–92 From Plutarch's *De communibus notitiis,* 1083 d. See Schoell, p. 238. Parrott noted the source for a practically identical passage in *Caesar and Pompey,* I. ii. 272–277.

87 *dissite*) Situated distant. Cf. Chapman, *Od.,* VII, 270.

97 *those you reckon Homicides*) See *And. Lib.,* 487–496 and note.

103–118 The argument of this passage and the quotation in the gloss to 111 are taken from Ficino's commentary on the *Symposium, Oratio* VI, cap. xiv. See Schoell, pp. 17–18, except that Chapman's text reads "Audacior autem" instead of "Audacior quidem," and omits the "autem" after "credelior."

119 *Bound to a barraine rocke*) See *And. Lib.,* 143 and note.

128–129 and gloss. This gloss and gloss 7 of *H. in N.* are the only two times Chapman mentions Comes by name. For his great debt to the *Mythologiae,* see notes to *S. of N.,* and *And. Lib., passim.*

PRO VERE, / AVTVMNI / LACHRYMAE. / Inscribed To The Immortal / Memorie of the most Pious and Incom- / parable Souldier, Sir Horatio Vere, / Knight: *Besieged, and distrest in* / Mainhem. /

Pers: Sat: IV.

———— ——— *da verba & decipe neruos*

By Geo: Chapman.

(*chain line; type device; chain line*)

LONDON, / Printed by *B. Alsop* for *Th. Walkley*, and are / to be sold at his shop at the Signe of the *Eagle* and *Child* in *Britaines Burse*. / 1622. /

A–B⁴; C². 4to.

Contents: (A₁ʳ) Title; A₂ʳ–A₃ᵛ "To the Most Worthily Honored . . . Robert, Earle of Somerset;" (A₄ʳ)–C₁ᵛ "Pro Vere, Autumni Lachrymae;" C₂ blank.

Entered: 8 no.

Copies Used: British Museum   Huth 84   Victoria and Albert   Dyce 2049   Harvard College 14424. 14. 80* (White copy)

Punctuation Revised.

Ep. Ded. 1 Comma instead of semicolon after *Good*   9 Final comma instead of period

Pro Vere. 24 Final period deleted   42 *Danger)* *Danger* instead of *Danger* (*Danger*

The circumstances which lay behind this appeal to King James to send aid to Sir Horace Vere are described by Clements R. Markham in *The Fighting Veres*, Part II, Ch. 3. The trouble had started in 1619, when the Bohemians, dissatisfied with their Hapsburg rulers, had offered the crown to the Elector Palatine, Frederic V, who, as prince, had married Elizabeth, daughter of King James of England, in 1613. (See Chapman's *Hymn to Hymen*.) The crowning of Frederick and Elizabeth as King and Queen of Bohemia had roused all Catholic Germany with the determination to take Frederick's hereditary dominions from him. At the same time it was arranged between the Emperor and the Archdukes "that a Spanish army under Spinola should march from Brussels and overrun the Palatinate." James reluctantly consented to let Count Dohna, Frederick's envoy, raise a body of volunteers in England for the defence of the Palatinate. Sir Horace Vere was offered the command of a very distinguished regiment, limited to 2,200 men. On 29 October, 1620, Frederick and Elizabeth were made fugitives by the Battle of Prague, and since James refused to let his daughter come home to England, Prince Maurice received them at the Hague. Winter set in and Vere was intrenched at Manheim whence he sent home for help to keep his position. This help was refused, and by the spring of 1621 Vere and his men were left entirely deserted. Frederick visited Manheim and Heidelberg early in 1622, but on 13 June, 1622, he left Manheim for good, following on the failure of Lord Chichester's negotiations with Tilly for a truce. This left the English force to its fate, divided between the garrisons of Manheim, Heidelberg, and Frankenthal, under the leadership of Vere, Sir Gerard Herbert, and Sergeant-major General Burrough. Heidelberg was first besieged and fell Aug.–Sept., then Manheim, which was occupied by 1,400 men without money or supplies. Vere capitulated at the end of September. "He and his brave garrison marched out with all the honors of war," and retired to the Hague. Burrough held out at Frankenthal till April 14, 1623, when he capitulated on receiving orders from home. Chapman's poem, therefore, was written and printed in the summer of 1622. For further details of the situation, see Grimestone's *General History of the Netherlands* (ed. 1627, p. 1467).

Epistle Dedicatory.

This is Chapman's first greeting to Somerset after his release from the Tower.

3 Lord Somerset and Lady Frances were retired to their country estate.

Pro Vere.

2 This play of words on "Vere" as "Spring" is carried through to the end of the poem: 1.95. The phrase "spring of man" was used of Prince Henry in *Epic.*, 461.

2–3 The printer has dropped out at least one couplet between these lines; the omission is marked with asterisks.

7 *This*) That England can not furnish others like Vere.

30 *Gadcs*) Tartessus, a city in southwest Spain.

36–38 and gloss. 1) *Lord Norris.* It would seem that "Lord Norris" must be a mistake. Sir John Norris (1547?-1597) was the soldier fit to be grouped with the Veres. His father, Henry Norris, baron Norris of Rycote (d. 1601) was not a military man. He was succeeded by his grandson, Francis, who was made Viscount Thame and Earl of Berkshire 28 Jan., 1620–21, an irascible man but not a warrior, who shot himself 29 Jan., 1622–23.

2) Sir *Francis Vere* (d. Aug. 1609). See *H. in C.*, 334–347 and note.

3) Sir *Horatio Vere*, brother to Sir Francis (d. 2 May, 1635). He was the first peer created by Charles I: Lord Vere, Baron of Tilbury.

49–64 From Plutarch's *De fortuna Romanorum*, 317 e. See Schoell, pp. 221–222 and 239; also, Parrott's note to *Caesar and Pompey*, II. iv. 129–142, where the same elaborate simile appears.

55 PAPHIAN *Queene*) Venus.

56 *still-giglet*) Still wanton.

59 *Ceston*) Venus' girdle: the word taken straight from the Latin Plutarch.

81 SARDANAPALIAN *Sties*) The conventional legendary picture, now exploded, of the court life surrounding Sardanapalus (or Asurbanipal), the most successful and prosperous ruler of ancient Assyria.

A Iustification / OF A / STRANGE ACTION OF / NERO; / In burying with a solemne / FVNERALL, / One of the cast HAYRES of his / Mistresse POPPAEA. / (*chain line*) / Also a iust reproofe of a Romane smell- / Feast, being the fifth Satyre of / IVVEN- ALL. / (*chain line*) / Translated by *George Chapman.* / (*type line*) / Imprinted at London by THO. HARPER. / M.DC.XXIX. /

A–D⁴. 4to.

Contents: (A₁ʳ) Title; A₂ʳ–A₃ʳ Epistle to Richard Hubert, Esq.; A₃ᵛ–(A₄ᵛ) "To the Reader;" B₁ʳ–C₁ᵛ The Funerall Oration; C₂ʳ–(D₄ᵛ) D. . . . Iuuenalis, Lib. 1. Sat. 5. pp. (8)+24. Pagination starts B₁ʳ.

Not entered.

Copies Used: British Museum C.30.e.5.   Victoria and Albert   Dyce 2050   Bodleian   Mason H. 69.   Harvard College 14424. 14. 45*

Epistle Dedicatory.

The only Richard Hubert I have been able to discover is the brother of Sir Francis Hubert, who dedicated to Richard his poetical *Historie of Richard the Second* in the same year that this book of Chapman's was published (1629). Both dedications make R.H. seem a sober man "of parts," but there is no means of establishing the identity of Chapman's friend.

10–11 *the great defender of little labours*) Vergil, *Georgics*, IV. 6.

18 *following Translation*) The Fifth Satire of Juvenal, not included in the present edition.

21–22 *a preparation to the iustification of my ensuing intended Translations*) There is no record of what translations Chapman was engaged in so late in life, but it sounds as if they were to be in the realm of satire.

The Funerall Oration.

Poppaea was born 31 A.D. She was married 1) to Rufus Crispinus, 2) to Otho, Nero's friend, 3) to Nero. She was a dazzling and sophisticated lady, six or seven years older than Nero, who became acquainted with her when he was about twenty. Her hair was famous for its glorious amber colour. She died 65 A.D., reputedly of a kick that Nero gave her when she was annoyed at him for coming home later than she expected; the kick brought about a miscarriage. Their baby daughter had died, and they had no heirs.

34 Quotation from Seneca, found in the *Adages* of Erasmus. (Schoell, p. 44.) Erasmus had it from the *Sentences* of Publius Syrus.

46 seq. *I am not ignorant that hayre is noted by many as an excrement*) A current conception, as in Burton's *Anat. of Mel.*, when he is defining "Expulsion," (Part 1, Sect. 1, Mem. 11, Subs. v): "*Expulsion* is a power of *nutrition*, by which it expels all superfluous excrements, and reliques of meat and drink, by the guts, bladder, pores; as by purging, vomiting, spitting, sweating, urine, hairs, nails, &c." Cf. *Merchant of Venice*, 111. ii. 87.

57 *Sublimate*) Mercury sublimate.

75–82 Compare Vicary's *Anatomy* where the same explanation is given of the formation of hair: a hardening of excess vapor from the brain.

119 *the purple hair of Nisus*) Nisus, king of Megara and father of Scylla. The story is that "Scylla having fallen in love with Minos when the latter was besieging Megara, pulled out the purple or golden hair which grew on the top of her father's head, and on which his life depended. Nisus thereupon died, and Minos obtained possession of the city. Minos, however, was so horrified at the conduct of the unnatural daughter, that he ordered her to be fastened to the poop of his ship, and drowned her in the Saronic Gulf." See Comes, *Myth.*, VIII, xii, "De Scylla & Charybdi."

(To the Author of *Nennio*)

This complimentary sonnet is attached to the volume bearing the following title-page:

NENNIO / Or / A Treatise of Nobility: / Wherein is discoursed what true / Nobilitie is, with such qualities as are requi / red in a perfect Gentleman. / Written in Italian by that famous Doctor / and worthy Knight Sir John Bap- / tista Nenna of Bari. / Done into English by William / Iones Gent. / (*device*) / Printed by P.S. for Paule Linley, and Iohn / Flasket, and are to be sold at their shop in *Paules* / churchyard, at the Signe of the / blacke Beare, 1595.

A–Cc⁴; Dd²; extra leaf unsigned; ¶².
Chapman's sonnet appears on the extra leaf at the end, *recto*.

This treatise is an allegorical debate between certain ladies and gentlemen on the character of true nobility, in which judgment is finally given "that the nobilitie of the minde, is farre more true, and far more perfect, then the nobility of blood conioyned with riches."
William Jones, the translator, also translated Lipsius, "Six books of Politickes on Civil Doctrine, . . . " 1594.

1. *Nennio*) Was one of the gentlemen of the company which was disputing the nature of nobility. He was "indifferently chosen by them, for that purpose, who after he had heard the reasons debated on both sides, shoulde by his wisdome, giue iudgement and sentence, from which they promised they would not appeale, but friendly rest satisfied therewith."

4 *French*) I have not located the French translation of *Nennio*.

De Guiana.

These verses are prefixed to the volume:

A Relation of the / second Voyage to / Guiana. / Perfourmed and written in the yeare 1596. / By Lawrence Keymis, Gent. / (*device*) / Imprinted at London by Thomas Dawson, / dwelling at the three Cranes in the Vintree, / and are there to be solde. / 1596.

A^4; A^4–G^4. 4to.

Chapman's poem is printed in the second A signature. A_1^v–(A_4^r). The poem is only signed "G.C." and was first ascribed to Chapman by George Steevens, see Nichols' *Literary Illustrations*, Vol. VII, p. 121, and there seems no doubt as to the correctness of the ascription. For the three copies examined, the following symbols are used to note variants in the printing of Chapman's poem:

British Museum G.7169 A	C.32.g.36 B	Bodleian 4°L 80 Art C
77 that deserueth nought; A, C		that deserues not ought; B
80 hide,	A	hide B, C
103 rage,	A	rage: B, C
111 store,	A	store; B, C
114 combine.	A	combine; B, C

B is the corrected version throughout, and is here followed. The punctuation is more characteristic, and line 77 is revised to avoid a repetition of the last word in the line.

Punctuation Revised.

68 Final comma instead of period semicolon instead of comma semicolon instead of period instead of parenthesis after *this*   73 Final semicolon instead of period   77 Final comma instead of semicolon   166 Final parenthesis added   75 Final   94 Final   167 Comma

Lawrence Keymis, to whose account of the 1596 voyage to Guiana Chapman prefixes these verses, was a student of geography and mathematics as well as an explorer. He had accompanied Raleigh to Guiana in 1595 and led the expedition of 1596; he was imprisoned with Raleigh in 1603. His end was tragic. In 1618, having led the expedition up-country in Guiana during which Raleigh's son was killed, he was rebuked by Raleigh on his return to the coast, and killed himself.

Chapman's plea to Queen Elizabeth to accept Guiana arises from the fact that she would not see Raleigh after his return nor interest herself at all in his voyage or in giving money for the colonization of Guiana. Since he had done no plundering while he was there, some people even said he had never been there.

The poem is unique among Chapman's for being in blank verse.

18 *seq.* These lines rephrase Keymis' chief argument for England's acceptance of Guiana. "For the plentie of golde that is in this countrey, beeing nowe knowen and discovered, there is no possibilitie for them to keepe it: on the one side they coulde feele no greater miserie, nor feare more extremitie, then they were sure to finde, if the Spaniards prevayled, who perforce doe take all things from them, using them as their slaves, to runne, to rowe, to bee their guides, to cary their burthens, and that which is worst of all, to bee content, for safetie of their lives, to leave their women, if a Spaniard chance but to set his eye on any of them to fancie her: on the other-side they could hope for, nor desire no better state and usage, then her Majesties gracious government, and Princely vertues doe promise, and assure unto them. . . . The case then so standing, is it not meere wretchedness in us, to spend our time, breake our sleepe, and waste our braines, in cavilling false title to defraud a neighbour of halfe an acre of lande: whereas here whole shires of fruitfull rich grounds, lying now waste for want of people, do prostitute themselves unto us, like a faire and beautifull woman, in the pride and floure of desired yeeres."

19 Chapman repeated this image two years later in *Hero & Leander*, V. 197–198: Neptune up-rose, "for haste his forehead hit Gainst heauens hard Christall." Cf. Horace, *Odes*, I. i. 36, "Sublimi feriam sidera vertice;" also Robert Herrick, *The bad season makes the poet sad*, 14, "Knock at a star with my exalted head."

41 *squint-eyd Enuies feet,*) Cf. *Iliads:* "To the Reader," 77, and *And. Lib.:* Ep. Ded., 174–175. The epithet for Envy had been used by Sylvester in his translation of Du Bartas (ed. 1608, p. 284). The idea comes from Plutarch's essay, *De invidio et odio.* "But envy has only one sort of object, the felicity of others. Whence it becomes in-

finite, and, like an evil or diseased eye, is offended with everything that is bright."
Prosperity, being compared with the sun, Envy retires unable to face it.

56–62 Parrott points out Chapman's repetition of this image in *Byron's Consp.*, I. i. 183–
192, and *Chabot*, v. i. 16–19. The image, with variations, is one of Chapman's favor-
ites: cf. also *O.B. of S.*, stanzas 44–45; *In Seianum*, 33–44; *Friendship*, 6–10; *Epic.*,
349–351; *Eug.*, 349–354. Chapman is very likely to have been impressed by Sylvester's
treatment of the same image in the Third Day of the First Weeke (ed. 1608, pp. 66–67).

> And all the highest Heav'n-approaching Rocks
> Contribute hither with their snowie locks:
> For, soon as *Titan*, having run his Ring,
> To th'ycie climates bringeth back the spring;
> On their rough backs he melts the hoarie heaps,
> Their tops grow green; and down the water leaps
> On every side, it foames, it roars, it rushes,
> And through the steep and stony hills it gushes,
> Making a thousand Brooks; whereof, when one
> Perceives his fellow striving to be gone;
> Hasting his course, he him accompanies;
> After, another and another hies,
> All in one race; ioynt-losing all of them
> Their Names and Waters in a greater Stream:
> And he that robs them, shortly doth deliver
> Himself and his into a larger River:
> And that, at length, how ever great and large
> (Lord of the Plain) doth in some Gulf discharge
> His parent-tribute to *Oceanus*,
> According to th'Eternall *Rendez-vous*.

65 *triple worlde*) Earth, sea, and hell. See *H. in C.*, 2–3.

123–144 He is describing Raleigh. As Miss Bradbrook says in *The School of Night*, p. 142,
"Here Raleigh is the soul of England: and England's disregard of him is like the cor-
ruption of natural gifts by perverted senses."

159 *Argolian*) From Argo, the name of the famous ship which carried Jason on his expedi-
tion to recover the Golden Fleece.

161 Cf. Keymis: "The rivers, as also others neerer Raleana, doe fall out of the plaines of
this empire over rocks, as the river Caroli doeth into Raleana."

Peristeros: or the male Turtle.

This poem is one of the "Poeticall Essaies" attached to Robert Chester's allegorical poem
Loves Martyr (1601). The subject of the allegory and of the "essaies" following is the
Phoenix and the Turtle; and since the contributors numbered among themselves such dis-
tinguished persons as William Shakespeare, Ben Jonson, John Marston, and George Chap-
man, the volume is one of considerable fame, and the identity of the Phoenix and the Turtle
a matter of most interesting conjecture. The second part of the volume is now readily
accessible as reprinted in The Shakespeare Head Quartos VII, edited by Bernard H. Newdi-
gate (1937). The only original copy of the book now existing in England (British Museum)
is a re-issue of 1611, and bears the following title-page for the second part, on (Z₁ʳ).

HEREAFTER / FOLLOW DIVERSE / Poeticall Essaies on the former Sub- / iect; viz:
the Turtle and Phoenix. / Done by the best and chiefest of our / moderne writers, with
their names sub- / scribed to their particular workes: neuer before extant. / And (now first)
consecrated by them all generally, / to the loue and merite of the true-noble Knight, / Sir
Iohn Salisburie. / Dignum laude virum Musa vetat mori. / (*Device:* Anchora spei) / MDCI.

Chapman's poem, *Peristeros: or the male Turtle*, comes on p. 176, Aa₂ᵛ.

The theme of Chester's allegorical poem is the mating of the Phoenix and the Turtle so that another Phoenix may spring from them. As the symbol of the turtle indicates, it is a poem in honor of conjugal fidelity, and the identity of the married couple here celebrated has been variously guessed: see Shakespeare, *Poems*, Variorum, ed. Hyder Rollins, pp. 566–583. The problem of interpretation is still unsolved, despite Newdigate's recent studies plausibly identifying the Phoenix with Lucy Harington, Countess of Bedford. The poems were probably written by 1600: Jonson's Epode certainly that early since its last line was quoted in *England's Parnassus*, printed that year.

Punctuation Revised.

8 Final parenthesis added

Title: *Peristeros*, the masculine form of the Greek word for pigeon, περιστερά.

8, 11, and 12 The quotation marks before these lines set them apart as *sententiae*.
17 *Analisde*) Resolved, reduced to its elements. The first illustration in the *N.E.D.* of this use of the ppl.a. Cf. *H. & L.*, VI. 256.

(Sonnet to Walsingham: *All Fools*.)

Considerable doubt has existed as to the authenticity of this sonnet which appears only in the Wrenn copy of *All Fools* (1605), University of Texas Library. In that copy it is inserted between A₂ and A₃, and the leaf is smaller than the others, so that its margins have been extended to the required size, framed by a later stiffer paper. This copy was the one from which Collier worked when preparing the play for the new edition of Dodsley, *Select Collection of Old Plays* (1825), and the sonnet is there reprinted for the first time. Thomas Marc Parrott, in his edition of Chapman's *Comedies* (1914), follows T. J. Wise in considering the sonnet a Collier forgery and hence prints it only in his textual notes: see pp. 725–727, and his articles in *Notes and Queries*, May 6, 1906, and *Athenaeum*, July 27, 1908. However, Professor Parrott now writes me that he has come to accept the sonnet as genuine and suggests that it might have been written for *May-Day* (1611) or *The Widow's Tears* (1612). He makes this suggestion to account for Chapman's statement in the prose dedication to Walsingham of *The Conspiracy and Tragedy of . . . Byron* (1608) that he knows Walsingham to dislike "these unprofitable rites of Dedication (which disposition in you hath made me hitherto dispense with your right in my other impressions)." He would scarcely have made this remark if he had already dedicated *All Fools* to Walsingham.

After considerable hesitation, I am including this sonnet in the present edition of Chapman's *Poems* for the perhaps over-simple reason that it sounds so very much like Chapman. Constant reading of his verse over an extended period of time makes it sound more and more authentic rather than anything cooked up out of his customary diction and phrases. One may cite, for instance, the similarity of the image in the second line in the sonnet, "The least allow'd birth of my *shaken braine;*" to the first line of the "Corollarium ad Principem," *Teares of Peace*, "Thus *shooke* I this abortiue from my *Braine;*" a similarity which seems to arise from a genuine individuality in habits of thought rather than a wilful imitation which would have struck a closer correspondence of phraseology.

Bibliographically, however, this sonnet stands on as uncertain ground as ever. The paper is of the right period, but that is saying very little. It is only a personal guess that the sonnet probably was first printed as an extra leaf for some other quarto than the one in which it is now found and was cut down some time when that quarto was bound, that subsequently it was transferred to its present position. The content of the sonnet seems to indicate that it was prefixed to a comedy, certainly to one of Chapman's lighter compositions as distinct from his Homeric translations which he was always proud to present to possible patrons. Parrott's suggestion of *May-Day* or *The Widow's Tears* would fit. The printing of extra leaves of dedicatory sonnets is not without precedent in Chapman's career: see notes to the sonnets to Cranborne, Philips, and Rochester, *Iliads* (1611). In the present edition the sonnet is printed under the caption of *All Fools* only for purposes of convenience, because it is only known as included in the Wrenn quarto of that play. As Mr. Greg says, the problem could probably be settled finally in favor of the authenticity of the sonnet only if it turned up in some other Chapman quarto, but so far no one has succeeded in finding it elsewhere. Nor is there any great likelihood that, even if the sonnet is genuine, it will be found elsewhere, for—after all—there are only a few known copies of the *Iliads* containing the three extra dedicatory sonnets just mentioned. It may even have been that the sonnet was printed only for a single copy of a Chapman quarto, that which he intended to present to Walsingham himself.

For Chapman's relations with Walsingham, see the dedications by him and Blount of *Hero and Leander* (1598) and his dedication of *The Conspiracy and Tragedy of . . . Byron* (1608).

In Seianum.

These verses are prefixed to the volume:

SEIANUS / HIS FALL. / Written / by / BEN: IONSON. /

> Mart. Non hic Centaures, non Gorgonas, Harpyasq, /
> Inuenies: Hominem pagina nostra sapit. /

AT LONDON / Printed by G. Elld, for Thomas / Thorpe. 1605. /

This play was entered 2 Nov. 1604 to Edward Blount, and was transferred 6 Aug. 1605 to Thorpe. It was certainly printed before 27 Nov. 1605, when Northumberland was committed to the Tower.

¶⁴; A–M⁴; N². Chapman's poem is printed on ¶₃ʳ–A₁ᵛ.
The title page exists in two states: the first with the spelling "Elld," and the second with "Ellde."

Herford and Simpson used seven copies of the play in preparing their edition of *Ben Jonson*. They note (IV, 33), "The changes in the preliminary sheet are in Chapman's long poem of commendation, and show Jonson's scrupulous care to reproduce the punctuation and emphatic capitals of the manuscript." The corrections certainly seem to be more carefully made than in any texts for which Chapman was himself responsible. In noting these changes, the designation of the copies made by Herford and Simpson is here followed.

British Museum 644.b.53, used as a basis for the present text	A	T. J. Wise, on large paper	C
Bodleian, Malone 222.7	B₁	Dyce Collection, Heber copy	D₁
Bodleian, Malone 189.6	B₂	Dyce Collection	D₂
		Dyce Collection, Roxburghe copy	D₃

To which group is here added the Yale University Library copy, Y

B₁, D₂, D₃, Y	A, B₂, C, D₁		B₁, D₂, D₃, Y	A, B₂, C, D₁
¶₃ᵛ (6) 30 Semicircle	Semi-circle	¶₄ʳ (21) 81 others	Others
(7) 31 Sphaere	Sphaere,	(29) 89 one	One
(8) 32 Liues,	Liues:	(30) 90 another	Another
(18) 42 And . . . waters	And, . . . waters,	(31) 91 life,	Life
¶₄ʳ (3) 63 eye . . . flame	eye, . . . flame,	knowne.	knowne:
(5) 65 truly,	truly	(32) 92 Degrees,	Degrees.
(6) 66 inspireth,	inspireth:	(36) 96 deseruing.	deseruing:
(7) 67 vnduly,	vnduly		

To this list, given by Herford and Simpson in *Ben Jonson*, IV, pp. 33–34, should be added:

¶₃ᵛ (30) 54 presence	Presence
¶₄ʳ (28) 88 emminence	emminence,

The second group of copies (A, B₂, C, D₁) is the corrected version.

See Herford and Simpson, *Ben Jonson: The Man and his Work*, II, pp. 4–5, for the argument that Chapman was the "second pen" in the first, unpublished, version of *Sejanus*.

1–4 Jonson used a great stock of classical sources for this play, though the chief may be said to be the *Annals* of Tacitus.

30 *The Semi-circle of Seianus life,*) Since Sejanus was killed, his life did not come full circle.

33–44 See note to *De Guiana*, 56–62.

49–52 *Seianus* was Jonson's first surviving tragedy, performed at the Globe in 1603. In the "Apologetic Dialogue" of the *Poetaster* (1601) he had announced his intention of turning to tragedy.

53–80 From Plutarch's essay *De profect. virtut. sent.*, 77 b, 81 c, d, e, in Xylander's translation, including the reference to Aeschylus. See Schoell, pp. 228–239.

85–92 From the same essay, 78 d. See Schoell, p. 229.

107 *expiscation*) The act of fishing out. This is the first illustration of the word in the *N.E.D.*

113 *CYRRHAN poet*) Apollo. See *O.B. of S.*, 2.1 and marginal gloss.

123–134 From Plutarch's *Symposiacon*, Lib. 1, *Quaestio octava*, 626 b. See Schoell, p. 70.

124 *the Sensor of our Sense*) The nose, which does the sensing. Cf. *O.B. of S.*, 31.3 and note.

136 *Arachnean*) Cf. *H. & L.*, IV. 121 and note.

137 *Diadems*) In the meaning of "monarchs," not given in the *N.E.D.*

140 *Chancelor*) Ellesmere, Lord Egerton. See sonnet to *Iliads* (1609–11).

141 *Treasurer*) Thomas Sackville, first Earl of Dorset, author of the *Induction* and co-author of *Gorboduc*.

142 *Northumber*) Henry Percy, Ninth Earl: the scholarly gentleman who had been referred to once by Chapman in his Epistle to Roydon, *Shadow of Night*. On the 27 Nov. 1605 he was sent to the Tower, not to be released till 1621.

143 *Worc'ster*) Edward Somerset, Fourth Earl, who in 1601 had become the patron of the former Pembroke's Men when they settled at the Rose under Henslowe and took Worcester's name.

144 *Northampton*) Henry Howard. See notes to sonnet, *Iliads* (1609–11). He turned out to be Jonson's chief enemy in the Sejanus affair rather than his friend.

145 *Deuonshire*) Charles Blount, Eighth Lord Mountjoy, created Earl of Devonshire in 1604 two years before his death. At the time of this poem he was enveloped in the scandal attendant on his marriage with Lady Rich, Penelope d'Evereux.

147 *Salisburie*) Robert Cecil who, with Suffolk, came to the help of Chapman and Jonson later in the same year. See sonnet, *Iliads* (1609–11).

151 *Suffolke*) Thomas Howard, Lord Chamberlain, who came to the help of Jonson and Chapman at the time of the *Eastward Ho* imprisonment later in this year, 1605. But it is clear from these lines that Chapman already owed him a debt of gratitude for having intervened in some theatrical trouble. If one is inclined to wonder at Chapman's later blind devotion to Somerset and his Lady, it may be well to recall this double indebtedness to the Countess of Somerset's father, Thomas Howard.

To his deare Friend, Beniamin Ionson his Volpone.

These verses are prefixed to the volume:

BEN: IONSON / his / VOLPONE / Or / THE FOXE. / —Simul & iucunda, & idonea dicere vitae. / Printed for Thomas Thorppe. / 1607. /

Chapman's poem appears on (A₃ʳ).

To . . . M. Io. Fletcher concerning his Pastorall.

These verses were prefixed to *The Faithful Shepherdess* in all five editions of the play: 1609 (?), 1629, 1634, 1656, 1665. The title-page of the first edition is as follows:

THE / FAITHFVLL / Shepheardesse. / By IOHN FLETCHER. / (*device*) / Printed at

London for R. Bonian / and H. Walley, and are to be sold at / the spred Eagle over against the / great North dore of S. Paules. / n.d.

1609 is arrived at as the date for the first edition of this play because of the dedicatory poem to Sir William Skipworth who died in May 1610. In this edition Chapman's poem appears on the third unsigned leaf *verso* in the first folding.
(So Harvard and Dyce copies.)

The editors, Glover and Waller, of *Beaumont and Fletcher* (Cambridge, 1909), II, 520, take their text of the poem from the first edition, noting the following variants:
Title: concerning . . . play: omitted edd. 3, 4, 5
13 fals) fall,   edd. 3, 4, 5   18 limme) limbe,   edd. 4, 5

However, other variants that might be noted between the first and second editions are:
1 suerties) sureties   be taken) betaken (3rd ed. goes back to 1st)   7 thats) that's   8 whiffler) Wiffler (3rd ed. goes back to 1st)   12 art) Art   18 art) Art   22 pastorall;) Pastorall;   23 semi-Gods,) semi-gods,

8 *whiffler*) An attendant, armed with insignia of office, who makes way for a procession or spectacle. Cf. *Mons. d'Ol.*, III. ii. 167, and *Widow's Tears*, II. iv. 104.
16 Cf. *Ep. to Roydon, O.B. of S.*, Poetry . . . "which euery Cobler may sing to his patch."
17 *nifles*) Trifles.

(To Byrd, Bull, and Gibbons, on *Parthenia*.)

This sonnet, not before reprinted, is prefixed to the following volume of music:

Parthenia / or / the Maydenhead / of the first musicke that / euer was printed for the Virginalls. / Composed By three famous Masters: William Byrd, Dr: Iohn Bull, & Orlando Gibbons, / Gentilmen of his Maties: most Illustrious Chappell. / Ingrauen by William Hole. / for / Dorothie Euans. / Cum Priuilegio. / (*Engraved picture of lady at virginals.*) / Printed at London by G. Lowe and are to be soulde at his howse in Loathberry. / n.d. 1611?

I am indebted to Mr. Percy Simpson for calling my attention to this poem. There are no signatures in the volume, and Chapman's sonnet appears on the leaf following the title-page, along with one by Hugh Holland. The two sonnets are engraved in script with many contractions which have been expanded in this copy.

To . . . Nat. Field, and his Wether-cocke Woman.

These verses are prefixed to the following volume:

A / Woman is a Wea- / ther-cocke. / A New Comedy, / As it was acted before the King in WHITE-HALL. / And diuers times Priuately at the / White-Friers, By the Children of her / Maiesties Reuels. / Written by NAT: FIELD. / Si natura negat faciat Indignatio versum. / (*device:* HEB-DDIM-HEB-DDIEU-) / Printed at London, for Iohn Budge, and are to be sold at / the great South doore of Paules, and at Brittaines / Bursse. 1612. /

Chapman's poem is printed (A₄ʳ).

The names of Chapman and Field are primarily associated in the history of *Bussy d'Ambois*. Field's first recorded part is Chapman's Bussy. According to Parrott, Chapman first wrote this play in 1603 or 1604 for the Children of the Chapel, and about 1610 revised it for a new production at Whitefriars. Nat. Field acted in the later performance, and was probably responsible for transferring the revised version in MS. to the King's Men. (See *Tragedies*, p. 541.)

4 *Homers Sea-man*) Proteus.

A Hymne to Hymen.

Although this poem has been reprinted by Parrott along with the *Masque of the Middle Temple* on the marriage of the Princess Elizabeth in his edition of the *Comedies*, p. 458, it is repeated in the present volume of Chapman's poems as an independent poem. The wedding *Masque* and *Hymne* appeared in two editions, n.d. 1613–14. See notes on these two quartos, Parrott, *Comedies*, pp. 832–834. The title of the earlier edition, entered 27 January, 1613, is as follows:

The / Memorable Maske / of the two Honorable Houses or Inns of / Court; the Middle Temple, and / Lyncolns Inne. / As it was / performd before the King, at / White-Hall on Shroue Munday at night; / being the 15. of February. 1613. / At the Princely celebration of the most Royall / Nuptialls of the Palsgraue, and his thrice gratious / Princesse Eliza-beth. &c. / With a description of their whole show; in the manner / of their march on horse-backe to the Court from / the Maister of the Rolls his house: with all / their right Noble consorts, and most / showfull attendants. / Inuented, and fashioned, with the ground, and / speciall structure of the whole worke, / By our Kingdomes most Artfull and In-genious / Architect Innigo Iones. / Supplied, Aplied, Digested, and written, By Geo: Chapman. / At London, / Printed by G. Eld, for George Norton and are to be sould at his shoppe neere Temple-bar. /

The *Hymne* appears (E₄ʳ)–F₁ᵛ.

In the second edition, the title notes the change of printer: "Printed by F. K. for George Norton." The following variants are the only ones of any interest:

Eld	*F. K(ingston)*	*Eld*	*F. K(ingston)*
6 Dilating,	Dilating;	32 com close	come close
14 Midnights	Mid-nights	71 Twynn	Twyn
17 Loue-scorch't	Loue scorch't	74 Brests	Brest
31 richest weedes:	richest weedes;	82 styr;	styr,

In lines 17 and 74 the readings of the Eld printing are accepted; otherwise the text follows that of the Kingston edition.

Punctuation Revised.

81 Final semicolon instead of period.

For the sources of this poem, see Schoell's article, "George Chapman and the Italian Neo-Latinists," in *Mod. Phil.*, Vol. XIII, where it is shown that Chapman took his poem from two epithalamia written in the fifteenth century by the Italian poet, Jovianus Pontanus, for his daughters Aurelia and Eugenia, the third and fourth pieces in the third book of *De Amore Conjugali*. A widely issued edition of the works of Pontanus, in four volumes, was printed at Bale in 1556. Lines 9–31 of Chapman's hymn are a free translation from the epithalamium of Aurelia; the last 53 lines are chiefly from the epithalamium of Eugenia.

1–8 and the last two lines of the poem, which repeat the first, are the only lines in the poem to which Chapman can lay original claim.

2 *Parcaes tears*) The recent mourning for Prince Henry.

71 *These two, One Twyn are;*) See the *Masque* itself, 316–331 and marginal glosses, where much is made of the couple being twins because they were of one age and because the poet wished them to be as reciprocally sympathetic as the twins of which Hippocrates wrote; see also *A good woman*, 59 and note.

(To Christopher Brooke on his *Ghost of Richard the Third*.)

These verses are prefixed to the play:

The / Ghost / of / Richard / The Third. / Expressing himselfe in these / three Parts. /

    1. His Character.
    2. His Legend.
    3. His Tragedie.

Containing more of him then hath heretofore / shewed,; (*sic*) / either in Chronicles, Playes, or Poems. / Laurea Desidia praebetur nulla. / Printed by G. Eld: for L. Lisle: and are to be sold / in Paules Church-yard at the signe of the / Tygers head. 1614. /

Chapman's poem is printed on pp. 1–2, (A₂). It was not reprinted by Shepherd in his edition of Chapman's poems, but appeared in Payne Collier's edition of Brooke's poem for the Shakespeare Society, 1844.

Christopher Brooke is chiefly known as a member of Lincoln's Inn and the personal friend of John Donne. He numbered in his acquaintance most of the wits of the day and wrote verses, including the long poem, *The Ghost of Richard the Third*, which were collected and edited for the *Worthies Library* by Dr. Grosart, 1872. It is easy to believe that Christopher Brooke might really have been a "much lou'd Friend" of Chapman. The first stanza of his "Funerall Elegie on the Prince," 1613, is much attune with Chapman, both in sentiment and language:

> Those baser mindes, vnknowing, sensuall, rude,
> That measure contraries indifferently;
> Whose *Summum Bonum* is their sleepe and food,
> Preferring moments, to Eternitie;
> That GOOD, in ILL; and Soule, in Sence include;
> And beare no part in publique Miserie:
> May well bee call'd that many-headed Beast;
> The spawne of Earth, and lump but indigest.

1 *Smithfield*) The great London cattle market.

3 *swish swash Rippiers*) An obscure phrase, though not in its scornful implication. "Swish swash," (the sound of splashing water); "Rippiers," (peddlers who sell fish inland).

5 The meaning of the first sentence is saved by the correction of "House" to "Houre" in this line. The pronoun "they" refers to the Hackney ware, cheap poems, which if read carefully for only half an hour tire the discriminating reader.

10 *Bush Muse*) Muse of the ale-house.
    Hedge wine) Common wine.

11 *Will sell like good old Gascoigne*.) Payne Collier notes, "Chapman here seems to play upon the word, 'Gascoigne,' as the name of a wine, and as the name of our old English poet, George Gascoigne, who died in 1577, and whose poetical works were collected and published about 1572, and still more completely in 1587, 4to."

12 *Red-Oker men*) Men stained with red ochre, or reddle: reddle-men, dealers in reddle for staining sheep. The figure is in contrast to the poet who is trying to sell the royal purple matter of a king's life and death.

13 Cf. *To Fletcher*, 16, and *Ep. to Roydon, O.B. of S.* The chimney-sweep heralds his approach with a horn: note the dramatic use which Chapman makes of this fact in showing Lorenzo disguised as a sweep in *May-Day*.

22 *Orsadine*) The only illustration in the *N.E.D.* of this variant of "Arsedine," a gold colored alloy of copper and zinc, rolled into tinfoil for ornamental purposes.

(To Grimestone on his translation of Coeffetau's *Table of Humaine Passions*.)

These verses are prefixed to the volume:

A Table of Humaine / Passions. / With their Causes and Effects. / Written by yᵉ Reuerend Father in / God F. N. Coeffetau, Bishop of / Dardania, Councellor to yᵉ French / King in his Councels of Estate, / Suffragane and Administrator ge- / nerall of ye Bishopricke of Metz. / Translated into English by / Edw: Grimeston / Sergiant at Armes. / London, Printed by Nicholas Okes. / 1621

Chapman's poem is printed on a⁸. It was not reprinted in Shepherd's edition of Chapman's poems.

See F. S. Boas 1) "Edward Grimestone," *Mod. Phil.*, III, No. 4 (April, 1906), for a bibliographical sketch and detailed description of Grimestone's numerous works. 2) *Athenaeum*, Jan. 10, 1903, for the discovery of the influence of Grimestone's translation of Jean de Serre's *Inventaire Général de l'Histoire de France* (1607) on Chapman's historical plays.

12 *Dolon*) Trojan spy, *Iliad*, x.

(On the Tragic History of Hipolito and Isabella.)

These verses are prefixed to the volume:

THE / True History of the / Tragicke Loves of / HIPOLITO and JSABELLA / Neapolitans. / Englished / London Printed by Tho: Harper, and Nath: Feild, / 1628. / (Engraved title page.)

The poem is printed on A₂ʳ and is retained in the second edition of 1633: Thomas Harper. The second edition has the following variants: 2 line,) liue, 3 life,) life-Presse;) Presse, 8 Orbs,) Orbs Mooue:) moue. 10 Octauius;) Octauius,

An account of this book will be found in Mary Augusta Scott's *Elizabethan Translations from the Italian* (M.L.A., 1895–99). It is the source of Middleton's tragedy, *Women beware Women*.

10 *Sell (great Octauius;) and Augustus be,)* Referring to the promotion of the first Roman emperor from his original name of Octavius, to Augustus, the title given him by the senate. Chapman is still referring to the book itself, not the book-sellers.

Untraced quotations in England's Parnassus.

The excerpts are attributed to Chapman by the editors of the poetical phrase-book *England's Parnassus* (1600). If the ascription is correct, they show that in the nineties Chapman had tried his hand at using blank verse for poems of an amorous nature. These selections are not taken from any published work, and may simply have been written into the copy-book of some friend.

Epicures frugallitie and An Invective . . . against Mr. Ben: Johnson.

These poems appear in a manuscript book, dating about 1638, in the Bodleian Library, Ashmole 38. The date is ascertained by the tracing of leaves on ff. 165 and 166 "which J Nicholas Burghe did gather in St Johns wood by marribone parke pale on the 3d of June 1638—in the presence of mʳ Roger Dalton." Nicholas Burghe is described in the Ashmole Catalogue as having been a Poor Knight of Windsor in 1661, but nothing else is known about him.

The poem *Epicures frugallitie* appears on f. 10, and the *Invective* on ff. 16–18. The present copy follows as closely as possible the details of the original except in the capitalization of the first letters of the lines which, in the manuscript, is entirely haphazard. The cesural punctuation is reproduced from the manuscript; the punctuation at the ends of the lines has been added. Any exceptions are recorded in the notes.

In addition to these two poems, there is copied on ff. 5–6 a pair of poems, *The bodie* and *The Minde*, ascribed to "Geo: Chapman." These poems, however, were printed two years later than this copy book was put together in Ben Jonson's *Underwood* (1640), where they are part of a series of poems called *Eupheme*, addressed to the memory of Sir Kenelme Digby's wife. On f. 190 is copied the quatrain found on the folded engraving which accompanied the *Epicede*. (See that poem.) It bears the heading, "On Prince Henry," and is signed "G⁰: Chapman."

On f. 180 appear some humorous verses ascribed to "G C," but they do not sound like anything we know of Chapman. The rhyme runs as follows:

> On Habel Task a Contentious Solicitor Hauing
> A Great beard, and A wart on his nose and affectes
>   the word, Rationall,
>
> Here lies the beard, the wart and all
> of Habell Task the Rationall
> whether he's gone J cannott tell
> To heauen J hope? but yff to hell
> Questionles, by this his Jorney
> Heele gaine to bee the Diuells Atturney
> And then Finds looke fo't for he swears
> yee shall together all by'th eares
> And weare Hell richer then they fabell
> Beggard all should be by habell
>   finis G C:

This commonplace book contains the only known manuscript version of any poems by Chapman. Nicholas Burghe must either have got *Epicures frugallitie* and the *Invective* from a friend of the poet, or have been a young friend himself, for the *Invective* ends with the statement, "More then this neuer came to my hands, but lost in his sickenes."

Epicures frugallitie.

7 *Johnson*) Ben Jonson, thus proving the verses to be of late composition, after Chapman turned against his old friend in the mood of the *Invective*.

An Invective . . . against Mr. Ben: Johnson.

There is no way of dating this poem with any certainty. It could have been written any time after 1623, the year when the contents of Jonson's desk were destroyed by fire, and he wrote his *Execration Vpon Vulcan*. An invective such as this is highly unlikely to have been written on a death-bed, particularly when one knows the poet to have had Jonson's poem in hand as he wrote (see lines 98–107). Hence the final notation in the manuscript, "More then this neuer came to my hands, but lost in his sickenes," probably means nothing more than that whoever extricated the manuscript from Chapman's possessions at the time of his illness found no more than the portion here copied—if indeed, there ever had been any more of it. The poem reads like a fulmination written soon after reading Jonson's *Execration*, hence probably in 1623 or 1624. It has always been painful for biographers of both poets to consider this bitter conclusion of a friendship that had been so close in the early decade of the century. Even as late as 1618 Jonson was making favorable comments about Chapman to Drummond of Hawthornden. It seems not unlikely, however, that Johnson's scholarly strictures on the critical dicta contained in Chapman's preface to his *Whole Works of Homer* (1616) had come to Chapman's attention. If there was anything Chapman could not abide, it was being challenged on his scholarly information, and in this matter Jonson had the right of it. His reproving, though semi-affectionate, marginal notes are to be found in his copy of the *Homer* in the Fitzwilliam Museum, Cambridge.

The picture of arrogance and selfish conceit corresponds with the complaint which Inigo Jones held against Jonson as collaborator in the invention of court masques. It is possible that in writing this invective, Chapman was definitely taking sides with Jones. (Jones had prepared the pageant for *The Masque of the Middle Temple*.) The final quarrel between

478 THE POEMS OF GEORGE CHAPMAN

Jones and Jonson did not occur until 1631, but it had been brewing for a long time before.

21 *Admires*) Admirers'. Cf. l. 134. The final dash is in the MS. (See general introductory note to the manuscript poems on the handling of the punctuation.)

37 Question mark added after "redounds."

45 *a dust*) The adjective, "adust," in the physiological sense of dry or atrabilious.

51 *standing lakes*) See note to *Hymn to our Sauiour*, 108–109.

55 Cf. *A Fragment of the Teares of peace*, 23 and note.

61 The semicolon is in the MS.

80 *highest*) Emended from "Highes."

86 *ther*) Emended from "their."

98–107 These lines are a résumé of Jonson's own description of the contents of his desk, often in his own phrases. See *An Execration Vpon Vulcan*, 85–114.

> But in my Deske, what was there to accite
>   So ravenous, and vast an appetite?
> I dare not say a body, but some parts
>   There were of search, and mastery in the Arts.
> All the old *Venusine*, in *Poëtrie*,
>   And lighted by the *Stagerite*, could spie,
> Was there made English: with the Grammar too,
>   To teach some that, their Nurses could not doe,
> The puritie of Language; and among
>   The rest, my journey into *Scotland* song,
> With all th'adventures; Three bookes not afraid
>   To speake the Fate of the *Sicilian* Maid
> To our owne Ladyes; and in storie there
>   Of our fift *Henry*, eight of his nine yeare;
> Wherein was oyle, beside the succour spent,
>   Which noble *Carew, Cotton, Selden* lent:
> And twice-twelve-yeares stor'd up humanitie,
>   With humble Gleanings in Diuinitie;
> After the Fathers, and those wiser Guides
>   Whom Faction had not drawne to studie sides.

99 *Mastrie Jn the Artes;*) At this point in the MS. there is a marginal note which states, "Wm then Lord Chamberlayne and Earl of Pemb. made him Mr of Arts wth his Letter." The ceremony of his induction took place at Oxford, July 19, 1619.

100 *his English Grammare*) Finally written in the early thirties.

103 *his Journye Jnto Scotland*) 1618.

124 *Hercules Furens*) Seneca's tragedy.

125 *Biting the grene-cloth*) i.e. Defying the board of control of the king's household.

129 *wings*) Emended from "wing."

131 *Jmp*) Repair, as one does a bird's wings.

137 *two*) Emended from "tow."

142 *Candle Rents*) Rents from house-property, that constantly deteriorates. Cf. Chapman's translation of *Hesiod* 1, 584, and *May-Day*, I. i. 343.

167 *Wounder*) Wonder: speaking of the popularity and profit derived from Jonson's plays and publications.

169 *on*) One.

(To *M. Harriots*, accompanying *Achilles Shield*.)

This poem comes at the end of the volume which bears the following title-page:

ACHILLES / SHIELD. / Translated as the other seuen Bookes / of Homer, out of his eighteenth / booke of Iliades. / By George Chapman Gent. / (*device*: CONTRAHIT AVARITIA BELLVM) / LONDON / Imprinted by Iohn Windet, and are to be sold / at Paules Wharfe, at the signe of the / Crosse Keyes. 1598. /

A–D⁴. 4to. (14)+11+(7). The poem to Harriot is printed D₁ᵛ–(D₄ʳ).

Copies Used: British Museum C.39.d., 54, 8773   Victoria and Albert, Dyce 4894
    Yale University, Elizabethan Club   Harvard University, Widener Collection

Not entered.

Punctuation Revised.

46 Final semicolon instead of period   48 Final period added   49 Final colon instead of period   50 Final semicolon instead of colon   80 Comma added after *reuerence* Final comma deleted   88 Final period added   96 Final comma instead of period   97 Final comma deleted   98 Final colon instead of period   141 Final comma instead of period   142 Final period added   153 Final colon added   155 Final comma added   164 Final period instead of commas

Harriots) Thomas Harriot, the notable philosopher and astronomer, a member of Sir Walter Raleigh's household, who—with Matthew Roydon, Warner, and Raleigh himself—was implicated in the charges of blasphemy made against Christopher Marlowe. The slim quarto, *Achilles Shield*, in which this poem to Harriot appears is dedicated (like the *Seauen Bookes of the Iliads* which had been printed earlier, in June or July of the same year) to the Earl Marshal, The Earl of Essex. It is evident from the dedication that Essex had not paid any attention to the earlier volume and Chapman wanted to strike again while the iron was hot. It seems most unlikely that the argument in the poetic address to Harriot here printed would have helped his cause any! For an elaborate but unconvincing argument relating this poem to Shakespeare's *Troilus and Cressida*, see Arthur Acheson's *Shakespeare's Sonnet Story;* for a more sober discussion of the poem, Miss Bradbrook's *School of Night*, pp. 143–145.

41 *perfect eye*) Harriot's telescope.

46 *this fowle Panther earth*) Cf. the allegory of *H. in C.*, 243 seq. Chapman likens earth to the panther because that animal was supposed to attract by its sweet breath and then destroy.

99 *fortune-glossed Pompists*) Doubtless, wealthy men who make an ostentatious show. The word "pompist" is not in the *N.E.D.* and appears to have been invented by Chapman.

113 *this despisde, inuerted world*) Chapman sees his personification as actually moving upside down. Cf. *Coronet*, 5.5–6 and note.

145 *Since it is made a Courtly question now*) That is, whether Chapman is to receive help at court, from Essex, for his translation.

146 *partles*) Impartial. A sense not given in the *N.E.D.*

(Epistle Dedicatory to Prince Henry: *The Iliads*.)

This Epistle appears in the *Twelue Bookes* of the *Iliads*, n.d., 1609; the complete *Iliads*, n.d. 1611; and the *Whole Works of Homer* (1616), in which edition the unsold quires of the 1611 printings of the *Iliads* are bound with the *Odysseys*, n.d. 1615. The title-page of the *Whole Works* is here given, and the text follows the edition of 1611. The title-page is an elaborate engraving by William Hole which follows in conception his earlier, and smaller, engraving for the title of the *Twelue Bookes*.

THE / WHOLE WORKS / OF / HOMER; / PRINCE OF POETTS / In his Iliads, and / Odysses. / Translated according to the Greeke, / By / Geo: Chapman. /

De Ili: et Odiss: /
Omnia ab his: et in his sunt omnia: /
siue beati /
Te decor eloquij, seu rerū pondera /
tangunt,   Angel: Pol: /

At London printed for Nathaniell Butter. / William Hole sculp: /

On the back of the title-page is a large engraved portrait of Chapman which is used as a frontispiece to the present edition of his poems.

Entered: 2 no. 1614

The epistle to Prince Henry is printed *2ʳ–*4ʳ (misprinted A4).
Copies Used: British Museum 11315 i. 6

>   Trinity College, Cam. Capell F.4
>   vi 4.17
>   Fitzwilliam Museum
>   Bodleian   Malone 9

The punctuation in this edition follows closely that of 1609, and there are no verbal differences in the poem.

Punctuation Revised.

14 *empire: you* instead of *empire. You*   26 Final semicolon instead of period
   89 Final semicolon instead of period   151 Final colon instead of period (As in
   ed. 1609.)   ed. 1609.)

Chapman had been a sewer-in-ordinary in Prince Henry's household for five or six years and doubtless had received a tacit promise of the Prince's support before resuming his translation of Homer which had been in abeyance for eleven years. That the Prince acknowledged his Homer after the publication of the *Twelue Bookes*, and commanded him to proceed with the rest of the translation, we know from the "Corollarium ad Principem" at the end of *The Teares of Peace*.

41 Cf. l. 16 of the passage from Silius Italicus translated at the beginning of the address "To the Reader," *Iliads;* and the sonnet to Salisbury, l. 10.
114–147 For this image of circles in water, see *O.B. of S.*, 99.1–4 and note.

(Memorial verses to Prince Henry: *Whole Works of Homer*.)

Since Prince Henry died before the *Iliads* and *Odysseys* were issued together in 1616, an engraved plate was added to the volume, inscribed with two Corinthian columns, the Prince of Wales' plume and motto, and the verses here printed.
It is clear from these verses that the four years which had elapsed between Prince Henry's death and the issue of the *Whole Works* had not brought forth any posthumous fulfilment at court of the Prince's promises of financial assistance to Chapman.

(An Anagram on Henrye: The Iliads.)

This anagram appears on *4ᵛ (misprinted A4) of the *Iliads*.
The anagram consists of the words: OVR SVNN, HEYR, PEACE, LIFE, the letters being taken from HENRYE PRINCE OF WALES, V counting for W. In composing this anagram and sonnet, Chapman was following the precedent of the Homeric scholar, Johannes Spondanus, from whose great Greco-Latin edition of Homer with notes he made his own translation. Spondanus had included in his prefatory matter an anagram on the name of his patron, King Henry III of Navarre.

(Sonnet to Queen Anne: *Iliads*.)

This sonnet appears both in the *Twelue Bookes* of the *Iliads* and in the complete *Iliads* where it is printed *6ʳ.

(*To the Reader: Iliads.*)

This epistle appears both in the 1609 edition of the *Twelue Bookes* and the 1611 complete *Iliads* where it is printed (*₆ʳ)–A₂ᵛ. The edition of 1611 makes two verbal corrections:
l. 8 of the lines prefacing the three translated passages, "saies" to "saith."
l. 122 of the epistle, "as earth, in him" to "as earth's in him."

Punctuation Revised.

62 Final semicolon instead of period

Introductory Lines.

2 *prejudicacies*) Preconceived opinions. There is no illustration of this word in the *N.E.D.* before 1636.

Translated Passages.

The three passages with which Chapman prefaces his epistle are all translated from Latin selections presented in the same order in the prolegomena of Spondanus' Homer. See note to *Anagram on Henrye*, and Schoell, p. 171.

Silius Italicus
16 This line is adopted in the *Epistle to Henry*, 41, and the sonnet to Salisbury.
26 *Æacides*) Achilles.

Angelus Politianus
For Chapman's further acquaintance with this scholar, see *Epistle to Somerset, Odysseys* introductory lines, 17–52 and note.

Epistle, "To the Reader."

This epistle is notable for providing the "due praise of your mother tongue above all others, for Poesy," which Chapman promised his public in the preface to his *Seauen Bookes* of the *Iliads* (1598).
1–6 Amplification of Spondanus' remark on concluding his testimonies from authors. See Schoell, l. 172.
8–43 This passage summarizes the theory of translation which Chapman retained throughout his career as a translator from the dedication of the *Seauen Bookes* (1598), to the epistle "To the Reader" prefixed to his last translation, Juvenal's satire, 1629.
46 *Valla*) Laurentius Valla, who translated Homer into Latin prose, 1474.
  Hessus) Eobanus Hessus, who translated Homer into Latin verse, 1540. These two translators are frequently quoted by Chapman in notes to his translation, always with the most extreme scorn.
47 *Messines*) La Badessa Messinese who translated the first five books of the *Iliad* into Italian, 1564, probably known to Chapman only through Spondanus.
49 *Salel*) Hugues Salel who translated the first ten books of the *Iliad* into French, 1555, a work that was completed by A. Jamyn, 1580.
61–64 This poem on the mysteries in Homer, as far as we know, was never written.
75–80 Chapman had already discussed the propriety of using the fourteener in poems of long scope in his preface to *Achilles Shield* (1598). He was to change his mind and turn the *Odyssey* to heroic couplets, a change that Jonson would have approved: see Conversations with Drummond of Hawthornden where he remarked "that the translations of Homer and Vergill in Long Alexandrines were but Prose." But note Chapman's general preference for the heroic couplet expressed in *H. in C.*, 86–94.
77 *squint-ey'd Enuie*) See note to *De Guiana*, 41.

81–82 Chapman is not consistent in his stand on this controversial subject of the reform of the English language. See the "Address to the Understander," *Achilles Shield* (1598), where he defends his "beyond-sea manner of writing."

86–96 Compare the technique of these lines with that of Pope in the *Essay on Criticism:*

> These equal syllables alone require,
> Tho' oft the ear the open vowels tire;
> While expletives their feeble aid do join;
> And ten low words oft creep in one dull line.

Both poets illustrate their attack in the process of making it.

88–96 Chapman had already written of the superiority of the English tongue to French, Italian, and Spanish as a vehicle for translation in his dedication to *Achilles Shield* (1598), though the argument about monosyllables is new.

120 *Bernacle*) Wild goose.

(Dedicatory Sonnets: *Iliads*.)

The *Twelue Bookes* of the *Iliads* (1609) contained sixteen sonnets in addition to those to Prince Henry and Queen Anne. Those that are retained in the complete *Iliads* of 1611 are here presented from the later text, with variants of 1609 recorded. The sonnets of 1609 which were later dropped are especially indicated, as well as those which were added in 1611. The compliments in these dedicatory sonnets are generalized, and there is no reason to suppose that Chapman was intimately associated with any of the noblemen or women whom he addressed. In the edition of 1609 they are printed 2Dd, 4Ee, 1Ff; in the edition of 1611 they are printed Gg₄ʳ–Gg₇ᵛ, and in a few copies, especially noted, on two extra eaves at the end.

Duke of Lennox. Ludovic Stuart, who was too important a person for Chapman to have risked overlooking, and the only one of the lot to whom he seems actually to come begging. It is possible that Chapman had appealed to him for help at the time of his trouble over the Byron plays just the year before (1608), probably without success. See his letters to Mr. Crane, the Duke's secretary, and comments by Bertram Dobell, *Athenaeum*, April 6, 1901.

The Lord Chancellor. Ellesmere, Thomas Egerton. Chapman approached the Chancellor on one other occasion in his life, date unknown, when he petitioned him to grant an injunction restraining John Woolfall from proceeding with a suit. See *Athenaeum*, March 23, 1901.

The Lord Treasurer. Earl of Salisbury, Robert Cecil, another nobleman too important to miss. He, with Suffolk, had helped rescue Chapman and Jonson from prison at the time of *Eastward Ho.* Jonson sized up his character with the remark that "he never cared for any man longer than he can make use of him." Perhaps Chapman felt this same reservation about his character, for though he paid him a pretty compliment, not only in this sonnet but also in his lines *In Seianum* (1605), his chief praise and gratitude in that poem are reserved for Suffolk.

Ed. 1609 does not have the anagram.

10 From Silius Italicus, see passage prefixed to "To the Reader," *Iliads*, 16.

Earl of Suffolk. Thomas Howard. Although this sonnet is impersonal in tone, Chapman owed a real debt of gratitude to Suffolk which he had expressed most warmly on an earlier occasion. See *In Seianum*, 149–158 and note. He was the father of Frances, Lady Essex, later Countess of Somerset. See notes to *Andromeda Liberata.*

Earl of Northampton. Henry Howard, a second son of the poet Surrey, High Stewart of Oxford, Chancellor of Cambridge, 1612. He was a notorious intriguer and had been the principal accuser in summoning Ben Jonson before the Council on the charge of "popery and treason" in *Sejanus.* Hence we may well believe that Chapman cherished no affection for this nobleman. Northampton's charge against Jonson was part of his ostentatious anti-

Catholic activity, conducted through a course of years in order to detract attention from his own Catholic leanings. It was Northampton to whom, as Lord of the Privie Seale, Chapman had to turn when, left destitute by the death of Prince Henry, he found it necessary to make appeals to important people whom he hoped might be persuaded to fulfil the Prince's dying promises. See *Athenaeum*, April 6, 1901.

Earl of Arundell. Thomas Howard, the second Earl of Arundell, known primarily as the first important collector of art in England. In 1609 he travelled in the Low Countries, where he seems to have acquired his love of art, though he did not do much collecting until after 1615. He was a friend of the chief antiquaries of that time, and is said to have discovered the talent of Inigo Jones.

In the edition of 1609 Arundell came last of the people addressed, Ff₁ʳ. Hence the sonnet took an entirely different form, and runs as follows:

"To conclude, and accomplish the right Princely Traine of *our most excellent* Prince, HENRIE, *&c. In entertainment of all the vertues brought hither, by the preseruer,* Homer, *&c. His diuine worth solicits the right Noble and vertuous Heroe the Earle of* ARUNDELL, &c.

> The end crownes all: and therefore though it chance,
>> That here, your honor'd Name be vsde the last;
> Whose worth all Right should (with the first) aduance,
>> Great Earle, esteeme it, as of purpose past.
> Vertue had neuer her due place in earth;
>> Nor stands shee vpon Forme; for that will fade:
> Her sacred substance (grafted in your birth)
>> Is that, for which she calls you to her aide.
> Nor could she but obserue you with the best
>> Of this Heroicall, and Princely Traine;
> All following her great Patron to the Feast
>> Of *Homers* soule, inuiting none in vaine.
> Sit then, Great Earle, and feast your soule, with his:
>> Whose food, is knowledge; and whose knowledge, blisse.
>> *Subscrib'd by the most true obseruant of*
>> *all your Heroicall vertues,*
>>> Geo. Chapman.

Earl of Pembroke. William Herbert, the third Earl of Pembroke, son of the famous patroness, the Countess of Pembroke, a self-centered, pleasant, and futile sort of individual. He had incurred Elizabeth's wrath by his intrigue with Mary Fitton, but had been rescued from retirement by James I. He is known to have sent Ben Jonson twenty pounds every New Year with which to buy books.

One is struck by the number of sonnets in this series addressed to members of the Sidney-Pembroke family. Chapman seems intent on capturing the attention of a family so notably generous to men of letters. His hopes very likely took rise from an earlier connection with this family: namely, the patronage of Sir Thomas Walsingham, cousin to Sir Francis, the father-in-law of Sir Philip Sidney. See dedication to *Hero and Leander.* For Sir Thomas' personal aversion to receiving dedications, see the dedication to *Byron's Conspiracy* (1608). The six members of the family here addressed are the earls of Pembroke, Montgomery, the Countess of Montgomery, Lord Lisle, Lady Mary Wrothe, and Lucy Countess of Bedford. Lord Wotton, an old family friend, also really belongs in this group.

Earl of Montgomery. Philip Herbert, more promising as a patron than his older brother, the Earl of Pembroke. He was the patron of Massinger and was one of the seven noblemen to whom Jonson addressed letters of appeal at the time when he was incarcerated with Chapman for the offence of *Eastward Ho.* There is no evidence in this sonnet, however, that Chapman felt indebted to him.

Lord Lisle. Sir Philip Sidney's brother, Robert, a very old man and unlikely to be encouraged into patronizing a "work in progress." The nephews mentioned in the sonnet were the Lords Pembroke and Montgomery.

In the ed. of 1609, line 14, "stand" reads "sticke."

Countess of Montgomery. Philip Herbert's wife. She had been Lady Susan Vere, and Chapman signed the sonnet when it first appeared as an after-thought on an extra leaf in 1609 as an admirer of her father, Edward Vere, the seventeenth Earl of Oxford. I have not located the "friend" whom he refers to as having recently dedicated work to her.

Lady Wrothe. Mary Wrothe, the daughter of Lord Lisle. She was a great friend of Jonson at this period, and he dedicated the *Alchemist* to her. Author of *Urania*, a pastoral romance, 1621.

Countess of Bedford. Lucy, first cousin of Sir Philip Sidney and Lady Pembroke. She was the patroness and friend of Donne, Drayton, and Jonson, and her home at Twickenham was a well known center for men of letters. One might therefore think that Chapman would consider her his most likely entry into the favor of the Sidney-Pembroke family, but—if so—the haughty and puritanical tone of this sonnet was most unfortunately taken.

Earl of Southampton. Henry Wriothesley, Shakespeare's famous patron. If Chapman had ever entertained any hope of rivalling Shakespeare in his patronage, a theory occasionally mentioned in these notes, his hopes must have long since died, for the sonnet is as impersonal as the rest.

In the ed. of 1609, line 2 read: (Fit, those aforesaid Monsters to conuince.   Line 11 read: Crimes:

Earl of Sussex. Robert Ratcliffe, who had been Queen Elizabeth's proxy at the baptism of Prince Henry, an occasion alluded to in the sonnet.

Lord of Walden and *Sir Thomas Howard.* These two sonnets appear for the first time in 1611. They are both to members of the Howard family, before represented by Suffolk, Arundell, and Northampton. Now Chapman adds the brothers Theophilus Howard, Earl of Walden, and Sir Thomas Howard, sons of the Earl of Suffolk and brothers to Lady Frances who was soon to become Somerset's wife. The sonnet addressed to the younger of the two, Sir Thomas Howard, the father of Dryden's wife, is more personal in tone than many of the sonnets, and would seem to indicate an acquaintance with the young man.

Vicount Cranborne. William Cecil, son of the Earl of Salisbury. This sonnet and the two following, to Rochester and Phillips, were printed on two extra leaves for the 1611 edition of the *Iliads*. These leaves are found only in very rare copies: 1) Malone Collection, Bodleian, F. II. 30; 2) Trinity College, Cambridge; 3) Chapin Collection, Williams College, Williamstown, Mass.; 4) Harvard College Library, GL 62.819. In the Malone copy the first leaf is bound between Gg₆ and Gg₇ and the second after Gg₇; in the Trinity College and Harvard copies they follow the sonnet to Queen Anne in the first folding; in the Chapin copy they follow Gg₇ before an original blank leaf which still bears the faint impress of the two sonnets on Gg₇ᵛ to Walden and Howard. This last is doubtless the proper arrangement.

Vicount Rochester. Robert Carr who was created Viscount Rochester on 25 March, 1611. The two extra leaves must, then, have been printed between that date and 3 Nov. 1613 when he was created Earl of Somerset. This sonnet is Chapman's first bid for favor to the man who was to become his final Homeric patron; hence, it was the only one which may be supposed to have profited him at all. It reflects the court gossip of the day, only to defend Rochester against it, a trust which probably genuinely gratified the court favorite. For Chapman's further relations with Somerset, see notes to *Andromeda Liberata, Justif. of And. Lib., Pro. Vere,* and *Ep. to Somerset, Hymns of Homer.*

Sir Edward Phillips. Prince Henry's Chancellor to whom Chapman dedicated in the following year *Petrarch's Seuen Penitentiall Psalmes,* and in 1613 his *Masque of the Middle Temple.* He had succeeded to the position of Master of the Rolls in 1611, and died in 1614.

Lady Arabella. Arabella Stuart, cousin of James I, and great-grand-daughter of Margaret Tudor and her second husband, the Earl of Angus, a lady whom many Englishmen favored as a successor to Queen Elizabeth. This sonnet appeared in the 1609 edition of the *Twelue*

Bookes, but was withdrawn from the final edition of the *Iliads*. Lady Arabella was evidently a woman "of parts" but certainly of no influence, for, being of the royal blood both of England and of Scotland, she was suspect under the reign of James, as she had been under Elizabeth. The same year as this sonnet, 1609, saw her clandestine marriage with William Seymour for which she was committed to the Tower, only to die there six years later in a state of idiocy.

Lord Wotton. Edward Wotton, created Lord, 1603, chiefly known as an old friend of Sir Philip Sidney. This sonnet appeared in the 1609 edition of the *Twelve Bookes*, but was withdrawn, for no ascertainable reason, from the final edition of the *Iliads*. In 1616 he was appointed Treasurer of the Household.

(Epistle to Somerset: Odysseys.)

This prose and verse epistle appeared both in the edition of the *Twelve Books* of the *Odysseys*, A₃ʳ–(A₆ʳ), and in the complete *Odysseys*, bound with the *Iliads* to make up the *Whole Works of Homer*. The title-page of the *Twelve Books* is engraved and bears the following title:

Homer's Odysses. / Translated according to yᵉ Greeke / by Geo: Chapman / (*verses from Propertius*) / Jmprinted at London by / Rich: Field, for Nath- / aniell Butter. / n.d.

This book, which was registered as "Odisses 24 bookes" by Nathaniell Butter on the 2 Nov., 1614, was printed at the end of that year. This date is ascertained by the fact that Somerset was not made Lord Chamberlain until 1614; the book is entered that November, and is presented to him as a New Year's gift. The address at the beginning of the epistle read for this edition:

To the Most Noble,
Now liuing restorer
of the Vlyssean Temper;
Of solide Vertue
The most open, profest, and Heroicall Contemner;*
Of all true Honor
The most Truth-like, vnalterable, and inuincible Deseruer,
Robert, Earle of Somerset,
Lord Chamberlaine, etc.
His Lords
Euer most deseruedly deuoted
Geo. Chapman
Humbly celebrates this New-years Light; with discouerie
of that long hidden Relict; for whose presentment
Macedon would haue giuen a kingdome;
Homer reuiued:

The *Odysseys* were then brought out complete in 1615, with the same title-page. A₃, bearing the above inscription and reference to the New Year, was cancelled and replaced by the leaf bearing the address as found in this edition. In rare copies (such as those in the Fitzwilliam Museum, Cambridge, and in the possession of Mr. Hugh Macdonald) the engraved title-page is retained when the *Odysseys* were bound with the *Iliads* to make the *Whole Works*. In some other copies there is a new title printed by Harper:
Homers / Odysses. / Translated according / to the Greeke. / By George Chapman. / (*motto*) / (*device*) / London, Printed for Nathaniel Butter. / n.d.
The reference to the New Year, on account of which A₃ was cancelled in the final edition, is retained, however, in the prose interlude between the concluding lines of verse, 17–18, and in lines 43–46.

* Contemner is obviously a misprint, possibly for "Contender."

Punctuation Revised.

Prose 75 Colon added after *induction*   Concluding lines 2 Final semicolon instead of
    period   3 Final comma instead of semicolon

In 1614 Somerset had been made Lord Chamberlain and Keeper of the Privy Seal. (He
had married Lady Frances Howard in 1613.) By the time of writing this epistle the scandal
about his marriage had reached its height, and Chapman had already written the tactless
Andromeda Liberata and its *Justification*. Hence Chapman was now addressing a man who,
though loaded with public honors, was tottering on the brink of a downfall. He was in
general ill repute as a result of his marriage, and his hold on the king was slipping. Before
the year 1615 was out, Somerset was being held in durance and the first manoeuvres of the
famous Overbury trial were under way. Thus Chapman lost his second real patron.

Introductory verses.

17–52 *Ex Angeli Politiana Ambra*) Angelus Politianus (1454–98), professor of Greek and
    Latin studies at the "studio" in Florence, and friend of Lorenzo de Medici, who gained
    for himself the nickname of "l'Omerico Giovinetto" by translating a small portion of
    the *Iliad* into Latin hexameters at the age of sixteen. Chapman had quoted from him
    before in the address "To the Reader," *Iliads*, but there he was translating a passage
    found in Spondanus. Schoell writes about the passage here translated (*Mod. Phil.*,
    Vol. xiii): "The passage chosen by Chapman . . . is taken from the *Ambra*, which
    stands third among the *Sylvae*, and was written in 1485. This poem, an easy, graceful
    eulogy of Homer, is mainly a verse-replica of Politianus' earlier prose-work: *Oratio in
    expositionem Homeri*, which is itself largely adapted from the elaborate Greek essays
    of Pseudo-Plutarch and Pseudo-Herodotus. Chapman's choice fell upon the somewhat
    high-flown periods with which the poem opens." He has expanded a 19-line passage
    into 35 lines.

Prose.

The prose section of this epistle is particularly interesting as the only passage in any of his
prefaces in which Chapman refers specifically to the allegory of the Homeric epics. His
own sentiment on allegorical poetry in general is expressed in the prose *Justification of
Andromeda Liberata*.

1–9 The comparison of the *Iliad* and *Odyssey* is taken from Spondanus' prolegomena, but
    it stems from Plutarch.
12 In a manuscript note Schoell gives the source of the Greek quotation: *Phaedrus* 267 a.
31 *aesture*) Boiling. A word invented by Chapman.
68–86 This description of the two sorts of poetic ecstasy comes from Ficino, *In Platonis
    Ionem, vel de furore poetico*. See Schoell, p. 5. It was one of Chapman's favorite con-
    cepts; compare the defense of the *Masque of the Middle Temple*, and note on the 12th
    book of the *Od*.
96 *Besogne*) A raw recruit. Cf. *Widow's Tears*, i. iii. 24.

Concluding verses.

5–11 echo Chapman's early description of the poetic process in the *Ep. to Roydon, O.B. of S.*
7–9 Parrott compares *Byron's Trag.*, v. iii. 68.
12–14 In the "Preface to the Reader," *Iliads* (1609), Chapman had promised to write a
    poem on the "mysteries revealed in Homer," but so far as we know he never got be-
    yond the intention. Fundamentally, he was not interested in the analysis of "mys-
    teries," but in the interpretation of Homer's poems as moral documents.
17 *the brazen head*) Of Rumor.
43–46 See introductory note to this Epistle.
59 *Clients*) Is possessive.

Certaine ancient Greeke Epigrammes.

These epigrams are printed on (A₆ᵛ) of the *Odysseys*, and are taken from the prolegomena of Spondanus.

(Epilogue to the Odysseys.)

These lines are printed (Ii₆ᵛ–Ii₇ᵛ) of the *Odysseys*. *Ad Deum* also appears (Ii₇ʳ).

Punctuation Revised.

8 Final comma instead of period.

(Epistle to Somerset: *Hymns*.)

This epistle appears in the *Crowne of all Homers Workes*, Chapman's translation of the *Batrachomyomachia*, the *Hymns*, and *Epigrams*, ascribed to Homer. This is the most sumptuous of any volume of Chapman's works, and was printed by John Bill, probably in 1624. The title is set in an elaborate engraving signed, *Will: Pass*, and is as follows:

the / CROWNE of all HOMERS Workes / Batrachomyomachia / *Or the Battaile of Frogs and Mise.* / His Hymn's—*and*—Epigrams / Translated according to ye Originall / By George Chapman. / LONDON, *Printed by* Iohn Bill, his MAIESTIES *Printer.*

Not entered.

Copies Used: British Museum G 8837   Chapin Collection, Williams College, Mass.
Lambeth Palace Library   Sion College   Trinity College, Cambridge vi. 4. 17
Widener Collection, Harvard

The epistle to Somerset is printed ¶(1)ʳ–¶₃ᵛ, (pp. 5–10).

The engraved title-page exists in two versions. In the first we have the spelling "Worckes" instead of "Works," and the pages of the book in Homer's hand are blank; in the second they have been engraved with a Greek phrase.

An interesting copy now in the Widener Collection at Harvard University bears Chapman's autograph inscription to Henry Reynolds on the back of the title-page, and contains textual changes, also apparently in his hand-writing. The presumption that Chapman corrected this copy before giving it to his friend Reynolds is strengthened by the curious revisions made in ink on the engraved title-page (first state). The beard on the engraved portrait of Chapman has been trimmed down, evidently to approximate more closely its real size and shape, and the hair on Apollo's head which in Pass' engraving frizzes up rather wildly is made to curl downwards in longer more poetical locks. A number of revisions, presumably made by Chapman himself, are penned into the text. The correction made in the epistle dedicatory is here retained: ¶₁ᵛ, (l. 26),

All
Borne to ∧ Heauen, to take of Earth, no part

Punctuation Revised.

1–3 Bracket added   81 Final semicolon instead of period   81–83 Bracket added
118 Final comma instead of period   119 Final colon added

The dedication to Somerset makes it certain that this book was published after 1622, the date of Somerset's release from the Tower. In this year Somerset and the Lady Frances were allowed to retire to a country estate, but their freedom of action was limited to a three mile radius. In 1624, the year of the king's death, their pardon was made complete. But they still, wisely, preferred to live "the life retired" which Chapman refers to in the opening lines of his poem. For the poet's previous relations with Somerset, see particularly the introductory note to *Andromeda Liberata.*

29–30 Shepherd compared these lines with *Byron's Tragedy*, III. i. 127–129.

39 *Heauens seuenfold Carr*) A pun on Somerset's name, Robert Carr, and the seven stars of the constellation called the Wain (or Great Bear).

41 *Erymanthian Beare*) The star Arctos, or the Bear, which Zeus had created after the she-bear into which he had metamorphosed the Arcadian nymph, Callisto, who had been slain by Artemis.

84-104 and gloss. I have combed the well-known histories of the War in the Netherlands, without success, for an account of this engagement. Sir John Norris (1547?-97) was an important soldier in these wars, a man trusted by Elizabeth and feared by Leicester. Chapman also describes him in *Byron's Conspiracy*, II. ii. 216. This passage picks up a trail of interest in the Netherlands which Chapman had first evinced in 1594: see *H. in C.* and notes.

117-121 This sentence, which was originally two, but which has been emended by two changes in punctuation (see table) means that Somerset will find the "Doctrine" of all Chapman has been saying in the *Batrachomyomachia* and *Hymns* of Homer as well as in the *Odysses* which Chapman had also dedicated to him. The *Odyssey* itself is described as the "glasse" of Homer's mind in which he reveals the "body," or actual life and adventures of Odysseus.

131 Chapman had used this line before: *Eug.*, 261, and *Epic.*, 612.

132 135 and gloss. This reference to the ancients' understanding of poetry is paraphrased from Ficinus, *In Platonis Ionem, vel de furore poetico*, in which commentary Chapman also finds the quotation he gives in his gloss, *Ion* 533 e. (See Schoell, p. 5.)

(Epilogue to the *Hymns*.)

These lines appear at the conclusion of the volume just described, Aa₁ʳ-Aa₂ᵛ. In the Widener copy Chapman has penned in two corrections: one to line 17 of the poem, and one to the Latin poem which follows. Both of these revisions are retained in the present text.

Tumor
Aa₁ʳ All is extuberance, and ~~exuberant~~ All,

Aa₂ᵛ vt nobis Adiuneto sis;
In "Adiuneto" a third minim is added to the *n* to make *m*, and an *n* inserted before the *t*, so that it reads "Adiumento."

33-42 This passage seems to me to belie Anthony Wood's statement, generally accepted, that Chapman spent some time in Oxford where he "was observed to be most excellent in the Latin and Greek tongues." If he had studied the ancient tongues at Oxford, surely he would never have boasted that he was self-taught. He had evidently often been twitted for his lack of a formal education in the classics, and if he could truthfully have said so, he would have been the first to retaliate indignantly with a reminder of his university training.

Prayer.

The prayer at the end is the one with which Simplicius concludes his commentary on Epictetus' *Encheiridion*. Chapman had used it before in his postscript to the *Iliads* (1611) where we hear that it was his "daily and nightly prayer."